Adobe® Flex™ 3
Training from the Source

Jeff Tapper
Michael Labriola
Matthew Boles
with James Talbot
Foreword by Matt Chotin, Flex Product Manager

Adobe

Adobe Flex 3: Training from the Source

Jeff Tapper, Michael Labriola, and Matthew Boles with James Talbot

Adobe Press books are published by

Peachpit
1249 Eighth Street
Berkeley, CA 94710
510/524-2178
510/524-2221 (fax)

Find us on the Web at: www.peachpit.com

To report errors, please send a note to errata@peachpit.com

To learn more about Adobe Press books, go to www.adobepress.com

Project Editor: Victor Gavenda
Editor: Robyn G. Thomas
Technical Editor: Josh Berling
Production Coordinator: Becky Winter
Copy Editors: Dan Foster and Mark Goodin
Compositors: Rick Gordon, Emerald Valley Graphics / Debbie Roberti, Espresso Graphics
Indexer: Jack Lewis
Cover Design: Peachpit Press
Proofreader: Soledad Decosta

Notice of Rights

Trademarks

Notice of Liability

Printed and bound in the United States of America

ISBN 13: 978-0-321-52918-3
ISBN 10: 0-321-52918-9

9 8 7 6 5 4 3

Bios

Jeff Tapper is a Senior Technologist at Digital Primates IT Consulting Group. He has been developing Internet-based applications since 1995 for a myriad of clients including Morgan Stanley, Conde Nast, Toys R Us, IBM, Dow Jones, American Express, M&T Bank, Verizon, and many others. He has been developing Flex applications since the earliest days of Flex 1. As an instructor, Jeff is certified to teach all of Adobe's courses on Flex, ColdFusion, and Flash development. He is also a frequent speaker at Adobe Development Conferences and user groups. Digital Primates IT Consulting Group provides expert guidance on rich Internet application development and empowers clients through mentoring.

Michael Labriola is a Founding Partner and Senior Consultant at Digital Primates IT Consulting Group. He has been developing Internet applications since 1995 and has been working with Flex since its 1.0 beta program. Michael is an Adobe Certified Instructor, Community Expert, Flex Developer Champion, and international speaker on Flex and AIR topics who has consulted for three of the world's 10 most recognized brands.

As a consultant, he mentors software development teams using emerging technologies and designs enterprise applications with high business impact. His free time is spent escaping from technology through wine and food.

Matthew Boles is the Technical Lead for the Adobe Customer Training group and has been developing and teaching courses on Flex since the 1.0 release. Matthew has a diverse background in web development, computer networking, and teaching in both professional computer classes and the public schools. In addition to this book, Matthew coauthored a version of the Certified ColdFusion Developer Study Guide. He has also developed official Allaire/Macromedia/Adobe curricula in both ColdFusion and Flash development content areas.

Acknowledgments

I would like to thank Mike, Matt, and Josh for all their hard work, which has helped shape this book. Special thanks go to the team at Adobe/Macromedia, which has made this all possible, especially the efforts of David Mendels, Phil Costa, and Matt Chotin. Thanks to Tad Staley of Adobe Consulting, who has given me more opportunities than anyone else to work on Flex projects. Thanks to the editorial staff at Adobe Press, who was faced with the Herculean task of making our writings intelligible. Finally, thanks to the 2004 and 2007 World Series Champion Boston Red Sox.

—Jeff Tapper

Thanks to Jeff, Matt, Josh, and James for their work and dedication on this project. Many thanks to Robyn for her continued patience and diligence, and to Victor for his work on our behalf at Peachpit. Thanks to all of the team members at Digital Primates that picked up the slack when this book took a little more time than expected. Thanks to my clients for the interesting work and inspiration to keep learning these technologies. And, as always, continuing thanks to Matt for dragging me into this adventure. Finally, thanks to my wife Laura who is the real reason I accomplish anything at all.

—Michael Labriola

Thanks to Jeff, Mike, Josh and Robyn for the great work getting this book out.

—Matthew Boles

Contents

Foreword xiv

Introduction xvi

LESSON 1 **Understanding Rich Internet Applications** 2

Understanding the Evolution of Computer Applications. 4

Breaking Away from Page-Based Architecture 6

Identifying the Advantages of Rich Internet Applications 7

Business Managers. 7

IT Organizations 8

End Users. 8

RIA Technologies 8

Asynchronous JavaScript and XML (AJAX) 9

Flash. 10

Flex 10

The Windows Presentation Foundation, XAML, Silverlight,
and Expression 12

LESSON 2 **Getting Started** 14

Getting Started with Flex Application Development 16

Creating a Project and an MXML Application 16

Understanding the Flex Builder 3 Workbench. 21

Running Your Application 23

Creating a Second Application Page and Working in Design Mode 30

Getting Ready for the Next Lesson. 35

LESSON 3 **Laying Out the Interface.** 38

Learning About Containers 40

Laying Out the E-Commerce Application Using Design Mode 41

Working with Constraint-Based Layouts 47

Using Constraints with the Parent Container 47

Using Enhanced Constraints. 52

Working with View States 55

Controlling View States 57

Laying Out an Application in Source Mode 59

Adding and Controlling View States with MXML. 63

LESSON 4 **Using Simple Controls** **68**

Introducing Simple Controls. 70

Displaying Images 71

Building a Detail View 75

Using Data Binding to Link a Data Structure to a Simple Control 78

Using a Form Layout Container to Lay Out Simple Controls. 80

Adding Radio Buttons and Date Fields to the Dashboard 85

LESSON 5 **Handling Events and Data Structures** **88**

Understanding Event Handling. 90

Understanding a Simple Example 90

Handling the Event with an ActionScript Function 91

Passing Data when Calling the Event Handler Function 92

Building a Data Structure on the creationComplete Event. 93

Using Data from the Event Object 96

Building a Custom ActionScript Class 101

Building a Value Object. 101

Building a Method to Create an Object. 106

Building Shopping Cart Classes. 109

LESSON 6 **Using Remote XML Data with Controls** **114**

Retrieving XML Data with HTTPService. 116

Creating an HTTPService Object 117

Invoking the send() Method. 117

Using the Returned Data. 117

Understanding Security Issues 119

Retrieving XML Data via HTTPService. 119

Populating an ArrayCollection with HTTPService Data 122

Using ArrayCollections 122

Using Collections as Data Providers 123

Populating a ComboBox Control and Programmatically Adding an Option. . . 125

Using XML Data with a Tree Control 129

Understanding E4X Operators 129

Populating a Tree Control with XML Data 134

Retrieving XML Data and Transforming It into an ArrayCollection

   of Custom Objects. 141

Using Data Binding with Complex Data Structures 145

Manipulating Shopping Cart Data 147

Adding Items to the Cart. 147

Sorting Items in an ArrayCollection 148

Adding an Item or Updating the Quantity. 150

Using a Cursor to Locate a ShoppingCart Item 152

Adding a Remove Button. 160

LESSON 7   **Creating Components with MXML** **164**

Introducing MXML Components 166
  Understanding the Basics of How to Create a Custom Component 167
  Creating a Custom Component Step by Step 168
  Using Custom Components in the Application Architecture 169
Creating an Update/Delete Product Component and Instantiating It. 171
Popping Up Product Information When Clicking the Update and
  Delete Buttons 175
Creating Another Value Object 182
Creating a Data Manager Component for All Three Applications 184
Using the New Data Manager Component 191
Implementing Add Product Functionality 195
Creating and Using a Component for the Dashboard Application. 196

LESSON 8   **Using Controls and Repeaters with Datasets** **200**

Using Datasets 202
  Understanding HorizontalList and TileList Components 203
  Implementing a labelFunction 204
  Implementing an itemRenderer 205
Displaying the Categories Using a HorizontalList and an itemRenderer 207
Displaying Grocery Products Based on Category Selection 211
  Using a Repeater to Loop Over a Dataset 211
  Retrieving Data from Repeated Components. 212
  Addressing Components Built by a Repeater 214
  Understanding Performance Differences Between TileList and Repeater . . 215
  Displaying Grocery Items Based on Category. 215
Coding States to Display Detailed Product Information 223
Placing Products in the Shopping Cart 225

LESSON 9   **Using Custom Events** **230**

Understanding the Benefits of Loosely Coupled Architecture 233
Dispatching Events. 233
Declaring Events for a Component. 235
Identifying the Need for Custom Event Classes. 236
Building and Using the CategoryEvent 237
Creating and Using the ProductEvent Class 241
  Using ProductEvent to Remove a Product from the Cart. 245
  Using ProductEvent to Add a Product to the Cart 247
Understanding Event Flow and Event Bubbling 250

LESSON 10   Creating Custom Components with ActionScript 3.0 . . . . **256**

Introducing Building a Component with ActionScript 3.0 258

Creating the Structure of the Class. 258

Overriding the createChildren() Method 261

    Creating a Button in ActionScript 262

    Using the addChild() Method to Add the Button to Your Component 262

    Understanding chrome and rawChildren 263

    Using addChild() on rawChildren to Add Elements to the Chrome 264

Sizing and Positioning in Flex. 268

Understanding the measure() Method 269

Overriding the updateDisplayList() Method 270

LESSON 11   Using DataGrids and Item Renderers **278**

Introducing DataGrids and Item Renderers 281

Adding a Generic DataGrid to ChartPod 281

Adding HTTPService Calls to Dashboard 283

Displaying the Shopping Cart with a DataGrid 287

    Add Inline Editing Control for DataGridColumn 289

    Create an MXML Item Renderer for Displaying the Product. 290

    Create an Inline MXML Item Renderer for Displaying

        the Remove Button 292

    Update ShoppingCartItem with Set and Get Functions 298

Using the AdvancedDataGrid 299

    Sorting the AdvancedDataGrid. 299

    Sorting in Expert Mode. 301

    Styling the AdvancedDataGrid 302

    Grouping Data 306

    Displaying Summary Data 312

LESSON 12   Using Drag and Drop **322**

Introducing the Drag and Drop Manager 324

Dragging and Dropping Between Two DataGrids 325

Dragging and Dropping Between a DataGrid and a List 328

Using a Nondrag-Enabled Component in a Drag-and-Drop Operation. 333

Dragging a Grocery Item to the Shopping Cart. 339

LESSON 13   Implementing Navigation. **346**

Introducing Navigation. 348

Using a TabNavigator in the DataEntry Application 351

Adding a Home Page and Checkout Page in the E-Commerce Application . . . 354

Creating the First Step of the Checkout Process Displayed by a ViewStack . . . 358

Completing the Checkout Process Using the ViewStack 365

LESSON 14 **Using Formatters and Validators**. **372**

Introducing Formatters and Validators 374

Using a Formatter Class to Display Currency Information in the
    E-Commerce Application. 375

Using Validator Classes 378

Using Regular Expressions to Validate Data (Part 1) 382

Using Regular Expressions to Validate Data (Part 2) 384

Building a Custom Validator Class 386

LESSON 15 **Implementing History Management and Deep Linking** **392**

Introducing History Management 394

Implementing History Management within a Navigator Container 396

Building a Custom History Manager. 398

Introducing Deep Linking 403

    Implementing Flex 3 Deep Linking 403

    Adding Deep Linking to Your Application 403

LESSON 16 **Customizing the Look and Feel of a Flex Application**. **410**

Applying a Design with Styles and Skins. 413

Applying Styles 413

    Setting Styles Inline with Tag Attributes 414

    Understanding Style Inheritance. 416

    Setting Styles with the <mx:Style> Tag. 417

    Using Flex Builder Tools for Working with CSS 419

    Setting Styles with CSS Files. 421

Changing CSS at Run Time. 431

    Benefits of Run-Time CSS. 432

    Creating a SWF from a CSS File 432

    Loading a CSS SWF with StyleManager. 433

    Overriding Styles with a Loaded CSS 433

Skinning Components 433

    Graphical Skins 434

    Importing Skins Created in CS3. 434

    Programmatic Skins 437

LESSON 17 **Working with Web Services** **444**

Introducing Server Communication. 447

Using the Event Model Remote Server Calls. 448

Configuring an Application to Work Locally 448

Using a Web Service in the Dashboard 450

    Handling Web Service Results. 453

    Calling Web Service Methods 456

Using a Web Service in the DataEntry Application. 458

Using the Web Service Introspection Wizard 463

Using the Generated Code in Your Application 465

Refactoring with Flex Builder 467

Completing the Integration of the Generated Code 469

Updating and Deleting Products 470

LESSON 18   Accessing Server-Side Objects **472**

Uploading Files to the Server 475

Integrating the FileUpload Component with DataEntry 479

Using RemoteObject to Save an Order 481

Update Flex Compiler Command 483

Dispatch an Order Confirmed Event in the Checkout Process 484

Create and Call Remote Object 485

Pass ShoppingCart into the Checkout Component 488

Change the Application State Back to Welcome 489

Mapping ActionScript Objects to Server Objects 490

The Flex Builder Data Wizards 492

Creating a Server Project 493

LESSON 19   Visualizing Data **498**

Exploring Flex Charting Components 500

Chart Types 500

Chart Packaging 500

Parts of a Chart 501

Laying Out Initial Charts 502

Populating Charts 504

Specifying the Charts' Series 504

Adding Horizontal and Vertical Axes to Line and Column Charts 510

Adding Legends to Charts 517

Limiting the Labels Shown on an Axis 518

Interacting with Charts 520

Mouse-Over Events 520

Click Events 520

Selection Events 520

Adding Chart Events 520

Adding Animations to Charts 525

Customizing Chart Appearance with Styles 527

LESSON 20   Creating Modular Applications **530**

Introducing Modular Applications in Flex 3 532

Using Flex Modules 533

Using the Module Class 534

Replacing the Checkout Code with a ModuleLoader Tag 535

Understanding Runtime Shared Libraries (RSLs) 537

Understanding the Linker 539

Using the Flex Framework RSL Caching. 540
    Understanding the Purpose of the Framework Cache 541
    Using Signed vs. Unsigned RSLs 541
    Examining the Current Size of the Applications 542
    Configuring Your Application to Use the Framework RSL 542
    Examining the Difference Made by the Framework RSL 544
Creating a Library Project. 544
    Adding Classes and Assets to the Library 545
    Using the FlexGrocerLibrary within the FlexGrocer Application 546

LESSON 21   **Deploying Flex Applications. 548**
Compiling a Deployment Version of Your Application 550
Breaking Out of the Browser with the Adobe Integrated Runtime (AIR) 550
    Getting Started with AIR 551
    Installing the AIR Runtime 551
    Installing a First Application 552
Creating an AIR Application 553
    Creating a New AIR Project 553
    Making the Dashboard Application into an AIR Application 555
    Customizing the Application with the Application.xml file 557
    Exporting the AIR File 559

LESSON 22   **Creating Transitions and Behaviors 566**
Introducing Behaviors and Transitions 568
    Using Behaviors on Components 568
    Using Transitions on View States 570
Implementing Effects on a Component. 572
Adding Effects to View States 574

LESSON 23   **Printing from Flex 576**
Introducing Flex Printing. 579
Printing for the First Time from Flex 579
Using the PrintDataGrid in a Nonvisible Container. 582
Building the Printable View in a Separate Component 585
Scaling the Printed Output. 589
Printing a Receipt from the Checkout Process 591

LESSON 24   **Using Shared Objects. 596**
Introducing Shared Objects 598
    Creating Shared Objects 599
    Reading Shared Objects 600
Building a SharedObject to Store Shopping Cart Data 601
Reading Data from an Existing Shared Object 604

LESSON 25 **Debugging Flex Applications** **608**

Introducing Debugging Techniques. 610
Watching Client/Server Data Exchange. 610
Learning More About the Debugger 611
    Learning More Details About Setting Breakpoints. 612
    Inspecting Variables and Their Associated Values in the Debugger 613
Handling Errors with try-catch 619
    Using the try-catch Syntax. 620
    Understanding the Error Types 622
    Using Multiple catch Blocks 622
    Example Using Only One catch Block. 622
    Example Showing Bad Practice of Using the Error Base Class in
        the First catch Block. 623
    Using the finally Statement 624
    Using the throw Statement 625
    Creating Your Own Error Classes 625

LESSON 26 **Profiling Flex Applications** **630**

Flash Player Memory Use. 632
    Flash Player Memory Allocation 632
    Passing by Reference or Value. 632
    Flash Player Garbage Collection 633
    Garbage Collection 636
Memory Profiling a Flex Application. 639
    Reviewing the ProfilerTest Application 639
    Profiling the ProfilerTest Application 642
    Fixing the ImageDisplay Class. 647
Performance Profiling a Flex Application. 648
    Profiling the ProfilerTest Application 648
    Fixing the ProfilerTest Class 651

APPENDIX A **Setup Instructions** **652**

Hardware Requirements 652
Software Requirements. 653
Software Installation. 653
Installing Flex Builder 654
Installing Lesson Files 654
Installing the ColdFusion Server 655
Starting the ColdFusion Server 655
Installing Flash Debug Player 656

Index **657**

Foreword

It was the beginning of the decade when Macromedia coined the term "rich Internet application" (RIA) to describe the future of applications. An RIA is a web experience that is engaging, interactive, lightweight, and flexible. RIAs offer the flexibility and ease of use of an intelligent desktop application, and to add the broad reach of traditional web applications. Adobe Flex has established itself as the premiere platform for delivering these experiences.

It is a great time to be a Flex developer. In June 2006 Adobe released Flex 2—a lineup of developer tools, libraries, and run-time services that enable developers everywhere to build and deploy RIAs that take advantage of Flash Player run time. Flex 2 has been hugely successful with tens of thousands of new developers, a vibrant community that shares tips, tricks, code, dozens of commercial and open source components, add-ons, and of course hundreds of new applications built, with more coming online every day. In the short lifetime of Flex 2, Flash Player 9 has followed the traditional penetration pattern of previous Flash Players reaching 90% by June 2007). Flex won its second Jolt Award, this year in the web development category.

We've also seen great success with LiveCycle Data Services, which enables developers to build applications that are not only rich in terms of user interface, but also in terms of how data flows between tiers, *and* also in terms of the innovative services these applications can offer. With features like LiveCycle ES application integration, PDF document generation, and integration with frameworks such as Hibernate and Spring, LiveCycle Data Services ES provides the ultimate solution for connecting RIAs to J2EE infrastructure.

With the latest release of Flex, Flex 3, we've decided to move to an open source model for the Flex SDK. Making Flex open source helps the platform reach the largest audience and allows the community to participate in all aspects of its development. The Flex community is fantastic, and its contributions to the product benefit all users.

All of this may be why you're here; it's time for you to learn how to use Flex to create great things. Fortunately, getting started with Flex is easy! Flex has a declarative markup language called MXML to help structure your application, and uses ActionScript 3.0 (an implementation of ECMAScript 4) to add all of the programming power you need. Your UI can even be customized using CSS. Although all of this can be coded by hand with your favorite text editor, Adobe Flex Builder 3 is a fantastic IDE that can help build a lot of your functionality faster.

In addition to learning the languages used by Flex (and when to use each), you'll want to learn about the powerful component library and the best way to leverage it in your applications. Flex provides layout containers, form controls, formatters and validators, an animation library, and much more to allow you to quickly build a powerful UI. And when Flex doesn't provide something out of the box, it's easy to build it yourself by extending what does exist.

It's not enough to have a pretty interface, your application needs to actually be functional, and often that means manipulating data. You'll find that Flex offers a variety of ways to connect to your backend data sources, from XML over HTTP, to SOAP web services, to an efficient remoting protocol called AMF. Flex also offers tight integration with LiveCycle Data Services, a powerful offering that makes it easy to manage large sets of data, especially when that data is shared among many users.

Flex 3 also introduces support for the Adobe Integrated Runtime, or AIR. AIR allows you to take the power of a web application and bring it to the desktop. With powerful HTML support and great integration with the desktop, like drag and drop, local file system access, and even an embedded SQL database, you'll be able to build RIAs like never before.

Finally, it's not enough to simply know about the pieces that make up a Flex application; you have to know how to use them well. *Adobe Flex 3: Training from the Source* draws from the expertise of its authors to present a number of lessons that will not only introduce you to the concepts of Flex, but help you use best practices. The topics move from introductory to advanced, but you'll be helped every step of the way with comprehensive step-by-step instructions and explanations.

I'd like to welcome you to the exciting world of Flex development. You'll find yourself quickly building applications that look better and do more than anything you've done before. But to get there you may need a guide, and you've chosen a fantastic one in *Adobe Flex 3: Training from the Source*.

We at Adobe can't wait to see what you build!

Matt Chotin
Product Manager
Adobe Systems, Inc.

Introduction

In March 2002, Macromedia coined the term *rich Internet application*. Back then, the idea felt somewhat futuristic; but, all that has changed. Rich Internet applications (RIAs) are today's reality.

Macromedia introduced Flex in 2004 to make it possible for developers to write applications for the nearly ubiquitous Flash platform. These applications can benefit from improved design, usability, and portability, dramatically changing the user experience for web applications. This is a cornerstone of the concept of Web 2.0, a new generation of Internet applications focused on creativity and collaboration.

Since then, Macromedia—and now Adobe—has released versions 1.5, 2, and 3 of Flex. With each subsequent version, creating rich, compelling, intuitive applications has gotten easier, and the bar has been raised on users' expectations of web applications. Countless organizations have discovered the benefits of Flex and have successfully built and deployed applications that run on top of the Flash platform.

But, despite the early Flex successes, Flex 1 and 1.5 were most definitely not a mass market product. The pricing, lack of IDE, limited deployment options, and other factors meant that the early versions of Flex were targeted specifically for larger and more complex applications, as well as for more sophisticated developers and development. However, with the new releases of the Flex product line, all this has changed.

Flex 2 was released in 2006 and made Flex development a possibility for many more people, as it included a free software development kit (SDK). With the open sourcing of Flex 3, and the announcement of free versions of Flex Builder for students, Flex development should be within the grasp of any developer with enough foresight to reach for it.

It is very easy to get yourself started with Flex. Flex itself is composed of two different languages: MXML, an XML-based markup language; and ActionScript, the language of Flash Player. MXML tags are easy to learn (especially when Flex Builder writes many of them for you). ActionScript has a steeper learning curve, but developers with prior programming and scripting experience will pick it up easily. But there is more to Flex development than MXML and ActionScript.

There are many concepts that need to be understood to be a successful Flex developer, including the following:

- How Flex applications should be built (and how they should not)

- Relationships between MXML and ActionScript, and when to use each

- Various ways to interact with back-end data, and the differences between each

- How to use the Flex components, and how to write your own

- Performance implications of the code you write and how to write it

- Best practices to write code that is scalable, manageable, and reusable (there is definitely more to Flex than MXML and ActionScript)

Developing these skills is where this book comes in. As the authors, we have distilled our hard-earned Flex expertise into a series of lessons that will jump-start your own Flex development. Starting with the basics, and then incrementally introducing additional functionality and know-how, the author team guides your journey into the exciting world of RIAs, ensuring success every step of the way.

Flex is powerful, highly capable, fun, and incredibly addictive. And *Adobe Flex 3: Training from the Source* is the ideal tour guide on your journey to the next generation of application development.

Adobe Flex 3: Training from the Source is an update to the extremely popular *Adobe Flex 2: Training from the Source*. Of course, we have done more than just tweak a few lines of code to ensure the same lessons work in the newest version; in fact, we have removed chapters that are now less applicable, and added several new ones on features such as modules, the Adobe Integrated Runtime (AIR), and the advanced DataGrid.

It is our sincere intention that both readers of the earlier book, as well those who are first exploring Flex with this book, will find this content equally compelling. Since the release of our previous book, several new announcements have come from Adobe about Flex, including:

- The release of the Flex 3 SDK under an open source license

- The introduction of BlazeDS, which contains many of the most frequently used features from LiveCycle Data Services (formerly Flex Data Services). BlazeDS will also be available under an open source license

- The introduction of AIR, which allows you to deploy both Flex and HTML/JS applications as standard desktop applications

- A greatly improved designer and developer workflow

- And much more

It's an incredible time to be an RIA developer, and we hope that this book provides you with all the tools you need to get started as a Flex Developer.

Prerequisites

To make the most of this book, you should at the very least understand web terminology. This book isn't designed to teach you anything more than Flex, so the better your understanding of the World Wide Web, the better off you'll be. This book is written assuming that you are comfortable working with programming languages and are probably working with a server-side language such as Java, .Net, PHP, ColdFusion, or a similar technology. Although knowledge of server-side technologies is not required to succeed with this book, there are many comparisons and analogies made to server-side web programming. This book is not intended as an introduction to programming or as an introduction to object-oriented programming (OOP). Experience with OOP is not required, although if you have no programming experience at all, you might find the materials too advanced.

Outline

As you'll soon discover, this book mirrors real-world practices as much as possible. Where certain sections of the book depart from what would be considered a real-world practice, every attempt has been made to inform you. The exercises are designed to get you using the tools and the interface quickly so that you can begin to work on projects of your own with as smooth a transition as possible.

This curriculum should take approximately 40–42 hours to complete and includes the following lessons:

Lesson 1: Understanding Rich Internet Applications
Lesson 2: Getting Started
Lesson 3: Laying Out the Interface
Lesson 4: Using Simple Controls
Lesson 5: Handling Events and Data Structures
Lesson 6: Using Remote XML Data with Controls
Lesson 7: Creating Components with MXML
Lesson 8: Using Controls and Repeaters with Datasets
Lesson 9: Using Custom Events
Lesson 10: Creating Custom Components with ActionScript 3.0
Lesson 11: Using DataGrids and Item Renderers
Lesson 12: Using Drag and Drop
Lesson 13: Implementing Navigation
Lesson 14: Using Formatters and Validators
Lesson 15: Implementing History Management and Deep Linking

Lesson 16: Customizing the Look and Feel of a Flex Application
Lesson 17: Working with Web Services
Lesson 18: Accessing Server-Side Objects
Lesson 19: Visualizing Data
Lesson 20: Creating Modular Applications
Lesson 21: Deploying Flex Applications
Lesson 22: Creating Transitions and Behaviors
Lesson 23: Printing from Flex
Lesson 24: Using Shared Objects
Lesson 25: Debugging Flex Applications
Lesson 26: Profiling Flex Applications
Appendix A: Setup Instructions

Technical Notes

Before getting started, you should follow the setup instructions in the appendix to ensure that you have the environment set up properly for use with this book.

Much of the data for the hands-on exercises is retrieved from www.flexgrocer.com. Of course, you must have an Internet connection to access this site. In lieu of this, you can start the ColdFusion server instance, as detailed in the appendix, "Setup Instructions," and change the URL from http://www.flexgrocer.com/ to http://localhost:8300/ and access the data locally. For example, in Lesson 6, "Using Remote XML Data with Controls," simply replace http://www.flexgrocer.com/units.xml with http://localhost:8300/units.xml to access the same XML data without an Internet connection.

Throughout the book, we use this wording: "Data type the function as void" or "Data type the function as String." This is just to make the instructions simpler; the authors realize the function itself is not data typed—what is really being data typed is the value the function returns.

Who Is This Book For?

All the content of this book should work equally well for users of Flex Builder 3 on Windows, Macintosh, or Linux.

The Project Application

Adobe Flex 3: Training from the Source includes many comprehensive tutorials designed to show you how to create a complete application using Flex 3. This application is an online grocery store that displays data and images and then submits completed orders to the server. It includes an executive Dashboard to enable store managers to view real-time graphs showing sales details, as well as a data-entry application for adding or editing the products sold by the grocery.

By the end of the book, you will have built an entire website using Flex. You will begin by learning the fundamentals of Flex and understanding how Flex Builder can be used to aid in developing applications. In the early lessons, you will make use of Design mode to begin laying out the application, but as you progress through the book and become more comfortable with the languages used by Flex, you will spend more and more time working in Source mode, which gives you the full freedom and flexibility of directly working with code. By the end of the book, you should be fully comfortable working with the Flex languages and could probably be able to work without Flex Builder by using the open source Flex SDK and its command-line compiler.

Standard Elements in the Book

Each lesson in this book begins by outlining the major focus of the lesson at hand and introducing new features. Learning objectives and the approximate time needed to complete all the exercises are also listed at the beginning of each lesson. The projects are divided into exercises that explain the importance of each skill you learn. Every lesson will build on the concepts and techniques used in the previous lessons.

 TIP: Alternative ways to perform tasks and suggestions to consider when applying the skills you are learning.

✳ NOTE: Additional background information to expand your knowledge and advanced techniques you can explore to further develop your skills.

▼ CAUTION: Information warning you of situations you might encounter that could cause errors, problems, or unexpected results.

Boldface text: Words that appear in **boldface** are terms that you must type while working through the steps in the lessons.

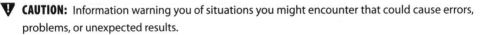

Boldface code: Lines of code that appear in boldface within code blocks help you easily identify changes in the block to be made in a specific step in an exercise.

```
<mx:HorizontalList dataProvider="{dp}"
    labelFunction="multiDisplay"
    columnWidth="130"
    width="850"/>
```

Code in text: Code or keywords appear slightly different from the rest of the text so you can identify them.

Code block: To help you easily identify ActionScript, XML, and HTML code within the book, the code has been styled in a special font that's unique from the rest of the text. Single lines of code that are longer than the margins of the page allow wrap to the next line. They are designated by an arrow at the beginning of the continuation of a broken line and are indented under the line from which they continue. For example:

```
public function Product (_catID:Number, _prodName:String, _unitID:Number,
    ➡ _cost:Number, _listPrice:Number, _description:String,_isOrganic:Boolean,
    ➡ _isLowFat:Boolean, _imageName:String)
```

Italicized text: Words that appear in *italics* are either for *emphasis* or are *new vocabulary*.

Italics are also used on placeholders, in which the exact entry may change depending on your situation. For example: *driveroot*:/flex3tfs/flexGrocer, where the *driveroot* is dependent on your operating system.

Menu commands and keyboard shortcuts: There are often multiple ways to perform the same task in Flex Builder. The different options will be pointed out in each lesson. Menu commands are shown with angle brackets between the menu names and commands: Menu > Command > Subcommand. Keyboard shortcuts are shown with a plus sign between the names of keys to indicate that you should press the keys simultaneously; for example, Shift+Tab means that you should press the Shift and Tab keys at the same time.

Appendix: This book includes one appendix that will guide you through the steps to set up the working environment required to execute the exercises in this book.

CD-ROM: The CD-ROM included with this book includes all the media files, starting files, and completed projects for each of the lessons in the book. These files are located in the assets, start, or complete directories, respectively. Lesson 1, "Understanding Rich Internet Applications," does not include tasks; however, the CD-ROM includes media in the directory Lesson01. This media provides the flexGrocer directory for your project. At any point if you need to return to the original source material, you can restore the flexGrocer project. Some lessons include an intermediate directory, which contains files in various stages of development in the lesson. Any time you want to reference one of the files being built in a lesson to verify that you are correctly executing the steps in the exercises, you will find the files organized on the CD-ROM under the corresponding lesson. For example, the files for Lesson 4 are located on the CD-ROM in the Lesson04 folder.

The directory structure of the lessons you will be working with is as follows:

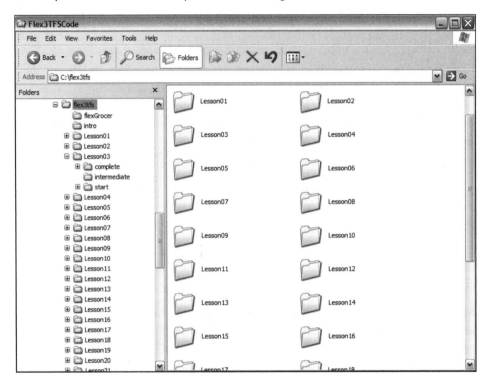

Adobe Training from the Source

The *Adobe Training from the Source* and *Advanced Training from the Source* series are developed in association with Adobe and reviewed by the product support teams. Ideal for active learners, the books in the *Training from the Source* series offer hands-on instruction designed to provide you with a solid grounding in the program's fundamentals. If you learn best by doing, this is the series for you. Each *Training from the Source* title contains hours of instruction on Adobe software products. They are designed to teach the techniques that you need to create sophisticated professional-level projects. Each book includes a CD-ROM that contains all the files used in the lessons, completed projects for comparison, and more.

Adobe Authorized Training and Certification

This book is geared to enable you to study at your own pace with content from the source. Other training options exist through the Adobe Authorized Training Partner program. Get up to speed in a matter of days with task-oriented courses taught by Adobe Certified Instructors. Or learn on your own with interactive online training from Adobe University. All these sources of training will prepare you to become an Adobe Certified Developer.

For more information about authorized training and certification, check out www.adobe.com/training/.

What You Will Learn

You will develop the skills you need to create and maintain your own Flex applications as you work through these lessons.

By the end of the course, you will be able to:

- Use Flex Builder to build Flex applications
- Understand MXML, ActionScript 3.0, and the interactions of the two
- Work with complex sets of data
- Load data from a server using XML, web services, and Remote objects
- Handle events to allow interactivity in an application
- Create your own custom events
- Create your own components, either in MXML or ActionScript 3.0
- Apply styles and skins to customize the look and feel of an application
- Add charts to an application
- Deploy your apps to the web or the desktop
- And much more…

Minimum System Requirements

Windows

- Intel Pentium 4 processor

- 1 GB of RAM recommended

- Microsoft Windows XP (with Service Pack 2) or Microsoft Vista Home Premium or higher

- 500 MB (stand-alone) of available hard-disk space to install

- Java Virtual Machine: Sun JRE 1.4.2, Sun JRE 1.5 (included), IBM JRE 1.5, Sun JRE 1.6 or later

- Flash Player 9 (9.0.30) or higher

Macintosh

- G4 1.25 GHz PowerPC or Intel-based Mac

- OS X 10.4.7 or later

- 1 GB of RAM recommended

- 500 MB of available hard-disk space to install

- Java Virtual Machine: JRE 1.5 or JRE 1.6 from Apple

- Flash Player 9 (9.0.30) or higher

The Flex line of products is extremely exciting, and we're waiting to be amazed by what you will do with it. With a strong foundation in Flex, you can grow and expand your set of skills quickly. Flex is really not too difficult to use for anyone with programming experience. With a little bit of initiative and effort, you can fly through the following lessons and be building your own custom applications and sites in no time.

What You Will Learn

In this lesson, you will:

- Explore alternatives to page-based architecture
- See the benefits of rich Internet applications (RIAs)
- Compare RIA technologies

Approximate Time

This lesson takes approximately 30 minutes to complete.

Lesson Files

Media Files:

None

Starting Files:

None

Completed Files:

None

Understanding Rich Internet Applications

Computers have played a role in business environments for more than four decades. Throughout that time, the roles of the client and server have constantly evolved. As businesses and their employees have become more comfortable delegating responsibilities to computers, the look, feel, and architecture of computerized business applications have changed to meet the new demands. This evolving process continues today, as businesses are demanding faster, lighter, and richer Internet applications. In this lesson, you will learn about this evolving nature and understand the business requirements that push us to build rich Internet applications (RIAs).

You will use Flex to build the FlexGrocer application seen here.

Understanding the Evolution of Computer Applications

In the earliest days of computerized business applications, all processing took place on mainframes, with the client having no role other than displaying information from the server and accepting user input. This was largely dictated by the high cost of processing power. It simply was not affordable to spread powerful clients throughout the enterprise, so all processing was consolidated, and "dumb terminals" provided the user interaction.

As memory and processing power became cheaper, dumb terminals were replaced by microcomputers (or personal computers). With the added power available, more desktop applications, such as word processors and spreadsheets, could run as stand-alone applications, so no server was necessary. One challenge faced by organizations with microcomputers was a lack of centralized data. Although the mainframe era had everything centralized, the age of the microcomputer distributed data, adding many challenges for centralizing business rules and synchronizing data across the enterprise.

To help resolve this issue, several vendors released platforms that sought to combine the strengths of the microcomputer with those of the mainframe, which led to the birth of client/server systems. These platforms afforded end users the power and ease of microcomputers while allowing for business logic and data to be stored and accessed from a centralized location—which solved the problems of the day. The new challenge introduced with the client/server systems was distribution. Any time changes needed to be made to client applications, IT departments had to manually reinstall or upgrade the software on every single desktop computer. Many companies found they needed a full-time IT staff whose primary responsibility was keeping the software on the end users' desktops current.

With the explosive growth of the Internet in the 1990s, a new model for business applications became available. This model worked by having a web browser act as a thin client, whose primary job was to render HTML and send requests back to an application server that dynamically composed and delivered pages to the client. This is often referred to as a "page-based architecture." This model successfully solved the distribution problem of the client/server days; the application was downloaded from the server each time an end user needed it, so updates could be made in a single centralized place and automatically distributed to the entire user base. This model was and continues to be successful for many applications; however, it also creates significant drawbacks and limitations. In reality, Internet applications bore a great resemblance to mainframe applications, in that all the processing was centralized at the server, and the client only rendered data and captured user feedback. The biggest problems with this surrounded the user interface (UI). Many of the conveniences that end users grew to accept over the previous decade were lost, and the UI was limited by the capabilities of HTML. For example, desktop software as well as client/server applications frequently use the drag-and-drop feature. However, HTML (Hypertext Markup Language) applications almost never use the feature, due to the complexities and lack of cross-browser support for the DHTML (Dynamic HTML) elements which are required to implement drag-and-drop in a pure HTML/DHTML solution.

In most cases, the overall sophistication of the solutions that could be built and delivered was greatly reduced. Although the web has offered great improvements in the ease and speed of deploying applications, the capabilities of web-based business applications took a big step backward because browser-based applications had to adapt to the limitations of the web architecture: HTML and Hypertext Transport Protocol (HTTP).

Today, the demands for Internet-based applications continue to grow and are often quite different from the demands of the mid-1990s. End users and businesses are demanding more from their investments in Internet technology. The capability to deliver true value to users is forcing many companies to look toward richer models for Internet applications—models that combine the media-rich power of the traditional desktop with the deployment and content-rich nature of web applications.

As Internet applications begin to be used for core business functionality, the maintainability of those applications becomes more crucial. The maintainability of an application is directly related to the application's architecture. Sadly, many web applications were built with little thought about the principles of application architecture and are therefore difficult to maintain and extend. Today, it is easier to build a solid architecture for an application by providing a clean separation between the business, data access, and presentation areas. With the introduction of elements such as Web Services, the concept of a service-oriented architecture (SOA) has become more feasible for web-based applications.

To meet the demands of businesses, RIAs should be able to do the following:

- Provide an efficient, high-performance runtime for executing code, content, and communications. In the next section of this lesson, you will explore the limitations of the standard HTML-based applications and learn that traditional page-based architectures have a number of performance-related challenges.

- Provide powerful and extensible object models to facilitate interactivity. Web browsers have progressed in recent years in their capability to support interactivity through the Document Object Model (DOM) via JavaScript and DHTML, but they still lack standardized cross-platform and cross-browser support. Building RIAs with these tools so they will work on a variety of browsers and operating systems involves creating multiple versions of the same application.

- Enable using server-side objects via Web Services or other similar technologies. The promise of RIAs includes the capability to cleanly separate presentation logic and user interfaces from the application logic housed on the server.

- Enable use of Internet applications when "offline." As laptops and other portable devices continue to grow in popularity, one of the serious limitations of Internet applications is the requirement that the machine running the application be connected to the Internet. Although users can be online the vast majority of the time, business travelers know there are times when an Internet connection is not possible. A successful RIA should enable users to be productive with or without an active connection.

Breaking Away from Page-Based Architecture

For experienced web developers, one of the biggest challenges in building RIAs is breaking away from a page-based architecture. Traditional web applications are centered on the concept of a web page. Regardless which server-side technologies (if any) are used, the flow goes something like this:

1. User opens a browser and requests a page from a web server.

2. Web server receives request.

3. (optional) Web server hands request to an application server to dynamically assemble page, or

4. (optional) Web server retrieves static page from file system.

5. Web server sends page (dynamic or static) back to browser.

6. Browser draws page in place of whatever was previously displayed.

Even in situations when most of the content of the previous page is identical to the new page, the entire new page needs to be sent to the browser and rendered. This is one of the inefficiencies of traditional web applications: each user interaction requires a new page loading in the browser. One of the key goals of RIAs is to reduce the amount of extra data transmitted with each request. Rather than download an entire page, why not download only the data that changed and update the page the user is viewing? This is the way standard desktop or client/ server applications work.

Although this goal seems simple and is readily accepted by developers taking their first plunge into RIA development, often web developers bring a page-based mindset to RIAs and struggle to understand how to face the challenges from the page-based world, such as how to "maintain state." For example, after users log in, how do we know who they are and what they are allowed to do as they navigate around the application?

Maintaining state was a challenge introduced by web-based applications. HTTP was designed as a stateless protocol, in which each request to the server was an atomic unit that knew nothing about previous requests. This stateless nature of the web allowed for greater efficiency and redundancy because a connection did not need to be held open between the browser and server. Each new page request lasted only as long as the server spent retrieving and sending the page, allowing a single server to handle far more simultaneous requests.

The stateless nature of the web added challenges for application developers. Usually, applications need to remember information about the user: login permissions, items added to a shopping cart, and so on. Without the capability to remember this data from one request to the next, true application development would not be possible. To help solve this problem, a series of solutions was implemented, revolving around a unique token being sent back to the server with each request (often as cookies, which are small text files containing application-specific identifiers for an individual user) and having the server store the user's information.

Unlike traditional web applications, RIAs can bypass many of these problems. Because the application remains in client RAM the entire time it's used (instead of being loaded and unloaded like a page-based model), variables can be set once and accessed throughout the application's life cycle.

A different approach to handling state is just one of many places in which building applications requires a slightly different mindset than web application development. In reality, web-based RIAs bear more resemblance to client/server applications than they do to web applications.

Identifying the Advantages of Rich Internet Applications

Unlike the dot-com boom days of the mid-to-late 1990s, businesses are no longer investing in Internet technologies simply because they are "cool." To succeed, a new technology must demonstrate real return on investment and truly add value. RIAs achieve this on several levels: They reduce development costs and add value throughout the organization.

Business Managers

By making it easier for users to work with software, the number of successful transactions is increasing. This increase occurs across many industries and can be quantified by businesses with metrics, such as increased productivity using intranet applications or increased percentage of online shoppers who complete a purchase. More productive employees can drastically reduce labor costs while growing online sales increase revenue and decrease opportunities lost to competitors.

IT Organizations

Breaking away from page-based architectures reduces the load on web servers and reduces overall network traffic. Rather than transmitting entire pages over and over again, the entire application is downloaded once; then, the only communication back and forth with the server is the data to be presented on the page. By reducing server load and network traffic, infrastructure costs can be noticeably reduced. RIAs developed using sound architectural principles and best practices can also greatly increase the maintainability of an application as well as greatly reduce the development time to build the application.

End Users

End users experience the greatest benefits of RIAs. A well-designed RIA greatly reduces users' frustration levels because they no longer need to navigate several pages to find what they need nor have to wait for a new page to load before continuing to be productive. Additionally, the time users spend learning how to use the application can be greatly reduced, further empowering them. Today, there are a number of excellent applications that would not be possible without the concepts of an RIA, such as the Harley Davidson Motorcycle Configurator and Virtual Ubiquity's Buzzword applications. These easy-to-use applications provide excellent examples of the ease of use an RIA can offer an end user.

RIA Technologies

Today, developers have several technology choices when they start building RIAs. Among the more popular choices are HTML-based options, such as AJAX (Asynchronous JavaScript and XML), as well as plug-in-based options, such as Adobe Flash, Adobe Flex, and others that run in Flash Player. Also, new options from Microsoft have arrived, as Windows Presentation Foundation (WPF), Silverlight, and XAML (Extensible Application Markup Language) are now a reality.

There are four different runtimes on which the current RIA landscape is based: AJAX, Flash Player, Windows Presentation Foundation (WPF), and Java, which is used by AWT (Active Window Toolkit), Swing, and Eclipse RCP. It seems that both the Java and WPF solutions are taking aim at desktop applications rather than RIAs, although they could be used for RIAs as well. More recently, Adobe announced Flash Player support for desktop applications with the upcoming Adobe Integrated Runtime (AIR), which is discussed in more detail in Lesson 21, "Deploying Flex Applications to the Desktop."

Asynchronous JavaScript and XML (AJAX)

One of the easier choices to understand (but not necessarily to implement) is AJAX, the acronym for Asynchronous JavaScript and XML. AJAX is based on tools already familiar to web developers: HTML, DHTML, and JavaScript. The fundamental idea behind AJAX is to use JavaScript to update the page without reloading it. A JavaScript program running in the browser can insert new data into the page or change its structure by manipulating the HTML DOM without reloading a new page. Updates may involve new data loaded from the server in the background (using XML or other formats) or in response to user interaction, such as a click or hover.

Early web applications used Java applets for remote communication. As browser technologies developed, other means, such as the use of IFrames, replaced the applets. In recent years, XMLHttpRequest was introduced into JavaScript, facilitating data transfers without the need for a new page request, applet, or IFrame.

In addition to the benefit of AJAX using elements already familiar to many web application developers, AJAX requires no external plug-in to run. It works purely on the browser's capability to use JavaScript and DHTML. However, the reliance on JavaScript poses one of the new liabilities of AJAX: It fails to work if the user has JavaScript disabled in the browser.

Another issue with AJAX is that it has varying levels of support for DHTML and JavaScript in different browsers on different platforms. For applications in which the target audience can be controlled (such as intranet applications), AJAX can be written to support a single browser on a particular platform (many businesses today have standardized browsers and operating systems). However, when applications are opened to larger audiences (such as extranet and Internet applications), AJAX applications need to be tested (and often modified) to ensure that they run identically in all browsers on all operating systems.

AJAX is not likely to go away any time soon, and each day increasingly more high-profile AJAX applications are launched with great acclaim (such as Google Maps).

It should be noted that AJAX is not actually a programming model in and of itself. It is really a collection of various JavaScript libraries. Some of these libraries include reusable components designed to make common tasks easier. Although AJAX lacks a centralized vendor, integrating these libraries introduces dependencies on third parties, which assumes a certain amount of risk.

Flash

One of the key competitive runtimes in the RIA space is the Adobe Flash Platform. The Flash Platform is currently the key competitor to AJAX for RIAs. Originally written as a plug-in to run animations, Flash Player has evolved over the years, with each new version adding new capabilities while still maintaining a very small footprint. Over the past decade, Flash Player has gained near ubiquity, with some version of it installed in more than 97 percent of all web browsers. Since 2002, Macromedia (now part of Adobe) began focusing on Flash as more than an animation tool. And with the Flash 6 release, Macromedia began providing more capabilities for building applications. Macromedia found that with the combination of the ubiquity of the player and the power available from its scripting language (ActionScript), developers could build full browser-based applications and get around the limitations of HTML.

By targeting Flash Player, developers could also break away from browser and platform incompatibilities. One of the many nice features of Flash Player is that content and applications developed for any particular version of Flash Player will (usually) run on any platform/browser that supported that version of the player. With very few exceptions, that remains true today.

Historically, the biggest drawback of building applications for the Flash Player was the authoring environment, which was clearly built as an animation tool for users creating interactive content. Many developers who wanted to build RIAs for Flash Player were thwarted by the unfamiliarity of the tools. This, coupled with the scant materials available in 2002 for learning to use Flash as an application platform, kept many serious developers from successfully building Flash applications.

Although Flash Player remains an excellent platform for RIAs, the introduction of solutions such as Flex have greatly simplified the development process and reduced the number of RIAs developed solely in Flash Studio.

Flex

Sensing the need for more developer-friendly tools for building RIAs, Adobe (then Macromedia) developed a language and compiler that enabled developers to work with familiar languages from which their compiler could create applications to run in Flash Player. In 2004, Macromedia released Flex 1.0 (followed by Flex 1.5 in 2005). Adobe continued this cycle releasing Flex 2.0 and Flex 3.0 in 2006 and 2008, respectively. Architecturally, Flex applications are similar to AJAX applications, in that both are capable of dynamic updates to the user interface and both include the ability to send and load data in the background.

Flex now provides the next generation of developer tools and services that enable developers everywhere to build and deploy RIAs on the Flash platform.

Flex consists of several pieces:

- **ActionScript 3.0**—A powerful object-oriented programming language that advances the capabilities of the Flash platform. ActionScript 3.0 is designed to create a language ideally suited for building RIAs rapidly. Although earlier versions of ActionScript offered the power and flexibility required for creating engaging online experiences, ActionScript 3.0 further advances the language, improving performance and ease of development to facilitate even the most complex applications with large datasets and fully object-oriented, reusable code.

- **Flash Player 9 (FP9)**—Building on Flash Player 8, this next generation of Flash Player focuses on improving script execution. To facilitate this improvement, FP9 includes a brand new, highly optimized ActionScript Virtual Machine (AVM), known as AVM2. AVM2 is built from the ground up to work with ActionScript 3.0, the next generation of the language that powers Flash Player. The new virtual machine is significantly faster and supports runtime error reporting and greatly improved debugging. Flash Player 9 will also contain AVM1, which executes ActionScript 1.0 and 2.0 code for backward compatibility with existing and legacy content. Unlike applications built using JavaScript, Flash Player is capable of using a Just In Time (JIT) compilation process, which enables it to run faster and consume less memory.

- **Flex SDK**—Using the foundation provided by FP9 and ActionScript 3.0, the framework adds an extensive class library to enable developers to easily use the best practices for building successful RIAs. Flex uses an XML-based language called MXML to provide developers with a declarative way to manage the elements of an application. Developers can get access to Flex framework through Flex Builder or the free Flex SDK, which includes a command-line compiler and debugger, allowing developers to use any editor they prefer and still be able to access the compiler or debugger directly. In 2007, Adobe announced the road map to open sourcing the Flex SDK, which should be complete some time in 2008.

- **Flex Builder 3**—Building on the success of Flex Builder 2, which provides developers with an environment specifically built for building RIAs, Flex Builder 3 takes the IDE to the next level. Built on top of the industry standard, open-source Eclipse project, Flex Builder 3 provides an excellent coding and debugging environment, is a rich and useful design tool, and promotes best practices in coding and application development. Another benefit of the Eclipse platform is that it provides a rich set of extensibility capabilities, so customizations can easily be written to extend the IDE to meet specific developers' needs or preferences.

The Windows Presentation Foundation, XAML, Silverlight, and Expression

Microsoft has released a set of tools to help developers build RIAs on the Windows platform. The new system consists of the following:

- **WPF**—The Windows Presentation Foundation (formerly code-named Avalon). WPF is analogous to the Flash Player and Flex frameworks.

- **XAML**—Extensible Application Markup Language. The XML-based language in which you can build WPF applications. XAML is analogous to Flex's MXML language.

- **Silverlight**—A web-based subset of WPF, which allows for the use of XAML and Java-Script for creating rich web applications.

- **Microsoft Expression**—A professional design tool designed to work with XAML and enable interaction designers to create the user interface and visual behavior for WPF applications. This is roughly analogous to Flash Studio, as a design tool for WPF applications.

With these tools, Microsoft is promoting a workflow in which designers create compelling user interfaces with Expression (using WPF or Silverlight), and then developers can implement the business and data access logic using Visual Studio.

While Microsoft has publicly stated it will provide support for other platforms (specifically with Silverlight), specific information, such as which browsers and platforms will be supported, has not been forthcoming. It is encouraging to see Microsoft finally promising to provide tools for platforms other than Windows, but it's too soon to see how they will live up to that promise.

Assuming that the cross-platform promise is met, Silverlight may someday offer a very compelling platform, in that developers can leverage integration with Visual Studio, which many developers already use. Microsoft also has a separate design tool specifically for designers, called Expression. It is also worth noting that it is likely to be a long time before WPF reaches any kind of ubiquity—even on Windows—because of the large download required. WPF is available for Windows XP, but requires an external install of the .Net framework 3, and is available natively in Windows Vista.

What You Have Learned

In this lesson, you have:

- Explored the evolution of computer applications (pages 4–6)
- Explored alternatives to page-based architecture (pages 6–7)
- Explored the benefits of RIAs (pages 7–8)
- Compared RIA technologies (pages 8–12)

What You Will Learn

In this lesson, you will:

- Create a new project and three main application files
- Understand the different parts of the Flex Builder workbench: editors, views, and perspectives
- Code, save, and run application files
- Use some of the features in Flex Builder 3 that make application development faster and easier, such as code hinting and local history
- Work in both Source mode and Design mode
- Use various views, such as the Navigator view, Components view, and Flex Properties view

Approximate Time

This lesson takes approximately 1 hour and 30 minutes to complete.

Lesson Files

Media Files:

None

Starting Files:

None

Completed Files:

Lesson02/complete/DataEntry.mxml
Lesson02/complete/Dashboard.mxml
Lesson02/complete/EComm.mxml

LESSON 2

Getting Started

You're ready to start your adventure of learning Adobe Flex, and the first thing to do is become familiar with the environment in which you will be developing your applications. This environment is Adobe Flex Builder 3, which is based on the Eclipse platform. The Eclipse platform is an open source, integrated development environment (IDE) that can be extended. Flex Builder 3 has extended and customized Eclipse for building Flex applications.

In this lesson, you become familiar with Adobe Flex Builder 3 by building the main application files of the FlexGrocer application that you will be working on throughout this book. By building the three basic files of the FlexGrocer application, you will learn about the Flex Builder 3 interface and how to create, run, and save application files. You will also discover some of the many features Flex Builder 3 offers to make application development easier.

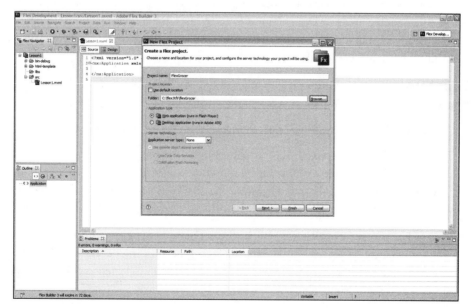

Creating a new Project in Flex Builder 3

Getting Started with Flex Application Development

Before a building can be built, the foundation must be laid. This lesson is that foundation for further Flex development. You will finish this lesson knowing how to manipulate the Flex Builder 3 workbench in ways that make the process of Flex development easier and faster. Along the way you will create the three main application files that define the major sections of the FlexGrocer application.

Part of the study of any new body of knowledge is learning a basic vocabulary, and in this lesson you will learn the basic vocabulary of both Flex development and Flex Builder. You will understand terms such as *view*, *perspective*, and *editor* in relationship to the Flex Builder workbench. You also will understand the terms describing the processes—and the processes themselves—that transform the text entered in Flex Builder into the type of file you can view with your browser using Flash Player.

Creating a Project and an MXML Application

In this first exercise, you will create a Flex application. To do so, you must first create a project in Flex Builder. A project is nothing more than a collection of files and folders that help you organize your work. All the files you create for the FlexGrocer application will be in this project. You'll also see that you have two choices when working with an application file: You can work in either Source mode or Design mode. In most cases, the mode you choose will be a personal preference, but there are times when some functionality will be available to you only when you are in a particular mode.

Also in this exercise, you will run the Flex application. You'll discover how the MXML code you write is turned into a SWF file that is viewed in a browser.

1 Start Flex Builder 3 by choosing Start > Programs > Adobe > Adobe Flex Builder 3.

This is most likely the way you will start Flex Builder. There is a possibility that you have Eclipse already installed on your computer and that you have previously added the Flex functionality using the plug-in configuration. In that case, you need to open Eclipse as you have before.

2 Choose File > New > Flex Project. For the Project name, enter **FlexGrocer**. Deselect the "Use default location" check box, and for the Folder location enter ***driveroot:/flex3tfs/flexGrocer***. Be sure that the Web Application radio button is selected and the Application server type is set to None, then click Next.

NOTE: *driveroot* is a placeholder for the root drive of the operating system you are using, either Windows or Mac. Replace *driveroot* with the appropriate path. Also, note that the directory name is case sensitive.

The project name should reflect the files contained in the project. As you continue your work with Flex Builder, you'll soon have many projects, and the project names will help remind you which files are in each project.

Do not accept the Default location entry. The default uses your My Documents directory and places files very deep in the directory structure. For simplicity's sake, you are putting your working files right on the root drive.

Flex Builder 3 allows you to choose whether to use the most recent compiler (the default choice), or one from a previous version. For this application, you should use the most recent compiler.

3 Leave the output folder for the Compiled Flex application as bin-debug. Then click Next.

At this time, there is no need to change this default.

4 For the Main application file enter **DataEntry.mxml**.

By default, Flex Builder gives the main application file the same name as your project name. You do not want that in this case. Flex Builder automatically creates the main application file for you and includes the basic structure of a Flex application file.

✲ NOTE: MXML is a case-sensitive language. Be sure to follow the case of filenames in tags shown in this book. At the end of this lesson, there will be a short discussion on how object-oriented programming affects some of the case usage for filenames, tags, and properties.

5 Click Finish and see the project and application file that were created.

Here you see your first Flex application. Currently the application is displayed in Source mode. Later in this lesson, you will also look at this application in Design mode.

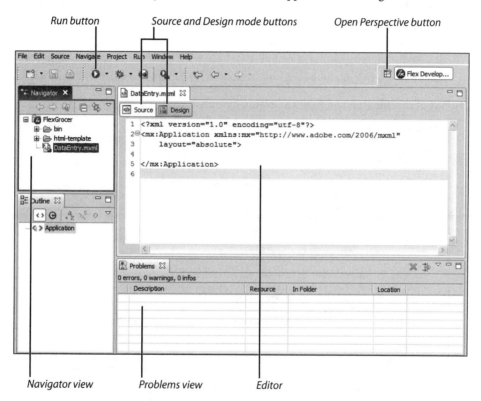

Run button   Source and Design mode buttons   Open Perspective button

Navigator view   Problems view   Editor

The default application file contains some elements you need to understand. The first line of code (<?xml version="1.0" encoding="utf-8"?>) is an XML document type declaration. Because MXML is an XML standard language, the document declaration must be included.

The second line of code (<mx:Application xmlns:mx="http://www.adobe.com/2006/ mxml"layout="absolute">) defines a Flex main application page. The <mx:Application> tag represents the outside container, or holder of all the content in the Flex application. You can have only one <mx:Application> tag per Flex application.

Inside the <mx:Application> tag, the attribute/value pair that appears to hold the URL xmlns:mx="http://www.adobe.com/2006/mxml" is defining a namespace for your Flex tags.

This code defines the mx prefix to be associated with a set of tags. The value of the attribute that looks like a URL is actually what is referred to as a Universal Resource Identifier (URI) in XML terminology. In a configuration file like flex-config.xml, an association is made between this URI and what is called a manifest file. The manifest file contains all the legal tags that can be used with the mx prefix. In a standard Flex Builder on a PC, the manifest file is found at this location: *installationdirectory*/Adobe/Flex Builder 3/ sdks/3.0.0/frameworks/mxml-manifest.xml. On a Mac, the manifest file is found at: *installationdirectory*/Adobe Flex Builder 3/sdks/3.0.0/frameworks/mxml-manifest.xml.

Part of that file is shown in the following figure.

```
mxml-manifest.xml  ✕
<?xml version="1.0"?>
<componentPackage>

    <component id="Accordion" class="mx.containers.Accordion"/>
    <component id="AddChildAction" class="mx.effects.AddChildAction"/>
    <component id="AnimateProperty" class="mx.effects.AnimateProperty"/>
    <component id="Application" class="mx.core.Application"/>
    <component id="ApplicationControlBar" class="mx.containers.ApplicationControlBar"/>
    <component id="ArrayCollection" class="mx.collections.ArrayCollection"/>
    <component id="Blur" class="mx.effects.Blur"/>
    <component id="Box" class="mx.containers.Box"/>
    <component id="Button" class="mx.controls.Button"/>
    <component id="ButtonBar" class="mx.controls.ButtonBar"/>
    <component id="Canvas" class="mx.containers.Canvas"/>
    <component id="CheckBox" class="mx.controls.CheckBox"/>
    <component id="ColorPicker" class="mx.controls.ColorPicker"/>
    <component id="ComboBox" class="mx.controls.ComboBox"/>
    <component id="Container" class="mx.core.Container"/>
    <component id="ControlBar" class="mx.containers.ControlBar"/>
    <component id="CurrencyFormatter" class="mx.formatters.CurrencyFormatter"/>
    <component id="CurrencyValidator" class="mx.validators.CurrencyValidator"/>
    <component id="CreditCardValidator" class="mx.validators.CreditCardValidator"/>
    <component id="DataGrid" class="mx.controls.DataGrid"/>
```

Finally, layout="absolute" defines how this application page laid out its children or what is on the page. With an *absolute* layout you specify *x*- and *y*-coordinates to position all children of the application. Other valid choices for the layout's value are vertical and horizontal. A *vertical* layout means all children of the application run vertically down the application's page, and *horizontal* means they run horizontally across the application's page. As you continue to develop in Flex you will use a combination of layouts to gain the look you want.

Understanding the Flex Builder 3 Workbench

Before you do any more work on your application file, you should first become more familiar with the Flex Builder *workbench*, which is all you see in Flex Builder. There are a number of terms you should become familiar with concerning this interface. For instance, you will learn in this exercise what *views*, *editors*, and *perspectives* mean in the workbench.

1 Close the current editor by clicking the *x* on the right side of the DataEntry.mxml editor tab. All editors will have a tab on the top left of the editor area.

Whenever you have a file open, it is opened in the workbench in what is called an editor. You just closed the editor containing the DataEntry.mxml file. You can have many editors open at once in the workbench, and each will contain a file with code in it.

2 Open the editor containing the DataEntry.mxml file from the Navigator view by double-clicking the filename.

You can also open the file by right-clicking the filename and choosing Open.

3 Make the editor expand in width and height by double-clicking the editor tab.

There will be times when you want to see as much of your code as possible, especially because Flex Builder does not wrap text. Simply double-clicking the editor tab expands the editor in both width and height, showing as much code as possible.

4 Restore the editor to its previous size by double-clicking the tab again.

As you see, you can easily switch between expanded and nonexpanded editors.

5 Click the Design mode button in the editor to view the application in Design mode.

The workbench looks radically different in Design mode, which allows you to drag and drop user interface controls into the application. You will also be able to set property values in Design mode. Obviously, Design mode also lets you see your application more as it will look to an end user.

6 Return to Source mode by clicking the Source button in the editor.

Most frequently, you will be using Source mode in this book, but some tasks are better performed in Design mode.

7 Close the Navigator view by clicking the *x* on the Navigator tab. Just like editors, all views also have tabs in the top left of the particular view.

In Flex Builder 3, the different sections displaying content are all called *views*.

8 Reopen the Navigator view by choosing Window > Project Navigator.

After you close a view you can reopen that view from this menu. There are many views; in fact, if you choose Window > Other Views you'll see a window with many of the views displayed.

9 Click the Open Perspective button just above the top right of the editor, and choose the Flex Debugging perspective.

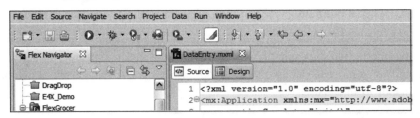

A *perspective* is nothing more than a layout of views that you want to use repeatedly. Flex Builder comes with built-in Flex Development and Flex Debugging perspectives. You can create a layout from your own set of views and save it as a perspective that can be recalled at any time.

10 Return to the Flex Development perspective.

As you can see, it is easy to switch between perspectives. Later in the book, you'll be using the Debugging perspective and discovering its many helpful options.

11 If they are not showing, turn on code line numbers by choosing Window > Preferences. In the dialog box, click the plus signs (+) in front of General and then Editors. Finally, click Text Editors and click the check box for Show Line Numbers.

Line numbers are useful because Flex Builder reports errors using line numbers.

> **TIP:** You can also turn on line numbers by right-clicking in the marker bar of the editor and selecting Show Line Numbers. The marker bar is the area just to the left of where the code is displayed in the editor.

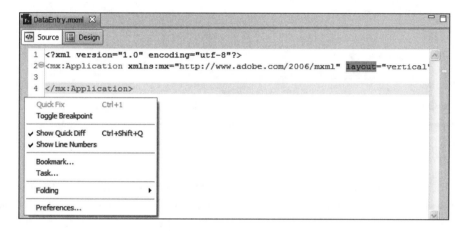

Running Your Application

In the first exercise, you created your project and an application page. Before you had a chance to run the application, the second exercise took you on a tour of the Flex Builder workbench. You will now get back to your application. You will run it, add code to it, and learn the basics of file manipulation.

1 Open the Project menu. Be sure the Build Automatically option has a checkmark in front of it.

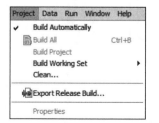

When Build Automatically is selected, Flex continually checks your saved files, compiles them upon saving, and prepares them to run. Syntax errors are flagged even before you run your application, which does not occur if Build Automatically is not selected.

> **TIP:** As your applications grow more complex, you might find that having this setting selected takes too much time, in which case you should deselect this setting, and the build will happen only when you run your application.

2 Run your application by clicking the Run button. You will not see anything in the browser window when it opens.

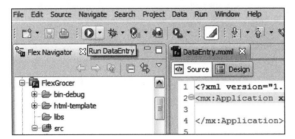

You have now run your first Flex application, and it wasn't that interesting. In this case, the skeleton application contained no tags to display anything in the browser. But you did see the application run, and you saw the default browser open and display the results, as uninteresting as it was.

> **NOTE:** What exactly happened when you pushed the Run button? Actually, a number of processes occurred. First, the XML tags in the application file were translated to ActionScript. ActionScript was then used to generate a SWF file, which is the format Flash Player understands. The SWF file was then sent to Flash Player in the browser.

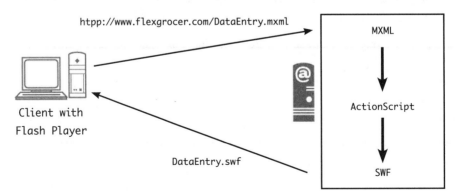

3 Close the browser and return to Flex Builder.

4 Add an <mx:Label> tag by placing the pointer between the <mx:Application> tags; enter the less-than sign (<) and then enter **mx**, followed by a colon (:). You will see a long list of tags. Press the letter **L** (upper or lower case) and select Label by highlighting it and pressing Enter or double-clicking it.

This is an example of code hinting, which is a very helpful feature of Flex Builder that you should take advantage of.

5 Press the spacebar, and you'll see a list of options, including properties and methods, which you can use with the <mx:Label> tag. Press the letter **t** and then the letter **e**; then select the text property.

Not only can you select tags with code hinting but you can also choose attributes that belong to those tags.

✱ NOTE: In these two instances of code hinting, both the desired options happened to be at the top of the list. If the options were not at the top, you would either select the desired option by pressing the down arrow key and then pressing Enter or by double-clicking the selection.

6 Enter **My first Flex application** for the value of the text property. Be sure that the text is in the quotes supplied by code hinting.

Proper XML formatting dictates that the value of the attribute be placed in quotes.

7 End the tag with a slash (/) and a greater-than sign (>).

Check to be sure that your code appears as follows:

```
<?xml version="1.0" encoding="utf-8"?>
<mx:Application xmlns:mx="http://www.adobe.com/2006/mxml"
   layout="absolute">

   <mx:Label text="My first Flex application"/>

</mx:Application>
```

✱ NOTE: The code in this example places the layout="absolute" attribute/value pair of the Application tag on a separate indented line. The entire </mx:Application> tag could have been on one line; whether or not to add line breaks to code is a matter of personal preference. Some developers like the look of placing each attribute/value pair on a separate indented line.

Proper XML syntax gives you two ways to terminate a tag. One of them you just used—to place a slash at the end of the tag. The other option is to use the slash in front of the tag name that is completely typed out again, as follows:

```
<mx:Label text="My first Flex application">
</mx:Label>
```

You usually use the slash at the end of the tag unless there is a reason to place something inside a tag block. For example, if you want to place the </mx:Label> tag inside the <mx:Application> tag block, you have to terminate the </mx:Application> tag on a separate line.

8 Save the file and run it. The text "My first Flex application" appears in your browser.

Finally, you get to see something appear in your new Flex application.

The <mx:Application> tag comes with a default look summarized in this table:

Default Application Styles	
Style	**Default**
backgroundImage	A gradient controlled by the fillAlphas and fillColors
fillAlphas	[1.0,1.0], a fully opaque background
fillColors	[0x9CB0BA,0x68808C], a gray background slightly darker at the bottom
backgroundSize	100%
paddingTop	24 pixels
paddingLeft	24 pixels
paddingBottom	24 pixels
paddingRight	24 pixels
horizontalAlign	Centered

If you do not want any of these defaults and want to start with the simplest possible look, you can set the styleName property equal to plain, as shown here:

```
<mx:Application xmlns:mx="http://www.adobe.com/2006/mxml"
   layout="vertical"
   styleName="plain"/>
```

With the style set to plain, you get the look summarized in this table:

Plain Application Styles	
Style	**Description**
backgroundImage	None
backgroundColor	White
paddingTop	0 pixels
paddingLeft	0 pixels
paddingBottom	0 pixels
paddingRight	0 pixels
horizontalAlign	Left

9 Change the value of the text property from "My first Flex application" to **new text**. Save the file and run it.

The next step shows another helpful feature of Flex Builder, but to see this feature you must have at least two saved versions of the file, which is why you changed the text and saved another version of the file.

10 Right-click in the editor and from the context menu choose Replace With > Local History.

A large dialog box should appear.

11 Compare the current version of your file, which is located on the left side of the dialog box, to the older version on the right. A history of the last 50 versions of your file is kept at the top of the dialog box. Click Replace to bring back your original text, which reads "My first Flex application".

You will find this feature very helpful when you want to roll back to a previous version of code.

> **TIP:** You can alter the settings for Local History by choosing Window > Preferences; then from the dialog box choose General > Workspace and click Local History.

12 Purposely introduce an error into the page by changing the <mx:Label> tag to <mx:Labe>, save the file, and then view where the error is reported.

After you save the file, the Build Automatically setting checks your code. The error is found and reported in two ways. First, a small white *x* in a red circle will appear next to the line of code in which the coding mistake is located. Also, a listing of the error appears in the Problems view.

> **TIP:** You can place the pointer over the description of the error to see the complete description. You can also double-click the error listed in the Problems view, and the pointer is placed at the appropriate line of code in the editor.

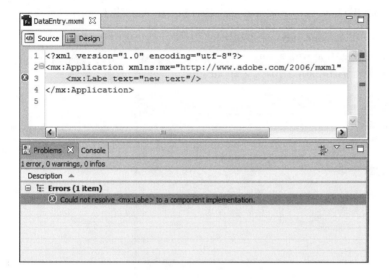

13 Run the application. You will see the following warning, telling you there are errors in your project and prompting you to confirm continuing the launch. In this case, click No so the launch does not continue.

If you click Yes in this dialog box, Flex Builder will run your last successfully compiled version of your application.

14 Correct the error, save the file, and run it to be sure that everything is again working properly. Close the file after it successfully runs.

You are now ready to move on to the next exercise.

Creating a Second Application Page and Working in Design Mode

Up to this point, you have been working with the file in Source mode. Although you might prefer to look only at the code, there are some tasks that are much easier in Design mode; for instance, laying out the visual appearance of a page.

1 Choose File > New > MXML Application. In the dialog box that opens, enter the filename **Dashboard**. From the Layout drop-down list, select horizontal. Click Finish.

Flex Builder remembers your previous choice for the layout next time you create an application. Remember that with a horizontal layout all the controls you add to the application appear horizontally across the application.

NOTE: You do not have to enter the .mxml extension; Flex Builder automatically adds the extension.

2 Click the Design mode button in the editor to open the new file in Design mode. Notice that a number of new views open when you change to Design mode.

Examine the following figure to see some of the key views you will use when working in Design mode.

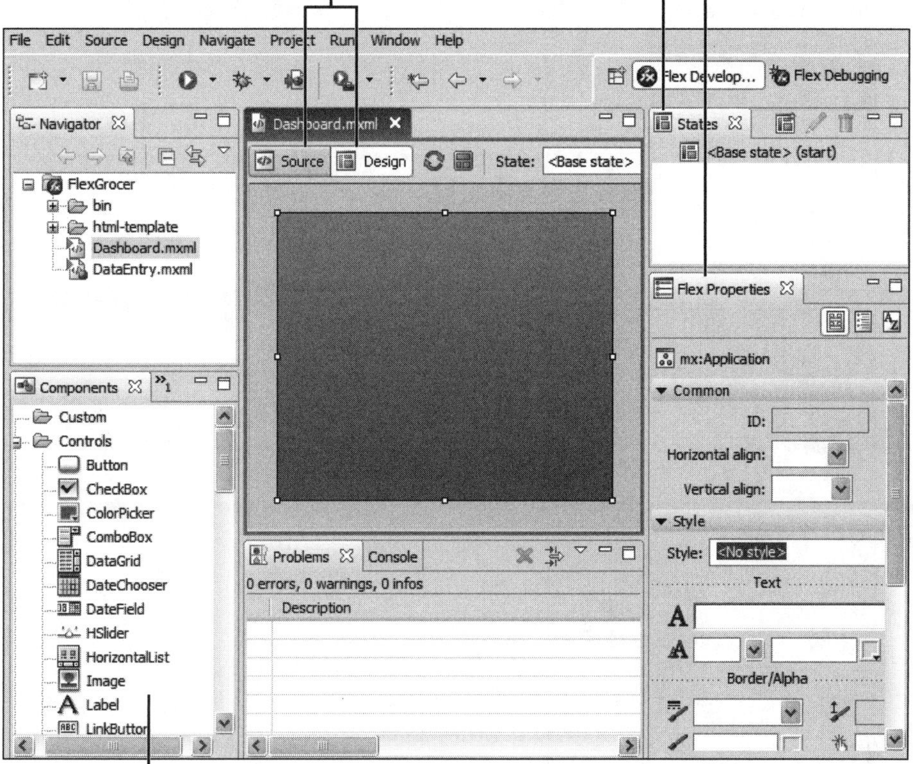

Source and Design mode buttons

States view

Flex Properties view

Components view

3 In the Components view, locate the Controls folder. Drag a Text control and position it in the upper portion of the editor. The Text control centers itself because you are in horizontal layout.

The Components view contains the components you will use in your Flex applications. This view, which is available only in Design mode, permits you to drag and drop components into your application. You'll see in a later lesson that you can also position the controls using a constraint-based layout.

4 Locate the States view in the upper right of the editor. Click the minimize icon to minimize the States view.

Next, focus on using the Flex Properties view.

5 Click anywhere in the editor so the Text control is not selected and the application
is selected. The name of the currently selected object appears at the top of the Flex
Properties view. Be sure it reads mx:Application. Locate the Layout section of the
Flex Properties view. Choose absolute from the Layout drop-down list.

When the layout is horizontal, you can't specify the position of the Text control using *x*- and *y*-coordinates, which you want to practice here. Absolute layout does allow this.

6 Select the Text control and enter **160** for the *x*-coordinate value and **180** for the *y*-coordinate value.

You have now positioned the Text control by setting values in the Flex Properties view.

7 Click the Text control and move it to the top left of the screen. Note that the *x*- and *y*-coordinates have changed.

You have now positioned the Text control by dragging and dropping it in Design mode.

8 At the top of the Flex Properties view locate the Common section. For the value of the text property, enter the string **I am using the Flex Properties view**. Press Enter and you see that the Text control contains the string you just entered.

You have now seen two ways to enter values for properties. In Source mode, you enter the values in quotes following the property name and an equals sign. In Design mode, you select the control to which property values should be supplied and then use the Flex Properties view to enter property values. A third way to change the value of the text displayed is to double-click the control in Design mode and enter or change the text.

✳ **NOTE:** One difference between the Label control and the Text control is that the Text control can contain multiple lines of text. This is not true for the Label control you used in Source mode; it can contain only one line of text.

9 Switch back to Source mode. You see the code that represents what you have done in Design mode. You have a Text control with text, x, and y properties with values that you assigned in the Flex Properties view.

You will most likely develop a preference for which mode you work in: Source or Design. You have seen that you can do many of the same things in both views.

10 Run the application by picking Dashboard.mxml from the drop-down list that appears when you click the down arrow next to the Run button. You see the text from the Text control appear in the browser.

When you run the application, the text is positioned in the browser as you positioned it in Design mode.

Congratulations! You have now run your second Flex application.

✱ **NOTE:** There can be only one <mx:Application> tag per Flex application. At this point, both DataEntry.mxml and Dashboard.mxml contain an <mx:Application> tag. By using multiple <mx:Application> tags, you created two different Flex applications.

11 Back in Flex Builder, remove the Text control in the Dashboard application. Also change the layout back to horizontal.

You need to change this file to prepare it for work in later lessons.

Getting Ready for the Next Lesson

The total FlexGrocer application will consist of three Flex application files. You have created two of them: DataEntry.mxml and Dashboard.mxml. The final application, which is called EComm.mxml, is created in this exercise.

1 Choose File > New > MXML application. In the dialog box that opens, enter the filename **EComm**. Set the layout property to be absolute. Click Finish.

This application allows customers to order from FlexGrocer. DataEntry.mxml defines where new grocery items are added to the inventory and quantities updated in the application. Dashboard.mxml defines where product sales can be analyzed.

2 Be sure that all three files contain nothing more than the skeleton code inserted when the file was automatically generated. You need to remove a Label control from DataEntry.mxml. The layout property of DataEntry.mxml and EComm.mxml should be set to absolute, whereas the layout property of Dashboard.mxml should be set to horizontal.

The only code in all three of the files should be what appears here, with the appropriate value for the layout:

```
<?xml version="1.0" encoding="utf-8"?>
<mx:Application xmlns:mx="http://www.adobe.com/2006/mxml"
   layout="absolute">

</mx:Application>
```

3 Save each file, run it, and then close it to get ready for the next lesson.

You have built the three main application files that you will be working with for the rest of the book.

✳ NOTE: Teaching object-oriented programming is not the focus of this book, but to be an effective Flex developer you must have at least a basic understanding of object-oriented terminology and concepts. For instance, the tags you have seen—such as <mx:Application>, <mx:Label>, and <mx:Text>—actually refer to classes. The *Adobe Flex 3 MXML and ActionScript Language Reference* (sometimes referred to as *ASDoc*) is the document that lists these classes, their properties, their methods, and much more.

✳ NOTE: Object-oriented programming standards have influenced how you named the files in this lesson. Traditionally, class names always start with an uppercase letter, and every class must be stored in a separate file in Flex. The three files you created in this lesson are classes named DataEntry, Dashboard, and EComm, respectively. Each of these classes is a subclass, or child, of the Application class, so they also start with an uppercase letter.

What You Have Learned

In this lesson, you have:

- Created a project to organize your application files (pages 16–20)
- Toured the pieces of the Flex Builder 3 workbench (views, editors, and perspectives) used to create application files (pages 21–23)
- Created and run application files while using code hinting and local history to produce the code for those files (pages 23–29)
- Worked in both Source mode and Design mode from within an editor (pages 30–36)

What You Will Learn

In this lesson, you will:

- Use containers
- Lay out an application in Design mode
- Work with constraint-based layouts
- Use enhanced constraints
- Work with view states
- Control view states
- Lay out an application in Source mode

Approximate Time

This lesson takes approximately 1 hour and 30 minutes to complete.

Lesson Files

Media Files:

None

Starting Files:

Lesson03/start/EComm.mxml
Lesson03/start/Dashboard.mxml

Completed Files:

Lesson03/complete/EComm.mxml
Lesson03/complete/Dashboard.mxml

LESSON 3

Laying Out the Interface

Every application needs a user interface, and one of the strengths of Adobe Flex Builder 3 is that it is simple for developers to use it to lay out the interface for their applications. In this lesson, you will learn about many of the containers in Flex, what differentiates them, and how to use them when laying out your applications. Using states, you can then make the applications dynamically change to react to users!

The user interface (UI) for the e-commerce application

Learning About Containers

All layout in Flex is done using containers. In the last lesson, you created three applications; each had an <mx:Application> tag, which is in fact a container. Each container has a set of rules that determines how any child tags are laid out. The following table shows commonly used containers and the rules they use to lay out their children.

Container Layout Rules	
Container	**Rule**
VBox	Children are laid out vertically; each child is drawn lower on the screen than the previous child.
HBox	Children are laid out horizontally; each child is drawn to the right of the previous child.
Canvas	Children are drawn at the *x*- and *y*-coordinates specified by the developer. If not specified, all children are drawn in the top-left corner of the container. For example, if you add a Button control to a Canvas container and do not specify *x*- and *y*-coordinates, the button is rendered in the top left of the canvas at the default 0,0 position.
Application	Can be set to behave as a VBox, HBox, or Canvas container through the use of the layout attribute.
Tile	Lays out its children in one or more vertical columns or horizontal rows, starting new rows or columns as necessary. All Tile container cells have the same size. Flex arranges the cells of a Tile container in a square grid, in which each cell holds a single child. The direction property is used to determine the layout.
Panel	A subclass of the Box container, a Panel container can act as either an HBox, VBox, or a Canvas container, depending on the layout attribute specified (you use layout="absolute" to have it behave as a Canvas container, which is the default). In addition to containing its children, the Panel container also provides a title bar area, which can contain a title for the Panel container and a status message.
ControlBar	The ControlBar container is used to dock a toolbar to the bottom of a Panel container or TitleWindow container. The ControlBar container can act as either an HBox container or a VBox container, depending on the direction attribute specified (horizontal is the default).
ApplicationControlBar	Can act as either an HBox container or a VBox container, depending on the direction attribute specified (horizontal is the default). The ApplicationControlBar container is used to hold components that provide access to elements used throughout an application. If specified as the first child of an <mx:Application> tag, and if the dock attribute is set to true, the ApplicationControlBar container docks at the top of the application's drawing area, extends the full width of the application, and does not scroll with the application.

Laying Out the E-Commerce Application Using Design Mode

The e-commerce application of FlexGrocer is how customers shop for groceries. The top region of the user interface of this application displays the store logo as well as links that are available throughout the application. Below that is a series of clickable icons that users can use to browse the various categories of groceries (dairy, meat, fruit, and so on). Below the icons is an area for displaying products.

1 Open the EComm.mxml file that you created in the previous lesson.

If you didn't complete the previous lesson, you can open EComm.mxml from Lesson03/ start and save it in your flexGrocer/src directory.

2 Switch Flex Builder to Design mode.

To switch between Design mode and Source mode in Flex Builder, use the buttons in the title bar at the top of the window.

3 In the Components view, open the Layout folder. Drag an ApplicationControlBar container to the top of the application. Set Dock to true, set the width of the ApplicationControlBar container to 100%, set the height to 90, and remove any entries for the *x*- and *y*-coordinates.

TIP: A blue bar will appear, indicating where you can drop the component.

Once the ApplicationControlBar container is placed, you should see a light gray bar stretching across the top of the page.

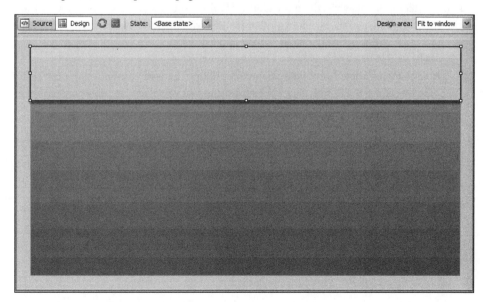

4 In the Components view, drag a Canvas container into the ApplicationControlBar container. In the Flex Properties view, set the canvas width and height to 100%.

Inserting a Canvas container inside the ApplicationControlBar container enables you to specify the exact positioning of the elements within it. By setting the canvas width and height to 100%, you are telling the canvas to be as wide and tall as the container it is in, which is the ApplicationControlBar container.

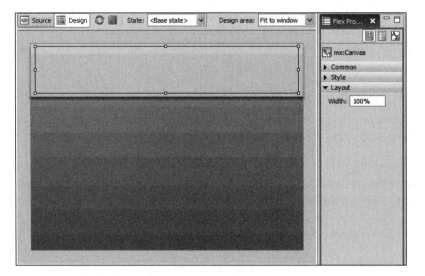

5 In the Components view, open the Controls folder and drag a Label control into the Canvas container in the ApplicationControlBar container. In the Flex Properties view, set the text property for the label to **Flex** and set the *x*- and *y*-coordinates to 0.

▶ **TIP:** Clicking the Show Surrounding Containers button (between the Refresh button and State combo box above the Design area) can help ensure that you place the Label control in the proper container.

This Label control will hold the company name: Flex GROCER.

The company name, Flex GROCER, will be split into two labels. In the next lesson, you will learn that a Label control can hold only a single line of text, and the Flex GROCER logo has the company name split across two lines.

6 From the open Controls folder, drag another Label control into the Canvas container, placing this one just below the first label. In the Flex Properties view, set the text property for the label to be **GROCER**, set the x-coordinate to 0, and set the y-coordinate to 41.

Later in the book, you will apply styles to set the company logo colors and size. For now, you are just placing the text in the appropriate position.

7 With the Controls folder still open, drag a Button control into the Canvas container so the Button control is positioned near the right edge of the container. In the Flex Properties view, give the Button control an ID of btnViewCart and a label of **View Cart.**

Don't worry about the exact placement. Later in this lesson, you will learn how to use a constraint-based layout to position the button so its right edge is always 10 pixels from the right edge of the application.

8 Drag a second Button control into the Canvas container, just to the left of the first Button control. In the Flex Properties view, give the Button control an ID of btnCheckout and a label of **Checkout**.

The users will use this button to indicate that they are finished shopping and want to complete the purchase of the selected products. Again, the exact placement will happen later in this lesson, when you learn about constraint-based layout.

9 Drag a Label control from the Controls folder and place it near the bottom-right edge of the screen. Double-click the label and set the text property to **(c) 2006, FlexGrocer**.

Much like the buttons you just added, you needn't worry about the exact placement because it will be handled later with constraints.

10 Drag an HBox container from the Layout folder of the Components view and place it in the large area below the ApplicationControlBar container. As you drop it, the Insert HBox dialog box appears. Set the height and width to 100% and click OK. In the Flex Properties view, set the *x*- and *y*-coordinates to 0, and set the ID of the HBox container to be bodyBox.

This HBox container will hold the product details and shopping cart for the application. Remember that an HBox container displays its children horizontally, so you can have products shown on the left and the shopping cart on the right.

11 Drag a VBox container from the Layout folder of the Components view and drop it inside the HBox container (you can use Outline view or the Show Surrounding Containers button to verify that you have the VBox container in the HBox container). In the Insert VBox dialog box, assign a height and width of 100% and click OK. In the Flex Properties view, give the VBox container an ID of products.

This VBox container will hold the details for a product.

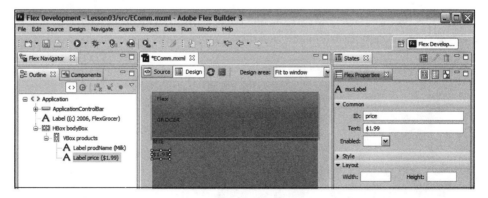

12 Drag a Label control into the new VBox container. Set the ID of the Label control to be prodName and the text to be **Milk.** Drag a second Label control below the first one. Give the second one an ID of price and set **$1.99** as the text.

Because they are children of the VBox container, the product name appears vertically above the price of the product.

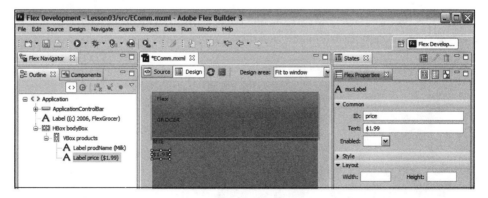

⦿ **TIP:** If you open the Outline view, you can see the hierarchy of your application. The root is the <mx:Application> tag, which contains an ApplicationControlBar container and an HBox container as children. You can also see the various children of the ApplicationControlBar container. This is a useful view if you want to make a change to a component. It can be difficult to select just the ApplicationControlBar container in Design mode in the Editor. You can easily select it by clicking it in the Outline view.

13 Add a Button control below the two labels, with an ID of *add* and the Label **Add To Cart.**

For each product, you want the name of the product and its price to be displayed. The Add To Cart button gives users the ability to add a product to their shopping carts. Because the two Label controls and the Button control are in a VBox container, they appear one above the other. The functionality for the Button control will be added in a later lesson.

14 Save the file and click Run.

As this runs, you can clearly see the difference between elements in the ApplicationControlBar container and those in the body.

Working with Constraint-Based Layouts

Flex supports constraint-based layouts, which enable you to arrange elements of the user interface with the freedom and pixel-point accuracy of absolute positioning while being able to set constraints to stretch or move the components when the user resizes the window. This method of controlling the size and position of components is different than the nested layout of containers (like the VBox and HBox containers in the previous exercise).

There are two approaches to constraint-based layouts. The first approach positions and sizes everything in relation to the edges of a Canvas container or other containers that allow absolute positioning, such as the Application or Panel container. The second approach uses enhanced constraints, where rows and columns are set up in a container that allows absolute positioning. In the first approach, you are always constraining to the parent container; the second approach allows you to constrain to siblings.

Using Constraints with the Parent Container

The Canvas container requires that elements be positioned to absolute coordinates; however, layout constraints allow users to dynamically adjust the layout based on the window size of their browsers. For example, if you want a label to always appear in the bottom-right corner of an application regardless of the browser size, you can anchor the control to the right edge of the Canvas container. Set the control's position is always maintained relative to the right edge of the Canvas container.

Layout anchors are used to specify how a control should appear relative to the edge of the Canvas container. To ensure that a control is a certain distance from the bottom and right edges, select the check boxes below and to the right of the control in the Constraints area in the Layout section of the Flex Properties view, and use the text boxes to specify the number of pixels away from the edge of the Canvas you want the control constrained to.

Flex allows constraints from the top, vertical center, bottom, left, horizontal center, or right of a canvas container.

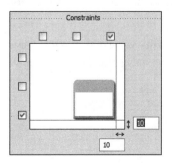

▶ **TIP:** All constraints are set relative to the edges of the container, so long as it allows absolute positioning. They cannot be set relative to other controls or containers.

1 Open the EComm.mxml file that you used in the previous exercise.

Alternately, you can open EComm_layout.mxml from Lesson03/intermediate and save it in the flexGrocer/src directory as **EComm.mxml**.

2 Find and select the Checkout button. In the Constraints area of the Layout section, add a constraint so the right edge of the button is 10 pixels away from the right edge of the container. If you don't set it, the y property will use a default value of 0.

To set a constraint from the right edge, click the rightmost check box above the button icon in the Constraints area. In the text box that appears, enter the number of pixels away from the edge you want the button to be.

3 Find and select the View Cart button. Add a constraint so the right edge of the button is 90 pixels from the right edge of the container.

If you don't otherwise set it, the y property will use a default value of 0. You now have it set so that, regardless of the width of the browser, the two navigation buttons are always anchored relative to the top-right edge of the container.

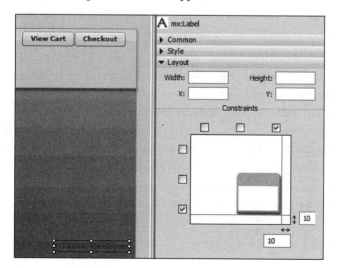

4 Find and select the label with the copyright notice. Constrain this label so that it is 10 pixels above the bottom and 10 pixels away from the right edge of its container. Click the check box in the top-right corner of the Constraints area, and enter **10** in the text box below. Also, click the bottom check box and enter **10** in the text box

Because the copyright label is below other containers, it is probably easiest to select it using the Outline view. These settings ensure that, regardless of the width of the Label control, its bottom-right edge will always be 10 pixels above and 10 pixels to the left of the bottom-right corner of the application.

If you switch to Source mode, the entire file should look similar to the following:

```
<?xml version="1.0" encoding="utf-8"?>
<mx:Application xmlns:mx="http://www.adobe.com/2006/mxml"
    layout="absolute">
    <mx:ApplicationControlBar dock="true" width="100%" height="90">
        <mx:Canvas width="100%" height="100%">
            <mx:Label x="0" y="0" text="Flex"/>
            <mx:Label x="0" y="41" text="GROCER"/>
            <mx:Button label="View Cart" id="btnViewCart" right="90" y="0"/>
            <mx:Button label="Checkout" id="btnCheckout" right="10" y="0"/>
        </mx:Canvas>
    </mx:ApplicationControlBar>
    <mx:Label text="(c) 2006, FlexGrocer" right="10" bottom="10"/>
    <mx:HBox x="0" y="0" width="100%" height="100%" id="bodyBox">
        <mx:VBox width="100%" height="100%" id="products">
            <mx:Label text="Milk" id="prodName"/>
            <mx:Label text="$1.99" id="price"/>
            <mx:Button label="Add To Cart" id="add"/>
        </mx:VBox>
    </mx:HBox>
</mx:Application>
```

Your code may differ slightly, depending on the order you added the items and the positions to which you dragged the various components. Don't worry; the order is not particularly important in this case. Every container and control that you added in Design mode is represented by a tag in Source mode. When you add elements inside a container, they appear as child tags to the container's tag. Also note that the layout constraints are set as attributes of the related component.

5 Switch back to Design mode and insert a second VBox container in the bodyBox HBox container. In the Insert VBox dialog box, leave the width empty and set the height to 100%. Set the ID of the new VBox to cartBox.

If you have difficulty setting the new VBox container inside the HBox container, it might help to turn on Show Surrounding Containers. The Show Surrounding Containers button is located between the Refresh button and the State combo box above the Design area. Then you can click the HBox container and be sure to insert the VBox into the correct container. If you accidentally place the VBox in the wrong container, the easiest fix is to switch to Source mode and move the tags yourself. The code in Source mode should look like this:

```
<mx:HBox x="0" y="0" width="100%" height="100%" id="bodyBox">
    <mx:VBox width="100%" height="100%" id="products">
        <mx:Label text="Milk" id="prodName"/>
        <mx:Label text="$1.99" id="price"/>
        <mx:Button label="Add To Cart" id="add"/>
    </mx:VBox>
```

```
  <mx:VBox height="100%" id="cartBox">
  </mx:VBox>
</mx:HBox>
```

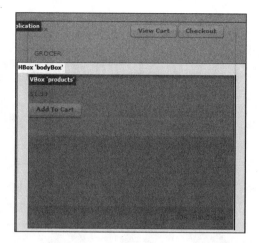

6 Switch to Design mode and add a Label control in the cartBox container with the text property set to **Your Cart Total: $**.

To the right of the products, there will always be a summary of the shopping cart, indicating whether there are items in the cart and what the current subtotal is.

7 From the Controls folder of the Components view, drag a LinkButton control below the newest Label control and set the label of the link to **View Cart**.

This link will be used to show the user the full contents of their shopping cart.

8 Save the file and click Run.

As the application runs you can resize the browser and see that the buttons and bottom text are always properly constrained.

Using Enhanced Constraints

Although you can accomplish much using constraints as shown in the previous section, you may also want to constrain objects to a sibling and not always to the parent container. You accomplish this using enhanced constraints, implemented with the ConstraintRow and ConstraintColumn classes.

Just as normal constraints must be used in containers that allow absolute positioning (Canvas, Panel, Module, and Application), so must enhanced constraints. Enhanced constraints divide a container's space into rows and columns that can then be used to position other components constrained to those row and column boundaries. You define horizontal regions using the ConstraintRow class and vertical regions using the ConstraintColumn class.

Here is a simple example of using enhanced constraints:

```
<?xml version="1.0" encoding="utf-8"?>
<mx:Application xmlns:mx="http://www.adobe.com/2006/mxml" layout="absolute">

    <mx:constraintColumns>
        <mx:ConstraintColumn id="col1" width="33%"/>
        <mx:ConstraintColumn id="col2" width="33%"/>
        <mx:ConstraintColumn id="col3" width="33%"/>
    </mx:constraintColumns>
```

```
<mx:constraintRows>
    <mx:ConstraintRow id="row1" height="50%"/>
    <mx:ConstraintRow id="row2" height="50%"/>
</mx:constraintRows>

<mx:TextArea id="ta1" text="TextArea 1"
    left="col1:5" right="col1:5"
    top="row1:10" bottom="row1:20"
    backgroundColor="yellow"
    fontSize="20"/>

<mx:TextArea id="ta2" text="TextArea 2"
    left="col1:5" right="col2:5"
    top="row2:10" bottom="row2:10"
    backgroundColor="red"
    fontSize="20" color="white"/>

<mx:TextArea id="ta3" text="TextArea 3"
    left="col3:5" right="col3:5"
    top="row1:10" bottom="row2:10"
    backgroundColor="green"
    fontSize="20" color="white"/>

</mx:Application>
```

Notice first that the application's layout property is set to absolute, which means absolute positioning will be used—a requirement for using constraints.

Next, the constraintColumns property is used to contain the data associated with the three ConstraintColumns. Instance names of col1, col2, and col3 are used. You must give the columns instance names because you will reference those names when constraining to them. In this case, the columns' widths are all set to 33%, so each column will use one-third of the available screen width. This means that when the application is resized, the widths of the objects will grow or shrink appropriately because they are constrained left and right to the columns.

The ConstraintRow objects are instantiated inside of the application's constraintRows property. The rows' heights are defined using percentages. This means that when the application is resized, the heights of objects grow or shrink appropriately because they are constrained top and bottom to the rows.

Two TextArea controls are constrained to the column and row constraints. The TextArea controls are used just for an example—any component could have been used.

The first TextArea control's left constraint is constrained to col1 and is 5 pixels away. The reference to the column uses the syntax columnName:pixels. If no reference is made to a column or row constraint, the constraint is to the parent object, which is what you did in the previous section.

The results of the application appear as follows:

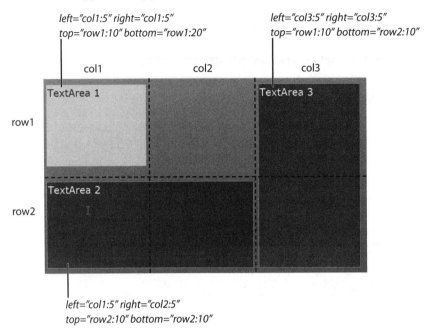

> [*] **NOTE:** TextArea controls can span multiple constraint columns and rows.

In the example code previously given, all the constraint rows and constraint columns were given percentage widths. This is not required nor always an optimal choice. You have three options when sizing enhanced constraints:

- **Percent:** Uses a calculated percentage of the parent container
- **Fixed:** Uses a fixed region of the parent container
- **Content:** Uses the region of the parent container based on the region used by the largest child

When using percent- or content-sized columns or rows, you can control how the regions grow and shrink by specifying minimum and maximum sizes with the `minHeight`, `minWidht`, `maxHeight` and `maxWidth` properties.

> [*] **NOTE:** There is no way to set up enhanced constraints in Design mode, as you can do when constraining to parent containers.

Working with View States

You can use Flex Builder to create applications that change their appearance based on the task the user is performing. For example, the e-commerce application starts by showing users the various products they can buy. When they start adding items to the cart, you want to add something to the view so users can get a feel for what is currently in the cart, such as total cost. Finally, users need a way to view and manage the full contents of the shopping cart.

In Flex, you can add this kind of interactivity with view states. A *view state* is one of several views that you define for an application or a custom component. Every MXML page has at least one state, referred to as the *base view state*, which is represented by the default layout of the file.

Additional states are represented in the MXML as modified versions of the base view state or of other states.

1 Open the EComm.mxml file you used in the previous exercise.

or

Open EComm_constraint.mxml from Lesson03/intermediate and save it in your flexGrocer/src directory as **EComm.mxml**.

2 If it is not already open, open the States view in Flex Builder 3.

If you don't currently see the States view when you look at Flex Builder in Design mode, you can add it to the view by choosing Window > States. Notice that there is already one state created to represent the default layout of the application.

3 Create a new state named cartView, which will be based on <Base state>.

You can create a state by clicking New State at the top of the States view or by right-clicking in the view and selecting the New State option. The cartView state will show users the details of all the items they have added to their cart.

4 With the new cartView state selected, click the Products container and set its height and width to 0; then, choose the cartBox container and set its height and width to 100%.

For the Cart view, the shopping cart will entirely replace the products in the center of the screen; so, you will resize the products container to take up no space and resize the container named cartBox to take up all space available.

5 Still with the cartView state selected, drag a DataGrid control from the Controls folder of the Components view and drop it below the View Cart link. Set the ID of the DataGrid control to dgCart, and set the DataGrid control's width to 100%.

In a later lesson, the DataGrid control will be used to show the user the full contents of the cart.

Be careful to ensure you are adding the DataGrid control into the cartBox container. Your application and code will look a bit different if you accidentally add the DataGrid control before the cartBox container.

If you look at the file in Source mode, you should see that the following code has been added:

```
<mx:states>
    <mx:State name="cartView">
        <mx:SetProperty target="{products}" name="width" value="0"/>
        <mx:SetProperty target="{products}" name="height" value="0"/>
        <mx:SetProperty target="{cartBox}" name="width" value="100%"/>
        <mx:AddChild relativeTo="{cartBox}" position="lastChild">
            <mx:DataGrid id="dgCart" width="100%">
                <mx:columns>
                    <mx:DataGridColumn headerText="Column 1" dataField="col1"/>
                    <mx:DataGridColumn headerText="Column 2" dataField="col2"/>
                    <mx:DataGridColumn headerText="Column 3" dataField="col3"/>
                </mx:columns>
            </mx:DataGrid>
        </mx:AddChild>
    </mx:State>
</mx:states>
```

6 Save the file.

Testing the file now shouldn't show any differences because you haven't added any ability for the user to toggle between the states. In the next exercise, you will add that navigational ability.

Controlling View States

Each MXML page has a property called currentState. You can use this property to control which state of the application is shown to a user at any given time.

1 Open the EComm.mxml file that you used in the previous exercise. Switch to Design mode if you are not already there.

or

Open EComm_states.mxml from Lesson03/intermediate, and save it in your flexGrocer/src directory as **EComm.mxml**.

2 If it is not already open, open the States view in Flex Builder and set the chosen state to <Base state> (start).

You will add functionality to the base view state so that users can navigate to the other states of the application.

3 Choose the View Cart LinkButton control from the cartBox container. In the Flex Properties view, set its On click: property to this.currentState='cartView'.

Events such as the button click will be explored in detail in Lesson 5, "Handling Events and Data Structures." The important thing to understand now is that when the user clicks the link, the view will change to the cartView state.

 CAUTION! The state name is case sensitive and must exactly match the name as you typed it in the previous exercise. You must use single quotes around the state name when entering it in Design mode.

▶ **TIP:** You can also enable the View Cart LinkButton in the ApplicationControlBar by adding the same code for its click event handler as well.

4 Switch to the cartView state. Add a new LinkButton control below the DataGrid control with the label set to **Continue Shopping** and the click property set to this.currentState=''.

Setting currentState to an empty string resets the application to its initial state.

5 Delete the View Cart LinkButton from the cartView state.

When the user is viewing the cart, there is no need for a link to the cart. You can delete the link by selecting it in Design mode and pressing Delete.

The completed cartView state block of code shown in Source mode should read as follows:

```
<mx:states>
  <mx:State name="cartView">
    <mx:SetProperty target="{products}" name="width" value="0"/>
    <mx:SetProperty target="{products}" name="height" value="0"/>
    <mx:SetProperty target="{cartBox}" name="width" value="100%"/>
    <mx:AddChild relativeTo="{cartBox}" position="lastChild">
      <mx:DataGrid id="dgCart" width="100%">
        <mx:columns>
          <mx:DataGridColumn headerText="Column 1" dataField="col1"/>
          <mx:DataGridColumn headerText="Column 2" dataField="col2"/>
          <mx:DataGridColumn headerText="Column 3" dataField="col3"/>
        </mx:columns>
      </mx:DataGrid>
    </mx:AddChild>
    <mx:RemoveChild target="{linkbutton1}"/>
    <mx:AddChild relativeTo="{cartBox}" position="lastChild">
      <mx:LinkButton label="Continue Shopping" click="this.currentState=''"/>
    </mx:AddChild>
  </mx:State>
</mx:states>
```

6 Save and test the application. You can now navigate between the states by clicking the buttons and links to which you added code.

Your file should resemble the code found in Lesson03/complete/EComm.mxml.

Laying Out an Application in Source Mode

Now that you have seen how to lay out an application with Design mode, you can look a little more deeply at the code and create your second application using Source mode. In this next exercise, you will lay out the Dashboard application, which is designed to give the FlexGrocer executives a quick high-level view of how sales are going for their company.

1 Open the Dashboard.mxml file created in the previous lesson.
or
Open Dashboard.mxml from Lesson03/start and save it in your flexGrocer/src directory.

2 Switch Flex Builder to Source mode.

To switch between Design mode and Source mode in Flex Builder, use the buttons in the title bar at the top of the window.

3 In Source mode, add an <mx:ApplicationControlBar> tag, and set the dock property to true. Add four <mx:LinkButton> tags as children to the ApplicationControlBar container, with labels reading **All**, **Sales**, **Categories**, and **Comparison**.

A bit later in this exercise, you will add code to use these links to toggle between the different states. The completed code should read as follows:

```
<?xml version="1.0" encoding="utf-8"?>
<mx:Application xmlns:mx="http://www.adobe.com/2006/mxml"
    layout="horizontal">
  <mx:ApplicationControlBar dock="true">
    <mx:LinkButton label="All"/>
    <mx:LinkButton label="Sales"/>
    <mx:LinkButton label="Categories"/>
    <mx:LinkButton label="Comparison"/>
  </mx:ApplicationControlBar>
</mx:Application>
```

Remember, you want the <mx:ApplicationControlBar> tag to be the first visible child of the <mx:Application> tag so that it will be docked to the top of the application.

4 After the </mx:ApplicationControlBar> tag, add a Panel container with an ID of sales, a title of **Sales Chart**, and a height and width of 100%.

By setting the height and width to 100%, this view will use all available space within the application. This will become particularly important as you add states to the application. By setting the height and width of the other items in the application to 0, the Panel container will use all the space.

```
<mx:Panel id="sales"
    width="100%" height="100%"
    title="Sales Chart">
</mx:Panel>
```

5 Between the open and close <mx:Panel> tags, add a ControlBar container. All you need to do is create an opening and closing <mx:ControlBar> tag.

```
<mx:Panel id="sales"
    width="100%" height="100%"
    title="Sales Chart">
  <mx:ControlBar>
  </mx:ControlBar>
</mx:Panel>
```

The Dashboard will continue to be a work in progress for the next several lessons. In the next lesson, you will add buttons to the control bar. Later, you will add a DataGrid control to view the data for that panel; much later, you will use the graphing controls to show a visual representation of that data.

6 After the closing tag for the Panel container, add a VBox container with an id of rightCharts, and width and height each set to 100%. All this requires is the addition of an <mx:VBox id="rightCharts" width="100%" height="100%"> </mx:VBox> tag, as shown in bold in the code below.

```
<mx:Panel id="sales"
    width="100%" height="100%"
    title="Sales Chart">
    <mx:ControlBar>
    </mx:ControlBar>
</mx:Panel>
<mx:VBox id="rightCharts"
    width="100%" height="100%">
</mx:VBox>
```

A VBox container is added so that two items can be shown on the right of the application, one above the other. Because the VBox container is also set to use 100% for its height and width, it uses any space inside the application not used by the other sales Panel container.

✱ NOTE: Flex enables you to assign more than 100 percent total width for a container. In the previous code, you assigned 100 percent width of the bodyBox to both the Sales view and the rightCharts VBox container. Clearly, an HBox container doesn't have 200 percent width to allocate. The Flex Layout Manager takes this into account and divides the space proportionally based on the requested percentages. Because two times more space was requested than is available, each request for a relative width is divided by 2, so they are each allocated 50 percent. If any elements were assigned a fixed width (that is, a number of pixels instead of a percentage), the fixed size requests are subtracted from the available space before any relative size requests are allocated.

7 Inside the VBox container, add a Panel container with an id of type, a title of **Category Chart**, and a height and width each of 100%. Add an empty ControlBar container to that view. After the type Panel container, but still in the VBox container, add a second Panel container with an id of comp, a title of **Comparison Chart**, and height and width each set to 100%.

You now have containers for all the charts that will get added in Lesson 19, "Visualizing Data."

```
<mx:VBox id="rightCharts"
    width="100%" height="100%" >
    <mx:Panel id="type"
        width="100%" height="100%"
        title="Category Chart">
        <mx:ControlBar>
        </mx:ControlBar>
    </mx:Panel>
    <mx:Panel id="comp"
        width="100%" height="100%"
        title="Comparison Chart">
        <mx:ControlBar>
        </mx:ControlBar>
    </mx:Panel>
</mx:VBox>
```

8 Save and test the application.

You should see the views laid out properly. The next steps are to add states to the application and the ability for users to navigate between the states.

Adding and Controlling View States with MXML

In Flex, states are defined in an <mx:states> block. Each state is represented by an <mx:State> tag, with attributes indicating the name of the state as well as any other state it might be based on. For example, review the states in the e-commerce layouts from earlier in this lesson:

```
<mx:states>
    <mx:State name="cartView">
        <mx:SetProperty target="{products}"
            name="width"
            value="0"/>
        <mx:SetProperty target="{products}"
            name="height"
            value="0"/>
        <mx:SetProperty target="{cartBox}"
            name="width"
            value="100%"/>
        <mx:AddChild relativeTo="{cartBox}"
            position="lastChild">
            <mx:DataGrid id="dgCart"
                width="100%">
                <mx:columns>
                    <mx:DataGridColumn headerText="Column 1"
                        dataField="col1"/>
                    <mx:DataGridColumn headerText="Column 2"
                        dataField="col2"/>
                    <mx:DataGridColumn headerText="Column 3"
                        dataField="col3"/>
                </mx:columns>
            </mx:DataGrid>
        </mx:AddChild>
        <mx:AddChild relativeTo="{cartBox}"
            position="lastChild">
            <mx:LinkButton label="Continue Shopping"
                click="this.currentState=''"/>
        </mx:AddChild>
        <mx:RemoveChild target="{linkbutton1}"/>
    </mx:State>
</mx:states>
```

First, you defined the cartView state that uses the <mx:SetProperty> tag four times: once to set the height of the products container to 0; once to set its width to 0; once to set the height of the container named cartBox to 100%; and once more to set the width of the container named cartBox to 100%.

The <mx:AddChild> tag is then used to add a DataGrid control and link, and the <mx:RemoveChild> tag is used to remove a link.

▶ **TIP:** When using the <mx:AddChild> tag, specify the relativeTo and position attributes. The target attribute is the container to which the child will be added; position indicates where in that container the child will be added. Possible values are before, after, firstChild, and lastChild. The default value is lastChild. The child to be added is most often specified between the open and closing <mx:AddChild> tags.

1 Open the Dashboard.mxml file that you used in the previous exercise.

or

Alternately, you can open Dashboard_layout.mxml from the Lesson03/intermediate and save it in your flexGrocer/src directory as **Dashboard.mxml**.

2 After the closing <mx:ApplicationControlBar> tag, but before the <mx:Panel id="sales" …> tag, add an <mx:states> tag pair.

Because the <mx:states> tag doesn't represent a visual element in the application, states could really be defined anywhere in the application.

3 Between the open and closing <mx:states> tags, add an <mx:State> tag to define a new state named fullSales. Because this will be based on the base view state, there is no need to specify a basedOn attribute.

```
<mx:states>
   <mx:State name="fullSales">
   </mx:State>
</mx:states>
```

4 Use the <mx:SetProperty> tag to define the fullSales state to set the height and width of the rightCharts VBox container to 0.

The body of the application has only two children, both of which initially requested 100% width. By setting the other child (rightCharts) to use 0 pixels for its width, the first child (the Sales view) will expand to fill 100% of the space.

```
<mx:states>
   <mx:State name="fullSales">
      <mx:SetProperty target="{rightCharts}"
         name="width" value="0"/>
      <mx:SetProperty target="{rightCharts}"
         name="height" value="0"/>
   </mx:State>
</mx:states>
```

▶ **TIP:** Remember that the target needs to be specified as a binding; that is, it needs to be the name of the component placed within curly brackets. Binding will be discussed in detail in the next lesson.

5 Define a second state named fullType after the end tag for the fullSales state. The fullType state should use the <mx:SetProperty> tag to set the height and width of the sales component to 0, and the height and width of the comp component to 0.

When the Dashboard shows the type chart fully, the sales chart and comparison charts both need to be minimized; hence, for the fullType state, you are setting 0 for the height and width of both of the other charts. Because all three charts were initially set up to take 100% for both height and width, when the other two charts no longer use any space, the type chart is free to use the whole screen.

```
<mx:State name="fullType">
   <mx:SetProperty target="{sales}"
      name="width"
      value="0"/>
   <mx:SetProperty target="{sales}"
      name="height"
      value="0"/>
   <mx:SetProperty target="{comp}"
      name="width"
      value="0"/>
   <mx:SetProperty target="{comp}"
      name="height"
      value="0"/>
</mx:State>
```

6 Define a third state named fullComp, which sets the height and width of both sales and type components to be 0 pixels.

This directly mirrors the work you did for the fullType state, so that to show the comparison chart fully, you will set the sales and type charts to take up 0 pixels for their height and width. The new fullComp state block of code should read like this:

```
<mx:State name="fullComp">
   <mx:SetProperty target="{sales}"
      name="width"
      value="0"/>
   <mx:SetProperty target="{sales}"
      name="height"
      value="0"/>
   <mx:SetProperty target="{type}"
      name="width"
      value="0"/>
   <mx:SetProperty target="{type}"
      name="height"
      value="0"/>
</mx:State>
```

7 Add click events for the LinkButton controls in the `<mx:ApplicationControlBar>` tag to toggle the `currentState` property, as shown in the following code.

```
<mx:ApplicationControlBar dock="true">
  <mx:LinkButton label="All"
    click="this.currentState=''"/>
  <mx:LinkButton label="Sales"
    click="this.currentState='fullSales'"/>
  <mx:LinkButton label="Categories"
    click="this.currentState='fullType'"/>
  <mx:LinkButton label="Comparison"
    click="this.currentState='fullComp'"/>
</mx:ApplicationControlBar>
```

8 Save and test the Dashboard. You should be able to control the states using the links on the menu bar at the top of the application window.

You can now navigate and see that each of the panels uses the full stage to display its contents.

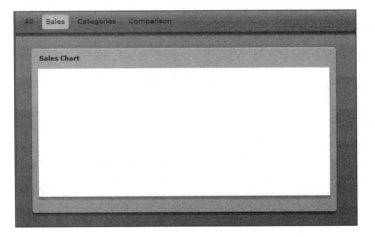

What You Have Learned

In this lesson, you have:

- Used containers (page 40)
- Laid out an application in Design mode (pages 41–46)
- Worked with constraint-based layouts (pages 47–52)
- Used enhanced constraints (pages 52–54)
- Worked with view states (pages 55–56)
- Controlled view states (pages 57–59)
- Laid out an application in Source mode (pages 59–66)

What You Will Learn

In this lesson, you will:

- Define the user interface (UI) for the e-commerce application of FlexGrocer

- Use simple controls such as the Image control, text controls, and CheckBox control

- Define the UI for the administrative tool that allows users to update data

- Use the Form container to lay out simple controls

- Use data binding to connect controls to a data model

Approximate Time

This lesson takes approximately 45 minutes to complete.

Lesson Files

Media Files:

Lesson04/start/assets/dairy_milk.jpg

Starting Files:

Lesson04/start/EComm.mxml
Lesson04/start/DataEntry.mxml
Lesson04/start/Dashboard.mxml

Completed Files:

Lesson04/complete/EComm.mxml
Lesson04/complete/DataEntry.mxml
Lesson04/complete/Dashboard.mxml

LESSON 4

Using Simple Controls

In this lesson, you will add user interface elements to enable the end user to work with grocery items. An important part of any application is the user interface, and Adobe Flex contains elements such as buttons, text fields, and radio buttons that make building interfaces easier. Simple controls can display text and images and also gather information from users. You can tie simple controls to underlying data structures, and they will reflect changes in that data structure in real time using data binding. You are ready to start learning about the APIs (application programming interfaces) of specific controls, which are available in both MXML and ActionScript. The APIs are fully documented in the ASDOC, which is available at www.adobe.com/go/flex3_livedocs.

There are many tools within the Flex framework that make laying out simple controls easier. All controls are placed within containers (see Lesson 3, "Laying Out the Interface"). In this lesson, you will become familiar with simple controls by building the basic user interface of the application you will develop throughout this book. You will also learn about time-saving functionality built into the framework such as data binding, using the Form layout container, and using focus management to optimize the user experience.

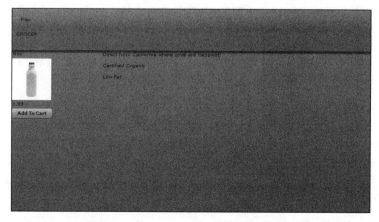

FlexGrocer with an Image and Text control bound to a data structure

Introducing Simple Controls

Simple controls are provided as part of the framework and help make rich Internet application (RIA) development easy. Using controls, you can easily define the look and feel of your buttons, text, combo boxes, and much more. Later in this book you'll learn how to customize controls to provide your own unique look and feel. Controls provide a standards-based methodology that makes learning how to use them easy. Controls are the foundation of any RIA.

Flex includes an extensive class library for both simple and complex controls. All these classes can be instantiated via an MXML tag or as a standard ActionScript class, and their APIs are accessible in both MXML and ActionScript. The class hierarchy also includes other classes that define the new event model, as well as the display attributes that all simple controls share.

You place the visual components of your Flex application inside containers, which provide bounding boxes for text, controls, images, and other media elements (you learned about containers in the last lesson). All simple controls have events that can be used to respond to user actions, such as clicking a button, or system events, such as drawing another component (events will be covered in detail in the next lesson). You will also learn in later lessons how to build your own custom events. Custom events are a fundamental concept used to build easily maintainable applications that reduce the risk of a change to one portion of the application forcing a change in another. This concept is often referred to as building a "loosely coupled" application.

Most applications need to display some sort of text, whether it be static or dynamically driven from a database. Flex has a number of text controls that can be used to display editable or noneditable text. You have already used the Label control to display single lines of text. The Label control cannot be edited by an end user, so if you need that functionality you can use a TextInput control. The TextInput control, like the Label control, is limited to a single line of text. The Text control is used to display multiple lines of text, but is not editable and does not display scroll bars if the usable space is exceeded. The TextArea component is useful for displaying multiple lines of text, either editable or noneditable, with scroll bars if the available text exceeds the screen space available. All text controls support HTML 1.0 and a variety of text and font styles.

To populate text fields at runtime, you must assign an id to the control. Once you have done that, you can access the control's properties; for example, all the text controls previously mentioned have a `text` property. This property can be used to populate the control with plain text using either an ActionScript function or by doing it inline using data binding. The following code demonstrates assigning an ID to the label, which enables you to reference the Label control in ActionScript:

```
<mx:Label id="myLabel"/>
```

You can populate any text control at runtime using data binding, which is denoted by curly bracket syntax in MXML. The following code will cause your Label control to display the same text as the myLabel control in the previous example:

```
<mx:Label id = "yourLabel" text = "{myLabel.text}"/>
```

Data binding can also be used to bind a simple control to underlying data structures. For example, if you have XML data, which might come from a server-side dataset, you can use the functionality of data binding to connect a simple control to the data structure. When the underlying data changes, the controls are automatically updated to reflect the new data. This provides a powerful tool for the application developer.

The Flex framework also provides a powerful container for building the forms that will be covered in this lesson. The Form container allows developers to create efficient, good-looking forms with minimal effort. The heading, spacing, and arrangement of form items are handled automatically by Flex.

Displaying Images

In this exercise you will be displaying images of grocery products. To do this, you must use the Image control to load images dynamically. The Image control has the capability to load JPG, SVG, GIF, SWF, and PNG files at runtime. You also have the ability to use an alpha channel with GIF and PNG files that enable you to create transparencies in images. If you are developing an offline application that will not access the Internet, you can use the @Embed directive to include the Image control in the completed SWF file.

1 Open the EComm.mxml file you worked with in the previous lesson. If you didn't complete the previous lesson, you can open EComm.mxml from Lesson04/start and save it in your flexGrocer/src directory.

2 Switch Flex Builder to Design mode by clicking the Design mode button.

3 Be sure that the Components view is open. If not, choose Window > Components.

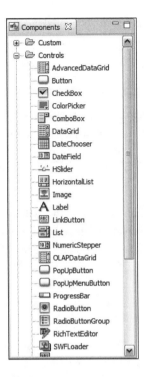

4 Select the Image control and drag and drop the control between the Milk and 1.99 Label controls you already added.

When you drag the Image control from the Components view to the container, Flex Builder automatically adds the MXML to place the Image control on the screen and position it where you indicated when you dropped it.

5 Be sure that the Flex Properties view is open. If not, choose Window > Flex Properties.

The Flex Properties view shows important attributes of the selected component—in this case, the Image control. You can see the Source property, which specifies the path to the Image file. The ID of the Image control is used to reference the instance created from the `<mx:Image>` tag or Image class in ActionScript.

6 Click the Source folder button and navigate to the assets directory. Select the dairy_milk. jpg image and click Open. You see the image appear in Design mode.

The image you selected in Design mode is displayed. The source property will also be added to the MXML tag.

7 Click the Scale content drop-down list and change the value to true.

In an ideal world, all the images that you use in the application would be a perfect size, but this is not always the case. Flex has the capability to set the width and height of images and can scale the image to fit the size of the Image control.

8 Switch back to Source mode and notice that Flex Builder has added an `<mx:Image>` tag as well as the attributes you specified in the Flex Properties window.

As you can see, it is easy to switch between Source mode and Design mode, and each one has its own advantages.

```
            </mx:AddChild>
            <mx:AddChild relativeTo="{cartBox}" position="lastChild">
                <mx:LinkButton label="Continue Shopping" click="this.currentState='
            </mx:AddChild>
            <mx:RemoveChild target="{linkbutton1}"/>
        </mx:State>
    </mx:states>
    <mx:ApplicationControlBar dock="true" width="100%" height="90">
        <mx:Canvas width="100%" height="100%">
            <mx:Label x="0" y="0" text="Flex"/>
            <mx:Label x="0" y="41" text="GROCER"/>
            <mx:Button label="View Cart" id="btnViewCart" right="90" y="0"/>
            <mx:Button label="Checkout" id="btnCheckout" right="10" y="0"/>
        </mx:Canvas>
    </mx:ApplicationControlBar>
    <mx:Label text="(c) 2006, FlexGrocer" right="10" bottom="10"/>
    <mx:HBox x="0" y="0" width="100%" height="100%" id="bodyBox">
        <mx:VBox width="100%" height="100%" id="products">
            <mx:Label text="Milk" id="prodName"/>
            <mx:Image source="assets/dairy_milk.jpg" scaleContent="true"/>
            <mx:Label text="$1.99" id="price"/>
            <mx:Button label="Add To Cart" id="add"/>
        </mx:VBox>
        <mx:VBox height="100%" id="cartBox">
```

9 In the <mx:Image> tag that you added, add an @Embed directive to the Image control:

<mx:Image source="@Embed('assets/dairy_milk.jpg')" scaleContent="true"/>

The @Embed directive causes the compiler to bake the JPG into the SWF file at compile time. This technique has a couple of advantages over the default of loading the image at runtime. First, the image is loaded at the start of the application; so, the user doesn't have to wait for the image to be displayed. Also, this technique can be useful if you are building offline applications that do not access the Internet because the appropriate images are included in the SWF file and will be correctly displayed. Remember, though, that using this technique greatly increases the size of your SWF file.

10 Save and compile the application, and then click Run.

You should see that the Image and Label controls and button fit neatly into the layout container.

Building a Detail View

In this exercise, you will use a rollover event to display a detailed state of the application. You will explore the use of different simple controls to display text and review how application states work.

1 Be sure that you are still in Source mode in Flex Builder. Locate the `<mx:Image>` tag that displays the image you added in the previous section. Add a mouseOver event to the tag that will change the currentState to expanded.

```
<mx:Image source="@Embed('assets/dairy_milk.jpg')" scaleContent="true"
    mouseOver="this.currentState='expanded'"/>
```

mouseOver simply means that when the user rolls the mouse anywhere over the dairy_milk.jpg image tag, the ActionScript will be executed. In this ActionScript, you are referring to the expanded state, which will be created later in this lesson. You will modify this state so it displays more information about the item the user is interested in purchasing.

2 In the same `<mx:Image>` tag, add a mouseOut event that will change the currentState back to the default or original state. The beginning view state of the application is expressed as "" or " inline.

```
<mx:Image source="@Embed('assets/dairy_milk.jpg')" scaleContent="true"
    mouseOver="this.currentState='expanded'"
    mouseOut="this.currentState=''"/>
```

When the user moves the mouse away from the dairy_milk.jpg image, the detailed state is no longer displayed, and the application displays only the images and labels for the control, which is the default and expressed with an empty string.

3 Switch back to Design mode. Be sure to click the Refresh button to make sure all your changes in code have been applied.

4 Be sure that the States view is open. If not, choose Window > States. Click the New State button and create a new state with the name of **expanded**. Be sure that this state is based on the `<Base state>` state.

You want the product description to appear when the user rolls the pointer over the <mx:Image> tag that shows the image associated with each grocery item.

5 Return to Source mode, and locate the expanded state. Add an <mx:AddChild> tag, and inside of that tag add an <mx:VBox> tag. You will see that Flex automatically adds the <mx:State name="expanded"/> tag; however, it used the single tag syntax described in Lesson 2, "Getting Started." You need to change this to an open and close tag, as shown:

```
<mx:State name="expanded">
   <mx:AddChild>
      <mx:VBox>

      </mx:VBox>
   </mx:AddChild>
</mx:State>
```

You will place all the controls to display the item detail inside a VBox container so that you can position the controls all at once.

6 Set the x property of the VBox container in the expanded state to 200. Also, set the width property to 100%, as follows.

```
<mx:VBox x="200" width="100%">
```

This places the controls in the <mx:VBox> tag in a better position—easier for users to view when they roll over the grocery product.

7 Switch back to Design mode. Ensure that the expanded state is selected in the States view and drag an instance of the Text control from the Controls folder in the Components view to the VBox container you just modified in the previous step.

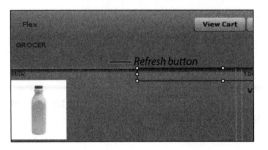

The Text control enables you to display multiple lines of text, which you will do when you display the product description, which will ultimately come from a database. You will use data binding in the next section to make this Text control functional. For now, you are just setting up the layout. All the text must use the same styling unless you specify it as HTML text.

8 Drag an instance of the Label control from the Components view to the bottom part of the VBox container you created. Populate the text property with the words **Certified Organic**.

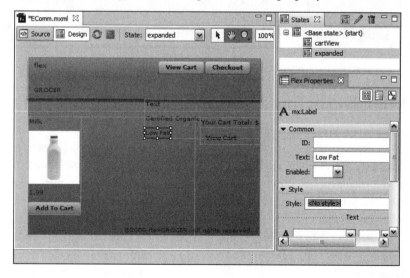

The Label control allows you to display a single line of text. Later on, you will modify the visible property of this component to be displayed only when a grocery item is certified organic.

9 Drag an instance of the Label control from the Components view to the bottom part of the VBox container you created. Populate the text property with the words **Low Fat**.

Later, you will set the visible property of this label to true if the grocery item is low fat or false if it is not.

10 Switch back to Source mode. Notice that Flex Builder has added the Text and two Label controls you added in Design mode.

Note that all the code created in Design mode is displayed in the code in Source mode.

11 Locate the <mx:Text> tag in the expanded state and set the width property of the Text control to 50%.

```
<mx:Text text="Text" width="50%"/>
```

12 Save and run the application.

When you roll the pointer over the milk bottle image, you see the Text and Label controls you created in the expanded state.

Using Data Binding to Link a Data Structure to a Simple Control

Data binding enables you to connect controls, such as the text controls that you have already worked with, to an underlying data structure. Data binding is incredibly powerful because if the underlying data changes, the changes are reflected in the control. For example, suppose that you created a text control that displayed the latest sports scores and was connected to a data structure in Flex. When a score changed in that data structure, the changes would also be reflected in the control that the end user views. In this task, you will connect a basic data structure in an <mx:Model> tag to simple UI controls to display the name, image, and price associated with each grocery item. Later in the book, you will learn more about data models, the effective use of a model-view-controller architecture on the client, and how to actually connect these data structures with server-side data.

1 Be sure that EComm.mxml is open, and add an <mx:Model> tag directly below the <mx:Application> tag at the top of the page.

The <mx:Model> tag allows you to build a client-side data model. This tag converts an XML data structure into a format Flex can use.

2 Directly below the opening <mx:Model> tag, and before the closing <mx:Model> tag, add the following XML data structure. Your <mx:Model> tag should look as shown:

```
<mx:Model>
    <groceries>
        <catName>Dairy</catName>
        <prodName>Milk</prodName>
        <imageName>assets/dairy_milk.jpg</imageName>
        <cost>1.20</cost>
        <listPrice>1.99</listPrice>
        <isOrganic>true</isOrganic>
        <isLowFat>true</isLowFat>
        <description>Direct from California where cows are happiest!</description>
    </groceries>
</mx:Model>
```

You have defined a very simple data structure inline inside of an <mx:Model> tag.

3 Assign the <mx:Model> tag an ID of groceryInventory. The first line of your <mx:Model> tag should look as shown:

```
<mx:Model id="groceryInventory">
```

By assigning an ID to the <mx:Model> tag, you can reference the data using dot syntax. For example, to access the list price of the item, you could simply use groceryInventory.listPrice. In this case, that would resolve to 1.99.

4 Switch Flex Builder to Design mode.

In Design mode, you can easily set up the bindings between the data structure and the controls. You can also set up the bindings in Source mode.

5 Select the Text control in the expanded state and be sure that the Flex Properties view is open. Modify the text property to **{groceryInventory.description}**.

The data binding is indicated by the curly brackets {}. Whenever the curly brackets are used, you use ActionScript instead of simple strings. Data binding is extremely powerful because the UI control will be updated if the data structure changes, which will become increasingly important as you begin to work with server-side data.

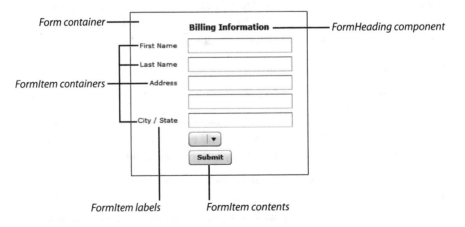

6 Save and run the application.

You should see that the description you entered in the data model appears when you roll the pointer over the grocery item.

Using a Form Layout Container to Lay Out Simple Controls

Forms are important in most applications that collect information from users. You will be using the Form container to enable an administrator to update the inventory for the grocery store. The administrator can add new items, delete old items, and update existing items. The Form container in Flex will handle the layout of the controls in this form, automating much of the routine work. With a Form container, you can designate fields as required or optional, handle error messages, and perform data checking and validation to be sure the administrator follows designated guidelines. A Form container uses three separate tags: an <mx:Form> tag, an <mx:FormHeading> tag, and an <mx:FormItem> tag for each item on the form.

1 Open DataEntry.mxml and switch to Source mode. After the <mx:Application> tag, add a new <mx:Model> tag, assign it an ID of **prodModel**, and add the data structure as follows:

```
<mx:Model id="prodModel">
   <groceries>
      <catName>Dairy</catName>
      <prodName>Milk</prodName>
      <imageName>assets/dairy_milk.jpg</imageName>
      <cost>1.20</cost>
      <listPrice>1.99</listPrice>
      <isOrganic>true</isOrganic>
      <isLowFat>true</isLowFat>
      <description>Direct from California where cows are happiest!</description>
   </groceries>
</mx:Model>
```

You will use this application to build an interface so administrators can update and add information in a database. Later in the book, you will use a server-side dataset from an actual database to populate the fields.

2 Below the <mx:Model> tag, use the <mx:Form> tag to define the outermost container of the form.

```
<mx:Form>
</mx:Form>
```

The Form container, which is the outermost tag of a Flex form, always arranges its children in a vertical fashion and left-aligns them. All your form elements will be defined within this container.

3 Within the Form container, use the <mx:FormHeading> tag to define a heading for the current category. Use data binding to set up the binding between the label property and the catName property of the data model.

```
<mx:FormHeading label="{prodModel.catName}"/>
```

The <mx:FormHeading> tag enables you to specify a label for a group of FormItem containers. This is perfect for your application because the user will be updating items from a specific category, such as produce or bakery. It is possible to have multiple <mx:FormHeading> tags, with the left side of the label in the <mx:FormHeading> aligning with the left side of the form.

4 After the FormHeading container, use the <mx:FormItem> tag to define the product name. Inside the <mx:FormItem> tag, add an <mx:TextInput> tag with an ID of product that will be populated with the name of the actual item from the data model. Use data binding to reference the prodName property inside the model.

```
<mx:FormItem label="Product Name">
   <mx:TextInput id="product" text="{prodModel.prodName}"/>
</mx:FormItem>
```

The <mx:FormItem> tag will automatically specify one Label control with one or more form elements, such as TextInput controls. A label displaying Product Name is automatically added with the appropriate spacing and alignment relative to the TextInput control.

5 After the last <mx:FormItem> tag, insert another <mx:FormItem> tag, set the label to ProductNameUnit, and specify the direction property as horizontal. Inside the FormItem container, place a ComboBox control and a TextInput control. Leave the ComboBox and TextInput controls blank for now; you will come back to them in a later lesson.

```
<mx:FormItem label="ProductNameUnit" direction="horizontal">
   <mx:ComboBox/>
   <mx:TextInput/>
</mx:FormItem>
```

By default, all the controls in a FormItem container are laid out vertically to the right of the Label control. By using the direction attribute in the <mx:FormItem> tag, you can specify that the controls should be laid out horizontally instead of vertically. If the children are laid out horizontally and do not fit into a single row, they are divided into multiple rows with equal-sized columns.

6 After the last <mx:FormItem> tag, add three more <mx:FormItem> tags that define the cost, the list price, and the description of the item. Place TextInput controls with the binding to the text property, inside each FormItem container:

```
<mx:FormItem label="Cost">
   <mx:TextInput id="cost" text="{prodModel.cost}"/>
</mx:FormItem>
<mx:FormItem label="List Price">
   <mx:TextInput id="listPrice" text="{prodModel.listPrice}"/>
</mx:FormItem>
<mx:FormItem label="Description">
   <mx:TextInput id="Description" text="{prodModel.description}"/>
</mx:FormItem>
```

This code will add more information to the form that the user needs when updating, adding, or deleting product.

7 After the last `<mx:FormItem>` tag, add two more `<mx:FormItem>` tags that define whether the product is organic or low fat. Use a CheckBox control with the `selected` attribute, and be sure to get this data from the data model tag.

```
<mx:FormItem label="Organic">
   <mx:CheckBox id="isOrganic" selected="{prodModel.isOrganic}"/>
</mx:FormItem>
<mx:FormItem label="Is Low Fat?">
   <mx:CheckBox id="isLowFat" selected="{prodModel.isLowFat}"/>
</mx:FormItem>
```

The CheckBox control can contain a checkmark or be left unchecked (empty). When the user clicks the check box, the CheckBox control changes its state from checked to unchecked or vice versa. This is accessed through the `selected` property, which is a Boolean value (true or `false`).

8 After the last `<mx:FormItem>` tag, add another `<mx:FormItem>` tag that will display two items in a horizontal box: the first is the path of the image in the data model in a TextInput control, and the second is a button that will allow users to browse for the image.

```
<mx:FormItem label="Image Path">
   <mx:TextInput id="imageName" text="{prodModel.imageName}"/>
   <mx:Button label="Browse"/>
</mx:FormItem>
```

You will add functionality to the Browse button in the next step using the FileReference class, so users can upload data from the client to a server.

9 Add an `<mx:Script>` block to the top of the application, immediately after the existing `<mx:Model>` tag. Note that a CDATA tag is automatically added for you by Flex Builder. Import the FileReference class and then create a function with the name of `fileBrowse()` that instantiates a new instance of the FileReference class and calls the `browse()` function.

```
<mx:Script>
<![CDATA[
import flash.net.FileReference;
public function fileBrowse():void{
   var myFileRef:FileReferenceList = new FileReferenceList();
   myFileRef.browse();
}
]]>
</mx:Script>
```

The file upload process will be completed in Lesson 18, "Accessing Server-Side Objects."

You have used MXML to lay out your application and will now use ActionScript to add functionality and provide logic. The first line of code enables you to make use of the existing FileReference class. The second line of code declares a new function. The void keyword indicates that the function is not expected to return a value to the caller. The first line of the function creates a new object: myFileRef from the FileReference class you imported. It is important to specify the type of all objects that you create. Here you type the object to FileReferenceList. By typing objects, you will receive better error messages to debug your application and get faster performance. The second line in the function calls the browse() method of the FileReference class, which will cause a window to pop up when the user clicks the Browse button. Mac users will see a similar window, although styled with their specific operating system chrome.

10 Return to the Browse button and add a click event that will call the fileBrowse() method you wrote in the last step.

```
<mx:Button label="Browse" click="fileBrowse()"/>
```

This code will call the method that you wrote in the script block and cause the pop-up window to appear. You will learn later in the book how to send the data to a server.

11 After the last <mx:FormItem> tag, add another <mx:FormItem> tag that will display two buttons, one with the label of Update and the other with the label of Delete, in an HBox.

```
<mx:FormItem>
  <mx:HBox>
    <mx:Button label="Update"/>
    <mx:Button label="Delete"/>
  </mx:HBox>
</mx:FormItem>
```

12 Save and run the application.

> **TIP:** If you tab through the various components of the form, you might wonder whether there is a way to control which components receive the user focus. The form itself (and each top-level container), has a built-in focus manager. The focus manager contains a getFocus() method that will return the component that currently has the focus. You can use the setFocus() method to set the focus to another component. Using the Focus Manager class is the preferred method to control selection in a Flex application.

13 Close the current editor by clicking the X.

Adding Radio Buttons and Date Fields to the Dashboard

Radio buttons in Flex work differently than in HTML. When you have more than one radio button and you want the user to be able to select only one, you must define a RadioButtonGroup. Only one radio button in a RadioButtonGroup can be selected at a time. You will define a RadioButtonGroup in the Dashboard application, enabling the user to view data for either gross sales or net sales, but not both.

1 Open Dashboard.mxml and locate the <mx:ApplicationControlBar> tag. Immediately after the comparison <mx:LinkButton> tag (the last one), add an <mx:Spacer> tag and set the width to 100%.

```
<mx:Spacer width="100%"/>
```

This tag will simply add space between the current LinkBar control and the RadioButton controls that you will add.

2 Immediately after the `<mx:Spacer>` tag, add an `<mx:Label>` control, set the `text` property to **Start Date**, and add an `<mx:DateField>` tag with an ID of **startDate**.

```
<mx:Label text="Start Date"/>
<mx:DateField id="startDate"/>
```

This will create a new date field that the end user can click, causing a calendar date chooser to appear.

3 Add another `<mx:Label>` control, and set the `text` property to **End Date**. Add an `<mx:DateField>` tag with an ID of **endDate**.

```
<mx:Label text="End Date"/>
<mx:DateField id="endDate"/>
```

This will create another new date field that the end user can click to cause calendar date chooser to appear.

4 Add a new `<mx:RadioButtonGroup>` tag and assign it an ID of **grossOrNetGroup**.

```
<mx:RadioButtonGroup id="grossOrNetGroup"/>
```

This will define a new RadioButtonGroup. You will add two new radio buttons to this group in the next step. Because both buttons will belong to the same group, the user can choose only one radio button.

5 Immediately after the `<mx:RadioButtonGroup>` tag, add a new `<mx:RadioButton>` tag and assign it an ID of **gross**. Assign the `groupName` property to the ID of the `RadioButtonGroup` you created, defined previously as `grossOrNetGroup`. Assign it a `label` of **Gross Sales**, a `data` property of **GROSS**, and set the `selected` property to **true**.

```
<mx:RadioButton id="gross"
    groupName="grossOrNetGroup"
    label="Gross Sales"
    data="GROSS"
    selected="true"/>
```

This creates a new radio button on the screen that belongs to the `grossOrNetGroup`. You have assigned a label of Gross Sales. You can tell which radio button the user has selected through the `data` property. Because you have set the `selected` property to `true`, this radio button will be selected by default.

6 Immediately after the `<mx:RadioButton>` tag, add a new `<mx:RadioButton>` tag and assign it an ID of **net**. Assign the `groupName` property to the ID of the RadioButtonGroup you created, defined previously as `grossOrNetGroup`, and assign it a `label` of **Net Sales**. Also, assign the `data` property as `NET`.

```
<mx:RadioButton id="net"
    groupName="grossOrNetGroup"
    label="Net Sales"
    data="NET"/>
```

7 Save and run the application.

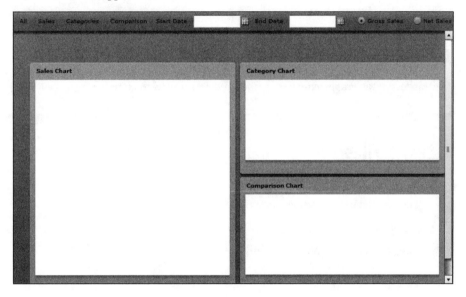

What You Have Learned

In this lesson, you have:

- Learned how to load images at runtime with the Image control (pages 71–74)

- Learned how to display blocks of text (pages 75–78)

- Learned how to link simple controls to an underlying data structure with data binding (pages 78–80)

- Learned how to build user forms with a minimum of effort using the Form container (pages 80–85)

- Learned how to use radio buttons (pages 85–87)

What You Will Learn

In this lesson, you will:

- Understand that Flex uses an event-based programming model

- Handle both user and system events with ActionScript functions

- Understand that an event object is created every time an event is dispatched and use the event object's properties

- Create ActionScript classes for use as value objects

Approximate Time

This lesson takes approximately 1 hour and 15 minutes to complete.

Lesson Files

Media Files:

Lesson05/start/assets/inventory.xml

Starting Files:

Lesson05/start/Dashboard.mxml
Lesson05/start/DataEntry.mxml
Lesson05/start/EComm.mxml
Lesson05/eventObject/start/src/EventTest.mxml

Completed Files:

Lesson05/complete/valueObjects/ShoppingCartItem.as
Lesson05/eventObject/complete/src/EventTest.mxml

LESSON 5

Handling Events and Data Structures

An important part of building a rich Internet application (RIA) is building effective client-side architecture. When you use Flash Player to build an application, you have the ability to use an event-based programming model, build rich client-side data models, and create a logical application following good object-oriented best practices. This type of development is very different for web application developers, because it does not use a page-based, flow-driven development model. Ultimately, using this client-side, event-based architecture results in better-performing applications that consume less network traffic because page refreshes are no longer needed. During this lesson, you will use Flex's event-based programming model with custom ActionScript classes.

```
package valueObjects
{
    [Bindable]
    public class Product
    {
        public var catID:Number;
        public var prodName:String;
        public var unitID:Number;
        public var cost:Number;
        public var listPrice:Number;
        public var description:String;
        public var isOrganic:Boolean;
        public var isLowFat:Boolean;
        public var imageName:String;

        public function Product (_catID:Number, _prodName:String, _unitID:Number, _cost:
            catID = _catID;
            prodName =_prodName;
            unitID =_unitID;
            cost = _cost;
            listPrice = _listPrice;
            description = _description;
            isOrganic = _isOrganic;
            isLowFat =  _isLowFat;
```

The finished FlexGrocer data structure built in ActionScript 3.0 and integrated into the application

Understanding Event Handling

Flex uses an event-based, or event-driven, programming model. This means events deter-mine the flow of the application. For example, a user clicking the mouse button or data being returned from a web service determines what should happen next in the application.

These events come in two types: user events and system events. User events are just what you'd most likely guess—a user clicking a mouse or pressing a key. System events include the application being instantiated and displayed as well as a component changing from invisible to visible. The Flex developer determines what should happen when a certain event occurs. The developer handles these events and writes code for what should happen.

> ● **TIP:** Many server-side developers are accustomed to a flow-driven programming model, in which the developer determines the flow of the application rather than having to react to events generated by the user or system.

The following general steps occur when a developer wants something to happen based on a user event:

1. The user interacts with the application.

2. The object on which the user interacts dispatches a user event.

3. The event is listened for and handled.

4. Code associated with a corresponding event handler executes.

Understanding a Simple Example

Let's examine a concrete example to aid our understanding. In this example, the user will click a button and text will appear in a label. The code below makes this happen.

```
<mx:Label id="myL"/>

<mx:Button id="myButton"
    label="Click Me"
    click="myL.text='Button Clicked'"/>
```

A button appears with the label "Click Me." When the user clicks the button, the click event is dispatched. In this case the ActionScript myL.text='Button Clicked' is executed. The text property of the label is assigned the Button Clicked string value. This code contains nested values and, therefore, nested single and double quotes are necessary. The double quotes sur-round the entire line of code, and the nested single quotes delineate the string.

Up to now, when you have assigned values to properties you supplied one of two types of values: scalar values or bindings. Scalar values are simple data types like strings, numbers, or Boolean values. You have used these values when setting, for example, x and y values, widths, and label values. You have also used bindings for properties. This was done whenever you used braces ({}) in a value. Remember from the last lesson that the braces let you enter ActionScript for the value of a property.

When supplying a value to an event, it is understood by the Flex compiler to be ActionScript. So you can enter ActionScript directly for the value of the event without using braces. You see this done in the previous example code, click="myL.text='Button Clicked'".

Just as code hinting assisted you when entering property names, so will code hinting assist with event names. In the following figure, you see the change and click events displayed with the lightning bolt icon in front of them, which designates events.

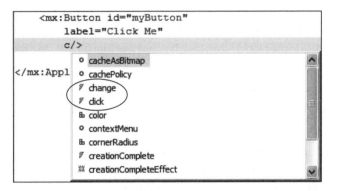

Handling the Event with an ActionScript Function

The code used earlier to place text in a label when a button was clicked worked well. But a problem with this approach soon develops when you have more than one or two lines of ActionScript you want executed when the event is handled. You would have to place many lines of code after the click event separated by semicolons, which, although it works, is messy and not a best practice. Also, you may have the same lines of code you want executed for several events. In the approach shown earlier, you would have to copy and paste the same code into several places, which leads to multiple changes if edits ever need to be made.

A better approach would handle the event in an ActionScript function. The function will be built in an <mx:Script> block, which simply tells the Flex compiler that the code in the Script block is ActionScript. So instead of placing the actual ActionScript to be executed as a value for the click event, you will call a function instead. Following is the code that does the exact same thing as the code examined earlier, except using the best practice of placing the code to be executed when the event occurs in a function.

```
<mx:Script>
  <![CDATA[
    private function clickHandler():void
    {
        myL.text="Button Clicked";
    }
  ]]>
</mx:Script>

<mx:Label id="myL"/>

<mx:Button id="myButton"
    label="Click Me"
    click="clickHandler()"/>
```

 NOTE: The <![CDATA[ ]]> block inside the Script block marks the section as character data. This tells the compiler that the data in the block is character data, not well formed XML, and should not show XML errors for this block.

So now when the button is clicked, the function clickHandler() is called, and the string is written to the label. In this case, because no quotes were nested, double quotes were used around the string.

The function itself is data typed as void. This means that the function will not return a value. It is a best practice to always data type the functions you build, even if using void to indicate no data will be returned. You will be given a warning by the compiler if you do not data type the function.

Passing Data when Calling the Event Handler Function

You may wish to pass data when calling the function. This works in ActionScript just as you'd expect. You place the data to pass inside the parentheses following the function name, and then modify the event handler to accept the parameter. Just as you will always data type your function itself, you also need to data type the parameter the function will accept.

In the following code example, the application is modified so the string to be displayed in the label is passed to the event handler.

```
<mx:Script>
  <![CDATA[
    private function clickHandler(toDisplay:String):void
    {
        myL.text=toDisplay;
    }
  ]]>
</mx:Script>
```

```
<mx:Label id="myL"/>

<mx:Button id="myButton"
    label="Click Me"
    click="clickHandler('Value Passed')"/>
```

In this case, when the button is clicked, the string Value Passed is sent to the event handler function. The function accepts the parameter in the toDisplay parameter, which is data typed as String. The value stored in the toDisplay variable is then displayed in the label's text property.

Building a Data Structure on the creationComplete Event

In general, the creationComplete event is dispatched when a component has been instantiated and properly placed in the application. The component will be visible in the application when creationComplete is dispatched unless its visible property is set to false. The creationComplete event on the Application object is dispatched when the children (all the components in the Application container) have broadcast their creationComplete events.

Let's examine the following code snippet:

```
<?xml version="1.0" encoding="utf-8"?>
<mx:Application xmlns:mx="http://www.adobe.com/2006/mxml"
    creationComplete="addToTextArea('Application creationComplete')">

    <mx:Script>
        <![CDATA[
            private function addToTextArea(eventText:String):void
            {
                var existingText:String=reportEvents.text;
                reportEvents.text=existingText+eventText+"\n";
            }
        ]]>
    </mx:Script>

    <mx:TextArea editable="false"
        height="100"
        width="200"
        borderStyle="solid"
        id="reportEvents" />

    <mx:HBox creationComplete="addToTextArea('HBox creationComplete')">
        <mx:Label creationComplete="addToTextArea('Label creationComplete')"/>
        <mx:Button creationComplete="addToTextArea('Button creationComplete')"/>
    </mx:HBox>

</mx:Application>
```

First look at the event handler named *addToTextArea*. This event handler simply accepts a parameter named eventText and places it in a TextArea, followed by a return so the text doesn't all run together. In each component, which includes an Application, HBox, Label, and Button, a creationComplete event is used. When each component finishes its completion process, the event is dispatched and the corresponding string is sent to the event handler for display in the TextArea.

Flex does not create from top to bottom; rather, you can think of its creation from inside out. So, first the Label and Button dispatch creationComplete events; then, since the HBox's children are finished, the HBox dispatches creationComplete. Finally, with all the Application's children created, the Application dispatches creationComplete.

The results displayed in the TextArea appear as shown here.

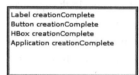

Armed with this knowledge, you can now understand why the creationComplete event on the Application object is often used for data retrieval. Once all the children of the Application are created, it is an appropriate time to request data from an outside source and use the data.

In this next task, you will make two major changes. The first is to reference an external file for the source of the data that is now embedded in the application. Then you will use an event handler to be sure the data is retrieved correctly by tracing part of the data.

In this task, you will first specify an external XML model for your <mx:Model> tag. You will then use the creationComplete event to call a method or function that will eventually build individual value objects using a custom ActionScript class.

1 In Flex Builder, open the file src/assets/inventory.xml.

This file is the data you used in the last lesson, except now it is in an external file.

2 Open the EComm.mxml file you worked with in the last lesson. If you didn't complete the previous lesson, you can open EComm.mxml from Lesson05/start and save it in your flexGrocer/src directory.

3 Remove the child nodes from the <mx:Model> tag and also remove the closing </mx:Model> tag.

4 Add a closing slash to the end of the <mx:Model> tag as follows:

```
<mx:Model id="groceryInventory" />
```

5 In the <mx:Model> tag, point to the external XML file by specifying the source attribute value as "assets/inventory.xml", as follows:

```
<mx:Model id="groceryInventory" source="assets/inventory.xml"/>
```

The <mx:Model> tag will automatically parse the data from this external XML file into a native ActionScript data structure—in this case, an object. In Lesson 6, "Using Remote XML Data with Controls," you will learn about more complex data structures.

6 In the <mx:Application> tag, add the creationComplete event and have it call an event handler function named prodHandler(), as follows:

```
<mx:Application xmlns:mx="http://www.adobe.com/2006/mxml"
    layout="absolute"
    creationComplete="prodHandler()">
```

As you have learned, when the creationComplete event is on the <mx:Application> tag, it is dispatched only after all the children of that tag have been created. It is useful because it means that everything in the entire application is ready for use.

7 Pass to the prodHandler() the data structure created by the <mx:Model> tag, groceryInventory, as follows:

```
<mx:Application xmlns:mx="http://www.adobe.com/2006/mxml"
    layout="absolute"
    creationComplete="prodHandler(groceryInventory)">
```

The id of your <mx:Model> tag is groceryInventory. The <mx:Model> tag automatically created a simple ActionScript object from the XML file and can be used for data binding.

> **TIP:** If a variable or function has been created, you can get tag help when typing it. For instance, when entering the variable name **groceryInventory** as the function parameter, you could have typed **gr**, then pressed Ctrl-Space and selected the variable from a drop-down list.

8 Add an <mx:Script> block immediately after the existing <mx:Model> tag. Note that a CDATA tag is automatically added for you by Flex Builder. At the top of the script block, define a private function with the name of prodHandler(), data typed as void. The function must accept a parameter named theItems data typed as an Object.

```
<mx:Script>
    <![CDATA[
        private function prodHandler(theItems:Object):void
        {
        }
    ]]>
</mx:Script>
```

This prodHandler() function is the event handler for the creationComplete event. You have specified that this function is private, which means it can be accessed only from inside the class, that it will take a single parameter of type Object, and it will not return anything because you have specified void as the return type.

9 Inside the prodHandler() function, add two trace statements that will display the name and the price of the items being passed to it.

```
private function prodHandler(theItems:Object):void
{
   trace (theItems.prodName);
   trace (theItems.cost);
}
```

10 Click the Debug tool to compile the application. Return to Flex Builder.

This displays the results of your trace statements in the Console view. You should see the product name and the product price displayed in the console. You will need to minimize the browser that pops open and choose Window > Console if the console is not open.

```
Console
EComm (1) [Flex Application] file:/C:/flex3tfs/FlexGrocer2/bin-debug/EComm.html
[SWF] C:\flex3tfs\FlexGrocer2\bin-debug\EComm.swf - 978,560 bytes after decompression
Milk
1.2
```

Using Data from the Event Object

Flex creates an Event object each time an event is dispatched. This object contains information about the event that occurred. The event object is created automatically, even if you choose not to use it. But, you will use it often. Very commonly, you will pass the event object to the event handler and access properties from the object in the event handler.

There are many different kinds of event objects you can use. The generic Event object is defined in an ActionScript class. But this generic version will not work for all events. For instance, you can probably guess that the vital information returned from a drag-and-drop event will vary from the vital information returned when a web service call is completed. Because of this, the generic Event class is the basic building block for many other event classes. In fact, the following figure from the documentation shows how many other event classes are based on, or subclassed from, the generic Event object.

Package	flash.events
Class	public class Event
Inheritance	Event → Object
Subclasses	ActivityEvent, ADGHeaderShiftEvent, ADGItemSelectEvent, AdvancedDataGridEvent, AIREvent, AutomationEvent, AutomationRecordEvent, AutomationReplayEvent, BrowserChangeEvent, CalendarLayoutChangeEvent, ChannelEvent, ChartSelectionChangeEvent, ChildExistenceChangedEvent, CloseEvent, CollectionEvent, ColorPickerEvent, ContextMenuEvent, CubeEvent, CuePointEvent, DataGridEvent, DateChooserEvent, DividerEvent, DRMAuthenticateEvent, DRMStatusEvent, DropdownEvent, DynamicEvent, EffectEvent, FileEvent, FileListEvent, FlexEvent, FocusEvent, HTMLUncaughtJavaScriptExceptionEvent, HTTPStatusEvent, IndexChangedEvent, InvokeEvent, ItemClickEvent, KeyboardEvent, ListEvent, ListItemSelectEvent, LogEvent, MenuShowEvent, MessageEvent, MessageFaultEvent, MetadataEvent, MouseEvent, MoveEvent, NativeWindowBoundsEvent, NativeWindowDisplayStateEvent, NetStatusEvent, NumericStepperEvent, OutputProgressEvent, ProgressEvent, PropertyChangeEvent, ResizeEvent, ScrollEvent, SliderEvent, SQLEvent, SQLUpdateEvent, StateChangeEvent, StatusEvent, SyncEvent, TextEvent, TextSelectionEvent, TimerEvent, ToolTipEvent, TreeEvent, TweenEvent, ValidationResultEvent, VideoEvent

Why the need for all these different event objects? Well, you want an object that contains all the needed information, but no excess information.

The generic Event object contains properties included in all the event type objects. Two properties easily understood are the type and target. The type of the event is a string that contains the name of the event handled—for instance, click or creationComplete. The target is the component that dispatched the event—for instance, a Button component if the button is what was clicked to generate the event.

 NOTE: Target may seem like an odd name for this property because it was the event that broadcast the event, seemingly not the target of anything. This property name will make more sense once you finish Lesson 9, "Using Custom Events," and learn about event flow.

Examine the following code that sends an event object, in this case a MouseEvent object, to the event handler.

```
<mx:Script>
  <![CDATA[
    private function clickHandler(event:MouseEvent):void
    {
        trace(event.type);
    }
  ]]>
</mx:Script>

<mx:Label id="myL"/>

<mx:Button id="myButton"
  label="Click Me"
  click="clickHandler(event)"/>
```

In the code, an event is passed to the event handler and the word "click" will be displayed in the Console view when the application is debugged.

Although the Event object is not used at this point in any of the applications you are building, understanding the Event object is mandatory in an introduction to event handling. So, although it is not added to the existing code of the three applications, you will still explore the Event object in the following task.

1 Choose File > New > Flex Project. Set the Project name to be EventObject.

2 Set the Project location to be flex3tfs/Lesson05/eventObject/start.

3 For the Application type select Web application.

4 Set the Server technology to None, then click Next.

5 Leave the Output folder as bin-debug, then click Next.

6 Leave the Main source folder as src.

7 Browse for the Main application file and select EventTest.mxml. Click Finish.

You have now created a project. You can run the application that is used to experiment with the event object. This file is just a skeleton of an application with a Script block added.

8 Add a Button between the closing `</mx:Script>` tag and the end of the application. Give the Button the instance name `myButton` using the id property. Add a `label` property with a value of **Click To Debug**. Add a `click` event and have it call an event handler named doClick(), passing the event object as a parameter, as follows:

```
<mx:Button id="myButton" label="Click To Debug" click="doClick(event)"/>
```

When the button is clicked, the doClick() function will be called, and the event object passed to it.

9 In the script block, add a private function named doClick() data typed as void. Accept a parameter named event data typed as `MouseEvent`, as shown here:

```
private function doClick(event:MouseEvent):void
{

}
```

▶ **TIP:** You may wish to name your event handlers consistently. For instance, in this lesson you've seen a click event handled by event handlers named clickHandler() and doClick(). There is no "right" way to name event handlers, but you may wish to pick a naming convention and stick with it.

In the next step you will use the debugger built into Flex Builder in a very simple way. Lesson 25, "Debugging Flex Applications," discusses the debugger in depth. Here you will use it to examine the event object.

10 Add a breakpoint on the closing brace of the function by double-clicking in the marker bar just to the left of the code and line numbers. A small blue dot will appear in the marker bar indicating where program execution will halt. You can examine values at this point.

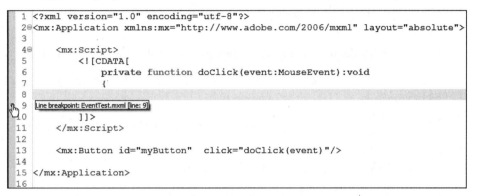

```
 1 <?xml version="1.0" encoding="utf-8"?>
 2 <mx:Application xmlns:mx="http://www.adobe.com/2006/mxml" layout="absolute">
 3
 4     <mx:Script>
 5         <![CDATA[
 6             private function doClick(event:MouseEvent):void
 7             {
 8
 9             Line breakpoint: EventTest.mxml [line: 9]
10         ]]>
11     </mx:Script>
12
13     <mx:Button id="myButton"  click="doClick(event)"/>
14
15 </mx:Application>
16
```

The debugger is immensely helpful in understanding what is happening in your Flex application. Use it often to get a sense of what is going on "under the hood" of the application.

11 In the Flex Builder interface, click the Debug button.

12 In the browser, click the button labeled Click To Debug. In Flex Builder, you will be prompted to use the Debugging perspective. You should select it.

13 Double-click the tab of the Variables view to use the full screen.

There will be lots of information and a full screen will make viewing easier.

14 You will see two variables displayed, this and event, as shown here:

Variables ✕	Breakpoints	Expressions
Name	**Value**	
⊞ ● this	EventTest (@e4b10a1)	
⊞ ● event	flash.events.MouseEvent (@e487769)	

The this variable represents the entire application. If you click the plus sign in front of the variable, you will see many properties and associated values. The event variable represents the event variable local to the function where the breakpoint was placed. The letter "L" in the icon in front of event indicates it is a local variable.

15 Click the + sign in front of the event variable and then the + sign in front of the [inherited] set of properties. Locate the target property. Notice that the target is the component that broadcasts the event Button. Also notice the type property has the value click.

From the earlier discussion, neither of those property values should be a surprise.

16 Click the + sign in front of the target, then click the + sign in front of the [inherited] set of properties, and locate the id property.

Notice that the property's value is myButton, which is what you assigned in the code.

17 Double-click the Variables tab again to restore it. Click the red box on either the Debug or Console view to terminate the debugging session.

Don't forget to terminate debugging sessions. It is possible to have one debugging session running inside another. You might want to do this in special cases, but not normally.

18 Return to the Development perspective by clicking the chevron (>>) in the top-right of your screen and then selecting Flex Development.

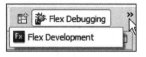

▶ **TIP:** If you place the cursor to the left of the Open Perspective icon, the sideways arrow will appear. You can click and drag to the left to increase the space allotted for perspectives. You will be able to see both the Development and Debugging perspectives and will be able to click their tabs to switch between them.

| ←→ 🗂 | 📄 Flex Develop... | 🐞 Flex Debugging |

19 Close the EventObject project and return to the FlexGrocer project.

Building a Custom ActionScript Class

As mentioned at the end of Lesson 2, "Getting Started," this book does not aspire to teach object-oriented programming (OOP), but every Flex developer needs at least a working knowledge of OOP terminology. So if you are not familiar with terms like *class*, *object*, *property*, and *method*, now is a good time to take advantage of the hundreds, if not thousands, of OOP introductions around the web and in books.

You have already been building custom ActionScript classes in this book but may not have been aware of it because Flex has hidden them from you. When you build an application in MXML, you are actually creating a new ActionScript class. Your MXML is combined with the ActionScript in the script block and a pure ActionScript class is created, which is then compiled into a .swf file for Flash Player to use. So in the last task when you created EventTest.mxml, a file named EventTest-generated.as was created that contained the following code:

```
public class EventTest extends mx.core.Application
```

You extended the Application class when you built EventTest.mxml, and all other applications that you've created in this book.

> **TIP:** If you wish to see the ActionScript created, you can add a compiler argument in Flex Builder. Navigate to Project > Properties > Flex Compiler > Additional compiler arguments and add to the end of the existing arguments the text **-keep-generated-actionscript**. A folder named generated will be created automatically in your project, and lots of ActionScript files will be placed there. Your actual application files will be in the form Name-generated.as. Don't forget to remove the compiler argument when you've finished exploring.

In this section of this lesson, you will build ActionScript classes directly in ActionScript, without relying on Flex to convert MXML into ActionScript.

A good question to ask is why would you want to do this? The answer is that building ActionScript classes will be required for some tasks you will perform in this book, including creating your own custom event classes and building value objects. You've just learned about the event object; in Lesson 9, you will build custom event objects to hold specific data, and you'll need to build custom ActionScript classes.

Building a Value Object

Value objects, also called data transfer objects (DTO), or just transfer objects, hold only data related to an object, are free of implementation detail and business logic, and are implemented as ActionScript classes.

The name data transfer object comes from the fact that DTOs are often used for data transfer to the back end of an application, often for permanent storage in a database. In this lesson, you will build value objects for a grocery product, a product when it is moved into a shopping cart, and the shopping cart itself.

Before you get started, the basics of building an ActionScript class need to be understood. A very simple class is shown here, and labeled for discussion:

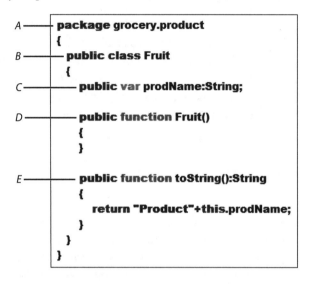

```
A ——— package grocery.product
       {
B ———   public class Fruit
         {
C ———      public var prodName:String;

D ———      public function Fruit()
             {
             }

E ———      public function toString():String
             {
                 return "Product"+this.prodName;
             }
         }
       }
```

In line A, the package represents the directory structure where the class is stored. In this example, you know the file is stored in a "grocery/product" directory structure in relation to the application.

In line B, the class is named Fruit. This must also correspond to the name of the file, Fruit.as.

In line C, the properties of the class are declared. Of course, multiple properties may be declared.

Line D contains the constructor of the class. The constructor is called automatically when a new object is instantiated from the class. The name of the constructor function must match the name of the class, which matches the name of the file. This function must be public and cannot be data typed.

In line E, the methods of the class are defined. Of course, multiple methods may be declared.

Throughout the FlexGrocer application, you will need to manage large amounts of typed data and send this data to other applications. In this task, you will build a value object to hold information about a grocery product.

1 Create a new ActionScript class file by choosing File > New > ActionScript class. Set the Package to **valueObjects**, which causes Flex Builder to automatically create a folder with the same name. Name the class **Product** and leave all other fields with the defaults. Click Finish to create the file.

This process creates a file for you, named Product.as, with the basic structure of an ActionScript class. The words package and class are both keywords used in defining this class. Remember that this class will be a blueprint for many objects that you will use later to describe each grocery product.

2 In the file you've just created before the class keyword, but after the package keyword, add a [Bindable] metadata tag. Inside the Product class definition, add a public property with the name of catID and a data type of Number.

```
package valueObjects{
   [Bindable]
   public class Product{
      public var catID:Number;
   }
}
```

The [Bindable] metadata tag, when specified in front of the class keyword, means that every property in the class can be used in a binding (be bound to controls or other data structures). Instead of specifying the whole class as [Bindable], you can specify individual properties. In the case of the FlexGrocer application, we want every property to be bindable.

3 Create public properties with the names of prodName (String), unitID (Number), cost (Number), listPrice (Number), description (String), isOrganic (Boolean), isLowFat (Boolean), and imageName (String). Your class should appear as follows:

```
package valueObjects{
   [Bindable]
   public class Product{
      public var catID:Number;
      public var prodName:String;
      public var unitID:Number;
      public var cost:Number;
      public var listPrice:Number;
      public var description:String;
      public var isOrganic:Boolean;
      public var isLowFat:Boolean;
      public var imageName:String;
   }
}
```

You are creating a data structure to store inventory information for the grocery store. You have now created all the properties that will be used in the class.

4 Within the braces for the Product class, after the imageName property, define the constructor function of the class and specify the parameters that will be passed to this function. The parameters should match the data type of the properties you already defined, and the names should match but begin with an underscore in order to avoid *name collision* (when the same name could refer to two separate variables) between parameters and properties. Be sure that the name of the function matches the class name and that the constructor is public. You cannot data type the constructor function.

```
public function Product (_catID:Number, _prodName:String, _unitID:Number,
   ➡ _cost:Number, _listPrice:Number, _description:String,_isOrganic:Boolean,
   ➡ _isLowFat:Boolean, _imageName:String){
}
```

The constructor function is called automatically every time an object is created from a class. You can create an object from a class by using the new keyword and passing the class parameters. Eventually, you will pass values from your <mx:Model> tag or database to the constructor parameter.

5 Inside the constructor function, set each property to the value passed to the constructor function.

```
public function Product (_catID:Number, _prodName:String, _unitID:Number,
   ➡ _cost:Number, _listPrice:Number, _description:String,_isOrganic:Boolean,
   ➡ _isLowFat:Boolean, _imageName:String)
   {
```

```
    catID = _catID;
    prodName = _prodName;
    unitID = _unitID;
    cost = _cost;
    listPrice = _listPrice;
    description = _description;
    isOrganic = _isOrganic;
    isLowFat = _isLowFat;
    imageName = _imageName;
}
```

This code will set each class property to the parameter value passed to the constructor.

> **TIP:** Each property listed to the left of the equals sign could have had a `this.` prefix on it, for example `this.catID = _catID;`. Such a prefix is sometimes added when developers wish to use the same names for both properties and parameters while still avoiding name collision. The `this` prefix refers to the class itself.

6 Create a new method directly below the constructor function with the name of toString(), which will return the string [Product] and the name of the product.

```
public function toString():String
{
    return "[Product]"+this.prodName;
}
```

This method will return the name of the current product and will be handy for retrieving the name when you need it. Building methods to access properties is good practice because if the property name ever changes, you still call the same function, potentially saving much legacy code. The toString() method is automatically invoked by Flex framework any time an object is traced. This can be very useful for debugging and displaying data structures.

7 Return to the EComm.mxml file and locate the script block at the top of the page. Just below the CDATA tag, import the Product class from the valueObjects folder.

```
import valueObjects.Product;
```

To use a custom class, Flex Builder needs an `import` statement that references the location or package in which the class is located. When you write a custom class, you need to import a class explicitly so it is available to Flex framework. You do this by using the `import` keyword.

8 In the script block following the `import` statement and above the function, declare a private variable named theProduct data typed as Product. Add a [Bindable] metadata tag.

```
[Bindable]
private var theProduct:Product;
```

All MXML files ultimately compile to an ActionScript class. You must follow the same conventions when creating an MXML file as when creating an ActionScript class. For example, you must import any classes that are not native to the ActionScript language, such as the Product class you have built, and you must declare any properties that you will use in your MXML file. This is done in a script block. The [Bindable] metadata tag ensures that this property's value can be used in binding expressions.

9 Within the prodHandler() function, but above the trace statements, create a new instance of the Product class with the name theProduct, and populate and pass the parameter to the constructor function with the information from the <mx:Model> tag, as follows:

```
theProduct = new Product(theItems.catID, theItems.prodName,
    ➥ theItems.unitID, theItems.cost, theItems.listPrice,
    ➥ theItems.description, theItems.isOrganic, theItems.isLowFat,
    ➥ theItems.imageName);
```

Here you are using the new class you built and instantiating an object of that class type. You are passing the data from the <mx:Model> tag as values for the properties.

10 Delete the two trace statements from the prodHandler() function and replace them with a new trace statement. This statement will automatically retrieve the information you specified in the toString() method.

```
trace(theProduct);
```

11 Save and debug the application.

You should see [Product]Milk in the console window, which indicates that you have created a Product value object.

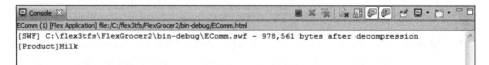

```
Console ✕
EComm (1) [Flex Application] file:/C:/flex3tfs/FlexGrocer2/bin-debug/EComm.html
[SWF] C:\flex3tfs\FlexGrocer2\bin-debug\EComm.swf - 978,561 bytes after decompression
[Product]Milk
```

Building a Method to Create an Object

As you just did in the previous exercise, you can instantiate an instance of the Product class by passing all the values to the constructor method as parameters. In this task, you will build a method that will accept an object which contains all the property/value pairs, and return an instance of the Product class. Note that for this method to function correctly, the object passed to the method must contain property names that correspond exactly to the property names you used in the class.

1 Be sure the Product class in the valueObjects folder is open. Locate the toString() method and after this method add the skeleton of a new public, static method called buildProduct(). Be sure that the return type of the method is set to Product, and that it accepts a parameter named o data typed as Object, as shown:

```
public static function buildProduct(o:Object):Product
{
}
```

A static method can be called without having to first create an object from the class. Instance methods, like those we have used so far, can be used only with objects instantiated from the class. Methods declared as static can be used directly from the class. Static methods are useful for utilities such as the buildObject() static method you are creating here because you want to access this method without having to create an object first. Used appropriately, static methods can increase performance because you do not have to first create an object that uses space in memory. To reference a static method with the name of getName() from the Product class, you would use the code Product.getName(), which uses the class name before the method, not the name of an object instantiated from the class.

2 Inside the buildProduct() method, instantiate an instance of the Product class with the name of p by using the new keyword. Set the catID, prodName, unitID, cost, listPrice, description, isOrganic, isLowFat, and imageName properties as parameters to the constructor. You will need to cast the isOrganic and isLowFat variables to Boolean.

```
var p:Product = new Product(o.catID, o.prodName, o.unitID, o.cost,
  ➥ o.listPrice, o.description, Boolean(o.isOrganic),
  ➥ Boolean(o.isLowFat), o.imageName);
```

Remember that the data used here is retrieved from the <mx:Model> tag. When data is retrieved this way, all the data is untyped, so the true and false values are just treated as simple strings. Casting a variable tells the compiler to treat a given value as a specific data type. In this example, you are telling the compiler that you, the developer, know that the isOrganic and isLowFat properties will contain Boolean data and by casting them to this type, the newly created object will have Boolean values for the isOrganic and isLowFat properties.

3 Return the object you just created by using the return keyword with the name of the object, p. Your final buildProduct() method should appear as follows:

```
public static function buildProduct(o:Object):Product{
   var p:Product = new Product(o.catID, o.prodName, o.unitID,
     ➥ o.cost, o.listPrice, o.description, Boolean(o.isOrganic),
     ➥ Boolean(o.isLowFat), o.imageName);
   return p;
}
```

This code will return a Product value object created by passing a generic object to the method.

4 Save the Product.as file.

The class file is saved with the new method. No errors should appear in the Problems view.

5 Return to EComm.mxml. In the `prodHandler()` method, remove the code that builds `theProduct` and replace it with code that uses the static method to build `theProduct`. Remember to remove the `new` keyword.

```
theProduct = Product.buildProduct(theItems);
```

This code calls the static method that builds an instance of the Product class, which returns a strongly typed Product value object from an object that was not typed.

6 Locate the first VBox layout container in the expanded state, which displays the product description, whether the product is organic, and whether the product is low fat. Change the `text` property of `<mx:Text>` tag to reference the theProduct object you created in the `prodHandler()` method. Also, add a `visible` property to both labels, and bind each to the appropriate theProduct object properties, as shown in the following code.

> **TIP:** Remember now that Product is a class and imported, you can get code hinting for both the class name and its properties. When you are in the braces creating the binding, press Ctrl-spacebar to get help for inserting the Product instance, theProduct. Then, after you enter the period, you will get the properties listed.

```
<mx:VBox x="200" width="100%">
    <mx:Text text="{theProduct.description}" width="50%"/>
    <mx:Label text="Certified Organic"
        visible="{theProduct.isOrganic}"/>
    <mx:Label text="Low Fat"
        visible="{theProduct.|}"/>
</mx:VBox>
:AddChild>                        o  catID
te>                               ◇  constructor
                                  o  cost
ionControlBar dock="true" wid    o  description
as width="100%" height="100%"    o  imageName
Label x="0" y="0" text="Flex"    o  isLowFat
Label x="0" y="41" text="GROC    o  isOrganic
Button label="View Cart" id="    o  listPrice
                                  o  prodName
```

```
<mx:VBox x="200" width="100%">
   <mx:Text text="{theProduct.description}"
      width="50%"/>
   <mx:Label
      text="Certified Organic"
      visible="{theProduct.isOrganic}"/>
   <mx:Label
      text="Low Fat"
      visible="{theProduct.isLowFat}"/>
</mx:VBox>
```

You are now referencing the value object you created.

7 Save and debug the application.

You should see that the trace performs just as before, and the data binding should still work when you roll over the image.

Building Shopping Cart Classes

In this task, you will build a new class for items added to the shopping cart. The new class will need to keep track of which product was added and its quantity. You will build a method that calculates the subtotal for that item. You will also build the skeleton for a ShoppingCart class that will handle all the logic for the shopping cart, including adding items to the cart.

1 Create a new ActionScript class file by choosing File > New > ActionScript class. Set the Package to valueObjects, which automatically adds this class to the folder you created earlier. Enter **ShoppingCartItem** as the name and leave all other fields with default values.

In this class, you will calculate the quantity of each unique item as well as the subtotal.

2 Within the class definition, define a public property with the name of product and a data type of Product, as shown:

```
package valueObjects {
    public class ShoppingCartItem {
        public var product:Product;
    }
}
```

An important piece of the shopping cart is which item has been added. You have already created the Product class to track all this data, so it makes perfect sense to use an instance of this class in the ShoppingCartItem class.

3 Define a public property with the name of quantity and a data type of uint, as shown:

```
package valueObjects {
    public class ShoppingCartItem {
        public var product:Product;
        public var quantity:uint;
    }
}
```

The uint data type means unsigned integer, which is a non-fractional, non-negative number (0, 1, 2, 3, …). The quantity of an item added to the shopping cart will be either zero or a positive number, so it makes sense to type it as a uint.

4 Define a public property with the name of subtotal and a data type of Number, as shown:

```
package valueObjects {
   public class ShoppingCartItem {
      public var product:Product;
      public var quantity:uint;
      public var subtotal:Number;
   }
}
```

Each time a user adds an item to the shopping cart, you will want the subtotal for that item to be updated. Eventually, you will display this data in a visual control.

5 Immediately after the subtotal property, define the signature of the constructor function of the class and specify the parameters that will be passed to this function. These parameters include product data typed as Product and quantity data typed as uint. Because the constructor is called only on a product creation, set the quantity to 1 in the parameter list.

```
public function ShoppingCartItem(product:Product, quantity:uint=1)
{
}
```

Remember that constructor functions must be public and cannot be data typed.

6 In the constructor, assign the class properties the parameter values. In this case the names used are the same, so prefix the properties on the left side of the equal sign with this. Also assign the subtotal property the value of the product's listPrice multiplied by the quantity.

```
public function ShoppingCartItem(product:Product, quantity:uint=1){
   this.product = product;
   this.quantity = quantity;
   this.subtotal = product.listPrice * quantity;
}
```

Remember that the constructor function is called automatically every time an object is created from a class. The constructor will set the properties that are passed in—in this case, an instance of the Product class, and the quantity, which is automatically set to 1 as a default. This method will be used only when an item is added to the shopping cart, so it makes sense to define the initial quantity as 1.

7 Create a public method with the name of recalc() that will calculate the subtotal of each item by multiplying the listPrice of the product by the quantity, as follows:

```
public function recalc():void{
   this.subtotal = product.listPrice * quantity;
}
```

When the user adds items to the shopping cart, you need to perform calculations so that the total can be updated. You also need to check to see whether the item has been added to the cart already; if so, update the quantity. You will learn how to do this in the next lesson.

8 You will now create another new class. Start by choosing File > New > ActionScript class. Set the Package to valueObjects, which will automatically add this class to the valueObjects folder you created earlier. Name the class ShoppingCart and leave all other fields with default values.

You are creating a new class that will be the actual shopping cart, filled with shopping-CartItem objects. This class will handle the manipulation of the data in the shopping cart. You have already created the visual look and feel of the shopping cart, and you will place all your business logic in the ShoppingCart class. This business logic includes adding an item to the cart, deleting an item from the cart, updating an item in the cart, and so on.

9 Add an `import` statement that will allow you to use Flash utilities such as the `trace` statement within the class, as shown:

```
package valueObjects{
    import flash.utils.*
    public class ShoppingCart{
    }
}
```

Just as you have to import your own custom classes for use, you need to import the appropriate classes from the framework to use them. You will use a `trace()` function and other utilities, which require the import of these classes.

10 Create the skeleton of a public `addItem()` method, data typed as `void`, that accepts a parameter named item, data typed as ShoppingCartItem. In the method, add a `trace` statement that will trace the product added to the cart:

```
package valueObjects{
    import flash.utils.*
    public class ShoppingCart{
        public function addItem(item:ShoppingCartItem):void{
            trace(item.product);
        }
    }
}
```

This is the method in which you will add a new item to the shopping cart. You will add much more business logic to this method in later lessons. For now, you will just trace the name of the item added to the cart. Remember that the `toString()` function you wrote earlier is called automatically whenever an instance of the Product class is traced.

11 Open EComm.mxml in Flex Builder and locate the script block. Just below the Product `import` statement, import the ShoppingCartItem and ShoppingCart classes from the valueObjects folder, as shown:

```
import valueObjects.ShoppingCartItem;
import valueObjects.ShoppingCart;
```

To use a class, Flex Builder needs an `import` statement that references the location or package in which the class is located.

12 Just below the `import` statements, instantiate a public instance of the ShoppingCart class, name the instance `cart`, and add a `[Bindable]` metadata tag, as follows:

```
[Bindable]
public var cart:ShoppingCart = new ShoppingCart();
```

When the user clicks the Add To Cart button, you want to call the `addItem()` method of the ShoppingCart class you just created. You will pass the `addItem()` method an instance of the ShoppingCartItem class. By instantiating the class here, you ensure that you have access to it throughout the application.

13 Locate the `prodHandler()` method in the `<mx:Script>` block. Immediately after this method, add a skeleton of a new private method with the name `addToCart()` data typed as `void`. Have the method accept a parameter named `product` data typed as Product, as shown:

```
private function addToCart(product:Product):void {
}
```

This method will be called when the user clicks Add, and you will pass the Product value object that the user selected. This is a method of the MXML file and will not be called outside of this file. Therefore, you can use the identifier private, which means that the method cannot be accessed from outside the class and helps to provide better data protection.

14 Inside the `addToCart()` method, create a new instance of the ShoppingCartItem class with the name of `sci` and pass the constructor the `product` parameter:

```
var sci:ShoppingCartItem = new ShoppingCartItem(product);
```

15 Inside the `addToCart()` method, call the `addItem()` method of the `cart` instance of the ShoppingCart class. Be sure to pass to the method the `sci` object you just created, as follows:

```
cart.addItem(sci);
```

This code will call the addItem() method of the ShoppingCart class you built earlier. In the next lesson, you will learn how to loop through the data structure to see whether the item is added. For now, this method simply traces the name of the product added to the cart.

16 Add a click event to the Add To Cart button. Call the addToCart() method, passing the method an instance of theProduct:

```
<mx:Button id="add" label="Add To Cart"
    click="addToCart(theProduct)"/>
```

Remember, the addToCart() method creates an instance of the ShoppingCartItem class and then the object is added to the shopping cart.

17 Save and debug the application.

Each time you click the Add To Cart button, you should see [Product]Milk appear in the Console view.

What You Have Learned

In this lesson, you have:

- Gained an understanding of event handling (pages 90–93)
- Handled a creationComplete event on the <mx:Application> tag to build a data structure (pages 93–96)
- Explored the event object to understand what it is and used two properties of that object (pages 96–101)
- Gained an understanding of the basic structure of an ActionScript class (page 101)
- Created ActionScript classes that are value objects (pages 101–106)
- Created properties, methods, and static methods of ActionScript classes (pages 106–113)

What You Will Learn

In this lesson, you will:

- Create an HTTPService object that returns data as an ArrayCollection
- Use an ArrayCollection as a data provider for ComboBox and List controls
- Understand security issues involved with retrieving data into Flash Player
- Create an HTTPService object that returns data as an XMLListCollection
- Use an XMLListCollection to populate a Tree control
- Use the ArrayCollection's cursor to locate, retrieve, and remove data in an ArrayCollection

Approximate Time

This lesson takes approximately 2 hours and 30 minutes to complete.

Lesson Files

Media Files:

None

Starting Files:

Lesson06/start/EComm.mxml
Lesson06/start/valueObjects/ShoppingCartItem.as
Lesson06/start/valueObjects/ShoppingCart.as
Lesson06/start/valueObjects/Product.as
Lesson06/start/Dashboard.mxml
Lesson06/start/DataEntry.mxml
Lesson06/e4xdemo/src/E4X_Demo.mxml

Completed Files:

Lesson06/complete/EComm.mxml
Lesson06/complete/valueObjects/ShoppingCartItem.as
Lesson06/complete/valueObjects/ShoppingCart.as
Lesson06/complete/valueObjects/Product.as
Lesson06/complete/DataEntry.mxml
Lesson06/complete/Dashboard.mxml

LESSON 6

Using Remote XML Data with Controls

In this lesson, you will begin to connect the grocery applications to remote data. In the e-commerce application, you will access and use remote XML data to populate the grocery item interface you created in earlier lessons. In the DataEntry application, you will use a Tree control to enable users to easily display details of grocery items. In the Dashboard application, you will dynamically populate a ComboBox control with remote XML data.

A Tree control populated with remote XML data and used to display details from a particular node of the Tree

You will populate the control by using the HTTPService class to load remote XML data. The data could exist on a remote server, or in external files on the same server, but the data is remote to the application. The data will be transmitted through the HTTP protocol. You will work with this XML data in several formats. By default, the data is parsed into an ArrayCollection, which is a special featured array. You will also use functionality from the ECMAScript for XML (E4X) implementation that implements XML as a native data type in ActionScript.

To put this data to actual use, you will use it as a source for controls that take complex data structures as their data provider. These controls enable you to easily display complex datasets and enable the user to navigate these datasets. You will use the List, ComboBox, and Tree data provider controls in this lesson.

Retrieving XML Data with HTTPService

In the last lesson, you embedded XML in a SWF file by specifying the source attribute of the `<mx:Model>` tag and pointing to an external XML file. This method can be a bad practice because the XML is compiled into the SWF file, increasing the file size. The XML is also not readily updateable; you would have to recompile the SWF every time the data changed. This is not practical for data that will change or for large datasets. In actual practice, you will rarely embed XML data; it is a much better practice to load the XML at runtime using the HTTPService class.

Simply stated, the HTTPService component provides access to URLs and returns data viewed at those URLs. Most often the data on the URLs will be formatted as XML. The data is returned, and you can choose the format in which you wish to use the returned data. In this lesson you will use the returned data in two different formats.

To use the HTTPService you do the following:

1. Create an HTTPService object.

2. Invoke the send() method of the object.

3. Use the returned data.

Creating an HTTPService Object

You create the HTTPService object just like you created other objects in MXML. When you create the object, you need to specify the URL that the service should view, and also specify the result event. The result event is broadcast when data is successfully returned by the HTTPService object. An example of using the HTTPService object is shown here:

```
<mx:HTTPService id="unitData"
   url=http://www.flexgrocer.com/unitData.xml
   result="resultHandler(event)"/>
```

> **TIP:** The url property could also point to a file on the file system that contains XML data.

Invoking the send() Method

Creating the HTTPService object does not automatically cause the data to be retrieved. You must also invoke the send() method of the object in response to some event. In many cases, you will want to retrieve data upon application startup. Remember from the last lesson that the creationComplete event attached to the Application tag is dispatched only when all other children in the application are also creationComplete. This is an ideal time to retrieve remote data—any components that are supposed to use the data will then be created and ready to go.

Using the Returned Data

The returned data can be used in two different ways. The first is to use the data directly in a binding *not* using a result handler. When you do this, the data is stored in a variable named lastResult. In the next section you will see specifically the data structure used to store the data, but first you will learn how to access the data. To get to the data, use the following to build an expression:

1. The instance name of the HTTPService

2. The lastResult property

3. The path in the XML structure to point to the repeated node of the XML

For example, in the next task you have an HTTPService defined as

```
<mx:HTTPService id="unitRPC"
   url="http://www.flexgrocer.com/units.xml"/>
```

and retrieving the following XML:

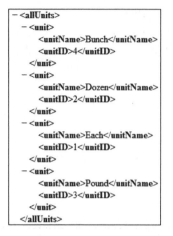

```
- <allUnits>
  - <unit>
      <unitName>Bunch</unitName>
      <unitID>4</unitID>
    </unit>
  - <unit>
      <unitName>Dozen</unitName>
      <unitID>2</unitID>
    </unit>
  - <unit>
      <unitName>Each</unitName>
      <unitID>1</unitID>
    </unit>
  - <unit>
      <unitName>Pound</unitName>
      <unitID>3</unitID>
    </unit>
  </allUnits>
```

To access the unit nodes in the XML data you would use the following code:

```
unitRPC.lastResult.allUnits.unit
```

This is the instance name of the HTTPService (unitRPC), followed by the lastResult property, followed by the path in the XML to the repeated node (unit).

Most likely you will very rarely use the lastResult property to access the data returned by the HTTPService, although you will see an example of doing this later in this lesson. The reason you seldom use lastResult is that you will usually want to use a result event handler with the HTTPService. When you do this you do not access the data using lastResult but rather by using the event.result property in the event handler.

If you are using an HTTPService created as follows:

```
<mx:HTTPService id="unitRPC"
    url="http://www.flexgrocer.com/units.xml"
    result="unitRPCResult(event)"/>
```

the returned XML is also available in the event handler. Given a result handler with the following signature:

```
private function unitRPCResult(event:ResultEvent):void{
}
```

you could access the unit XML data in the body of the function by specifying event.result.allUnits.unit.

The returned data is in event.result. To point to the repeating node of the XML, simply append allUnits.unit.

Understanding Security Issues

Flex is subject to the *security sandbox restrictions* of Flash Player, which means that an application on one domain is prevented from loading data from another domain. To automatically give an application loaded from www.mysite.com access to data on www.yoursite.com, you must use a *cross-domain policy file*. This file, named crossdomain.xml, specifies which domains have access to resources from Flash Player and is placed on the root of the web server that the SWF file is calling. Here is an example of a cross-domain policy file that would enable any SWF to access resources available on the web server where it resides:

```
<cross-domain-policy>
<allow-access-from domain="*"/>
</cross-domain-policy>
```

 TIP: Browse the URL www.flexgrocer.com/crossdomain.xml to see the cross-domain file that allows you to retrieve data from your data source for this book. Also check www.cnn.com/crossdomain.xml to see who CNN allows to syndicate their content using Flash Player.

More information about the sandbox restrictions of Flash Player is available in the tech note on the Adobe site: www.adobe.com/cfusion/knowledgebase/index.cfm?id=tn_14213.

Before deploying a cross-domain security file like this to a server, be sure to understand all the ramifications.

Retrieving XML Data via HTTPService

In this task, you will use an HTTPService object to retrieve XML data that contains the units of measure in which the grocery items are sold—such as pounds or dozens. You will verify that the data is returned correctly by using the debugger to see the data in the event object.

1 Open a web browser and go to the following URL:

www.flexgrocer.com/units.xml

Notice the structure of the XML. This is the data you will retrieve using the HTTPService.

2 Open DataEntry.mxml. In the existing script block, import the following classes:

```
mx.rpc.events.ResultEvent
utils.Util
```

You need these classes for the additions you will make to the DataEntry application in this lesson. The ResultEvent class will be used when data is successfully retrieved by the HTTPService. The Util class has been custom built for this book.

3 Directly below the <mx:Script> block, add an <mx:HTTPService> tag. Give it an id of unitRPC, and specify the url property to http://www.flexgrocer.com/units.xml. Specify the result handler to call the unitRPCResult event handler and be sure to pass the event object, as follows:

```
<mx:HTTPService id="unitRPC"
url="http://www.flexgrocer.com/units.xml"
result="unitRPCResult(event)"/>
```

You are specifying the URL of the HTTPService to point to the XML you examined in step 1. In the next step, you will write an event handler with the name of unitRPCResult() that will be called when the data has been retrieved.

4 In the script block below the existing function, add a new private function with the name of unitRPCResult(), data typed as void. Accept a parameter named event, data typed as ResultEvent. At this point the function is empty.

```
private function unitRPCResult(event:ResultEvent):void{
}
```

The event object is created when the result event is dispatched. Remember from the last lesson that this object should be strictly typed to the type of event occurring; in this case, a ResultEvent.

5 In the <mx:Application> tag, add a creationComplete event that has the unitRPC HTTPService call its send() method.

```
<mx:Application xmlns:mx="http://www.adobe.com/2006/mxml"
   layout="absolute"
   creationComplete="unitRPC.send()">
```

The object created from the HTTPService class, with the id of unitRPC, must invoke its send() method to actually make the call to the URL.

6 Add a breakpoint on the closing brace of the function by double-clicking in the marker bar just to the left of the code and line numbers. A small blue dot will appear in the marker bar indicating the spot where program execution will halt. You can examine values at this point.

Placing a breakpoint here gives you the chance to examine the data returned by the HTTPService.

7 Debug the application. Return to Flex Builder and be sure you are in the Debugging perspective. Double-click the tab on the Variables view. Drill down to the returned data by clicking on the plus sign in front of event > result > allUnits > unit. Here you see the four unit measurement values in brackets [0], [1], [2], and [3] when you expand them.

Name	Value
⊞ ● this	DataEntry (@b1880a1)
⊟ ◉ event ◄———	mx.rpc.events.ResultEvent (@b17ec41)
⊞ ◆ [inherited]	
◦ headers	null
⊟ ◦ result ◄———	mx.utils.ObjectProxy (@b1c67d9)
⊟ ◦ allUnits ◄———	mx.utils.ObjectProxy (@b1c6701)
⊞ ◦ object	Object (@b0a6589)
◦ type	null
◦ uid	"5E4CD380-1D0F-09FE-0718-2716ABD1C7BD"
⊟ ◦ unit ◄———	mx.collections.ArrayCollection (@b1e6a41)
⊞ ◆ [inherited]	
⊟ ● [0]	mx.utils.ObjectProxy (@b1c6ca1)
⊞ ◦ object	Object (@b0a6b01)
◦ type	null
◦ uid	"97511F12-94EC-0D46-5453-2716D7D33F9C"
◦ unitID	4
◦ unitName	"Bunch"
⊟ ● [1]	mx.utils.ObjectProxy (@b1c6989)
⊞ ◦ object	Object (@b1ec499)
◦ type	null
◦ uid	"32D342C4-3FDF-88AD-1518-2716E0CC1772"
◦ unitID	2
◦ unitName	"Dozen"
⊞ ● [2]	mx.utils.ObjectProxy (@b1c69d1)
⊞ ● [3]	mx.utils.ObjectProxy (@b1c6a19)

Here you see that the data has been returned in the event handler in the expression event.result.allUnits.unit. In the next section you will learn more about the format in which the data has been returned.

8 Double-click the tab on the Variables view to return it to its normal size. Terminate the debugging session by clicking the red block in either the Debug or Console view. Finally, return to the Development perspective.

You have now used an HTTPService object to retrieve data, and you used debugging techniques to confirm it has actually been returned to the application. Next, you will put the data to use.

Populating an ArrayCollection with HTTPService Data

You now know how to use the HTTPService to retrieve XML data from a URL. Now you need to learn how to use that data once it has been returned to your application. In this section you will see some of the strengths of using an ArrayCollection for the returned data, and later in this lesson you will learn why ArrayCollections are such useful data structures.

Using ArrayCollections

In the debugging information from the last exercise, the returned data is placed into an ArrayCollection. By default, complex data structures are returned in an ArrayCollection.

(x)= Variables ⊠ ● Breakpoints Expressions	
Name	**Value**
⊞ ● this	DataEntry (@b1880a1)
⊟ ⓘ event	mx.rpc.events.ResultEvent (@b17ec41)
⊞ ◆ [inherited]	
● headers	null
⊟ ● result	mx.utils.ObjectProxy (@b1c67d9)
⊟ ● allUnits	mx.utils.ObjectProxy (@b1c6701)
⊞ ● object	Object (@b0a6589)
● type	null
● uid	"5E4CD380-1D0F-09FE-0718-2716ABD1C7BD"
⊟ ● unit	mx.collections.ArrayCollection (@b1e6a41)
⊞ ◆ [inherited]	
⊞ ● [0]	mx.utils.ObjectProxy (@b1c6ca1)
⊞ ● [1]	mx.utils.ObjectProxy (@b1c6989)
⊞ ● [2]	mx.utils.ObjectProxy (@b1c69d1)
⊞ ● [3]	mx.utils.ObjectProxy (@b1c6a19)
⊞ ● source	Array (@b1a3c49)

> ✱ **NOTE:** Plain old arrays are useful for storing data in Flex, but if you intend to use the data to populate controls, or if you're going to manipulate the data by filtering or sorting, the ArrayCollection is the data structure to choose.

In the next task you will use data from an ArrayCollection to populate a List box. This process shows off one of the strengths of the ArrayCollection: it is very useful as a data provider for components. When an ArrayCollection used in a data binding is changed, the visual display automatically updates when the underlying data changes.

> ▼ **CAUTION!** This is not true if you use a regular Array object as the data provider. It will populate the component the first time but will not update the component if the Array's data should change.

Using Collections as Data Providers

There are multiple controls that enable you to display complex data structures using the dataProvider property. The list-based controls—which include List, Tree, DataGrid, TileList, and ComboBox, among others—use a dataProvider property.

A data provider is simply a collection of objects, much like an Array or ArrayCollection. You can think of a dataProvider property as a client-side data model and the Flex components as views of the model. A data provider control displays a complex data structure to the end user. For example, the dataProvider property of a ComboBox control can be set to an ArrayCollection. The labelField property of the data provider controls which dataProvider property is displayed to the end user. The code in the following example would result in a ComboBox displayed with three items: Fruit, Meat, and Dairy:

```
<mx:ComboBox id="myCombo" labelField ="type">
  <mx:dataProvider>
    <mx:ArrayCollection>
      <mx:Object type="Fruit" id="zero"/>
      <mx:Object type="Meat" id="one"/>
      <mx:Object type="Dairy" id="two"/>
    </mx:ArrayCollection>
  </mx:dataProvider>
</mx:ComboBox>
```

The data provider controls have multiple advantages: you can populate multiple controls with the same data, you can switch out data providers at runtime, and you can modify a data provider so changes in it are reflected by all controls using it.

Now you will place the data returned from the HTTPService into an ArrayCollection and use it to populate a List component.

1 Open DataEntry.mxml. In the existing script block, import the following class:

```
mx.collections.ArrayCollection
```

You need to import the ArrayCollection class to use it in your application.

2 Below the `import` statements, but above any function declarations, add a bindable, private variable named `units`, data typed as ArrayCollection and set it equal to a new ArrayCollection.

```
[Bindable]
private var units:ArrayCollection=new ArrayCollection();
```

You will bind an ArrayCollection to the List control. As a best practice, it makes sense to use an ArrayCollection for data binding with a complex data structure because you want it to update when any changes are made to the data structure.

3 In the script block, locate the `unitRPCResult` event handler. In the function, set the `units` variable equal to the returned results, specified by the expression `event.result.allUnits.unit`.

```
private function unitRPCResult(event:ResultEvent):void{
    units=event.result.allUnits.unit;
}
```

Remember from the previous section that when in an event handler for the HTTPService, you access the returned data in `event.result`, then use the path to the repeating node of the data.

4 Locate the second FormItem whose `label` is ProductNameUnit. Change the `label` to just Unit and remove the `direction="horizontal"` property assignment.

You will replace the ComboBox and TextInput with just a List, so the `direction` property is no longer needed.

5 Remove both the ComboBox and TextInput controls nested in the FormItem tags. In their place, insert a List control with an `id` of `unitID` and set the `rowCount` variable to 4. Bind the `dataProvider` property to the `units` ArrayCollection and specify the `labelField` as `unitName`. Your FormItem should appear as follows:

```
<mx:FormItem label="Unit">
    <mx:List id="unitID"
        rowCount="4"
        dataProvider="{units}"
        labelField="unitName"/>
</mx:FormItem>
```

This will create a List control that will display the units of measurement for the administration tool. You needed to specify the `labelField` because each item in the XML data contained both a unitName and unitID field.

6 Save and run the application.

You should see that the List control is populated with the units, as shown.

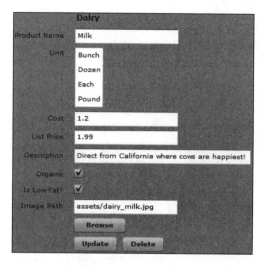

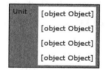 **TIP:** If you forget to specify a `labelField` property, Flash Player will not know which property to display from the object. Flash Player will indicate you are using an object where a simple value is required by displaying the following:

7 Close the file.

You will work with a different application in the next task.

Populating a ComboBox Control and Programmatically Adding an Option

In this task, you will work on the Dashboard application. You will make a call to an HTTPService that returns all the grocery categories and IDs and uses the returned data to populate a ComboBox control. This exercise differs from the last in that you will perform the common practice of adding an "All" type selection to the ComboBox control. Seldom will the XML or database table contain an "All" type selection for the user interface control that consumes the data. In this case you use the `addItemAt()` method of the ArrayCollection class to add such an option.

1 Open a web browser and browse to the following URL:

www.flexgrocer.com/category.xml

Notice the structure of the XML. Your goal in this task is to populate a ComboBox control with this information. The XML contains a repeating node, category, which contains the information you need to populate the ComboBox control.

2 Open Dashboard.mxml. Add a script block directly below the `<mx:Application>` tag, and add two `import` statements that will import the ArrayCollection class from the mx.collections package, and include the `ResultEvent` from the mx.rpc.events package. Add a [Bindable] ArrayCollection property with the name of `categories`, and set it equal to a new ArrayCollection.

```
<mx:Script>
    <![CDATA[
        import mx.collections.ArrayCollection;
        import mx.rpc.events.ResultEvent;
        [Bindable]
        private var categories:ArrayCollection=new ArrayCollection();
    ]]>
</mx:Script>
```

You will bind an ArrayCollection to the ComboBox control. As you just learned, the ArrayCollection is the best data structure for that task. To use an ArrayCollection, you need to import the class. You will also use a ResultEvent with the HTTPService class, so you need to import it as well.

3 Directly below the script block, add an `<mx:HTTPService>` tag. Assign it an `id` of `catRPC` and specify the `url` property as http://www.flexgrocer.com/category.xml. Specify the result handler to call `catHandler()` and be sure to pass the event object, as follows:

```
<mx:HTTPService id="catRPC"
    url="http://www.flexgrocer.com/category.xml"
    result="catHandler(event)"/>
```

You are specifying the URL of the HTTPService to point to the XML you examined in step 1. Later you will write a result handler with the name of `catHandler` that will be called when the data has been retrieved.

4 Move to the top of the application and add a `creationComplete` event that calls the `catRPC` HTTPService using the `send()` method.

```
<mx:Application xmlns:mx="http://www.adobe.com/2006/mxml"
    layout="horizontal"
    creationComplete="catRPC.send()">
```

To actually have the HTTPService retrieve the data, you must invoke the send() method. Just adding the tag does not retrieve the data.

5 Returning to the script block, add a new private method with the name catHandler(), data typed as void. The method must accept a parameter named event, data typed as ResultEvent. Populate the ArrayCollection, categories, with the event.result.catalog.category ArrayCollection returned from the HTTPService and stored in the event object.

```
private function catHandler(event:ResultEvent):void{
   categories = event.result.catalog.category;
}
```

As in the first task, you have retrieved data and placed the returned ArrayCollection in the categories variable.

6 Now you will programmatically add another option to the ComboBox control. Start by creating a new object with the name of catObj just below where you assigned categories a value in catHandler(). Set a property as name with the value of **All**, and set another property as categoryID with a value of 0. Your code should appear as follows:

```
private function catHandler(event:ResultEvent):void{
   categories = event.result.catalog.category;
   var catObj:Object = new Object();
   catObj.name = "All";
   catObj.categoryID = 0;
}
```

Here you created the Object that will be added to the ArrayCollection, and hence the ComboBox, in the next step.

7 Now add the object to the first index of the ArrayCollection by using the addItemAt() method and specifying catObj and the first index, which is 0. Finally, set the selectedIndex of the ComboBox to 0 so the new item in the collection is selected at startup. Your code should appear as follows:

```
private function catHandler(event:ResultEvent):void{
   categories = event.result.catalog.category;
   var catObj:Object = new Object();
   catObj.name = "All";
   catObj.categoryID = 0;
   categories.addItemAt(catObj, 0);
   catCombo.selectedIndex = 0;
}
```

Because the data structure from the server does not include an All property, you need to add it manually in the result event handler, and then make it the selected item. If you did not set the selectedIndex property to 0, the selected item in the ComboBox would be the first item returned from the HTTPService, with "All" at the top of the list but not selected.

 TIP: The ArrayCollection also contains a method named addItem(object). This method adds the object passed as a parameter to the end of the ArrayCollection.

8 Locate the ApplicationControlBar. After the endDate DateField and above the <mx:RadioButtonGroup> tag, add a ComboBox control and assign it an id of catCombo. Bind the dataProvider property to the categories ArrayCollection, as follows:

```
<mx:ComboBox id="catCombo"
   dataProvider="{categories}"/>
```

You are binding the dataProvider for the ComboBox to be the categories ArrayCollection created earlier.

9 In the <mx:ComboBox> tag, add a labelField property to the control. Specify the value of name for the property, as follows:

```
<mx:ComboBox id="catCombo"
   dataProvider = "{categories}"
   labelField = "name"/>
```

If you compile the application without adding the labelField property, the ComboBox would not know which property or field to use as the label property. You can specify any of the field names in the data structure as the labelField property. In this case, you specify the name field because you want the names of all the categories to display.

10 Save and run the application.

You should see that the ComboBox has been populated with the XML data you examined in the first step, as well as the word "All" in the first index.

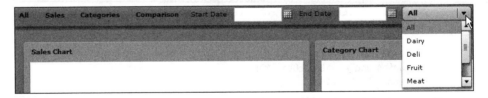

11 Close the file.

Using XML Data with a Tree Control

In this section, you add functionality to the DataEntry application. You will use an HTTPService to access the data and use this data to populate a Tree control. You will use the Tree control to easily navigate the complex data structure and populate the form you created in Lesson 4, "Using Simple Controls."

ActionScript 3.0 contains native XML support in the form of ECMAScript for XML (E4X). This ECMA standard is designed to give ActionScript programmers access to XML in a straightforward way. E4X uses standard ActionScript syntax with which you should already be familiar, plus some new functionality specific to E4X.

> **▼ CAUTION!** The XML class in ActionScript 3.0 is not the same as the XML class in ActionScript 2.0. That class has been renamed to XMLDocument so that it does not conflict with the XML class now part of E4X. The old XML document class in ActionScript is not covered in this book. You should not need to use this class except when working with legacy projects.

Understanding E4X Operators

In this task and through the rest of this lesson, you will use E4X functionality. The new E4X specification defines a new set of classes and functionality for working with XML data. These classes and functionality are known collectively as E4X.

First, for a very basic, very quick review of XML terminology, examine the XML object as it would be defined in ActionScript:

```
private var groceryXML:XML = new XML();
groceryXML=
<catalog>
  <category name="vegetables">
    <product name="lettuce" cost="1.95">
      <unit>bag</unit>
      <desc>Cleaned and bagged</desc>
    </product>
    <product name="carrots" cost="2.95">
      <unit>pound</unit>
      <desc>Baby carrots, cleaned and peeled</desc>
    </product>
  </category>
  <category name="fruit">
    <product name="apples" cost="1.95">
      <unit>each</unit>
      <desc>Sweet Fuji</desc>
    </product>
```

code continues on next page

```
      <berries>
        <product name="raspberries" cost="3.95">
          <unit>pint</unit>
          <desc>Firm and fresh</desc>
        </product>
        <product name="strawberries" cost="2.95">
          <unit>pint</unit>
          <desc>Deep red and juicy</desc>
        </product>
      </berries>
    </category>
 </catalog>;
```

The following statements describe the XML object, with the XML terminology italicized:

- The *root node* (or element) is catalog.

- There are two category *nodes*, sometimes also referred to as elements.

- The product node has two *child* nodes, called unit and desc.

- The product node has two *attributes*, name and cost.

> ✱ **NOTE:** Both berry products are nested inside a <berries> node. This is done intentionally to show the power of the E4X operators you will soon see. The data you will work with in the application does not have this extra node around any of the products.

Now that you understand the basic XML terminology, you can start using some of the powerful E4X operators. A small application has been written for you to test some of these operators.

1 Choose File > New > Flex Project. Set the Project name as **E4X_Demo**.

2 Set the Project location to flex3tfs/Lesson06/e4xdemo.

3 For the Application type, select Web application.

4 Set the Application server type to None, then click Next.

5 Leave the Output folder set to bin-debug, then click Next.

6 Leave the Main source folder and Main application file with the values src and E4X_Demo, respectively, and then click Finish.

You have now created a project so you can run the application, which demonstrates some of the E4X operators.

7 Run the E4X_Demo application.

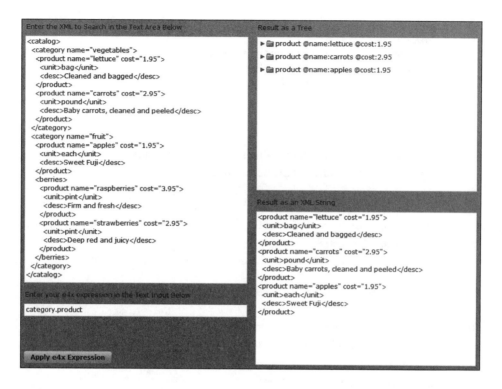

On the top left you see the XML that will be operated on. The top right shows the returned XML in a Tree view. The bottom right shows the returned XML as an XML string. The bottom left contains Text Input where you will enter E4X expressions and the button to apply them on the displayed XML.

8 Click the button to apply the default expression `category.product`.

▶ **TIP:** When using E4X expressions, the root node (in this case `category`) is not used in statements.

This expression uses the *dot* (.) operator. This is one way to access data in the XML document. The dot operator behaves much like the dot in `object.property` notation, which you are familiar with. You use the dot operator to navigate to child nodes. The expression yields the following results:

```
<product name="lettuce" cost="1.95">
  <unit>bag</unit>
  <desc>Cleaned and bagged</desc>
</product>
```

code continues on next page

```
<product name="carrots" cost="2.95">
    <unit>pound</unit>
    <desc>Baby carrots, cleaned and peeled</desc>
</product>
<product name="apples" cost="1.95">
    <unit>each</unit>
    <desc>Sweet Fuji</desc>
</product>
```

The dot operator retrieves all the products that are direct children of category. Notice that the products that are children of the berries node did not appear.

9 Now enter the expression category.product.unit and click the button to apply it.

Here the dot operator again navigates the XML and returns the unit node for the three products retrieved in step 8.

```
<unit>bag</unit>
<unit>pound</unit>
<unit>each</unit>
```

10 Enter and apply the expression category.product[1]. This demonstrates that you can apply your knowledge of array notation in E4X. Here you get the second (based on a zero-indexed list) product.

```
<product name="carrots" cost="2.95">
    <unit>pound</unit>
    <desc>Baby carrots, cleaned and peeled</desc>
</product>
```

This again shows that E4X lets you use familiar notation to work with XML. In previous versions of ActionScript, you had to use specific methods to access data in XML.

11 Enter and apply the expression, category.product.(unit=="bag"). This limits the products returned to those where the unit node is bag. You limit the data returned by putting a filter on what you want returned using the parentheses operator.

```
<product name="lettuce" cost="1.95">
    <unit>bag</unit>
    <desc>Cleaned and bagged</desc>
</product>
```

The parentheses operator implements what is referred to as *predicate filtering*. This gives you a way to filter the returned data.

12 Enter and apply the expression `category.product.(@cost=="1.95")`. You get two product nodes returned.

```
<product name="lettuce" cost="1.95">
   <unit>bag</unit>
   <desc>Cleaned and bagged</desc>
</product>
<product name="apples" cost="1.95">
   <unit>each</unit>
   <desc>Sweet Fuji</desc>
</product>
```

You have now performed predicate filtering on an attribute—hence the use of the attribute operator (@) in the parentheses, `(@cost=="1.95")`. Also notice that if multiple nodes match the filter, you simply get multiple nodes returned—in this case both the lettuce and apples products.

13 Enter and apply the expression `category.product.(@cost=="1.95").(unit=="each")`. This expression demonstrates that you can apply predicate filtering multiple times. This results in only one product being returned.

```
<product name="apples" cost="1.95">
   <unit>each</unit>
   <desc>Sweet Fuji</desc>
</product>
```

14 Finally, to see the berry products get involved, select the expression `category..product`. You see that all products are returned, regardless of where they are in the XML.

```
<product name="lettuce" cost="1.95">
   <unit>bag</unit>
   <desc>Cleaned and bagged</desc>
</product>
<product name="carrots" cost="2.95">
   <unit>pound</unit>
   <desc>Baby carrots, cleaned and peeled</desc>
</product>
<product name="apples" cost="1.95">
   <unit>each</unit>
   <desc>Sweet Fuji</desc>
</product>
<product name="raspberries" cost="3.95">
   <unit>pint</unit>
   <desc>Firm and fresh</desc>
</product>
<product name="strawberries" cost="2.95">
   <unit>pint</unit>
   <desc>Deep red and juicy</desc>
</product>
```

This is an example of the very powerful *descendant accessor* operator, represented by two dots (..). This operator navigates to descendant nodes of an XML object, no matter how complex the XML's structure, and retrieves matching nodes. The descendant accessor operator searches through the entire XML object and returns all the product nodes.

15 Enter and apply the expression `category..product.(@cost>2)`. This combines two operators and returns three products.

```
<product name="carrots" cost="2.95">
   <unit>pound</unit>
   <desc>Baby carrots, cleaned and peeled</desc>
</product>
<product name="raspberries" cost="3.95">
   <unit>pint</unit>
   <desc>Firm and fresh</desc>
</product>
<product name="strawberries" cost="2.95">
   <unit>pint</unit>
   <desc>Deep red and juicy</desc>
</product>
```

Here both predicate filtering and the descendant accessor are in use. E4X searched all the XML, regardless of position, and found three matches.

You have now seen just a slice of the very powerful E4X implementation in ActionScript 3.0. For more information, see "Working with XML" in the Programming ActionScript 3.0 documentation that comes with Flex.

Return to the FlexGrocer project.

Populating a Tree Control with XML Data

Just as you used an ArrayCollection to populate List and ComboBox controls in the last two tasks, you will use an XMLListCollection to populate a Tree control. The XMLListCollection has many of the same characteristics of the ArrayCollection that make it an excellent choice for components that use an XML data provider, like the Tree control.

1 Using a web browser, browse to the following URL:

www.flexgrocer.com/categorizedProducts.xml

The grocery items used for the store inventory are displayed in the XML structure. You see that products are grouped by category, and all property data is assigned as attributes.

```
- <catalog>
    + <category name="Meat" catName="Meat" catID="1"></category>
    - <category name="Vegetables" catName="Vegetables" catID="2">
        <product name="Broccoli" prodName="Broccoli" prodID="14" unitName="Pound" cost="2.16"
        listPrice="3.19" imageName="veg_broccoli.jpg" description="Firm and no bitterness" isOrganic="Yes"
        isLowFat="Yes" unitID="3" catName="Vegetables" catID="2"/>
        <product name="Vine Ripened Tomatoes" prodName="Vine Ripened Tomatoes" prodID="3"
        unitName="Pound" cost="1.69" listPrice="3.15" imageName="veg_tomato.jpg" description="Juicy and
        tender tomatoes, ripened on the vine" isOrganic="No" isLowFat="Yes" unitID="3"
        catName="Vegetables" catID="2"/>
        <product name="Yellow Peppers" prodName="Yellow Peppers" prodID="1" unitName="Pound"
        cost="1.25" listPrice="1.99" imageName="veg_pepper_yellow.jpg" description="Yellow Peppers
        cleaned and ready to eat." isOrganic="Yes" isLowFat="Yes" unitID="3" catName="Vegetables"
        catID="2"/>
    </category>
    + <category name="Fruit" catName="Fruit" catID="3"></category>
    + <category name="Dairy" catName="Dairy" catID="4"></category>
    + <category name="Deli" catName="Deli" catID="5"></category>
    + <category name="Seafood" catName="Seafood" catID="6"></category>
</catalog>
```

2 Open DataEntry.mxml.

3 Remove the existing `<mx:Model>` tag block.

You will populate the form with dynamic data from the HTTPService class instead of with static XML data embedded in the SWF file.

4 Directly below the existing HTTPService call, add another `<mx:HTTPService>` tag, assign it an id of prodByCatRPC, and specify the url property as http://www.flexgrocer.com/categorizedProducts.xml. Specify the resultFormat as e4x.

```
<mx:HTTPService id="prodByCatRPC"
    url="http://www.flexgrocer.com/categorizedProducts.xml"
    resultFormat="e4x"/>
```

The Tree control easily handles E4X data. In this case, you are transforming the XML in the file into ActionScript XML objects. In the next steps, you will use this data in the Tree control.

5 Directly after the `<mx:HTTPService>` tag, add an `<mx:XMLListCollection>` tag, specify the id as foodColl, and specify the source as prodByCatRPC.lastResult.category.

```
<mx:XMLListCollection id="foodColl"
    source="{prodByCatRPC.lastResult.category}"/>
```

The XMLListCollection is very much like the ArrayCollection except it is used for XML data. Just as it is a best practice to use an ArrayCollection over an Array for data binding, so it is a best practice to bind to an XMLListCollection instead of native XML objects.

6 Move to the top of the application and add to the existing creationComplete event so it calls the prodByCatRPC HTTPService using the send() method.

```
<mx:Application xmlns:mx="http://www.adobe.com/2006/mxml"
    layout = "absolute"
    creationComplete="unitRPC.send();prodByCatRPC.send()">
```

This actually executes the HTTPService call. You need to add a semicolon to separate the two lines of ActionScript code.

✱ **NOTE:** The next eight steps change the form so you can bind the XML data to the UI controls, and also make some aesthetic changes.

7 In the Form, remove the text properties from the five <mx:TextInput> tags.

8 In the Product Name FormItem, change the id property of the <mx:TextInput> tag to prodName.

9 Remove the <mx:FormHeading> tag.

10 Change the Description's <mx:TextInput> to an <mx:RichTextEditor>. Set the id to description and set the height of the control to 200.

```
<mx:FormItem label="Description">
   <mx:RichTextEditor id="description" height="200"/>
</mx:FormItem>
```

The <mx:RichTextEditor> allows users to mark up the text entered into the control. With this control, users can change the font family, color, size, and style, and other properties such as text alignment, bullets, and URL links of text entered.

11 Group the isLowFat and isOrganic <mx:CheckBox> tags into one <mx:FormItem> tag. The label of the combined FormItem should be Specialties. Remove the selected properties, and add label properties with the text "Is Low Fat" and "Is Organic."

```
<mx:FormItem label="Specialties">
   <mx:CheckBox id="isLowFat" label="Is Low Fat"/>
   <mx:CheckBox id="isOrganic" label="Is Organic"/>
</mx:FormItem>
```

12 Change the label of the <mx:FormItem>, which is currently Image Path, to Image Name.

13 To this <mx:FormItem>, add a direction property set equal to horizontal.

```
<mx:FormItem label="Image Name" direction="horizontal">
   <mx:TextInput id="imageName"/>
<mx:Button click="fileBrowse()" label="Browse"/>
</mx:FormItem>
```

14 Check to be sure your finished form appears as follows:

```
<mx:Form>
  <mx:FormItem label="Product Name">
    <mx:TextInput id="prodName"/>
  </mx:FormItem>
  <mx:FormItem label="Unit">
    <mx:List id="unitID"
      rowCount="4"
      dataProvider="{units}"
      labelField="unitName"/>
  </mx:FormItem>
  <mx:FormItem label="Cost">
    <mx:TextInput id="cost"/>
  </mx:FormItem>
  <mx:FormItem label="List Price">
    <mx:TextInput id="listPrice" />
  </mx:FormItem>
  <mx:FormItem label="Description">
    <mx:RichTextEditor id="description" height="200"/>
  </mx:FormItem>
  <mx:FormItem label="Specialties">
    <mx:CheckBox id="isLowFat" label="Is Low Fat"/>
    <mx:CheckBox id="isOrganic" label="Is Organic"/>
  </mx:FormItem>
  <mx:FormItem label="Image Name" direction="horizontal">
    <mx:TextInput id="imageName"/>
    <mx:Button click="fileBrowse()" label="Browse"/>
  </mx:FormItem>
  <mx:FormItem>
    <mx:HBox>
      <mx:Button label="Update" />
      <mx:Button label="Delete" />
    </mx:HBox>
  </mx:FormItem>
</mx:Form>
```

You will populate the form from the Tree control instead of accessing the data directly, and the changes you made to the form allow this to happen.

15 Add a Tree control directly above the existing form. Assign it an id of productTree, a height of 100%, a dataProvider of foodColl, a labelField of @name, and a change event of populateForm, passing the event object as a parameter.

```
<mx:Tree id="productTree"
  height="100%"
  dataProvider="{foodColl}"
  labelField="@name"
  change="populateForm(event)"/>
```

The user can use the Tree to find the product they are interested in updating or deleting.

16 Surround both the Tree control and the Form container with an HBox so the two elements will be arranged horizontally.

17 Create the skeleton of a new private function with the name of populateForm(), data typed as void. The function should accept a parameter named event, data typed as Event. Inside of the method, create a variable with the name of selectedNode, data typed as Object. Set this variable equal to the selectedItem of the event.target object, which is the selected node from the Tree control.

```
private function populateForm(event:Event):void{
    var selectedNode:Object=event.target.selectedItem;
}
```

Because you specified that this method would be called on a change event, the populateForm() method is called when the user clicks a node in the Tree control. The selectedItem property of the Tree control enables you to access the node that the user has selected.

18 Add conditional logic that checks to make sure that the XML attribute prodName in that node is defined. Add an else statement that will call the resetForm() method if there is no prodName attribute in the XML data structure.

```
private function populateForm(event:Event):void{
    var selectedNode:Object=event.target.selectedItem;
    if(selectedNode.@prodName != undefined)
    } else {
        resetForm();
    }
}
```

The conditional logic checks to see if the user clicked on a product or a category. If the user clicked on a product, you will populate the form; if the user clicked on a category, you will clear the form using the resetForm() method. You will write the resetForm() method in an upcoming step.

19 Set the text property of the prodName field to the corresponding attribute value of the selectedNode using E4X notation. Set the text property of the cost field, listPrice, description, and imageName using the same syntax. Set the selected property of the isOrganic and isLowFat CheckBoxes to the appropriate value. These are stored in the XML data as yes/no values; you need to use the Util class's yesNoToBoolean() method to convert these values into Booleans. The method should look as follows:

```
private function populateForm(event:Event):void{
   var selectedNode:Object=event.target.selectedItem;
   if(selectedNode.@prodName != undefined){
      prodName.text = selectedNode.@prodName;
      cost.text = selectedNode.@cost;
      listPrice.text = selectedNode.@listPrice;
      description.text = selectedNode.@description;
      isOrganic.selected = Util.yesNoToBoolean(selectedNode.@isOrganic);
      isLowFat.selected = Util.yesNoToBoolean(selectedNode.@isLowFat);
      imageName.text = selectedNode.@imageName;
   } else {
      resetForm();
   }
}
```

This populates the form fields with the product the user clicked.

20 As the first line of code in the if block, use the presetList() method of the Util class to prepopulate the List. Specify the first parameter as unitID, the second parameter as "unitID", and use E4X syntax to obtain the unitID property from the selectedNode.

```
Util.presetList(unitID,"unitID",selectedNode.@unitID);
```

This code selects the correct unit in the List control based on the product selection. The other units are still displayed if the user wishes to change the units.

21 Your completed populateForm() method should appear as follows:

```
private function populateForm(event:Event):void{
   var selectedNode:Object=event.target.selectedItem;
   if(selectedNode.@prodName != undefined){
      Util.presetList(unitID,"unitID",selectedNode.@unitID);
      prodName.text = selectedNode.@prodName;
      cost.text = selectedNode.@cost;
      listPrice.text = selectedNode.@listPrice;
      description.text = selectedNode.@description;
      isOrganic.selected = Util.yesNoToBoolean(selectedNode.@isOrganic);
      isLowFat.selected = Util.yesNoToBoolean(selectedNode.@isLowFat);
      imageName.text = selectedNode.@imageName;
   } else {
      resetForm();
   }
}
```

22 Build the private resetForm() method that will set all the values back to blank if the user selects a category and not a product.

```
private function resetForm():void{
    prodName.text = "";
    unitID.selectedIndex = -1;
    cost.text="";
    listPrice.text="";
    description.text="";
    isOrganic.selected = false;
    isLowFat.selected = false;
    imageName.text = "";
}
```

To represent that no items are selected in a list-based control, the selectedIndex of the control is set to -1.

23 Save and run the application. You should see that the Tree control is populated with data. When you drill down through the data, it is displayed on the form you created earlier.

This provides a great way for users to navigate a complex data structure and easily find the information they need.

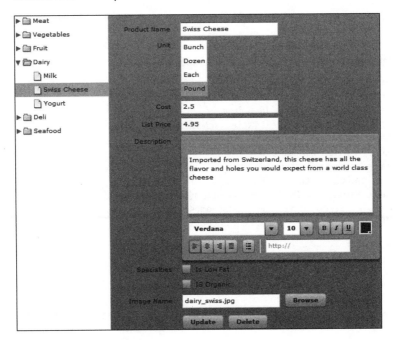

24 Close the file.

Retrieving XML Data and Transforming It into an ArrayCollection of Custom Objects

Once you have retrieved data from the HTTPService, you may want to put this data into a specific format for an application. In this task you will use E4X functionality to parse the XML data returned and place it into an array of Product objects.

The basic approach to what will be performed in this task is shown in the following diagram.

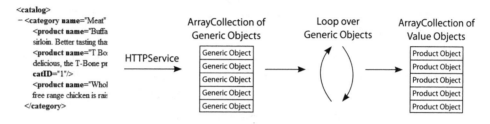

1 Using a web browser, browse to the following URL:

www.flexgrocer.com/categorizedProducts.xml

This is the same categorized grocery item data used in the last task.

2 Open EComm.mxml.

3 Remove the `<mx:Model>` tag.

```
<mx:Model id="groceryInventory" source="assets/inventory.xml")/>
```

Instead of defining your data by embedding an external XML file in the SWF file, you will use the HTTPService class to load in XML data at runtime.

4 Immediately after the current script block, add an `<mx:HTTPService>` tag and assign it an id of `prodByCatRPC`. Specify the URL property to be the URL of the page that you browsed in the first step.

```
<mx:HTTPService id="prodByCatRPC"
    url="http://www.flexgrocer.com/categorizedProducts.xml"/>
```

This creates an object with the name of prodByCatRPC from the HTTPService class. Remember that creating this object does *not* automatically make the request for the data. You need to actually execute the request, which you will do soon.

5 Specify the `result` handler of the HTTPService to call the `prodHandler()` function. Pass the result handler the event object. Specify the `resultFormat` as e4x. The `<mx:HTTPService>` tag should now look as follows:

```
<mx:HTTPService id="prodByCatRPC"
    url="http://www.flexgrocer.com/categorizedProducts.xml"
    result="prodHandler(event)"
    resultFormat="e4x"/>
```

You will use ECMAScript E4X functionality to convert the returned XML into an array of Product objects needed in this application. By specifying e4x as the result format, you are returning native ActionScript XML objects.

6 In the `creationComplete` event on the `<mx:Application>` tag, remove the current call to the `prodHandler()` method, and invoke the `send()` method of the prodByCatRPC HTTPService object. The `<mx:Application>` tag should now look as shown here:

```
<mx:Application xmlns:mx="http://www.adobe.com/2006/mxml"
    layout="absolute"
    creationComplete="prodByCatRPC.send()">
```

Creating the HTTPService object is only the first step in retrieving data. You must also invoke its `send()` method to actually get the data.

7 At the top of the script block, add an `import` statement that will import the ResultEvent class.

```
import mx.rpc.events.ResultEvent;
```

You need the ResultEvent class to data type the parameter used in the `result` event handler.

8 In the script block, locate the `prodHandler()` method. Change the parameter of the `prodHandler()` method to accept a parameter named event, data typed as `ResultEvent`. Remove all the other code in the method and add a `trace` statement that will display the `result` property of the event object. The `prodHandler()` method should appear as follows:

```
private function prodHandler(event:ResultEvent):void{
    trace(event.result);
}
```

You changed the function to now be the event handler for the `result` event of the HTTPService object.

9 Debug the application. You should see the XML in the Console view from the `trace`
statement that represents the ActionScript XML objects returned by the HTTPService.
Be sure to terminate the debugging session when done viewing the data.

```
<catalog>
  <category name="Meat" catName="Meat" catID="1">
    <product name="Buffalo" prodName="Buffalo" prodID="7" unitName="Pound" cost="4" listPrice="6.5" imageName="mea
    <product name="T Bone Steak" prodName="T Bone Steak" prodID="17" unitName="Pound" cost="6" listPrice="9.98" im
    <product name="Whole Chicken" prodName="Whole Chicken" prodID="6" unitName="Pound" cost="1.5" listPrice="2.99"
  </category>
  <category name="Vegetables" catName="Vegetables" catID="2">
    <product name="Broccoli" prodName="Broccoli" prodID="14" unitName="Pound" cost="2.16" listPrice="3.19" imageNa
    <product name="Vine Ripened Tomatoes" prodName="Vine Ripened Tomatoes" prodID="3" unitName="Pound" cost="1.69"
    <product name="Yellow Peppers" prodName="Yellow Peppers" prodID="1" unitName="Pound" cost="1.25" listPrice="1.
  </category>
  <category name="Fruit" catName="Fruit" catID="3">
    <product name="Bananas" prodName="Bananas" prodID="5" unitName="Bunch" cost="0.95" listPrice="1.98" imageName=
    <product name="Grapes" prodName="Grapes" prodID="4" unitName="Bunch" cost="1.34" listPrice="2.15" imageName="f
    <product name="Strawberries" prodName="Strawberries" prodID="2" unitName="Pound" cost="2.5" listPrice="3.95" i
  </category>
  <category name="Dairy" catName="Dairy" catID="4">
    <product name="Milk" prodName="Milk" prodID="8" unitName="Each" cost="0.99" listPrice="1.59" imageName="dairy_
    <product name="Swiss Cheese" prodName="Swiss Cheese" prodID="15" unitName="Pound" cost="2.5" listPrice="4.95"
    <product name="Yogurt" prodName="Yogurt" prodID="9" unitName="Each" cost="0.99" listPrice="1.19" imageName="da
  </category>
  <category name="Deli" catName="Deli" catID="5">
    <product name="Honey Roasted Ham" prodName="Honey Roasted Ham" prodID="10" unitName="Pound" cost="2.16" listPr
    <product name="Roast Beef" prodName="Roast Beef" prodID="16" unitName="Pound" cost="3.46" listPrice="5.99" ima
    <product name="Roasted Turkey" prodName="Roasted Turkey" prodID="11" unitName="Pound" cost="2" listPrice="3" i
  </category>
  <category name="Seafood" catName="Seafood" catID="6">
    <product name="Alaskan King Crab" prodName="Alaskan King Crab" prodID="18" unitName="Pound" cost="8.5" listPri
    <product name="Maine Lobster" prodName="Maine Lobster" prodID="12" unitName="Pound" cost="8.99" listPrice="18.
    <product name="Salmon Filet" prodName="Salmon Filet" prodID="13" unitName="Each" cost="4.55" listPrice="6.99"
  </category>
```

10 In the `prodHandler()` method, remove the `trace` statement and create a new instance of an
ActionScript array named `prodArray`. The `prodHandler()` method should look as follows:

```
private function prodHandler(event:ResultEvent):void{
    var prodArray:Array = new Array();
}
```

The Array class is a native ActionScript data structure that can be used to store complex
data. In this case, you will build an array of Product objects, using the value object pattern you worked with in the previous lesson. To do this, you will need to build a simple
loop that loops through the returned ActionScript XML objects.

11 Still in the `prodHandler()` method, immediately after the Array is declared, build a new
`for each..in` loop that iterates through the attributes or properties in the XML objects,
as follows:

```
for each (var p:XML in event.result..product){
}
```

The `for each..in` loop is used to iterate over XML objects. In this case you use the descendant accessor operator to extract all product nodes from the XML. The variable p acts as
the iterant in the loop and represents a different product in each iteration of the loop.

12 Within the `for each..in` loop, create a new instance of the Product value object with the name of `prod` and pass it the attributes of the `p` XML object for the required property values. Be sure to cast each attribute to the appropriate data type. Also note that on the `isOrganic` and `isLowFat` properties you must do a comparison to the string Yes to convert it to a Boolean.

```
var prod:Product = new Product
(
Number(p.@catID),
String(p.@prodName),
Number(p.@unitID),
Number(p.@cost),
Number(p.@listPrice),
String(p.@description),
Boolean(p.@isOrganic=="Yes"),
Boolean(p.@isLowFat=="Yes"),
String(p.@imageName));
```

Within the XML there is no mechanism for casting each attribute required by the value object class, so it must be done as the class is instantiated.

> ✱ **NOTE:** Where you did the comparison to the string "Yes" in creating the new Product, you could have also used the `Util.yesNoToBoolean` static method. The method is a bit smarter in that it does not care about the case of the string, but the same outcome is achieved either way; `true` or `false` is placed in the property value instead of Yes or No.

13 Still inside the `for` loop, but outside of the Product object declaration, use the `push()` method of the Array object to add the `prod` object, which is an instance of the Product class, to the array, as follows:

```
prodArray.push(prod);
```

The `push()` method of the Array object adds an element to the end of the Array. When the loop terminates, you will have pushed all the Product value objects into the array.

14 Immediately after the loop, add a `trace` statement that will trace the `prodArray` data structure you just created. The final `prodHandler()` method should appear as follows:

```
private function prodHandler(event:ResultEvent):void{
    var prodArray:Array = new Array();
    for each (var p:XML in event.result..product){
        var prod:Product = new Product(
        Number(p.@catID),
        String(p.@prodName),
        Number(p.@unitID),
        Number(p.@cost),
        Number(p.@listPrice),
        String(p.@description),
```

```
        Boolean(p.@isOrganic=="Yes"),
        Boolean(p.@isLowFat=="Yes"),
        String(p.@imageName));
        prodArray.push(prod);
    }
    trace(prodArray);
}
```

15 Save the file and debug the application. Be sure to terminate the debugging session.

In the Console view, you should see the toString() method of the Product class display the literal text [Product], followed by the name of each product in the Array. A partial display is shown here:

```
[Product]Buffalo,[Product]T Bone Steak,[Product]Whole Chicken,[Product]Broccoli
```

Using Data Binding with Complex Data Structures

In this task, you will use data bindings to display the information from the array of Product value objects. Remember, for data binding it is a best practice to use the ArrayCollection class because it will automatically update the visual controls if the underlying data structure changes, which is not true of the normal Array class.

1 Return to EComm.mxml. At the top of the script block, add an import statement that will import the ArrayCollection class from the mx.collections package.

```
import mx.collections.ArrayCollection;
```

This will give you access to the ArrayCollection class for use in the application.

2 In the <mx:Script> block below the import statements, declare a bindable, private variable named groceryInventory as an ArrayCollection.

```
[Bindable]
private var groceryInventory:ArrayCollection;
```

This declares a private ArrayCollection that you can use throughout the application. You can now use the data binding functionality of the ArrayCollection class.

3 In the prodHandler() method, remove the trace statement and in its place assign the groceryInventory variable a new ArrayCollection object. Pass the prodArray as a parameter to the ArrayCollection constructor.

```
groceryInventory=new ArrayCollection(prodArray);
```

This code takes the local array, prodArray, and places it in the ArrayCollection with the name of groceryInventory.

4 Near the bottom of the file, locate the first VBox that displays product information. Modify the code in the VBox to bind the appropriate data to the new ArrayCollection you just created, groceryInventory, rather than displaying static data. Use the getItemAt() method of the ArrayCollection and pass the number 0 to this method, which represents the first index of the Array. When you pass the object to the addToCart() method, be sure to cast it as a Product.

```
<mx:VBox id="products" width="100%" height="100%">
  <mx:Label id="prodName" text="{groceryInventory.getItemAt(0).prodName}"/>
  <mx:Image source="{'assets/'+groceryInventory.getItemAt(0).imageName}"
    scaleContent="true"
    mouseOver="this.currentState='expanded'"
    mouseOut="this.currentState=''"/>
  <mx:Label id="price" text="{groceryInventory.getItemAt(0).listPrice}"/>
  <mx:Button id="add" label="Add To Cart"
    click="addToCart(groceryInventory.getItemAt(0) as Product)"/>
</mx:VBox>
```

You have changed all the data binding to use an ArrayCollection. Data binding will now work and display the appropriate controls and images.

The getItemAt() method of collections is defined to return an Object. The addToCart() function is defined to accept a Product as a parameter. If you did not cast the returned Object, you would get the "implicit coercion" error. By using "as" to cast the returned item, you tell the compiler you understand the difference exists and you want the compiler to ignore it in this case.

5 In the defined view state, locate the expanded state. Bind the appropriate data to the new ArrayCollection you just created: groceryInventory.

```
<mx:VBox width="100%" x="200">
  <mx:Text text="{groceryInventory.getItemAt(0).description}"
    width="50%"/>
  <mx:Label text="Certified Organic"
    visible="{groceryInventory.getItemAt(0).isOrganic}"/>
  <mx:Label text="Low Fat"
    visible="{groceryInventory.getItemAt(0).isLowFat}"/>
</mx:VBox>
```

This code will bind to the controls the property values of the Product object at array position 0 in the ArrayCollection.

6 Save and run the application.

You should see that the data is now bound to the controls. Be sure to roll over the Buffalo item to see the description in the view state.

Manipulating Shopping Cart Data

The next four tasks all deal with manipulating data in the shopping cart. You will use features of the ArrayCollection extensively to perform these tasks.

Adding Items to the Cart

In this next exercise you will write code to add items to the shopping cart.

1 Open the ShoppingCart.as file in the src/valueObjects folder.

Alternatively, you can open ShoppingCart.as from your Lesson06/start/valueObjects directory, and save it into your flexGrocer/src/valueObjects directory.

2 After the existing `import` statement, import the ArrayCollection class from the package mx.collections.

```
import mx.collections.ArrayCollection;
```

This enables you to use the ArrayCollection class in the ShoppingCart class that you are defining here.

3 Right after the `class` keyword, define a `[Bindable]` public property with the name of *aItems*, data typed as ArrayCollection and set equal to a new ArrayCollection.

```
public class ShoppingCart {
   [Bindable]
   public var aItems:ArrayCollection = new ArrayCollection();
```

This instantiates an ArrayCollection object with the name of *aItems*. You will use this ArrayCollection to track all the objects in the shopping cart.

4 Define a `[Bindable]` public property with the name of `total`, data typed as Number. It will be used as the default value for an empty shopping cart, so set the value to 0, as shown:

```
[Bindable]
public var total:Number=0;
```

Any time a user adds an item to the cart, you will update this variable with the price of the item. This will enable you to track the total cost of the end user's order.

5 Locate the `addItem()` method of the ShoppingCart class and remove the `trace` statement. Use the `addItem()` method of the ArrayCollection class to add the ShoppingCartItem to the *aItems* ArrayCollection:

```
public function addItem(item:ShoppingCartItem):void{
   aItems.addItem(item);
}
```

In the last lesson, you built a ShoppingCartItem class to hold any data associated with items in a shopping cart. This class has properties to hold the Product (an instance of the Product class), the quantity (an integer) and the subtotal (a number derived by multiplying the quantity by the price). When the user clicked the Add To Cart button, you passed the ShoppingCartItem to this method and placed it in the ArrayCollection using addItem().

 TIP: In the next step you will be asked to locate a specific VBox instance. Use the Outline view to find named object instances.

6 Switch back to EComm.mxml and locate the cartBox VBox. Directly after the LinkButton control, add a List control. Assign the List control an id of cartView, specify cart.aItems as the dataProvider, and set the width to 100%.

```
<mx:List id="cartView"
    dataProvider="{cart.aItems}"
    width="100%"/>
```

This List control is what the user will see as the shopping cart. Because you have not specified which property to display using the label property, at this point you will only see that ShoppingCartItem objects have been added.

7 Save and run the application. Click the Add To Cart button for the Buffalo.

You should see the items that you click appear in the cart, as shown in the following example:

Your Cart Total: $
View Cart
[object ShoppingCartItem]
[object ShoppingCartItem]

Sorting Items in an ArrayCollection

To sort an ArrayCollection you will use both the Sort and SortField classes. You will use the following steps to sort an ArrayCollection, with code examples supplied that will be further explained later in the task:

1. Create a new Sort object.

2. Create one or more SortField objects.

3. Assign the `fields` property of the Sort object an array of SortField objects (created in step 2).

4. Assign the Sort object to the ArrayCollection's `sort` property.

5. Apply the sort by calling the `refresh()` method of the ArrayCollection.

Here is sample code that performs the steps to sort the items in an ArrayCollection.

```
var prodSort:Sort = new Sort();
var sortField:SortField = new SortField("prodName");
prodSort.fields=new Array(sortField);
myArrayCollection.sort = prodSort;
myArrayCollection.refresh();
```

 TIP: If only one SortField object is used, you often see steps 2 and 3 combined as follows
`prodSort.fields=[new SortField("prodName")];`

In the sample code, a SortField object was created to sort on the `prodName` property. When creating SortField objects you have multiple parameters you can use. Only one is required: the property name of the objects to sort on. In this case the sort will be on the `prodName` property. Three other optional parameters are available:

- Case sensitivity (false by default)
- Ascending versus descending (descending by default)
- Numeric versus alphabetic (alphabetic by default)

A Sort object can have several sort fields (for example, you could sort by category then price), which is why the `fields` property of the Sort class requires that an array of `SortFields` be specified. If you want to sort only on a single field, create an array with only one `SortField` within it, as the example does.

 TIP: When specifying multiple SortFields, the order in the array is the order in which the sort fields would be applied. If you sort by category and then price, your code would look like this:

```
var prodSort:Sort = new Sort();
var sortField1:SortField = new SortField("catID");
var sortField2:SortField = new SortField("listPrice");
prodSort.fields=new Array(sortField1, sortField2);
```

In this next task you will write a sort function that you will use later when adding items to the users shopping cart.

1 In the ShoppingCart.as file below the existing function, build the skeleton for a function named sortItems, data typed as void.

```
private function sortItems():void{
}
```

2 In the sortItems() method, instantiate a new Sort object with the name of prodSort. Next, instantiate a new SortField instance with the name of sortField, set it equal to a new SortField, and pass the product property as a parameter. Finally, set the fields property of the prodSort object equal to a new Array passing the SortField as the parameter.

```
private function sortItems():void{
   var prodSort:Sort = new Sort();
   var sortField:SortField = new SortField("product");
   prodSort.fields=new Array(sortField);
}
```

> **TIP:** Flex Builder should have automatically imported both the Sort and SortField classes when you created this function. If it did not, be sure to import mx.collections.Sort and mx.collections.SortField.

This sort will be performed on the properties of the shopping cart items, which are stored in an ArrayCollection named aItems. You will create this ArrayCollection later in this lesson.

3 Still in the sortItems() method, add the Sort to the sort property of the aItems ArrayCollection, then call the refresh() method of the aItems ArrayCollection. The final sortItems() method should appear as follows:

```
private function sortItems():void{
   var prodSort:Sort=new Sort();
   var sortField:SortField=new SortField("product");
   prodSort.fields=new Array(sortField);
   aItems.sort=prodSort;
   aItems.refresh();
}
```

When this method is called, it defines how the collection will be sorted, and then executes the sort.

Adding an Item or Updating the Quantity

The code you are about to write implements placing an item in the shopping cart, and is not difficult line by line, but the logic involved may seem complex at first. To be sure you understand the big picture before you try to implement the details, let's walk through the following code and diagram.

Code walkthrough

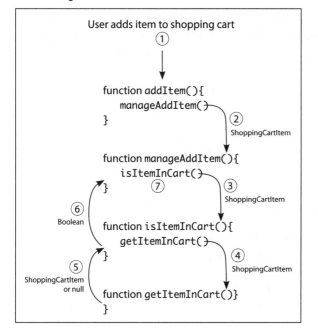

1. The user clicks a button to add an item to the shopping cart.

2. The addItem() method calls the manageAddItem() method, passing it a ShoppingCartItem.

3. The manageAddItem() method calls the isItemInCart() method, passing it a ShoppingCartItem.

4. The isItemInCart() method calls the getItemInCart() method, passing it a ShoppingCartItem.

5. The getItemInCart() method tries to find the item. If it is found, the function returns the found ShoppingCartItem. If it is not found, the function returns null.

6. The isItemInCart() method returns false if null is returned or returns true if the ShoppingCartItem is returned from the getItemInCart() method.

7. The manageAddItem() method updates the ShoppingCartItem if the Boolean value returned is true, or adds the ShoppingCartItem if the Boolean value returned is false.

As you begin to code each method you will see a note giving you pseudocode showing the logic that method will implement.

 TIP: Pseudocode is simply a compact and informal high-level description of the code that will be written.

Using a Cursor to Locate a ShoppingCart Item

A key point in the logic in this task is determining if a newly selected ShoppingCartItem is already in an existing ArrayCollection of ShoppingCartItems. The ability to perform this is achieved using the concept of a cursor. A cursor is a position indicator within the collection class, which allows direct access to any particular item in the collection. This allows for easy manipulation of items within the collection. Once you have a cursor created in a collection, you can

- Move the cursor backward and forward

- Find specific items with the cursor

- Retrieve the item at the cursor location

- Add and remove items at the cursor position

All of this functionality is available natively to the ArrayCollection class, meaning you do not need to write verbose loops to achieve any of these goals.

> ✴ **NOTE:** Cursors are not unique to ArrayCollections; they are available to any class that implements the ICursorView interface. For more information on interfaces, please refer to the "About Interfaces" section of the "Creating and Extending Flex 3 Components" documentation.

The general steps to using a cursor in a collection class are:

1. Create a cursor in the ArrayCollection using the `createCursor()` method.

2. Sort the ArrayCollection.

3. Use the `findFirst()`, `findAny()`, `moveNext()` methods of the cursor to move the cursor and find items in the ArrayCollection.

Each time you click an item, List control is updated automatically because of the data binding to the underlying ArrayCollection. Right now, even if the identical item is added multiple times, you get the same behavior.

Checking to see if an item needs to be added or updated

The desired behavior is to have only new items added to the cart. If an item is clicked more than once, it should update the quantity of the item. You will use the `IViewCursor` as part of the solution implementation.

1 In the ShoppingCart.as file, add another `import` statement that will import the IViewCursor interface from the package mx.collections.

```
import mx.collections.IViewCursor;
```

The cursor is available through the use of the IViewCursor interface. To work with a cursor, you must have access to this interface.

2 Define a private property with the name of cursor, data typed as IViewCursor. The ShoppingCart class should appear as follows:

```
public class ShoppingCart {
    [Bindable]
    public var aItems:ArrayCollection = new ArrayCollection();
    [Bindable]
    public var total:Number=0;
    private var cursor:IViewCursor;
    public function addItem(item:ShoppingCartItem):void{
        aItems.addItem(item);
    }
    private function sortItems():void{
        var prodSort:Sort=new Sort();
        var sortField:SortField=new SortField("product");
        prodSort.fields=new Array(sortField);
        aItems.sort=prodSort;
        aItems.refresh();
    }
}
```

IViewcursor is an interface available from the collections package, which includes the ArrayCollection class. By defining a private variable here, you can use the methods of this interface.

3 Still in the ShoppingCart.as file, locate the addItem() method. Delete the existing code inside this method and call the manageAddItem() method. Pass the item parameter to the manageAddItem() method.

```
public function addItem(item:ShoppingCartItem):void{
    manageAddItem(item);
}
```

Each time the user clicks the Add To Cart button, the cart needs to determine whether or not the Product is already in the cart. If the Product isn't already there, the item should be added, but if it is there, the quantity of the ShoppingCartItem should be incremented.

Rather than having an unwieldy block of code for all of this logic in the addItem() method, you will instead create a number of smaller methods to implement this logic. The manageAddItem() method will be the gateway into the logical process.

✱ **NOTE:** The pseudocode for the *manageAddItem()* method is:

```
if item is in cart{
   update item;
}else{
   add item;
}
```

4 Add a new private method with the name of manageAddItem(), data typed as void. The method should accept an argument named item, data typed as ShoppingCartItem. Within the method, add conditional logic that tests whether the item is already in the cart. The logic to search through the cart will be implemented in a method you will soon write called isItemInCart(). If the item is not in the cart, call the addItem() method of the ArrayCollection as you did previously. If it is, call another soon to be written method, called updateItem().

```
private function manageAddItem(item:ShoppingCartItem):void{
   if (isItemInCart(item)){
      updateItem(item);
   }else{
      aItems.addItem(item);
   }
}
```

This demonstrates good architecture, in which you set up different functionality in different methods to foster code reuse.

Returning a Boolean value with an item already in the cart

The manageAddItem() method is asking the isItemInCart() method to return a Boolean value depending on whether or not an item is in the cart.

✱ **NOTE:** The pseudocode for the *isItemInCart()* method is:

```
get item;
if item is null{
   return false;
}else{
   return true;
}
```

1 Create the isItemInCart() method, data typed as Boolean. The function will accept an argument named item, data typed as ShoppingCartItem. Within the method, create a new variable local to the method with the name of sci, which will hold a matched ShoppingCartItem, returned by the getItemInCart() method.

```
private function isItemInCart(item:ShoppingCartItem):Boolean{
   var sci:ShoppingCartItem = getItemInCart(item);
}
```

When you write the getItemInCart() method, you will build it so that if it finds the item, it returns it; otherwise, it will return null.

Next, you need to create the getItemInCart() method, which will use a cursor to find an item already in the collection.

2 Insert an if-then-else statement in the method. If sci is null, isItemInCart() should return false. If sci is not null, it will return true.

```
private function isItemInCart(item:ShoppingCartItem):Boolean{
   var sci:ShoppingCartItem = getItemInCart(item);
   if(sci == null){
     return false;
   } else {
     return true;
   }
}
```

The isItemInCart() method will now return true if the added item is in the cart and false if the added item was not found in the cart.

Checking whether an item is already in the cart

The isItemInCart method returns a Boolean value based on whether an item is already in the cart. The getItemInCart actually does the checking to see if the item is in the cart.

✱ NOTE: The pseudocode for the *getItemInCart()* method is:

```
create the cursor;
sort the ArrayCollection;
find the item;
if item found{
   return ShoppingCartItem cursor is pointing to;
}else{
   return null;
}
```

1 Create the getItemInCart() method, data typed as ShoppingCartItem. Have it accept an argument named item, data typed as ShoppingCartItem. Within this method, create the cursor property you defined earlier, using the createCursor() method of the ArrayCollection.

```
private function getItemInCart(item:ShoppingCartItem):ShoppingCartItem{
   cursor = aItems.createCursor();
}
```

You need to search through the entire cart to check whether the item the user is adding is already in the cart. The ShoppingCartItem that the user wants to add is being passed to this method; if it is already in the cart, the method will return the item to the calling function.

2 Below the cursor creation code, call the `sortItems()` method you created in the previous task.

```
private function getItemInCart(item:ShoppingCartItem):ShoppingCartItem{
   cursor = aItems.createCursor();
   sortItems();
}
```

Remember that to use a cursor in an ArrayCollection, the collection must be sorted. In this case, you coded `sortItems()`method to sort on the product property.

3 After the call to the `sortItems()` method, pass the `item` parameter to the cursor's `findFirst()` method, and store the results in a Boolean variable named `found`.

```
var found:Boolean = cursor.findFirst(item);
```

In this step, you use the `findFirst()` method of the cursor to search through the collection of ShoppingCartItems looking for a match. The `findFirst()` method requires an object be passed to it. The property within the object is used to determine the name of the property in the item, on which you are looking for a match. The value of the object's property specifies the value to match. In this case, you are instructing the cursor to search through the product properties of each ShoppingCartItem, and to find the first Product object whose value matches the Product object in the passed in ShoppingCartItem. If a match is found, the method will return a value of `true`. If no match is found, a value of `false` will be returned. Importantly, the cursor will stop on the matching record.

> **TIP:** In addition to `findFirst()`, the cursor also has the `findAny()` and `findLast()` methods. Any of these three could be used in the code, but because your logic will ultimately prevent more than one ShoppingCartItem for each Product from being added, `findFirst()` seems a logical choice.

4 In the `getItemInCart()` method, add a conditional statement to test if `found` is `true`. If true, create a new ShoppingCartItem with the name of `sci`, which references the `current` property of the cursor. Add an `else` statement that will return a value of `null`. After the conditional, return `sci`.

```
if(found){
   var sci:ShoppingCartItem = cursor.current as ShoppingCartItem;
}else{
   return null;
}
return sci;
```

The current property of the cursor will return the entire object at the present position of the cursor, which will be the ShoppingCartItem you found using the cursor's findFirst() method. If findFirst() was successful, the cursor will stop on that record, and the current property will remain at that position. The final getItemInCart() method should look like this:

```
private function getItemInCart(item:ShoppingCartItem):ShoppingCartItem{
    cursor = aItems.createCursor();
    sortItems();
    var found:Boolean = cursor.findFirst(item);
    if(found){
        var sci:ShoppingCartItem = cursor.current as ShoppingCartItem;
    }else{
        return null;
    }
    return sci;
}
```

Updating the quantity if the item is already in the cart

Once it has been determined that an item is already in the cart, the item's quantity should be updated rather than adding the item to the cart again.

> ✱ **NOTE:** The pseudocode for the *updateItem()* method is:
>
> ```
> assign to a variable the ShoppingCartItem the cursor is pointing to;
> update the quantity ordered;
> recalculate shopping cart totals;
> ```

1 Create a skeleton for the updateItem() method, data typed as void. Have it accept an argument named item, data typed as ShoppingCartItem. On the first line of the method, define a local variable with the name of sci, data typed as a ShoppingCartItem, which is equal to cursor.current cast as a ShoppingCartItem.

```
private function updateItem(item:ShoppingCartItem):void{
    var sci:ShoppingCartItem = cursor.current as ShoppingCartItem;
}
```

Because the cursor has not been moved since it was used to check if the item was in the cart, cursor.current still refers to the matched item. The sci variable will always be populated because this method is called only if there has already been a match in the cart. If the sci variable is null, this method will not be called, and a new item will be added to the cart using the addItem() method.

The cursor.current object must be cast as a ShoppingCartItem instance because in the ActionScript definition the IViewCursor's current property is data typed as Object.

2 Still in the updateItem() method, update the quantity property of the sci object to its current value plus the value located in the existing aItems ArrayCollection.

```
sci.quantity += item.quantity;
```

Remember, whenever a new item is added to the cart, you hardcoded the quantity value in the ShoppingCartItem to 1.

3 Still in the updateItem() method and immediately after you set the quantity, call the reCalc() method of the sci ShoppingCartItem class. The final updateItem() method should look like this:

```
private function updateItem(item:ShoppingCartItem):void{
   var sci:ShoppingCartItem = cursor.current as ShoppingCartItem;
   sci.quantity += item.quantity;
   sci.recalc();
}
```

When you first created the ShoppingCartItem class, you added a method with the name of reCalc() that created a subtotal property with the price of each product multiplied by each product. When you built the method, you hardcoded the quantity to 1. It now makes sense to recalculate that value, because you have just updated the quantity property to however many items the user has in their cart.

❋ **NOTE:** The pseudocode for the *calcTotal()* method is:

```
loop over all items in shopping cart and create grand total;
```

4 Directly after the updateItem() method, create a skeleton for the calcTotal() method, data typed as void. In the method, set the initial value of the total variable you declared previously to 0.

```
private function calcTotal():void{
   this.total = 0;
}
```

In this method, you will loop over the entire shopping cart and update a total text field with the entire total of the end user's purchases. Initially, you need to set the value of the total variable to 0.

5 Still in the calcTotal() method, create a skeleton of a for loop that will loop through the aItems ArrayCollection. Use the variable i as the iterant for the loop, with a data type of int. Use the length property of aItems to return the length of the ArrayCollection for use in the terminating condition, and use the ++ operator to increment the iterant.

```
for(var i:int=0;i<aItems.length;i++){
}
```

This builds a simple loop that enables you to loop through the entire shopping cart. The loop will continue to execute as long as i (the iterant) is less than the length of the array. Each time the loop executes, the iterant is increased by 1 (++ is shorthand for this increase).

6 Inside the loop, update the total variable with the subtotal of each item stored in the aItems array. Be sure to use the += operator so it will add the new value to the existing one. Use the getItemAt() method and pass it the value i to get a reference to each ShoppingCartItem. Your final calcTotal() method should appear as follows:

```
private function calcTotal():void{
   this.total = 0;
   for(var i:int=0;i<aItems.length;i++){
      this.total += aItems.getItemAt(i).subtotal;
   }
}
```

This loops through the entire shopping cart, and updates the total variable by adding the subtotal (price * quantity) of each item in the cart to the current total. Now any time you need to calculate the total price of all the items, you can simply call this method.

7 Locate the addItem() method and call the calcTotal() method you just wrote. The final addItem() method should look as follows:

```
public function addItem(item:ShoppingCartItem):void{
   manageAddItem(item);
   calcTotal();
}
```

After a new item is added to the cart, it makes sense to update the total field, which is bound to the total text field that displays to the end user.

8 Return to EComm.mxml and locate the cartBox VBox. Immediately after the Label control that says "Your Cart Total," add another Label control whose text property is bound to the total property in the cart object. Add an <mx:HBox> tag around the two Label controls.

```
<mx:HBox>
   <mx:Label text="Your Cart Total: $"/>
   <mx:Label text="{cart.total}"/>
</mx:HBox>
```

This will create another Label control directly above the cart that will display the total cost of the cart, which you set in your calcTotal() method. Remember that you instantiated the ShoppingCart class as cart in an earlier lesson.

9 Save and run the application. Add Buffalo to the cart, and you will see that the cart total increases, as the item is added only once. Later, you will use a DataGrid to actually display more information (such as price, quantity, and subtotal) for each item.

Adding a Remove Button

In this task, you will add a Remove button to remove an item from the shopping cart. This method will search through the entire shopping cart for the item the user wants to remove. In this task, you will see how the architecture of encapsulating the functionality into separate methods, as you did in the previous task, makes coding this functionality easier. You can use the already built search method to search through the entire shopping cart to find the item you wish to delete.

1 Return to EComm.mxml and locate the products VBox. Just below the Add To Cart button, add another button with the label of Remove From Cart and add a click event that will call the deleteProd() method. Pass to the event handler the first object (at index 0) from the groceryInventory ArrayCollection using the getItemAt() method. The object must be cast as a Product, as follows.

```
<mx:Button label="Remove from Cart"
    click ="deleteProd(groceryInventory.getItemAt(0) as Product)"/>
```

This will call a method you will soon write in the EComm.mxml file and pass it the product that should be deleted. Be aware that at this point you are hardcoding this to use only the first product. In a later lesson, when you are creating all the products dynamically, you will update this so it can delete any product you have in the cart.

2 Still in EComm.mxml, locate the script block and add a new method with the name of deleteProd, data typed as void. Have it accept a single argument, named product, data typed as Product. Inside this method, call the soon to be written removeItem() method from the cart object. The deleteProd() method should appear as follows:

```
private function deleteProd(product:Product):void{
    cart.removeItem(product);
}
```

This method asks the cart to remove the specified product.

3 Return to the ShoppingCart class and add a new method with the name of removeItem, data typed as void. Have it accept an argument named prod, data typed as Product. Inside this method, create a new ShoppingCartItem variable, with the name of item, which contains the prod.

```
public function removeItem(prod:Product):void{
   var item:ShoppingCartItem = new ShoppingCartItem(prod);
}
```

Remember, earlier, you wrote the getItemInCart() method to find any particular Product in the cart; but, it requires that you pass it a ShoppingCartItem, not just a product. To be able to use that method, you are temporarily creating a new ShoppingCartItem, which contains that product.

4 Create a second ShoppingCartItem instance, with the name of sci, and set it equal to the results of a call to your getItemInCart() method. Use an if statement to check if the sci variable is not equal to null. If it is, use the cursor's remove() method to delete the product at that cursor location. Finally, call the calcTotal() method of the cart. The finished removeItem() method should look as follows:

```
public function removeItem(prod:Product):void{
   var item:ShoppingCartItem = new ShoppingCartItem(prod);
   var sci:ShoppingCartItem = getItemInCart(item);
   if(sci != null){
      cursor.remove();
   }
   calcTotal();
}
```

Remember that the getItemInCart() method that you wrote earlier searches the cart for a ShoppingCartItem that contains a particular product and returns that item. When you call that method, the cursor will move to the matching location in the aItems ArrayCollection. Once the cursor is there, you can use the cursor's remove() method to delete the item at that location.

As a best practice, you should verify whether the item being passed in matches the item found in the cart. If the result (sci) of getItemInCart() is null, no product is matched, so it cannot be removed. If you omitted this conditional, and clicked the Remove button when there were no items in the cart, a runtime error would be thrown. With this conditional logic in place, you are preventing a potential error.

Finally, you need to recalculate all the items in the cart. Call the calcTotal() method so the interface can continue to show the new correct total.

5 Save and run the application. Add Buffalo to the cart. You should see that you can click the Remove from Cart button to delete Buffalo from the cart and that the total field is updated each time you do this.

What You Have Learned

In this lesson, you have:

- Retrieved remote XML data using the `<mx:HTTPService>` tag and used it as a data provider for a List control (pages 116–122)

- Programmatically added an item to an ArrayCollection built from remote XML data and used the ArrayCollection as a data provider for a ComboBox control (pages 122–128)

- Explored E4X operators (pages 129–134)

- Populated a Tree control with XML data (pages 129–140)

- Transformed XML data into an ArrayCollection of custom value objects (pages 141–145)

- Used an ArrayCollection of custom objects in data bindings (pages 145–146)

- Sorted an ArrayCollection (pages 148–150)

- Implemented shopping cart functionality using a cursor with an ArrayCollection (pages 150–160)

- Created a method to remove shopping cart items (pages 160–162)

What You Will Learn

In this lesson, you will:

- Understand the need for components and how they can fit into a bigger application architecture scheme
- Understand the class hierarchy used in Flex
- Build both visual and nonvisual components
- Instantiate and use custom components
- Create properties and methods in custom components
- Create a pop-up window and learn how to close it
- Create a value object ActionScript class

Approximate Time

This lesson takes approximately 3 hours to complete.

Lesson Files

Media Files:

Lesson07/assets/AddProduct.mxml

Starting Files:

Lesson07/start/Dashboard.mxml
Lesson07/start/DataEntry.mxml
Lesson07/start/EComm.mxml

Completed Files:

Lesson07/complete/Dashboard.mxml
Lesson07/complete/DataEntry.mxml
Lesson07/complete/EComm.mxml
Lesson07/complete/managers/CategorizedProductManager.mxml
Lesson07/complete/valueObjects/Category.as
Lesson07/complete/views/dashboard/ChartPod.mxml
Lesson07/complete/views/dataEntry/AddProduct.mxml
Lesson07/complete/views/dataEntry/ConfirmScreen.mxml
Lesson07/complete/views/dataEntry/UpdateDeleteProd.mxml

LESSON 7

Creating Components with MXML

You have used many components while building the three applications to their current state. Every time you use an MXML tag, you are actually using a component. In fact, Flex is considered to be a component-based development model. In this lesson you'll learn how to create your own components. The custom components you build will either extend functionality of components or group functionality of components.

Up to this point, you did not have a way to break up your application pages. The application would continue to get longer and longer and become more difficult to build, debug, and maintain. It would also be very difficult for a team to work on one large application page. Components let you divide the application into modules, which you can develop and maintain separately. With careful planning, these components can become a reusable suite of application functionality.

```
1  <?xml version="1.0" encoding="utf-8"?>
2  <mx:Panel xmlns:mx="http://www.adobe.com/2006/mxml"
3      layout="vertical">
4
5      <mx:ControlBar>
6
7      </mx:ControlBar>
8
9  </mx:Panel>
10
```

A simple component

You will need to learn two things in this lesson. The first is how to build components. You must learn the syntax and rules for creating and using the custom components you build. Second, you need to learn why you'd want to do this and how components can affect your overall application architecture. The "Introducing MXML Components" section provides an overview of how to build components. Then in the tasks throughout the rest of the lesson, you will reinforce your component-building skills and continue to learn more and more details about building custom components. The beginning of this lesson includes a theoretical discussion of why you would want to use components. The rest of the lesson will use an architectural approach to implementing components.

Introducing MXML Components

All Flex components and all the components you will build are actually ActionScript classes. The base class for the visual components you have been using and the MXML components you will build in this lesson is UIComponent. This means that in a hierarchy of components, UIComponent is at the top, and all the other components inherit from it.

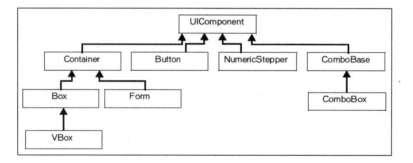

There are general groupings of these classes based on their functionality, such as component, manager, and data service classes. Most of the classes you have been using up to this point have been component classes, such as Application, HBox, and TextInput, which have visual representations. You also used the HTTPService tag, which does not descend from UIComponent because it is a nonvisual component—a data service.

Package	mx.rpc.http.mxml
Class	public class HTTPService
Inheritance	HTTPService → HTTPService → AbstractInvoker → EventDispatcher → Object
Implements	IMXMLObject, IMXMLSupport

✱ **NOTE:** You can examine a complete description of the class hierarchy in the Flex ActionScript and MXML API reference, referred to as ASDoc.

Understanding the Basics of How to Create a Custom Component

When you build your own component, you basically want to do one of two things: add functionality to a predefined component or group numerous components together.

The basic steps to build a component are as follows:

1 Create a new file with the filename you want for your component. Because you're building a class, the name should start with an uppercase letter. Also, remember that these names will be case sensitive, like Flex is in general.

2 Make the first line of code the XML document type definition you have been using for the main application files.

```
<?xml version="1.0" encoding="utf-8"?>
```

3 As the first MXML tag, insert the root tag of your component, which will reflect what you want to do in the component. If it is a container, you most likely want to group several components' functionality into one easier-to-use component. If it is not a container, you most likely want to extend the functionality of a predefined component or further extend the functionality of a custom component.

```
<mx:VBox xmlns:mx="http://www.adobe.com/2006/mxml">

</mx:VBox>
```

4 In the body of the component, add the functionality needed. This will vary depending on what functionality you want the component to provide.

5 In the file that will instantiate the component, add an XML namespace so you can access the component. It is considered a best practice to group components in subdirectories according to their purpose. For instance, you will create a directory called views; then under that directory you will add another three subdirectories, one for each of the applications you are building: Dashboard, DataEntry, and EComm. Later in this lesson, you will add a namespace, using the letter *v* as the prefix, to have access to all the custom components in the views/dataEntry directory. The statement will appear as follows:

```
xmlns:v="views.dataEntry.*"
```

6 Instantiate the component as you would a predefined component. For instance, if you created a file component called MyComp.mxml, using the namespace just created, you would instantiate that component as follows:

```
<v:MyComp/>
```

Creating a Custom Component Step by Step

Now that you know the general approach to building a component, here is a simple example of adding functionality to a predefined component. Assume that you want to build a List that will automatically display three grocery categories. Your component will use <mx:List> as its root tag. Up to now, all the MXML pages you've built use the <mx:Application> tag as the root tag. Components cannot use the <mx:Application> tag as the root tag because it can be used only once per application. Here are the six steps for creating a simple component:

1. Create a file named MyList.mxml. (You don't need to actually do this, just follow along with the logic.)

2. The first line of the component will be the standard XML document declaration
   <?xml version="1.0" encoding="utf-8"?>.

3. Because you are extending the functionality of the <mx:List>, you will use it as the root tag. Your skeleton component will appear as follows:

   ```
   <?xml version="1.0" encoding="utf-8"?>
   <mx:List xmlns:mx="http://www.adobe.com/2006/mxml">

   </mx:List>
   ```

4. The functionality to add to the body of the component is to display three <mx:String> tags in the <mx:List>. You know you need to use an <mx:dataProvider> tag to supply data to an <mx:List>, so here is the finished component:

   ```
   <?xml version="1.0" encoding="utf-8"?>
   <mx:List xmlns:mx="http://www.adobe.com/2006/mxml">

       <mx:dataProvider>
           <mx:String>Dairy</mx:String>
           <mx:String>Produce</mx:String>
           <mx:String>Bakery</mx:String>
       </mx:dataProvider>

   </mx:List>
   ```

5. Assume that a file named CompTest.mxml is created at the root of the project. Also, the component is created in a directory called myComps. Use the letter *c* as the prefix for the components in this folder. Therefore, the XML namespace to add to the <mx:Application> tag is xmlns:c="myComps.*".

6. Finally, instantiate the component in the main application file:

```xml
<?xml version="1.0" encoding="utf-8"?>
<mx:Application xmlns:mx="http://www.adobe.com/2006/mxml"
    xmlns:c="myComps.*">

    <c:MyList/>

</mx:Application>
```

✳ NOTE: You will see shortly that Flex Builder makes this process of creating the skeleton of the component very easy.

The CompTest.mxml output would appear as shown here.

Using Custom Components in the Application Architecture

You now know the basic mechanics of creating custom components. You might ask yourself, so now what? How does this affect what I have been doing? Why should I use them? How do I use them?

The advantages of components mentioned in the opening pages of this lesson should now be more clear:

- Components make applications easier to build, debug, and maintain.
- Components ease team development.
- With planning, components can lead to a suite of reusable code.

To facilitate the use of components as reusable code, you should make them independent of other code whenever possible. The components should operate as independent pieces of application logic with a clear definition of what data must be passed into them and what data will be returned from them. The object-oriented programming term *loosely coupled* is often applied to this kind of architecture.

Suppose you have a component that uses an `<mx:List>` to display some information. You later learn of a new component that would be a better way to display that data. If built correctly, you should be able to switch the display component used in your custom component and not need to make any other changes. You would have changed the inner workings of the custom component, but the data going into the component and what came out would not change, so no changes to the rest of the application were needed.

Now, you need to think about how components fit into the bigger picture of application architecture. Although this book is not meant to be a discourse on Flex application architectures, it would be negligent not to show how components can fit into the bigger picture. In the applications you are building in this book you will implement a simple form of model-view-controller (MVC) architecture.

MVC is a design pattern or software architecture that separates the application's data, user interface, and control logic into three distinct groupings. The goal is to implement the logic so changes can be made to one portion of the application with minimal impact to the others. Short definitions of the key terms are as follows:

- **Model:** The data the application uses. It manages data elements, responds to queries about its state, and manages instructions to change the data.

- **View:** The user interface. The view is responsible for presenting model data to the user and gathering information from the user.

- **Controller:** Responds to events—typically user events, but also system events. The events are interpreted and the controller invokes changes on the model and view.

Generally, the flow of MVC is as follows:

1. The user interacts with the user interface (a view), such as clicking a button to add an item to a shopping cart.

2. The controller handles the input event.

3. The controller accesses the model, maybe by retrieving or altering data.

4. A view then uses the model data for appropriate user presentation.

Consider the e-commerce application you are building. Eventually your EComm.mxml main application page will be the controller. There will be views that do the following:

- Display the different grocery item categories

- Display the items in the shopping cart

- Display a detailed view of a particular grocery item

- Display all the grocery items in a particular category

All of these views will be fronted by the controller, which in your case is the main application page: EComm.mxml. The model will start as an <mx:Model> tag.

Now the stage is set, and you're ready to get started building components and enhancing the architecture and functionality of the applications you are building.

Creating an Update/Delete Product Component and Instantiating It

This first task will not add any functionality from the user's point of view; the exercise will improve the overall architecture of the DataEntry application. In fact, you'll want the application to appear exactly as it did before you started. You will pull the visual elements of the application into a component, which is a view in terms of MVC architecture. DataEntry.mxml will begin to transform into the controller.

1 Right-click the FlexGrocer project and create a folder named views. Right-click the views folder and create another folder named dataEntry.

It is a best practice to organize your components. In this case, the views folder will contain the views for all three of your application sections. Within the views folder, the dataEntry folder will be where you will create your first component.

2 Right-click the dataEntry folder and then choose New > MXML Component. In the New MXML Component dialog box, set the filename as **UpdateDeleteProd.mxml** and the base component as an HBox, remove any width and height values, and then click Finish.

In this case, you are using an <mx:HBox> as your root tag, which means the children you insert in this component will be aligned beside each other.

3 Insert an <mx:Script> block just after the <mx:HBox> tag.

You will have a large <mx:Script> block in this component. Some of the code you will copy from the old DataEntry.mxml file, whereas other code you will write new.

4 Import the following three classes at the top of the <mx:Script> block:

flash.net.FileReference

utils.Util

mx.collections.ArrayCollection

These are all classes you will use in this component that you used previously in DataEntry.mxml. Feel free to copy the import statements from the DataEntry.mxml file.

5 From the DataEntry.mxml file, copy the bindable private variable `units` and paste it below the `import` statements in the component. Remove the instantiation of the new ArrayCollection from `units` and change the access modifier from private to public. Create another bindable public variable named `foodColl`, data typed as XMLListCollection.

```
[Bindable]
public var units:ArrayCollection;
[Bindable]
public var foodColl:XMLListCollection;
```

✱ **NOTE:** When you data type the `foodColl` variable, Flex Builder will automatically import that class, which is mx.collections.XMLListCollection.

When you copied the variable into the component, and created the second, they actually became properties of the component. Simply by using the `var` statement and defining the variables to be public, you create properties of the components that can have data passed into them.

This is no small matter. The basic building blocks of object-oriented programming are objects, properties, and methods. So knowing how to create properties is a very important piece of information.

Later in this lesson, you will add public functions to a component. Just as public variables are properties, public functions are the methods of your components.

6 Copy the three functions `fileBrowse()`, `populateForm()`, and `resetForm()` from the DataEntry.mxml page and paste them in the `<mx:Script>` block below the variable declarations.

You actually could have cut the three functions from the DataEntry.mxml page, because they will no longer be needed there after this component is built. But for now, you will leave them there and remove them later.

7 Copy the `<mx:Tree>` tag and the complete Form from the DataEntry.mxml page and paste them below the `<mx:Script>` block but above the closing `<mx:HBox>` tag in the component.

You can see that you are moving the functionality that displayed information in the main application page into this component. In the main application page, the Tree and Form were surrounded by an HBox. That is why an `<mx:HBox>` tag was used as the root tag for your new component.

8 Save the file.

You have now created your first MXML component. Now that the component is built, you will remove code no longer needed in the main application page and then instantiate the new component.

9 Return to the DataEntry.mxml file and remove all the `import` statements except for the following:

```
import mx.collections.ArrayCollection;
import mx.rpc.events.ResultEvent;
```

The removed `import` statements were needed for code that you placed in the component.

10 After you are sure that they have been copied correctly to the new component, remove the `fileBrowse()`, `populateForm()`, and `resetForm()` functions from the `<mx:Script>` block.

As mentioned earlier, these functions were left in until they had been copied correctly.

11 Remove the Tree and Form and the HBox that contained them.

This functionality has been moved into the component.

12 Add a namespace, using the letter *v* as a prefix, which allows you to use the components in the views/dataEntry folder. The code should appear as follows and be placed in the `<mx:Application>` tag:

```
xmlns:v="views.dataEntry.*"
```

There is currently only one component in the dataEntry folder, so you could have specified the name of that one component rather than using the *. Later in this lesson, you will create another component in the dataEntry folder and will want to use it as well, and using the * enables use of all components in the directory.

13 Just above the closing `</mx:Application>` tag, instantiate the new component using the prefix defined in the namespace, the letter *v*. The code should appear as follows:

```
<v:UpdateDeleteProd />
```

You have now created and instantiated your first custom MXML component. Notice that the invocation of your custom component looks very similar to instantiating one of the built-in components. You use the prefix (in this case the letter v instead of `mx`) and then the name of the component, followed by />. It is important to remember that the components you build are just as valid as the components that ship with Flex and are used in similar ways.

14 Return to the UpdateDeleteProd.mxml component and note the name of the two properties defined in the component: units and foodColl.

These two properties must be passed values for the component to work correctly, which
means that in the invocation of the component in the main application page you use
these property names and bind values to them.

15 Return to DataEntry.mxml and add two property/value pairs to the instantiation of the
component. To the left of the equal signs will be the properties defined in the component,
and to the right of the equal signs will be the bindable variables created on this page. In
this case, they are intentionally the same:

```
<v:UpdateDeleteProd
    units="{units}"
    foodColl="{foodColl}"/>
```

The property names and the variables bound to them do not have to be named the same,
but your coding will be simpler if you follow this practice.

16 Change the layout property in the <mx:Application> tag so it is set equal to vertical.

You will create another component later in this lesson and will want the two to display
vertically.

17 Save the file and check to be sure that your code for that DataEntry.mxml file appears
as follows:

```
<?xml version="1.0" encoding="utf-8"?>
<mx:Application xmlns:mx="http://www.adobe.com/2006/mxml"
    layout="vertical"
    creationComplete="unitRPC.send();prodByCatRPC.send()"
    xmlns:v="views.dataEntry.*">

    <mx:Script>
      <![CDATA[
        import mx.collections.ArrayCollection;
        import mx.rpc.events.ResultEvent;

        [Bindable]
        private var units:ArrayCollection =new ArrayCollection();

        private function unitRPCResult(event:ResultEvent):void{
            units = event.result.allUnits.unit;
        }
      ]]>
    </mx:Script>
```

```
<mx:HTTPService id="unitRPC"
    url="http://www.flexgrocer.com/units.xml"
    result="unitRPCResult(event)"/>

<mx:HTTPService id="prodByCatRPC"
    url="http://www.flexgrocer.com/categorizedProducts.xml"
    resultFormat="e4x"/>

<mx:XMLListCollection id="foodColl"
    source="{prodByCatRPC.lastResult.category}"/>

<v:UpdateDeleteProd
    units="{units}"
    foodColl="{foodColl}"/>

</mx:Application>
```

You see that the main application page is a much smaller than it was and is now acting more like a controller. The main application page is now retrieving model data and instantiating the views.

18 Run the DataEntry.mxml file. You see that creating the component has not changed the functionality.

The purpose of this first task was not to add functionality to the application but to rearchitect it. As the functionality of the DataEntry application continued to grow, the main application page would have become much too long and complex. Using components gives you the chance to break it up into manageable application modules.

Popping Up Product Information When Clicking the Update and Delete Buttons

Right now, nothing happens in the DataEntry application when you click the Update/Delete buttons. You will change this now. You will not yet actually write data back to the server; that comes in a later lesson. Now you will display in a pop-up window the product information you will deal with later at the server level.

You will be creating a *modal* pop-up window. This means that a window will appear with the product information in it, and you will not be able to interact with any other components in the Flex application until you close the pop-up window. To build this functionality, you will use the TitleWindow class for the root tag in your component. You will also use the

PopUpManager class—in particular, the createPopUp() and removePopUp() methods. Your application will appear as follows with a pop-up window open.

1. Right-click the views/dataEntry folder. Choose New > MXML Component. The filename should be **ConfirmScreen.mxml**, and the base component should be TitleWindow. After you select TitleWindow, set the layout to vertical, remove any width and height values, and then click Finish.

   In this case, you chose the `<mx:TitleWindow>` tag as the base tag for your component. In the component you built earlier, you chose an `<mx:HBox>`. Your decision for the base tag should be driven by what you want the component to do.

2. Add a close event to the `<mx:TitleWindow>` tag. The ActionScript for this close event should call the static method of the PopUpManager class removePopUp(), in which the argument for the method is this. Also set the showCloseButton property equal to true.

```
<mx:TitleWindow xmlns:mx="http://www.adobe.com/2006/mxml"
    layout="vertical"
    close="PopUpManager.removePopUp(this)"
    showCloseButton="true">
```

The TitleWindow class is well-suited for use as a pop-up window because you can choose to display a close button, and when the user clicks that button the close event will handle that action and close the pop-up window.

Notice that the removePopUp() method is used. It is invoked directly from the class name—in this case, PopUpManager. Hence, you know it must be a static method. You did not have to create an instance of the PopUpManager class to use the removePopUp() method.

The argument of the removePopUp() method, this, refers to the instance of the TitleWindow itself. So in fact you are telling the TitleWindow to close itself.

3 Add an <mx:Script> to the block below the <mx:TitleWindow> tag. In the <mx:Script> block, import two classes: mx.managers.PopUpManager and valueObjects.Product. Also create a bindable public variable named prod, data typed as Product.

```
<mx:Script>
  <![CDATA[
      import mx.managers.PopUpManager;
      import valueObjects.Product;

      [Bindable]
      public var prod:Product;
  ]]>
</mx:Script>
```

The PopUpManager must be imported because you have used it in the handler for the close event. You will pass a Product object to be displayed in this pop-up window; hence the need for the bindable prod variable. And because that variable is of type Product, you must also import that class.

4 Below the <mx:Script> block, create an <mx:Form> to display all the pertinent data about the product passed to this component, as shown here:

```
<mx:Form>
    <mx:FormItem label="Category ID">
      <mx:Label text="{prod.catID}"/>
    </mx:FormItem>
    <mx:FormItem label="Product Name">
      <mx:Label text="{prod.prodName}"/>
    </mx:FormItem>
    <mx:FormItem label="Unit">
      <mx:Label text="{prod.unitID}"/>
    </mx:FormItem>
    <mx:FormItem label="Cost">
      <mx:Label text="{prod.cost}"/>
    </mx:FormItem>
    <mx:FormItem label="List Price">
      <mx:Label text="{prod.listPrice}"/>
    </mx:FormItem>
    <mx:FormItem label="Description">
      <mx:Text htmlText="{prod.description}"/>
```

code continues on next page

```
      </mx:FormItem>
      <mx:FormItem label="Organic">
         <mx:Label text="{prod.isOrganic}"/>
      </mx:FormItem>
      <mx:FormItem label="Low Fat">
         <mx:Label text="{prod.isLowFat}"/>
      </mx:FormItem>
      <mx:FormItem label="Image Name">
         <mx:Label text="{prod.imageName}"/>
      </mx:FormItem>
   </mx:Form>
```

The purpose of this component is to display the updated or deleted product. The
`<mx:Form>` will show the pertinent data in this modal window.

5 Save the file.

You have completed the building of your second component. You will now return to
UpdateDeleteProd.mxml and write the code to instantiate this component when needed.
Don't forget that this component is a class, which is a child of the TitleWindow class,
which you have now added to your Flex application for use whenever needed.

6 In UpdateDeleteProd.mxml, import mx.managers.PopUpManager and
valueObjects.Product. Also declare a private variable named win, data typed
as ConfirmScreen, the class which your new component creates.

You will need the PopUpManager class to create the pop-up window, and because you
will pass a variable of type Product, you'll also need to import the Product class. The win
variable will be used in popping up the confirm screen.

7 Just below the `<mx:Script>` block, add an `<mx:Model>` tag with an id of prodModel. In the
body of the `<mx:Model>` tag, create properties for all pertinent information gathered in the
Form. The only value not gathered in the form is the catID. This value can be retrieved
from the selected item from the Tree.

```
<mx:Model id="prodModel">
   <product>
      <catID>{productTree.selectedItem.@catID}</catID>
      <prodName>{prodName.text}</prodName>
      <unitID>{unitID.selectedItem.unitID}</unitID>
      <cost>{Number(cost.text)}</cost>
      <listPrice>{Number(listPrice.text)}</listPrice>
      <description>{description.text}</description>
      <isOrganic>{isOrganic.selected}</isOrganic>
      <isLowFat>{isLowFat.selected}</isLowFat>
      <imageName>{imageName.text}</imageName>
   </product>
</mx:Model>
```

It is a very common practice to bind form data to a Model, which takes the individual pieces of form data gathered in each control and puts them into an object you can more readily use. In this case, you will soon use the prodModel object to build an object of type Product that can be passed to your new component.

TIP: The <mx:Model> tag must have a root node, as <product> is in the Model shown. The name of the root node is not important.

8 Locate the two buttons at the bottom of the Form. Add a click event to the Update button; in the event handler, call a function named doProdUpdate(). Add a click event to the Delete button; in the event handler, call a function named doProdDelete().

```
<mx:Button label="Update" click="doProdUpdate()"/>
<mx:Button label="Delete" click="doProdDelete()"/>
```

You are calling ActionScript functions when an event occurs.

9 At the bottom of the <mx:Script> block, create the skeleton of a private function named showPopUp(), data typed as void. It should accept two parameters: prod, data typed as Product, and title, data typed as String.

```
private function showPopUp(prod:Product,title:String):void{
}
```

You will call this function in both the update and delete functions to display the product that is being acted upon.

10 As the first line of code in the function, set the win variable created earlier (remember that it is data typed as ConfirmScreen) equal to win=ConfirmScreen(PopUpManager. createPopUp(this,ConfirmScreen,true)).

This line of code is a bit tricky and will take some work to understand. First, examine what is inside of the parentheses. Here you are calling the static method createPopUp(). This method accepts three parameters:

- The first parameter is the parent of the pop-up window; in this case, this refers to the current component. The pop-up will appear in front of its parent.

- The second parameter is the class to be created for the pop-up window. Here you are using the component you just built: the ConfirmScreen class.

- The last parameter specifies whether the pop-up window should be modal or not.

If you were not passing data to the component, the code inside the parentheses would display a window, and you would not need any other code to perform the pop-up.

The rest of the code on this line is treating one object as a different type than it actually is. This is sometimes referred to as *casting*, or *coercing*, the object. You need to tell the compiler that the expression in parentheses is a ConfirmScreen object instance. You will now explore what this means and why it is possible.

If you did not cast the object to a ConfirmScreen object you would receive the following error:

```
Implicit coercion of a value with static type mx.core:IFlexDisplayObject to a
possibly unrelated type views.dataEntry:ConfirmScreen
```

The Adobe Flex 3 Language Reference (sometimes referred to as ASDoc), states that the createPopUp() method returns an object of type IFlexDisplayObject. You are trying to assign this object to a variable data typed as a ConfirmScreen—hence the compiler error indicating that they might be unrelated. By surrounding the expression with Confirm-Screen and parentheses, you have told the compiler they can be the same type.

11 When you call the showPopUp() function, you will pass it two parameters, named prod and title, which hold data to be displayed in the pop-up. As the last two lines of code in the function, assign those parameters to like named properties of the win object.

```
private function showPopUp(prod:Product,title:String):void{
   win=ConfirmScreen(PopUpManager.createPopUp(this,ConfirmScreen,true));
   win.prod=prod;
   win.title=title;
}
```

The reason you worked so hard to create and understand the win variable is because you needed it to pass data to the pop-up window. You can use the prod property you defined when you created the component as one way to pass data to the pop-up window. The title property is part of the TitleWindow class (actually it is a property inherited from the TitleWindow's parent class, Panel).

Now that you have created the showPopUp() function, you will use it in your update and delete functions.

12 At the bottom of the <mx:Script> block, build the skeleton for a private function named doProdUpdate(). Because the function will not return a value, data type it as void.

This is the function called when the user clicks the Update button.

13 In the function, use the `var` statement to create a variable named `prod`, data typed as Product. This variable should be set equal to an invocation of the static `buildProduct()` method of the Product class, passing the object built in the `<mx:Model>` tag, `prodModel`, as a parameter.

```
var prod:Product=Product.buildProduct(prodModel);
```

The variable created in this statement will be passed as a Product object to be displayed in the `showPopUp()` function.

14 As the last line of code in the function, call the `showPopUp()` function you built earlier. The first parameter should be the `prod` variable. The second parameter should be a concatenated string that displays the word "product," followed by the product name, followed by the word "updated." Your completed function should appear as follows:

```
private function doProdUpdate():void{
    var prod:Product=Product.buildProduct(prodModel);
    showPopUp(prod,"product "+ prod.prodName +" updated");
}
```

Remember that the code in this function will be replaced after you learn how to send data back to the server. At that time, you'll invoke the remote method to actually update the record in the database.

15 Now create a `doProdDelete()` function. The easiest way to do this is to simply copy the function you just created and change the name of the function as well as the word "updated" in the concatenated string.

```
private function doProdDelete():void{
    var prod:Product = Product.buildProduct(prodModel);
    showPopUp(prod,"product "+ prod.prodName +" deleted");
}
```

With these two functions now created, you're ready for testing.

16 Be sure that the ConfirmScreen and UpdateDeleteProd components are saved. Run the DataEntry.mxml main application page.

To test the functionality, select a product from one of the categories, and you will see the form filled. Click either the Update or Delete button, and you will see the modal pop-up window appear. Close the pop-up window. Be sure to test both the Update and Delete buttons.

Creating Another Value Object

In this task, you will build a simple value object. Up to this point, you have retrieved only product information, but, as the application continues to grow, it will also be important to retrieve information about the categories in which the products are grouped. For this reason, you need a Category value object that will hold the category name and a category ID, which is the primary key field for the category.

1 Right-click the valueObjects folder. Choose New > ActionScript Class. In the New ActionScript Class dialog box, be sure that the Package Name is valueObjects and supply the Name of the new class as **Category**. Also, be sure that the only modifier checked is public, and then click Finish. You should see that the code automatically generated for the class appears as follows:

```
package valueObjects
{
   public class Category
   {
   }
}
```

This creates the skeleton for the new Category value object class.

✱ **NOTE:** The positioning of opening braces is purely a style issue. Some developers like the opening brace at the end of the preceding line of code. For instance, the skeleton class code generated by Flex Builder is just as valid with the open braces positioned at the end of the preceding lines of code:

```
package valueObjects{
   public class Category{
   }
}
```

2 Make the class bindable because the two properties in the class both need to be bindable. In the class, create two public properties: the first is catID, data typed as int; the second is catName, data typed as String.

```
package valueObjects{
   [Bindable]
   public class Category{
      public var catID:int;
      public var catName:String;
   }
}
```

When dealing with the categories, there are obviously times when you want to see the category name—hence the need for the catName property. You will also retrieve products based on their category, which will be done by category ID. Hence the reason for the catID property.

3 Below the variable declarations, build the constructor function so it accepts two parameters: the first is id, data typed as int; the second is catName, data typed as String. In the constructor function, assign the catID property the value of the parameter id and assign the catName property the value of the parameter name.

```
public function Category(id:int,catName:String){
    this.catID=id;
    this.catName=catName;
}
```

When the property names match the parameter names, the class's properties must be preceded by the this prefix when assigning the values in the constructor. So, in this case, only the catName property had to use the this prefix because the name of the property and the name of the parameter are the same.

4 Create a public toString() function data typed as String. In the function, return the word Category in square brackets, followed by a space, and then the category name.

```
public function toString():String{
    return "[Category] "+ catName;
}
```

It is always a good idea to create a toString() function for a value object in case the object is ever used in a trace statement.

5 Check to be sure your completed Category value object appears as follows:

```
package valueObjects{
    [Bindable]
    public class Category{
        public var catID:int;
        public var catName:String;

        public function Category(id:int,catName:String){
            this.catID=id;
            this.catName=catName;
        }
        public function toString():String{
            return "[Category] "+ catName;
        }
    }
}
```

With the category value object now created, you can begin work on the nonvisual data manager component.

Creating a Data Manager Component for All Three Applications

In the first task, you rearchitected part of the application without adding any functionality. In the second task, you added functionality while building more components. This task is like the first, in which you are rearchitecting the application without adding any visible functionality for the user.

All three applications—DataEntry, EComm, and Dashboard—share the same data. In this task, you will build an MXML component that can be thought of as a data manager. This component will provide certain types of data to all the applications when they need it. This data manager component will be different from other components you've built in this lesson in that it will not have any visible representation that a user will see. These components are referred to as nonvisual components.

The advantage of building a data manager component is that it will centralize data requests. For instance, rather than having many HTTPService requests on different application pages and components, you can centralize them in this data manager component.

1 Create a new folder named managers under the FlexGrocer project.

   Because this new component is neither a value object nor a view, a new folder is needed.

2 Right-click the managers folder and then choose New > MXML Component. In the New MXML Component dialog box, set the filename as **CategorizedProductManager.mxml** and set the base component as a UIComponent; then click Finish.

   The UIComponent is the lightest-weight component you can use when creating an MXML component.

3 Insert an `<mx:Script>` block into the component. Add the following three `import` statements needed for this class:

```
import mx.rpc.events.ResultEvent;
import valueObjects.Product;
import valueObjects.Category;
```

   These statements are needed because there will be a `result` event from an HTTPService, and you will also build arrays of Products and Categories.

4 Just below the `import` statements in the `<mx:Script>` block, create three new private variables. The first is named `categorizedProducts`, data typed as Object, and set equal to a new Object. The second is named `aCats`, data typed as an Array, and set equal to a new Array. And the last is named rawData, data typed as XML. It does not have to be set equal to anything.

```
private var categorizedProducts:Object = new Object();
private var aCats:Array = new Array();
private var rawData:XML;
```

5 Open the EComm.mxml file and copy the <mx:HTTPService> tag whose id is prodByCatRPC and paste it under the <mx:Script> block you just created in the CategorizedProductManager component. Change the name of the result event handler from prodHandler to prodByCategoryHandler.

You're building this component to act as a data manager for other components. So, of course, some data will be retrieved in this component.

6 Add to the <mx:UIComponent> tag a creationComplete event and call the send() method of the prodByCatRPC HTTPService.

This is an easy piece of code to forget to add. Remember, setting up the HTTPService does not automatically call the send() method.

7 Again from the EComm.mxml file, copy the entire prodHandler() function and paste it just above the closing <mx:Script> tag in the CategorizedProductManager component. Change the name of the function from prodHandler to prodByCategoryHandler.

With some modifications, the existing function you just copied can supply not only an array of products but also an array of categories and products by category.

8 Remove the following three lines of code from the function:

```
var prodArray:Array=new Array();
prodArray.push(prod);
groceryInventory=new ArrayCollection(prodArray);
```

This code is no longer needed in the new function.

9 As the first line of the function, set the rawData variable equal to event.result and cast it to XML using the as operator as shown:

```
rawData = event.result as XML;
```

When populating the Tree, a function will be called to send back this raw data.

10 Surround the existing for each..in loop with another for each..in loop. The iterant in the new loop should be a local variable named c, data typed as XML. The loop should look in the event.result XML object for the category nodes. Change the nested for each..in loop, so instead of looking in the event.result XML object, it looks in the iterant from the outer loop, c, for product nodes:

```
for each (var c:XML in event.result..category){
    for each (var p:XML in c..product){
        var prod:Product = new Product(
            Number(p.@catID),
            String(p.@prodName),
            Number(p.@unitID),
            Number(p.@cost),
            Number(p.@listPrice),
            String(p.@description),
            Boolean(p.@isOrganic=="Yes"),
            Boolean(p.@isLowFat=="Yes"),
            String(p.@imageName));
    }
}
```

You now have a scenario in which you can build an array of Category objects between the beginnings of the for each..in loops.

11 Between the beginnings of the for each..in loops, create a variable local to the function named category, data typed as Category. Set that equal to a new Category in which you pass two parameters. The first parameter will be the catID attribute of the c iterant, and the second will be the catName attribute of the c iterant. The catID value needs to be cast as int, and the catName value needs to be data typed as String.

```
var category:Category = new Category(int(c.@catID), String(c.@catName));
```

The data types of the parameter values must be data typed because the data is untyped from the XML object.

12 Below the line of code you just created, push the category object onto the aCats array:

```
aCats.push(category);
```

The aCats array was declared earlier and will be the data returned in a function you will build later in this task. The array holds six Category objects, each containing the catID and catName properties as shown in the following figure from the debugger:

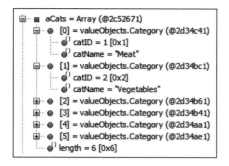

13 Below the line of code you just created, add a new property of the categorizedProducts object using the c iterant's catID attribute in square bracket notation as the property name, and set this equal to a new Array.

```
categorizedProducts[c.@catID] = new Array();
```

You are building a complex data structure here, and depending on your computer language background, you might understand it as a hashmap, or associative array. In categorizedProducts, there will be a property for each category, identified by its category ID. Each of these properties will hold an array of all the products in that category, as shown in the following figure from the debugger:

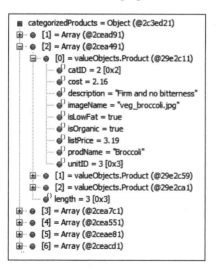

You must use square bracket notation to create the property. What you are using for the property name contains a dot itself. The compiler would not understand if you used this notation: categorizedProducts.c.@catID.

14 In the inner loop, just after where the Product object is built, push the new prod Product object on to the array you just created.

```
categorizedProducts[c.@catID].push(prod);
```

15 After the close of the two loops, just above the closing brace for the function, insert the following if statement:

```
if(this.parentDocument.categorizedProductDataLoaded != null){
   this.parentDocument.categorizedProductDataLoaded(aCats);
}
```

This if statement code is a bad practice. You are reaching into the parent document and running a function, thus coupling this component to another, which was stated earlier as a bad practice.

That being said, why are you doing this? The function ensures that data is loaded from the <mx:HTTPService> tag. You have not yet learned the best-practice way to handle this, so for now know that this does the needed job. In a later lesson, you will learn about dispatching custom events, which is the best practice method for handling this situation.

16 Check that the function you just built appears as follows:

```
private function prodByCategoryHandler(event:ResultEvent):void{
   rawData=event.result as XML;
   for each(var c:XML in event.result..category){
      var category:Category = new Category(int(c.@catID),String(c.@catName));
      aCats.push(category);
      categorizedProducts[c.@catID] = new Array();
      for each (var p:XML in c..product){
         var prod:Product = new Product(Number(p.@catID),
            String(p.@prodName),
            Number(p.@unitID),
            Number(p.@cost),
            Number(p.@listPrice),
            String(p.@description),
            Boolean(p.@isOrganic=="Yes"),
            Boolean(p.@isLowFat=="Yes"),
            String(p.@imageName));
         categorizedProducts[c.@catID].push(prod);
      }
   }
   if(this.parentDocument.categorizedProductDataLoaded != null){
      this.parentDocument.categorizedProductDataLoaded(aCats);
   }
}
```

To be sure that you still have the big picture in mind, here is a recap of the three things this function has done. This function has:

- Built an array named aCats that contains all the category objects.

- Built an object named categorizedProducts that contains a property for each category, and each property contains an array of all the products for that particular category.

- Used a not-best-practice way to be sure data is loaded. This bad practice will be corrected in Lesson 9, "Using Custom Events."

17 Just under the variable declarations, create a public function named getProdsForCat(), data typed as an Array. It should accept a parameter named catID, data typed as an int.

This is the first of three functions you will build to complete this component. All three functions return data to invoking pages. In this case, the function will return a set of products based on the category ID passed to the function.

This is also an example of creating public functions that will be methods that can be called after the component is instantiated on a calling page. For instance, if the component is instantiated as shown here,

```
<m:CategorizedProductManager id="prodMgr"/>
```

you could then invoke the method as follows:

```
prodMgr.getProdsForCat(4);
```

18 As the single line of code in the function, return the categorized products for the catID parameter:

```
public function getProdsForCat(catID:int):Array{
   return categorizedProducts[catID];
}
```

19 Create another public function named getCats(), data typed as an Array. In this function, return the aCats array that was built in the prodByCategoryHandler() function.

```
public function getCats():Array{
   return aCats;
}
```

20 Create another public function named getCategorizedProducts(), data typed as XML. In this function, return the rawData XML object that was built in the prodByCategoryHandler() function.

```
public function getCategorizedProducts():XML{
   return rawData;
}
```

21 Check to be sure that your component appears as follows:

```
<?xml version="1.0" encoding="utf-8"?>
<mx:UIComponent xmlns:mx="http://www.adobe.com/2006/mxml"
   creationComplete="prodByCatRPC.send()">

   <mx:Script>
     <![CDATA[
        import mx.rpc.events.ResultEvent;
        import valueObjects.Product;
        import valueObjects.Category;

        private var categorizedProducts:Object = new Object();
        private var aCats:Array = new Array();
        private var rawData:XML;

        public function getProdsForCat(catID:int):Array{
           return categorizedProducts[catID];
        }
        public function getCats():Array{
           return aCats;
        }
        public function getCategorizedProducts():XML{
           return rawData;
        }
        private function prodByCategoryHandler(event:ResultEvent):void{
           rawData=event.result as XML;
           for each (var c:XML in event.result..category){
              var category:Category=new Category(int(c.@catID),String(c.@catName));
              aCats.push(category);
              categorizedProducts[c.@catID]=new Array();
              for each (var p:XML in c..product){
                 var prod:Product = new Product(
                 Number(p.@catID),
                 String(p.@prodName),
                 Number(p.@unitID),
                 Number(p.@cost),
                 Number(p.@listPrice),
                 String(p.@description),
```

```
                    Boolean(p.@isOrganic=="Yes"),
                    Boolean(p.@isLowFat=="Yes"),
                    String(p.@imageName));
                categorizedProducts[c.@catID].push(prod);
            }
        }
        if(this.parentDocument.categorizedProductDataLoaded != null){
            this.parentDocument.categorizedProductDataLoaded(aCats);
        }
    }
    ]]>
</mx:Script>

<mx:HTTPService id="prodByCatRPC"
    url="http://www.flexgrocer.com/categorizedProducts.xml"
    result="prodByCategoryHandler(event)"
    resultFormat="e4x"/>

</mx:UIComponent>
```

Now the data manager component is finished, and it's time to put it to use in the next task.

Using the New Data Manager Component

This will be the first of several times you use the new data manager component to retrieve data for an application. In this case, you'll remove the <mx:HTTPService> tag from the main application, DataEntry.mxml, and instead instantiate the new data manager component. With the new data manager component instantiated, you will then use it to get both a list of categories and a list of categorized products. The list of categorized products is used immediately in the UpdateDeleteProd component, and the list of categories will be used later, when you build yet another component in this lesson.

1 Open DataEntry.mxml. Remove the <mx:HTTPService> tag that has the id property of prodByCatRPC. Also remove the invocation of the send() method for the remote procedure call (RPC) in the creationComplete event of the <mx:Application> tag. Finally, remove the <mx:XMLListCollection> tag.

Here you are removing all the code associated with the <mx:HTTPService> tag that retrieved categorized product information. This will be replaced by instantiating the new data manager component.

2 Check that your DataEntry.mxml page appears as follows:

```
<?xml version="1.0" encoding="utf-8"?>
<mx:Application xmlns:mx="http://www.adobe.com/2006/mxml"
   layout="vertical"
   creationComplete="unitRPC.send()"
   xmlns:v="views.dataEntry.*">

   <mx:Script>
     <![CDATA[
        import mx.collections.ArrayCollection;
        import mx.rpc.events.ResultEvent;

        [Bindable]
        private var units:ArrayCollection=new ArrayCollection();

        private function unitRPCResult(event:ResultEvent):void{
           units =event.result.allUnits.unit;
        }
     ]]>
   </mx:Script>

   <mx:HTTPService id="unitRPC"
      url="http://www.flexgrocer.com/units.xml"
      result="unitRPCResult(event)"/>

   <v:UpdateDeleteProd
      units="{units}"
      foodColl="{foodColl}"/>

</mx:Application>
```

Make sure that you have a clean base to start with before adding in new code that uses the new data manager component.

3 Add the following namespace definition in the `<mx:Application>` tag:

```
xmlns:m="managers.*"
```

After working so hard to build the new data manager component, this code will allow you to access it.

4 Near the bottom of the file, just above the closing `</mx:Application>` tag, instantiate the new data manager component, named CategorizedProductManager, and assign the id property as prodMgr. Remember that you'll need to use the m: prefix to instantiate this.

```
<m:CategorizedProductManager id="prodMgr"/>
```

The fruits of your labor are beginning to pay off. You have now instantiated the new component from which you can invoke methods to retrieve data.

5 In the `<mx:Script>` block, add a bindable private variable named `categories`, data typed as an ArrayCollection. Add another bindable private variable named `foodColl`, data typed as XML.

The `categories` variable will be used to store the array of categories retrieved from the data manager component. The `foodColl` variable will be used to store the grocery items stored by category.

6 Just above the end of the `<mx:Script>` block, create a public function named `categorized ProductDataLoaded()`. Have the function accept a parameter named `aCats`, data typed as an Array, and data type the function itself as void.

```
public function categorizedProductDataLoaded(aCats:Array):void{
}
```

This is the function called from the data manager component. Remember that this is a bad practice that will be remedied later.

7 As the first line of code in the function, set the `categories` variable equal to a new ArrayCollection with an argument of `aCats`:

```
categories = new ArrayCollection(aCats);
```

8 Also in the function, set the `foodColl` variable equal to the invocation of the `getCategorizedProducts()` method of the `prodMgr` component instance.

```
foodColl= prodMgr.getCategorizedProducts();
```

9 Be sure that the main application file DataEntry.mxml appears as follows:

```
<?xml version="1.0" encoding="utf-8"?>
<mx:Application xmlns:mx="http://www.adobe.com/2006/mxml"
    layout="vertical"
    creationComplete="unitRPC.send()"
    xmlns:v="views.dataEntry.*"
    xmlns:m="managers.*">

    <mx:Script>
        <![CDATA[
            import mx.collections.ArrayCollection;
            import mx.rpc.events.ResultEvent;
```

code continues on next page

```
    [Bindable]
    private var units:ArrayCollection=new ArrayCollection();
    [Bindable]
    private var categories:ArrayCollection;
    [Bindable]
    private var foodColl:XML;

    private function unitRPCResult(event:ResultEvent):void{
       units = event.result.allUnits.unit;
    }
    public function categorizedProductDataLoaded(aCats:Array):void{
       categories = new ArrayCollection(aCats);
       foodColl= prodMgr.getCategorizedProducts();
    }
  ]]>
</mx:Script>

<mx:HTTPService id="unitRPC"
   url="http://www.flexgrocer.com/units.xml"
   result="unitRPCResult(event)"/>

<v:UpdateDeleteProd
   units="{units}"
   foodColl="{foodColl}"/>

<m:CategorizedProductManager id="prodMgr"/>

</mx:Application>
```

Now the new data manager component is built and is being used, so it's time for testing.

✱ **NOTE:** When you save DataEntry.mxml, you will get an error that is corrected in the next step by changing a data type of a public variable.

10 Open UpdateDeleteProd.mxml and change the data type of the public variable foodColl from XMLListCollection to XML. Remove the import of the XMLListCollection class. The variable declaration should appear as follows:

```
public var foodColl:XML;
```

You are now passing XML instead of an XMLListCollection, so this data type must be updated.

✱ **NOTE:** You do not need to import the XML class to replace the XMLListCollection because it is imported automatically as part of the Top Level package. You can see this by looking in ASDoc at the Package information.

11 Locate the instantiation of the Tree component. Add the showRoot property to the Tree and set it equal to false. Also set the width of the Tree equal to 200 pixels.

```
<mx:Tree id="productTree"
   height="100%" width="200"
   dataProvider="{foodColl}"
   labelField="@name"
   change="populateForm(event)"
   showRoot="false"/>
```

The foodColl data used in the dataProvider binding has a root node of catalog that you do not want to be visible. You hide the root node by setting the showRoot property to false.

12 Run DataEntry.mxml. Select a product from the Tree and you should see that the form fills correctly.

After all the work in the last two tasks, you might be a little disappointed that no new functionality appears to the user. Remember that the last two tasks were for rearchitecting the application, not for adding functionality. You now have a component to provide product and category data whenever you need it throughout the three applications.

Implementing Add Product Functionality

If you open the file flex3tfs/Lesson07/assets/AddProduct.mxml, you will see there is nothing in this file that is new to you, so you do not need to spend the time typing the code for the new component. AddProduct.mxml contains the following major sections, all of which you have experience with:

- Building a data model with <mx:Model>
- Creating a form and binding the form data to the model
- Displaying a pop-up on form submission

You will not write the new component, just use it.

1 Copy the AddProduct.mxml component from Lesson07/assets to your flexGrocer/src/views/dataEntry directory. Open the file and note the two public properties defined, named units and cats.

Even though you are not writing this component, you still must have it in the correct location to use it properly.

2 Open the main application file DataEntry.mxml.

This is the file in which you will instantiate the AddProduct.mxml file.

3 Below the instantiation of the UpdateDeleteProd component, instantiate the AddProduct component using the v prefix, which is defined in an XML namespace. You need to bind the categories variable to the cats property and bind the units variable to the units property.

```
<v:AddProduct
    cats="{categories}"
    units="{units}"/>
```

You are passing data to the two properties you examined in step 1 of this task. Remember that the categories data is retrieved from the data manager component you built, and the units data is retrieved from the HTTPService call in this file.

4 Run the application DataEntry.mxml. You will see the update/delete product functionality on the top of the page and the add product functionality below that. Fill in the form for the add product functionality and click Add. You should see the new data appear in a pop-up window. Close the pop-up window.

The look of the page is not optimal with the two kinds of functionality appearing on the same page. In Lesson 13, "Implementing Navigation," you will learn about navigator containers and place these two components in what is called a TabNavigator.

5 Get ready for the next task by closing any open editors.

The next task uses different files than you have been working with up to this point in the lesson.

Creating and Using a Component for the Dashboard Application

In the Dashboard application there are three Panels that currently exist and will eventually display charting data. In this lesson, you abstract those Panels into components. In a later lesson, you will abstract those components even further to add functionality such as maximizing and minimizing.

1 Open Dashboard.mxml and run it.

You will rearchitect this application. In the end, you must be sure to have the same results as when you start, so give it a look now to refresh your memory.

2 Create a folder named dashboard under the views folder.

The views for each application will be stored in separate locations.

3 Right-click the dashboard folder and then choose New > MXML Component. In the New MXML Component dialog box, set the filename as **ChartPod.mxml** and set the base component as a Panel. After you have selected Panel, the layout option appears. Set the layout to vertical and remove any width and height values, then click Finish.

```
<?xml version="1.0" encoding="utf-8"?>
<mx:Panel xmlns:mx="http://www.adobe.com/2006/mxml" layout="vertical">

</mx:Panel>
```

You are using a Panel as your root tag for this component because it will be used to replace some Panel tags in the main application file.

4 In the new component, insert a `<mx:ControlBar>` tag set.

Because the `<mx:Panel>` tags you are replacing with this component had ControlBars, the component also needs them.

5 Check that your new component appears as follows:

```
<?xml version="1.0" encoding="utf-8"?>
<mx:Panel xmlns:mx="http://www.adobe.com/2006/mxml"
    layout="vertical">

    <mx:ControlBar>

    </mx:ControlBar>

</mx:Panel>
```

At this time you are just creating the component, not putting any content into it.

6 Return to Dashboard.mxml and insert a new namespace in the `<mx:Application>` tag so the new component can be used. Set the letter *v* as the prefix:

```
xmlns:v="views.dashboard.*"
```

Remember that you must use the XML namespace so the new component can be located correctly.

7 Locate the three Panels near the bottom of the file. Remove the three sets of `<mx:ControlBar>` tags.

You will replace three instances of the Panel with instances of your new component, which now contains a ControlBar.

8 Replace <mx:Panel> with <v:ChartPod> in the six places you see it. Do not change any other properties or associated values. Both opening and closing tags should be modified:

```
<v:ChartPod id="sales"
   width="100%" height="100%"
   title="Sales Chart">
</v:ChartPod>
<mx:VBox id="rightCharts"
   width="100%" height="100%" >
   <v:ChartPod id="type"
      width="100%" height="100%"
      title="Category Chart">
   </v:ChartPod>
   <v:ChartPod id="comp"
      width="100%" height="100%"
      title="Comparison Chart">
   </v:ChartPod>
</mx:VBox>
```

That finishes up the creation of the component and its use in the Dashboard application.

9 Run the Dashboard.mxml and you should see no difference in the look of the application.

Again, this was a rearchitecting change, with no new functionality added from the user's point of view.

What You Have Learned

In this lesson, you have:

- Gained a theoretical understanding of why components should be used and how they fit into a simple implementation of MVC architecture (pages 166–171)

- Built a component that moved the visual elements from a main application page to the component and then instantiated the component in the main application page (pages 171–175)

- Subclassed the TitleWindow component to create a component that can be used as a pop-up window (pages 175–181)

- Used the UIComponent for the root tag of a nonvisual data manager component that provides category and product information to other applications (pages 182–195)

- Instantiated an AddProduct component that started the implementation of functionality to add new grocery products (pages 195–196)

- Created a now-empty component for the Dashboard application that uses the <mx:Panel> tag as the root tag for the component (pages 196–198)

What You Will Learn

In this lesson, you will:

- Populate a HorizontalList with a dataset and display the information using a `labelField`, `labelFunction`, and `itemRenderer`

- Create an MXML component to be used as an `itemRenderer`

- Loop over a dataset using a Repeater component

- Use the `currentItem` and `currentIndex` properties and the `getRepeaterItem()` method with a Repeater

- Reference controls built by a Repeater using array notation

- Instantiate a custom component in a Repeater

Approximate Time

This lesson takes approximately 2 hours to complete.

Lesson Files

Media Files:

None

Starting Files:

Lesson08/start/EComm.mxml

Completed Files:

Lesson08/complete/EComm.mxml
Lesson08/complete/views/ecomm/Cart.mxml
Lesson08/complete/views/ecomm/CategoryView.mxml
Lesson08/complete/views/ecomm/FoodList.mxml
Lesson08/complete/views/ecomm/GroceryDetail.mxml
Lesson08/complete/views/ecomm/TextAndPic.mxml
Lesson08/complete/as/ecomm.as

Using Controls and Repeaters with Datasets

In this lesson, you will expand your skill set in working with datasets. You often get a dataset from a back-end service in the form of a complex data structure, such as an object, an array, or an array of objects. Up to this point, you have learned few ways to display, manipulate, or loop over these datasets (although you did loop over XML data using a **for each..in** loop).

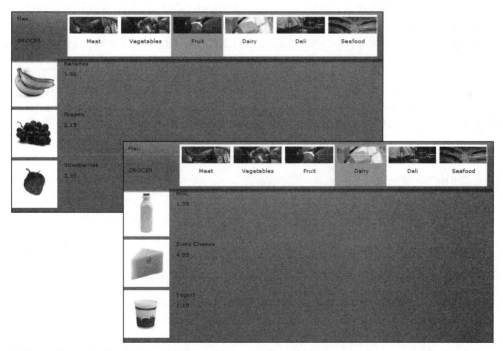

A dataset is used with a HorizontalList to display grocery categories and a Repeater to display the grocery items from that category.

One focus of this lesson is to supply a dataset to list-based components, especially the HorizontalList and TileList components. These components enable you to display data for each object in the dataset in various ways. You will also see that you can override the default behavior of these components, which enables only text to be displayed, by using an **itemRenderer**. This functionality enables you to define a component to display whatever kind of data you choose when using list-based controls.

Another focus of this lesson is using a Repeater component, which enables you to loop over the objects in a dataset using MXML. During the looping you can instantiate components, including custom components using data from the dataset. For instance, in one of the tasks in this lesson, you will loop over a custom component that displays grocery items from a certain category of groceries.

Using Datasets

In this lesson, you will learn two approaches to dealing with datasets. One is to loop over the data using a Repeater in MXML; the other is to use the dataset as a *dataProvider* for a special collection of controls. From these two basic approaches you will find many options and learn to determine the best choice for different situations.

First, consider the group of list-based controls, which enable a user to scroll though a list of items and select one or more items from the list. All Flex list-based components inherit from the ListBase class and include the following:

- DataGrid
- HorizontalList
- List
- ComboBox
- TileList
- Tree

All these components take a data provider, which in most cases will be a dataset. You have already used the Tree and List. In this lesson, HorizontalList and TileList will be discussed. DataGrids are covered in a later lesson.

Another way to think of these components ties back to the architecture discussion on model-view-controller (MVC) in Lesson 7, "Creating Components with MXML." The components represent the view on the model (the underling data), and provide an abstraction between the data and the components used to display that data. This enables you to do the following (among other things):

- Populate multiple components from the same data model

- Switch data providers at runtime

- Make a change to a model and have it immediately reflected in all components that use that data

Understanding HorizontalList and TileList Components

Both HorizontalList and TileList components display a list of items; the exact information displayed about each item is controlled by you. HorizontalList displays items horizontally (no surprise there, hopefully) and, if needed, places scroll bars along the bottom of the list for viewing all the items.

TileList lays out items in dynamically created rows and columns of equal-sized tiles. You can use the `direction` property to lay out the items horizontally or vertically. If needed, a scroll bar can be added to one axis for viewing all the items.

Most likely, you will display data that comes from an object. The question is, how do you choose what data from the object to display? Looking at some code will help clear this up.

First, assume that you want to display just one property of the object that contains text. To do that, you specify the property name in the labelField property of HorizontalList.

```
<mx:Script>
  <![CDATA[
    import mx.collections.ArrayCollection;

    private var arrayData:Array=[
      {name:"banana",cat:"fruit",cost:0.99},
      {name:"bread",cat:"bakery",cost:1.99},
      {name:"orange",cat:"fruit",cost:0.52},
      {name:"donut",cat:"bakery",cost:0.33},
      {name:"apple",cat:"fruit",cost:1.05}];

    private var dp:ArrayCollection=new ArrayCollection(arrayData);
  ]]>
</mx:Script>

<mx:HorizontalList dataProvider="{dp}"
  labelField="name"
  columnWidth="100"
  width="600"/>
```

The code would create the display as shown here:

banana	bread	orange	donut	apple

So by specifying the name property of the object, you display those property values in the list.

Implementing a labelFunction

Next is the situation in which you want to display combined text from a number of the properties. To do this, you must write a function that specifies how to format the text and use the return statement. Instead of using the labelField property, you use the labelFunction property. In the function, you accept a parameter of data type Object. This parameter represents the object currently displayed by the HorizontalList. Convention is to call this parameter item, but it is not necessary to use that parameter name. Because the function returns a String, you must data type the function as String. The following code shows an example of a labelFunction:

```
<mx:Script>
  <![CDATA[
    import mx.collections.ArrayCollection;
```

```
      private var arrayData:Array=[
         {name:"banana",cat:"fruit",cost:0.99},
         {name:"bread",cat:"bakery",cost:1.99},
         {name:"orange",cat:"fruit",cost:0.52},
         {name:"donut",cat:"bakery",cost:0.33},
         {name:"apple",cat:"fruit",cost:1.05}];

      private var dp:ArrayCollection=new ArrayCollection(arrayData);

      private function multiDisplay(item:Object):String{
         return item.cat+": "+item.name+" $"+item.cost;
      }
   ]]>
</mx:Script>

<mx:HorizontalList dataProvider="{dp}"
   labelFunction="multiDisplay"
   columnWidth="130"
   width="850"/>
```

This code would create the display as shown here:

fruit: banana $0.99   bakery: bread $1.99   fruit: orange $0.52   bakery: donut $0.33   fruit: apple $1.05

For each item in the HorizontalList, the function is called. The currently displayed object is passed to the function, the string is built, returned from the function, and displayed.

 NOTE: Even though the function is defined to accept a parameter (private function multiDisplay(item:Object):String), you do nothing to pass it in the labelFunction property (labelFunction="multiDisplay"). Flex automatically passes the correct object to the function.

Implementing an itemRenderer

By default, both HorizontalList and TileList permit only text to be displayed, as you have just seen in the example code. This default can be overridden by using an itemRenderer property. For this lesson, you can think of an itemRenderer as an MXML file you create to display an item's data in the way you choose, and not have the display limited to text only. For example, it is common to display some text and an image from the HorizontalList.

 NOTE: There are actually a number of ways to implement an itemRenderer, and you will see more ways in Lesson 11, "Using DataGrids and ItemRenderers."

When using an itemRenderer with the HorizontalList or the TileList, you specify an external file in the itemRenderer property, which can be either an MXML or AS file. This itemRenderer file is then used for each object in the dataProvider. For instance, if you have an array of 14 objects as a data provider, the itemRenderer would be used 14 times. In the itemRenderer, all the particular item's data being rendered is available in a variable called data.

In the following code example, the objects hold an image name instead of a price. This first code example contains the HorizontalList control.

```
<mx:Script>
  <![CDATA[
      import mx.collections.ArrayCollection;

      private var arrayData:Array=[
        {name:"banana",cat:"fruit",imgName:"banana.jpg"},
        {name:"grape",cat:"fruit",imgName:"grape.jpg"},
        {name:"strawberry",cat:"fruit",imgName:"strawberry.jpg"},
        {name:"tomato",cat:"vegetable",imgName:"tomato.jpg"},
        {name:"broccoli",cat:"vegetable",imgName:"broccoli.jpg"}];

      private var dp:ArrayCollection=new ArrayCollection(arrayData);
  ]]>
</mx:Script>

<mx:HorizontalList dataProvider="{dp}"
    itemRenderer="Thumbnail"
    width="600"/>
```

The next code example is the itemRenderer. The <mx:VBox> tag was selected as the root tag of the renderer because the text should appear above the image, but a renderer need not be a VBox.

```
<?xml version="1.0" encoding="utf-8"?>
<mx:VBox xmlns:mx="http://www.adobe.com/2006/mxml"
    width="100"
    height="120">

    <mx:Label text="{data.name}"/>
    <mx:Image source="{data.imgName}"/>

</mx:VBox>
```

The code would create the display as shown here:

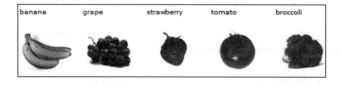

Displaying the Categories Using a HorizontalList and an itemRenderer

In a grocery application, there would be many, many grocery items. So many, in fact, that it would not be reasonable to display minimal information and a thumbnail image for each item without making the user do lots of scrolling to see them. To ease the process, you can use categories of items.

The first step of getting this functionality to work is to display the categories. In a later task, you will make the categories clickable and display corresponding grocery items, but, for now, you will just get the categories to display. At this point in the application, the categories will display as text and will be clickable using a HorizontalList control.

Putting to work what you learned in Lesson 7, "Creating Components with MXML," you will build a component to display the categories and then instantiate it where you want the categories to display.

1 In the FlexGrocer project, locate the views folder. Create a subfolder named ecomm.

2 Right-click on the ecomm folder and choose New > MXML Component. In the New MXML Component dialog box, name the file **CategoryView.mxml,** set the base component to a HorizontalList, then click Finish.

3 Below the <mx:HorizontalList> tag, insert an <mx:Script> block. In the <mx:Script> block, import the mx.collections.ArrayCollection class. Also in the <mx:Script> block, create a bindable public variable named cats, data typed as an ArrayCollection:

```
<mx:Script>
  <![CDATA[
    import mx.collections.ArrayCollection;

    [Bindable]
    public var cats:ArrayCollection;
  ]]>
</mx:Script>
```

To reiterate an important concept from Lesson 7: when you used the var keyword and public access modifier, you created the cats property of the CategoryView class.

4 Add the dataProvider property to the HorizontalList and bind it to the cats ArrayCollection.

```
<mx:HorizontalList xmlns:mx="http://www.adobe.com/2006/mxml"
  dataProvider="{cats}">
```

When you instantiate this component, you will pass to it an ArrayCollection that contains all the category information. This information is the category name, named `catName`, and that category primary key value, named `catID`.

5 In the `<mx:HorizontalList>` tag, set the `itemRenderer` equal to views.ecomm.TextAndPic.

```
<mx:HorizontalList xmlns:mx="http://www.adobe.com/2006/mxml"
    dataProvider="{cats}"
    itemRenderer="views.ecomm.TextAndPic">
```

Remember that when you supply the value for the `itemRenderer`, you do not include the filename's extension, which could be either .mxml or .as. Include the path to the `itemRenderer` from the location of the main application file: EComm.mxml.

6 Set the `horizontalScrollPolicy` to off.

```
<mx:HorizontalList xmlns:mx="http://www.adobe.com/2006/mxml"
    dataProvider="{cats}"
    itemRenderer="views.ecomm.TextAndPic"
    horizontalScrollPolicy="off">
```

The tolerances of the images displayed are tight, and horizontal scroll bars are not needed.

7 Right-click on the ecomm folder and choose New > MXML Component. In the New MXML Component dialog box, name the file **TextAndPic.mxml** and set the base component to a VBox. Set the `width` to 100 pixels and the `height` to 75 pixels; then click Finish.

```
<?xml version="1.0" encoding="utf-8"?>
<mx:VBox xmlns:mx="http://www.adobe.com/2006/mxml"
    width="100" height="75">

</mx:VBox>
```

This is the skeleton of your `itemRenderer`.

8 In the `<mx:VBox>` tag, set the `horizontalAlign` to center.

```
<mx:VBox xmlns:mx="http://www.adobe.com/2006/mxml"
    width="100" height="75"
    horizontalAlign="center">
```

9 In the body of the component, display an image. The image is a JPEG file located in the assets folder. The name of the file is the same as the category name with the string nav_ in front of the name and a .jpg extension. Remember that the data passed to this itemRenderer is in an object called data, and the category name is in a property called catName. You need to use string concatenation in the binding for the source property to create the correct path to the image. Also set the `height` of the image to 31 pixels and the `width` of the image to 93 pixels.

```
<mx:Image source="{'assets/nav_'+data.catName+'.jpg'}"
  height="31" width="93"/>
```

 TIP: Adding words together is referred to as *string concatenation*. In ActionScript, you simply use the plus sign (+) to perform string concatenation operations. Notice that when using string concatenation in a binding, the braces surround the entire expression. Alternatively, you could have used the following syntax: `source="assets/nav_{data.catName}.jpg"` where the braces are around only the variable name and you do not need the plus signs.

The HorizontalList will use this renderer component once for each category object in the `dataProvider`, so a unique image displays for each category.

10 Under the image, use an `<mx:Label>` tag to display the category name. Again, the data passed to this `itemRenderer` is an object called data, and the category name is in a property called `catName`. Set the `width` of the Label control to 100%.

```
<mx:Label text="{data.catName}" width="100%"/>
```

This is all your renderer file will do: display an image associated with the category and under that display the category name.

11 Open EComm.mxml. Add the following XML namespaces to the `<mx:Application>` tag so you can use the files you've just built in this lesson as well as the data manager component built in the previous lesson:

```
xmlns:v="views.ecomm.*"
xmlns:m="managers.*"
```

12 Create a bindable private variable named `categories`, data typed as ArrayCollection.

This variable will store the category information when retrieved from the data manager component.

13 Just above the end of the `<mx:Script>` block, create a public function named `categorizedProductDataLoaded()`. Have the function accept a parameter named `aCats`, data typed as Array, and data type the function itself as void.

```
public function categorizedProductDataLoaded(aCats:Array):void{

}
```

This is the function called from the data manager component. Remember that this is a bad practice that will be remedied in the next lesson.

14 As the first line of code in the function, set the `categories` variable created in step 12 equal to a new ArrayCollection with an argument of *aCats*:

```
public function categorizedProductDataLoaded(aCats:Array):void{
   categories=new ArrayCollection(aCats);
}
```

This assigns an array of categories built in the data manager component to your `categories` variable.

15 At the bottom of the page, just above the closing `<mx:Application>` tag, instantiate the data manager component named CategorizedProductManager, and set the `id` property to catProds. Remember that you'll need to use the `m:` prefix so the component can be located.

```
<m:CategorizedProductManager id="catProds"/>
```

You are now seeing the benefit of building the data manager component in the previous lesson. Rather than having to write all the functionality that retrieves the category data, you can just instantiate the data manager component and use data from it.

16 Locate the ApplicationControlBar. Below the two Labels that display the text Flex GROCER, insert the CategoryView component. Set the `id` to catView, the `width` to 600 pixels, the `left` property to 100 pixels, and bind the `cats` property to the `categories` ArrayCollection.

```
<mx:Label x="0" y="0" text="Flex"/>
<mx:Label x="0" y="41" text="GROCER"/>
<v:CategoryView id="catView"
   width="600"
   left="100"
   cats="{categories}"/>
```

17 In the `<mx:Canvas>` tag that contains the CategoryView, set both the `horizontalScrollPolicy` and `verticalScrollPolicy` to off.

```
<mx:Canvas width="100%" height="100%"
   horizontalScrollPolicy="off"
   verticalScrollPolicy="off">
```

You do not want scroll bars anywhere in the ApplicationControlBar, and this will ensure that none appear.

18 Run your EComm.mxml main application file, and you should see the categories displayed.

Displaying Grocery Products Based on Category Selection

You just passed a dataset to a HorizontalList control and had an item display for each object in the dataset. In addition to this functionality, at some point you will want to loop over the dataset. For instance, you might need to loop over the dataset and display a radio button or check box for each object in the dataset. In this task, you will add functionality—when the category is clicked, appropriate grocery items will display.

Using a Repeater to Loop Over a Dataset

You can loop over a dataset in MXML using a Repeater component. Just as HorizontalList created one item for each object in the dataset, the Repeater will loop once for each object in a dataset. You have access to the data in the objects when the Repeater initially loops and when the user interacts with the application.

The general syntax for a Repeater is as follows:

```
<mx:Repeater id="instanceName" dataProvider="{data}">
</mx:Repeater>
```

A Repeater loops over a dataset and enables you to access each item of that set. Two properties help you access this data while looping. The currentItem property is a reference to the particular piece of data in the set that you are currently processing, and currentIndex is a zero-based counter that specifies this item's order in the dataset.

The following code example creates radio buttons for each object in a dataset. You will use data from the objects for the radio button label. The code would appear as follows:

```
<mx:Script>
  <![CDATA[
    import mx.collections.ArrayCollection;

      private var arrayData:Array=[
        {name:"banana",cat:"fruit",imgName:"banana.jpg"},
        {name:"grape",cat:"fruit",imgName:"grape.jpg"},
        {name:"strawberry",cat:"fruit",imgName:"strawberry.jpg"},
        {name:"tomato",cat:"vegetable",imgName:"tomato.jpg"},
        {name:"broccoli",cat:"vegetable",imgName:"broccoli.jpg"}];

      private var dp:ArrayCollection=new ArrayCollection(arrayData);

    ]]>
</mx:Script>

<mx:Repeater id="myRepeater" dataProvider="{dp}">
  <mx:RadioButton label="{myRepeater.currentItem.name}"/>
</mx:Repeater>
```

The result of this code would appear as follows:

Note that you use the *name* property from the objects being repeated over for the *label* of the radio buttons. Also notice that there are five objects in the array, and there are five buttons created by the Repeater. The values of the *currentItem* and *currentIndex* properties are meaningful only during the actual looping. For example, after the Repeater has finished looping, *currentIndex* contains the value -1.

Retrieving Data from Repeated Components

The next problem to solve is how to use data from the controls created in the Repeater after the looping is finished. You have already learned that *currentItem* and *currentIndex* will be of no value except during the looping. For example, how can you retrieve costs associated with each grocery item using the preceding example code? Repeated components have a *getRepeaterItem()* method that returns the item in the *dataProvider* property that was used to produce the object. When the Repeater component finishes repeating, you can use the *getRepeaterItem()* method to determine what the event handler should do based on the *currentItem* property.

Assume that you want to expand the code example by filling a Label control with the price of the grocery item when a radio button is selected. You do this by adding a *click* event to the radio button and using the *event.target.getRepeaterItem()* method to get the data. The code would appear as follows:

```
<mx:Script>
  <![CDATA[
    import mx.collections.ArrayCollection;

      private var arrayData:Array=[
        {name:"banana",cat:"fruit",cost:.99},
        {name:"bread",cat:"bakery",cost:1.99},
        {name:"orange",cat:"fruit",cost:.52},
        {name:"donut",cat:"bakery",cost:.33},
        {name:"apple",cat:"fruit",cost:1.05}];

      private var dp:ArrayCollection=new ArrayCollection(arrayData);

    ]]>
</mx:Script>
```

```
<mx:Label id="priceLabel" text="Price Here"/>

<mx:Repeater id="myRepeater" dataProvider="{dp}">
   <mx:RadioButton label="{myRepeater.currentItem.name}"
      click="priceLabel.text=event.target.getRepeaterItem().cost"/>
</mx:Repeater>
```

Although this works, you have learned it is a better practice to call a function on an event. When using a function, the code appears as follows:

```
<mx:Script>
   <![CDATA[
      import mx.collections.ArrayCollection;

         private var arrayData:Array=[
            {name:"banana",cat:"fruit",cost:0.99},
            {name:"bread",cat:"bakery",cost:1.99},
            {name:"orange",cat:"fruit",cost:0.52},
            {name:"donut",cat:"bakery",cost:0.33},
            {name:"apple",cat:"fruit",cost:1.05}];

         private var dp:ArrayCollection=new ArrayCollection(arrayData);

         private function displayCost(repeaterItem:Object):void{
            priceLabel.text=repeaterItem.cost;
         }
   ]]>
</mx:Script>

<mx:Label id="priceLabel" text="Price Here"/>

<mx:Repeater id="myRepeater" dataProvider="{dp}">
   <mx:RadioButton label="{myRepeater.currentItem.name}"
      click="displayCost(event.target.getRepeaterItem())"/>
</mx:Repeater>
```

You pass the object retrieved by event.target.getRepeaterItem() to the function as a parameter and then fill the Label control with the cost property of that object.

The result of this code would appear as follows:

Addressing Components Built by a Repeater

Another issue that needs to be clarified when using a Repeater is how to address the repeated components after they have been instantiated in the loop. Up to this point, you used the id property to uniquely identify each object. When you use an id property on a component within a Repeater, you seemingly would have many components with the same instance name. This is not the case because Flex creates an array of these components when they are repeated over. You actually use array syntax to address each of the components individually. For example, if you repeat it over a check box four times, and that check box had an id of myCheck, you address those four controls as myCheck[0], myCheck[1], myCheck[2], and myCheck[3].

The following code uses this array notation to change the label of radio buttons when the user clicks a button. When the button is clicked, a function is called, and two labels are changed:

```
<mx:Script>
  <![CDATA[
    import mx.collections.ArrayCollection;

      private var arrayData:Array=[
          {name:"banana",cat:"fruit",cost:0.99},
          {name:"bread",cat:"bakery",cost:1.99},
          {name:"orange",cat:"fruit",cost:0.52},
          {name:"donut",cat:"bakery",cost:0.33},
          {name:"apple",cat:"fruit",cost:1.05}];

      private var dp:ArrayCollection=new ArrayCollection(arrayData);

      private function displayCost(repeaterItem:Object):void{
          priceLabel.text=repeaterItem.cost;
      }

      private function changeLabels():void{
          myButtons[0].label="New Banana";
          myButtons[3].label="New Donut";
      }

    ]]>
</mx:Script>

<mx:Label id="priceLabel" text="Price Here"/>

<mx:Repeater id="myRepeater" dataProvider="{dp}">
   <mx:RadioButton id="myButtons"
      label="{myRepeater.currentItem.name}"
      click="displayCost(event.target.getRepeaterItem())"/>
</mx:Repeater>

<mx:Button label="Change Radio Buttons"
   click="changeLabels()"/>
```

The result of this code would appear as follows:

```
0.33
○ New Banana
○ bread
○ orange
◉ New Donut
○ apple
[ Change Radio Buttons ]
```

Understanding Performance Differences Between TileList and Repeater

You should always consider performance when developing an application, and you have a performance decision to make when presenting data in a tiled look. Earlier in the book, you used a Tile container. You could place a Repeater inside the Tile container, and the resulting display would look very much like using the TileList, which you learned about earlier in this lesson. Which is the better option?

Generally speaking, you should probably use the TileList control because TileList control instantiates objects when they are displayed, whereas a Repeater inside of a Tile container instantiates all the objects in the entire dataset, whether they are initially displayed or not. Depending on the size of the dataset, this could result in a long delay before the page is displayed in Flash Player.

One point to consider in this decision is scrolling. Because the TileList control must instantiate each object as the user is scrolling, you might see better scrolling performance using a Repeater inside of the Tile container when all the objects are initially instantiated.

If the dataset is quite small, you will most likely not see any performance difference between the two options.

Displaying Grocery Items Based on Category

In this task, a Repeater will be used to instantiate a custom component numerous times. The data provider of the Repeater will contain all the grocery items that belong to one particular category.

1 In the component CategoryView.mxml in the `<mx:Script>` block, add a bindable public variable named `catSelected`, data typed as int.

This variable will be used to store the category ID. That value will then be used to retrieve all the grocery items belonging to that category. Datatyping as int is the best choice because the category ID is always an integer.

2 Also in the <mx:Script> block, create a private function named categorySelect() and data type it as void. In the function, assign the catSelected variable the catID from the selectedItem of the <mx:HorizontalList>, which is the root tag of the component.

```
private function categorySelect():void{
   catSelected=this.selectedItem.catID;
}
```

This stores the category ID value that can later be used to retrieve the corresponding products.

 TIP: You cannot assign an id to the root tag of a component, so you could not have added the id property to the <mx:HorizontalList> tag and used the instance name (instead of this) in the code in the function. The function will work correctly without adding the this prefix, but use it if you feel it makes the code more readable.

3 In the <mx:HorizontalList> tag, add a click event to call the categorySelect() function, which will assign the selected category's ID to the catSelected variable.

4 Right-click on the views/ecomm folder and choose New > MXML Component. In the New MXML Component dialog box, name the file **FoodList.mxml**, set the base component to a VBox, and remove any width and height values; then click Finish.

5 Add an XML namespace, using the letter v as the prefix, to access components in the views/ecomm folder:

```
xmlns:v="views.ecomm.*"
```

6 In an <mx:Script> block, import mx.collections.ArrayCollection and then create a bindable public variable named prodByCategory, data typed as ArrayCollection.

```
<mx:Script>
  <![CDATA[
     import mx.collections.ArrayCollection;

     [Bindable]
     public var prodByCategory:ArrayCollection;
  ]]>
</mx:Script>
```

This is the property to which you will pass the products of a certain category.

7 Below the <mx:Script> block, insert an <mx:Repeater> tag block. Set the id to foodRepeater, and also set the width and height to 100%. Finally, bind the dataProvider to the prodByCategory property.

```
<mx:Repeater id="foodRepeater"
    width="100%" height="100%"
    dataProvider="{prodByCategory}">

</mx:Repeater>
```

The Repeater will loop once for each product in the result set passed to the component.

8 In the Repeater, instantiate a component named GroceryDetail, which you will begin writing in the next step. Give the component an id of prod and set the width to 80%. Pass the currentItem of the Repeater to a property that you will name groceryItem.

```
<mx:Repeater id="foodRepeater"
    width="100%" height="100%"
    dataProvider="{prodByCategory}">
        <v:GroceryDetail id="prod"
            width="80%"
            groceryItem="{foodRepeater.currentItem}"/>
</mx:Repeater>
```

The GroceryDetail component will be instantiated once for each product looped over in the Repeater.

9 Create another component in the views/ecomm folder named GroceryDetail.mxml and use a Canvas tag as the base tag. Remove any width and height values.

This creates the skeleton of the component that will display grocery items.

10 In the <mx:Canvas> tag, set both the horizontalScrollPolicy and verticalScrollPolicy to off to ensure no scroll bars appear.

11 Add an <mx:Script> block and import valueObjects.Product.

The object passed to this component is a Product, so you need to import this class so you can use it as a data type.

12 Create a bindable public variable named `groceryItem`, data typed as Product.

```
<?xml version="1.0" encoding="utf-8"?>
<mx:Canvas xmlns:mx="http://www.adobe.com/2006/mxml"
    horizontalScrollPolicy="off"
    verticalScrollPolicy="off">

    <mx:Script>
      <![CDATA[
          import valueObjects.Product;

          [Bindable]
          public var groceryItem:Product;
      ]]>
    </mx:Script>

</mx:Canvas>
```

This is the property that accepts an object passed to the component from the `currentItem` of the Repeater.

13 In the body of the component, insert an `<mx:Image>` tag with an `id` set to `pic` and the source set to the `imageName` of the `groceryItem`. Remember that the images are in the assets folder.

```
<mx:Image id="pic"
    source="{'assets/'+groceryItem.imageName}"/>
```

This will display the image of each grocery item in the selected category.

14 Below the image, insert a Label control to display the `prodName` of the `groceryItem`. Set the `id` to `prodName`, the x position to 100, and the y position to 0.

```
<mx:Label id="prodName"
    text="{groceryItem.prodName}"
    x="100" y="0"/>
```

The product name will appear with the image. It is important to understand that the x and y values supplied here position the Label relative to the top-left corner of the Canvas location, *not* the 0,0 position of the Application. So this Label control will be positioned right 100 pixels and down 0 pixels from the top-left corner of where the Canvas is positioned.

15 Below the first Label, insert another Label control to display the `listPrice` of the `groceryItem`. Set the `id` to `price`, the x position to 100, and the y position to 20.

```
<mx:Label id="price"
    text="{groceryItem.listPrice}"
    x="100" y="20"/>
```

The product price will display after the product name.

16 Below the Label controls, add a Button with an id of add and a label of Add To Cart. On the click event, call a function named itemAdded(), passing the groceryItem as a parameter. Also, position the Button at *x*, *y* values 100, 40.

```
<mx:Button id="add"
    label="Add To Cart"
    click="itemAdded(groceryItem)"
    x="100" y="40"/>
```

Clicking the button calls the function that will eventually start the process of adding the product to the shopping cart.

17 At the bottom of the `<mx:Script>` block, create a private function named itemAdded(). The function should accept a parameter named prod, data typed as Product. Because the function does not return a value, data type the function itself as void. In the function, simply trace the prod parameter. The function is highlighted in the completed component:

```
<?xml version="1.0" encoding="utf-8"?>
<mx:Canvas xmlns:mx="http://www.adobe.com/2006/mxml"
    horizontalScrollPolicy="off"
    verticalScrollPolicy="off">

    <mx:Script>
      <![CDATA[
        import valueObjects.Product;

        [Bindable]
        public var groceryItem:Product;

        private function itemAdded(prod:Product):void{
           trace(prod);
        }
      ]]>
    </mx:Script>

    <mx:Image id="pic"
      source="{'assets/'+groceryItem.imageName}" />
    <mx:Label id="prodName"
      text="{groceryItem.prodName}"
      x="100" y="0"/>
    <mx:Label id="price"
      text="{groceryItem.listPrice}"
      x="100" y="20"/>
    <mx:Button id="add"
      label="Add To Cart"
      click="itemAdded(groceryItem)"
      x="100" y="40"/>

</mx:Canvas>
```

At this point, you will simply trace the product. Later in this lesson, you will add code to the function to place the product in a shopping cart.

 TIP: Remember that the Product is an ActionScript value object you built. The reason you can trace it is because you wrote a toString() method that displays just the product name.

18 In EComm.mxml, some cleaning up needs to be done. Some functionality then needs to be added to display products by category, which is the whole point of this task. Start by removing the creationComplete event from the <mx:Application> tag.

You will retrieve categorized product information from the data manager component, so this HTTPService will not be needed.

19 Remove the bindable private property groceryInventory. Don't forget to remove the [Bindable] metadata tag with the variable declaration.

This variable was used to store grocery product information. It is no longer needed because this data will now be pulled in from the data manager component.

20 Remove the entire function named prodHandler().

This function-supplied data is now retrieved from the data manager component.

21 Remove the <mx:HTTPService> tag with the id of prodByCatRPC.

The data manager removes the need for this HTTPService.

 TIP: In the next step you will be asked to locate a specific VBox instance. Use the Outline view to find named object instances.

22 Locate the VBox with an id of products. Remove that VBox and the five children it contains.

The main point of functionality added in this task is to display grocery items based on product selection. These VBox containers will be replaced by a custom-built component to do just that.

23 In the single remaining State named cartView, locate the two <mx:SetProperty> tags.

```
<mx:SetProperty target="{products}" name="width" value="0"/>
<mx:SetProperty target="{products}" name="height" value="0"/>
```

These tags reference the VBox that was removed, so they must be altered.

24 Change the target of the two `<mx:SetProperty>` tags so they bind to an object named prodTile instead of products.

```
<mx:SetProperty target="{prodTile}" name="width" value="0"/>
<mx:SetProperty target="{prodTile}" name="height" value="0"/>
```

You will create the prodTile object later in this task.

25 Locate the `<mx:State>` block named expanded and remove it.

The details shown in this State will be added to the GroceryDetail component later in this lesson.

Now, you will start implementing the functionality of displaying grocery items by category.

26 Locate the instantiation of the CategoryView component in ApplicationControlBar. Add a click event and call a function named displayProdByCategory():

```
<v:CategoryView id="catView"
    width="600"
    left="100"
    cats="{categories}"
    click="displayProdByCategory()"/>
```

This will call the function that actually displays the products identified when a user clicks one of the categories.

27 In the `<mx:Script>` block, create a bindable private variable named prodByCategory, data typed as ArrayCollection.

This variable will store the products grouped by category.

28 At the bottom of the `<mx:Script>` block, insert a private function named displayProdByCategory(), data typed as void. In the function, create a variable local to the function named prodArray, data typed as Array. Remember that in the component in which you are now working, the data manager component has an instance name of catProds. Assign the prodArray variable the value returned by calling the getProdsForCat() method from the data manager component, passing the catView.catSelected value as a parameter.

```
private function displayProdByCategory():void{
    var prodArray:Array=catProds.getProdsForCat(catView.catSelected);
}
```

This retrieves an array of products based on the category selected from the data manager component and assigns them to a variable.

The parameter is the value from the CategoryView component, which holds the category ID of the selected category. What is done here is a bad practice that will be corrected in the next lesson. It is a bad practice because it requires knowledge of the inner workings of the CategoryView component, which is unnecessary.

29 As the second line of code in the function, assign the prodByCategory variable a new ArrayCollection object using the prodArray variable as data for the constructor:

```
private function displayProdByCategory():void{
    var prodArray:Array=catProds.getProdsForCat(catView.catSelected);
    prodByCategory=new ArrayCollection(prodArray);
}
```

The prodByCategory variable now holds the array of products of a certain category, based on the category the user clicks. In the next step, you will pass the data to the FoodList component, which you built earlier.

 TIP: In the next step you will be asked to locate a specific HBox instance. Use the Outline view to find named object instances.

30 Locate the HBox with an id of bodyBox. It is near the end of the file, just below the ApplicationControlBar.

31 As the first child in this HBox, just above the existing VBox, instantiate the FoodList component. Set the id to prodTile, and set the width and height to 100%. Bind the prodByCategory property of FoodList to the prodByCategory variable from this file.

```
<v:FoodList id="prodTile"
    width="100%" height="100%"
    prodByCategory="{prodByCategory}"/>
```

Remember that FoodList in turn calls the GroceryDetail component that actually displays product information, which at this point is nothing more than the product name and price.

32 Debug EComm.mxml. Click a category and a list of products should appear. Click one of the Add To Cart buttons and then return to Flex Builder. In your Console view, you should see the trace of the product added to the cart. Be sure to terminate the debugging session by clicking the red box on the top of the Console view.

▶ **TIP:** You must debug the application to see the results of trace statements.

Coding States to Display Detailed Product Information

You have a simple display of the grocery products generated by selecting a category. You will now write code to implement a state that shows detailed product information on a user event.

1 Return to GroceryDetail.mxml.

2 At the bottom of the <mx:Script> block, insert a private function named toggleState(), data typed as void. The function should accept a parameter named state data typed as String. In the function, insert an if..else statement and for the condition check to see whether the parameter state is equal to closed. If the condition is true, set the currentState equal to the empty string, which is the base state. If the condition is false, set the currentState equal to expanded:

```
private function toggleState(state:String):void{
   if(state == "closed"){
      this.currentState = "";
   } else {
      this.currentState = "expanded";
   }
}
```

As you can see from the code, you will create a state named expanded, which shows details of the product. This function will be used to switch the state between the normal view and the product details view based on user interaction.

3 Surround the Image, two Labels, and the Button in an <mx:Canvas> tag block.

You are nesting this <mx:Canvas> tag inside the root tag Canvas to control the mouse events.

4 In the new <mx:Canvas> tag, add a mouseOver event that calls the toggleState() function passing the String open.

```
mouseOver="toggleState('open')"
```

When the user does a mouseOver of product information, the details will be displayed by showing the expanded state.

5 In the new <mx:Canvas> tag, add a mouseOut event that calls the toggleState() function passing the String closed.

```
mouseOut="toggleState('closed')"
```

When the user does a mouseOut of product information, the details will disappear.

6 Above the start of the Canvas block you just inserted (not the base tag), insert an `<mx:states>` block. Set up the basic infrastructure for the state by nesting an `<mx:State>` block inside the `<mx:states>` block, and set the name property to expanded. Then, nested inside of the `<mx:State>` block, add an `<mx:AddChild>` block. Finally, nested in the `<mx:AddChild>` block, add a VBox container with the width set to 100% and the x property set to 200.

```
<mx:states>
   <mx:State name="expanded">
      <mx:AddChild>
         <mx:VBox width="100%" x="200">
         </mx:VBox>
      </mx:AddChild>
   </mx:State>
</mx:states>
```

As you remember from Lesson 3, "Laying Out the Interface," this is the basic structure for using a VBox in a state.

7 In the VBox, insert an `<mx:Text>` tag. Assign the following properties the associated values to display the product description:

```
text:    {groceryItem.description}
width:   50%
```

```
<mx:Text text="{groceryItem.description}"
   width="50%"/>
```

8 Below the `<mx:Text>` tag, insert an `<mx:Label>` tag. Assign the following properties the associated values:

```
text:    Certified Organic
visible: {groceryItem.isOrganic}
```

```
<mx:Label text="Certified Organic"
   visible="{groceryItem.isOrganic}"/>
```

You use the Boolean value of isOrganic to determine whether or not the Label should display. This way the Label displays only when a product is organic.

9 Insert another `<mx:Label>` to display if the product is low fat. Position this Label at *x, y* values 100, 60.

```
<mx:Label text="Low Fat"
   x="100" y="60"
   visible="{groceryItem.isLowFat}"/>
```

10 In the Add To Cart button, set the visible property to false.

Initially, you want the Button to not be visible because it will be part of the product details.

11 Just below the closing `<mx:AddChild>` tag and just above the closing `<mx:State>` tag, use an `<mx:SetProperty>` tag to have the Add To Cart Button's `visible` property set to `true`. You set the `target` by binding the Button's instance name of *add*.

```
    </mx:AddChild>
    <mx:SetProperty target="{add}"
        name="visible"
        value="true"/>
</mx:State>
```

This will make the Button visible when the expanded state is active.

12 Run the EComm.mxml application file and test the product details functionality.

When you move the mouse pointer over existing product information, you should see more product details. The text "Certified Organic" or "Low Fat" should appear only for certain products, and no extra space should be left if they are not organic or low fat.

Placing Products in the Shopping Cart

In this task, you improve how the products are placed in the shopping cart. You create a shopping cart component and use that when products are added to the cart.

1 Create another component in the views/ecomm folder named Cart.mxml and use a VBox tag as the base tag. Remove any width and height values.

This will eventually be your shopping cart display component.

2 In an `<mx:Script>` block, import the following three classes from the valueObjects folder: ShoppingCart, ShoppingCartItem, and Product.

3 Create a bindable public variable named *cart*, data typed as ShoppingCart.

This is the property to which the shopping cart data will be passed.

4 Create a private function named `renderLabel()`, data typed as String. The function should accept a parameter named *item*, data typed as ShoppingCartItem.

This function will create and return a String value that will be added to the List component that is currently the shopping cart display.

5 In the function, return the item quantity, product name, and subtotal, concatenated as a single String. There should be a space between the quantity and name, and a colon between the name and subtotal:

```
return String(item.quantity)+" "+item.product.prodName+":"+String(item.subtotal);
```

This will populate the shopping cart as follows:

```
1 Swiss Cheese:4.95
2 T Bone Steak:19.96
```

Because the quantity and subtotal are numeric, you should cast them as Strings to be concatenated, although it is not required.

6 Below the <mx:Script> block, insert an <mx:List> tag. Give the List an id of cartView, bind the dataProvider to the aItems array of the cart property, and set the labelFunction property equal to the renderLabel function you just created.

```
<mx:List id="cartView"
    dataProvider="{cart.aItems}"
    labelFunction="renderLabel"/>
```

Each time an item is added to the shopping cart, the cart property of this component will update, causing the dataProvider to change, and the List is updated.

7 Return to EComm.mxml and locate the <mx:DataGrid> tag in the cartView state.

8 Replace the <mx:DataGrid> tag with an instantiation of your Cart.mxml component. Set the id equal to shoppingCart, set the width to 100%, and bind the cart property to the cart variable:

```
<v:Cart id="shoppingCart"
    width="100%"
    cart="{cart}"/>
```

Notice the binding. This means that any time the cart variable changes on this page (items added or removed from the cart, for instance) the binding will be redone, and the changes rippled into your Cart component.

9 In GroceryDetail.mxml, locate the itemAdded() function in which you currently trace the product. Replace the trace statement with an invocation of the addToCart() method of the EComm.mxml application file. Pass the prod variable as a parameter. To reference the EComm.mxml file, use the mx.core.Application.application property:

```
mx.core.Application.application.addToCart(prod);
```

What you are doing here is not a best practice. You will find in the next lesson a better way to pass the product to the addToCart() function.

✱ NOTE: To access properties and methods of the top-level application, you can use the `application` property of the mx.core.Application class. This property provides a reference to the Application object from anywhere in your Flex application. Although this is possible, you should carefully consider its use because it will lead to tightly coupled components and might not be a best practice.

10 In EComm.mxml, change the access modifier of the `addToCart()` function from private to public.

This has to be done because you are accessing the method from outside the file itself.

11 Test the new functionality by running EComm.mxml.

After you add some items to the cart, click the View Cart button to see your shopping cart. You will see two shopping carts, one of which you will remove from a State in the next step.

12 In EComm.mxml, look for an `<mx:RemoveChild>` tag in the State in which the linkbutton1 object is the target. Add another `<mx:RemoveChild>` tag under the existing one in which the `target` removed is `cartView`.

```
<mx:RemoveChild target="{cartView}"/>
```

This prevents the two shopping carts, the one you created in the Cart component and the one in the `bodyBox` HBox near the end of the file, from being displayed at the same time.

13 Create a new folder in the flexGrocer/src directory named as.

14 Right-click on the new as directory and choose New > ActionScript File. In the New ActionScript File dialog box, name the file **ecomm.as**; then click Finish. Remove any comments in the new file.

15 In EComm.mxml, cut all the ActionScript code between the character data tags in the `<mx:Script>` block and paste the code into the ecomm.as file.

You have moved this code into a separate file to keep the size of the MXML file more manageable.

▶ TIP: To remove the excess tabs, highlight all the code and press the Shift+Tab key combination three times to move the appropriate code to the left margin.

16 In EComm.mxml, remove the `<mx:Script>` block and replace it with an `<mx:Script>` tag that uses the source property to point to the new ActionScript file just created:

```
<mx:Script source="as/ecomm.as"/>
```

Specifying a source property to include the ActionScript file works just as if the Action-Script were still in the MXML file. Again, this is not required; this is just to make file sizes more manageable.

17 Test EComm.mxml; you should see no differences in functionality after moving the `<mx:Script>` block into a separate ActionScript file.

What You Have Learned

In this lesson, you have:

- Displayed various kinds of data using the HorizontalList (pages 203–204)
- Created a custom component that extends the functionality of the HorizontalList (pages 204–205)
- Built and used an `itemRenderer` (pages 205–206)
- Used a HorizontalList and itemRenderer to display categories (pages 207–210)
- Used a Repeater to instantiate a custom component multiple times in a loop (pages 211–223)
- Displayed product details using a state (pages 223–225)
- Implemented shopping cart functionality using a custom component (pages 225–228)

What You Will Learn

In this lesson, you will:

- Understand the benefits of loosely coupled architecture
- Dispatch events
- Declare events for a component
- Identify the need for custom event classes
- Create event subclasses
- Create and use a CategoryEvent class
- Create and use a ProductEvent class
- Use ProductEvent to remove a product from the cart
- Use ProductEvent to add a product to the cart
- Use event bubbling

Approximate Time

This lesson takes approximately 2 hours to complete.

Lesson Files

Media Files:

None

Starting Files:

Lesson09/start/DataEntry.mxml
Lesson09/start/EComm.mxml
Lesson09/start/as/ecomm.as
Lesson09/start/managers/CategorizedProductManager.mxml
Lesson09/start/valueObjects/Category.as
Lesson09/start/valueObjects/Product.as
Lesson09/start/valueObjects/ShoppingCart.as
Lesson09/start/valueObjects/ShoppingCartItem.as
Lesson09/start/views/dataEntry/UpdateDeleteProd.mxml
Lesson09/start/views/dataEntry/AddProduct.mxml
Lesson09/start/views/ecomm/Cart.mxml
Lesson09/start/views/ecomm/CategoryView.mxml
Lesson09/start/views/ecomm/FoodList.mxml
Lesson09/start/views/ecomm/GroceryDetail.mxml

Completed Files:

Lesson09/complete/DataEntry.mxml
Lesson09/complete/EComm.mxml
Lesson09/complete/as/EComm.as
Lesson09/complete/events/CategoryEvent.as
Lesson09/complete/events/ProductEvent.as
Lesson09/complete/managers/CategorizedProductManager.mxml
Lesson09/complete/utils/Util.as
Lesson09/complete/valueObjects/Category.as
Lesson09/complete/valueObjects/Product.as
Lesson09/complete/valueObjects/ShoppingCart.as
Lesson09/complete/valueObjects/ShoppingCartItem.as
Lesson09/complete/views/dataEntry/UpdateDeleteProd.mxml
Lesson09/complete/views/dataEntry/AddProduct.mxml
Lesson09/complete/views/ecomm/Cart.mxml
Lesson09/complete/views/ecomm/CategoryView.mxml
Lesson09/complete/views/ecomm/FoodList.mxml
Lesson09/complete/views/ecomm/GroceryDetail.mxml

LESSON 9

Using Custom Events

In the last few lessons, you worked with events from built-in objects, such as the click of a Button or the change of a List. As you get deeper into application development, you will often find a need to dispatch your own custom events. In this lesson, you will learn how to create an event object, set the metadata for the object, and dispatch it.

This lesson presents an overview of how to dispatch custom events within your application, and how to create new Event classes by creating a subclass of Event.

The shopping cart allows you to add and remove items.

Understanding the Benefits of Loosely Coupled Architecture

At the end of Lesson 7, "Creating Components with MXML," you were left with a bad practice, having the CategorizedProductManager component reach into its parent document to inform the parent that the category data had been loaded. This created a *tightly coupled* application, in that the CategorizedProductManager component can work only if it knows the parent has a certain method. A far better practice—and better object-oriented design—is to use *loosely coupled* architecture made possible by using events to notify other components of changes instead of requiring components to know information about the rest of the application. With loosely coupled architecture like this, components can be reused across multiple applications without requiring a particular structure to the applications.

Dispatching Events

To broadcast an event from a component, you need to use the dispatchEvent() method. This method is defined in the flash.events.EventDispatcher class, which is a superclass in the hierarchy from which UIComponent inherits.

The following is the inheritance hierarchy of the UIComponent class:

```
mx.core.UIComponent extends
flash.display.Sprite extends
flash.display.DisplayObjectContainer extends
flash.display.InteractiveObject extends
flash.display.DisplayObject extends
flash.events.EventDispatcher
```

The dispatchEvent() method takes a single argument, which is an event object to be dispatched. When an event is dispatched, anything listening for that event is notified, and the specified event handlers are executed. This offers a much better alternative to tightly coupled architectures.

1 Open CategorizedProductManager.mxml from your flexGrocer/src/managers directory.

   If you skipped the lesson when this was created, you can open this file from the Lesson09/start/managers directory, and save it in your flexGrocer/src/managers directory.

2 At the end of the prodByCategoryHandler() method, find and delete the lines of code that explicitly call categorizedProductDataLoaded() in the parent. The lines to remove are as follows:

```
if(this.parentDocument.categorizedProductDataLoaded != null){
   this.parentDocument.categorizedProductDataLoaded(aCats);
}
```

Here, you are eliminating the bad practice of tightly coupling this component to its parent.

3 Create a new instance of the event object, with a type `catDataLoaded`.

```
var e:Event = new Event("catDataLoaded");
```

This creates the new event object, which will be used in place of the tight coupling.

4 Just after creating the event object, dispatch it. Save this component.

```
this.dispatchEvent(e);
```

This dispatches the event so that any listening components can hear and respond to it.

5 Open DataEntry.mxml from your flexGrocer/src directory.

6 Find the instantiation of the CategorizedProductManager component. Listen for the `catDataLoadedEvent` and call the `categorizedProductDataLoaded()` method to handle the event.

```
<m:CategorizedProductManager id="prodMgr"
    catDataLoaded="categorizedProductDataLoaded()"/>
```

Don't be alarmed if you see a problem listed in the Problems panel when you save the file; it will be explained in step 8 and fixed in the next exercise.

7 Find the `categorizedProductDataLoaded()` method in the `<mx:Script>` block. Make the function private and remove the argument from it. Change the line setting of the categories property so that it's set to an ArrayCollection based on `prodMgr.getCats()` instead of on the argument you removed.

```
private function categorizedProductDataLoaded():void{
    categories=new ArrayCollection(prodMgr.getCats());
    foodColl=prodMgr.getCategorizedProducts();
}
```

You are now repurposing the method you wrote in Lesson 8, "Using Controls and Repeaters with Datasets." You are no longer explicitly calling this method from the data manager; instead, this method is being invoked as a handler for the `catDataLoaded` event. As such, it no longer needs to be public. The array of categories is not passed into this method, so the array collection will be created using the `getCats()` method of the manager.

> **TIP:** Following best practices, if a method or property doesn't need to be public, it should not be.

As mentioned in the previous step, if you save DataEntry.mxml now, you will see an error listed in the Problems panel. This is completely expected and will be explained in the next step and fixed in the next exercise.

8 Save DataEntry.mxml. Look at the Problems panel and notice that an error exists.

The Problems panel is now showing an error: `Cannot resolve attribute 'catDataLoaded' for component type managers.CategorizedProductManager`. This error occurs because you are referring to an attribute of the `CategorizedProductManager` tag named `catDataLoaded`, but the compiler doesn't recognize any properties or events of that component with the name `catDataLoaded`.

For the compiler to know what `catDataLoaded` means, you need to add metadata to the component, specifically declaring any events that the component will dispatch.

Declaring Events for a Component

Every component must explicitly declare the events it can dispatch. Components that are sub-classes of other components can also dispatch any events that their superclasses have declared. In Flex, events can be declared with metadata tags. This is done with the `[Event]` metadata tag, which is used to declare the event publicly so that the MXML compiler recognizes it. In MXML, an event declaration looks like this:

```
<mx:Metadata>
[Event(name="catDataLoaded",type="flash.events.Event")]
</mx:Metadata>
```

The `<mx:Metadata>` tag declares that the child elements are all metadata. Next, any metadata is declared. Notice that the tags are enclosed within square bracket. Details for these tags are defined within parentheses. In this example, you can see a `catDataLoaded` event declared. This event will be an instance of the flash.events.Event class. In this exercise, you will fix the error from the previous exercise by declaring a custom event for the CategorizedProductManager component.

1 Open CategorizedProductManager.mxml from your flexGrocer/src/managers directory.

Alternately, you can open CategorizedProductManager_dispatch.mxml from Lesson09/intermediate/ and save it as **CategorizedProductManager.mxml** in your flexGrocer/src/managers directory.

2 Before the `<mx:Script>` block, add a metadata block to declare the `catDataLoaded` event.

```
<mx:Metadata>
   [Event(name="catDataLoaded")]
</mx:Metadata>
```

The type is omitted, so the event must be an instance of the flash.events.Event class.

3 Save CategorizedProductManager.mxml. Run the DataEntry application.

The errors should now be gone, and the DataEntry application should run as it always did.

4 Open EComm.mxml from your flexGrocer/src directory.

5 Find the instantiation of the CategorizedProductManager component. Listen for the catDataLoadedEvent and call the categorizedProductDataLoaded() method to handle the event.

```
<m:CategorizedProductManager id="catProds"
   catDataLoaded="categorizedProductDataLoaded()" />
```

6 Open ecomm.as from your flexGrocer/src/as directory.

If you prefer, you can open this file from your Lesson09/start/as directory, and save it in your flexGrocer/src/as directory. If you recall, in the previous lesson you moved the ActionScript for EComm.mxml into an external script file.

7 Find the categorizedProductDataLoaded() method. Make the function private and remove the argument from it. Change the line setting of the categories property so that it's set to an ArrayCollection based on catProds.getCats() instead of on the argument you removed.

```
private function categorizedProductDataLoaded():void{
   categories=new ArrayCollection(catProds.getCats());
}
```

8 Save both ecomm.as and EComm.mxml. Run the EComm application.

It should continue to run as it did at the end of the last lesson, although now it uses better, loosely coupled architecture.

Identifying the Need for Custom Event Classes

In the previous exercise, custom events were used to notify other parts of the application about a change in data. In addition to notifications, you sometimes need to pass data around with events. The base flash.events.Event class doesn't support this, but you can create an event subclass that does. The applications you have been building need a few different custom events to function properly. When all is said and done, several user tasks will generate events, as follows.

In the DataEntry application:

- Adding a new product
- Updating an existing product
- Deleting a product

In the Ecomm application:

- Browsing for products by category
- Adding a product to a shopping cart
- Removing a product from a shopping cart

If you analyze these events carefully, you will see they all are events that need to pass along data so the system can react properly (which product to add to the cart, which category to show, and so on). In fact, all these specifically have either a Category or a Product as their data. To facilitate this, you will create two event classes, ProductEvent and CategoryEvent.

So far, all the events you have used are instances of the built-in flash.events.Event class, which does not have a property to enable you to pass data along with an event; it has properties for things, such as a type to uniquely identify the event, and bubbles, which will be discussed later in this lesson.

As you saw earlier, you can broadcast an event from a component using the `dispatchEvent()` method.

Considering that `dispatchEvent()` accepts an event instance as an argument, any custom event classes you create should be a subclass of Event. You can add any methods or properties you need to your event, but you are required to override the `clone()` method. Overriding a method allows you to redefine a method from the superclass for your new subclass. This provides the flexibility to use the functionality you want from the superclass as well as the ability to define custom functionality for your class. When you override a method, it needs to match the name, access modifier (public, protected, internal, etc.), return type, and argument list of the method from the superclass you are overriding. The `clone()` method returns a new copy of the Event object with the same values by setting the properties in the `clone()` method. Typically, you define the `clone()` method to return an instance of your newly created event class.

Building and Using the CategoryEvent

The first place you will use a custom event is for browsing products by categories. If you remember how the application was left at the end of Lesson 7, there was a tight coupling between the CategoryView component and the e-commerce application. When a user chose a category, this method fired:

```
private function displayProdByCategory():void{
    var prodArray:Array=catProds.getProdsForCat(catView.catSelected);
    prodByCategory=new ArrayCollection(prodArray);
}
```

The bold code shows the main application file reaching into the CategoryView component to pull out data. Again, this tight coupling is undesirable. A far better solution is for the CategoryView to notify its controller (in this case, the EComm application) that a category had been selected. This event will want to carry an instance of the Category class to indicate which one was selected.

1 Right-click on the FlexGrocer project and create a folder named events. Right-click the events folder and create a new ActionScript class. Name the class **CategoryEvent**, deselect the "Generate constructor from superclass" checkbox, and set its superclass to Event.

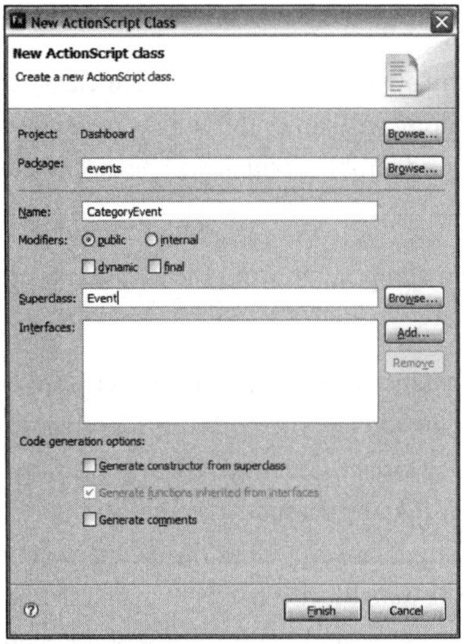

```
package events{
    import flash.events.Event;
    public class CategoryEvent extends Event {
    }
}
```

Filling out the dialog box automatically creates the skeleton of the class seen here.

2 Inside the class definition, create a public property named cat to hold an instance of the valueObjects.Category class.

```
public var cat:Category;
```

If you use the code-completion feature, the import for the Category class will be automatically added; if not, you need to manually add the following:

```
import valueObjects.Category;
```

3 Create a constructor, which takes a Category and a string, defining the `type` as arguments. Pass the type to the superclass and set the `cat` property with the passed-in Category.

```
public function CategoryEvent(cat:Category, type:String){
   super(type);
   this.cat = cat;
}
```

Like all constructors in ActionScript 3.0, this one is also public. The two arguments will be used to populate the event. The `cat` property will be used to hold the data about the Category on which the event is acting. The `type` defines what is happening with the Category in this event. Because the constructor of the Event class is defined as accepting an event `type` as an argument, you can pass the `type` directly to the superclass to set it.

4 Override the `clone()` method so it returns a new instance of the CategoryEvent class.

```
public override function clone():Event{
   return new CategoryEvent(cat, type);
}
```

When you override a method in ActionScript 3.0, the method must be defined exactly like the method of the superclass and must include the `override` keyword. Therefore the `clone()` method needs to be defined as public override, it must take no arguments, and it must return an instance of the Event class.

The complete CategoryEvent class should look like the following code block:

```
package events{
   import flash.events.Event;
   import valueObjects.Category;
   public class CategoryEvent extends Event {
      public var cat:Category;
      public function CategoryEvent(cat:Category, type:String){
         super(type);
         this.cat = cat;
      }
      public override function clone():Event{
         return new CategoryEvent(cat, type);
      }
   }
}
```

5 Open CategoryView.mxml from your src/views/ecomm directory.

Alternatively, you can open it from your Lesson09/start/views/ecomm directory and save it in your flexGrocer/src/views/ecomm directory.

6 Inside the <mx:Script> block, find the method called categorySelect(), delete its contents, and write a line that builds a CategoryEvent based on the selectedItem from the HorizontalList, cast as a Category. As a second argument, pass the string categorySelect as the event name.

```
private function categorySelect():void{
   var e:CategoryEvent = new CategoryEvent(this.selectedItem
     ➥ as Category, "categorySelect");
   this.dispatchEvent(e);
}
```

The class definition for the selectedItem of a HorizontalList declares that it is of type Object. You need to tell the compiler that this particular Object is a Category, so that it will accept the value as a valid argument to the CategoryEvent constructor. If you used the code-completion feature, imports for both Category and CategoryEvent will be added to your class automatically; otherwise, you will need to manually add imports for both of them.

```
import valueObjects.Category;
import events.CategoryEvent;
```

7 Before the <mx:Script> block, use metadata to declare the new event for the CategoryView component.

```
<mx:Metadata>
   [Event(name="categorySelect",type="events.CategoryEvent")]
</mx:Metadata>
```

Because the event is an instance of events.CategoryEvent, not directly an instance of flash.events.Event, the type declaration of the metadata is required.

Your CategoryView component is now fully equipped to be loosely coupled as it broadcasts an instance of the CategoryEvent class. All that remains to use it is to have the EComm.mxml application listen for and handle this event.

8 Open EComm.mxml from your flexGrocer/src directory and ecomm.as from your flexGrocer/src/as directory.

9 Find the instantiation of the CategoryView component. Remove the click handler and replace it with a categorySelect handler, passing the event object to the displayProdByCategory() method.

```
<v:CategoryView id="catView"
   width="600"
   left="100"
   cats="{categories}"
   categorySelect="displayProdByCategory(event)"/>
```

Here you are instructing the EComm application to listen for the `categorySelect` event from CategoryView. When the event is heard, the resulting event object is passed to the `displayProdByCategory()` method.

10 Find the `displayProdByCategory()` method in ecomm.as. Accept an argument containing a CategoryEvent. Remove the reference to `catView.catSelected` and replace it with the `id` of the selected `Category` in the `CategoryEvent`.

```
private function displayProdByCategory(event:CategoryEvent):void{
   var prodArray:Array=catProds.getProdsForCat(event.cat.catID);
   prodByCategory=new ArrayCollection(prodArray);
}
```

If the `import` statement for the CategoryEvent class was not automatically imported, then you will need to explicitly import that class.

```
import events.CategoryEvent;
```

11 Save and run the EComm application. It should run as it did earlier.

Creating and Using the ProductEvent Class

In this next exercise, you will create an event subclass called ProductEvent. ProductEvent will add a single property to the Event class named `product`, which will hold an instance of the Product value object (defined in Lesson 5, "Handling Events and Data Structures"). This procedure follows the same structure as the CategoryEvent class you created in the last exercise.

1 Right-click the events folder and create a new ActionScript class. Name the new class **ProductEvent**, ensure that the Package is set to events, set Event as the superclass, and deselect the "Generate constructor from superclass" check box.

The skeleton for your new class should look like this:

```
package events {
   import flash.events.Event;

   public class ProductEvent extends Event {

   }
}
```

2 Create a property of your new class, named `product`, with a data type Product.

If you use code completion and choose the Product class from the list, the import state-ment for valueObjects.Product will be added automatically; if not, you will need to manually import the class.

```
package events {
   import flash.events.Event;
   import valueObjects.Product;

   public class ProductEvent extends Event {
      public var product:Product;
   }
}
```

3 Create a constructor for your class, which takes two arguments. The first argument is an instance of the Product class; the second is a String that indicates the type for the event.

```
public function ProductEvent(prod:Product, type:String){
   super(type);
   product = prod;
}
```

4 Override the base class's clone() method. This method will return a new instance of the ProductEvent class with the same type and product.

```
public override function clone():Event{
   return new ProductEvent(product, type);
}
```

5 Save the ProductEvent class and verify that there are no errors in the Problems panel.

The class should currently look like this:

```
package events {
   import flash.events.Event;
   import valueObjects.Product;
   public class ProductEvent extends Event {
      public var product:Product;
      public function ProductEvent(prod:Product, type:String){
         super(type);
         product = prod;
      }
      public override function clone():Event{
         return new ProductEvent(product, type);
      }
   }
}
```

6 Open UpdateDeleteProd.mxml from your flexGrocer/src/views/dataEntry directory.

Alternately, you can open this file from the Lesson09/start/views/dataEntry directory, and save it in your flexGrocer/src/views/dataEntry directory.

7 Add a new private method named broadcastEvent(), which takes two arguments: the first an instance of the Product class; the second a String that describes the event type. Inside this method, create a new instance of the ProductEvent class with the two passed-in arguments and dispatch it.

```
private function broadcastEvent(prod:Product, type:String):void{
    var e:ProductEvent = new ProductEvent(prod,type);
    this.dispatchEvent(e);
}
```

Rather than having redundant logic in both AddProduct and UpdateDeleteProduct—both of which show a pop-up to confirm adding, editing, and deleting a product—both components will dispatch a ProductEvent and use an event type to indicate whether the product is being added, updated, or deleted.

If not automatically added by the code-completion feature, manually add the import statement for the ProductEvent class to the top of the <mx:Script> block:

```
import events.ProductEvent;
```

8 Find the doProdUpdate() method. Remove the call to showPopUp(). In its place, call the broadcastEvent() method and pass it the product and the string productUpdate.

```
broadcastEvent(prod,"productUpdate");
```

9 Find the doProdDelete() method. Remove the call to showPopUp(). In its place, call the broadcastEvent() method, and pass it the product and the string productDelete.

```
broadcastEvent(prod,"productDelete");
```

10 Add metadata to declare that UpdateDeleteProd.mxml will dispatch events named productUpdate and productDelete. Declare both events to be of type events.ProductEvent.

```
<mx:Metadata>
    [Event(name="productUpdate",type="events.ProductEvent")]
    [Event(name="productDelete",type="events.ProductEvent")]
</mx:Metadata>
```

11 Open AddProduct.mxml from your flexGrocer/src/views/dataEntry directory.

Alternately, you can open this file from the Lesson09/start/views/dataEntry directory and save it in your flexGrocer/src/views/dataEntry directory.

12 Find the doProdAdd() method. Remove the line calling the showPopUp() method, and instead create a new instance of the ProductEvent class using the product created on the previous line and the string productAdded.

```
private function doProdAdd():void{
   var prod:Product = Product.buildProduct(prodModel);
   var o:ProductEvent = new ProductEvent(prod,'productAdded');
   this.dispatchEvent(o);
}
```

Just as you did with UpdateDeleteProd, you are now preparing AddProduct to dispatch an event using the ProductEvent class.

If not automatically added, you will need to manually add the import statement for the ProductEvent class to the top of the <mx:Script> block:

```
import events.ProductEvent;
```

13 Add metadata to declare that AddProduct.mxml will dispatch an event named productAdded. Declare the event to be of type events.ProductEvent.

```
<mx:Metadata>
   [Event(name="productAdded",type="events.ProductEvent")]
</mx:Metadata>
```

14 Delete the the showPopUp() method from UpdateDeleteProd. Copy and delete the showPopUp() method from AddProduct.

This method will be implemented in DataEntry instead.

15 Open DataEntry.mxml from your flexGrocer/src directory. After the imports, create a private property named win of type ConfirmScreen.

```
private var win:ConfirmScreen;
```

This will hold the instance of the window that is launched. If you use the code-completion feature, the import will be added automatically for you.

16 Inside the <mx:Script> block, paste the showPopUp() method you copied in step 14.

```
private function showPopUp(prod:Product, title:String):void{
   win = ConfirmScreen(PopUpManager.createPopUp(this, ConfirmScreen, true));
   win.prod = prod;
   win.title = title;
}
```

17 At the top of the `<mx:Script>` block, add imports for valueObjects.Product and mx.managers.PopUpManager.

```
import valueObjects.Product;
import mx.managers.PopUpManager;
```

You just added calls to these classes in the previous step. Because you were pasting code, there was no chance to use code completion and have the imports automatically added, so you need to manually import the classes.

18 Call your newly created `showPopUp()` method as the event handler for `productUpdate`, `productDelete`, and `productAdded`.

```
<v:UpdateDeleteProd
    units="{units}"
    foodColl="{foodColl}"
    productUpdate="showPopUp(event.product,'Product Updated')"
    productDelete="showPopUp(event.product,'Product Deleted')"/>
<v:AddProduct
    cats="{categories}"
    units="{units}"
    productAdded="showPopUp(event.product,'Product Added')"/>
```

Now, the DataEntry application is solely responsible for showing confirmation pop-ups. You no longer have to handle them in each child component. If you save and test the application, it will continue to behave as it did in the previous lesson, but it is built in a far more maintainable and reusable manner.

Using ProductEvent to Remove a Product from the Cart

At the end of Lesson 8, you had the ability to add items to your shopping cart, but no means to remove them from the cart. The same ProductEvent class that you wrote for the DataEntry application can be used any time an event needs to carry a Product with it. One such case is when the user decides to remove a product from the shopping cart. In this next exercise, you will use the same ProductEvent class to facilitate removing items from the cart.

1 Open Cart.mxml from flexGrocer/src/views/ecomm.

Alternatively, you can open the file from Lesson09/start/views/ecomm and save it in your flexGrocer/src/views/ecomm directory.

2 Add a Button after the List, with the label Remove, and add a `click` event handler that will call a soon-to-be-written method called `removeItem()`.

```
<mx:Button label="Remove"
    click="removeItem();"/>
```

This will allow the user to choose an item in the List and click this button to remove it.

3 Create a new method called `removeItem()`. This method should use the `selectedItem` property of the List control to find the ShoppingCartItem, which is selected. Using the ShoppingCartItem, you can find the product for the selected item.

```
private function removeItem():void{
   var item:ShoppingCartItem = cartView.selectedItem as ShoppingCartItem;
   var prod:Product = item.product;
}
```

Currently, this method extracts the product from the `selectedItem` of the cart List. Knowing the product, you can now create a ProductEvent for it. Remember that if you want to treat the `selectedItem` as a member of the ShoppingCartItem class, you need to use casting to remind the compiler that the `selectedItem` of this List is a ShoppingCartItem.

> **TIP:** These two lines:
>
> ```
> var item:ShoppingCartItem = cartView.selectedItem as ShoppingCartItem;;
> var prod:Product = item.product;
> ```
>
> could be combined into a single line if you prefer:
>
> ```
> var prod:Product = (cartView.selectedItem as ShoppingCartItem).product;
> ```

4 At the end of the `removeItem()` method, create an instance of the ProductEvent class with the selected product and a type of productRemoved. Dispatch the event instance.

```
var e:ProductEvent = new ProductEvent(prod,"productRemoved");
this.dispatchEvent(e);
```

If not added automatically, you will need to specifically add the `import` statements for the ProductEvent class.

```
import events.ProductEvent;
```

> **TIP:** These two lines:
>
> ```
> var e:ProductEvent = new ProductEvent(prod, "productRemoved");
> this.dispatchEvent(e);
> ```
>
> could be combined into a single line:
>
> ```
> this.dispatchEvent(new ProductEvent(prod, "productRemoved"));
> ```
>
> Or you can combine the code with the previous tip:
>
> ```
> this.dispatchEvent(new ProductEvent(ShoppingCartItem(
>     cartView.selectedItem).product, "productRemoved"));
> ```

However, it is easier to understand (and therefore maintain), if you leave the code as four lines:

```
var item:ShoppingCartItem = cartView.selectedItem as ShoppingCartItem;
var prod:Product = item.product;
var e:ProductEvent = new ProductEvent(prod,"productRemoved");
this.dispatchEvent(e);
```

5 Add metadata to declare the `productRemoved` event as an instance of the events.ProductEvent class.

```
<mx:Metadata>
    [Event(name="productRemoved",type="events.ProductEvent")]
</mx:Metadata>
```

All that remains is to have the EComm.mxml application listen for this event and remove the product when the event is heard.

6 Open EComm.mxml from your flexGrocer/src directory. Find the instantiation of Cart. Listen for the `productRemoved` event and handle it by passing the event.product object to the `deleteProd()` method.

```
<v:Cart id="shoppingCart"
    width="100%"
    cart="{cart}"
    productRemoved="deleteProd(event.product)"/>
```

The event you are receiving here is a ProductEvent, which, as you defined earlier, has a property called `product`. Because the `deleteProd()` method was already written to accept a `product` as an argument, you can reuse the same method without changing it by just passing it the `product` from the event. If you save and run the application, you will find it is still functioning properly, and is built with a much more sound architecture.

▶ **TIP:** If you click the Remove button without first selecting an item in the List, a runtime error will occur. In Lesson 25, "Debugging Flex Applications," you will learn about different strategies for catching and handling this error.

Using ProductEvent to Add a Product to the Cart

The ProductEvent class can also be put to use to add products to the shopping cart. At the end of Lesson 8, items were added to the shopping cart from the GroceryDetail component with this line of code:

```
mx.core.Application.application.addToCart(prod);
```

This is tightly coupling the GroceryDetail so that it can be used only in an application that has a method named *addToCart()* in the root application file. A far better practice is for the component to dispatch an event and pass along the product to be added.

1 Open GroceryDetail.mxml from flexGrocer/src/views/ecomm.

Alternatively, you can open the file from Lesson09/start/views/ecomm and save it in your flexGrocer/src/views/ecomm directory.

2 Find the itemAdded() method and remove the mx.core.Application.application.addToCart line. Instead, create an instance of the ProductEvent class that uses the same product and has its type set to itemAdded. Then dispatch that event.

```
private function itemAdded(prod:Product):void{
    var e:ProductEvent = new ProductEvent(prod,"itemAdded");
    dispatchEvent(e);
}
```

Again, the tightly coupled references are removed and replaced with event-based architecture. Determine if you need to specifically add the import for the ProductEvent class.

```
import events.ProductEvent;
```

3 Add metadata to indicate that GroceryDetail will dispatch an event called itemAdded() of type events.ProductEvent.

```
<mx:Metadata>
    [Event(name="itemAdded",type="events.ProductEvent")]
</mx:Metadata>
```

Now that GroceryDetail is dispatching the event, you want its parent, FoodList, to listen for and handle the event.

▶ **TIP:** In the next section, you will see how event bubbling can simplify this process, enabling the event to pass through FoodList without FoodList explicitly redispatching it.

4 Open FoodList.mxml from flexGrocer/src/views/ecomm.

5 Find where GroceryDetail is instantiated. Add an event handler for the itemAdded event and pass the event object to a method you will add shortly, named addItem().

```
<v:GroceryDetail id="prod"
    width="80%"
    groceryItem="{foodRepeater.currentItem}"
    itemAdded="addItem(event)"/>
```

Here, you are listening for the itemAdded event and handling it with the addItem() method.

6 Create a new private method called addItem(), which accepts an argument named event as an instance of the ProductEvent class. The method should return void. Inside the function, use the dispatchEvent() method to rebroadcast the event.

```
private function addItem(event:ProductEvent):void{
    this.dispatchEvent(event);
}
```

Determine if you need to add the import statement for the ProductEvent class.

```
import events.ProductEvent
```

7 Add metadata to indicate that this method will dispatch an event called itemAdded that will be an instance of the events.ProductEvent class.

```
<mx:Metadata>
    [Event(name="itemAdded",type="events.ProductEvent")]
</mx:Metadata>
```

You can actually cut and paste this from GroceryDetail if you prefer, because the metadata is identical there.

8 Open EComm.mxml from your directory.

Alternatively, you can open EComm_remove.mxml from Lesson09/intermediate and save it as **EComm.mxml** in your flexGrocer/src directory.

9 Find the instantiation of FoodList. Listen for the itemAdded event and handle it by passing the event.product object to the addToCart() method.

```
<v:FoodList id="prodTile"
    width="100%" height="100%"
    prodByCategory="{prodByCategory}"
    itemAdded="addToCart(event.product)"/>
```

The event you are receiving here is the ProductEvent you dispatched from the GroceryDetail. Because the addToCart() method was already written to accept a product as an argument, you can reuse the same method without changing it by just passing it the product from the event.

If you save the files and run the EComm application now, it should continue to run as it did.

Understanding Event Flow and Event Bubbling

It might be helpful to understand how Flash Player handles events. Whenever an event occurs, Flash Player dispatches an event. If the event target is not a visible element on the screen, Flash Player can dispatch the event object directly to the designated target. For example, Flash Player dispatches the result event directly to an HTTPService component. However, if the target is a visible element on the screen, Flash Player dispatches the event and it travels from the outermost container (the Application container), down through the target component, and then back up to the Application container.

Event flow is a description of how that event object travels through an application. As you have seen by now, Flex applications are structured in a parent–child hierarchy, with the Application container being the top-level parent. Earlier in this lesson, you saw that flash. events.EventDispatcher is the superclass for all components in Flex. This means that all objects in Flex can use events and participate in the event flow; they can all listen for an event with the addEventListener() method, but will hear the event only if the listening object is part of the event flow.

When an event occurs, an event object makes a round trip from the root application through each of the containers on the way to the component that was responsible for the event (known as the *target* of the event). For example, if a user clicks a Button named button, Flash Player will dispatch an event object whose target is button. Although the target of an event is constant throughout the flow, an event object also has a currentTarget property, which indicates which element in the flow currently has the event object.

The event flow is conceptually divided into three parts:

- The *capture phase* comprises all the containers from the base application to the one containing the event's target.

- The *target phase* consists solely of the target node.

- The *bubbling phase* comprises all the elements encountered on the return trip from the target back to the root application.

The following image describes a branch of an application, in which a Button is contained within an HBox, which is contained by a Panel, which sits in the root Application. For the context of this example, other elements in the application are moot.

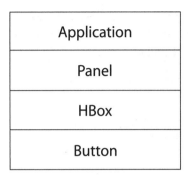

If a user clicks the Button, Flash Player dispatches an event object into the event flow. The object's journey starts at the Application, moves down to the Panel, moves to the HBox and finally gets to the Button. The event object then "bubbles" back up to Application, moving again through the HBox and Panel on its way up.

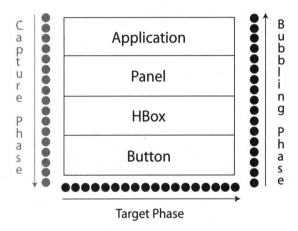

Target Phase

In this example, the capture phase includes the Application, Panel, and HBox during the initial downward journey. The target phase comprises the time spent at the Button. The bubbling phase comprises the HBox, Panel, and Application containers as they are encountered during the return trip.

This event flow offers far more power and flexibility to programmers than the event model of previous versions of ActionScript. Prior to Flex 2, event listeners had to be assigned directly to the object that generated an event. In Flex 2 and Flex 3, you can still do this, or you can register event listeners on any node along the event flow.

All instances of the Event class have a `bubbles` property that indicates whether that event object will participate in the bubbling phase of the event flow. You can look to the API documentation to find out whether a particular event type will bubble.

In practicality, this means that an event can occur in a child component and be heard in a parent. Consider this simple example:

```
<?xml version="1.0" encoding="utf-8"?>
<mx:Application xmlns:mx="http://www.adobe.com/2006/mxml"
  click="showAlert(event)" >
<mx:Script>
    import mx.controls.Alert;
    private function showAlert(event:Event){
        var msg:String = event.target.toString() +" clicked";
        Alert.show(msg);
    }
</mx:Script>
<mx:Panel id="panel"
    click="showAlert(event)" >
    <mx:HBox id="hbox"
        click="showAlert(event)" >
        <mx:Button id="button"
            click="showAlert(event)"/>
    </mx:HBox>
</mx:Panel>
</mx:Application>
```

In this case, there is a Button control inside an HBox, inside a Panel, inside an Application. When the button is clicked, the `click` event of the Button control is heard from the event handler of the Button, HBox control, Panel, and Application, and therefore four Alert boxes pop up, all saying the following:

```
Application4.panel:Panel.hbox:HBox.button:Button clicked
```

The `click` event of the Button control can be captured at the Button control itself or in any of the parent containers of the Button instance. This happens because `click` is a bubbling event. The `bubbles` property of the Event class is Boolean, which indicates whether an event should bubble. By default, `bubbles` is set to `false` on newly created events (although it is preset to `true` for some built-in events, such as `click`). When you create event instances or event subclass instances, you can decide whether you want to enable bubbling for the event. If you leave the bubbling to the default `false` value, the event can be captured only at the source of the event (the Button control in the preceding example). However, if bubbling is set to `true`, the event can be captured by a parent of the dispatching component (such as the HBox, Panel, and Application).

Currently, in the EComm application, when the itemAdded event is dispatched from the GroceryDetail component, you are capturing the event in FoodList and then redispatching it. However, if the ProductEvent could optionally be set to bubble, there would be no need for the FoodList to capture and rebroadcast the event—it could be handled directly in the EComm application.

1 Open ProductEvent.as from your flexGrocer/src/events directory.

Alternatively, you can open ProductEvent_initial.as from Lesson09/intermediate and save it in your flexGrocer/src/events directory as **ProductEvent.as**.

2 Add a third argument to the constructor: bubbles—of data type Boolean with a default value of false.

```
public function ProductEvent(prod:Product, type:String, bubbles:Boolean=false){
```

Throughout this lesson, you have created instances of the ProductEvent class that did not bubble. So you don't need to go back to all of them and specify false as the third argument to the constructor. A default value of false is used. Therefore, when only two values are passed, the bubbles argument comes through as false.

3 Inside the constructor, pass the bubbles argument to the constructor of the superclass. You should also pass the bubbles parameter in the call to create a new ProductEvent in the clone() method.

```
package events{
    import flash.events.Event;
    import valueObjects.Product;
    public class ProductEvent extends Event{
        public var product:Product;
        public function ProductEvent(prod:Product, type:String,
            ➥ bubbles:Boolean=false){
            super(type, bubbles);
            product = prod;
        }
        public override function clone():Event{
            return new ProductEvent(product, type, bubbles);
        }

    }
}
```

The flash.events.Event class takes an optional second argument to its constructor that indicates whether the event should bubble. If not provided, the default value of false is used.

Save and close ProductEvent.as. It is now ready to creating bubbling instances when requested.

4 Open GroceryDetail.mxml from flexGrocer/src/views/ecomm.

Alternatively, you can open GroceryDetail_event from Lesson09/intermediate and save it as **GroceryDetail.mxml** in your flexGrocer/src/views/ecomm directory.

5 Inside the itemAdded() method, add true as the third argument when creating the ProductEvent instance.

```
private function itemAdded(prod:Product):void{
   var e:ProductEvent = new ProductEvent(prod,"itemAdded",true);
   dispatchEvent(e);
}
```

This one instance of the ProductEvent class is told to bubble. Now you no longer need to capture the event in FoodList; you can instead capture it directly in EComm.

Save and close GroceryDetail.mxml.

6 Open FoodList.mxml from src/views/ecomm.

Alternatively, you can open FoodList_event from Lesson09/intermediate and save it as **FoodList.mxml** in your views/ecomm directory.

7 Remove the itemAdded event handler from the instantiation of the GroceryList component. Also delete the addItem() method from this file.

The remaining code in FoodList.mxml should look like this:

```
<?xml version="1.0" encoding="utf-8"?>
<mx:VBox xmlns:mx="http://www.adobe.com/2006/mxml"
   xmlns:v="views.ecomm.*">
   <mx:Metadata>
      [Event(name="itemAdded",type="events.ProductEvent")]
   </mx:Metadata>
   <mx:Script>
      <![CDATA[
         import mx.collections.ArrayCollection;
         import events.ProductEvent;
         [Bindable]
         public var prodByCategory:ArrayCollection;
      ]]>
   </mx:Script>
   <mx:Repeater id="foodRepeater"
      width="100%" height="100%"
      dataProvider="{prodByCategory}">
      <v:GroceryDetail id="prod"
         width="80%"
         groceryItem="{foodRepeater.currentItem}"/>
   </mx:Repeater>
</mx:VBox>
```

You no longer need to capture and redispatch the itemAdded event here. You do, however, need to have the Event metadata for itemAdded so the compiler will enable EComm to listen to this component for the event.

Save and close FoodList.mxml. Run EComm.mxml and notice that items are still properly added to the cart.

What You Have Learned

In this lesson, you have:

- Understood the benefits of loosely-coupled architecture (page 233)
- Dispatched events (pages 233–235)
- Declared events for a component (pages 235–236)
- Identified the need for custom event classes (pages 236–237)
- Created and used a CategoryEvent class (pages 237–241)
- Created and used a ProductEvent class (pages 241–245)
- Used ProductEvent to remove a product from the cart (pages 245–247)
- Used ProductEvent to add a product to the cart (pages 247–249)
- Learned about event bubbling (pages 250–255)

What You Will Learn

In this lesson, you will:

- Create a class for your component

- Embed images in ActionScript

- Instantiate Flex components in ActionScript

- Override the `createChildren()` and `updateDisplayList()` methods

- Understand the mechanism used by Flex to determine size and positioning

Approximate Time

This lesson takes approximately 1 hour and 30 minutes to complete.

Lesson Files

Media Files:

None

Starting Files:

Lesson10/start/Dashboard.mxml
Lesson10/start/views/dashboard/ChartPod.mxml

Completed Files:

Lesson10/complete/Dashboard.mxml
Lesson10/complete/views/Dashboard/ChartPod.mxml
Lesson10/complete/views/MaxRestorePanel.as

Creating Custom Components with ActionScript 3.0

In Lesson 7, "Creating Components with MXML," you learned how to build custom components using MXML. There are times when you will need even more flexibility than MXML can offer. For these occasions, you can create components in ActionScript 3.0.

In this lesson, you will create a new component called MaxRestorePanel, which extends the Panel component and adds icons to the title bar with which users can maximize or restore the panel.

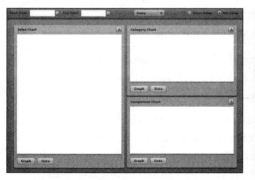

The Dashboard will use your new component instead of the panel.

Here you see the MaxRestorePanel in its maximized state.

Introducing Building a Component with ActionScript 3.0

In an earlier lesson, you learned that any code written in MXML is first translated into ActionScript before being compiled into a SWF file. In reality, every Flex component is an ActionScript class, regardless of whether it's a UI control, a container, or some other type of component. Anything you might create in MXML can also be created in ActionScript, and there are things you can do with ActionScript that are not available purely from MXML. It is possible to create custom components in MXML, as you explored in Lesson 7, or you can develop more advanced components purely in ActionScript 3.0, as you will learn in this lesson.

The steps you will take in creating an ActionScript 3.0 component are very similar to the steps for building any ActionScript 3.0 class. First, determine what (if any) superclass your new class will extend. Then, determine what properties you need to declare for your class. Next, determine any new methods you might need to implement. You will also need to declare any events your component will dispatch. If your component is a visual class, you will likely need to override `createChildren()` and `updateDisplayList()` because they are the methods that Flex components use to create, size, and lay out any child elements of the components.

Creating the Structure of the Class

To create a component with ActionScript 3.0, you will define the component as an ActionScript class. You must decide what superclass you will use for the class. This decision will often be based on the functionality you want for your new component. In the case of the MaxRestorePanel class that you are building here, you want the general look, feel, and behavior of the Panel class, so you can use that as your superclass.

1 In Flex Builder 3, choose File > New > ActionScript Class. Set the package to views, the name of the class to MaxRestorePanel, and the superclass to Panel. Save this file as **flexGrocer/src/views/MaxRestorePanel.as**.

This class is created in the views directory because it is not specific to any of the three applications but can be used by any or all of them. Panel was chosen as a superclass because the intention is to create a component that looks like a Panel, with the addition of a Button for the user to maximize the Panel, or to restore it to its original state.

2 After the package declaration, but before the class declaration, add imports for the flash.events.Event and mx.controls.Button classes.

The import for mx.containers.Panel was automatically added by the wizard when you chose Panel as the superclass. The completed class will need to broadcast events to let a containing MXML file know that the user has requested that the Panel be maximized or restored, so you will need the Event class. The button, which the user will click to change the state of the Panel, will be an instance of the mx.controls.Button class, so it also needs to be imported.

```
package views {
    import mx.containers.Panel;
    import mx.controls.Button;
    import flash.events.Event;
    public class MaxRestorePanel extends Panel {

    }
}
```

3 Inside the class definition, create a private property named state, which will hold a value representing whether or not the Panel is currently maximized. Set its default value to 0.

```
private var state:int = 0;
```

A value of 0 indicates that the Panel is in its normal state; a value of 1 indicates that it is maximized. Your Panel will start in a normal (non-maximized) state, so the initial value is 0.

> **TIP:** Because there will be only two states for the panel, you could use a Boolean property instead; however, in the future you might want to further extend this component with other states, such as minimized, so this is being set as an int.

4 Create another private property named btStateUp as an instance of the Button class.

```
private var btStateUp: Button;
```

btStateUp will be a reference to the button a user can click to request that the Panel be maximized.

5 Create one more private property named btStateDown as an instance of the Button class.

```
private var btStateDown: Button;
```

btStateDown will be a reference to the button a user can click to request that the Panel be restored.

Next, you need to embed the images that will be used for the buttons. In Lesson 4, "Using Simple Controls," you learned about the @Embed directive for embedding images from MXML. You can use the same strategy, with slightly different syntax, for embedding images in an ActionScript 3.0 class. In ActionScript 3.0, the [Embed("path to file")] meta-data tag is used to embed an asset. On the line immediately following the @Embed directive, a variable should be created (of the type Class) to hold a reference to the embedded asset.

6 After the other property definitions, use an [Embed] metadata tag to embed upArrow.gif.

```
[Embed("../assets/upArrow.gif")]
```

When using the [Embed] metadata tag, the path to the file is relative to the component into which the asset is embedded. Many other things you do in Flex (such as defining XML namespaces) are relative to the application's root. The [Embed] tag does not follow this model; it uses a relative reference from the component that is using it.

7 On the next line, create a variable named buttonUpIcon of the type Class.

```
private var buttonUpIcon:Class;
```

By declaring this variable right after the [Embed] tag, the Flex compiler knows to use this variable as a reference to the embedded image.

8 Create another [Embed] metadata tag, this time referencing downArrow.gif. Create a variable for this asset, named buttonDownIcon of the type Class.

```
[Embed("../assets/downArrow.gif")]
private var buttonDownIcon:Class;
```

9 At the top of the class, after the import statements but before the class definition, declare metadata tags for the Maximize and Restore events.

```
[Event(name="restore")]
[Event(name="maximize")]
```

As discussed in the previous lesson, when a component broadcasts custom events, the events should be enumerated explicitly with metadata. Because these events are both of the default flash.events.Event type, the type attribute of the [Event] metadata tag does not need to be specified.

10 Create a new private method setState(), which takes an int as an argument and returns void. This method will take the argument and set the component instance's state property equal to the value passed in. Then it will check the value and dispatch either a restore event or maximize event, depending on whether the value is 0 or 1, respectively.

```
private function setState(state:int):void{
   this.state=state;
   if (state==0){
      this.dispatchEvent(new Event('restore'));
   } else {
      this.dispatchEvent(new Event('maximize'));
   }
}
```

This method will dispatch the events you defined, which gives you a single method solely responsible for informing any listeners that the user has clicked the Maximize or Restore buttons. When you add the buttons later in this lesson, the event handlers for each of the buttons will call this method to handle the event dispatching.

11 Save your class file.

There is no need to test the class at this point because you haven't yet created any visual elements for your new component. At the end of the next exercise, you will have the ChartPod.mxml component use your new class.

At this point, the class definition for your MaxRestorePanel should read like this:

```
package views{
    import mx.containers.Panel;
    import mx.controls.Button;
    import flash.events.Event;
    [Event(name="restore")]
    [Event(name="maximize")]
    public class MaxRestorePanel extends Panel{
        private var state:int = 0;
        private var btStateUp: Button;
        private var btStateDown: Button;
        [Embed("../assets/upArrow.gif")]
        private var buttonUpIcon:Class;
        [Embed("../assets/downArrow.gif")]
        private var buttonDownIcon:Class;
        private function setState(state:int):void{
            this.state=state;
            if (state==0){
                this.dispatchEvent(new Event('restore'));
            } else {
                this.dispatchEvent(new Event('maximize'));
            }
        }
    }
}
```

Overriding the createChildren() Method

When creating a component in MXML, elements can be added to the component using standard MXML tags. These tags are not available to you when you create components in ActionScript, so to create children of your component, you need to override the createChildren() method of your component's superclass. The createChildren() method is called automatically during the initialization sequence of a Flex component.

The initialization sequence is the following:

```
Constructor
createChildren()
commitProperties()
measure()
updateDisplayList()
```

The four methods after the constructor are initially implemented in `mx.core.UIObject`. Virtually any ActionScript 3.0 component you create will need to override the `createChildren()` and `updateDisplayList()` methods, as you will do in the next few exercises. The `commitProperties()` method needs to be overridden only if you need to set properties dependant on other properties that are already set, or if you want to explicitly pass in properties to be set on newly created components. After all the children of a component are created, `commitProperties()` is called to set all the properties passed in. By waiting until this method is called, you know that the children have already been successfully instantiated before their properties are set. The `measure()` method exists to enable you to manually calculate the height and width of all created children, if necessary. This method often needs to be overridden for creation of new containers with unique layout rules. In the case of the MaxRestorePanel, the `commitProperties()` and `measure()` methods of the superclass (Panel) are adequate and therefore do not need to be overridden.

Creating a Button in ActionScript

When working with ActionScript 3.0 components, you need a way to instantiate child components. Fortunately, Flex 3 and ActionScript 3.0 enable you to do this just like any other class you instantiate by using the `new` keyword. To create a new instance of the Button component, you would simply declare the following:

```
import mx.controls.Button;
var myButton:Button = new Button();
```

After you instantiate the Button, you can set any properties on it, just as you would with any other object, such as the following:

```
myButton.label = "click me";
myButton.addEventListener("click",doClick);
myButton.width=150;
```

Using the addChild() Method to Add the Button to Your Component

Merely creating a component does not add it to the interface. As you learned earlier, user interface elements in Flex must be shown within a container. To add an element to a container, you need to use the container's `addChild()` method. The mx.core.Container class implements the addChild() method that will append the new child in the container. Depending on the type of container, this may impact where in the container the child is shown. For example, a VBox shows its children in order vertically, so the first child is shown on top, the next below the first, and so on. So, in the following example, the order in which the children are added dictates the order in which they appear.

```
package {
    import mx.containers.VBox;
    import mx.controls.Label;
    public class Test extends VBox{
        protected override function createChildren(): void {
            var a:Label = new Label();
            a.text = "label one";
            this.addChild(a);
            var b:Label = new Label();
            b.text = "label two";
            this.addChild(b);
            var c:Label = new Label();
            c.text = "label three";
            this.addChild(c);
        }
    }
}
```

Had this class instead been based on the Canvas class, all three labels would be stacked on top of each other, as they would all be placed at an *x* and *y* of 0.

▶ **TIP:** You can declare explicitly where you want a child created by using addChildAt() instead of addChild(). Both methods are available to all containers.

Understanding chrome and rawChildren

Flex containers have two distinct sections: the layout area, in which their children are drawn; and the chrome, which consists of all the other elements, such as borders, backgrounds, margins, scrollbars, headers, footers, and so on. In the Panel class, the title bar of a panel is implemented as chrome.

The base class flash.display.DisplayObjectContainer does not draw any distinction between child components and chrome—they are all accessible using the getChildAt and numChildren properties. However, the mx.core.Container class (the superclass for all Flex containers) overrides several methods, including getChildAt() and numChildren(), to give the appearance that the container's only children are the child components. To gain access to all the elements, you need to use the rawChildren property. Likewise, to add elements to the chrome (as you will do in the next exercise when you add a Maximize and Restore button), they need to be added to the rawChildren property. With a Panel, any children added with addChild() will be rendered below the title bar. If you want to add elements to the title bar, you must use rawChildren.addChild().

Using addChild() on rawChildren to Add Elements to the Chrome

In this exercise, you will add two buttons to the chrome of your MaxRestorePanel.

1 Open the MaxRestorePanel.as file you created earlier in this lesson.

This file contains the skeleton of the new class you wrote earlier.

2 Create a new protected function named createChildren(), which overrides the function from the superclass.

```
protected override function createChildren(): void {
}
```

As mentioned in Lesson 9, "Using Custom Events," any method overriding a method from a superclass must have exactly the same signature; therefore, your createChildren() method must be protected and must have the same argument list (in this case, none), and the same return type: void.

3 Inside the new function, call the superclass's createChildren() method.

```
super.createChildren();
```

You still need the rest of the Panel's chrome to be created, so you should explicitly invoke the createChildren() method of the superclass, so those elements will still be created.

4 Create the new btStateUp button.

```
btStateUp = new Button();
```

In the property definitions at the top of the class, you declared variables for two buttons: btStateUp and btStateDown. This step is instantiating a button into the first of these two.

5 Create the new btStateDown button.

```
btStateDown = new Button();
```

6 Set event listeners on each button. Clicking btStateUp should fire a soon-to-be-written method called doMaximize(); clicking btStateDown should fire a soon-to-be-written method called doRestore().

```
btStateUp.addEventListener("click",doMaximize);
btStateDown.addEventListener("click",doRestore);
```

7 Use the buttons' setStyle() methods to set the embedded graphics as the icons for the buttons.

```
btStateUp.setStyle("overIcon",buttonUpIcon);
btStateUp.setStyle("downIcon",buttonUpIcon);
btStateUp.setStyle("upIcon",buttonUpIcon);
btStateDown.setStyle("overIcon",buttonDownIcon);
btStateDown.setStyle("downIcon",buttonDownIcon);
btStateDown.setStyle("upIcon",buttonDownIcon);
```

You will learn about the setStyle() method in detail in Lesson 16, "Customizing the Look and Feel of a Flex Application." For now, it's worthwhile to understand that you can use the setStyle() method to specify an icon to use for each of the states. The up state is the normal default appearance; the over state is how the button appears when the mouse is over it; the down state is how the button appears when the mouse is clicked on the button. For now, you are setting all three states to be the same, so the button will not change its appearance when the user moves their mouse over it or clicks it.

8 Set the initial visibility of the buttons so that btStateUp is visible and btStateDown is not visible when the application starts.

```
btStateUp.visible =true;
btStateDown.visible =false;
```

In a few steps, you will add code to ensure that only one button is seen whenever it's clicked. The previous line ensures that the MaxRestorePanel starts with only a single button visible as well.

9 Add the newly created buttons to the rawChildren property.

```
rawChildren.addChild(btStateUp);
rawChildren.addChild(btStateDown);
```

At this point, the createChildren() method should look like this:

```
protected override function createChildren(): void {
   super.createChildren();
   btStateUp = new Button();
   btStateDown = new Button();
   btStateUp.addEventListener("click",doMaximize);
   btStateDown.addEventListener("click",doRestore);
```

code continues on next page

```
    btStateUp.setStyle("overIcon",buttonUpIcon);
    btStateUp.setStyle("downIcon",buttonUpIcon);
    btStateUp.setStyle("upIcon",buttonUpIcon);
    btStateDown.setStyle("overIcon",buttonDownIcon);
    btStateDown.setStyle("downIcon",buttonDownIcon);
    btStateDown.setStyle("upIcon",buttonDownIcon);
    btStateUp.visible =true;
    btStateDown.visible =false;
    rawChildren.addChild(btStateUp);
    rawChildren.addChild(btStateDown);
}
```

10 Create a doMaximize() method, which will set the state property to 1; toggle the visibility of the buttons, so that btStateDown is visible and btStateUp is not.

```
private function doMaximize(event:Event) :void{
    setState(1);
    btStateUp.visible = false;
    btStateDown.visible = true;
}
```

This method will call the setState() method you wrote earlier, and pass it the value 1. This tells your Panel it should become maximized. When you set the state to maximized, the btStateUp button is hidden, and the btStateDown button is shown.

11 Create a doRestore() method to set the current state to 0; toggle the visibility of the buttons, so that btStateUp is visible and btStateDown is not.

```
private function doRestore(event:Event) :void{
    setState(0);
    btStateUp.visible = true;
    btStateDown.visible = false;
}
```

This method will call the setState() method you wrote earlier and pass it the value 0, which tells your Panel that it should be restored to its initial state. When you set the state to restored, the btStateUp button is shown, and the btStateDown button is hidden.

12 Open the ChartPod.mxml file from src/views/dashboard directory.

13 Set the ControlBar id to controls. Add two buttons inside the <mx:ControlBar> tag: one with an id of btGraph and a label of Graph and the other with the id of btData and the label set to Data.

```
<mx:ControlBar id="controls">
    <mx:Button id="btGraph"
        label="Graph" />
    <mx:Button id="btData"
        label="Data" />
</mx:ControlBar>
```

14 Change the root node of ChartPod from <mx:Panel> to <v:MaxRestorePanel> and add an XML namespace to relate v: to the views directory.

```
<?xml version="1.0" encoding="utf-8"?>
<v:MaxRestorePanel
    xmlns:mx="http://www.adobe.com/2006/mxml"
    xmlns:v="views.*"
    layout="vertical">
    <mx:ControlBar id="controls">
        <mx:Button id="btGraph"
            label="Graph" />
        <mx:Button id="btData"
            label="Data" />
    </mx:ControlBar>
</v:MaxRestorePanel>
```

15 Save ChartPod.mxml and test the Dashboard application.

As the Dashboard application runs, you should see the up and down arrows placed on top of each other in the top-left corner of each Panel. As you click a button in a corner, it will toggle so that only one of the two arrows is visible. You might notice that the button is not showing a border or background, like buttons normally do; in the next exercise, you will set the size and position of the button so it can render itself properly with borders and background.

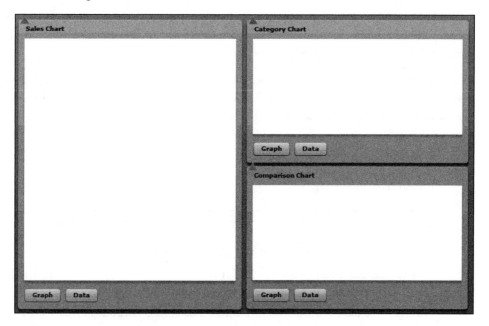

Sizing and Positioning in Flex

You now have a new Flex component, based on a Panel, which displays buttons for maximizing and minimizing. Before you add more code to move these buttons into position, it is worthwhile to discuss how Flex sizes and positions children in containers and the methods involved in this process.

So far you have used a variety of layout containers, including VBox and HBox, to arrange your component on the screen. For some of these components, you have provided explicit sizes by providing a fixed number for their height or width. For other components, you have provided relative sizes by providing a percentage for the height or width property. However, you have left the decision of sizing the majority of your components and containers to the Flex Layout Manager.

Every HBox, Label, or Button that does not have an explicit or relative size specified must be assigned a size before it can appear on the screen. Flex components must be able to provide a recommendation of an appropriate size in this case. Each component provides this recommendation in a unique way. For example, the HBox looks at all its children and determines how much space they will require. The Label takes the size of its text into account, and the Button examines both its text and icon, if present. The method inside each component that provides this recommendation is called measure().

When the Layout Manager needs to determine how to lay out a Flex application, it first asks all the components for their explicit or recommended sizes, starting with the most deeply nested and working toward the Application container.

Once the Layout Manager understands the required sizes, it works from the outermost container, the Application container, toward the most deeply nested component, assigning sizes and moving components to the appropriate place on the screen.

The following narrative based on this diagram will help illustrate this layout mechanism.

The Flex Layout Manager asks the Application how much space it requires on the screen. Before the Application can respond, it must first ask the ApplicationControlBar and HBox how much space they each require. Unfortunately, the HBox needs to ask the VBox and Canvas before it can respond. In turn the VBox must ask the Label.

This means that the deepest nested child must determine its size before any of the components that contain it. Once the Label provides its size, the VBox, HBox, and eventually the Application can respond to the Layout Manager's request.

So far we have referred to the sizes provided by each of these components as a recommendation. Ultimately, the sizes recommended by each of these components may add up to more than the total space available on the user's screen, so another pass through the components is required to size them appropriately.

The Layout Manager informs the Application container of the actual usable width and height. In turn, the Application container decides how much of that space to give to the ApplicationControlBar and how much to give to the HBox. When the HBox receives its sizing information, it decides how much is provided to the VBox and how much to the Canvas. Finally, the VBox determines how much space to allocate to the Label. Immediately after each component determines the size of its children, it also determines where they should be placed within the component based on the layout rules implicit in their type (HBox lays out its children horizontally; VBox vertically.) The method inside each component that is responsible for sizing and positioning children is called updateDisplayList().

The passes up and down the component hierarchy occur every time the application is resized. Based on the amount of work required, it becomes easy to see why a developer should limit unnecessary container nesting.

Understanding the measure() Method

You just learned about sizing and positioning of components within an application. You also learned that finding the recommended size of each component is crucial to this process. Determining the recommended (often called the default) size is the job of the measure() method.

The measure() method works differently for each component. The VBox, for instance, needs to understand the collective height of all of its children, whereas the HBox cares more about the collective width. Ultimately, the measure method is responsible for providing a value to four distinct properties present in every UIComponent.

```
measuredHeight
measuredWidth
measuredMinHeight
measuredMinWidth
```

The measuredHeight and measuredWidth are the sizes requested by this component in the ideal case where plenty of space is available. The measuredMinHeight and measuredMinWidth are the smallest sizes the component recommends to display correctly. The Flex layout containers will never size a component smaller than the minimum sizes. However, as you will see in the next exercises, when writing your own components, you can ignore these recommendations and size a component in any way you see fit.

As mentioned in the beginning of this lesson, the default measure() method provided by the Panel class will suffice for this component, as our addition of two buttons does not change the amount of space required on the screen by the Panel.

While we will not need to write a custom measure() method, we will still need to deal with the sizing of these new buttons and their positioning. This happens in the updateDisplayList() method.

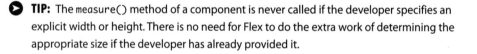 **TIP:** The measure() method of a component is never called if the developer specifies an explicit width or height. There is no need for Flex to do the extra work of determining the appropriate size if the developer has already provided it.

Overriding the updateDisplayList() Method

At this point, you have created the bulk of the ActionScript 3.0 component. You defined the class, instantiated the children, and added them to the chrome. All that remains is to size and position them appropriately. For this, you will override the updateDisplayList() method. This method is invoked automatically each time the component is redrawn, such as when it changes size or when the browser is resized. When you override this method, you should first call the super.updateDisplayList() method to ensure that the Panel's layout is also done properly. Each time this method is called, it is passed two attributes, unscaledHeight and unscaledWidth, which are the actual height and width allotted to the component regardless of any scaling that may have been applied.

1 Open the MaxRestorePanel.as file you created in the previous exercise.

This file contains the class you created earlier in this lesson, with the buttons added to the chrome of the Panel.

2 Override the updateDisplayList() function, which will accept two numeric arguments (call them unscaledWidth and unscaledHeight) and return void.

```
protected override function updateDisplayList(unscaledWidth: Number,
    ➥ unscaledHeight:Number):void {
}
```

3 As the first line inside updateDisplayList(), call updateDisplayList() in the superclass and pass in the same two arguments received by your function.

```
super.updateDisplayList(unscaledWidth, unscaledHeight);
```

To ensure that the updateDisplayList() method of the superclass (Panel) is run properly, you need to call it explicitly in your override method. The unscaledWidth and unscaledHeight attributes tell the function the exact pixel width and height of your MaxRestorePanel. Because you want to place the buttons near the top-right corner of the Panel, knowing the actual width is required, so the button can be placed relative to the right side.

4 Add a conditional statement to set the component's visible property to true if the unscaledWidth parameter is greater than 0. Add an else block to set the visible property to false when it isn't.

```
if(unscaledWidth > 0){
    this.visible = true;
} else {
    this.visible = false;
}
```

When one of your panels is maximized, you'll set the height and width of the other panels to 0. This conditional statement enables you to determine whether the instance of the component has a nonzero size. If so, you will add all the necessary logic to render the component; otherwise, you will simply hide it.

5 Call the setActualSize() method for both buttons, passing in the values returned by the button's getExplicitOrMeasuredWidth() and getExplicitOrMeasuredHeight() methods.

```
btStateUp.setActualSize( btStateUp.getExplicitOrMeasuredWidth(),
    btStateUp.getExplicitOrMeasuredHeight() );
btStateDown.setActualSize( btStateDown.getExplicitOrMeasuredWidth(),
    btStateDown.getExplicitOrMeasuredHeight() );
```

The getExplicitOrMeasuredWidth() and getExplicitOrMeasuredHeight() methods are available on all UIComponents. They return either the explicit width or height specified by the developer through the width and height properties, or, if those properties are not set, the sizes that the component recommends.

The setActualSize() method accepts a width and height and resizes the component to these parameters. setActualSize() is used with the updateDisplayList() method. In other situations you would use the width and height properties to set these same values.

6 Save the component and run Dashboard.mxml.

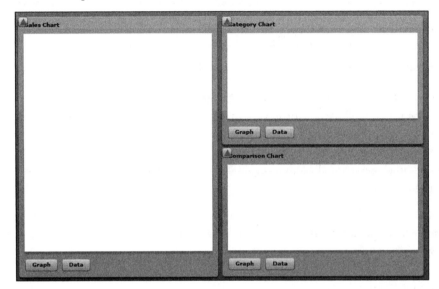

The buttons are now sized to their default recommended size. However, as the developer, you are free to ignore this recommendation and provide your own size. Next, you will resize these buttons to take up less space in the Panel.

7 Just after the conditional statement added in step 4, create a reference to the graphics used for btStateUp and btStateDown by using the buttons' getChildByName() method.

```
var upAsset:DisplayObject = btStateUp.getChildByName("upIcon");
var downAsset:DisplayObject = btStateDown.getChildByName("upIcon");
```

The getChildByName() method of a component is specified as an instance of the DisplayObject class. This class is a superclass of all Flex components, and implements the properties height and width, among others. Because this is the first time you are using the DisplayObject class, you should add it to the imports at the beginning of the class, if it wasn't added automatically when you created the variable.

```
package views {
    import flash.events.Event;
    import mx.containers.Panel;
    import mx.controls.Button;
    import flash.display.DisplayObject;
```

8 Just after the variable declarations for upAsset and downAsset, create a variable named margin, of data type int, with a value of 4.

```
var margin:int = 4;
```

You will use this variable when computing the size of the buttons to provide a few pixels of space between the icon and border of the button. Here, the value of 4 allows for 2 pixels on each side of the button.

9 Replace the parameters of the setActualSize() methods for each button, passing in the width and height of the icons plus the margin.

```
btStateUp.setActualSize(upAsset.width+margin, upAsset.height+margin);
btStateDown.setActualSize(downAsset.width+margin, downAsset.height+margin);
```

In this case, you are not asking the button for default or recommended sizes. Instead you have determined that you want the button to be 4 pixels bigger than the icon it displays.

Because the assets are 14 by 14, this will set the size of the buttons to be 18 by 18—giving a 2-pixel border to the top, left, right, and bottom of the button. This allows room for the border to be drawn and to show some area for a background.

10 Save the component and run Dashboard.mxml. Note the new size of the buttons.

The buttons are now appropriately sized. Now, you need to position them.

11 Just after the two setActualSize() calls, define variables to indicate the width of the button and the distance that it should be rendered from the top and right edges.

```
var pixelsFromTop:int = 5;
var pixelsFromRight:int = 10;
var buttonWidth:int=btStateUp.width;
```

Because both buttons have the same width, it isn't necessary to create a different variable for each button's width. If you were building a system in which each button might have a different width, you would need to explicitly capture each button's width. If you hadn't set the size of the component in the earlier step, btState.width would be equal to 0 (meaning the buttons would be invisible).

12 Create a variable that will compute the *x* coordinate for the buttons by subtracting the unscaledWidth from the buttonWidth; then subtract the pixelsFromRight variable.

```
var x:Number = unscaledWidth - buttonWidth - pixelsFromRight;
```

This sets the button's position relative to the right edge of the Panel. Because the *x* coordinate indicates the left edge of the button, subtract the width of the panel (`unscaledWidth`) from the button's width and then subtract the `pixelsFromRight` to offset the button from the edge of the Panel.

13 Create a variable *y* equal to the `pixelsFromTop` variable.

```
var y:Number = pixelsFromTop;
```

14 Move both buttons to the newly computed *x* and *y* coordinates.

```
btStateDown.move(x, y);
btStateUp.move(x, y);
```

The `move()` method, like the `setActualSize()` method, is used primarily within the `updateDisplayList()` method. In other situations, you would use the x and y properties to set these same values.

Both buttons are set to the same coordinate because only one of the two will be seen at any given time.

15 Save **MaxRestorePanel.as** and run Dashboard.mxml.

As the Dashboard runs, you should see that the buttons are rendered in the correct place and toggle properly when clicked. All that remains to make this functional is to have the main application (Dashboard.mxml) listen to each of the components for the `maximize` or `restore` events and to toggle the states appropriately.

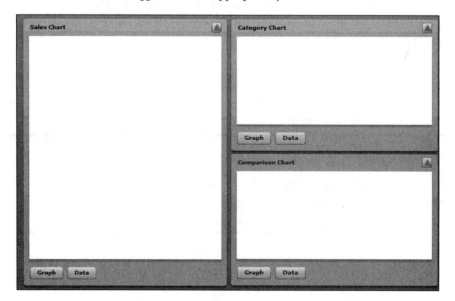

Your completed updateDisplayList() method should read like this:

```
protected override function updateDisplayList(unscaledWidth: Number,
  ➥ unscaledHeight:Number):void {
  super.updateDisplayList(unscaledWidth, unscaledHeight);
  if(unscaledWidth > 0){
    this.visible = true;
  } else {
    this.visible = false;
  }
  var upAsset:DisplayObject = btStateUp.getChildByName("upIcon");
  var downAsset:DisplayObject = btStateDown.getChildByName("upIcon");
  var margin:int = 4;

  btStateUp.setActualSize(upAsset.width+margin, upAsset.height+margin);
  btStateDown.setActualSize(downAsset.width+margin, downAsset.height+margin);
  var pixelsFromTop:int = 5;
  var pixelsFromRight:int = 10;
  var buttonWidth:int=btStateUp.width;
  var x:Number = unscaledWidth - buttonWidth - pixelsFromRight;
  var y:Number = pixelsFromTop;
  btStateDown.move(x, y);
  btStateUp.move(x, y);
}
```

16 Open the Dashboard.mxml file.

You can also copy Lesson10/start/Dashboard.mxml to your flexGrocer/src directory if you choose.

17 Remove the four LinkButton controls and the Spacer control from the ApplicationControlBar. Add two new <mx:Spacer> tags—one between the end-Date DateField and the ComboBox, and another between the ComboBox and the RadioButtonGroup—to force the remaining controls to occupy the entire ApplicationControlBar.

```
<mx:ApplicationControlBar dock="true">
  <mx:Label text="Start Date"/>
  <mx:DateField id="startDate"/>
  <mx:Label text="End Date"/>
  <mx:DateField id="endDate"/>
  <mx:Spacer width="100%"/>
  <mx:ComboBox id="catCombo"
    dataProvider="{categories}"
    labelField = "name"/>
  <mx:Spacer width="100%"/>
  <mx:RadioButtonGroup id="grossOrNetGroup"/>
```

code continues on next page

```
      <mx:RadioButton id="gross"
         groupName="grossOrNetGroup"
         label="Gross Sales"
         data="GROSS"
         selected="true"/>
      <mx:RadioButton id="net"
         groupName="grossOrNetGroup"
         label="Net Sales"
         data="NET"/>
   </mx:ApplicationControlBar>
```

You no longer need the links, as each panel now has a button you can use to maximize it.

18 Add an attribute to the first <mx:ChartPod> tag, which will set the currentState to fullSales when the maximize event occurs. Add another attribute to reset the currentState when the restore event occurs.

```
<v:ChartPod id="sales"
   width="100%" height="100%"
   title="Sales Chart"
   maximize="this.currentState='fullSales'"
   restore="this.currentState=''">
```

Remember, your MaxRestorePanel is the base class for ChartPod, so ChartPod will broadcast the maximize and restore events that you defined in MaxRestorePanel.

19 Handle the maximize and restore events for the other two ChartPods. The restore event handler will be identical for all three, the maximize event handler for the type pod will set the currentState to fullType, and the maximize event handler for the comp pod will set the currentState to fullComp.

```
<v:ChartPod id="type"
   width="100%" height="100%"
   title="Category Chart"
   maximize="this.currentState='fullType'"
   restore="this.currentState=''">
</v:ChartPod>
<v:ChartPod id="comp"
   width="100%" height="100%"
   title=" Comparison Chart"
   maximize="this.currentState='fullComp'"
   restore="this.currentState=''">
</v:ChartPod>
```

20 Save and run Dashboard.mxml. You should now be able to maximize or restore any of the three pods.

What You Have Learned

In this lesson, you have:

- Created a class for your component (pages 258–261)
- Embedded images in ActionScript (pages 259–260)
- Overridden the createChildren() method (pages 261–267)
- Instantiated Flex components in ActionScript (page 262)
- Used the rawChildren property of containers (pages 263–267)
- Learned about the Flex sizing and layout mechanisms (pages 268–269)
- Learned about the measure() method (pages 269–270)
- Overridden the updateDisplayList() method (pages 270–277)

What You Will Learn

In this lesson, you will:

- Define the viewable columns of a DataGrid through DataGridColumn

- Use a `labelFunction` and an itemRendererDisplay to display DataGridColumn information

- Create an MXML component to be used as an item renderer

- Create an inline custom item renderer for a DataGridColumn

- Raise events from inside an item renderer to the container MXML file of the DataGrid using `outerDocument`

- Sort the AdvancedDataGrid

- Style rows, columns, and cells in an AdvancedDataGrid

- Group data in an AdvancedDataGrid using both tags and ActionScript to manipulate the grid's data provider

- Display summary data in an AdvancedDataGrid using both tags and ActionScript

Approximate Time

This lesson takes approximately 2 hours and 30 minutes to complete.

Lesson Files

Media Files:

None

Starting Files:

Lesson11/start/Dashboard.mxml

Lesson11/start/views/dashboard/ChartPod.mxml

Lesson11/start/views/ecomm/Cart.mxml

Lesson11/start/valueObjects/ShoppingCartItem.as

Lesson11/adg/start/src/GroupWithActionScriptADG.mxml

Lesson11/adg/start/src/GroupWithTagsADG.mxml

Lesson11/adg/start/src/SortingADG.mxml

Lesson11/adg/start/src/SortingExpertADG.mxml

Lesson11/adg/start/src/StyleCellADG.mxml

Lesson11/adg/start/src/StyleColumnADG.mxml

Lesson11/adg/start/src/StyleRowADG.mxml

Lesson11/adg/start/src/SummaryWithActionScriptADG.mxml

Lesson11/adg/start/src/SummaryWithTagsADG.mxml

Completed Files:

Lesson11/complete/Dashboard.mxml

Lesson11/complete/views/dashboard/ChartPod.mxml

Lesson11/complete/views/ecomm/Cart.mxml

Lesson11/complete/valueObjects/ShoppingCartItem.as

Lesson11/complete/renderer/ecomm/ProductName.mxml

Lesson11/adg/complete/src/GroupWithActionScriptADG.mxml

Lesson11/adg/complete/src/GroupWithTagsADG.mxml

Lesson11/adg/complete/src/SortingADG.mxml

Lesson11/adg/complete/src/SortingExpertADG.mxml

Lesson11/adg/complete/src/StyleCellADG.mxml

Lesson11/adg/complete/src/StyleColumnADG.mxml

Lesson11/adg/complete/src/StyleRowADG.mxml

Lesson11/adg/complete/src/SummaryWithActionScriptADG.mxml

Lesson11/adg/complete/src/SummaryWithTagsADG.mxml

Lesson11/adg/complete/src/renderers/SummaryText.mxml

LESSON 11

Using DataGrids and Item Renderers

In Lesson 8, "Using Controls and Repeaters with Datasets," you learned about working with datasets and some controls that could be used to show the data. In this lesson, you will build upon that set of base controls and be introduced to the primary MXML component used to display and manipulate large datasets.

In this lesson, you will learn how to use the DataGrid component to display a dataset in an interactive way using rows and columns. Aside from using the DataGrid in its simplest form, you will learn how to override the default behavior of a particular column in the DataGrid by implementing a custom item renderer; do a custom sort of the data in a column; and change the editing controls, which manage underlying data. You will also use the sorting, styling, grouping, and summary data features of the AdvancedDataGrid.

Here, you see the shopping cart displayed in a DataGrid.

Introducing DataGrids and Item Renderers

Using a DataGrid as a way to display the data of your application provides the largest possible number of options for your users to interact with the data. At the simplest level, the DataGrid organizes the data in a column-by-row format and presents this to the user. From there, the DataGrid can be configured to allow you to modify the data it contains.

In this lesson, you will make modifications to two of the applications. The first is the Dashboard application, in which you will use the DataGrid for purely display purposes. The second is the EComm application, in which the DataGrid will give you a view of the cart and the ability to both update and remove items from the cart.

> **TIP:** Although the DataGrid does provide the most versatile manner of interacting with the data of your application, it does come with additional overhead (performance and size). It is wise to consider what you expect the user to do with the data or control before you automatically choose to use a DataGrid.

Adding a Generic DataGrid to ChartPod

This exercise will have you extending the current ChartPod.mxml, created in Lesson 10, "Creating Custom Components with ActionScript 3.0," in two ways. The first is to add a DataGrid, in which you can view sales data that is passed in. The second is to add a property to the MaxRestorePanel component to allow the containing MXML file to pass in the dataset that the component should use when displaying the data in the DataGrid. This exercise focuses on the base usage of the DataGrid, which allows for the DataGrid to get the definition of which columns it will use from the dataset.

1 Open the ChartPod.mxml file.

If you didn't complete Lesson 10 or if you were unhappy with the state of the application after that lesson, you can copy Lesson11/start/views/dashboard/ChartPod.mxml to your flexGrocer/src/views/dashboard directory.

2 Below the beginning <mx:MaxRestorePanel> tag, place an <mx:Script> block to enable you to declare attributes that can be passed into the component.

```
<mx:Script>
  <![CDATA[
  ]]>
</mx:Script>
```

This is needed to allow you to import classes and declare functions and properties for the ChartPod application.

3 Inside the script block, add an import for the mx.collections.ICollectionView class.

```
import mx.collections.ICollectionView;
```

The attribute passed into the component will be of type ICollectionView, so you need the import to data type the attribute.

4 Below the import, declare a public variable, named dp, which will hold the reference of the data passed into the component. Make it of type ICollectionView and make it [Bindable] so that the DataGrid can update its data as the property value changes.

```
[Bindable]
public var dp:ICollectionView = null;
```

A value of null is used to act as the initial state of the property until a value is passed in. The [Bindable] metadata is used to tell the compiler that this property is being watched by another part of the application.

5 Below the script block, insert an <mx:DataGrid> tag.

```
<mx:DataGrid />
```

It is not necessary for you to always define columns for a DataGrid. By not defining any columns in the DataGrid definition, the DataGrid implicitly creates a column for each column of the dataset that is assigned to it. Also, you don't need to worry about how the DataGrid is positioned relative to the ControlBar because of the ControlBar's behavior of placing itself at the bottom of the component.

6 In the <mx:DataGrid> tag, set the width and height to 100%.

```
<mx:DataGrid width="100%" height="100%" />
```

This means that the DataGrid should fill 100% of the width and height of its parent.

7 Bind the dataProvider attribute of the <mx:DataGrid> tag to dp.

```
<mx:DataGrid dataProvider="{dp}" width="100%" height="100%" />
```

This will set the dataset for the DataGrid to whatever is passed into the component.

8 Save the ChartPod.mxml file.

There is no need to test this component at this point because you don't have data being passed to it yet.

Adding HTTPService Calls to Dashboard

These next exercises have you returning to the Dashboard.mxml file, modifying it to retrieve the data from a HTTPService, and passing it to the modified ChartPod.mxml component. The data currently resides in static XML files that you will pull into the application to fill the DataGrids in your Dashboard. The data is already presorted.

1 Open the Dashboard.mxml file.

You can also copy Lesson11/start/Dashboard.mxml to your flexGrocer/src directory if you choose.

2 Insert three <mx:HTTPService> tags to retrieve sales information for the three pods in the Dashboard. Place them just below the script block.

```
<mx:HTTPService id="salesRPC"
    url="http://www.flexgrocer.com/rawSalesData.xml"
    result="salesRPCResult(event)"
    fault="showFault(event)"/>
<mx:HTTPService id="typeRPC"
    url="http://www.flexgrocer.com/categorySalesData.xml"
    result="typeRPCResult(event)"
    fault="showFault(event)"/>
<mx:HTTPService id="compRPC"
    url="http://www.flexgrocer.com/salesData.xml"
    result="compRPCResult(event)"
    fault="showFault(event)"/>
```

In Lesson 6, "Using Remote XML Data with Controls," it was discussed in detail how to use the <mx:HTTPService> tag and how to use the result handlers of the tag. Each tag has its own specific result handle method but uses one shared fault handle method.

3 In the script block at the top of the file, create a private salesRPCResult() method. This method will handle the result from the HTTPService that gets the sales data by taking the result and passing it along to the sales pod.

```
private function salesRPCResult(event:ResultEvent):void{
    sales.dp = event.result.salesData.dailySales;
}
```

This function takes the ResultEvent event passed in and assigns it to the sales component through the dp attribute that you defined earlier in the lesson.

4 Just like the last step, create a private typeRPCResult() method in the script block. This method will handle the result from the HTTPService that gets the sales type data by taking the result and passing it along to the type pod.

```
private function typeRPCResult(event:ResultEvent):void{
    type.dp = event.result.categorySalesData.categorySales;
}
```

This function takes the ResultEvent event passed in and assigns it to the type component through the dp attribute.

5 In the script block at the top of the file, create a private compRPCResult() method. This method will handle the result from the HTTPService that gets the sales type data by taking the result and passing it along to the comp pod.

```
private function compRPCResult(event:ResultEvent):void{
    comp.dp = event.result.salesData.dailySales;
}
```

This function takes the ResultEvent event passed in and assigns it to the comp component through the dp attribute.

6 Inside the script block, add an import for the mx.rpc.events.FaultEvent class.

```
import mx.rpc.events.FaultEvent;
```

You need this class to be able to capture errors that were made during your request for the XML files.

7 In the script block, create a private showFault() method. This method will trace out the fault codes that occur in the HTTPService call.

```
private function showFault(event:FaultEvent):void{
    trace(event.fault.faultCode+":"+event.fault.faultString);
}
```

8 Create a private method called getData(). It accepts no arguments and returns void.

```
private function getData():void{
}
```

This function will be called at application startup to fetch the data for the drop-down list and the three pods. In a later lesson, this function will be called when the filter criteria changes, which will request data from the server using the values the user specifies.

9 In the getData() method, call the three HTTPServices through their send() methods to fetch the data.

```
private function getData():void{
   salesRPC.send();
   typeRPC.send();
   compRPC.send();
}
```

As you may remember from an earlier lesson, we created a single method, called getData(), where the data is requested for the whole Dashboard application. Because you have three different outbound requests, you need to call them all from inside this method.

10 Create a private method called init(). It accepts no arguments and returns void.

```
private function init():void{
}
```

This function will hold your initialization routine the first time the application is started.

11 Inside the init() method, initialize the startDate DateField control to have a selectedDate of 4/1/2006 and the endDate DateField control to have a selectedDate of 5/1/2006.

```
private function init():void{
   startDate.selectedDate = new Date(2006,3,1);
   endDate.selectedDate = new Date(2006,4,1);
}
```

This will give a default start and end date of your date filter controls. You will use these in Lesson 18, "Accessing Server-Side Objects," when you start to interact with the server to get the data dynamically.

✱ NOTE: The constructor for the Date object allows you to quickly build a new date by specifying values such as the year, month, and day. However, in Flex, months are 0 based, meaning 0 represents January and 11 represents December. Specifying 2006, 3, and 1 to the constructor means April 1, 2006.

12 Move the HTTPService call responsible for getting the categories from the creationComplete event of the <mx:Application> tag to inside the init() method.

```
private function init():void{
   startDate.selectedDate = new Date(2006,3,1);
   endDate.selectedDate = new Date(2006,4,1);
   catRPC.send();
}
```

13 Make a call to the getData() method inside the init() method.

```
private function init():void{
   startDate.selectedDate = new Date(2006,3,1);
   endDate.selectedDate = new Date(2006,4,1);
   catRPC.send();
   getData();
}
```

This will retrieve the data for the Dashboard and make it available when the application starts up.

14 In the creationComplete event of the <mx:Application> tag, call the init() method.

```
<mx:Application xmlns:mx="http://www.adobe.com/2006/mxml"
   layout="horizontal"
   creationComplete="init();"
   xmlns:v="views.dashboard.*">
```

This sets the defaults for the filter controls and then initially loads the Dashboard data after the whole application is loaded.

15 Save and run your Dashboard.mxml, and see the data populated in the pods on the dashboard.

❋ **NOTE:** Sorting the data is part of the default behavior of the DataGrid. The data came back from the XML file already presorted, so there was no need to sort the data upon receipt. Lesson 18 will demonstrate how to pragmatically sort the data of a DataGrid.

Displaying the Shopping Cart with a DataGrid

When you left off in Lesson 8, you had the contents of your cart displayed in a List control with the ability to remove the current item you were viewing from the cart via a Remove button. You will switch this to use a DataGrid to display the contents of the cart. The DataGrid control supports the syntax to allow you to specify the columns explicitly through the DataGridColumn. This is done with the following syntax:

```
<mx:DataGrid … >
  <mx:columns>
    <mx:DataGridColumn dataField=""…>
    <mx:DataGridColumn…>
    <mx:DataGridColumn…>
  </mx:columns>
</mx:DataGrid>
```

The dataField is used to map the column in the dataset to a given column. The order in which the DataGridColumns are listed is the order you will see the columns from left to right in the DataGrid. This is useful when you need to specify a different order to the columns than specified in the dataset. Each DataGridColumn supports a large number of attributes that affect the DataGrid's rendering and interaction with the given column.

1 Open Cart.mxml from the flexGrocer/src/views/ecomm directory.

If you prefer, you can copy this file from the Lesson11/start/views/ecomm directory to your flexGrocer/src/views/ecomm directory.

2 Replace the `<mx:List>` tag with an `<mx:DataGrid>` tag. Set the width and height to 100%, set draggableColumns to false, and set editable to true.

```
<mx:DataGrid
   id="cartView"
   dataProvider="{cart.aItems}" width="100%" height="100%"
   editable="true" draggableColumns="false">
   <mx:columns>
   </mx:columns>
</mx:DataGrid>
```

You are specifying editable as true because you will allow one of the columns to be changed by the user. If it is set to false, the whole DataGrid becomes read-only. You no longer need the labelFunction attribute for data formatting on the base control because it is the DataGridColumns that will specify how each piece of data is shown. For now, leave the code in the script block that defined the label function; you will return to it in a few steps. The DataGrid will remain bound to the same dataset as before (cart.aItems). You also had to set the draggableColumns attribute to false because the default value is true, and you don't want the columns to be able to be moved around.

3 Define an <mx:DataGridColumn> for the product name, and place it at the top of the column list. Set dataField to product, editable to false, and headerText to Product.

```
<mx:DataGridColumn dataField="product" headerText="Product"
   editable="false" />
```

The headerText attribute specifies the text of the DataGridColumn header. If you don't specify this, it will take the value of the dataField attribute.

▶ **TIP:** You could have optionally set the dataField attribute to product.prodName because the product field is actually a complex object available as a property of ShoppingCartItem. The DataGridColumn can resolve property.property references.

Because the editable attribute is set to true on the <mx:DataGrid> tag, you need to set it to false for each column you don't want to use for editing.

4 Define an <mx:DataGridColumn> for displaying the quantity and place it after the last <mx:DataGridColumn>. Set dataField to quantity and headerText to Quantity.

```
<mx:DataGridColumn dataField="quantity" headerText="Quantity" />
```

This column will be used to allow users to change the quantity of a specific product they want to buy.

5 Define an <mx:DataGridColumn> for displaying subtotals for each item and place it after the last <mx:DataGridColumn>. Set dataField to subtotal, editable to false, and headerText to Amount.

```
<mx:DataGridColumn dataField="subtotal" headerText="Amount"
   editable="false" />
```

The column will show the cost for this specific product. You don't want the customer to be able to change this amount, so you are setting the editable attribute to false.

6 Save Cart.mxml. Run the EComm Application, add the Buffalo product to the shopping cart and click on View Cart.

You can see the cart shown in a DataGrid. Note the Product column is showing up as text in the DataGrid, even though it is a complex attribute in the dataset. This is because there is a toString() function declared on the Product value object. If this wasn't defined, you would see [Object Product]. You will look at how to better display a complex object later. For now, this is what you should see:

Add Inline Editing Control for DataGridColumn

In a DataGrid, you have the ability to specify that a column of the data shown can be changed by the user when focus is brought to the cell. This is done by setting the editable attribute to true. The default editing control for the column is a text field. It is possible to specify which editor to use when managing the data via the itemEditor attribute and the editorDataField. The editorDataField specifies the attribute of the editor control used to manage changing the value for the cell, as well as which attribute on that control the dataset should examine to get the changed value. The following are the built-in controls you can specify (full package names are needed unless imported into the containing page):

- Button
- CheckBox
- ComboBox
- DateField
- Image

- Label
- NumericStepper
- Text (Default)
- TextArea
- TextInput

> **TIP:** You can also specify your own control if you desire, as long as it implements the IDropInListItemRenderer interface in its class definition.

1 Open the Cart.mxml you created in the previous exercise.

If you didn't finish the previous exercise, you can open Cart_1.mxml from Lesson11/ intermediate and save it as **Cart.mxml** in your flexGrocer/src/views/ecomm directory.

2 In the <mx:DataGridColumn> tag that maps to the quantity, set the itemEditor to mx.controls.NumericStepper, editorDataField to value, and editable to true.

```
<mx:DataGridColumn dataField="quantity"
    itemEditor="mx.controls.NumericStepper"
    editorDataField="value" editable="true" headerText="Quantity" />
```

This now has the Quantity column being edited as a NumericStepper. The underlying value of the column is bound to the value attribute of the NumericStepper.

3 Save Cart.mxml. Run the EComm application, add the Buffalo product to the shopping cart, and click View Cart.

When you click in the Quantity column, you will notice that it doesn't open as a free-form text field, but rather as a NumericStepper control.

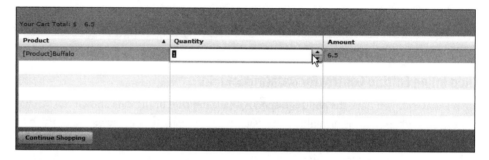

Create an MXML Item Renderer for Displaying the Product

The default behavior of the DataGrid is to convert every value of the dataset into a string and then display it. However, when you are dealing with a complex object that is stored in the dataset, another alternative is to create a custom item renderer that shows more information about the column. In this case, you are going to create a simple item renderer that shows the product's name and image.

When working with item renderers, you will find that there is an implicit public variable available to you in the item renderer called *data*, which represents the data of the row itself. You can use the data to bind your controls without having to worry about what column you are working with. When the DataGrid creates a column that has a custom item renderer associated with it, it creates a single instance of the cell renderer per row, so you don't have to worry about scoping between rows.

1 Create a new folder under the flexGrocer/src directory named renderer, and one under that called ecomm.

2 Right-click the ecomm folder you just created and choose New > MXML Component. In the New MXML Component dialog box, set the filename to **ProductName.mxml**, the base component to an HBox, remove any width and height values, and then click Finish.

This MXML file will define the layout of a given cell in the DataGrid. You are creating it in a separate file so that, if needed, it can be used on multiple DataGrid columns and/or multiple DataGrids.

3 Open ProductName.mxml.

The file should already be open in your Flex Builder workspace; if not, the file is located in your flexGrocer/src/renderer/ecomm directory.

4 In the <mx:HBox>, set the verticalScrollPolicy and horizontalScrollPolicy attributes to off.

```
<mx:HBox xmlns:mx="http://www.adobe.com/2006/mxml"
   verticalScrollPolicy="off" horizontalScrollPolicy="off">
```

This will keep the cell renderer from having scroll bars if the DataGrid is resized too small.

5 Place an <mx:Image> tag inside the <mx:HBox> to display the product's thumbnail image. You need to set the source attribute to a hard-coded directory location, but the filename should be bound to the imageName of the product. That will make it look like assets/ {data.product.imageName}.

```
<mx:Image source="{'assets/' +data.product.imageName}"/>
```

You do not need to specify the height or width of the image because it will resize the column to fit the image.

> **TIP:** The image location used is relative to the location where the main application is loaded from, not the location of the file that contains the <mx:Image> tag.

6 Place an <mx:Text> tag for the product name in the <mx:HBox> below the <mx:Image> tag. Bind the text attribute to data.product.prodName. Set the height and width to 100%.

```
<mx:Text text="{data.product.prodName}" width="100%" height="100%"/>
```

7 Save the ProductName.mxml file.

There is no need to test this component at this point because it is not assigned to the DataGrid yet.

8 Open the Cart.mxml you created in the previous exercise.

Alternately, you can open Cart_2.mxml from Lesson11/intermediate and save it as **Cart.mxml** in your flexGrocer/src/views/ecomm directory.

9 Update the <mx:DataGridColumn> with a dataField of product with a new attribute, itemRenderer, set to renderer.ecomm.ProductName.

```
<mx:DataGridColumn dataField="product" headerText="Product"
   itemRenderer="renderer.ecomm.ProductName" editable="false"/>
```

With the use of the `itemRenderer` attribute, you are overriding the default TextInput editor. You need to use the fully qualified class name to set your item renderer unless you have imported the class package that it exists in.

10 Update the `<mx:DataGrid>` with a new attribute `variableRowHeight` set to `true`.

```
<mx:DataGrid
   id="cartView"
   dataProvider="{cart.aItems}" width="100%" height="100%"
   editable="true" draggableColumns="false"
   variableRowHeight="true">
```

It is necessary for you to set the `variableRowHeight` to `true`, so that Flex resizes the row's height to accommodate the thumbnail image.

> **TIP:** This attribute can be used to allow for exploding details inside a DataGrid row. In this case, you can have summary data in one cell that if you click on an icon or button, the cell expands to show the new details.

11 Save Cart.mxml. Run the EComm Application, add the Buffalo product to the shopping cart and click View Cart.

Product		Quantity	Amount
	Buffalo	1	6.5

Your Cart Total: $ 6.5

Create an Inline MXML Item Renderer for Displaying the Remove Button

Another option for creating an item renderer is through the `<mx:itemRenderer>` tag, which allows you to declare and create the item renderer inline with the DataGridColumns. From a compiler perspective, doing an inline item renderer is the equivalent of building it in an external file (it actually compiles the code of the inline item renderer as a separate file internally). Inside the `<mx:cellRenderer>` tag, you will place an `<mx:Component>` tag, which defines the boundaries of the inline item renderer file from the rest of the page. Thus, the inside of the `<mx:Component>` tag will have its own scope for which you will need to do imports, function declarations, and the like.

▶ **TIP:** Although this will be very efficient from a coding perspective to build inline item renderers, it does not allow you to reuse the item renderers for other DataGrids. Good candidates are item renderers that are specific to one DataGrid only, such as action item controls.

Just like the item renderer you just created, this one will have access to the data variable, which will hold the reference to the row. In addition, you will also be able to communicate out of the inline cell editor back into the page through the outerDocument scope. Note, however, that all functions and variables in the containing page that you want to reference must be declared as public, because it is really a component talking to another component.

For this example, you will look to replace the Remove button that is outside the DataGrid with a Remove button inside each row.

1 Open the Cart.mxml you created in the previous exercise.

Alternately, you can open Cart_3.mxml from Lesson11/intermediate and save it as **Cart.mxml** in your flexGrocer/src/views/ecomm directory.

2 Create a new <mx:DataGridColumn> to hold a Remove button at the bottom of the DataGrid column list. Set editable to false; otherwise, the cell would be able to receive focus. You also do not need to specify dataField, because there is no data you are mapping directly to.

```
<mx:DataGridColumn editable="false">
</mx:DataGridColumn>
```

This will create the placeholder column in the DataGrid. We used a start and end <mx:DataGridColumn> tag because the item renderer definition will be placed inside it.

3 Place the <mx:itemRenderer> and <mx:Component> tags inside the <mx:DataGridColumn> tag.

```
<mx:itemRenderer>
    <mx:Component>
    </mx:Component>
</mx:itemRenderer>
```

4 Place an <mx:VBox> tag inside the <mx:Component> tag to provide a container for the Remove button.

```
<mx:itemRenderer>
    <mx:Component>
        <mx:VBox>
        </mx:VBox>
    </mx:Component>
</mx:itemRenderer>
```

When creating this inline item renderer we want to use the VBox to help us be able to center the button in the DataGrid no matter the size of the cell.

5 Place an <mx:Button> tag inside the VBox. Set the label to Remove and set the click event to call the removeItem() function on the containing page. You will need to use the outerDocument reference to call the function. An import statement for valueObjects. ShoppingCartItem should be added automatically to the inline component. If not, add an <mx:Script> block inside of the <mx:VBox> tag, and include the import statement.

```
<mx:VBox>
    <mx:Script>
      <![CDATA[
          import valueObjects.ShoppingCartItem;
      ]]>
    </mx:Script>
    <mx:Button
        label="Remove"
        click="outerDocument.removeItem(data as ShoppingCartItem);"/>
</mx:VBox>
```

In prior lessons, you used the Remove Button that was outside the List to remove an item from the shopping cart. The remove function could simply look at the selectedItem in the List to determine which product to remove. Because you are building an inline item renderer you will need to change the method signature of the removeItem() function to accept a ShoppingCartItem instance that the row is pointing to. It is necessary for you to do this because the DataGrid will not always have a concept of a selected row that the code can remove.

You need to fully qualify the casting of the data property into the ShoppingCartItem, as well as add the appropriate import statement, because the import statements made at the top of the file are in a different scope than the inline item renderer.

▶ **TIP:** As an alternative to the _eas_f operator, you can convert an object instance from one type to another (as long as they are compatible) by simply wrapping the desired object instance in the ClassNameToConvertTo(object) syntax.

6 Change the method signature of removeItem to accept a ShoppingCartItem as an argument. Also, change the method to public.

```
public function removeItem(cartItem:ShoppingCartItem):void{
```

When the button is clicked, the item renderer passes the cart item of the row it is on, so we need to add an argument to accept this cart item. We need to make this method public so that the code running inside the inline cell renderer can access it.

7 Change the first two lines of the removeItem() function so that the Product to be removed from the cart is set equal to the argument passed in.

```
var prod:Product = cartItem.product;
```

The whole function should now look like this:

```
public function removeItem(cartItem:ShoppingCartItem):void{
   var prod:Product = cartItem.product;
   var e:ProductEvent = new ProductEvent(prod,"productRemoved");
   this.dispatchEvent(e);
}
```

You no longer need to build the product item from the selected row because the row is now calling this method and passing in the specific cart item.

8 Inside the script block, add an import for the mx.controls.dataGridClasses.DataGrid-Column class.

```
import mx.controls.dataGridClasses.DataGridColumn;
```

You need to update the labelFunction that you had for the List control so that it will work with a DataGrid. The method signature for a labelFunction on a DataGrid is labelFunctionName(item:Object, dataField:DataGridColumn).

 TIP: In the Flex Builder integrated development environment (IDE), if you choose DataGridColumn from the list of classes that are presented after the colon (:) of your argument, the IDE will automatically import the class for you if it is not already present.

9 Add an argument to the end of the renderLabel() function to call dataField of type DataGridColumn.

```
private function renderLabel(item:ShoppingCartItem,
   _dataField:DataGridColumn):String{
```

Because the DataGrid has multiple columns that can each have its own labelFunction, as well as share the same labelFunction, the additional argument is used to distinguish between which labelFunction is being used. If you know that your function will only be used on just one column, you can ignore this argument in your code.

10 Update the renderLabel() function to just return the subtotal of the item formatted with a $. Change the name to renderPriceLabel().

For now, you want to put a simple mask on the price to represent the number as a dollar figure. The signature and functionality of the labelFunction is the same on the DataGrid as it is on the List.

```
private function renderPriceLabel(item:ShoppingCartItem,
    _dataField:DataGridColumn):String{
    return "$"+String(item.subtotal);
}
```

11 Update the <mx:DataGridColumn> with a dataField of subtotal with a new attribute of labelFunction set to renderPriceLabel.

```
<mx:DataGridColumn dataField="subtotal" headerText="Amount"
    labelFunction="renderPriceLabel" editable="false"/>
```

This will have the subtotal column use renderPriceLabel on each of the rows in the DataGrid.

12 Remove the old <mx:Button> that called the logic to remove items from the cart outside the DataGrid.

The final code for the Cart.mxml should look like the following:

```
<?xml version="1.0" encoding="utf-8"?>
<mx:VBox xmlns:mx="http://www.adobe.com/2006/mxml">
    <mx:Metadata>
        [Event(name="productRemoved",type="events.ProductEvent")]
    </mx:Metadata>
    <mx:Script>
        <![CDATA[
            import mx.controls.dataGridClasses.DataGridColumn;
            import events.ProductEvent;
            import valueObjects.ShoppingCart;
            import valueObjects.ShoppingCartItem;
            import valueObjects.Product;
            [Bindable]
            public var cart:ShoppingCart;
            private function renderPriceLabel(item:ShoppingCartItem, dataField:
        _DataGridColumn):String{
                return "$"+String(item.subtotal);
            }
            public function removeItem(cartItem:ShoppingCartItem):void{
                var prod:Product = cartItem.product;
                var e:ProductEvent = new ProductEvent(prod,"productRemoved");
                this.dispatchEvent(e);
            }
        ]]>
    </mx:Script>
```

```
<mx:DataGrid
    id="cartView"
    dataProvider="{cart.aItems}" width="100%" height="100%"
    editable="true" draggableColumns="false"
    variableRowHeight="true">
    <mx:columns>
        <mx:DataGridColumn dataField="product" headerText="Product"
            itemRenderer="renderer.ecomm.ProductName" editable="false"/>
        <mx:DataGridColumn dataField="quantity"
            itemEditor="mx.controls.NumericStepper"
            editorDataField="value" editable="true" headerText="Quantity"/>
        <mx:DataGridColumn dataField="subtotal" headerText="Amount"
            editable="false" labelFunction="renderPriceLabel"/>
        <mx:DataGridColumn editable="false">
            <mx:itemRenderer>
                <mx:Component>
                    <mx:VBox>
                        <mx:Script>
                            <![CDATA[
                                import valueObjects.ShoppingCartItem;
                            ]]>
                        </mx:Script>
                        <mx:Button
                            label="Remove"
                            click="outerDocument.removeItem(data as ShoppingCartItem);"/>
                    </mx:VBox>
                </mx:Component>
            </mx:itemRenderer>
        </mx:DataGridColumn>
    </mx:columns>
</mx:DataGrid>
</mx:VBox>
```

13 Save Cart.mxml. Run the EComm.mxml application, add the Buffalo product to the shopping cart, and click View Cart. Notice both the formatting on the Amount column and the Remove button in the shopping cart.

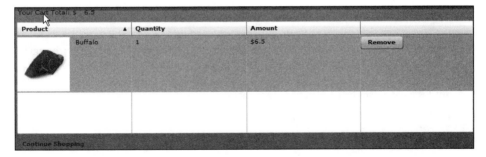

Update ShoppingCartItem with Set and Get Functions

One thing you might have noticed when you took the shopping cart out for a test run was that when you changed the quantity of the item in the cart, the pricing wasn't updated to reflect the change. This is because changes to either price or quantity are not triggering the `recalc()` function you created in the ShoppingCartItem class.

ActionScript enables you to declare some behind-the-scenes functions that will execute whenever you attempt to access a property of a class. These are called custom set and get functions. In the function, you will place the keyword of either `get` or `set` in your function declaration that has the same name as the property you are trying to mask. Also, you will change the property to be a private variable that is named differently than before. It is recommended that you prefix it with an underscore. The three parts will follow this brief structure:

```
private var _insVar:uint;
public function set insVar(qty:uint):Void
public function get insVar():uint
```

1 Open ShoppingCartItem.as from your flexGrocer/src/valueObjects directory.

If you prefer, you can copy this file from the Lesson11/start/valueObjects to your flexGrocer/src/valueObjects directory.

2 Change the `quantity` property declaration to have a prefix of an underscore (_) and change the access modifier to private.

```
private var _quantity:uint;
```

We changed this property to be private so that no one can directly access this property outside the class itself.

3 Add a set `quantity()` function declaration and have it call the `recalc()` function.

```
public function set quantity(qty:uint):void{
   _quantity = qty;
   recalc();
}
```

This will be called every time something changes the quantity of an item in the cart. This is where you want to call the `recalc()` function.

4 Add the get `quantity()` function declaration.

```
public function get quantity():uint{
   return _quantity;
}
```

5 Add a public function called toString() that will return type String. Have the function return a concatenation of the ShoppingCartItem quantity and its product's name.

```
public function toString():String{
   return this.quantity.toString() + ": " + this.product.prodName;
}
```

This function will be used if Flex is asked to display the contents of the ShoppingCartItem. Currently, this is done on the small cart view off the main product page.

6 Save ShoppingCartItem.as. Run the EComm.mxml application, add the Buffalo product to the shopping cart, and click View Cart. Change the quantity of the Buffalo item in your cart and see the subtotal change.

When you change the quantity of a cart item, you will see the updating of the price after you leave the column because the DataGrid is watching for changes to the dataset to which it is assigned. The reason that you need to leave the column is that the data that DataGrid is managing is not updated until after you are finished working with the column. This is to avoid constant broadcasting of every change made to the column until the user is finished editing the value. Be aware that the cart total above the cart does not change, just the price of the individual items in the cart. You will be updating the cart in a later lesson.

Using the AdvancedDataGrid

The AdvancedDataGrid, which is part of the Data Visualization package, expands the capabilities of the normal DataGrid. The AdvancedDataGrid control provides added features and greater control of data display, data aggregation, and data formatting. In this section not all features of the AdvancedDataGrid will be used. The less complex features can be easily discovered from documentation, so the space here will be used to demonstrate some of the more conceptually difficult capabilities.

At this point, the shopping application does not have a good use case for the AdvancedDataGrid, so smaller files to illustrate the learning points will be used for practice.

Sorting the AdvancedDataGrid

Using the AdvancedDataGrid, it is now possible to sort by multiple columns. This behavior differs according to the Boolean value assigned to the AdvancedDataGrid's sortExpertMode property. When that property is set to false, clicking the header area of a column makes that the first priority sort. Clicking in the multiple column sort area adds additional sort criteria. The numbers at the top of the columns indicate the sorting order. If you wish to reset the top-level sort, click the header area of a column and that column becomes the first priority sort.

Header areas   Multiple column sort areas

cat	1 ▲	cost	name	2 ▲	qty	
bakery		1.99	bread		3	
bakery		0.33	donut		2	
dairy		4.52	cheddar cheese		6	
dairy		3.05	colby cheese		4	
dairy		2.99	milk		2	
dairy		0.33	sour cream		2	
dairy		0.99	yogurt		5	
fruit		1.05	apple		4	
fruit		0.99	banana		2	
fruit		0.52	orange		4	

1 Choose File > New > Flex Project. Set the Project name to be **ADG**.

2 Set the Project location to be flex3tfs/Lesson11/adg/start.

3 For the Application type select Web application.

4 Set the Server technology to None, then click Next.

5 Leave the Output folder as bin-debug, then click Next.

6 Leave the Main source folder as src.

7 Click the Browse button for the Main application file, select SortingADG.mxml, and then click OK.

8 Click Finish.

You have now created a project so you can run the applications for AdvancedDataGrid.

9 Run the SortingADG.mxml application.

10 Click the cat header area to sort by product category, and note the number 1 appears in the multiple column sort area.

By clicking in the header area, you set sorting by category to be the first priority sort, and the 1 that appears confirms this.

11 Now click in the multiple column sort area for the name column to make it the secondary sort.

You see that the names are now sorted within categories and the number 2 that appears in the name column confirms this is the second-level sort.

12 Click the qty header area.

This changes the first priority sort to be on the quantity field.

13 Click the multiple column sort area. Note that the direction of the arrow in the area changes.

By clicking in the multiple column sort area, you toggle the sort from ascending to descending.

14 Close the browser, return to Flex Builder, and close the SortingADG.mxml file.

Sorting in Expert Mode

When you set the sortExpertMode property to true, sorting behaviors, as well as component visuals, change. You will not see the multiple column sort areas. To perform a multiple column sort in this mode, first click the column you want for the first priority sort. Then, Ctrl-click in the header area to add additional sort criteria. The numbers at the top of the columns indicate the sorting order. If you wish to reset the top-level sort, click (not CTRL-click) the header area of a column and that column becomes the first priority sort.

No multiple column sort areas available when sortExpertMode *set to* true

cat	1 ▲	cost	2 ▲	name	qty
bakery		0.33		donut	2
bakery		1.99		bread	3
dairy		0.33		sour cream	2
dairy		0.99		yogurt	5
dairy		2.99		milk	2
dairy		3.05		colby cheese	4
dairy		4.52		cheddar cheese	6
fruit		0.52		orange	4
fruit		0.99		banana	2
fruit		1.05		apple	4

1 Open the application SortingExpertADG.mxml and note the sortExpertMode property is set to true. Run the application.

Note that there are no multiple column sort areas displayed.

2 Click the cat column header to sort the AdvancedDataGrid by product category. Now, CTRL-click the name column header.

Note that when you CTRL-clicked the name column, the names were sorted by name within the category. Also, the number 2 appeared in the column header to indicate the sorting order.

3 CTRL-click again in the name header area.

CTRL-clicking again in a header that already has a sort applied toggles the sort from ascending to descending.

4 Click in the qty column.

This resets the top priority sort, in this case to the quantity field.

5 Close the browser, return to Flex Builder, and close the SortingExpertADG.mxml file.

Styling the AdvancedDataGrid

There are times when you will want to change the look of the AdvancedDataGrid. For instance, you may wish to draw attention to a particular row, column, or cell. A common example of this is to have negative numbers displayed in red. The AdvancedDataGrid allows you to write and apply styling functions to implement this functionality.

Styling columns

Your first task is to change the default look of the grid by applying a style to an entire column.

1 Open the application StyleColumnADG.mxml and run it.

Note that there is no special styling on the grid.

2 At the bottom of the script block, create a new public function named `myStyleFunc` and data type it as Object. The function should accept two parameters, the first named `data` is data typed as Object, and the second named `col` is data typed as AdvancedDataGridColumn.

Note that the signature of the style function must accept two parameters, the first being an Object and the second an AdvancedDataGridColumn. The first parameter represents the data for a particular row in the AdvancedDataGrid, and the second contains information about the column the `styleFunction`property is associated with.

The function must return an Object, which is usually one of two kinds of values. The first is `null`, which means you do not want any styling applied. The function can also return an Object composed of one or more style properties and associated values.

3 In the body of the function, return an object associating the `color` property with the hexadecimal value 0xFF0000, and the `fontWeight` property with the string value bold. Your style function should appear as shown here.

```
public function myStyleFunc(data:Object,col:AdvancedDataGridColumn):Object
{
    return {color:0xFF0000,fontWeight:"bold"};
}
```

The object returned will be used as a style sheet and applied to part of the AdvancedDataGrid.

4 In the `<mx:AdvancedDataGridColumn>` tag that displays the category information, add the `styleFunction` property and reference the function you just wrote, `myStyleFunc`.

`styleFunction="myStyleFunc"`

This will apply the style function you just wrote to the column.

5 Run the application and note the category column has red and bold text in it.

cat	name	cost
fruit	banana	0.99
bakery	bread	1.99
dairy	cheddar cheese	4.52
dairy	sour cream	0.33
fruit	orange	0.52
bakery	donut	0.33
dairy	yogurt	0.99
dairy	milk	2.99
fruit	apple	1.05
dairy	colby cheese	3.05

6 Close the StyleColumnADG.mxml file.

Styling rows

To change the style of a particular row, you also reference a function using the `styleFunction` property. To change a row, use the `styleFunction` property with the AdvancedDataGrid tag itself. Then add logic to the function to return the style object only when you want.

1 Open the application StyleRowADG.mxml. Note that the signature for the style function is included and returns null, so no error is reported. Run the application.

Note that there is no special styling on the grid.

2 Add the `styleFunction` property to the `<mx:AdvancedDataGrid>` tag and have it reference the style function named `myStyleFunc`.

```
<mx:AdvancedDataGrid dataProvider="{dp}"
    height="250"
    styleFunction="myStyleFunc">
    <mx:columns>
        <mx:AdvancedDataGridColumn dataField="cat"/>
        <mx:AdvancedDataGridColumn dataField="name"/>
        <mx:AdvancedDataGridColumn dataField="cost"/>
    </mx:columns>
</mx:AdvancedDataGrid>
```

Adding the style function to the AdvancedDataGrid tag itself causes the style function to be called for every row. For this reason you will add logic to the function so not all rows have the style applied.

3 In the style function, remove the `return` statement and add an empty `if-else` statement.

```
public function myStyleFunc(data:Object,col:AdvancedDataGridColumn):Object
{
   if()
   {

   }
   else
   {

   }
}
```

The `if-else` statement will be used to control which row will be styled.

4 For the condition of the `if-else` statement, check to see if the cost of the data in the current row is .99.

```
if(data["cost"]==.99)
```

Remember that the data parameter contains all the data of a particular row of the grid. So, the `if` statement is checking to see if the cost field for a particular row is .99.

5 If the condition is true, return the styling object {color:0xFF0000,fontWeight:"bold"}, and if the condition is false, return `null`.

```
public function myStyleFunc(data:Object,col:AdvancedDataGridColumn):Object
{
   if(data["cost"]==.99)
   {
      return {color:0xFF0000,fontWeight:"bold"}
   }
   else
   {
      return null;
   }
}
```

This is the completed style function.

6 Run the application and note the two rows with a cost of .99 are styled.

cat	name	cost
fruit	banana	0.99
bakery	bread	1.99
dairy	cheddar cheese	4.52
dairy	sour cream	0.33
fruit	orange	0.52
bakery	donut	0.33
dairy	yogurt	0.99
dairy	milk	2.99
fruit	apple	1.05
dairy	colby cheese	3.05

> **✱ NOTE:** The style function could be written more concisely, but it may not be as clear. You can take advantage of the fact that an if statement without braces({}) will only execute the next line of code. Also, once a function returns a value, it does not continue to execute any other code. Using this information, you could rewrite the function to appear as follows:

```
public function myStyleFunc(data:Object,col:AdvancedDataGridColumn):Object
{
    if(data["cost"]==.99)
        return {color:0xFF0000,fontWeight:"bold"};
    return null;
}
```

> Brevity is not always your goal when writing code, so use the approach that is clearest to you and your team.

7 Close the StyleRowADG.mxml file.

Styling cells

If you wish to style cells, you still use a style function. You move the property back to one of the AdvancedDataGridColumn tags and add logic to return a style only when certain criteria are met. For instance, you may wish to only style the cells that contain the value .99, not the whole row as was just shown.

1 Open the StyleCellADG.mxml file.

This contains the same code as the starting file used when styling a row.

2 Implement the same logic in the style function as you did in the last task.

```
public function myStyleFunc(data:Object,col:AdvancedDataGridColumn):Object
{
   if(data["cost"]==.99)
   {
      return {color:0xFF0000,fontWeight:"bold"}
   }
   else
   {
      return null;
   }
}
```

3 Add a `styleFunction` property to the `<mx:AdvancedDataGridColumn>` tag that displays the cost and references the `myStyleFunc` function.

```
<mx:AdvancedDataGridColumn dataField="cost" styleFunction="myStyleFunc"/>
```

This will apply the function only to this column of the grid.

4 Run the application and note only the cells containing .99 are styled.

cat	name	cost
fruit	banana	0.99
bakery	bread	1.99
dairy	cheddar cheese	4.52
dairy	sour cream	0.33
fruit	orange	0.52
bakery	donut	0.33
dairy	yogurt	0.99
dairy	milk	2.99
fruit	apple	1.05
dairy	colby cheese	3.05

5 Close the StyleCellADG.mxml file.

Grouping Data

Grouping data is an often requested feature of the DataGrid and is now implemented in the AdvancedDataGrid. The grouping feature allows you to select a data field and group data by that field in a Tree control-like manner. This feature lets you create what is sometimes called a

Tree DataGrid because the first column contains an expandable tree to determine which rows are visible in the grid, as shown here.

name	cost	qty
▼ 🗁 bakery		
🗋 donut	0.33	2
🗋 bread	1.99	3
▶ 🗀 dairy		
▼ 🗁 fruit		
🗋 banana	0.99	2
🗋 apple	1.05	4
🗋 orange	0.52	4

You have two approaches to implement this functionality, either through ActionScript or via tags nested in the AdvancedDataGrid tag itself. Both methods follow the same approach, which is manipulating the dataProvider of the AdvancedDataGrid.

Grouping data with tags

You will first implement grouping using tags.

1 Open the application GroupWithTagsADG.mxml and run it. Note that the category column has been removed, because this is the column you will be grouping on.

   Notice that all the data are displayed in nongrouped rows.

2 Remove the `dataProvider` property from the `<mx:AdvancedDataGrid>` tag, and insert an `<mx:dataProvider>` tag set just below the `<mx:AdvancedDataGrid>` tag.

```
<mx:AdvancedDataGrid
   height="200">
   <mx:dataProvider>

   </mx:dataProvider>
   <mx:columns>
      <mx:AdvancedDataGridColumn dataField="name"/>
      <mx:AdvancedDataGridColumn dataField="cost"/>
      <mx:AdvancedDataGridColumn dataField="qty"/>
   </mx:columns>
</mx:AdvancedDataGrid>
```

Grouping is implemented by manipulating the dataProvider of the grid.

3 In the dataProvider tag set, nest a GroupingCollection tag set, and specify an id property of myGroup. Bind the source property to the dp ArrayCollection.

```
<mx:dataProvider>
    <mx:GroupingCollection id="myGroup" source="{dp}">

    </mx:GroupingCollection>
</mx:dataProvider>
```

The GroupingCollection class permits you to group data. Its properties permit you to specify both the data to be grouped, as well as how it should be grouped and where it is displayed.

4 Nest an <mx:Grouping> tag set inside the GroupingCollection block. Inside the Grouping block, use the <mx:GroupingField> tag and set the name property to be **cat**, which specifies the field on which to group the data. The complete <mx:dataProvider> tag block should appear as shown here.

```
<mx:dataProvider>
    <mx:GroupingCollection id="myGroup" source="{dp}">
        <mx:Grouping>
            <mx:GroupingField name="cat"/>
        </mx:Grouping>
    </mx:GroupingCollection>
</mx:dataProvider>
```

The tag that actually specifies the field to group on is <mx:GroupingField>. The name property specifies the field on which to group.

5 Run the application.

Notice that no grouping has taken place. In fact, the grid is now not showing any data.

6 Add a creationComplete event to the AdvancedDataGrid and specify myGroup.refresh() to be executed.

```
<mx:AdvancedDataGrid creationComplete="myGroup.refresh()"
    height="200">
```

The refresh() method of the GroupingCollection class actually applies the grouping to the data.

7 Run the application again, and you will see the data grouped on the category field.

name	cost	qty
▶ 📁 bakery		
▼ 📁 dairy		
📄 yogurt	0.99	5
📄 sour crea	0.33	2
📄 milk	2.99	2
📄 colby che	3.05	4
📄 cheddar	4.52	6
▶ 📁 fruit		

8 Close the GroupWithTagsADG.mxml file.

Grouping data with ActionScript

Rather than add tags to the AdvancedDataGrid as you did in the last task, this exercise will now manipulate the dataProvider using ActionScript. The manipulation will take place in a function called initDG, whose skeleton is provided for you. You will later call the function from a creationComplete event on the AdvancedDataGrid.

1 Open the application GroupWithActionScriptADG.mxml and run it. Note that the category column has been removed, because this is the column you will be grouping on.

Notice that all the data is displayed in nongrouped rows.

2 In the script block, following the import of the ArrayCollection class, import the classes you used in the last task via tags: the GroupingField, Grouping, and GroupingCollection classes.

```
import mx.collections.ArrayCollection;
import mx.collections.GroupingField;
import mx.collections.Grouping;
import mx.collections.GroupingCollection;
```

You will be working with the same classes you did in the last exercise when you implemented grouping with tags, so you must import them. You could have also used the classes and Flex Builder would have made the appropriate imports automatically.

3 Inside the initDG function, whose skeleton was provided for you, create a new GroupingCollection object named myGroupColl.

```
var myGroupColl:GroupingCollection=new GroupingCollection();
```

The GroupingCollection class, and its supporting classes and properties, permits you to implement grouping.

4 Now assign the source property of the myGroupColl object the dataProvider of the AdvancedDataGrid, whose instance name is myADG.

```
myGroupColl.source=myADG.dataProvider;
```

Remember that grouping is basically implemented by manipulating the dataProvider of the grid, so this statement assigns the dataProvider of the AdvancedDataGrid to a property of the GroupingCollection so it can be manipulated.

5 Next, create a new Grouping object named **group**.

```
var group:Grouping=new Grouping();
```

The Grouping object will act as a holder for a GroupingField object that specifies the grouping specification.

6 Define the field on which to group by creating a new GroupingField object named **gf**. Pass as a parameter to the constructor the cat field.

```
var gf:GroupingField=new GroupingField("cat");
```

This GroupingField object specifies that the grouping will be implemented on the product category field.

7 Now assign the `fields` property of the Grouping object the GroupingField object using array notation.

```
group.fields=[gf];
```

The `fields` property of a Grouping object contains an array of GroupingField objects that specify the fields used to group the data. In this case, you designated the cat field as the grouping field, so this is what is assigned to the Grouping object's `fields` property.

8 To complete the creation of the grouping, assign the Grouping object, in this case group, to the GroupingCollection object's `grouping` property.

```
myGroupColl.grouping=group;
```

The creation of the grouping collection is complete, but the application will not run correctly without two more lines of code.

9 As the last two lines of the function, use the `refresh()` method to set the grouping on the GroupingCollection object, and then assign the GroupingCollection object back to the AdvancedDataGrid's dataProvider.

```
myGroupColl.refresh();
myADG.dataProvider=myGroupColl;
```

You must refresh the GroupCollection using the `refresh()` method, then assign the GroupingCollection object to the dataProvider of the AdvancedDataGrid before you will see any results in the application.

10 Be sure your `initDG` function appears as shown here.

```
private function initDG():void
{
    var myGroupColl:GroupingCollection=new GroupingCollection();
    myGroupColl.source=myADG.dataProvider;
    var group:Grouping=new Grouping();
    var gf:GroupingField=new GroupingField("cat");
    group.fields=[gf];
    myGroupColl.grouping=group;
    myGroupColl.refresh();
    myADG.dataProvider=myGroupColl;
}
```

You've built the function to implement grouping, but as of yet you have not called the function.

11 Add a `creationComplete` event to the `<mx:AdvancedDataGrid>` tag and call the `initDG` function.

```
<mx:AdvancedDataGrid id="myADG"
    dataProvider="{dp}"
    creationComplete="initDG()">
    <mx:columns>
        <mx:AdvancedDataGridColumn dataField="name"/>
        <mx:AdvancedDataGridColumn dataField="cost"/>
        <mx:AdvancedDataGridColumn dataField="qty"/>
    </mx:columns>
</mx:AdvancedDataGrid>
```

The function will now be called that manipulates the dataProvider to implement grouping.

12 Run the application and confirm that grouping on the product categories is working just as it did when implemented in the previous exercise with tags.

name	cost	qty
▼ 📂 bakery		
📄 donut	0.33	2
📄 bread	1.99	3
▶ 📁 dairy		
▶ 📁 fruit		

13 Close the GroupWithActionScriptADG.mxml file.

To review, here are the steps you just completed to group via ActionScript:

1. Create a GroupCollection object.

2. Assign the `source` property of the GroupCollection object the AdvancedDataGrid's dataProvider.

3. Create a new Grouping object.

4. Create a new GroupingField object that specifies the field on which to group.

5. Assign the `fields` property of the Group object an array of GroupingField objects.

6. Assign the `grouping` property of the GroupingCollection the Grouping object.

7. Refresh the GroupingCollection.

8. Assign the GroupingCollection to the dataProvider of the AdvancedDataGrid.

Displaying Summary Data

Often when displaying data in a table, you want to display summaries of that data. For instance, when displaying sales data by region, you may want to display summary data for each of the regions. This is now possible with the AdvancedDataGrid. Just as with the grouping of data, you can create summary data with tags or ActionScript. Because you can only display summary information for data represented by the GroupingCollection class, you will work with the code you finished in the previous tasks where grouping was correctly implemented.

The basic concept of summary data is shown in the following figure.

name	cost	qty
▼ 🗀 bakery		
donut	0.33	2
bread	1.99	3
Total number of items: 5		
▶ 🗀 dairy		
▶ 🗀 fruit		

Here the summary shows the number of bakery items purchased is 5.

Displaying summary data with tags

In this task, you will use the working grouping example and add summary data. You will implement summary information with tags, and in the next task, you will implement the same functionality using ActionScript.

1 Open the application SummaryWithTagsADG.mxml and run it. You see that grouping is functioning on the category field.

2 Add a fourth AdvancedDataGridColumn to display a field called **summary**, which you will create shortly.

```
<mx:AdvancedDataGridColumn dataField="summary"/>
```

This will add a column to contain the summary data. You will create the summary field using tags.

3 Change the GroupingField tag into a tag set with opening and closing tags.

```
<mx:GroupingField name="cat">

</mx:GroupingField>
```

The summary tags must be nested inside the GroupingField tag block.

4 Insert an <mx:summaries> tag set nested in the GroupingField block.

You create summary data about your groups by using the summaries property of the GroupingField class.

5 Insert an <mx:SummaryRow> tag set nested in the summaries block. Add to the opening SummaryRow tag a summaryPlacement property, set equal to last.

```
<mx:GroupingField name="cat">
<mx:summaries>
        <mx:SummaryRow summaryPlacement="last">

        </mx:SummaryRow>
    </mx:summaries>
</mx:GroupingField>
```

The summaryPlacement property specifies where the summary row appears in the AdvancedDataGrid control. Your options are:

- first: Create a summary row as the first row in the group.

name	cost	qty	summary
▼ 📁 bakery			
📄			5
📄 donut	0.33	2	
📄 bread	1.99	3	
▶ 📁 dairy			
▶ 📁 fruit			

- last: Create a summary row as the last row in the group.

name	cost	qty	summary
▼ 📁 bakery			
📄 donut	0.33	2	
📄 bread	1.99	3	
📄			5
▶ 📁 dairy			
▶ 📁 fruit			

- group: Add the summary data to the row corresponding to the group.

name	cost	qty	summary
▼ 🗁 bakery			5
🗋 donut	0.33	2	
🗋 bread	1.99	3	
▶ 🗀 dairy			19
▶ 🗀 fruit			10

 TIP: You can also specify multiple locations by using the property values separated by a space. For instance you could use the value `last group` to have the summary in two locations, as shown here.

name	cost	qty	summary
▼ 🗁 bakery			5
🗋 donut	0.33	2	
🗋 bread	1.99	3	
🗋			5
▶ 🗀 dairy			19
▶ 🗀 fruit			10

So, by specifying `last` as the option, the summary information will be displayed after all the products in a specific category.

6 In the SummaryRow block, nest an `<mx:fields>` tag pair. In that tag set, nest an `<mx:SummaryField>` tag. In the SummaryField tag, set the following three properties to the indicated values:

- dataField: qty

- operation: SUM

- label: summary

```
<mx:GroupingField name="cat">
    <mx:summaries>
      <mx:SummaryRow summaryPlacement="last">
        <mx:fields>
          <mx:SummaryField dataField="qty"
              operation="SUM"
              label="summary"/>
        </mx:fields>
      </mx:SummaryRow>
    </mx:summaries>
</mx:GroupingField>
```

The `fields` property of the SummaryRow class holds one or more SummaryField objects. The SummaryField objects define how the summary should be created. The `dataField` property defines on which data field the summary will be computed. The `operation` defines how the summary data should be computed. Valid values are:

- SUM
- MIN
- MAX
- AVG
- COUNT

> **TIP:** If those operations do not perform the calculation you need, you can use a `summaryFunction` property to specify a function to compute a custom data summary.

The `label` property associates the summary value to a property. In this case, the property name is `summary`, which corresponds to the fourth AdvancedDataGridColumn you added at the start of this exercise.

7 Check to be sure your AdvancedDataGrid appears as shown here.

```
<mx:AdvancedDataGrid creationComplete="myGroup.refresh()"
   height="200">
   <mx:dataProvider>
      <mx:GroupingCollection id="myGroup" source="{dp}">
         <mx:Grouping>
            <mx:GroupingField name="cat">
               <mx:summaries>
                  <mx:SummaryRow summaryPlacement="last">
                     <mx:fields>
                        <mx:SummaryField dataField="qty"
                                operation="SUM"
                                label="summary"/>
                     </mx:fields>
                  </mx:SummaryRow>
               </mx:summaries>
            </mx:GroupingField>
         </mx:Grouping>
      </mx:GroupingCollection>
   </mx:dataProvider>
   <mx:columns>
      <mx:AdvancedDataGridColumn dataField="name"/>
      <mx:AdvancedDataGridColumn dataField="cost"/>
      <mx:AdvancedDataGridColumn dataField="qty"/>
      <mx:AdvancedDataGridColumn dataField="summary"/>
   </mx:columns>
</mx:AdvancedDataGrid>
```

8 Run the application. You will see that summary is displaying as the last line of the category group. The sum of the quantities in that group is the summary information displayed.

name	cost	qty	summary
▼ 🗁 bakery			
🗋 donut	0.33	2	
🗋 bread	1.99	3	
🗋			5
▶ 🗁 dairy			
▶ 🗁 fruit			

9 Do not close the file at this time.

Changing the display using rendererProviders

You have displayed the summary information, but most likely not in the way in which you would choose. To display the data in a more readable format, you must use rendererProviders. Previously in this lesson, you used item renderers for the normal DataGrid and assigned them to individual columns. In the AdvancedDataGrid, you assign the renderers to the AdvancedDataGrid itself, and then specify where to use the renderers.

The first step is to build a simple renderer.

1 Right-click on the src directory, and create a new folder named renderers.

2 Right-click on the renderers folder and then select New > MXML Component. Enter **SummaryText** as the Filename and set the Based on component to be **Label**. Click Finish.

This creates the basis for the renderer you will create to display summary information.

3 Add a text property to the Label tag and enter `Total number of items: {data.summary}` for the property's value. The entire component should appear as follows.

```
<?xml version="1.0" encoding="utf-8"?>
<mx:Label xmlns:mx="http://www.adobe.com/2006/mxml"
    text="Total number of items: {data.summary}">
</mx:Label>
```

You access the summary information through the `data` property. Remember that the `data` property contains all the data for a particular row in the grid and is automatically passed to the component by Flex.

4 Return to the SummaryWithTagsADG.mxml file and just above the closing AdvancedDataGrid tag, insert an `<mx:rendererProviders>` tag set. In the rendererProviders tag block, insert an `<mx:AdvancedDataGridRendererProvider>` tag. In the AdvancedDataGridRenderProvider, set the following four properties to the values indicated.

```
dataField:    summary
columnIndex: 1
columnSpan:  2
renderer:     renderers.SummaryText
```

Your code should appear as shown here.

```
<mx:rendererProviders>
<mx:AdvancedDataGridRendererProvider
dataField="summary"
columnIndex="1"
columnSpan="2"
renderer="renderers.SummaryText"/>
</mx:rendererProviders>
```

In this case, the `rendererProviders` property contains only one definition of an AdvancedDataGridRenderProvider, but the property can contain one or more definitions. This particular renderer is tied to the `summary` field, and the `columnIndex` property will cause the renderer to be displayed in the first column, where columns are zero-indexed. The `columnSpan` property will cause the renderer to span two columns. The `renderer` property that indicates the component to use is in the renderers directory and is named SummaryText.

▶ **TIP:** When the `columnSpan` property is set to 0, the renderer spans all columns in the row.

✳ **NOTE:** You could have placed this block of code anywhere in the AdvancedDataGrid tag block as long as it wasn't nested in a tag set other than AdvancedDataGrid. For instance, the block of code could have also been placed just below the opening `<mx:AdvancedDataGrid>` tag or just above the `<mx:columns>` tag block.

5 Remove the column that displays the summary.

You no longer need this column because you specified where the renderer should be displayed. Leaving in this column would cause the summary data to be displayed by both the renderer and the column.

6 Run the application to see the renderer in action.

name	cost	qty
▶ 🗀 bakery		
▶ 🗀 dairy		
▼ 🗁 fruit		
🗋 banana	0.99	2
🗋 apple	1.05	4
🗋 orange	0.52	4
🗋	Total number of items: 10	

 TIP: If you do not like the document icon in front of each product, you can bind the default-LeafIcon to null to remove it.

```
<mx:AdvancedDataGrid creationComplete="myGroup.refresh()"
  defaultLeafIcon="{null}">
```

name	cost	qty
▶ 🗀 bakery		
▶ 🗀 dairy		
▼ 🗁 fruit		
banana	0.99	2
apple	1.05	4
orange	0.52	4
	Total number of items: 10	

7 Close the SummaryWithTagsADG.mxml file.

Displaying summary data with ActionScript

Just as you implemented grouping with both tags and ActionScript, you can implement summaries with both tags and ActionScript. Use as a starting file the code that implemented grouping with ActionScript, plus the AdvancedDataGridRenderProvider you just created.

1 Open the SummaryWithActionScriptADG.mxml application.

2 In the script block following the import of the ArrayCollection class and the grouping classes, import the SummaryField and SummaryRow classes you used in the last section via tags.

```
import mx.collections.ArrayCollection;
import mx.collections.GroupingField;
import mx.collections.Grouping;
import mx.collections.GroupingCollection;
import mx.collections.SummaryField;
import mx.collections.SummaryRow;
```

You could have also just used these classes, and Flex Builder would have imported them for you.

3 Inside the `initDG` function, locate where the GroupingCollection object, named myGroupColl, invokes the `refresh()` method. Create a few blank lines just above this code. This is where you must enter the code to create the summary information. In this location, create a SummaryRow instance named `sr` and a SummaryField instance named sf.

```
var sr:SummaryRow=new SummaryRow();
var sf:SummaryField=new SummaryField();
```

Both of these objects are needed, just as you needed them when implementing summaries with tags.

4 Now, assign the `sf` object the following three properties and associated values:

- `dataField`: qty
- `operation`: SUM
- `label`: summary

```
sf.dataField="qty";
sf.operation="SUM";
sf.label="summary";
```

These values are assigned for the same reasons mentioned when implementing summaries with tags.

5 Assign to the `fields` property of the SummaryRow object the SummaryField object, using array notation.

```
sr.fields=[sf];
```

The `fields` property of a SummaryRow object contains an array of SummaryField objects. These objects specify the fields used to compute summary information.

6 Set the `summaryPlacement` property of the SummaryRow object to the value `last`.

```
sr.summaryPlacement="last";
```

The values for the `summaryPlacement` property are the same as discussed when implementing summaries with tags.

7 As the last line of code needed to create a summary, assign the summaries property of the GroupingField object, in this case named gf, the SummaryRow object, using array notation.

```
gf.summaries=[sr];
```

The summaries property contains an array of SummaryRow instances that define the summaries to be created.

8 Check to be sure your initDG method appears as shown here, paying special attention to the code just added to implement summary information.

```
private function initDG():void
{
   var myGroupColl:GroupingCollection=new GroupingCollection();
   myGroupColl.source=myADG.dataProvider;
   var group:Grouping=new Grouping();
   var gf:GroupingField=new GroupingField("cat");
   group.fields=[gf];
   myGroupColl.grouping=group;

   var sr:SummaryRow=new SummaryRow();
   var sf:SummaryField=new SummaryField();
   sf.dataField="qty";
   sf.operation="SUM";
   sf.label="summary";
   sr.fields=[sf];
   sr.summaryPlacement="last";
   gf.summaries=[sr];

   myGroupColl.refresh();
   myADG.dataProvider=myGroupColl;
}
```

9 Run the application and you will see the summary information just as it appeared when using tags.

name	cost	qty
	Total number of items: 19	
▼ 📁 fruit		
📄 banana	0.99	2
📄 apple	1.05	4
📄 orange	0.52	4
	Total number of items: 10	

10 Close the SummaryWithActionScriptADG.mxml file.

What You Have Learned

In this lesson, you have:

- Displayed a dataset via a DataGrid (pages 281–282)

- Retrieve data from an HTTPService for the Dashboard application (pages 283–286)

- Defined the viewable columns of a DataGrid through DataGridColumn (pages 287–289)

- Created an MXML component to be used as an item renderer (pages 290–292)

- Created an inline custom item renderer for a DataGridColumn (pages 290–297)

- Displayed information from a DataGridColumn using a `labelFunction` and an item renderer (page 295)

- Learned how to raise events from inside an item renderer to the containing MXML file of the DataGrid using `outerDocument` (page 297)

- Learned how to create custom `set` and `get` functions on a class (pages 298–299)

- Sorted the AdvancedDataGrid in two different ways (pages 299–302)

- Applied custom styling to rows, columns, and cells of the AdvancedDataGrid (pages 302–306)

- Manipulated the dataProvider for an AdvancedDataGrid to group data in an AdvancedDataGrid (pages 306–312)

- Created summary information for data in an AdvancedDataGrid (pages 312–320)

What You Will Learn

In this lesson, you will:

- Learn the terminology associated with drag-and-drop operations in Flex
- Understand that the list-based components in Flex have enhanced drag-and-drop support built in
- Implement drag and drop on drag-enabled components
- Use various drag events
- Implement various methods of the DragSource and DragManager classes to implement drag and drop on nondrag-enabled components
- Use formats to allow dropping of drag proxy objects

Approximate Time

This lesson takes approximately 1 hour and 30 minutes to complete.

Lesson Files

Media Files:

None

Starting Files

Lesson12/start/EComm.mxml
Lesson12/start/as/ecomm.as
Lesson12/start/views/ecomm/GroceryDetail.mxml
Lesson12/dragDrop/start/src/Task1_DG_to_DG.mxml
Lesson12/dragDrop/start/src/Task2_DG_to_List.mxml
Lesson12/dragDrop/start/src/Task3_Label_to_List.mxml

Completed Files

Lesson12/complete/EComm.mxml
Lesson12/complete/as/ecomm.as
Lesson12/complete/views/ecomm/GroceryDetail.mxml
Lesson12/dragDrop/complete/src/Task1_DG_to_DG.mxml
Lesson12/dragDrop/complete/src/Task2_DG_to_List.mxml
Lesson12/dragDrop/complete/src/Task3_Label_to_List.mxml

LESSON 12

Using Drag and Drop

Drag and drop is a common user interface technique in desktop applications. Not so, however, in web applications until the idea and implementation of rich Internet applications (RIAs) came along. Flex and Flash Player permit you as a web developer to use drag and drop just as a desktop developer does.

Implementing drag and drop in a Flex application utilizes the Drag and Drop Manager and the tools it provides. The Drag and Drop Manager enables you to write a Flex application in which users can select an object, drag it over another, and drop it on the second object. All Flex components support drag-and-drop operations, and a subset has additional drag-and-drop functionality, in which implementation is little more than adding a single property.

In this lesson, you will implement drag and drop in your e-commerce application so a user can click on a product, drag it to the shopping cart, and drop it to add it to the shopping cart.

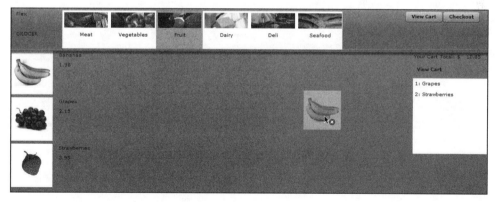

Dragging a grocery item to the shopping cart

Introducing the Drag and Drop Manager

The first step in understanding the Drag and Drop Manager is to learn the terminology surrounding it. The terminology is summarized in the following table.

Drag and Drop Manager Terminology	
Term	**Definition**
Drag initiator	Component or item from which a component is being dragged.
Drag source	Data being dragged.
Format	Property of the DragSource that allows an object to be dropped, or not, on another object. The data in the DragSource is also associated with the format. The data type of the formats are simple strings.
Drag proxy	Image displayed during the dragging process.
Drop target	Component the drag proxy is over.

The following figure gives you a visual representation of the terminology:

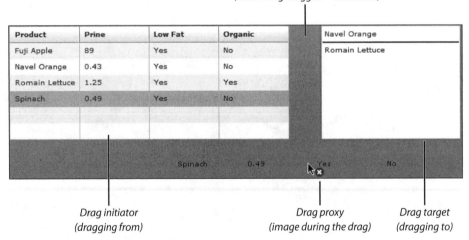

*Drag source
(data being dragged —nonvisual)*

*Drag initiator
(dragging from)*

*Drag proxy
(image during the drag)*

*Drag target
(dragging to)*

There are three phases to a drag-and-drop operation:

1. Initiating: A user clicks a Flex component or an item in a Flex component and then begins to move the component or item while holding down the mouse. The component or item is the drag initiator.

2. Dragging: While holding down the mouse button, the user moves the mouse around the screen. Flex displays an image called a drag proxy, and the associated nonvisual object called the drag source holds the data associated with the component or item being dragged.

3. Dropping: When the user moves the pointer over another component that will allow it, the item can be dropped onto a drop target. The data is then inserted into the new component in some way.

Flex components fall into two groups when it comes to drag-and-drop support: those with enhanced drag-and-drop functionality and those without. The following list-based controls have enhanced support for drag and drop:

- DataGrid
- PrintDataGrid
- Tree
- Menu
- List
- HorizontalList
- TileList

What this means to you as a developer is that your life will be a little bit easier when implementing drag and drop with those controls that have enhanced support. In fact, in many cases it might be no more than setting a single property value for each of the controls involved in the drag-and-drop operation.

Dragging and Dropping Between Two DataGrids

Your first foray into implementing drag-and-drop operations in Flex will be between two DataGrids. Because they are list-based components and have enhanced drag-and-drop support, this will require writing very little code on your part.

Two properties are important in this first phase: dragEnabled and dropEnabled. Here are their descriptions:

- dragEnabled: Assigned a Boolean value to specify whether the control is allowed to act as a drag initiator (defaults to false). When true, the user can drag items from the component.

- dropEnabled: Assigned a Boolean value to specify whether the control is allowed to act as a drop target (defaults to false). When true, the user can drop items onto the control using the default drop behavior.

Stated most simply, you set the dragEnabled property in the component from which you are dragging to true, and set the dropEnabled property in the component on which you are dropping to true.

So now you will put your drag-and-drop knowledge to use by implementing drag and drop from one DataGrid to another DataGrid.

1 Choose File > New > Flex Project. Set the Project name to be **DragDrop**.

2 Set the Project location to be flex3tfs/Lesson12/dragDrop/start.

3 For the Application type, select Web application.

4 Set the Server technology to None, then click Next.

5 Leave the Output folder as bin-debug, then click Next.

6 Leave the Main source folder as src.

7 Click the Browse button next to the Main application file option, and select the file Task1_DG_to_DG.mxml. Click OK and then click Finish.

You are creating a new project because some of the work in this lesson will not be directly involved with any of the three applications you are working on from the FlexGrocer site.

8 Examine the code in the Task1_DG_to_DG.mxml file, and then run it.

Note that the existing code does not use any concepts you have not already learned in this book. The file uses an HTTPService remote procedure call (RPC) to retrieve grocery info. The file then uses a result handler to place the data into an ArrayCollection, which is then used as a dataProvider in a DataGrid. When you run the application, you see you have a DataGrid populated with grocery product information and another DataGrid below it. Try to drag and drop between the DataGrids; you will see that this functionality is not yet working.

9 In the first DataGrid, set the dragEnabled property to true. Run the application; you can click one of the rows in the DataGrid and drag the drag proxy around the screen.

Setting this property did two obvious things: it enabled dragging and created the drag proxy, the image attached to the pointer when dragging. Another nonvisual event occurred at the same time: a DragSource object was created to hold the data. The data is associated with a format named items, as the following figure from the debugger shows:

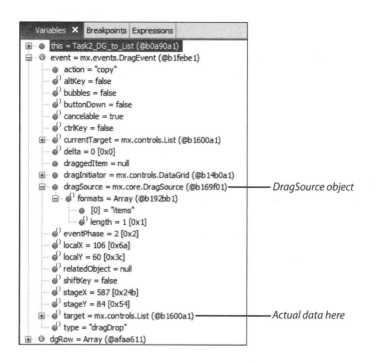

DragSource object

Actual data here

10 In the `<mx:Script>` block below the existing variable declaration, create a bindable private variable named `targetGridDP` of data type ArrayCollection and set it equal to a new ArrayCollection. Then bind this variable as the `dataProvider` of the second DataGrid, whose `id` is `targetGrid`.

These two steps initialize the `dataProvider` of the drop target DataGrid. This means it tells the control what the data type is of the data it will be dealing with. If you do not do this, you will get runtime errors.

11 In the second DataGrid, set the `dropEnabled` property to `true`. Your second DataGrid should appear as follows:

```
<mx:DataGrid id="targetGrid"
   dataProvider="{targetGridDP}"
   dropEnabled="true">
   <mx:columns>
      <mx:DataGridColumn dataField="name"
         headerText="Product"/>
      <mx:DataGridColumn dataField="category"
         headerText="Category"/>
   </mx:columns>
</mx:DataGrid>
```

You've done three basic steps so far to drag-and-drop enable the application:

- Added the dragEnabled property to the drag initiator
- Initialized the drop target's dataProvider
- Added the dropEnabled property to the drop target

Now you're ready to test.

12 Run the application and drag from the first DataGrid and drop onto the second.

Notice that the entire set of data for the row is dragged, not just the visible properties in the DataGrid. The category column is not displayed in the first DataGrid, but when dropped, that column is displayed in the second DataGrid. This shows you that all the data for the row is in the DragSource, not just the rows that happen to be displayed.

Product	Price	Low Fat	Organic
Fuji Apple	89	Yes	No
Navel Orange	0.43	Yes	No
Romain Lettuce	1.25	Yes	Yes
Spinach	0.49	Yes	No

Product	Category
Navel Orange	Fruit
Spinach	Vegetables
Fuji Apple	89	Yes	No

Dragging and Dropping Between a DataGrid and a List

In the previous exercise when describing the dropEnabled property the following sentence was used, "When true, the user can drop items onto the control using the default drop behavior." So what is this "default drop behavior"? Basically it means that Flex will try to figure out what should be dropped and do what it thinks is best, but that might not be what you want. In the last exercise it was clear to Flex that when dragging from one DataGrid to another, the columns in the drop target DataGrid should be filled with like-named properties from the DragSource data.

In this task you will drag from a DataGrid to a List component. In this case the "default drop behavior" won't know what data to drop into the List component and will dump the whole object into the List, which is not what you want.

You will use a drag event to get the data that you want into the List component. Here is a summary of the events for both the drag initiator and the drop target:

Drag Initiator Events	
Drag Events	**Description**
mouseDown and mouseMove (MouseEvent class)	Although not drag events, these MouseEvent class events are used to start the drag-and-drop process when not using dragEnabled components. The mouseDown event is broadcast when the user selects a control with the mouse and holds down the mouse button. The mouseMove event is broadcast when the mouse moves.
dragComplete event (DragEvent class)	Broadcast when a drag operation completes, either when the drag data drops onto a drop target or when the drag-and-drop operation ends without performing a drop operation.

Drag Target Events	
Drag Events (all events of the DragEvent class)	**Description**
dragEnter	Broadcast when a drag proxy moves over the target from outside the target.
dragOver	Broadcast while the user moves the pointer over the target, after the dragEnter event.
dragDrop	Broadcast when the mouse is released over the target.
dragExit	Broadcast when the user drags outside the drop target, but does not drop the data onto the target.

Now it is time to get to work.

1 Examine the code in the Task2_DG_to_List.mxml file, and then run it. Drag from the DataGrid to the List; you will see [object Object] appear in the List.

   The default drop behavior did not know what data you wanted placed in the List, so it dropped the whole data object in. Because the List cannot display the entire object, it lets you know what has happened by displaying [object Object]. The following figure shows the default behavior when dragging from DataGrid to the List.

Product	Prine	Low Fat	Organic	[object Object]
Fuji Apple	89	Yes	No	
Navel Orange	0.43	Yes	No	
Romain Lettuce	1.25	Yes	Yes	
Spinach	0.49	Yes	No	

2 Add a dragDrop event listener to the List, and call a function named doDragDrop() in the ActionScript executed when the event is broadcast. Pass the event object as a parameter to the function.

```
<mx:List id="targetList"
    width="200"
    dropEnabled="true"
    dataProvider="{targetListDP}"
    dragDrop="doDragDrop(event)"/>
```

The event is named dragDrop, and you have no control over that. The function name doDragDrop() is a good choice for the function name, but it can be named whatever you choose.

3 At the bottom of the <mx:Script> block, create a private function named doDragDrop() data typed as void. The function should accept a parameter named event data typed as DragEvent. Also import the class mx.events.DragEvent.

This function will be called when the user drops the drag proxy onto the List, which is the drop target in this application. Later in this task, you will write code in this function to display just the name of the product in the List.

4 As the first line of code in the function, create a variable local to the function named dgRow data typed as Object and set equal to a new Object.

```
var dgRow:Object=new Object();
```

This variable will be used to store information about the row dragged from the DataGrid and stored in the DataSource object.

5 As the second line of code in the function, set the dgRow variable equal to the data in the DragSource object associated with the items format. Use the dataForFormat() method.

```
dgRow=event.dragSource.dataForFormat("items");
```

The dataForFormat() method is a method of the DragSource class. It retrieves from the DragSource object the data associated with the particular format—in this case, items.

✱ **NOTE:** Remember that the format name associated with data in a DataGrid is always items.

6 Set a breakpoint at the closing brace of the doDragDrop() function. You do this by double-clicking in the marker bar just to the left of the line numbers in the editor. You will see a small blue dot appear to indicate the breakpoint was set.

The breakpoint will cause Flex Builder to halt execution at the marked line of code, and you will be able to check values of variables. You will learn more about the debugger in Lesson 25, "Debugging Flex Applications."

7 Debug the application and drag a row to the List. When you drop the drag proxy, the process flow will return to Flex Builder, and then you should view the Debugging perspective. Examine the dgRow variable value in the Variables view. You should then see that the variable contains all the data from that DataGrid row.

The following figure shows the row of data being dragged.

Notice that the variable contains an array of length 1, which means you have only 1 index, which is 0. Also note that the name property contains the name of the product.

▶ **TIP:** If you want to allow the user to drag multiple rows of data, set the DataGrid multipleSelection property equal to true.

8 Terminate the debugging session by clicking the red box in either the Debug or Console views. Return to the Development perspective by clicking the chevron (>>) in the upper-right corner of Flex Builder and selecting that perspective.

Normally, the Development perspective is best to work in because you can see so much more of your code.

9 As the third line of code in the function, add the name of the product to the List by using the addItem() method of the List's dataProvider. Remember that the dgRow variable contained an array of length 1, so use dgRow[0].name to reference the name.

```
targetList.dataProvider.addItem(dgRow[0].name);
```

This is a case in which viewing how the data is stored using the debugger is very helpful in retrieving the information.

10 Run the application and drag from the DataGrid to the List. You should see the product being placed in the List, but [object Object] also appears.

The event continued to do what it was supposed to do, even though you displayed some different data; hence, you still see the reference to the object.

Product	Prine	Low Fat	Organic		[object Object]
Fuji Apple	89	Yes	No		Fuji Apple
Navel Orange	0.43	Yes	No		
Romain Lettuce	1.25	Yes	Yes		
Spinach	0.49	Yes	No		

11 As the last line in the function, use the event class's preventDefault() method to cancel the event default behavior.

```
event.preventDefault();
```

In this case, you can cancel the default behavior. Not all events can be canceled; you must check the documentation for definitive answers on an event-by-event basis. By canceling this event, you prevent the display of [object Object] in the List.

12 Run the application. When you drag from DataGrid to List, only the name of the product appears in the List.

This wraps up our second task in this lesson on drag and drop.

Using a Nondrag-Enabled Component in a Drag-and-Drop Operation

So far, you have been taking advantage of enhanced functionality in list-based components when it concerns drag and drop. Now it is time to learn how to implement drag and drop on nonenhanced components. In this particular task, the use case is very simple: you want to drag a Label control to a List. Because the Label does not have enhanced drag-and-drop functionality, there is more of a burden on you as the developer in implementation.

Understanding what the list-based components did for you is a good place to start when having to write all the implementation yourself. Here is a list of mechanisms, hidden from you when using the list-based components, that you will need to use when implementing drag and drop without the help of the enhanced components:

- Assign the data to the DragSource object.
- Check to see whether the formats allow dropping onto the drop target.
- Use the data in the drop target (although in the second exercise you did some of this manually).
- Permit the component to be dragged.
- Actually accept the drop.

Although you have been using the DragSource class up to now in this lesson, you will need to dig deeper into the class when implementing all the functionality yourself. In this exercise, you use the following methods of the DragSource class:

DragSource Class Methods	
Method	**Description**
addData(data:*,format:String):void	Adds data to the associated format in the DragSource object; the * denotes the data can be of any data type.
hasFormat(format:String):Boolean	Returns true if the DataSource object contains a matching format of the drop target; otherwise, it returns false.
dataForFormat(format:String):Array of *	Retrieves the data for the specified format added by the addData() method; returns an Array of objects containing the data in the requested format; a single item is returned in a one-item Array.

These methods allow you to implement the first three hidden mechanisms. To implement the last two, you need to use methods of the DragManager class:

DragManager Class Methods	
Method	**Description**
doDrag(initiator:Component, ↪ dragSource:DragSource, ↪ mouseEvent:MouseEvent):void	Enables the initiator component to be initially dragged; often in an event handler for mouseDown or mouseMove.
acceptDragDrop(target:Component):void	Call this method in your dragEnter handler; often used in an if statement where the condition uses the hasFormat() method.

> ▶ **TIP:** The doDrag() method has a number of optional parameters to control the look of the drag proxy. You can find these parameters in the Class documentation for DragManager in the Adobe Flex 3 Language Reference.

Now you're ready to start writing code for this exercise.

1 Examine the code in the Task3_Label_to_List.mxml file, and then run it.

You see you have a Label with the text "Drag me" in it and an empty List below it. At this point, there is no drag-and-drop functionality.

2 Import the four classes shown here that you need in the application:

```
import mx.core.DragSource;
import mx.managers.DragManager;
import mx.events.DragEvent;
import mx.core.IUIComponent;
```

You could have also just used these classes as data types, and Flex Builder would have imported them for you automatically.

3 In the Label, add a mouseDown event and have the event call a function named dragIt(). The function call should pass four parameters; the first is the drag initiator, which in this case is the instance name of the Label: myLabel. The second parameter is the data you will later place in the DragSource object. In this case, just pass a string of "My data here". The third parameter is the event, which of course is just event. The last parameter is the format that will be associated with this data. In this task, use myFormat.

```
mouseDown="dragIt(myLabel,'My data here',event,'myFormat')"
```

This is the function that will be called to initiate the drag-and-drop operation. You need to pass the parameters because they are all needed in the function to allow:

- Dragging to start

- Placing the data in the DragSource object associated with the format

4 At the bottom of the <mx:Script> block, create a private function named dragIt(), data typed as void. The function should accept four parameters that, of course, correspond to the data passed to the function. Use the names and data types shown here:

```
initiator:Label
dsData:String
event:MouseEvent
format:String
```

Of these parameters, the initiator could be any kind of component, and the dsData could be nearly any kind of data you want to be dragged from one component to another. The event will often be the mouseDown MouseEvent or the mouseMove event, but that would not change either the event parameter name nor the data type used here. The format will always be a string.

5 As the first line of code in the function, create a variable local to the function named ds data typed as DragSource and set it equal to a new DragSource object.

```
var ds:DragSource=new DragSource();
```

This creates the DragSource object that will have data added to it.

6 Next in the function, use the addData() method of the ds DragSource object to add the data passed in the dsData parameter to the ds object. Associate it with the format passed in the format parameter.

```
ds.addData(dsData,format);
```

An important point here is that you can store data associated with multiple formats, which means you can use multiple addData() methods on the same DragSource object.

You might want to do this if you have multiple drop targets and want to drop different data in each drop target. The different drop targets would use different arguments in the dataForFormat() method to get the appropriate data.

7 As the last line of code in the function, permit the Label to be dragged by calling the static doDrag() method of the DragManager class. You pass it the three parameters initiator, ds, and event. Check to make sure your completed function appears as shown here:

```
private function dragIt(initiator:Label,dsData:String,event:MouseEvent,
    ➥ format:String):void{
    var ds:DragSource=new DragSource();
    ds.addData(dsData,format);
    DragManager.doDrag(initiator,ds,event);
}
```

Remember that a static method is one you can invoke directly from the class without first instantiating it.

8 Run the application and drag the Label. At this point there is no drop target that will accept the Label.

You now move on to coding the List to accept the drop of the Label and to display the data passed in the DragSource in the List.

9 In the List, add a dragEnter event and have it call a function named doDragEnter(). The function should pass two parameters. The first is the event, and the second is the format—which in this case should match the format used earlier: myFormat.

```
dragEnter="doDragEnter(event,'myFormat')"
```

You are passing data to the function that allows the initiator, the Label, to be dropped on the drop target, the List.

10 At the bottom of the <mx:Script> block, create a private function named doDragEnter(), data typed as void. The function should accept two parameters. Name the first parameter event, data typed as DragEvent, and the second parameter format, data typed as String.

Both these parameter values are needed to allow the dropping of the initiator.

11 Insert into the function an if statement that checks to see whether the formats of the two objects match. Use the hasFormat() method of the dragSource object, which is contained in the event object. The argument of the hasFormat() method should be the format parameter passed to the function.

```
if(event.dragSource.hasFormat(format)){
}
```

What is occurring is that the List is looking in the DragSource object and seeing whether a format exists that matches one of the formats it is allowed to accept. The hasFormat() function will return either true or false.

12 If the hasFormat() function returns true, use the DragManager's static function of acceptDragDrop() method to allow the dropping. The argument of the function should be the List itself, which is best referred to in this case as event.target.

```
DragManager.acceptDragDrop(event.target);
```

You could have actually replaced event.target with the instance name of the List, myList, and the function would have had the same result. The advantage of using the more generic event.target is that it makes this function more reusable. You can use the function for any dragEnter result handler—it will work correctly.

13 The acceptDragDrop() method is defined to accept an object of type IUIComponent. For this reason you need to cast event.target as an IUIComponent to satisfy the compiler.

The IUIComponent class defines the basic set of APIs that must be implemented to be a child of a Flex container or list.

14 Be sure that the new function appears as follows, and then run the application.

```
private function doDragEnter(event:DragEvent,format:String):void{
   if(event.dragSource.hasFormat(format)){
      DragManager.acceptDragDrop(IUIComponent(event.target));
   }
}
```

You should now be able to drag the Label. When it moves over the List, the red X disappears, and you can drop the drag proxy. At this point, nothing happens when you do the drop.

15 In the List, add a dragDrop event and have it call a function named doDragDrop(). The function should pass two parameters, the event and the format, which in this case should match the format used earlier: myFormat.

```
dragDrop="doDragDrop(event,myFormat')"
```

You are passing the data needed to have the data retrieved from the DragSource and have it displayed in the List.

16 At the bottom of the <mx:Script> block, create a private function named doDragDrop(), data typed as void. The function should accept two parameters. Name the first parameter event, data typed as DragEvent, and the second parameter format, data typed as String.

You need the event object in this function because it contains the DragSource object, and that is where the data is stored. Remember that you stored the String "My data here" in the DragSource object in steps 3–6 of this task. The format is needed because that is how you pull data from the DragSource object using the dataForFormat() method.

17 As the first line of code in the new function, create a variable local to the function named myLabelData, data typed as Object, and set it equal to a new Object.

```
var myLabelData:Object=new Object();
```

This is a temporary variable to hold the data when it is extracted from the DragSource object.

18 Use the dataForFormat() function to retrieve the data from the dragSource property of the event object. The argument of the function should be the format parameter passed to the function.

```
myLabelData=event.dragSource.dataForFormat(format);
```

Remember that you can store data associated with multiple formats, so you must specify which format's data to retrieve when retrieving data.

19 Display the data just retrieved in the List. You need to use the addItem() method on the List's dataProvider property to do this.

```
myList.dataProvider.addItem(myLabelData);
```

You have achieved your goal of moving the Label's data into the List.

20 Be sure that the new function appears as follows, and then run the application.

```
private function doDragDrop(event:DragEvent,format:String):void{
   var myLabelData:Object=new Object();
   myLabelData=event.dragSource.dataForFormat(format);
   myList.dataProvider.addItem(myLabelData);
}
```

Now when you drag and drop the Label onto the List, you will see that the data from the Label, the String "My data here", is displayed in the List. The following figure shows the List after successfully dropping the Label data.

Now that you have a solid background in drag and drop, you will implement drag-and-drop functionality in the e-commerce application of FlexGrocer.

Dragging a Grocery Item to the Shopping Cart

The culmination of your work in this lesson is to implement dragging a grocery item into the shopping cart, which you will do now. The exercises you have performed so far in this lesson have prepared you well for this final exercise; in fact, some of the code you have already written will be copied and pasted for use in this exercise.

In these steps, you will enable the user to click the grocery item, drag it to the small shopping cart, and then drop it in. The grocery item is displayed in a Canvas container, and the shopping cart is a List. Because the Canvas is not a drag-and-drop-enhanced component, you will have to pattern your code here after what you just wrote in the section, "Using a Nondrag-Enabled Component in a Drag-and-Drop Operation."

1 Open the file src/views/ecomm/GroceryDetail.mxml.

This is the component in which the grocery data is displayed; so this is where you will have to permit the data to be dragged.

➲ **TIP:** At first, you will drag all the data to the shopping cart and then write the code so that just the image of the item acts as the drag proxy.

2 In the `<mx:Canvas>` that is the root tag of the component, add a `mouseMove` event and have the event call a function named `dragIt()`. The function call should pass four parameters. The first is the drag initiator, which in this case is the component itself, which you reference as `this`. The second parameter is the data you will later place in the DragSource object. In this case, it is the instance of the Product class named `groceryItem`. The third parameter is the event, which is named `event`. The last parameter is the format that will be associated with this data. In this task, use `cartFormat`.

```
mouseMove="dragIt(this,groceryItem,event;cartFormat')"
```

By placing the mouseMove event on the root container tag of the component, it will enable the user to start the drag process by clicking any information about the grocery item.

3 Open the file Task3_Label_to_List.mxml and copy the dragIt() function from the <mx:Script> block of that file to the bottom of the <mx:Script> block of GroceryDetail. mxml. Change the data type of the first parameter, initiator, from Label to Canvas. Change the data type of the second parameter, dsData, from String to Product.

```
private function dragIt(
    ➥ initiator:Canvas,dsData:Product,event:MouseEvent,format:String):void{
    var ds:DragSource=new DragSource();
    ds.addData(dsData,format);
    DragManager.doDrag(initiator,ds,event);
}
```

The way in which you built this function in the previous section enabled you to bring it into this task almost unchanged. Because the initiator is a Canvas instead of a Label, and because the data you passed to it is an instance of a Product instead of a String, you had to change those data types and nothing else.

Recall that this function has two main purposes: to get data into the object being dragged and to permit the component to be dragged. The first line of code creates a new DragSource object; then the second line places the Product object passed to the function into the DragSource object and associates it with the format passed to the function. The third line of code actually enables the Canvas that contains the grocery item information to be dragged.

4 At the top of the <mx:Script> block, import the mx.managers.DragManager and mx.core.DragSource classes.

These classes are used in the function you just copied into the file.

5 Run the EComm.mxml application. You should be able to drag the grocery item data.

You see the drag proxy is the outline of the Canvas, or a big rectangular box. Later in this task, you will change the drag proxy to the image of the grocery item.

At this point there is no drop target, so you cannot drop the data anywhere.

6 Open the file EComm.mxml.

This file contains the List that is your shopping cart to which grocery items are dragged.

7 Locate the List with the id of cartView and add a dragEnter event to the List. In the ActionScript the event executes, call a doDragEnter() function and pass it two parameters: event and the String cartFormat.

```
dragEnter="doDragEnter(event;cartFormat')"
```

You pass the information to this function that will permit the drag initiator to be dropped on the List.

8 Open the file src/as/ecomm.as.

Remember that this file is actually what would be in the <mx:Script> block in EComm.mxml, but it was pulled out and placed in an external file.

9 From the file Task3_Label_to_List.mxml, copy the doDragEnter() function from the <mx:Script> block and paste it to the bottom of the ecomm.as file.

```
private function doDragEnter(event:DragEvent,format:String):void{
    if(event.dragSource.hasFormat(format)){
        DragManager.acceptDragDrop(IUIComponent(event.target));
    }
}
```

Because you wrote the function generically using only the parameters passed to the function, no changes need to be made in this function.

This function has only one purpose: to check whether formats enable the drag initiator to be dropped. The if statement determines whether there are matching formats; then the acceptDragDrop() method allows the actual dropping to take place.

10 At the top of the file, import the mx.managers.DragManager, mx.events.DragEvent and mx.core.IUIComponent classes.

These classes are used in the function you just copied into the file.

11 Run the EComm.mxml application. You should be able to drag the grocery item data; when you drag the pointer over the shopping cart List, you should see the red X disappear and you can drop the drag proxy.

At this point, nothing happens when you drop the drag proxy.

12 In EComm.mxml, locate the List with the id of cartView and add a dragDrop event to the List. In the ActionScript, the event calls a doDragDrop() function and passes it two parameters: event and the String cartFormat.

```
dragDrop="doDragDrop(event;cartFormat')"
```

You pass the information to this function, which will place data in the shopping cart.

13 In the file Task3_Label_to_List.mxml, copy the doDragDrop() function from the
<mx:Script> block of that file to the bottom of the ecomm.as file. Remove the code
in the body of the function so you are left with just the skeleton of the function.

```
private function doDragDrop(event:DragEvent,format:String):void{

}
```

In this case, the code in the function will completely change. You previously placed a
String in a Label; now you will be adding a ShoppingCartItem to a shopping cart, so none
of the existing code is applicable except the signature of the function.

▶ TIP: Open the file valueObjects/ShoppingCartItem.as and review that the constructor's
parameters are a Product object and an optional quantity.

14 As the first line of code in the function, create a variable local to the function named
prodObj, data typed as Product. Use the static buildProduct() method of the Product class
to set prodObj equal to a new Product object. The argument of the buildProduct() method
should be the object in the DragSource. Retrieve it using the dataForFormat() method.

```
var prodObj:Product=Product.buildProduct(
 ➥ event.dragSource.dataForFormat(format));
```

This Product object is needed to create a ShoppingCartItem in the next step of the task.

15 Next in the function, create a variable local to the function named sci, data typed as
ShoppingCartItem. Set that variable equal to a new ShoppingCartItem. The argument of
the ShoppingCartItem constructor should be the Product object created in the last step.

```
var sci:ShoppingCartItem = new ShoppingCartItem(prodObj);
```

Here is a quick review of how the Product object got in the DragSource:

- In steps 2 and 3 of this task, you passed a Product object to the dragIt() function.

- The function placed the Product object into the DragSource object using the addData()
  method and associated it with the cartFormat format.

- In this function, you retrieved that same Product object and will now place it in the
  shopping cart.

16 As the last line of code in the function, invoke the addItem() method of the cart ShoppingCart object and pass the sci ShoppingCartItem variable as a parameter. Check to be sure your function appears as shown here.

```
private function doDragDrop(event:DragEvent,format:String):void{
   var prodObj:Product=
      ➡ Product.buildProduct(event.dragSource.dataForFormat(format));
   var sci:ShoppingCartItem = new ShoppingCartItem(prodObj);
   cart.addItem(sci);
}
```

The method invocation actually places the ShoppingCartItem object in the shopping cart.

17 Run the application. You can now drag and drop grocery items into the shopping cart.

You see that the drag-and-drop operation is working, but the drag proxy is the whole container that surrounds the grocery item data. In the next step you add code so the drag proxy becomes just the image of the grocery item.

18 Return to GroceryDetail.mxml and locate the dragIt() function in the <mx:Script> block. At the top of the function create a new Image object local to the function named imageProxy. Use the load() method of the Image class to assign the current imageName in the groceryItem to the Image object. You can find the correct path for the image in the existing <mx:Image> tag currently displaying the grocery item. Finally, set both the height and width of the new Image object to 80.

```
var imageProxy:Image=new Image();
imageProxy.load("../assets/"+groceryItem.imageName);
imageProxy.height=80;
imageProxy.width=80;
```

The reason you must create a new Image object is because by default the drag-and-drop operation removes the drag proxy from its source. You could have simply given the image being displayed an instance name and used it as the drag proxy, but after dragging and dropping the image would no longer be shown with the other grocery item data. Also, the width and height are 0 by default when you create a new Image object in Action-Script, so you must set those property values for the image to be visible.

19 In the DragManager.doDrag() method invocation, add a fourth parameter of imageProxy.DragManager.doDrag(initiator,ds,event,imageProxy);

This fourth parameter represents the dragImage. Instead of the outline of the container of the grocery item data being the drag proxy, you have now specified that only the image of the item should be displayed when dragging is taking place.

20 Check to be sure that your dragIt() function appears as follows, and then run the application. You should be able to drag the image of the grocery item and drop it in the cart.

```
private function dragIt(initiator:Canvas,dsData:Product,event:MouseEvent,format:
String):void{
    var imageProxy:Image=new Image();
    imageProxy.load("assets/"+groceryItem.imageName);
    imageProxy.height=80;
    imageProxy.width=80;
    var ds:DragSource=new DragSource();
    ds.addData(dsData,format);
    DragManager.doDrag(initiator,ds,event,imageProxy);
}
```

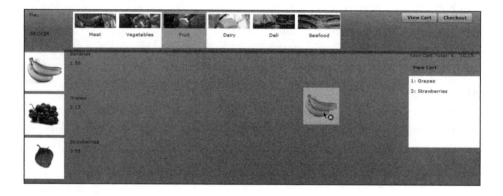

This completes the last exercise of the lesson.

What You Have Learned

In this lesson, you have:

- Implemented drag-and-drop operations between two drag-enabled components and used the default drop process (pages 324–328)

- Implemented drag-and-drop operations between two drag-enabled components and customized the drop process to use the data stored in the DragSource object (pages 328–332)

- Implemented drag-and-drop operations between nondrag-enabled components (pages 333–339)

- Implemented drag-and-drop operations between nondrag-enabled components and used a custom dragImage (pages 339–344)

What You Will Learn

In this lesson, you will:

- Use the ViewStack class as the basis for implementing navigation
- Use the ViewStack `selectedIndex` and `selectedChild` properties for navigation
- Use built-in tools to govern a ViewStack and normal Button controls
- Use the TabNavigator to place two different kinds of application functionality on different tabs
- Use and manipulate a Date control and the Date class

Approximate Time

This lesson takes approximately 1 hour and 30 minutes to complete.

Lesson Files

Media Files:

Lesson13/assets/CCInfo.mxml
Lesson13/assets/HomePage.mxml

Starting Files:

Lesson13/start/DataEntry.mxml
Lesson13/start/EComm.mxml
Lesson13/start/as/ecomm.as

Completed Files:

Lesson13/complete/DataEntry.mxml
Lesson13/complete/EComm.mxml
Lesson13/complete/as/ecomm.as
Lesson13/complete/events/ObjectDataEvent.as
Lesson13/complete/valueObjects/OrderInfo.as
Lesson13/complete/views/ecomm/BillingInfo.mxml
Lesson13/complete/views/ecomm/CCInfo.mxml
Lesson13/complete/views/ecomm/Checkout.mxml
Lesson13/complete/views/ecomm/HomePage.mxml
Lesson13/complete/views/ecomm/OrderConf.mxml

LESSON 13

Implementing Navigation

Imperative to any application is a navigation system. The user should be able to easily move around in an application and locate needed functionality. In technical terms, Flex implements navigation by using a special set of containers, called navigator containers, that control user movement through a group of child containers (for example, VBox, HBox, Canvas, and even other navigator containers).

Some navigation will be completely at the user's discretion, such as clicking a button to move to the home page or the checkout process. Other navigation can be tightly controlled by the developer—for example, a checkout process in which users cannot proceed to the next screen until certain conditions are met on an existing screen. In this lesson, you will implement both types of navigation.

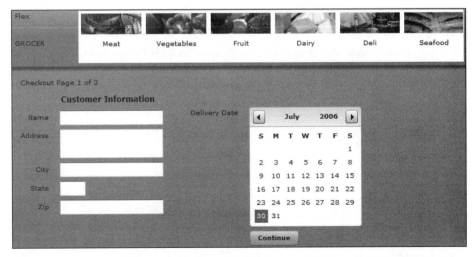

The checkout process will be controlled by a ViewStack, one of Flex's navigator containers.

Introducing Navigation

Navigation enables users to move through your application and (just as important) enables you to control user movement through the application. For an example of letting the user choose where to move in an application, you will add navigation to the data-entry application so the user can choose between adding a product and updating or deleting a product. Right now, functionality for both processes share the same crowded screen. There are also times when you want to control the user's movement through an application. You will do this in this lesson when implementing a checkout process to the e-commerce application. During this process, you need to control which screens users see and when they see them. Both approaches are easily implemented using Flex's navigator containers.

Navigator containers control user movement through the application by controlling which containers are displayed. You've used many containers so far (for example, Canvas, VBox, HBox, and Form); they enable you to add functionality to move among them. Here is a list of Flex's navigator components displayed in the Components panel:

At the heart of navigation in Flex is the ViewStack class, which is a Flex container component. The ViewStack is a collection of other containers, or children, that are stacked on top of each other so only one is visible at a time. Functionality must be added to control which child is visible at any one time. The ViewStack can have only other containers as children, including other navigator containers. If you use a non-container as a child of a ViewStack, a runtime error is produced. The following is a valid ViewStack because it contains only containers:

```
<mx:ViewStack id="myNav" height="100%" width="100%">
    <mx:HBox id="child0" label="Child 0">
        <mx:Label text="Zeroth child label 1" fontSize="40"/>
        <mx:Label text="Zeroth child label 2" fontSize="40"/>
    </mx:HBox>
    <mx:VBox id="child1" label="Child 1">
        <mx:Label text="First child label 1" fontSize="40"/>
        <mx:Label text="First child label 2" fontSize="40"/>
    </mx:VBox>
</mx:ViewStack>
```

The following generates a runtime error because the ViewStack contains a Label component, which is not a container:

```
<mx:ViewStack id="myNav" height="100%" width="100%">
    <mx:Label text="This will not work here"/>
    <mx:HBox id="child0" label="Child 0">
        <mx:Label text="Zeroth child label 1" fontSize="40"/>
        <mx:Label text="Zeroth child label 2" fontSize="40"/>
    </mx:HBox>
    <mx:VBox id="child1" label="Child 1">
        <mx:Label text="First child label 1" fontSize="40"/>
        <mx:Label text="First child label 2" fontSize="40"/>
    </mx:VBox>
</mx:ViewStack>
```

Although the ViewStack is the key element to implementing navigation in Flex, it does not intrinsically have a way to switch which child is visible; that must be done using another tool. You can use built-in tools to control the ViewStack or build your own.

An example of a built-in component to control the ViewStack is the LinkBar. If you set the dataProvider of the LinkBar to be the ViewStack, a link will appear for each child. Displayed on the link will be the label of the child container. For instance, code using a ViewStack and LinkBar is shown as follows, followed by its result when run. In the result, the middle link displaying the VBox container has been clicked.

```
<mx:LinkBar dataProvider="{myNav}" fontSize="30"/>
<mx:ViewStack id="myNav" height="100%" width="100%">
    <mx:HBox id="child0" label="Child 0">
        <mx:Label text="Zeroth child label 1" fontSize="20"/>
        <mx:Label text="Zeroth child label 2" fontSize="20"/>
    </mx:HBox>
    <mx:VBox id="child1" label="Child 1">
        <mx:Label text="First child label 1" fontSize="20"/>
        <mx:Label text="First child label 2" fontSize="20"/>
    </mx:VBox>
    <mx:HBox id="child2" label="Child 2">
        <mx:Label text="Second child label 1" fontSize="20"/>
        <mx:Label text="Second child label 2" fontSize="20"/>
    </mx:HBox>
</mx:ViewStack>
```

The following figure is of a ViewStack being used with a LinkBar (with the middle link selected).

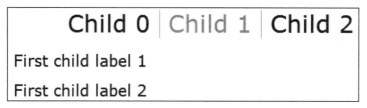

You might want to control navigation by implementing your own process, such as by using buttons. If you do this, two properties of the ViewStack are very important: selectedIndex and selectedChild. You use the selectedIndex to choose which child of the ViewStack should be displayed.

★ **NOTE:** The ViewStack is zero indexed, so the "first" child is numerated 0.

Use the selectedChild property if you would rather indicate which child of the ViewStack should be displayed by a logical name rather than numeric index. The selectedChild property will display the appropriate container in the ViewStack based on the instance name provided in the id property. The following example shows how to use plain Button components to control which child of the ViewStack is displayed using both the selectedChild and selectedIndex:

```
<mx:HBox>
   <mx:Button label="Child 0" click="myNav.selectedIndex=0"/>
   <mx:Button label="Child 1" click="myNav.selectedChild=child1"/>
   <mx:Button label="Child 2" click="myNav.selectedIndex=2"/>
</mx:HBox>
<mx:ViewStack id="myNav" height="100%" width="100%">
   <mx:HBox id="child0">
      <mx:Label text="Zeroth child label 1" fontSize="20"/>
      <mx:Label text="Zeroth child label 2" fontSize="20"/>
   </mx:HBox>
   <mx:VBox id="child1">
      <mx:Label text="First child label 1" fontSize="20"/>
      <mx:Label text="First child label 2" fontSize="20"/>
   </mx:VBox>
   <mx:HBox id="child2">
      <mx:Label text="Second child label 1" fontSize="20"/>
      <mx:Label text="Second child label 2" fontSize="20"/>
   </mx:HBox>
</mx:ViewStack>
```

This would create a result as shown here when run (with the middle button clicked). The following figure is of a ViewStack being used with buttons:

With this brief overview of the navigator containers, you are now ready to implement navigation in your applications.

Using a TabNavigator in the DataEntry Application

The ViewStack class has no built-in mechanism to control which child container is displayed or made active. A number of tools are supplied by Flex to control this—one of them is the TabNavigator. This class, which extends the ViewStack, builds tabs for each child container and uses the label property of the container to determine what should be displayed on each tab. When you click a tab, the content in the corresponding container will be displayed or made active. You simply replace the `<mx:ViewStack>` tags with `<mx:TabNavigator>` tags to use this navigator container, as shown here:

```
<mx:TabNavigator id="myNav" height="200" width="450">
   <mx:HBox label="Child 0">
      <mx:Label text="Zeroth child label 1" fontSize="20"/>
      <mx:Label text="Zeroth child label 2" fontSize="20"/>
   </mx:HBox>
   <mx:VBox label="Child 1">
      <mx:Label text="First child label 1" fontSize="20"/>
      <mx:Label text="First child label 2" fontSize="20"/>
   </mx:VBox>
   <mx:HBox label="Child 2">
      <mx:Label text="Second child label 1" fontSize="20"/>
      <mx:Label text="Second child label 2" fontSize="20"/>
   </mx:HBox>
</mx:TabNavigator>
```

This code generates the following when run (with the last tab clicked):

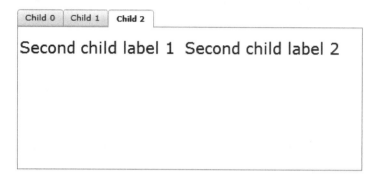

You will now use a TabNavigator component to place the two pieces of functionality in the DataEntry application, namely updating, deleting, and adding products, onto different tabs.

1 Open DataEntry.mxml.

In this file you instantiate two custom components: one to update and delete products and one to add products. Remember that UpdateDeleteProd.mxml is a subclass of the HBox class, and that AddProduct.mxml is a subclass of the VBox class. This is important because to use the TabNavigator with these custom components, they must be containers.

2 Locate the instantiation of the two custom components near the bottom of the file.

```
<v:UpdateDeleteProd units="{units}"
   foodColl="{foodColl}"
   productUpdate="showPopUp(event.product,'Product Updated')"
   productDelete="showPopUp(event.product,'Product Deleted')"/>

<v:AddProduct
   cats="{categories}"
   units="{units}"
   productAdded="showPopUp(event.product,'Product Added')"/>
```

The two implementations of functionality currently appear on the same page.

3 Surround both component instantiations with an <mx:TabNavigator> tag set. Set the width to 700 and the height to 600.

```
<mx:TabNavigator width="700" height="600">
   <v:UpdateDeleteProd units="{units}"
      foodColl="{foodColl}"
      productUpdate="showPopUp(event.product,'Product Updated')"
      productDelete="showPopUp(event.product,'Product Deleted')"/>
```

```
<v:AddProduct
    cats="{categories}"
    units="{units}"
    productAdded="showPopUp(event.product;Product Added')"/>
</mx:TabNavigator>
```

4 Run DataEntry.mxml.

You now see two tabs of the TabNavigator appear; you can click each tab to see the application functionality separated. Also note that because no `label` properties are set on the custom components, the tabs have no text on them.

5 Add a `label` property to the UpdateDeleteProd custom component with a value of Update/Delete Product. Add a `label` property to the AddProd custom component with a value of Add Product. Run the DataEntry.mxml application again; the label text is now displayed on the tabs.

Adding a Home Page and Checkout Page in the E-Commerce Application

Up to this point, the only functionality available in the e-commerce application was selecting products and adding them to the shopping cart, which is all implemented by using states. You will now add a home page and a checkout process. You will build a ViewStack and use Button components to navigate between the home page, product selection, and checkout screens.

1 Copy the file HomePage.mxml from Lesson13/assets to your flexGrocer/src/views/ ecomm folder.

Feel free to open this file to see that it contains no code that you haven't already worked with.

2 Open EComm.mxml and locate near the bottom of the file the HBox with the id of bodyBox.

You will add two more containers to this HBox in a ViewStack.

3 Just above the bodyBox HBox, instantiate the new HomePage.mxml component. Give it an id of homePage.

```
<v:HomePage id="homePage"/>
```

Because this will be the first child in the ViewStack, it will be the page displayed by default.

4 Create a new MXML component in the views/ecomm folder named Checkout.mxml and use a VBox as the base tag. Remove any width and height values.

This is the page that will control the checkout process.

5 In the component, use a Label to display the text "In the checkout component".

This is just temporary to test the navigation. Later in this lesson you will complete the checkout process.

6 In EComm.mxml (just below the closing tag for the bodyBox HBox and just above the instantiation of the CategorizedProductManager), instantiate the new Checkout.mxml component. Give it an id of checkout. Also set the width and height to 100%.

```
<v:Checkout id="checkout" width="100%" height="100%"/>
```

Later in this lesson this component will turn out to be a controller for the checkout process.

7 Run EComm.mxml and select a grocery category. You should see the home page, products, and text from the checkout component all stacked up on each other.

This mess will soon be cured with navigation.

8 Surround the HomePage, bodyBox HBox, and Checkout containers with an <mx:ViewStack> tag block, and give the ViewStack an id of ecommNav. Set the width and height to 100%. Run EComm.mxml; only the home page is displayed now.

```
<mx:ViewStack id="ecommNav"
  width="100%" height="100%" >
  <v:HomePage id="homePage"/>
  <mx:HBox x="0" y="0" width="100%" height="100%" id="bodyBox">
    <v:FoodList id="prodTile"
      width="100%" height="100%"
      prodByCategory="{prodByCategory}"
      itemAdded="addToCart(event.product)"/>
    <mx:VBox height="100%" id="cartBox">
      <mx:HBox>
        <mx:Label text="Your Cart Total: $"/>
        <mx:Label text="{cart.total}"/>
      </mx:HBox>
      <mx:LinkButton label="View Cart" click="this.currentState='cartView'"
        id="linkbutton1"/>
      <mx:List id="cartView"
        dataProvider="{cart.aItems}"
        width="100%"
        dragEnter="doDragEnter(event,'cartFormat')"
        dragDrop="doDragDrop(event,'cartFormat')"/>
    </mx:VBox>
  </mx:HBox>
  <v:Checkout id="checkout" width="100%" height="100%"/>
</mx:ViewStack>
```

9 Move the <mx:Label> tag that contains the FlexGrocer copyright information from directly above the newly added ViewStack to just below it and above the CategorizedProductManager.

As was demonstrated in step 7, Flex allows child tags and containers to occupy the same x- and y-coordinates on the page. Each child occupies a different depth (their place on the z-axis) initially determined by the order they are declared in MXML. Previous to this step, the <mx:Label> tag was placed on the screen, and was followed by the <mx:ViewStack>. Because they were not occupying the same x- and y-coordinates, they never formed the mess in step 7; however, as you continue to develop the application, there will be times when these two will occupy the same space. By moving the declaration for the <mx:Label> tag below the <mx:ViewStack>, we are ensuring that the label will be at a higher depth and always seen.

10 Add a click event to both Labels in the ApplicationControlBar to display the home page. Use the id, the selectedChild property of the TabNavigator, and the id of the HomePage component to accomplish this.

```
<mx:Label x="0" y="0" text="Flex"
   click="ecommNav.selectedChild=homePage"/>
<mx:Label x="0" y="41" text="GROCER"
   click="ecommNav.selectedChild=homePage"/>
```

This follows the convention that is used in many web applications of clicking the site name at the top of the page to return to the home page.

11 Add a click event to the Checkout button in the ApplicationControlBar to display the Checkout custom component when this button is clicked.

```
<mx:Button label="Checkout"
   id="btnCheckout"
   right="10" y="0"
   click="ecommNav.selectedChild=checkout"/>
```

This will make the Checkout component the active child of the ViewStack.

12 Add a click event to the View Cart button in the ApplicationControlBar. Have the event call a function named showCart().

```
<mx:Button label="View Cart"
   id="btnViewCart"
   right="90" y="0"
   click="showCart()"/>
```

You will follow the best practice of creating a function and calling it when you have multiple lines of code for an event handler.

13 Open ecomm.as. At the bottom of the file, insert a private function named showCart(), data typed as void, with the code needed to control the view state and navigation.

```
private function showCart():void{
   ecommNav.selectedChild=bodyBox;
   this.currentState='cartView';
}
```

Remember that you could have used the selectedIndex property instead of placing IDs on the containers and using the selectedChild property.

✱ **NOTE:** The selectedChild property has at least two advantages over selectedIndex. First, it is probably more intuitive for you to display the child of the ViewStack by name rather than number. Second, if you ever add a container anywhere except as the last child into the ViewStack, you do not have to renumber references to the children.

If you were to save and run the application now, you would see that this seems to work properly; however, a bug has now been introduced. If you run the application, and click the View Cart button, you will see a runtime error. This is happening because ViewStack natively uses a concept called *deferred instantiation*.

By default, the first container in a ViewStack is displayed and the others are hidden, so you will now see just the home page. Flex normally creates visual elements as they are needed. The home page would be created immediately; however, bodyBox and Checkout would be created only when the ViewStack changes the visible child.

The showCart method is now trying to change the visible child of the ViewStack to the bodyBox, and trying to change the state of the application to cartView. The problem lies in that the cartView state references children of bodyBox (prodTile, cartBox, cartView, and so on), and those children are not yet created. One solution to the problem would be to set creationPolicy="all" on the ViewStack. Although this would work, it is an extremely bad practice. Setting creationPolicy="all" turns off the deferred instantiation of the ViewStack, and tells Flash Player to create all the children at start-up, removing the efficiency gains of deferred instantiation. A better solution, which is just as easy to implement, is to disable the View Cart button until a product is added to the cart.

14 In EComm.mxml, set enabled="false" on the btnViewCart button.

```
<mx:Button label="View Cart"
id="btnViewCart"
right="90" y="0"
click="showCart()"
enabled="false"/>
```

This disables the View Cart button at start-up. Next, you will enable the button when an item is added to the cart.

15 In ecomm.as, add the line btnViewCart.enabled=true; to the addToCart() method.

```
btnViewCart.enabled=true;
```

This enables the View Cart button as soon as any product has been added to the cart. This will prevent any errors related to the deferred instantiation from the ViewStack.

16 In EComm.mxml, add a `click` event to the instantiation of the CategoryView component to call a function named `showProducts()`.

```
<v:CategoryView id="catView"
   width="600"
   left="100"
   cats="{categories}"
   categorySelect="displayProdByCategory(event)"
   click="showProducts()"/>
```

This ensures that when the user clicks the categories HorizontalList, the products are displayed.

17 Open ecomm.as and at the bottom of the file insert a private function named `showProducts()`, data typed as `void`, with the code needed to control the view state and navigation.

```
private function showProducts():void{
   ecommNav.selectedChild=bodyBox;
   currentState='';
}
```

This function ensures that the products are displayed when a user clicks a product category in the ApplicationToolbar.

18 Run EComm.mxml and navigate around the application to be sure that you are seeing the correct child of the ViewStack displayed as you click each button.

Creating the First Step of the Checkout Process Displayed by a ViewStack

After users have all the groceries they want in their shopping cart, they need to check out. You just implemented the mechanism to get to a checkout page, and in this exercise you will create a ViewStack that controls the steps the user will follow to check out.

The basic process is as follows:

- The user clicks a button to proceed to the checkout page (already done in the last exercise).

- The user fills in a form that supplies basic billing and shipping information such as name, address, and so on.

- The user clicks a button on the basic billing information page and is then taken to a credit card information form.

- The user fills in a form supplying credit card information.

- The user clicks a button to purchase the groceries and is then taken to an order confirmation page.

> ✷ **NOTE:** A button will exist on the order confirmation page to print the order confirmation. This functionality will be implemented in a later lesson.

1 Create a value object by right-clicking the valueObjects folder and selecting New > ActionScript Class. The name of the class should be **OrderInfo**. Click Finish.

This class will hold all the information about the order, including billing information about the user.

2 In the class, create the following public properties, using the data types shown. Make the entire class bindable.

- billingName:String
- billingAddress:String
- billingCity:String
- billingState:String
- billingZip:String

- cardType:String
- cardNumber:Number
- cardExpirationMonth:Number
- cardExpirationYear:Number
- deliveryDate:Date

You will later add a property to the shopping cart that holds the grocery items purchased.

> ✷ **NOTE:** The Date class is used here. The class hierarchy of the Date class is very simple; it has only the Object class as a parent. The Date class has many properties that hold date and time information, and many methods to get and set those properties. In this lesson, the key properties will be date, month, and fullYear.

3 Check to be sure that your complete class appears as follows:

```
package valueObjects{
    [Bindable]
    public class OrderInfo{
        public var billingName:String;
        public var billingAddress:String;
        public var billingCity:String;
        public var billingState:String;
        public var billingZip:String;
        public var cardType:String;
        public var cardNumber:Number;
        public var cardExpirationMonth:Number;
        public var cardExpirationYear:Number;
        public var deliveryDate:Date;
    }
}
```

This class looks very different from other classes you built earlier because this class has no constructor. In actuality, it does have a constructor, because ActionScript will automatically create a constructor for you if one is not written.

There is a reason to build the class this way. Because the property values will be gathered from different components, it is easy to instantiate an OrderInfo object. Whenever values are gathered from the user, you can simply assign them by using dot notation. If you wrote a constructor that needed all ten parameters at one time, it would be more difficult to populate the object in this particular case.

4 Open Checkout.mxml from the src/views/ecomm folder and remove the Label inserted in the last exercise.

The Label was used only temporarily to be sure the ViewStack implemented in the last exercise was working.

5 Insert an `<mx:ViewStack>` tag block with an `id` of `checkoutNav` and the `width` and `height` set to 100%.

You will have three components instantiated in this ViewStack that correspond to the steps of (1) gathering user information, (2) gathering credit card information, and (3) displaying a confirmation page.

6 Create a new MXML component in the views/ecomm folder named BillingInfo and use an HBox as the base tag. Remove the width and height values.

This is the form to gather user information such as name, address, and so on.

7 Add the following to gather user information:

```
<mx:VBox>
  <mx:Form>
    <mx:Label text="Checkout Page 1 of 3"/>
    <mx:FormHeading label="Customer Information"/>
    <mx:FormItem label="Name">
      <mx:TextInput id="billingName"/>
    </mx:FormItem>
    <mx:FormItem label="Address">
      <mx:TextArea id="billingAddress" width="160"/>
    </mx:FormItem>
    <mx:FormItem label="City">
      <mx:TextInput id="billingCity"/>
    </mx:FormItem>
    <mx:FormItem label="State">
      <mx:TextInput id="billingState" maxChars="2"/>
    </mx:FormItem>
```

```
        <mx:FormItem label="Zip">
            <mx:TextInput id="billingZip"/>
        </mx:FormItem>
    </mx:Form>
</mx:VBox>
<mx:VBox>
    <mx:Spacer height="40"/>
    <mx:Form>
        <mx:FormItem label="Delivery Date">
            <mx:DateChooser id="deliveryDate"/>
        </mx:FormItem>
        <mx:FormItem>
            <mx:Button label="Continue"/>
        </mx:FormItem>
    </mx:Form>
</mx:VBox>
```

The DateChooser control is used here for the first time in the book. It presents a calendar to the user, who can then choose a month, day and year. The DateChooser selectedDate property then holds the date value selected. The data type of the selectedDate is Date, a class discussed earlier in this lesson.

> **TIP:** Flex has another date selection control called DateField. This control has what appears to the user to be an empty TextInput box with a calendar icon beside it. The user can click the icon, and a calendar appears for date selection. After the selection, the date appears in the TextInput box.

8 Create the following Model just below the opening <mx:HBox> tag to group the form information into a single data structure:

```
<mx:Model id="checkoutInfo">
    <custInfo>
        <billingName>{billingName.text}</billingName>
        <billingAddress>{billingAddress.text}</billingAddress>
        <billingCity>{billingCity.text}</billingCity>
        <billingState>{billingState.text}</billingState>
        <billingZip>{billingZip.text}</billingZip>
        <deliveryDate>{deliveryDate.selectedDate}</deliveryDate>
    </custInfo>
</mx:Model>
```

As you have done before, you gather the form information into a Model. You will pass the Model information back to the checkout page later in this exercise.

9 Above the Model, use an `<mx:Metadata>` tag to create a custom event named billingInfoReturn of type ObjectDataEvent, which you will write in a following step.

```
<mx:Metadata>
   [Event(name="billingInfoReturn",type="events.ObjectDataEvent")]
</mx:Metadata>
```

What you will do in this component is gather the user information in the form, place that data in an object, and then dispatch a custom event containing that data. Here you create the name of the custom event.

10 Insert an `<mx:Script>` block under the `<mx:Metadata>` tag block and import the events. ObjectDataEvent custom event class.

```
import events.ObjectDataEvent;
```

You will build this class in the next step.

11 Right-click the events folder and select New > ActionScript class. Give it the name **ObjectDataEvent** and set the superclass to **flash.events.Event**. The custom class will have only one property, an Object named data, which will be passed into the custom event object as the second parameter of the constructor. Inside the constructor, pass the type to the superclass and set the data property with the passed-in object. Override the clone method to use your new constructor, and your class should appear as follows:

```
package events {
   import flash.events.Event;
   public class ObjectDataEvent extends Event{
      public var data:Object;
      public function ObjectDataEvent(type:String,data:Object){
         super(type);
         this.data = data;
      }
      override public function clone():Event {
         return new ObjectDataEvent(type, data);
      }
   }
}
```

This is a generic custom event class. You can use it whenever you want to use a custom event to pass a generic Object in the custom event object.

12 Back in BillingInfo.mxml, add a click event to the Continue button at the bottom of the form and call a function named process().

This function will eventually dispatch the custom event, along with the event object that contains the form data.

13 At the bottom of the `<mx:Script>` block, create the skeleton for a private function named process(), and data type the function itself as void. In the function, create a variable local to the function named o, data typed as ObjectDataEvent, and set it equal to a new ObjectDataEvent.

```
var o:ObjectDataEvent=new ObjectDataEvent();
```

You are building the custom event object that will be dispatched and handled in the Checkout component. You still have to add the event name and data to the object.

14 As parameters in the new ObjectDataEvent, pass the name of the custom component, the string `billingInfoReturn`, and the data to be returned, which is stored in the `checkOutInfo` Model.

```
var o:ObjectDataEvent=new ObjectDataEvent("billingInfoReturn", checkoutInfo);
```

The correct object is now created and ready for dispatching.

15 As the second—and last—line of code in the function, dispatch the ObjectDataEvent object just built. Verify that your function appears as follows:

```
private function process():void{
   var o:ObjectDataEvent=new ObjectDataEvent("billingInfoReturn", checkoutInfo);
   dispatchEvent(o);
}
```

This completes the BillingInfo component. You will now move back to the Checkout component and instantiate the new BillingInfo component. You will also handle the custom event and use the data sent back in the event object.

16 Return to Checkout.mxml. Add an XML namespace to the `<mx:VBox>` tag so you can use components in the views/ecomm folder. Use the letter v as the prefix.

```
xmlns:v="views.ecomm.*"
```

This permits you to use the BillingInfo component you just created.

17 In the `<mx:ViewStack>` block, instantiate the BillingInfo component. Give it an instance name of `billingInfo`, and set the width and height to 100%.

```
<v:BillingInfo id="billingInfo"
   width="100%" height="100%"/>
```

This is the first of three containers that will be in this ViewStack.

18 Handle the custom `billingInfoReturn` event in the component. In the ActionScript for the event, call a function named `doBillingInfoReturn()`. Pass the event object as a parameter.

```
billingInfoReturn="doBillingInfoReturn(event)"
```

If you happen to save at this point you will get an error because the custom event class is not yet imported.

19 Insert an `<mx:Script>` block and import the classes valueObjects.OrderInfo and events.ObjectDataEvent. Also create a public variable named `orderInfo`, data typed as OrderInfo, and set equal to a new OrderInfo object.

```
import valueObjects.OrderInfo;
import events.ObjectDataEvent;
[Bindable]
public var orderInfo:OrderInfo=new OrderInfo();
```

The whole point of the checkout process is to build an OrderInfo object to be sent to the back end for processing, so obviously you need that class and an instance of that class to place data in. An event object instance of the class ObjectDataEvent is passed to the function, so you need this class for data typing.

20 At the bottom of the `<mx:Script>` block, create a private function named `doBillingInfoReturn()` and data type the function as `void`. The function should accept a parameter named event data typed as ObjectDataEvent. In the function, assign the six properties passed in the custom event object to the orderInfo object instance, using the same property names.

```
private function doBillingInfoReturn(event:ObjectDataEvent):void{
    orderInfo.billingName=event.data.billingName;
    orderInfo.billingAddress=event.data.billingAddress;
    orderInfo.billingCity=event.data.billingCity;
    orderInfo.billingState=event.data.billingState;
    orderInfo.billingZip=event.data.billingZip;
    orderInfo.deliveryDate=event.data.deliveryDate;
}
```

▶ **TIP:** A great way to validate the data coming from the component is to use the debugger. For instance, before you added the six lines of code to assign property values, you could have marked a breakpoint in the empty function and then debugged the application. After you submitted the form, you would have seen in the Variables pane the data passed in correctly, as well as the exact object path to get to the data.

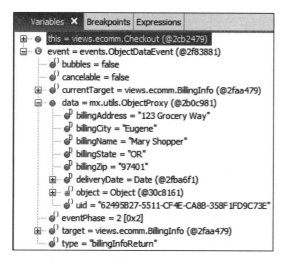

The data passed in the event object is stored in the *data* property because that is how it is named in the custom event class.

This concludes this exercise, and you now have the personal information from the user in the OrderInfo object. Next, you will use a component to get credit card information.

Completing the Checkout Process Using the ViewStack

In this exercise, your goal is to get credit card information into the OrderInfo object in the Checkout component and then display this information in a confirmation screen. In this case, you will use a component that is already built, because it is identical in logic to the BillingInfo component you just built. In the exercise, you will open the CCInfo component and examine its logic to see the similarities. You will then instantiate the component and manipulate the ViewStack to get the CCInfo component to appear. Finally, you will take all the order information and display it on an order confirmation screen.

1 Copy the file CCInfo.mxml from Lesson13/assets to your flexGrocer/src/views/ecomm folder. Open the file and examine the code.

As you look at the code, you will see that the logic is the same as in the BillingInfo component you just built. Note that the custom event name is ccInfoReturn. You will need this name to use the component correctly. Also note the property names of the data gathered in the Model:

- cardType
- cardNumber
- cardExpirationMonth
- cardExpirationYear

2 Open Checkout.mxml. In the <mx:ViewStack> block, under the BillingInfo component, instantiate the CCInfo component. Give it an instance name of ccInfo, and set the width and height to 100%.

This is the second of three containers that will be in the ViewStack.

3 Handle the custom ccInfoReturn event in the component. In the ActionScript for the event, call a function named doCCInfoReturn(). Pass the event object as a parameter, which must be data typed as ObjectDataEvent. Also handle the back custom event. In the ActionScript for the event, set the selectedChild of the checkoutNav ViewStack to billingInfo. Be sure that your instantiation appears as follows:

```
<v:CCInfo id="ccInfo"
    width="100%" height="100%"
    ccInfoReturn="doCCInfoReturn(event)"
    back="checkoutNav.selectedChild=billingInfo"/>
```

Review the CCInfo custom component to confirm what these two custom events do.

4 At the bottom of the <mx:Script> block, create a private function named doCCInfoReturn() and data type the function as void. The function should accept a parameter named event data typed as ObjectDataEvent. In the function, assign the four properties passed in the custom event object to the orderInfo object instance, using the same property names.

```
private function doCCInfoReturn(event:ObjectDataEvent):void{
    orderInfo.cardType=event.data.cardType;
    orderInfo.cardNumber=event.data.cardNumber;
    orderInfo.cardExpirationMonth=event.data.cardExpirationMonth;
    orderInfo.cardExpirationYear=event.data.cardExpirationYear;
}
```

At this point, your OrderInfo object should contain all the billing and credit card information collected from the user in the two custom components.

5 As the last line of code in the doBillingInfoReturn() function, make the CCInfo component be displayed in the ViewStack.

```
checkoutNav.selectedChild=ccInfo;
```

Until you add this code, there was no way to get to the CCInfo component. What happens now is when the user clicks the button in the billing information screen, the event is dispatched, the data is written into the OrderInfo object, and then the CCInfo component is displayed.

6 Run EComm.mxml. Click the Checkout button and fill in the billing information form. Click the Continue button and you will be shown the credit card information form. Fill in this form and click the Continue button. At this point, nothing happens. The Back button will take you back to the Customer Information screen.

You now have the customer information and credit card information in the single OrderInfo object.

> **TIP:** Use the debugger to confirm that all the data is in the orderInfo object. To do this, set a breakpoint at the end of the doCCInfoReturn() function and run EComm.mxml. Upon return to the Flex Builder debugger, add orderInfo as a Watched Expression in the Expressions pane.

7 Create a new MXML component in the views/ecomm folder named OrderConf, use a VBox as the base tag, and remove any width and height values.

This component will display the order information.

8 Insert an <mx:Script> block and import the OrderInfo value object. Also, create a bindable public variable named orderInfo data typed as OrderInfo.

```
import valueObjects.OrderInfo;
[Bindable]
public var orderInfo:OrderInfo;
```

This creates a property in the class. Order information will be passed to this property when the component is instantiated in the Checkout.mxml page.

9 Below the <mx:Script> block, insert the following form to display the order information to the user.

```
<mx:Form>
<mx:Label text="Checkout Page 3 of 3"/>
   <mx:FormHeading label="Billing Information"/>
   <mx:HBox>
     <mx:VBox>
       <mx:FormItem >
         <mx:Label text="{orderInfo.billingName}"/>
       </mx:FormItem>
       <mx:FormItem >
         <mx:Label text="{orderInfo.billingAddress}"/>
       </mx:FormItem>
```

code continues on next page

```
        <mx:FormItem >
           <mx:Label text="{orderInfo.billingCity}"/>
        </mx:FormItem>
        <mx:FormItem >
           <mx:Label text="{orderInfo.billingState}"/>
        </mx:FormItem>
        <mx:FormItem >
           <mx:Label text="{orderInfo.billingZip}"/>
        </mx:FormItem>
     </mx:VBox>
     <mx:VBox>
        <mx:FormItem label="Delivery Date">
           <mx:Label text="{orderInfo.deliveryDate.month+1}/
              {orderInfo.deliveryDate.date}/{orderInfo.deliveryDate.fullYear}"/>
        </mx:FormItem>
     </mx:VBox>
  </mx:HBox>
</mx:Form>
```

Note that you are displaying three properties of the Date class in the Delivery Date section. Because the month count is zero indexed (where 0 represents January,) you must add 1 to make the month value meaningful.

10 Below the form, insert the following buttons: Label and Spacer.

```
<mx:Button label="Complete Order"/>
<mx:Label text="* Clicking this button will bill your credit card and complete
this order"/>
<mx:Spacer height="20"/>
<mx:Button label="Edit Information" click="back()"/>
```

Functionality for the Complete Order button will be implemented in a later lesson. The event handler for the Edit Information button will be implemented in the next step.

11 Add an <mx:Metadata> block just under the opening <mx:VBox> tag and add a custom event named back.

```
<mx:Metadata>
   [Event(name="back")]
</mx:Metadata>
```

In this case, you do not have to supply the type, because the default type for an event is the Event class.

12 At the bottom of the `<mx:Script>` block, create a private function named back, data typed as void. Create an object named o, data typed as Event, and set it equal to a new event object, passing as a parameter the string "back". Dispatch the o object in the second line of the function.

```
private function back():void{
   var o:Event=new Event("back");
   dispatchEvent(o);
}
```

In this case, because you are *not* dispatching data in the custom event object, you did not need to create a custom event class.

13 Return to Checkout.mxml. At the bottom of the ViewStack, instantiate the newly created OrderConf component, and set the width and height to 100%. Set the orderInfo property equal to a binding of the like named variable from the Checkout component. Finally, handle the back event by setting the selectedChild of the checkoutNav ViewStack to billingInfo.

```
<v:OrderConf id="orderConf"
   width="100%" height="100%"
   orderInfo="{orderInfo}"
   back="checkoutNav.selectedChild=billingInfo"/>
```

This is the third and final component used in this ViewStack. At this point, the user has no way to see this component, which will be remedied in the next step.

14 As the last line of code in the doCCInfoReturn() function, make the orderConf component be displayed in the ViewStack.

```
checkoutNav.selectedChild=orderConf;
```

In this checkout process, you control when the different containers are displayed. The user cannot click, nor do anything else, to jump between these different screens. In a later lesson, you will see how validation ties into this navigation scheme, preventing users from moving to the next step until the form is filled out correctly.

❊ NOTE: You will receive warnings that data binding will not be able to detect assignments to the date, fullYear, and month items. You will correct this in the next lesson using a DateFormatter.

15 Run EComm.mxml and click the Checkout button. After you fill in the customer information screen and click the Continue button, you will be taken to the credit card information form. After filling in this form and clicking the Continue button, you will be shown the order confirmation screen with the data entered in earlier forms now displayed.

Your checkout process should mimic the one shown here. At this point, the Complete Order button is not functional. Following are the three steps of the checkout process. In a later lesson, you will format the left margins of the form.

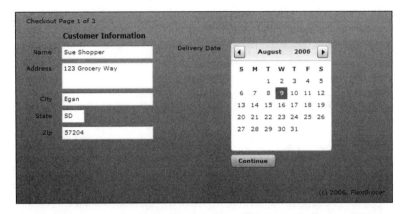

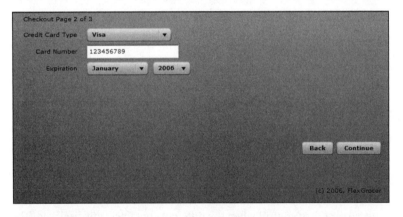

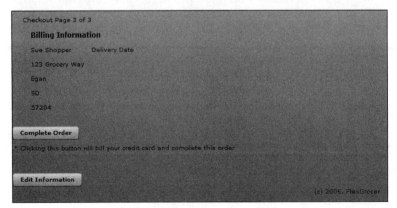

What You Have Learned

In this lesson, you have:

- Gained a general understanding of how Flex implements navigation and how the ViewStack is at the heart of this process (pages 348–351)

- Used a TabNavigator control to separate functionality from two components onto different tabs of the TabNavigator (pages 351–358)

- Implemented a checkout process using a ViewStack to control user progression through the process (pages 358–370)

What You Will Learn

In this lesson, you will:

- Create a new Validator object on the client machine
- Use the validator to check if the data is in a valid format
- Create a new formatter object on the client machine
- Use the formatter to format data

Approximate Time

This lesson takes approximately 1 hour and 30 minutes to complete.

Lesson Files

Media Files:

None

Starting Files:

Lesson14/start/EComm.mxml
Lesson14/start/views/dataEntry/AddProduct.mxml
Lesson14/start/views/ecomm/BillingInfo.mxml
Lesson14/start/views/ecomm/CCInfo.mxml
Lesson14/start/views/ecomm/GroceryDetail.mxml
Lesson14/start/views/ecomm/OrderConf.mxml

Completed Files:

Lesson14/complete/EComm.mxml
Lesson14/complete/utils/AddressValidator.as
Lesson14/complete/views/dataEntry/AddProduct.mxml
Lesson14/complete/views/ecomm/BillingInfo.mxml
Lesson14/complete/views/ecomm/CCInfo.mxml
Lesson14/complete/views/ecomm/GroceryDetail.mxml
Lesson14/complete/views/ecomm/OrderConf.mxml

Using Formatters and Validators

Flex provides many types of built-in validators and formatters that enable you to validate many types of user-supplied data such as dates, numbers, and currencies. Using the built-in data validators on the client side, you can make your application perform better by reducing calls to the server. You can also save development time by using the built-in formatters to automate the often repetitive process of formatting data.

Validating customer information

Introducing Formatters and Validators

Data validation is used to ensure that data meets specific criteria before the application uses it. Flex has a set of Validator classes that can be used to check data to ensure it has been entered correctly. You can use Validator classes either as MXML tags or instantiate them directly in ActionScript. With the Flex framework, it is possible to use validators to perform this checking at the client instead of when the data is submitted to the server. This is advantageous because it reduces the amount of data transmitted between the client and the server, which can result in a better-performing application. Of course, some types of secure data validation are best performed at the server, but using Validator classes at the client improves performance by offloading some validation to Flash Player.

All validators are a subclass of the Validator class. Some of the validators available as part of the Flex framework include the following:

- CreditCardValidator
- PhoneNumberValidator
- DateValidator
- SocialSecurityValidator
- EmailValidator
- StringValidator
- NumberValidator
- ZipCodeValidator

You often need to perform data validation that is beyond the capabilities of the built-in Validator classes, so Flex enables you to use the functionality of the Validator classes to build your own custom validators. For example, you might want to ensure that a user attaches a valid type of file to be uploaded. Or you might want to display only files to the user that have the word *Flex* in them. By creating a subclass of the Validator classes (also known as subclassing), you use a minimum of code to build a custom validator for any situation that might arise.

Flex also has a set of Formatter classes that can format raw data into a customized string. You can use the Formatter classes with data binding to automate data binding tasks and be able to apply the formatting to multiple fields simultaneously.

All formatters subclass the Formatter class; some of the formatters available include the following:

- mx.formatters.CurrencyFormatter
- mx.formatters.PhoneFormatter
- mx.formatters.DateFormatter
- mx.formatters.ZipCodeFormatter
- mx.formatters.NumberFormatter

Using a Formatter Class to Display Currency Information in the E-Commerce Application

In this exercise, you will apply a CurrencyFormatter class so all the price selections are displayed as U.S. dollars in the e-commerce application. There are multiple places in which prices are displayed in the application, including these:

- The list of grocery products displayed

- The total of the shopping cart

- The subtotal and list prices in the DataGrid that is in the user's shopping cart

The CurrencyFormatter adjusts the decimal rounding and precision and sets the thousands separator and the negative sign. You can specify the type and placement of the currency symbol used, which can contain multiple characters including blank spaces. The first step of using the CurrencyFormatter involves instantiating the Formatter class by using either MXML or ActionScript; the second step is calling the format method of the object and passing the number to be formatted to the method.

1 Open the GroceryDetail.mxml from the src/views/ecomm folder.

This is the component that is duplicated using the repeater control based on the grocery information retrieved from the server. All the information about each grocery product is displayed in this component.

2 Immediately after the script block, add an `<mx:CurrencyFormatter>` tag. Assign the tag an `id` of `curFormat` and specify the `currencySymbol` attribute as a dollar sign ($) and a precision of 2, as follows:

```
<mx:CurrencyFormatter id="curFormat"
    currencySymbol="$"
    precision="2"/>
```

The decimal rounding, the thousands separator, and the negative sign are properties that can be set on the CurrencyFormatter; we have left these at their defaults. You specified a precision of 2, meaning that two decimal places will always be displayed, and that a dollar sign be added to the formatted number. You could have specified any other character, for example, the character string *Yen*, for the currency symbol, including an empty space to be added between the symbol and the formatted number.

3 Locate the Label control a few lines down that displays the list price. Inside the data binding for the text property, call the format() method of the curFormat object, and pass the groceryItem.listPrice to the method, as follows:

```
<mx:Label id="price"
    text="{curFormat.format(groceryItem.listPrice)}"
    x="100"
    y="20"/>
```

The format() method takes the value and applies all the parameters you set on the <mx:CurrencyFormatter> tag. In this case, you are adding a dollar sign and specifying the precision, so two digits to the right of the decimal point will always be maintained.

4 Save the changes to GroceryDetail.mxml and run the application. Select some grocery items.

You should see that all the grocery items display correctly formatted list prices.

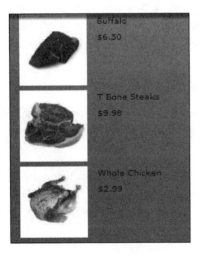

5 Open the EComm.mxml file.

EComm is where the total of the end user's shopping cart is displayed. You will apply a currency formatter to this field.

6 Immediately after the script tag, add an <mx:CurrencyFormatter> tag. Assign the tag an id of cartFormat, specify the currencySymbol as a dollar sign ($), and the precision as 2, as follows:

```
<mx:CurrencyFormatter id="cartFormat"
    currencySymbol="$"
    precision="2"/>
```

7 Locate the Label control (on approximately line 66) that displays "Your Cart Total". In place of the existing dollar sign, call the format() method of the cartFormat CurrencyFormat object, and pass the cart.total to the method. Remove the second Label control, which currently displays the cart.total, and delete the HBox that surrounds them both. The code for the remaining Label control should look as shown here:

```
<mx:Label text="Your Cart Total: {cartFormat.format(cart.total)}"/>
```

The format() method formats the cart.total according to the parameters you specified in the cartFormat object.

8 Save and run the application. Add some grocery items to the cart.

The total text field describing the contents of the shopping cart is displayed as currency with a dollar sign.

9 Open the OrderConf.mxml file from the src/views/ecomm directory.

In the last lesson, you concatenated portions of the date (month, day, and year) to format the delivery date for orders. Flex provides a built-in DateFormatter class. In this exercise, you will apply a DateFormatter to your class.

10 Directly below the existing <mx:Script> add an <mx:DateFormatter> tag. Assign the tag an id of orderFormat.

```
<mx:DateFormatter id="orderFormat"/>
```

A new object with the name of orderFormat is created. You can use this Formatter class to format dates throughout the application. Because you have not specified any properties, the default format "MM/DD/YYYY" is used. You can customize it by setting the formatString property.

11 While still in OrderConf.mxml, locate the Delivery Date form item. Change the `<mx:Label>` so the `text` property calls the `format()` method of the `orderFormat` DateFormatter on the `deliveryDate` property of the orderInfo data structure. Be sure to remove the manual date formatting from the last lesson. The `<mx:Label>` should look as shown here:

```
<mx:Label text="{orderFormat.format(orderInfo.deliveryDate)}"/>
```

This applies the DateFormatter object to the `deliveryDate` property and displays the date in the format "MM/DD/YYYY".

12 Save and run the application. Fill in the customer information fields and be sure to choose a delivery date. Note that the warnings are gone in the Problems section. Browse to the order confirmation section.

Note that the delivery date is formatted as shown in the following figure.

Using Validator Classes

In this task, you will use a ZipCodeValidator class to check whether a postal code is a valid U.S. zip code or Canadian postal code. Using a CreditCardValidator, you will also check whether a credit card number is valid during the checkout process.

1 Open BillingInfo.mxml from the src/views/ecomm directory.

This is the file that displays the billing information for the end user. It includes their name, address, and postal code.

2 Immediately after the `<mx:Model>` tag, add an `<mx:ZipCodeValidator>` tag and assign it an ID of zipV. Set up a binding to the source property as the billingZip input text box. Specify the property as text and specify the domain attribute as the US or Canada.

```
<mx:ZipCodeValidator id="zipV" source="{billingZip}"
    property="text" domain="US or Canada"/>
```

The `<mx:ZipCodeValidator>` validates that a string has the correct length for a five-digit zip code, a five-digit + four-digit U.S. zip code, or a Canadian postal code. The source attribute is simply the name of the control being validated and where the error message will appear. The property attribute is where the actual information that should be validated is stored.

3 Save and compile the application.

Click the Checkout button; enter some letters for the zip code in the billing information screen. When you exit the field, you should see a red highlight around the text field; when you move the pointer over the text field, you will see the default error message appear.

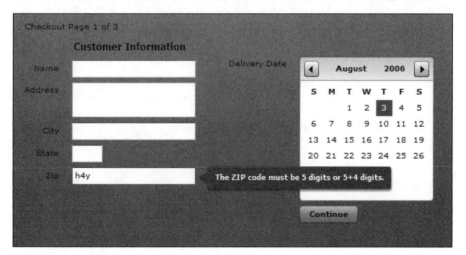

4 Open CCInfo.mxml from the src/views/ecomm directory.

This is the next step of the billing process: the user enters credit card information after filling out billing information.

5 Modify the dataProvider for the cardType ComboBox control. Change the data property of the dataProvider items to "American Express", "Diners Club", "Discover", "MasterCard", and "Visa".

```
<mx:ComboBox id="cardType">
  <mx:dataProvider>
    <mx:Object label="American Express"
      data="American Express"/>
    <mx:Object label="Diners Club" data="Diners Club"/>
    <mx:Object label="Discover" data="Discover"/>
    <mx:Object label="MasterCard" data="MasterCard"/>
    <mx:Object label="Visa" data="Visa"/>
  </mx:dataProvider>
</mx:ComboBox>
```

These constants that you have assigned indicate the type of credit card to be validated. In the next step, you will access these constants from the validator, which indicate which algorithm should be applied when using the validator.

6 Immediately after the `<mx:Model>` tag, add an `<mx:CreditCardValidator>` tag and assign it an id of ccV. Set up a binding between the CardTypeSource property and the cardType.selectedItem of the ComboBox control. Also specify the cardTypeProperty as data.

```
<mx:CreditCardValidator id="ccV"
  cardTypeSource="{cardType.selectedItem}" cardTypeProperty="data"/>
```

The type of card is being stored in a ComboBox control in the data property of the selectedItem. You specify the control in which the object is being stored by using the cardTypeSource property. In the last step, you specified that the information is being stored in the data property.

7 Still in the `<mx:CreditCardValidator>` tag, add another property with the name of cardNumberSource and set up a binding to the cardNumber text field. Specify the cardNumberProperty attribute as text. The final CreditCardValidator class should look as follows:

```
<mx:CreditCardValidator id="ccV"
  cardTypeSource="{cardType.selectedItem}"
  cardTypeProperty="data"
  cardNumberSource="{cardNumber}"
  cardNumberProperty="text"/>
```

The cardNumberSource property is the input text field in which the user has typed their credit card number. The number is stored in the text property of the input text field, which is why you specify the cardNumberProperty attribute.

8 In the <mx:Script> block, import the mx.events.ValidationResultEvent and declare a variable with the name of vResult as a ValidationResultEvent.

```
import mx.events.ValidationResultEvent;
private var vResult:ValidationResultEvent;
```

ValidationResultEvent will return either valid or invalid for the CreditCardValidator class. You must import these events to use them. If the credit card is valid, you want the user to continue with the checkout process. If it is not valid, you want the user to enter the appropriate credit card number.

9 In the <mx:Script> block, immediately inside the process() method, assign vResult to the value returned from the validate() method on the ccV validator. Surround the current code in the process() method with conditional logic that checks to see whether the vResult.type property is equal to the ValidationResultEvent.VALID. If it does match, place the code that continues the checkout process within the if statement. Add an else statement that will do nothing if the condition is not met.

```
vResult = ccV.validate();
if (vResult.type==ValidationResultEvent.VALID){
    ➥ var o:ObjectDataEvent=new ObjectDataEvent("ccInfoReturn",checkoutInfo);
    ➥ dispatchEvent(o);
} else {

}
```

The validate() method, which is part of the CreditCardValidator class, executes an algorithm that checks if a valid credit card number has been entered. The algorithm checks only that a valid card number was entered, not whether that card is actually active. After the validation is done, the method will return a ValidationResultEvent with a property of type set to the constant ValidationResultEvent.VALID if it looks like a credit card number. (You are adding logic that will test for this.) If so, continue with the checkout process; otherwise, do not continue.

10 Save and compile the application.

Click the Checkout button. Click the Continue button in the billing information screen to advance to the credit card section. Enter some letters into the credit card field and click the Continue button. You will see the text field display a red outline; roll the pointer over the text field and note the error message.

Using Regular Expressions to Validate Data (Part 1)

Regular expressions enable you to easily search through a text string without having to build complicated looping structures. Regular expressions are simply patterns that enable you to search and match other strings. They are created by using a special language—the regular expression language—which you will get a taste of in this exercise. The Flex framework has support for this language built in.

In this exercise, you will use regular expressions to build a custom validator to verify an image name the user has attached by dragging and dropping. You will check the file name to ensure that there is at least one character before the dot, and that the image they are attaching is a GIF file. There are lots of considerations that will make this validation more complicated. For example, you will have to consider all case possibilities when searching for the GIF string: GiF, gif, and even giF are all valid. You also need to search for the string GIF only at the end of the filename, after the dot. For example, you would not want a file with the name of gift.jpg to register as valid.

1 Open AddProduct.mxml from the src/views/dataEntry directory.

2 On the first line of the doProdAdd() method, create a new RegExp object with the name of pattern, as follows:

```
var pattern:RegExp = new RegExp();
```

The RegExp class is used to write regular expressions that can search for and replace text strings. The object stores the pattern that you use to search through these strings. The next step will take you through the syntax of the pattern.

3 Inside the parentheses for the RegExp() class, define the first character of the string as a period (.).

```
var pattern:RegExp = new RegExp(".");
```

The constructor for the RegExp class accepts a string to define the search pattern. The first step to defining your filename search is to ensure that at least one character appears directly before the period in the filename. In regular expressions syntax, a single valid character, also referred to as a wildcard, is represented by a period.

4 After defining the first period, define a literal search for a period using two backslashes and a period (\\.).

```
var pattern:RegExp = new RegExp(".\\.");
```

In step 3, you learned that a period represents any character in regular expressions. To make your search for an appropriate file type work, you need to be able to literally search for a period as well. This is accomplished using an escape character, which is a double backslash (\\) in Flex. The escape character tells the regular expression that you literally mean a period, and not another wildcard character.

5 After defining the search for the literal period, add searches for uppercase *G*, lowercase *g*, uppercase *I*, lowercase *i*, uppercase *F*, or lowercase *f*. To express this in a regular expression, you surround each of the upper- and lowercase character combinations in square brackets.

```
var pattern:RegExp = new RegExp(".\\.[Gg][Ii][Ff]");
```

This will check that the string ends with any variation of the capitalization of *GIF*.

6 Immediately after defining the pattern object, surround the rest of the method with conditional logic. Within the conditional logic, use the search() method of the String class to search the string located in prodModel.imageName with the RegExp pattern you completed in the last step. If the value is not equal to -1, execute the code.

```
if(prodModel.imageName.search(pattern) != -1){
   var prod:Product = Product.buildProduct(prodModel);
   var o:ProductEvent = new ProductEvent(prod,'productAdded');
   this.dispatchEvent(o);
}
```

The search() method of the String class will search the prodModel.imageName string for the regular expression that you defined in the pattern. It will look for a character before a period; for a period; and for the character *G*, *I*, or *F* in any case. If the string matching the pattern you defined is not found in the imageName, -1 is returned. If the string is found, the search method returns the position where the pattern begins in imageName.

7 Add an else statement that will display an Alert box if -1 one is returned. The final doProdAdd() method should look as follows:

```
private function doProdAdd():void{
   var pattern:RegExp = new RegExp(".\\.[Gg][Ii][Ff]");
   if(prodModel.imageName.search(pattern) != -1){
      var prod:Product = Product.buildProduct(prodModel);
      var o:ProductEvent = new ProductEvent(prod,'productAdded');
      this.dispatchEvent(o);
   }else{
      mx.controls.Alert.show("Please attach a GIF file");
   }
}
```

If the user has not attached a file with the extension gif, an Alert box is displayed, asking the user to attach a GIF file.

8 Save this file and run the DataEntry application. Click the Add Product tab and attempt to add a new image by typing some different combinations into the image field. Then click the Add Product button.

You should see only those combinations that have at least one character in front, a period, and an extension beginning with GIF add properly.

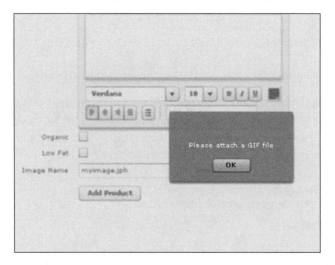

Using Regular Expressions to Validate Data (Part 2)

In this exercise, you will continue to use regular expressions and delve into some more complicated syntax. You will use regular expressions to be sure that an end user in the e-commerce application has entered a valid address. In reality, validating an address is difficult because there are many possible combinations; in this example you will verify that a street address starts with a number, contains a space, and then contains some more characters. This will work for the vast majority of U.S. addresses.

1 Open BillingInfo.mxml in the src/views/ecomm directory.

2 On the first line of the process() method, create a new RegExp object with the name of **pattern**, as follows:

```
var pattern:RegExp = new RegExp();
```

This creates a new `pattern` object that can store regular expression strings for searching.

3 Inside the constructor for the RegExp() object, define the search pattern as two backslashes and a d+.

```
var pattern:RegExp = new RegExp("\\d+");
```

The *d* indicates to search for a single digit. The plus sign (+) is referred to as a quantifier; it works with the *d* to indicate that you will accept one or more digits as a match.

4 After defining the expression that searches for the beginning digits, add an escape character (\\) and add an x20 character that represents a space.

```
var pattern:RegExp = new RegExp("\\d+\\x20");
```

This indicates that a space is required between the digits and the letters of the address.

5 In brackets, check for all lowercase and all uppercase letters using A-Z and a-z. Add a plus sign (+) after the brackets to allow for any length of those letters.

```
var pattern:RegExp = new RegExp("\\d+\\x20[A-Za-z]+");
```

This searches for any length of letters, in any case directly after the space. You have now built a pattern that checks for valid addresses.

6 Immediately after defining the Pattern object, surround the rest of the method with conditional logic. Within the conditional logic, use the search() method of the String class to search the checkoutInfo.billingAddress with the regular expression pattern you defined in the last step. If the value is not equal to -1, execute the code.

```
if(checkoutInfo.billingAddress.search(pattern) != -1){
    var o:ObjectDataEvent =
       ➥ new ObjectDataEvent ("billingInfoReturn",checkoutInfo);
    dispatchEvent(o);
}
```

The search() method of the String class will search the entire checkoutInfo.billingAddress string for the regular expression that you defined earlier.

7 Add an else statement that will display an Alert box if -1 is returned. The final process() method should look as follows:

```
private function process():void{
    var pattern:RegExp = new RegExp("\\d+\\x20[A-Za-z]+");
    if(checkoutInfo.billingAddress.search(pattern) != -1){
        var o:ObjectDataEvent =
            ➥ new ObjectDataEvent("billingInfoReturn",checkoutInfo);
        dispatchEvent(o);
    }else{
        mx.controls.Alert.show("Please enter a valid US address");
    }
}
```

8 Save and run the EComm application.

Type in some different combinations into the Address field. You should see that only those combinations that begin with numbers, have a space, and then have a sequence of letters are accepted.

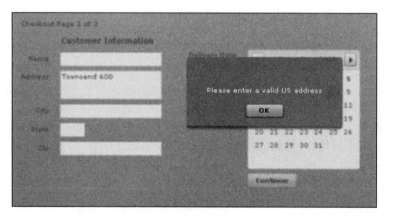

Building a Custom Validator Class

In this task, you will build a custom Validator class that can check for U.S. address formatting. In the last task you built the logic that can check whether a U.S. address is valid by using regular expressions. If the user types in a bad address, an Alert box is displayed. However, this does not take advantage of any of the built-in Validator class functionality. With the Validator class, you can offer the user visual cues to where the error is as well as display customized error messages. The Flex framework offers the ability to extend all the Validator classes and to add your application's functionality.

1 Create a new ActionScript class by right-clicking the utils folder and selecting New > ActionScript Class. The name of the class should be **AddressValidator**, ensure the package name is utils, and specify a superclass of **mx.validators.Validator** as shown.

This will be a new custom Validator class that will use the regular expression functionality you built in the last exercise.

2 Import the mx.validators.ValidationResult class.

```
package utils {
    import mx.validators.Validator;
    import mx.validators.ValidationResult;
```

The ValidationResult class contains several properties that enable you to record information about any validation properties, such as the error messages and codes that are generated from a failure.

3 Immediately inside the class definition, declare the private `results` array.

```
public class AddressValidator extends Validator{
   private var results:Array;
```

The `results` array will be returned from the `doValidation()` method that you will override.

4 Declare a public constructor with the name AddressValidator and call the base class constructor using super().

```
public class AddressValidator extends Validator{
   private var results:Array;
   public function AddressValidator(){
      super();
   }
```

The public constructor function invokes `super()` from the base Validator class. The base class can perform the check to ensure that data was entered into a required field.

5 Override the protected function `doValidation()` method, and set the parameter of the method to `Object`. The method will return an array.

```
override protected function doValidation(value:Object):Array{
}
```

The method on the AddressValidator class is now overriding the existing Validator class method, and you are defining a new `doValidation()` method. The `doValidation()` method will return an array of `ValidationResult` objects.

✳ **NOTE:** Public methods and properties are available to any object in the system. Private methods and properties are only available inside the class where they are defined. Protected methods and properties are available inside the same class and all derived classes, or subclasses.

6 Inside the method, clear the `results` array, and call the base class `doValidation()` method, passing it the value from the `doValidation()` method. Return the `results` array at the end of the method.

```
override protected function doValidation(value:Object):Array{
   results = [];
   results = super.doValidation(value);
   return results;
}
```

The results array is simply an array of ValidationResult objects, one for each field examined by the validator. If the validation is successful, the results array will remain empty. If the validation is not successful, one ValidationResult per each field is returned whether the validation of the individual field is successful or not. The isError property of the ValidationResult can be examined to determine whether the field passed or failed validation.

7 Immediately after calling the super.doValidation() method, add conditional logic to test if the value object passed into the AddressValidator doValidation() method is null.

```
override protected function doValidation(value:Object):Array{
    results = [];
    results = super.doValidation(value);
    if(value!=null){
    }
    return results;
}
```

You are about to search this value with your regular expression, but only if the value contains some data.

8 Return to the BillingInfo.mxml file and locate the process() method. Inside this method, remove the conditional logic and cut the definition of the pattern regular expression to the clipboard. Save the BillingInfo.mxml file. The final process() method should look as follows:

```
private function process():void{
    var o:ObjectDataEvent =
        ➥ new ObjectDataEvent("billingInfoReturn",checkoutInfo);
    dispatchEvent(o);
}
```

You will place this logic inside the new AddressValidator class that you are creating. You can still make sure that the user enters a valid U.S. address, and you will have all of the functionality of the Validator class.

9 Return to the AddressValidator class. Inside the conditional logic, paste the definition of the pattern regular expression. Add conditional logic that uses the search method of the String class to search value for the pattern and tests for -1, as follows:

```
if(value!=null){
    var pattern:RegExp = new RegExp("\\d+\\x20[A-Za-z]+", "");
    if(value.search(pattern) == -1){
    }
}
```

You have defined the same regular expression that will search for valid U.S. addresses, except now it is part of a new subclass of the Validator class. If a valid U.S. address is not found, the search method will return -1, and you will need to inform the user that the validation failed.

10 Inside the conditional logic that searches for the regular expression, call the push method of the Array object to add a new ValidationResult with the parameters: true, null, "notAddress", and "You must enter a valid US address" into the results array. Save the file. The final doValidation() method should appear as follows:

```
override protected function doValidation(value:Object):Array{
    results = [];
    results = super.doValidation(value);
    if(value!=null){
        var pattern:RegExp = new RegExp("\\d+\\x20[A-Za-z]+", "");
        if(value.search(pattern) == -1){
            results.push(new ValidationResult
                ➥ (true, null, "notAddress", "This is not a valid US address"));
        }
    }
    return results;
}
```

If the regular expression is not found in the string the user entered, a new ValidationResult error will be added to the results array. Remember that this is how the Validator class works: It displays error messages from the results array in the field that the user moves the pointer over. You can have more than one error message, so it needs to be an array. In this case, if the user entered a non–U.S. address, the error message "This is not a valid US address" is displayed.

11 Return to BillingInfo.mxml. Add a new namespace to the <mx:HBox> tag at the top of the page, with the name u, that will reference all files in the utils.* directory.

```
<mx:HBox xmlns:mx="http://www.adobe.com/2006/mxml"
    xmlns:u="utils.*">
```

This will enable you to reference the new customized AddressValidator class you created by using the namespace u.

12 Directly below the existing ZipCodeValidator class, add a new <u:AddressValidator> tag. Specify the id as addressV, the required property as true, the source as a binding to the billingAddress field, and the property as text.

```
<u:AddressValidator id="addressV" required="true"
    source="{billingAddress}" property="text"/>
```

This creates an instance of the new Validator class you have created. Because it is subclassing the existing Validator class, the properties are exactly the same as before.

13 Save and run the application.

Click the Checkout button and enter an address that begins with a letter (which is not valid in the United States). Using the Tab key, move focus off the Address field; the field is now highlighted in red, and you should see the error message you specified earlier when you roll the pointer over the field.

What You Have Learned

In this lesson, you have:

- Learned how to apply a formatter to incoming text (pages 374–378)
- Learned how to apply a validator to outgoing data (pages 378–381)
- Learned how to use regular expressions for validation of text (pages 382–386)
- Built a custom validator class (pages 386-391)

What You Will Learn

In this lesson, you will:

- Use standard history management
- Import the HistoryManagement classes
- Build a custom HistoryManager class for the CategoryView component
- Understand deep linking in Flex

Approximate Time

This lesson takes approximately 45 minutes to complete.

Lesson Files

Media Files:

None

Starting Files:

Lesson15/start/as/ecomm.as
Lesson15/start/views/ecomm/CategoryView.mxml

Completed Files:

Lesson15/complete/as/ecomm.as
Lesson15/complete/views/ecomm/CategoryView.mxml

Implementing History Management and Deep Linking

An important but often overlooked requirement for rich Internet applications is the capability to use the back and forward buttons in the browser. Most users of web-based applications are accustomed to navigating through web pages by using these buttons, and it makes sense to implement the same functionality in your Flex applications.

The FlexGrocer application with the back and forward buttons working within the browser.

The navigational components that you learned about in the Lesson 13, "Implementing Navigation," have this functionality automatically built in—including the Accordion, TabNavigator, and TabBar containers, and components that descend from the ViewStack container. Flex also offers the ability to implement this back/forward browser functionality via both the HistoryManager and the new deep linking features of Flex 3 (which will be introduced later in this lesson). In this lesson, you will enable the back and forward buttons in the FlexGrocer application using the HistoryManager class in a custom component, and you will enable users to link to individual product pages through the use of deep linking.

Introducing History Management

Using history management, the user can navigate through an application using the browser's back and forward buttons. For example, a user can click a tab in a TabNavigator or Accordion container and then move to the previous tab by clicking the back button in the browser.

Flex automatically supports history management for any navigator container without using any additional MXML or ActionScript tags. It is enabled by default for the Accordion and TabNavigator containers. If you want to turn off history management for these containers, simply specify the attribute historyManagementEnabled and set it to false, as follows:

```
<mx:TabNavigator historyManagementEnabled="false">
```

History management is disabled by default for the ViewStack container. You can turn on history management for the ViewStack container by specifying historyManagementEnabled and setting that attribute to true as follows:

```
<mx:ViewStack historyManagementEnabled="true">
```

When history management is turned on, as the user moves from state to state within the application, each navigation state is saved. When the browser's back or forward button is selected, the History Manager will load and display the next navigation state that was saved previously. Only the state of the actual navigator container is saved; if the navigator has any children, the states of these components are *not* saved unless history management is enabled for that container.

History management actually saves each state of the application by using the Adobe Flash Player navigateToURL() function. This function loads an invisible HTML frame into the current browser window. All the states of the Flex application are encoded into the URL parameters for the invisible HTML frame. A SWF file called history.swf, which is located in the invisible frame, decodes the query parameters and sends the navigation state information back to the HistoryManager class in Flex—where the saved data is displayed.

You can add history management to any custom component in which it is appropriate. For example, in the FlexGrocer application, you will add history management to the CategoryView component so the user can use the back and forward buttons in the browser to navigate between different food categories, as shown here:

There are six steps to implementing history management with a component that does not implement it by default:

1. Specify that your component will implement the IHistoryManagerClient interface.

2. Register the component with the HistoryManager class in Flex.

3. Implement the loadState() method in the custom component.

4. Implement the saveState() method in the custom component.

5. Implement the toString() method in the custom component.

6. Call the static methods of the HistoryManager class in Flex.

To implement the IHistoryManagerClient interface on a custom component, you add an implements property to the root node of your component and specify the interface name—in this case, mx.managers.IHistoryManagerClient. Specifying that a component implements a specific interface is like making a contract with the compiler. You are guaranteeing that your custom component will implement every method required by the interface. This contract tells the HistoryManager that it is safe to work with the component as the proper functionality is guaranteed to be in place.

To register a component with the HistoryManager class, you call the static register() method of the HistoryManager class and pass a reference to the component instance. This tells the HistoryManager that your component needs to know when the user navigates using the forward or back buttons in the browser. To fulfill your contract with the HistoryManager, your component must implement three methods of the mx.managers.IHistoryManagerClient interface—saveState(), loadState(), and toString()—with the following signature:

```
public function saveState():Object
public function loadState(state:Object):void
public function toString():String
```

The saveState() method returns an object that contains name–value pairs that represent the current navigational state of the component. These name–value pairs are often limited by the maximum URL size supported by the user's browser, which varies amongst browsers and platforms. Because the space available is limited, you should try to write the least amount of data possible.

The loadState() method of the component is activated when the user clicks the forward or back buttons in the web browser. The HistoryManager class passes a parameter to this method, which is identical to the object created by the saveState() method. Components that use the history management functionality must also implement the toString() method, but there is a default implementation of this method in the UIComponent class. This means that if the component descends from UIComponent, it already has a default toString() method. However, as you learned in Lesson 5, "Handling Events and Data Structures," it is still a good idea to write your own toString() method, specific to your class, as it helps significantly in debugging.

If you use history management in a custom HTML page (one not generated by Flex Builder), you must manually set up that HTML to support history management. This code is written for you if you are using Flex Builder to generate the HTML automatically.

You must include this HTML at the top of the page:

```
<script language='javascript' charset='utf-8'
   src='/flex/flex-internal?action=history_js'></script>
```

You then need to add the historyURL and iconId parameters to the flashVars variable in JavaScript as shown:

```
document.write("flashvars = 'historyUrl=
➥ %2Fflex%2Fflex%2Dinternal%3Faction%3Dhistory%5F html&Iconid=
➥ " + lc_id +"&versionChecked=true'");
```

Add the history iframe, as shown here:

```
<iframe src='/flex/flex-internal?action=history_html' name='_history'
   frameborder='0' scrolling='no' width='22' height='0'></iframe>
```

Implementing History Management within a Navigator Container

Due to security constraints, users of Microsoft Internet Explorer will not be able to build and preview the examples in this lesson as they have for previous lessons. History management does not work in Internet Explorer *when previewing a local file*, meaning that it does not work when previewing local files on your hard drive; however, it will work if the file is on a web server or accessed through an HTTP URL, as opposed to the file:/// URL used during normal development. If you are using Internet Explorer, you will need to preview these files from a web server. History management does work in Firefox, Netscape, and Safari browsers when previewing a local file.

In this exercise, you will examine how standard history management is implemented in the DataEntry application.

1 Open DataEntry.mxml and run the application. Navigate between the two tabs on the tab navigator on the first page. Note that the back and forward buttons are working within the browser.

As was mentioned earlier in this lesson, history management is turned on for the TabNavigator and Accordion components by default. If you want to turn off history management for these, you need to use the `historyManagementEnabled` property. If your navigation system uses a regular ViewStack component, you can turn on history management explicitly using this property. Notice that the back button is enabled because history management is turned on automatically.

2 Locate the TabNavigator component and add a `historyManagementEnabled` attribute to the tag and set it to `false`. Save and run the application.

Note that the back and forward buttons in the browser are no longer working when you move between the Update/Delete Product and Add Product tabs.

3 Locate the TabNavigator component and remove the `historyManagementEnabled` attribute.

If you save and run the application, the browser's back and forward buttons will work again.

Building a Custom History Manager

In this exercise, you will implement history management in the CategoryView.mxml component so that users can navigate between categories using the back and forward buttons in the browser.

1 Open CategoryView.mxml from the src/views/ecomm directory.

You will implement history management inside this component. When users click a category, they can return to the previous category by clicking the back button or move to the next category by clicking the forward button.

2 Run the application from EComm.mxml and click on the HorizontalList that contains the food categories.

Notice that the back and forward buttons are disabled. You will enable these buttons in the next steps.

3 Return to CategoryView.mxml. Inside the `<mx:Script>` block, import the mx.managers. IHistoryManagerClient interface and the mx.managers.HistoryManager class.

```
import mx.managers.IHistoryManagerClient;
import mx.managers.HistoryManager;
```

These classes are needed to use history management in Flex, as they interpret the information sent from the history.swf file. When the user moves back and forth using the browser buttons, the HistoryManager saves this information to the invisible frame in the HTML document mentioned earlier.

4 On the `<mx:HorizontalList>` tag at the top of the file, add an `implements` attribute that references the mx.managers.IHistoryManagerClient interface.

```
<mx:HorizontalList xmlns:mx="http://www.adobe.com/2006/mxml"
    dataProvider="{cats}"
    itemRenderer="views.ecomm.TextAndPic"
    horizontalScrollPolicy="off"
    click="categorySelect()"
    implements="mx.managers.IHistoryManagerClient">
```

Implementing the IHistoryManagerClient interface specifies that you will create two methods in this component, with the names `loadState()` and `saveState()`.

If you tried to compile the application at this point, you would receive an error because neither the `loadState()` method nor the `saveState()` method have been implemented. You will implement them in the next steps.

5 Call a new method with the name of `registerWithHistoryManager()` on the
creationComplete event of the HorizontalList control.

```
<mx:HorizontalList xmlns:mx="http://www.adobe.com/2006/mxml"
    dataProvider="{cats}"
    itemRenderer="views.ecomm.TextAndPic"
    horizontalScrollPolicy="off"
    click="categorySelect()"
    implements="mx.managers.IHistoryManagerClient"
    creationComplete="registerWithHistoryManager()">
```

You need to register this component with the HistoryManager to receive notice when the
user clicks the back or forward buttons in the browser. Encapsulating the work to register
the component into a separate method, `registerWithHistoryManager()`, is a good design
practice.

6 In the `<mx:Script>` block, create a new private method with the name of
`registerWithHistoryManager()` that returns void. Inside the method, call the static
`register` method of the HistoryManager and pass it a reference to the component,
as shown.

```
private function registerWithHistoryManager():void{
    HistoryManager.register(this);
}
```

This code registers the CategoryView component with the HistoryManager and enables
the forward and back buttons in the browser. The CategoryView component is referenced
from the `this` keyword.

7 Remaining in the `registerWithHistoryManager()` method, save the current state in the
HistoryManager using the static `save()` method. The final `registerWithHistoryManager()`
method should look like this:

```
private function registerWithHistoryManager():void{
    HistoryManager.register(this);
    HistoryManager.save();
}
```

The `save()` method of the HistoryManager saves the current state of the component.
When you first register a component, you must explicitly call this `save()` method.

8 Change the name of the `categorySelect()` method to `broadcastCategoryEvent()`. The
new `broadcastCategoryEvent()` method should look as follows:

```
private function broadcastCategoryEvent():void{
    var e:CategoryEvent = new CategoryEvent(this.selectedItem as
        Category, "categorySelect");
    this.dispatchEvent(e);
}
```

Remember that the `categorySelect` event is called when the user clicks a category in the HorizontalList control. You are moving the functionality of broadcasting an event into a separate method.

9 Create a new private method with the name of `categorySelect()` that returns void. On the first line of the method, call the static `save()` method of the HistoryManager class. On the second line, call the `broadcastCategoryEvent()` method you created in the last step to dispatch the event.

```
private function categorySelect():void{
   HistoryManager.save();
   broadcastCategoryEvent();
}
```

When the user clicks a category, this method saves the current state in the HistoryManager and broadcasts the event.

10 Within the `<mx:Script>` block, create a new public method with the name of `saveState()` that returns an `Object`. Inside the method, create a new local object with the name of state. Create a `selectedIndex` item property of the state object and set this property to the `selectedIndex` property of the component. Return the state object from the method. The method should look as follows:

```
public function saveState():Object{
   var state:Object = new Object();
   state.selectedIndex = this.selectedIndex;
   return state;
}
```

The HistoryManager class's `save()` method collects the state object returned by the `saveState()` method for each registered component. This method is required and saves the current `selectedIndex` of the HorizontalList control so you can easily come back to it later.

✳ **NOTE:** In previous lessons you were told that `selectedItem` is preferable to `selectedIndex` when working with controls. The `selectedChild` refers to the actual item selected, while the `selectedIndex` refers to the order of that item in the list, which can change if you reorder the elements. However, when working with history management, you can store only a limited amount of data. Storing a single number that indicates the position takes less storage space than the name of the selected child. Storing the index is a common practice in this scenario.

11 Remaining in the `<mx:Script>` block, create a new public method with the name of `loadState()`. The method should accept a parameter of state data typed as `Object`. Be sure that the method returns a type of void. On the first line of the method, declare a new variable named `newIndex` data typed as an `int`. Next, add conditional logic that checks for the existence of the state object. If it exists, set the value of the newIndex variable to the selectedIndex of the state object, cast as an int. Remember, the state object is the object that you created in the saveState() method.

```
public function loadState(state:Object):void{
    var newIndex:int;
    if (state) {
        newIndex = int( state.selectedIndex );
    }
}
```

This code resets the selectedIndex of the HorizontalList to the index that was saved earlier. The loadState() method is automatically called by the HistoryManager when the back or forward buttons in the browser are selected. The categorySelect event will fire when the previous state is selected.

12 Within the loadState() method, add an else statement that sets the value of newIndex to -1. After the closing brace of the previous conditional logic, use another if statement to check whether the value of the newIndex variable is different than the selectedIndex variable. If so, set the value of the selectedIndex variable to the value of the newIndex variable and call broadcastCategoryEvent(). Your final loadState() method should appear as follows:

```
public function loadState(state:Object):void{
    var newIndex:int;
    if (state) {
        newIndex = int( state.selectedIndex );
    }else{
        newIndex = -1;
    }
    if(newIndex != selectedIndex){
        selectedIndex = newIndex;
        broadcastCategoryEvent();
    }
}
```

The if statement, which checks if the state object is null, catches the case where you have selected only one category and then clicked the back button. In this case, you have set the newIndex variable equal to -1, which removes any selection from the HorizontalList. If the newIndex variable is not equal to the current selectedIndex, you set the HorizontalList control to display the previous category the user selected. You then call the broadcastCategoryEvent() method to inform other areas of the application that the category has changed. Remember, the loadState() method is called only when the back or forward buttons in the browser are selected.

13 Open ecomm.as from the src/as directory.

You need to make a change in ecomm.as to support the case when a category is not selected.

14 Find the displayProdByCategory() method. Add conditional logic around the existing contents of the method to check if event.cat is not equal to null. Add an else clause to the conditional logic and set the prodByCategory variable equal to a new ArrayCollection. Your displayProdByCategory() method should look as follows:

```
private function displayProdByCategory(event:CategoryEvent):void{
   if (event.cat != null){
     var prodArray:Array=
        catProds.getProdsForCat(event.cat.catID);
     prodByCategory=new ArrayCollection(prodArray);
   }else{
     prodByCategory=new ArrayCollection();
   }
}
```

If the category information passed to this method is not valid, the prodByCategory variable will be set to an empty ArrayCollection, which will cause the FoodList component to not display any items. If a user selects only one category and then clicks the back button, you will also be assured correct behavior.

15 Save and run the application. Click on different categories and navigate throughout the application using the back and forward buttons in the browser.

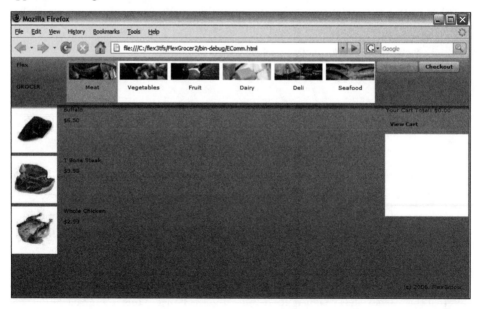

You should see that the back and forward buttons are enabled as you move through the application using the history management functionality.

Introducing Deep Linking

Deep linking is a phrase that describes support for URL-based navigation in applications that are traditionally served as a single URL. Unlike traditional HTML-based web applications, Flex applications are not inherently a disparate set of interlinked pages, each with its own URL. In the Flex world, it is far more likely that the entire application can be accessed via a single URL. This has posed some challenges for changing the URL in the browser. Normally, when the URL changes while a Flex application is running, the browser will unload the application and load the newly requested page. This makes it very difficult to email a customer a URL to a particular part of your application (for instance, you may want to email a link to the details of a product on sale this week) or to allow users to bookmark a particular place within the application. To help solve this problem, Flex 3 includes built-in support for deep linking.

Deep linking allows the URL to represent different "pages" in a Flex application without closing the application as you change the URL. This is accomplished by using named anchors (the parameters that follow the "#" in a URL that are normally used to navigate to different places within an HTML page.) By implementing deep linking with anchors, the main part of the URL is not changing, and therefore the browser will not attempt to unload the application and load a different one. Instead, all that changes is the anchor, which can be read and reacted to programmatically. The portion of the URL after the "#" is commonly known as a *fragment*. Each time you change the fragment, the previous fragment gets stored in the browser history, allowing users to use their back and forward buttons to step back and forth through the application.

Implementing Flex 3 Deep Linking

In Flex 3, deep linking is implemented via the BrowserManager class. The BrowserManager provides support for reading and writing to the fragment, as well as to the browser's title. It also provides notification when the fragment changes within your application. The URLUtils class offers a number of tools to help you convert an object full of name–value pairs to a fragment and vice versa.

Adding Deep Linking to Your Application

In this example, you will replace the history management you added earlier in this lesson with deep linking, which will allow distributing links to specific product categories within the application. You are removing the HistoryManager you added earlier because the HistoryManager also uses the BrowserManager and will interfere with your fragment processing.

1 Open CategoryView.mxml from the src/views/ecomm directory.

To avoid having the HistoryManager interfere with deep linking, you will first remove the custom history management from the application.

2 Remove the implements="mx.managers.IHistoryManagerClient" attribute and the creationComplete="registerWithHistoryManager()" event handler from the HorizontalList tag, which is the root node for CategoryView. Also change the event handler for the click event from categorySelect() to broadcastCategoryEvent(), as follows:

```
<mx:HorizontalList xmlns:mx="http://www.adobe.com/2006/mxml"
    dataProvider="{cats}"
    itemRenderer="views.ecomm.TextAndPic"
    horizontalScrollPolicy="off"
    click="broadcastCategoryEvent()">
```

The HorizontalList will no longer use the HistoryManager, so it is no longer necessary to implement any of the functionality required by the HistoryManager.

3 In the <mx:Script> block, remove the registerWithHistoryManager(), categorySelect(), saveState(), and loadState() methods. Also remove the two import statements specific to the HistoryManager (mx.managers.IHistoryManagerClient and mx.managers.HistoryManager).

While removing these imports is not technically required, it is always a best practice to remove code that is no longer in use. The remaining CategoryView.mxml file should look like this:

```
<?xml version="1.0" encoding="utf-8"?>
<mx:HorizontalList xmlns:mx="http://www.adobe.com/2006/mxml"
    dataProvider="{cats}"
    itemRenderer="views.ecomm.TextAndPic"
    horizontalScrollPolicy="off"
    click="broadcastCategoryEvent()">
    <mx:Metadata>
        [Event(name="categorySelect",type="events.CategoryEvent")]
    </mx:Metadata>
    <mx:Script>
    <![CDATA[
    import events.CategoryEvent;
    import valueObjects.Category;
    import mx.collections.ArrayCollection;
    [Bindable]
    public var cats:ArrayCollection;
    [Bindable]
    public var catSelected:int;
    private function broadcastCategoryEvent():void{
        var e:CategoryEvent = new CategoryEvent(this.selectedItem as Category,
            ➥ "categorySelect");
        this.dispatchEvent(e);
    }
    ]]>
    </mx:Script>
</mx:HorizontalList>
```

4 In the <mx:Script> block, add an `import` statement to import the mx.managers. IBrowserManager, mx.managers.BrowserManager, mx.events.BrowserChangeEvent, and mx.utils.URLUtil classes.

```
import mx.managers.IBrowserManager;
import mx.managers.BrowserManager;
import mx.events.BrowserChangeEvent;
import mx.utils.URLUtil;
```

You will need all four of these classes to update the browser with a URL for each category.

5 Still in the <mx:Script>block, add a variable named browserMgr, of type IBrowserManager, and set it equal to the results of a call to BrowserManager.getInstance()

```
private var browserMgr:IBrowserManager = BrowserManager.getInstance();
```

Here, you are creating a property called browserMgr and using it to hold an instance of the BrowserManager singleton.

6 Add a creationComplete event handler on the root node (mx:HorizontalList) that calls a soon-to-be-written function called initApp().

```
<mx:HorizontalList xmlns:mx="http://www.adobe.com/2006/mxml"
    dataProvider="{cats}"
    itemRenderer="views.ecomm.TextAndPic"
    horizontalScrollPolicy="off"
    click="broadcastCategoryEvent()"
    creationComplete="initApp()">
```

7 In the <mx:Script>block, create a new method named initApp(), which initializes the browser manager instance and listens to it for a browser URL change event.

```
private function initApp():void{
    browserMgr.init(",Flex Grocer");
    browserMgr.addEventListener(BrowserChangeEvent.BROWSER_URL_CHANGE, parseURL);
}
```

The init method takes two arguments: the first indicating the normal state of the URL (in this case, it should have no fragments) and the second argument indicating what the title of the browser should be. In this case, when there are no fragments, the browser title should be "Flex Grocer." Next, an event listener is set on the browser manager so that a soon-to-be-written method, called parseURL, will handle any changes to the URL. This ensures that when a user changes the browser fragment for an application, the application knows how to respond.

8 Create a new method named updateURL, which takes no arguments and returns void. Inside this method, create a new generic object and populate a property of the object named category using the selectedIndex of this class as the value. Using the URLUtil class's objectToString static method, create a string for the fragment based on the new object. Finally, call the browserManager.setFragment method, passing it the string for the fragment.

```
private function updateURL():void{
   var o:Object = new Object();
   o.category=selectedIndex;
   var s:String = URLUtil.objectToString(o);
   browserMgr.setFragment(s);
}
```

When updateURL() is called, it will find the index of the selected category and add it to the URL with a variable named category.

9 As the final line of the broadcastCategoryEvent() method, add a call to the updateURL() method.

```
private function broadcastCategoryEvent():void{
   var e:CategoryEvent = new CategoryEvent(this.selectedItem as Category,
      ➥ "categorySelect");
   this.dispatchEvent(e);
   updateURL();
}
```

This completes the loop, so that each time the user clicks on a category, the URL updates to reflect the selected category. Not only will this enable use of the browser's back button, but any of the URLs for the individual categories can now be distributed.

10 Create the parseURL() method, as shown:

```
private function parseURL(event:BrowserChangeEvent=null):void{
   var o:Object = URLUtil.stringToObject(browserMgr.fragment);
   if(!cats){
      callLater(parseURL);
      return;
   }
   if(o.category != null){
      selectedIndex = o.category;
broadcastCategoryEvent();
   }
}
```

This method defines the event handler for the `BrowserChangeEvent.BROWSER_URL_CHANGE` event. Whenever the event is detected, this method is called to determine how the application should respond. Note that while the method can accept a `BrowserChangeEvent` as an argument, it is made optional by setting the argument equal to `null`. This means that if the argument is not provided, a null value will be passed in rather than having a runtime error thrown.

Within the method, the first thing that happens is the URL fragment is parsed into an object, using the `URLUtil.stringToObject` method. Next, a quick null check is added to determine whether or not this component has its category data (named cats). When the application first starts, this `parseURL` method will likely be fired before the category data is parsed. To prevent related runtime errors, you will determine whether the `cats ArrayCollection` is set. If it isn't, try calling this method again on the next update cycle, with the `callLater()` method, and then abort this execution with a `return` statement. When this method is called via `callLater()`, no arguments are passed to the function, which is why the event argument for the method is optional.

The final conditional will fire only if the `cats ArrayCollection` has already been set and the `category` property exists in the object parsed from the fragment. In that case, the `selectedIndex` of this `HorizontalList` is set to the value from the URL, and the `broadcastCategoryChange()` method is called to update the rest of the application.

11 Save and test the application. Click on the various categories and notice how the URL changes.

With each click of a category, the fragment in the browser's URL bar changes, with the addition of `category=` followed by the number of the category. So for example, the browser reads `EComm.html#category=3` when the Dairy category is clicked.

12 Create a new method called `setTitle()`. Inside this method, create a variable (of type String) and set it equal to the literal string "Flex Grocer –" concatenated with the `catName` property of the selected category from the HorizontalList.

```
private function setTitle():void{
   var title:String = "Flex Grocer - "+(selectedItem as Category).catName
browserMgr.setTitle(title);
}
```

You now have one method that can be called from both `parseURL` and `updateURL`, both of which will properly set the browser's title based on the selected category.

13 Add a call to setTitle from both parseURL() and updateURL():

```
private function updateURL():void{
    var o:Object = new Object();
    o.category=selectedIndex;
    var s:String = URLUtil.objectToString(o);
    browserMgr.setFragment(s);
    setTitle();
}
private function parseURL(event:BrowserChangeEvent=null):void{
    var o:Object = URLUtil.stringToObject(browserMgr.fragment);
    if(!cats){
        callLater(parseURL);
        return;
    }
    if(o.category != null){
        selectedIndex = o.category;
        setTitle();
        broadcastCategoryEvent();
    }
}
```

Save and test the application. While the application is running, click on a category and notice that the URL has changed. Manually change the value of the category in the URL and notice how the application updates itself automatically.

In order for Deep Linking to work properly on all browsers, it needs to be served via a web server. If you save and run the application in Firefox or Safari, you can change the fragment in the URL (for instance from EComm.html#category=0 to EComm.html#category=2), and see the interface update itself accordingly. If you are testing it in another browser, and it doesn't seem to work, try serving it from a web server. The Javascript which enables the Flex application to react to the changes to the URL doesn't work in all browsers when the file is run from the local file system, but will work in all browsers if the file is run off of a web server.

What You Have Learned

In this lesson, you have:

- Turned history management on and off for the ViewStack components (pages 394–396)
- Turned history management on and off for the TabNavigator (pages 396–397)
- Used the HistoryManager in a custom component (pages 398–402)
- Worked with deep linking by using the BrowserManager (pages 403–408)

What You Will Learn

In this lesson, you will:

- Learn how Flex applications are styled
- Set styles via tag attributes
- Learn about inheritable style properties
- Set styles via the `<mx:Style>` tag
- Set styles via CSS files
- Create a custom skin for components

Approximate Time

This lesson takes approximately 1 hour and 30 minutes to complete.

Lesson Files

Media Files:

Lesson16/assets/flexGrocer.css

Starting Files:

Lesson16/start/EComm.mxml
Lesson16/start/views/ecomm/BillingInfo.mxml
Lesson16/start/views/ecomm/Cart.mxml
Lesson16/start/views/ecomm/CCInfo.mxml
Lesson16/start/views/ecomm/GroceryDetail.mxml
Lesson16/start/views/ecomm/Homepage.mxml
Lesson16/start/views/ecomm/OrderConf.mxml
Lesson16/start/views/ecomm/TextAndPic.mxml

Completed Files:

Lesson16/complete/EComm.mxml
Lesson16/complete/flexGrocer.css
Lesson16/complete/skins/OrangeOval.as
Lesson16/complete/views/ecomm/BillingInfo.mxml
Lesson16/complete/views/ecomm/Cart.mxml
Lesson16/complete/views/ecomm/CCInfo.mxml
Lesson16/complete/views/ecomm/GroceryDetail.mxml
Lesson16/complete/views/ecomm/Homepage.mxml
Lesson16/complete/views/ecomm/OrderConf.mxml
Lesson16/complete/views/ecomm/TextAndPic.mxml

Customizing the Look and Feel of a Flex Application

Out of the box, Flex provides a lot of functionality, but it has a rather generic look for an application. In this lesson, you will explore how to apply a design to a Flex application, both through the use of styles and by creating entirely new looks with skins.

The FlexGrocer e-commerce application you have been building all along gets a face-lift with styles and skins.

Applying a Design with Styles and Skins

There are two different approaches you can use to apply a design to your Flex applications: styles and skins.

You can modify the appearance of any Flex component through the use of *style* properties, which can be used for setting the font size, background color, and many other predefined style properties. In this lesson, you will explore the use of styles, learn about style inheritance, and see several different ways to apply styles to your application.

The other way to customize the look of a Flex application is by using *skins*, which are graphical elements (provided as files or drawn with ActionScript) that can be used to replace the default appearance of the varying states of a component. Although skinning is inherently more complex than applying styles, you will learn why you might need to do it, and how.

Applying Styles

As you have seen so far in your explorations, Flex development is done in a number of standards-based languages, such as MXML (based on XML) and ActionScript 3.0 (based on ECMAScript). It should be no surprise to learn that styles are also applied in a standards-based way through the use of Cascading Style Sheets (CSS). There are several different ways to apply a style: by setting a single style on a particular component; by using CSS class selectors to set several styles together, which can then be applied to various components; or by using a type selector to specify that all components of a particular type should use a set of styles.

In the next several exercises, you will have a chance to apply styles in all these different ways.

Regardless of which way a style is being applied, you need to know the style property that will affect the changes you want. ASDoc, also known as the *Adobe Flex 3 Language Reference* (which ships with Flex), has a complete listing of all styles available for every built-in component in Flex.

For example, any component showing text has the following styles:

- Color: Color of text in the component, specified as a hexadecimal number. The default value is 0x0B333C.

- disabledColor: Color of the component if it is disabled, specified as a hexadecimal number. The default value is 0xAAB3B3.

- fontFamily: Name of the font to use, specified as a string. Any font family name can be used. If you specify a generic font name (such as _sans), it will be converted to an appropriate device font. The default value is Verdana.

- `fontSize`: Height of the text, specified in pixels. The default value is 10.

- `fontStyle`: String indicating whether or not the text is italicized. Recognized values are `normal` and `italic`. The default is `normal`.

- `fontWeight`: String indicating whether or not the text is boldfaced. Recognized values are `normal` and `bold`. The default is `normal`.

- `marginLeft`: Number of pixels between the container's left border and the left edge of its content area. The default value for Text controls is 0, but different defaults apply to other components.

- `marginRight`: Number of pixels between the container's right border and the right edge of its content area. The default value for Text controls is 0, but different defaults apply to other components.

- `textAlign`: String indicating the alignment of text within its container or control. Recognized values are `left`, `right`, or `center`. The default value is `left`.

- `textDecoration`: String indicating whether or not the text is underlined. Recognized values are `none` and `underline`. The default value is `none`.

- `textIndent`: Offset of first line of text from the left side of the container, specified in pixels. The default value is 0.

Although these style properties are available for any component that has text, each component has its own unique list of style properties available, such as the `selectionColor` or `rollOverColor` (used in ComboBox, List, DataGrid, and so on), which accept a color as a hexadecimal value to indicate the color of the bar around an item when it is selected or has the mouse pointer positioned over it.

Setting Styles Inline with Tag Attributes

Styles can be applied to individual instances of a component by setting an attribute of the tag of the component with the name of the style property you want to set and the value to be set; for example, to make a label have a larger font size, you could specify the following:

```
<mx:Label text="Only a Test" fontSize="40"/>
```

In this exercise, you will set the `rollOverColor` and `selectionColor` for a ComboBox control in the second screen of the Checkout process (CCInfo.mxml).

1 Open CCInfo.mxml from your src/views/ecomm directory.

If you skipped the lesson when this was created, you can open this file from the Lesson16/start/views/ecomm directory and save it in your views/ecomm directory.

2 Find the declaration for the first ComboBox control with the id of cardType at about line 51. Add an attribute of the tag to specify the rollOverColor to be #AAAAAA.

```
<mx:ComboBox id="cardType" rollOverColor="#AAAAAA">
    <mx:dataProvider>
        <mx:Object label="American Express" data="AmericanExpress"/>
        <mx:Object label="Diners Club" data="DinersClub"/>
        <mx:Object label="Discover" data="Discover"/>
        <mx:Object label="MasterCard" data="MasterCard"/>
        <mx:Object label="Visa" data="Visa"/>
    </mx:dataProvider>
</mx:ComboBox>
```

It should be noted that letters used as part of a hexadecimal number (such as #AAAAAA) are not case sensitive; #aaaaaa works just as well.

3 Add another attribute to the same tag to specify the selectionColor as #EA800C.

```
<mx:ComboBox id="cardType" rollOverColor="#AAAAAA" selectionColor="#EA800C">
```

You are now telling this one ComboBox control that when a user puts the mouse pointer over one of the items, its color should be a pale gray (#AAAAAA) instead of the pale cyan (#0EFFD6), which is the default.

4 Save CCInfo.mxml. Open and run EComm.mxml. Click Checkout in the upper-right corner. On the Customer Information form, click the Continue button. Click the Credit Card Type combo box and notice the color of selected and rolled-over items.

You can easily compare this with the default look of the ComboBox control because you have changed only one of the three on this screen. Open either of the other two to see the default selectionColor and rollOverColor.

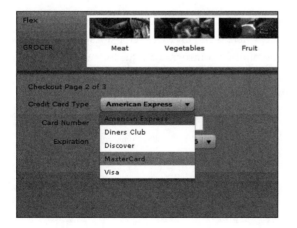

> **TIP:** It is also possible to set styles on individual instances in ActionScript using the `setStyle()` method. For example, the same style could have been applied with this code:

```
cardType.setStyle("selectionColor",0xEA800C);
cardType.setStyle("rollOverColor",0xAAAAAA);
```

> **NOTE:** When using `setStyle()`, colors are prefixed with 0x, which is the ECMAScript standard prefix for hexadecimal numbers. When applying a style in an attribute or `<mx:Style>` tag (as you will soon see), you can use a pound sign (#) instead of 0x. When set through ActionScript, numeric values (even those that are hexadecimal) do not have quotes around them.
>
> Although `setStyle()` is useful for times when styles need to change at runtime, it should be used sparingly because it is a processor-intensive operation.

Understanding Style Inheritance

As you look at the ASDoc on various components, you can see that each style has a yes or no property for something called CSS inheritance.

For example, in this figure you see a few styles of the ComboBox control—`selectionColor` and `rolloverColor`—do allow CSS inheritance, whereas `selectionDuration` does not. What this means is that if a parent container of a ComboBox control has a value for `selectionColor`, and the ComboBox control itself does not, the container's value will be used. However, because `selectionDuration` does not support inheritance, even if a parent container had a value set for `selectionDuration`, the ComboBox control would use the default value because it does not inherit the value.

Setting Styles with the <mx:Style> Tag

Many of you use CSS in web pages you build. You can also use many of the same CSS styles in your Flex applications. One way to do this is to add an <mx:Style> tag pair to any MXML document; you can write standard CSS style declarations between the open and close tags.

Standard CSS tends to have style properties whose names are all lowercase and uses hyphens as a separator between words:

```
background-color : #FFFFFF;
```

In the last exercise, you used multiword styles by declaring them with camel case syntax; that is, the style declaration started with a lowercase letter and each subsequent word started with an uppercase letter, with no spaces or hyphens used:

```
<mx:ComboBox rollOverColor="#AAAAAA"/>
```

The reason for the difference is that a hyphen is not a valid character for an XML attribute, and MXML tags are all XML tags. To work around this, when style names are set via attributes, they must be set with the ActionScript equivalent of the style name, so you use backgroundColor instead of background-color. The lowercase hyphenated versions of style properties are available only for properties that exist within traditional CSS. Any styles created specifically for Flex (such as rollOverColor) are available only in camel case. When you specify a style within an <mx:Style> tag, you can use either syntax, and it will be applied properly.

```
<mx:Style>
.customCombo{
   background-color: #AAAAAA;
   selectionColor: #EA800C;
}
</mx:Style>
```

Another choice you have when using CSS styles is the type of selector to use. Flex supports the use of CSS class selectors or CSS type (or Element) selectors.

A class selector defines a set of style properties as a single style class, which can then be applied to one or more components through the use of the component's styleName property.

```
<mx:Style>
.customCombo{
   color: #FF0000;
   selectionColor: #EA800C;
}
</mx:Style>
<mx:ComboBox styleName="customCombo"/>
```

> ● **TIP:** Unlike CSS for HTML, Flex does not support ID selectors.

Here, the ComboBox control is using the `customCombo` style class, which sets both the text color and the `selectionColor`.

A type selector enables you to specify a set of styles that will be applied to all instances of a type of component. In HTML applications, you can do this to define the look of an `<H1>` tag for your site. The same syntactic structure works to define a set of styles to be applied to all instances of a type of Flex control, as in the following:

```
<mx:Style>
ComboBox {
   color: #FF0000;
   selectionColor: #EA800C;
}
</mx:Style>
<mx:ComboBox id="stateProvenceCombo"/>
<mx:ComboBox id="countryCombo"/>
```

In this example, the `color` and `selectionColor` style properties are being applied to all ComboBox control instances.

> ● **TIP:** The terms *type* and *class selector* might seem counterintuitive if you haven't previously worked with CSS. These terms come from CSS standards. The confusion is that a type selector is what you would use to affect all instances of an ActionScript class; a class selector has no relation to any ActionScript class, but instead defines a style class that can be used on several elements.

In this next exercise, you will build a class selector and apply it to an `<mx:Form>` tag in CCInfo.mxml. This will not only showcase the use of a class selector, but you will also see style inheritance in use because the style will be inherited by all of the ComboBox controls in that form.

1 Open CCInfo.mxml from the previous exercise.

If you didn't finish the previous exercise, you can open CCInfo_inline.mxml from Lesson16/intermediate and save it as **CCInfo.mxml** in your views/ecomm directory.

2 Just after the root `<mx:Canvas>` tag, create an `<mx:Style>` tag pair.

```
<mx:Canvas xmlns:mx="http://www.adobe.com/2006/mxml">
   <mx:Style>
   </mx:Style>
   <mx:Metadata>
```

You now have an `<mx:Style>` block, in which you can create type or class selectors.

3 Inside the `<mx:Style>`block, create a class selector called `customCombo` that specifies a `selectionColor` of **#EA800C** and a `rollOverColor` of **#AAAAAA**.

```
<mx:Style>
   .customCombo{
       selectionColor:#EA800C;
       rollOverColor:#AAAAAA;
   }
</mx:Style>
```

As with traditional CSS, but unlike style properties set as attributes, no quotes are used around the values of the style properties.

4 Remove the `rollOverColor` and `selectionColor` attributes of the ComboBox control. Instead, specify a `styleName="customCombo"` as an attribute on that ComboBox control.

```
<mx:ComboBox id="cardType" styleName="customCombo">
```

If you save and test the application, the one ComboBox control should behave as it did before—with custom colors—whereas the other two show the default colors.

5 Cut the `styleName="customCombo"` from the ComboBox and instead paste it as an attribute of the `<mx:Form>` tag.

```
<mx:Form width="100%" styleName="customCombo">
```

Because the form contains three ComboBox controls, applying these cascading styles to the form will affect all the ComboBox controls within the form.

6 Save and run the application.

Verify that the style is now applied to all three ComboBox controls in the form.

Using Flex Builder Tools for Working with CSS

Flex Builder 3 offers a number of new tools to ease the process of applying a design to your application. Among these are two tools specific to working with cascading style sheets: the CSS Outline and CSS Design View.

When a CSS file is opened in Flex Builder 3, the Outline view now shows a hierarchical view of all the styles in the file. From within this view, you can now navigate to a particular node within a style definition with a single click. The following image shows the outline of the CSS file you will use throughout this lesson.

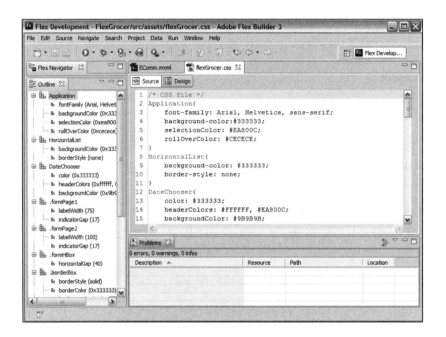

Another enhancement in Flex Builder 3 is the addition of a Design mode for CSS. Now, much like the Design mode you have for MXML files, you can also see the results of changes you make to the CSS in real time in a Design mode, as seen in the image that follows.

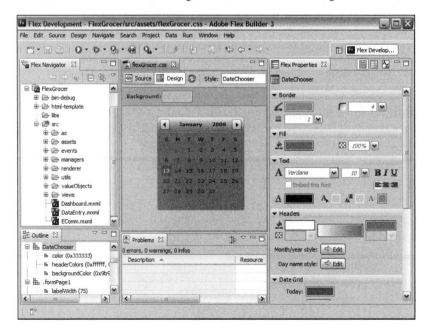

With these two new additions for working with CSS, it is much easier to build attractive, intuitive applications with Flex Builder.

Setting Styles with CSS Files

You can use an `<mx:Script>` tag to either define a block of code inline on the MXML document or you can use its `source` attribute to specify an external file to be compiled into the application. The `<mx:Style>` tag works in a similar way. Used as a tag pair, you can specify a series of styles inline in your MXML documents or you can use the `source` attribute to specify an external file:

```
<mx:Style source="path/to/file.css"/>
```

One great advantage of using an external file is that you can share CSS files between multiple Flex applications, or even between Flex and HTML applications. This is possible because CSS parsers in both Flex and HTML are smart enough to ignore any declarations they don't understand. So even if Flex supports only a subset of standard CSS, and in fact creates a number of its own custom declarations, neither your HTML nor your Flex applications will be hurt by declarations they cannot understand.

In this exercise, you will use a prebuilt CSS file to style the FlexGrocer application.

1 Copy flexGrocer.css from Lesson16/assets to your flexGrocer/src directory.

Open the file, and you will see a series of style definitions, some as type selectors (such as `Application`, `DateChooser`, and so on) and a number of class selectors (`.formPage1`, `.borderBox`, and so on). Styles that match traditional HTML styles (such as `background-color`, `font-family`, and so on) are all lowercase so they can work in both HTML and Flex applications, whereas any Flex-specific styles (`headerColors`, `hGridLines`, `alternatingRowColors`, and so on) are in only camel case.

2 Open the CCInfo.mxml file you worked on in the previous exercise and remove the `<mx:Style>` block you added.

As a best practice, all styles for the application are defined in a single style sheet. This way, if you want to change the look and feel of the application at a later time, you don't need to dig through the code to find all the places where styles were applied; instead, you can restyle the application by changing only one file!

3 Open EComm.mxml from your flexGrocer/src directory.

Alternatively, you can open this file from Lesson16/start and save it in your flexGrocer/src directory.

4 Just after the <mx:Application> tag, use an <mx:Style> tag with the source attribute to read in the CSS file.

```
<mx:Style source="flexGrocer.css"/>
```

This instructs the Flex compiler to read in the CSS file, making all those type and class declarations available to you.

5 Save the file and run the application.

Notice right away that any of the type selectors are automatically applied. This will become readily apparent as you notice that every ComboBox, DataGrid, List, and DateChooser control has the selectionColor and rollOverColor applied as they are specified in the Application type selector. This is because these two style properties are inheritable and they are applied at the topmost container (Application), so they will cascade to everything else within the application.

```
Application{
    font-family: Arial, Helvetica, sans-serif;
    background-color: #333333;
    selectionColor: #EA800C;
    rollOverColor: #CECECE;
}
```

Of course, more work needs to be done to the application because the default dark blue-green text on a dark gray background is nearly impossible to read. Don't worry—you will apply the other styles in the application to rectify it.

6 Still in EComm.mxml, find the labels for the logo in the ApplicationControlBar (at about lines 35 and 38). Set a styleName attribute of the first label to be logoTop and the second logo to be logoBottom.

```
<mx:Label x="0" y="0"
    text="Flex"
    styleName="logoTop"
    click="ecommNav.selectedChild=homePage"/>
<mx:Label x="0" y="41"
    text="GROCER"
    styleName="logoBottom"
    click="ecommNav.selectedChild=homePage"/>
```

The logoTop class selector specifies 40-point bold text with a #EA800C (orange) color. The logoBottom has the same color and bold, but with 19-point text instead.

7 Still in EComm.mxml, find the `<mx:ViewStack>` tag with an `id` of `ecommNav` (at about line 60). Set a `styleName` attribute of this tag to be `whiteBg`.

```
<mx:ViewStack id="ecommNav"
   width="100%" height="100%"
   styleName="whiteBg">
```

This sets a white (#FFFFFF) background for the body of the application. Because the ViewStack container is the outermost container for everything in the body, setting its background color to white will also create a white background for all its children.

8 Still in EComm.mxml, find the `<mx:Label>` that has the bottom branding (at about line 81). Set its `styleName` property to be `bottomBranding`.

```
<mx:Label text="(c) 2006, FlexGrocer. All rights reserved."
   right="10" bottom="10"
   styleName="bottomBranding"/>
```

The bottom text is set to be black, so it contrasts nicely with the white background.

9 Save and test the application.

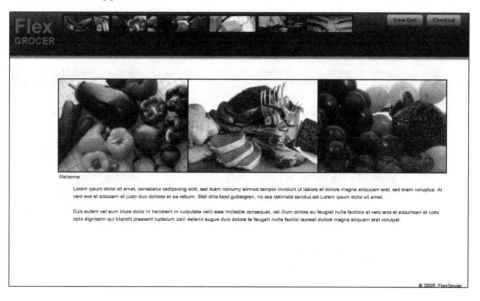

You should see a white background on the body, the orange logo, and the properly sized and colored bottom branding. After you have seen and tested it, you can close EComm.mxml. The rest of the styles you will be applying will be in child components.

10 Open Homepage.mxml from your src/views/ecomm directory.

Alternatively, you can open this file from the Lesson16/start/views/ecomm directory and save it in your src/views/ecomm directory.

11 Find the Label control with an `id` of `welcome`. Assign it a `styleName` of `homePageTitle`.

```
<mx:Label id="welcome"
     text="Welcome"
     left="{image.x}"
     top="{image.height+image.y}"
     styleName="homePageTitle"/>
```

The `homePageTitle` style class makes this label orange (#EA800C) with 90-point text, so it is very large.

12 Find the `<mx:Text>` tag with an `id` of `homePageText`. Assign it a `styleName` of `homePageText`.

```
<mx:Text width="{image.width-30}"
     left="{image.x+30}"
     top="{welcome.y + (welcome.height/2)}"
     styleName="homePageText">
```

The `homePageText` style class makes this text gray (#333333) with 13-point text.

13 Save Homepage.mxml and run the application.

You should now see the home page text styled properly. Notice that the labels under the category navigation are still too dark to read against the dark gray background. In the next set of steps, you will fix it.

After you see this rendering properly, you can save and close Homepage.mxml.

14 Open TextAndPic.mxml from your src/views/ecomm directory.

Alternatively, you can open this file from the Lesson16/start/views/ecomm directory and save it in your views/ecomm directory.

15 Find the `<mx:Label>` tag. Assign it a styleName of categoryText.

```
<mx:Label text="{data.catName}"
    width="100%"
    styleName="categoryText"/>
```

The categoryText style class makes this label white (#FFFFFF), 14-point, bold, and centered.

16 Save TextAndPic.mxml and run the application.

The category names should now be bigger, bolder, and white to make them visible against the dark background. However, if you click any of the categories, you will find that the text by each product seems very small, rendering in the default size of 10-point. You will address it next.

17 Open GroceryDetail.mxml from your src/views/ecomm directory.

Alternatively, you can open this file from the Lesson16/start/views/ecomm directory and save it in your flexGrocer/src/views/ecomm directory.

18 Find the `<mx:Label>` tag with an id of prodName (at about line 71). Assign it a styleName of standardOrange.

```
<mx:Label id="prodName"
    text="{groceryItem.prodName}"
    x="100" y="0"
    styleName="standardOrange"/>
```

The standardOrange style class will be used throughout the application when orange (#EA800C), nonbold, 12-point text is desired. When you finish the styling, GroceryDetail is one of four files that will use this style.

19 Find the <mx:Label> tag with an id of price (at about line 75). Assign it a styleName of standardBlackBold.

```
<mx:Label id="price"
    text="{curFormat.format(groceryItem.listPrice)}"
    x="100" y="20"
    styleName="standardBlackBold"/>
```

The standardBlackBold style class will be used throughout the application when black (#333333), bold, 12-point text is desired. This same style will also be used once in the BillingInfo component.

20 Find the <mx:VBox> tag added for the expanded state (at about line 51). Assign it a styleName of standardBlack.

```
<mx:states>
    <mx:State name="expanded">
        <mx:AddChild>
            <mx:VBox width="100%"
                x="200"
                styleName="standardBlack">
                ...
            </mx:VBox>
        </mx:AddChild>
        ...
    </mx:State>
</mx:states>
```

By applying the standardBlack (#333333, 12 point) style to the VBox, all the text contained by the VBox will use this style.

The last thing to do in GroceryDetail is to add a black border around the item when it is in its expanded state.

21 After the closing </mx:AddChild> tag that adds the <mx:VBox>, and before the <mx:SetProperty> tag that toggles the visibility of the Add button, add a new <mx:SetStyle> tag that sets the styleName property of the component to borderBox.

```
<mx:SetStyle
    name="styleName"
    value="borderBox"/>
```

Now, whenever the user moves the pointer over a product, in addition to showing the details, the borderBox style is also applied; it sets a dark gray (#333333) border around the entire component.

22 Save GroceryDetail.mxml and run the application.

As you run the application, clicking any of the categories should show all the styles now applied to the grocery details.

23 Open Cart.mxml from your src/views/ecomm directory.

Alternatively, you can open this file from the Lesson16/start/views/ecomm directory and save it in your views/ecomm directory. If you navigated to the fullCart state, the default look and feel of the DataGrid control feels a bit flat compared with the rest of the styled application. In these next steps, you will make the DataGrid control look more like the rest of the application.

24 Find the <mx:DataGrid> tag. Assign this a styleName of cartGrid.

```
<mx:DataGrid
    id="cartView"
    dataProvider="{cart.aItems}"
    width="100%" height="100%"
    editable="true"
    draggableColumns="false"
    variableRowHeight="true"
    styleName="cartGrid">
```

Looking back to the style sheet, you can see that the cartGrid style class sets the header colors to fade between white (#FFFFFF) and orange (#EA800C). Take a closer look at how the fade was specified.

```
.cartGrid{
    header-colors: #FFFFFF, #EA800C;
    horizontal-grid-lines: false;
    alternating-item-colors:#FFFFFF,#FFFFFF;
    vertical-grid-lines: false;
}
```

Notice that two of the styles (header-colors and alternating-item-colors) have comma-delimited lists of values specified. If you look to ASDoc for the definitions of these styles, you will see that they are both built to accept an array. Because CSS is not a programming language, nor really part of the ActionScript language, you can't use traditional approaches for creating an array (such as square brackets or the new Array() command). Instead, you specify an array in a CSS by providing a comma-delimited list of the elements. Another important thing to note is that alternating-item-colors needs at least two elements, even if they are the same. If this were defined only as alternating-item-colors: #EAEAEA; a run-time error would be thrown because Flash Player is looking to find an array and instead is finding only a single number.

▶ **TIP:** Elements that take an array, such as alternating-item-colors, are not limited to only two colors; you can usually specify several colors, and it will alternate between each of them.

25 Save Cart.mxml and run the application.

Choose a category, click the Add To Cart button for a few products, and then click the View Cart button. You should now see the Shopping Cart DataGrid control looking more like it belongs to this application.

All that remains to have styles from the style sheets applied to them are the pages of the checkout process.

26 Open BillingInfo.mxml from your src/views/ecomm directory.

Alternatively, you can open this file from the Lesson16/start/views/ecomm directory and save it in your views/ecomm directory.

27 On the root node of this document (an <mx:HBox> tag), apply a styleName of formPage1.

```
<mx:HBox xmlns:mx="http://www.adobe.com/2006/mxml"
    xmlns:u="utils.*"
    styleName="formPage1">
```

The `formPage1` style sets a `labelWidth` for all the form elements, so they now line up nicely and look less ragged than before. This also sets the `indicatorGap` style, which determines the space between the right edge of the label and the left edge of the controls.

28 Find the `<mx:Label>` tag, which tells the user they are on "Checkout Page 1 of 3", and apply a `styleName` attribute of `standardOrangeBold` to it.

```
<mx:Label text="Checkout Page 1 of 3"
   styleName="standardOrangeBold"/>
```

The `standardOrangeBold` style is the orange (#EA800C) version of the `standardBlackBold` style you applied to the price label in the GroceryDetail component.

29 On the next line, apply a `styleName` of `standardBlackBold` to the `<mx:FormHeading>` tag.

```
<mx:FormHeading label="Customer Information"
   styleName="standardBlackBold"/>
```

As was mentioned earlier, this style class sets black, 12-point bold text.

30 Save BillingInfo.mxml and run the application.

While running the application, click the Checkout button in the top-right corner of the screen. You should see the form items line up nicely, and have bold orange text for the step numbers and bold black text for the form heading. The `<mx:DateChooser>` control has had styles applied to it, too. (There is a type selector in the CSS file that sets the DateChooser control header colors, and it is inheriting the `selectionColor` and `rollOverColor` styles from the application.)

31 Open CCInfo.mxml from your src/views/ecomm directory.

Alternatively, you can open this file from the Lesson16/start/views/ecomm directory and save it in your views/ecomm directory.

32 Find the `<mx:Form>` tag (at about line 47). Replace the `styleName` attribute you set earlier (`customCombo`) with the value `formPage2`.

```
<mx:Form width="100%"
   styleName="formPage2">
```

The `formPage2` style is similar to the `formPage1` style you used in the previous document, except that it needs a larger `labelWidth` to accommodate longer text.

33 On the next line, set the `styleName` of the `<mx:Label>` to `standardOrangeBold`.

```
<mx:Label text="Checkout Page 2 of 3"
   styleName="standardOrangeBold"/>
```

Because you want to keep a consistent look and feel across the checkout process, the same style is used on the text to tell users where they are in the process.

34 Save CCinfo.mxml and run the application.

35 Open OrderConf.mxml from your src/views/ecomm directory.

Alternatively, you can open this file from the Lesson16/start/views/ecomm directory and save it in your flexGrocer/src/views/ecomm directory.

36 Find the `<mx:Form>` tag (at about line 23). Set its `styleName` attribute to `formPage1`.

```
<mx:Form styleName="formPage1">
```

This form, like the first, uses shorter labels; so the `formPage1` style is more appropriate for it.

Because you want to keep a consistent look and feel across the checkout process, in the next few steps you will add the same style to similar elements on the different pages to help the users know where they are in the process.

37 On the next line, set the styleName of the <mx:Label> to standardOrangeBold.

```
<mx:Label text="Checkout Page 3 of 3"
    styleName="standardOrangeBold"/>
```

38 On the next line, set the styleName of the <mx:FormHeading> to standardBlackBold.

```
<mx:FormHeading label="Billing Information"
    styleName="standardBlackBold"/>
```

39 On the next line, set the styleName of the <mx:HBox> to formHBox.

```
<mx:HBox styleName="formHBox">
```

This style sets only the horizontalGap of the HBox. On this page, it represents the distance between the first and second columns of data.

40 Save OrderConf.mxml and run the application.

```
Checkout Page 3 of 3

        Billing Information

        Jeff Tapper                Delivery Date    08/23/2006

        1 Radio Free Astoria Plaza

        Astoria

        NY

        11105

 Complete Order
 * Clicking this button will bill your credit card and complete this order


  Edit Information
```

Styles have now been consistently applied throughout the application. In order to see the changes on the third page, you will need to either comment out the credit card validation, or enter the number from a valid credit card. Don't worry, no information is actually being submitted, so there is no danger in entering your credit card information here.

Changing CSS at Runtime

One drawback to the CSS approach shown in the last section is that the CSS files are compiled into the application. This means that any changes to the application's style sheet require that the application be recompiled. A better approach is the ability to load CSS at runtime.

Benefits of Runtime CSS

There are a number of benefits to being able to change CSS at runtime. Chief among them is more rapid maintenance, in that a designer can simply deploy a new version of the CSS to the web server, eliminating the need to recompile and redeploy the application. Another benefit is it offers a much easier approach for deploying a single application that can be presented with multiple skins, without the need for separately deployed applications for each skin. For example, if Flex Grocer wanted to partner with local grocery stores and allow the stores to brand the application as their own, it is now possible to have a single deployed version of the application, which loads a different style sheet depending on the domain from which the application has been loaded.

Creating a SWF from a CSS File

As Flash Player doesn't natively have the ability to work with a runtime-loaded CSS file directly, Adobe has added a simple mechanism for converting an existing CSS style sheet into a SWF, with which Flash Player can easily interact. Using the SDK, you can use the MXMLC compiler to compile a CSS file to a SWF, or it can be done even easier within Flex Builder. All you need to do is right-click the CSS file in the Flex Navigator view, and choose the Compile To SWF option, as seen in the following figure.

Once the CSS has been compiled into a SWF, you can find the file named flexGrocer.swf in your bin-debug directory.

Loading a CSS SWF with StyleManager

Working with a CSS file compiled into a SWF is trivial; a single line of ActionScript is all you need to load and use that file:

```
StyleManager.loadStyleDeclarations("flexGrocer.swf");
```

This instructs the StyleManager to load the specified file and use any styles specified within it.

If you find the need to unload a CSS file loaded dynamically, there is another method on the StyleManager that will help with this: unloadStyleDeclaration

```
StyleManager.unloadStyleDeclaration("flexGrocer.swf");
```

Overriding Styles with a Loaded CSS

Making this even more powerful, it is possible to have multiple style sheets in play. These can be a combination of compiled and dynamically loaded style sheets. The fundamental rule to remember when dealing with multiple style sheets is that if any styles are defined in more than one style sheet, the one loaded last is the one that will be used. For example, if you have a CSS file compiled into the application with style definitions for Application, .boldText, and .formHeading, and you then load a CSS file at runtime that also has a definition for Application and .formHeading, the .boldText style from the compiled version will be used, as well as the Application and .formHeading style from the loaded style sheet—whichever is defined last is the one that is used.

Skinning Components

There are times when you might need to apply a design to a Flex application and you find that no style will easily fit your needs. In these cases, you need to use *skinning.*

Skinning is used to change the appearance of a component by modifying or replacing its visual elements. Unlike styles, which change values of the existing skins for a component, skinning enables you to actually replace the elements used. This can be done graphically with images and SWF files, or programmatically with class files and the drawing API.

Each component is made of several skins to represent the different visual looks of the component. For example, a button has a separate skin for its normal appearance (upSkin), for how it appears when the pointer is over it (overSkin), for when it is pressed (downSkin), and when it is disabled (disabledSkin). Each of the available skins for a component can be found in the styles section of that component's entry in ASDoc.

Graphical Skins

One way to apply skins to a component is to specify new graphical elements to be used in place of the default skins. If you are working with designers who have very specific graphic needs for the look and feel of components, you can use their graphical assets (JPG, GIF, PNG, or SWF files) as a replacement skin for any state of any component. Skins are actually applied as a style, they can be done inline, in an <mx:Style> block or CSS file, or via the setStyle() method. For example:

- Inline:

```
<mx:Button upSkin="@Embed('../assets/myFancyUpSkin.gif')"/>
```

- Setting in CSS Block (or file):

```
<mx:Style>
   Button {
      overSkin: Embed("../assets/images/myFancyOverSkin.gif");
   }
</mx:Style>
```

- Setting in ActionScript:

```
<mx:Script>
   [Embed("assets/myFancyDownSkin.gif")]
   var ds:Class;
   function initApp(){
      myButton.setStyle("downSkin",ds);
   }
</mx:Script>
```

Importing Skins Created in CS3

There are a number of different strategies for creating skins using Adobe's Creative Suite (CS3), which are nicely explained and detailed in the DevNet article here: www.adobe.com/devnet/flex/articles/flex_skins.html. Once these skins have been created, Flex Builder 3 offers a nice wizard for importing these skins and creating the cascading style sheets to make use of them.

▶ **TIP:** When creating skins in Flash Studio, be sure not to compress the movie (an option under the Publish Settings Screen). The wizard is unable to import assets from compressed SWFs.

To use the wizard to import images or SWFs, follow these steps:

1 In Flex Builder, choose File > Import. On the import menu, open the Flex Builder folder and choose Skin Artwork, then click next.

2 Choose the SWC or SWF file radio button, browse to the Lesson16/assets directory and choose skins.swf, then click next.

3 Click the Check All button, then fill in the appropriate Style Selector and Skin Part. All four skins will be used for the Button selector, as shown in the following figure. Then click the Finish button.

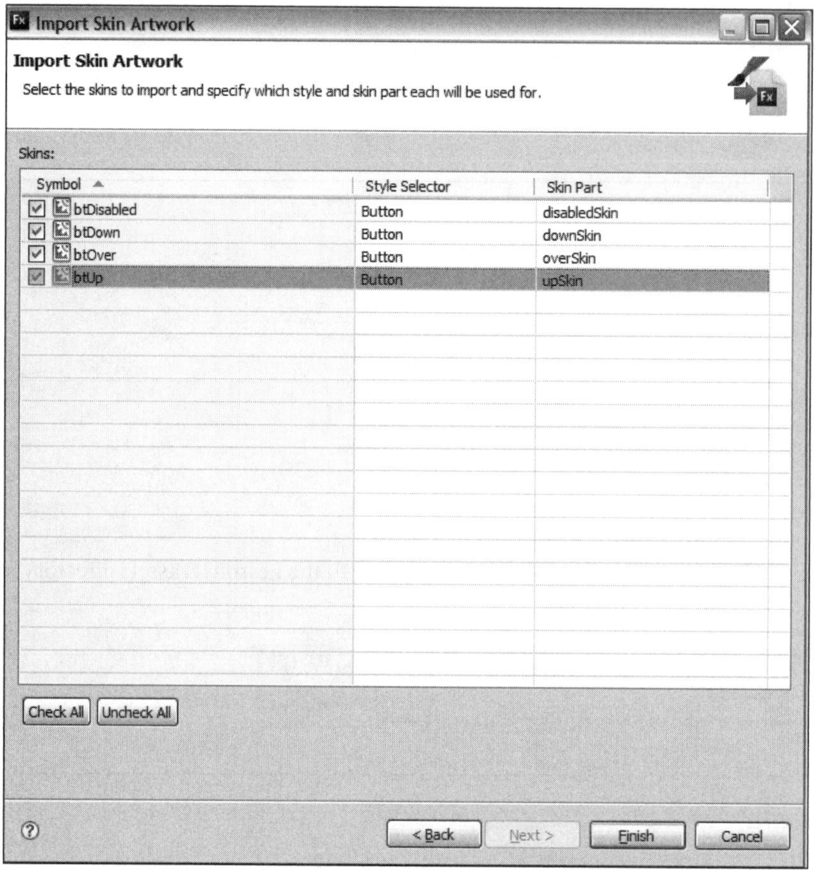

The wizard will copy the SWF into your project, and create a style sheet that associates the symbols from that SWF to the appropriate Skin Part, and associate the style sheet with the EComm.mxml file.

You can remove the line that includes skins.css, as you will learn a better option for this application in the next section.

Programmatic Skins

Rather than use graphical assets for skins, it is possible to use the drawing API of Flash Player (mostly found in the flash.display.Graphics class) to programmatically draw your own skins. To do this, you create a class file that defines the skin.

The main reason you might choose to use a programmatic skin instead of a graphical one is that you have much more control over skins when they are programmatic. Instead of embedding graphics of a fixed size, programmatic skins can easily be built to resize themselves, whereas a graphical skin does not resize so elegantly. Programmatic skins also tend to use less memory as they contain no external graphic files.

By drawing a skin programmatically, you have access to more flexibility than you would normally have by using styles. For example, a button has styles to allow a gradient fill by using the fillColors style property; however, you can't control the ratio of the fill. Imagine a gradient that was 20 percent red and 80 percent blue. The fillColors property applies an equal amount of each color, whereas the drawing API provides a beginGradientFill() method that not only allows you to specify the array of colors but also the percentages of each (as well as a matrix) to determine the direction of the fade.

To create a programmatic skin, you first need to choose a superclass for your new skin class. Flex provides three classes that you can choose from:

- **ProgrammaticSkin:** The ProgrammaticSkin class implements the `IFlexDisplayObject`, `ILayoutClient` and `IStyleable` interfaces. This is the lightest-weight class that can be used as the superclass for a skin.

- **Border:** The Border class extends the ProgrammaticSkin class and adds support for the `borderMetrics` property. If you are looking to implement a skin with a border that doesn't use a background image, this is the choice for you.

- **RectBorder:** The RectBorder class extends the Border class and adds support for the `backgroundImage` style.

The bulk of the work you will do to write a programmatic skin is to override the `updateDisplayList()` method. If you recall, during Lesson 10, "Creating Custom Components with ActionScript 3.0," you overrode this method when creating the MaxRestorePanel. This method is what is used to draw the visual elements of any class, so to create a new look for a skin, this method needs to be overridden.

If you choose to use one of the bordered classes (Border or RectBorder) as a superclass, you will also want to override the getter method for the `borderMetrics` property so it returns your custom metrics instead of the default values.

In this exercise, you will create a custom skin for the Button controls in your application. This skin will use an ellipse instead of the default rectangle as the shape for the skin.

1 In Flex Builder, create a new directory named **skins** as a subdirectory of your flexGrocer/src directory.

If you followed the default locations for your project, this new directory would be in your *driveroot*/flex3tfs/flexGrocer/src directory.

2 Create a new ActionScript class named **OrangeOval** in the skins package. The superclass for your skin should be mx.skins.ProgrammaticSkin. Make sure the "Generate constructor from superclass" check box is deselected, and click Finish.

```
package skins{
   import mx.skins.ProgrammaticSkin;

   public class OrangeOval extends ProgrammaticSkin{
   }
}
```

Because you don't need a border around your button, the ProgrammaticSkin class is an appropriate superclass for you.

3 Create the skeleton for your overridden `updateDisplayList()` method.

```
protected override function updateDisplayList(w:Number, h:Number):void{
}
```

Remember that an overridden method needs to exactly match the signature of the method in the superclass. Looking at ASDoc, you can find that this is a `protected` method, returning `void`, which accepts two numeric arguments.

4 Inside the `updateDisplayList()` method, create two local variables: an int named `lineThickness` with a value of 4 and a Number named `backgroundFillColor`.

```
var lineThickness:int=4;
var backgroundFillColor:Number;
```

When you draw the shape, these variables will be used with the drawing API.

5 Create a `switch` statement to determine which skin is being drawn. Assign the `backgroundFillColor` the appropriate value from the following table for each version of the skin.

Skin	Color
upSkin	0xEA800C
overSkin	0xF8B872
downSkin	0xB06109
disabledSkin	0xCCCCCC

```
switch (name) {
   case "upSkin":
      backgroundFillColor = 0xEA800C;
      break;
   case "overSkin":
      backgroundFillColor = 0xF8B872;
      break;
   case "downSkin":
      backgroundFillColor = 0xB06109;
      break;
   case "disabledSkin":
      backgroundFillColor = 0xCCCCCC;
      break;
}
```

The name property used in the switch statement is the current name of the skin. For a programmatic skin of a Button control, the name property could be any of the skin states. This method is automatically called each time the button is redrawn (such as when the Button control changes state), and Flex automatically updates the value of the name property.

6 Use the drawing API to clear any previously drawn elements.

```
graphics.clear();
```

The ProgrammaticSkin class has a property called graphics, which is an instance of the flash.display.Graphics class. This is the class that contains the drawing API. Because this same updateDisplayList() will be used to draw all four states, you want to remove the previously drawn elements before drawing the current state.

7 Use the beginFill() method of the Graphics class to set the background color to be drawn.

```
graphics.beginFill(backgroundFillColor);
```

When the shape for the skin is drawn, it will now be filled with the appropriate color determined from the switch statement.

8 Use the drawEllipse() method to draw the skin.

```
graphics.drawEllipse(0, 0, w, h);
```

This line does the actual drawing and creates an ellipse from the component's top left (0,0) to the height and width, as specified by the arguments automatically provided to the updateDisplayList() method.

9 End the fill.

```
graphics.endFill();
```

Flash Player waits until the endFill() method is called before actually drawing the fill on the screen.

10 Save and close OrangeOval.as.

The completed class file should read like this:

```
package skins{
   import mx.skins.ProgrammaticSkin;
   public class OrangeOval extends ProgrammaticSkin{
      protected override function updateDisplayList(w:Number,
         h:Number):void{
         var lineThickness:int=4;
         var backgroundFillColor:Number;
```

```
        switch (name) {
           case "upSkin":
              backgroundFillColor = 0xEA800C;
              break;
           case "overSkin":
              backgroundFillColor = 0xF8B872;
              break;
           case "downSkin":
              backgroundFillColor = 0xB06109;
              break;
           case "disabledSkin":
              backgroundFillColor = 0xCCCCCC;
              break;
        }
        graphics.clear();
        graphics.beginFill(backgroundFillColor);
        graphics.drawEllipse(0, 0, w, h);
        graphics.endFill();
     }
   }
}
```

11 Open flexGrocer.css.

If you didn't copy this file over earlier in the lesson, you can find it in the Lesson16/assets directory. Save it in your root directory.

12 At the bottom of the file, create a class selector named homePageButton that sets the upSkin, downSkin, overSkin, and disabledSkin style properties to use ClassReference('skins.OrangeOval');.

```
.homePageButton {
   upSkin:ClassReference('skins.OrangeOval');
   downSkin:ClassReference('skins.OrangeOval');
   overSkin:ClassReference('skins.OrangeOval');
   disabledSkin:ClassReference('skins.OrangeOval');
}
```

Programmatic skins can be applied in a CSS file by using the ClassReference directive. This directive takes a class name as the argument. It tells any button using the homePage-Button class selector to use your new skin class for all four states.

13 While still in the homePageButton class selector, add one more style declaration, setting the color property to white (#FFFFFF);

```
. homePageButton {
  upSkin:ClassReference('skins.OrangeOval');
  downSkin:ClassReference('skins.OrangeOval');
  overSkin:ClassReference('skins.OrangeOval');
  disabledSkin:ClassReference('skins.OrangeOval');
  color:#ffffff;
}
```

The white text makes the button easier to read.

14 Open EComm.mxml, then add a styleName="homePageButton" to the btnViewCart and btnCheckout buttons in the ApplicationControlBar.

```
<mx:Button label="View Cart"
  id="btnViewCart"
  right="90" y="0"
  click="showCart()"
  styleName="homePageButton"/>
<mx:Button label="Checkout"
  id="btnCheckout"
  right="10" y="0"
  click="ecommNav.selectedChild=checkout"
  styleName="homePageButton"/>
```

Setting this style name tells these two buttons to use the new style, which contains the OrangeOval skin.

15 Save all files and run the application.

The Button controls in the ApplicationControlBar are now rendered with the OrangeOval skin.

What You Have Learned

In this lesson, you have:

- Learned how Flex applications are styled (pages 413–414)
- Set styles via tag attributes (pages 414–416)
- Learned about inheritable style properties (page 416)
- Set styles via the <mx:Style> tag (pages 417–419)
- Set styles via CSS files (pages 419–433)
- Created and a graphical skin (pages 433–437)
- Created and used a programmatic skin (pages 437–443)

What You Will Learn

In this lesson, you will:

- Use the `<mx:WebService>` tag to retrieve data from the server
- Sort the collection returned from the server as a result of the web service call
- Declare specific operations on the `<mx:WebService>` tag
- Bind specific parameters to a Web Service operation
- Use the Web Service Introspection Wizard
- Use the Flex Builder Refactoring Tools

Approximate Time

This lesson takes approximately 1 hour and 30 minutes to complete.

Lesson Files

Media Files:

None

Starting Files:

Lesson17/start/Dashboard.mxml

Lesson17/start/DataEntry.mxml

Lesson17/start/managers/CategorizedProductManager.mxml

Lesson17/start/valueObjects/Product.as

Lesson17/start/views/dataEntry/UpdateDeleteProd.mxml

Completed Files:

Lesson17/complete/Dashboard.mxml

Lesson17/complete/DataEntry.mxml

Lesson17/complete/managers/CategorizedProductManager.mxml

Lesson17/complete/valueObjects/Product.as

Lesson17/complete/generated/webservices/AddProduct_request.as

Lesson17/complete/generated/webservices/AddProductResultEvent.as

Lesson17/complete/generated/webservices/ArrayOf_xsd_string.as

Lesson17/complete/generated/webservices/ArrayOfArrayOf_xsd_anyType.as

Lesson17/complete/generated/webservices/BaseProductManagerService.as

Lesson17/complete/generated/webservices/BaseProductManagerServiceSchema.as

Lesson17/complete/generated/webservices/CFCInvocationException.as

Lesson17/complete/generated/webservices/DeleteProduct_request.as

Lesson17/complete/generated/webservices/DeleteProductResultEvent.as

Lesson17/complete/generated/webservices/GetAllProds_request.as

Lesson17/complete/generated/webservices/GetAllProdsResultEvent.as

Lesson17/complete/generated/webservices/IProductManagerService.as

Lesson17/complete/generated/webservices/ProductManagerService.as

Lesson17/complete/generated/webservices/UpdateProduct_request.as

Lesson17/complete/generated/webservices/UpdateProductResultEvent.as

Lesson17/complete/generated/webservices/WebServiceProduct.as

Lesson17/completed/views/dataEntry/UpdateDeleteProd.mxml

LESSON 17

Working with Web Services

Until now, the data that you have been displaying (available products, categories, sales data, and so on) has come from XML feeds or was written into the application via MXML or ActionScript. In the real world, every application that you write will have three logic areas: the client, the business logic (logic that implements the requirement of the system), and the data it runs on.

Although Adobe Flex is a great platform for developing your rich-client interface and can also be used to write business logic, from an architectural standpoint it is sometimes best to put your core business logic outside your Flex application. For example, you could have the process that checks for available inventory reside on the server and be called by the client before completing a sale. Centralizing both the data access and business rules provides a system that is easier to secure and maintain.

Confirmation screen after adding a new product

In this lesson, you will learn to access web services on a server to retrieve data for the Dashboard application and create new products in the DataEntry application. You will also learn to use the new Web Service Introspection Wizard of Flex 3 to simplify the process of accessing and maintaining web service calls.

From this lesson forward, an increasing amount of the external data access from the Flex application will be using the local web server. Please refer to the "Setup Instructions" appendix to learn how to install, set up, and run the web server instance.

Introducing Server Communication

The need for clients to make calls to a server for business processing came about the first time multiple users could access the same system at the same time. The original calls were done over custom-defined protocols dubbed Remote Procedure Calls (RPCs). The first RPCs were primarily designed to work within a specific vendor's platform and product. They typically had a specific format for the data being passed (binary, encryption, what bit position referred to what piece of data, and so on). Today, the term *RPC* describes the most basic call between a client and a server instead of a specific protocol or message format.

The need for an enterprise to share the business logic written in one application with another quickly drove the need to standardize the way applications communicate. The emergence of Common Object Request Broker Architecture (CORBA) as an industry-maintained standard for exposing middle-tier server objects was a big step forward in the capability to share logic between applications. The big drawback was the difference in each vendor's implementation of CORBA and the mapping of data between different systems.

Java introduced Remote Method Invocation (RMI) as a more refined way of calling remote objects and passing data between the client and server tier. However, because of its complexity to implement, RMI was not heavily used by developers outside the Java world.

The latest way to interface between the client and the server, web services, leverages text-based XML to describe how the server objects are used as well as the format in which the communication is done. A web service can be thought of as a dynamic web page read by a client application. Even though web services are generally used (or consumed) by a client application, the data and description of that data remain human readable as XML. However, this strength is also a weakness. The human readable text is not as efficient as binary communication between the client and the server.

In Flash MX, Flash Remoting was introduced as a way to provide binary communication between the Flash client and the server. Flash Remoting is based on an open protocol called Action Message Format (AMF) that enables you to communicate with a variety of server technologies including Java, PHP, and ColdFusion. You will also learn to work with this protocol in Lesson 18, "Accessing Server-Side Objects."

Using the Event Model Remote Server Calls

When making calls to a server, you are calling logic that resides outside Flex. Just like the <mx:HTTPService> tag discussed in Lesson 6, "Using Remote XML Data with Controls," you do not have control over when the server will finish executing the request you made. Therefore, you need to use events and event listeners to understand when the server is finished with the request.

Flex broadcasts a result event if the server was able to process your request successfully, which may mean returning data from a query or simply performing an action on the server. Conversely, a fault event is broadcast if an error occurs communicating with the server or if the server encounters an error while processing your request. Both the result and fault event carry additional information, such as any data returned or an indication of why the fault occurred.

Throughout the remainder of the book, you will be using these events directly and indirectly to work with a ColdFusion server.

Configuring an Application to Work Locally

From this lesson forward, you will be using the local ColdFusion server for all data and remote objects that the application will use. With ColdFusion started and running, the next set of steps will have you update the application to point all the <mx:HTTPService> tags to the local ColdFusion server.

> ✳ **NOTE:** See the appendix, "Setup Instructions," for instructions on how to install and start the ColdFusion server. The ColdFusion server will receive requests from Flex to retrieve, add, and update data. You must have ColdFusion set up from this point forward to run the lessons.

1 If you have not done so already, start your local ColdFusion server.

If your ColdFusion server is installed according to the setup instructions in the appendix, you can start the server by executing the command jrun -start cfusion from a command prompt in the *driveroot*\cfusionFlexTFS\bin directory. Be sure to leave the command prompt open while using the server.

2 Open Dashboard.mxml.

Alternatively, you can open Dashboard.mxml from your Lesson17/start directory and save it to your flexGrocer/src directory.

3 Replace each incidence of http://www.flexgrocer.com/ in the url attribute of each <mx:HTTPService> tag with **http://localhost:8300/flexGrocer/xml/.**

```
<mx:HTTPService id="salesRPC"
    url="http://localhost:8300/flexGrocer/xml/rawSalesData.xml"
    result="salesRPCResult(event)"
    fault="showFault(event)"/>
<mx:HTTPService id="typeRPC"
    url="http://localhost:8300/flexGrocer/xml/categorySalesData.xml"
    result="typeRPCResult(event)"
    fault="showFault(event)"/>
<mx:HTTPService id="compRPC"
    url="http://localhost:8300/flexGrocer/xml/salesData.xml"
    result="compRPCResult(event)"
    fault="showFault(event)"/>
<mx:HTTPService id="catRPC"
    url="http://localhost:8300/flexGrocer/xml/category.xml"
    result="catHandler(event)"/>
```

4 Open DataEntry.mxml.

Alternatively, you can open DataEntry.mxml from your Lesson17/start directory and save it to your flexGrocer/src directory.

5 Replace each incidence of http://www.flexgrocer.com/ in the url attribute of each <mx:HTTPService> tag with **http://localhost:8300/flexGrocer/xml/** as the URL.

```
<mx:HTTPService id="unitRPC"
    url="http://localhost:8300/flexGrocer/xml/units.xml"
    result="unitRPCResult(event)"/>
```

6 Open CategorizedProductManager.mxml from your src/managers directory.

Alternatively, you can open CategorizedProductManager.mxml from your Lesson17/start/managers directory and save it to your flexGrocer/src/managers directory.

7 Replace each incidence of http://www.flexgrocer.com/ in the url attribute of each <mx:HTTPService> tag with **http://localhost:8300/flexGrocer/xml/.**

```
<mx:HTTPService id="prodByCatRPC"
    url="http://localhost:8300/flexGrocer/xml/categorizedProducts.xml"
    result="prodByCategoryHandler(event)"
    resultFormat="e4x"/>
```

8 Run the Dashboard, Data Entry, and Ecommerce applications. You should notice no difference in their functionality from what you saw at the end of Lesson 16, "Customizing the Look and Feel of a Flex Application." However, the data for these applications is now coming from your hard drive, as opposed to flexgrocer.com.

Using a Web Service in the Dashboard

In this exercise, you will replace the three `<mx:HTTPService>` tags with a single `<mx:WebService>` tag for retrieving the data for the Dashboard. The `<mx:WebService>` tag is pointing to a server object to retrieve the data that is needed.

There are two ways to call a web service in Flex. The first is tag based; the other is via ActionScript. You will use the `<mx:WebService>` tag in this exercise to create a WebService object against which you can call your methods.

1 If you have not done so already, start your local ColdFusion server.

2 Open Dashboard.mxml.

3 Below the script block, locate the first three `<mx:HTTPService>` tags (salesRPC, typeRPC, and compRPC) that get the XML data for the Dashboard, and replace them with a single `<mx:WebService>` tag. Set the id attribute to dashboardWS. Set the wsdl attribute to **http://localhost:8300/flexGrocer/cfcs/aggregate.cfc?wsdl**. Finally, leave the fault handler the same as what the `<mx:HTTPService>` used. Be sure to leave the HTTPService tag with the id catRPC in place.

```
<mx:WebService
    id="dashboardWS"
    wsdl="http://localhost:8300/flexGrocer/cfcs/aggregate.cfc?wsdl"
    fault="showFault(event)">
</mx:WebService>
```

The wsdl parameter of the WebService tag specifies the URL where Flex can find information about this server object's capabilities. It is defined in Web Service Description Language (WSDL). Flex will load this WSDL to understand the available methods on the server and how it can access them. Once the WSDL file is loaded successfully, the WebService tag broadcasts an event called load.

In Flex, you can use the methods on a web service in three ways:

- **Fully Declared Method:** You define the operation (method) and its arguments as a child of the `<mx:WebService>` tag via the `<mx:operation>` and `<mx:request>` tags. In effect, you are letting Flex know which methods you intend to call on the server object and which arguments you will be passing.

- **Declared Method:** You define the operation as a child of the `<mx:WebService>` tag via the `<mx:operation>` tag, but you do not define the arguments. This specifies the methods you intend to call, but does not specify the arguments to those methods. When you attempt to use the Web Service, Flex validates the arguments by looking into the WSLD.

- **Undeclared Method:** You use the `<mx:WebService>`, but do not specify the operations or arguments. When you attempt to use the Web Service, Flex looks at the loaded WSDL for both method and argument validation.

> ▶ **TIP:** Like the HTTPService tag that you used in earlier lessons, the WebService tag broadcasts fault or result events to indicate a failure or success, when retrieving data from the server. One of the benefits of declaring the methods and operations on a WebService tag is that you can have a specified fault and result handler for each operation.

4 In this example, you will use the Fully Declared Method. Create a child `<mx:operation>` tag inside the `<mx:WebService>` tag. Give it a name of getTypeSalesData and specify a result handler as the typeRPCResult() function, passing the event object as the only parameter.

```
<mx:operation name="getTypeSalesData" result="typeRPCResult(event)">
</mx:operation>
```

This lets Flex know that you intend to call a method named getTypeSalesData on the server object. Previously, you defined a function typeRPCResult() that dealt with the result (passed in as a variable called event) from the `<mx:HTTPService>`. You will modify this function later to handle the new data format returned by this web service.

5 In between the `<mx:operation>` tags, create an `<mx:request>` pair.

```
<mx:operation name="getTypeSalesData" result="typeRPCResult(event)">
    <mx:request>
    </mx:request>
</mx:operation>
```

6 Specify a tag for startDate that binds to startDate.selectedDate and a tag for endDate that binds to endDate.selectedDate.

```
<mx:request>
    <startDate>{startDate.selectedDate}</startDate>
    <endDate>{endDate.selectedDate}</endDate>
</mx:request>
```

This specifies that your getTypeSalesData() method on the server will accept two arguments representing the start and end date for the sales data you are retrieving. Using data binding ensures that the value of these arguments will be the last dates that the user selected from the startDate and endDate date fields.

> **TIP:** Specifying the arguments of the `WebService()` method and then having the values update via binding can be a very nice way to simplify your calls.

7 In the script block at the top of the file, add a bindable public variable called `selectedType` of type String. Default it to `All`.

```
[Bindable]
public var selectedType:String = "All";
```

This variable will be used to store the category selected in the ComboBox control. It is defaulted to `All`, the initial selection criteria. You will update this value later in the lesson.

8 Create another child `<mx:operation>` tag, under the close of the last `<mx:operation>` tag inside the `<mx:WebService>` tag. Give it a name of `getSalesData`, and specify the `result` handler as the `salesRPCResult()` function, passing it the event object.

```
<mx:operation name="getSalesData" result="salesRPCResult(event)">
</mx:operation>
```

This method will return the sales data summarized by each day for the selected category of food sold. You previously defined the function `salesRPCResult()` that processed the result from the `<mx:HTTPService>` tag. You will modify this function later to handle the new data format of this web service operation. This operation will provide data for two of the ChartPods in the Dashboard—sales and comparison. In lesson 19, "Visualizing Data," you will use this data for charting.

9 In between the `<mx:operation>` tags, create an `<mx:request>` pair.

```
<mx:operation name="getSalesData" result="salesRPCResult(event)">
    <mx:request>
    </mx:request>
</mx:operation>
```

10 In between the `<mx:request>` tags, specify a tag for `startDate` that binds to `startDate.selectedDate`, a tag for `endDate` that binds to `endDate.selectedDate`, and a `category` that binds to the public `selectedType` variable.

```
<mx:request>
    <startDate>{startDate.selectedDate}</startDate>
    <endDate>{endDate.selectedDate}</endDate>
    <category>{selectedType}</category>
</mx:request>
```

This specifies that the `getSalesData()` method has three arguments and sets their values according to the user's actions using data binding.

Handling Web Service Results

Web service requests are made to an external server, which requires an unknown amount of time to process your request and return the appropriate data. Therefore you need to "listen" for the result to arrive back from the server before attempting to act on the returned data.

The WebService class enables you to listen for the result of all methods returned from the server at once, or listen for the result of each individual method independently. You listen for your data (or find out that there was a failure) by creating event listeners for the result and fault events.

Once data is returned from the server successfully, you can manipulate or display it as needed. The web service results are not sorted in any particular way. Therefore, you are going to write a method to sort that data before passing it along for display.

1 Still in the Dashboard.mxml, create a private function called sortByDateField that returns an ArrayCollection. The first argument is called aSales of type ArrayCollection, the second argument is called colName and is of type String.

```
private function sortByDateField(aSales:ArrayCollection, colName:String):
    ➥ ArrayCollection{
}
```

The first argument will contain the results returned from the web service call. The second argument specifies the field you will use for sorting. Providing the second argument makes this method more reusable in multiple situations and gives you the flexibility to sort on different columns.

2 Create a local ArrayCollection variable called salesData, and assign it the passed in argument aSales.

```
private function sortByDateField
    ➥ (aSales:ArrayCollection, colName:String):ArrayCollection{
    var salesData:ArrayCollection = aSales;
}
```

This line of code does not create a new ArrayCollection. Rather, it simply provides us another way, called a pointer or reference, of accessing the same data.

3 Inside the script block, add an import for the mx.collections.Sort class.

```
import mx.collections.Sort;
```

4 Inside the sortByDateField() method, create a local Sort variable called sort.

```
private function sortByDateField
   _(aSales:ArrayCollection, colName:String):ArrayCollection{
   var salesData:ArrayCollection = aSales;
   var sort:Sort = new Sort();
}
```

You will use this variable to set up the sort definition for your local ArrayCollection.

5 Inside the script block, add an import for the mx.collections.SortField class.

```
import mx.collections.SortField;
```

6 Back inside the sortByDate() method, set the fields property of sort as an array with the first entry being a new SortField with two arguments passed to its constructor. The first is colName, which will specify the field name for the sort, and the second is true, which will make the sort case sensitive.

```
private function sortByDateField
   _(aSales:ArrayCollection, colName:String):ArrayCollection{
   var salesData:ArrayCollection = aSales;
   var sort:Sort = new Sort();
   sort.fields = new Array(new SortField(colName,true));
}
```

For each dataset that you use, you should specify the field name on which you are sorting.

7 Assign the local sort variable to the sort property of salesData, and refresh the salesData ArrayCollection.

```
private function sortByDateField
   _(aSales:ArrayCollection, colName:String):ArrayCollection{
   var salesData:ArrayCollection = aSales;
   var sort:Sort = new Sort();
   sort.fields = new Array(new SortField(colName,true));
   salesData.sort = sort;
   salesData.refresh();
}
```

8 Return the sorted salesData ArrayCollection from the function.

```
private function sortByDateField
   _(aSales:ArrayCollection, colName:String):ArrayCollection{
   var salesData:ArrayCollection = aSales;
   var sort:Sort = new Sort();
   sort.fields = new Array(new SortField(colName,true));
   salesData.sort = sort;
   salesData.refresh();
   return salesData;
}
```

9 Go to the salesRPCResult() function. Use the sortByDateField() function to sort event.result on the DTSALE field and assign the result to sales.dp. You will need to cast event.result into an ArrayCollection before you pass it into the function.

```
private function salesRPCResult(event:ResultEvent):void{
    sales.dp = this.sortByDateField(event.result as ArrayCollection, "DTSALE");
}
```

The salesRPCResult method is called when the result of the getSalesData web service method returns data successfully. The sales data returned by this method is an ArrayCollection, but the result property on the event object is a generic object. To use your function (which expects an ArrayCollection), you need to tell the Flex compiler that the data in event.result is an ArrayCollection. You do this by casting event.result as an ArrayCollection.

Your method returns the original collection, which has now been sorted by "DTSALE".

10 Go to the typeRPCResult() function. Cast the event.result value as an ArrayCollection.

```
private function typeRPCResult(event:ResultEvent):void{
    type.dp = (event.result as ArrayCollection);
}
```

The typeRPCResult method is called when the result of the getTypeSalesData web service method returns data successfully. The data returned by this method is an ArrayCollection, but the result property on the event object is a generic object. The dp property of the type object expects an ArrayCollection, so you need to tell the Flex compiler that the data in event.result is an ArrayCollection. You do this by casting event.result as an ArrayCollection.

11 Remove the compRPCResult() function completely. You will add the functionality from this method to the salesRPCResult() function as both sales.dp and comp.dp will now use the same data. Assign comp.dp to the same sorted results as is used to set sales.dp.

```
private function salesRPCResult(event:ResultEvent):void{
    sales.dp = this.sortByDateField(event.result as ArrayCollection, "DTSALE");
    comp.dp = this.sortByDateField(event.result as ArrayCollection, "DTSALE");
}
```

Because you no longer need the additional web service call to get the data for the Sales ChartPod, it makes sense to collapse the setting of the dp properties of the components into one method.

Calling Web Service Methods

You call a Web Service differently than an HTTP service. Further, the approach taken varies based upon how fully you decided to define the methods in the WebService tag.

When using the <mx: HTTPService> tag, you learned to call the send() method of the HTTP service to begin the process of retrieving data. The first approach you will learn for calling methods on a WebService tag also involves the send method; but, unlike the HTTPService, you call the send() method on a specific operation.

For example:

```
myHttpService.send();
myWebService.myOperation.send()
```

You will need to update your getData() function to call the WebService methods. Currently, getData() is only called on the initialization of the Dashboard. You have configured your Web Service operations to use a start date, an end date, and a category name as arguments to filter the results. Because these values change on the client, you will want to call the getData() function again to retrieve new information from the server.

1 Still in Dashboard.mxml, go to the getData() function. Replace the call to the three HTTPService send() functions with the calls to the Web Services' getTypeSalesData.send() and getSalesData.send() methods.

```
private function getData():void{
   dashboardWS.getTypeSalesData.send();
   dashboardWS.getSalesData.send();
}
```

2 Create a private function called setCat() that returns void. Have it accept one argument called event of type Event.

```
private function setCat(event:Event):void{
}
```

This function will capture any selection change in the ComboBox, set the selected category, and refresh the data of the Dashboard.

3 Set the public variable selectedType to the current category name, which is found in ComboBox(event.currentTarget).selectedItem.name. Then call the getData() function to refresh the data.

```
private function setCat(event:Event):void{
   selectedType = ComboBox(event.currentTarget).selectedItem.name;
   getData();
}
```

You need to first cast event.currentTarget to a ComboBox so that you can access the text property. In the text property, you will find the name of the current category name selected by the user.

4 On the change event of the catCombo ComboBox, call the setCat() function, passing along the event argument.

```
<mx:ComboBox id="catCombo"
   dataProvider="{categories}"
   change="setCat(event)"
   labelField="name"/>
```

5 On the startDate and endDate DateFields, call the getData() function on their change events.

```
<mx:Label text="Start Date"/>
<mx:DateField id="startDate" change="getData()"/>
<mx:Label text="End Date"/>
<mx:DateField id="endDate" change="getData()"/>
```

Remember, the start date, end dates, and selected type are bound to the arguments of your web service operations. As the user changes these fields, the web service arguments are automatically updated, but you still need to call the getData() function to ask the server for the newest data based on these arguments.

6 Save and run Dashboard.mxml. Notice that the data loads at start-up. Select a different start date and see how the data is refreshed. Do the same for the Category ComboBox and notice that the comparison pod changes (It is located in the bottom-right of the screen.).

When you run the Dashboard with a filter on Category, you should see the following figure.

Using a Web Service in the DataEntry Application

In this next set of tasks, you will access web services through ActionScript, as opposed to the <mx:WebService> tag used previously, to create a new product.

To create a new product, you will need to gather product data and then pass the product information back to the server. You will start by adding a new property to your Product valueObject, an ID that will uniquely identify each product in the system. You also need to update the code that creates and modifies these products to use this new ID.

1 If you have not done so already, start your local ColdFusion server.

2 Open Product.as from your valueObjects directory.

You can also copy Lesson17/start/valueObjects/Product.as to your flexGrocer/src/ valueObjects directory if you choose.

3 Add a public attribute called prodID typed as a Number.

```
public var prodID:Number;
```

From this point forward, you can use the prodID to uniquely identify the product.

4 Add a _prodID argument to the product() constructor, and set the product's prodID attribute with it.

```
public function Product(
    _prodID:Number,
    _catID:Number,
    _prodName:String,
    _unitID:Number,
    _cost:Number,
    _listPrice:Number,
    _description:String,
    _isOrganic:Boolean,
    _isLowFat:Boolean,
    _imageName:String){
        prodID = _prodID;
        catID = _catID;
        prodName = _prodName;
        unitID = _unitID;
        cost = _cost;
        listPrice = _listPrice;
        description = _description;
        isOrganic = _isOrganic;
        isLowFat = _isLowFat;
        imageName = _imageName;
    }
```

Your constructor accepts one argument per attribute. Adding the _prodID to the constructor arguments allows you to create a new product with an ID via a new Product(..) statement.

5 Update the buildProduct() function to look for o.prodID, and pass it into the new Product() method call.

```
public static function buildProduct(o:Object):Product{
    var p:Product = new Product(
        o.prodID,
        o.catID,
        o.prodName,
        o.unitID,
        o.cost,
        o.listPrice,
        o.description,
        Boolean(o.isOrganic),
        Boolean(o.isLowFat),
        o.imageName);
    return p;
}
```

6 Save the Product.as file.

7 Open CategorizedProductManager.mxml from your managers directory.

You can also copy Lesson17/intermediate/CategorizedProductManager.mxml to your flexGrocer/src/managers directory if you choose.

As you may remember, the CategorizedProductManager.mxml file retrieves product data and their categories. You will modify the code that instantiates new products to include the new ID field. You will also add a new method that instructs the manager to get the latest version of data from the server.

8 In the prodByCategoryHandler() function, locate where you are creating a new product. Add a new argument using the XML variable p.@prodID. Cast it as a Number.

```
for each (var p:XML in c..product){
    var prod:Product = new Product(
        Number(p.@prodID),
        Number(p.@catID),
        String(p.@prodName),
        Number(p.@unitID),
        Number(p.@cost),
        Number(p.@listPrice),
        String(p.@description),
        Boolean(p.@isOrganic=="Yes"),
        Boolean(p.@isLowFat=="Yes"),
        String(p.@imageName));
    ...
}
```

9 Create a public function called refetchData() that returns void. In this function have it make a call to the HTTPService prodByCatRPC to refetch the XML data.

```
public function refetchData():void{
    prodByCatRPC.send();
}
```

You can now call the refetchData() method to refresh the data from outside this file.

10 Replace the url attribute of the <mx:HTTPService> tag at the bottom of the page with http://localhost:8300/flexGrocer/xml/categorizedProducts.cfm.

```
<mx:HTTPService id="prodByCatRPC"
    url="http://localhost:8300/flexGrocer/xml/categorizedProducts.cfm"
    result="prodByCategoryHandler(event)"
    resultFormat="e4x"/>
```

The extension of this file changed from xml to cfm. The cfm extension is used by ColdFusion, the application server you started at the beginning of the lesson. From this point on, you will be able to add, update, and delete data, so a simple static XML file is no longer sufficient. This ColdFusion page will return a dynamically generated piece of XML, when requested, that contains the latest modifications made by the user.

11 Save the CategorizedProductManager.mxml file.

12 Open UpdateDeleteProd.mxml from your src/views/dataEntry directory and add the new prodID field to the the prodModel <mx:Model> tag.

```
<mx:Model id="prodModel">
    <product>
        <prodID>{productTree.selectedItem.@prodID}</prodID>
        <catID>{productTree.selectedItem.@catID}</catID>
        ..
        ..
    </product>
</mx:Model>
```

13 Save the UpdateDeleteProd.mxml file.

14 Open DataEntry.mxml.

You can also copy Lesson17/intermediate/DataEntry.mxml to your flexGrocer/src directory if you choose.

15 Inside the script block, add an import for the mx.rpc.soap.WebService class.

```
import mx.rpc.soap.WebService;
```

16 Create a new private function called addProduct(). Have it pass in an argument called product of type Product. This function does not return anything.

```
private function addProduct(product:Product):void{
}
```

17 Declare a local variable called ws of type WebService, and set it equal to new WebService(). Set the wsdl attribute to **http://localhost:8300/flexGrocer/cfcs/ ProductManager.cfc?wsdl**.

```
var ws:WebService = new WebService();
ws.wsdl = "http://localhost:8300/flexGrocer/cfcs/ProductManager.cfc?wsdl";
```

This code creates a WebService instance in ActionScript instead of the MXML <mx:WebService> tag. This is simply another way to accomplish the same goal.

18 Call the loadWSDL() function on the WebService instance.

```
ws.loadWSDL();
```

As you may remember, the WSDL file contains descriptions of the methods, arguments, and data returned by a particular web service. You must load the WSDL file before attempting to use a web service so Flex understands how to send and receive data.

▶ **TIP:** You can use the canLoadWSDL() function on the WebService instance to see whether it could load the WSDL.

19 Add a listener to the WebService instance for the result event and have it call the addProductResult() method when this event occurs. Add another listener to the WebService instance for the fault event that calls the addProductFault() method.

```
ws.addEventListener("result", addProductResult);
ws.addEventListener("fault", addProductFault);
```

Next, you will create the addProductResult() and the addProductFault() methods.

20 Create a new private function called addProductResult(). Have it pass in one argument called event of type ResultEvent. This function does not return anything.

```
private function addProductResult(event:ResultEvent):void{
}
```

21 Show a pop-up window with the results using the showPopUp() function. The showPopUp() function expects a Product instance and a title, so create a Product instance from the event.result using the Product.buildProduct() method.

```
showPopUp(Product.buildProduct(event.result),'Product Added');
```

The result from the Web Service is an object that you pass to the buildProduct() function to create a new product. The Object return type is defined by the WSDL file.

22 Call the `refetchData()` function on `prodMgr` to get the updated XML data.

```
prodMgr.refetchData();
```

There are several ways to deal with updating the list of products that populates the Tree component. Instead of adding this product to the collection (which is one option), you will simply ask the product manager to refetch all the data from the server when a new product is added. This was chosen for simplicity rather than as a best practice.

23 Create a new private function called `addProductFault()`. Have it pass in one argument called event of type `FaultEvent`. This function does not return anything.

```
private function addProductFault(event:FaultEvent):void{
}
```

Ensure that the `import` statement for `mx.rpc.events.FaultEvent` was added by Flex Builder, or add it manually to the top of the script block.

24 Add a `trace` statement to this function that sends the contents of the variable `event.fault.message` to the console in case of a fault.

```
trace( event.fault.message );
```

If a problem occurs accessing the ColdFusion server, a fault message is printed in your Flex Builder Console.

25 In the `addProduct()` function, call the `ws.addProduct()` method at the bottom and pass in an argument called `product`.

```
ws.addProduct(product);
```

Earlier you learned how to call a web service using the `send()` method when the methods are declared as part of the web service's definition. When you are using a WebService class defined in ActionScript, you will want to use an alternate syntax.

```
wsObject.methodName (arg1, arg2, …)
```

This calls a method on the web service and passes the arguments in line, as opposed to the data binding method used in MXML. In this case, you are calling the `addProduct()` method on the web service. The `product` will be the first argument to the method.

26 Look for the included `AddProduct` component. Change the `productAdded` event to call the `addProduct()` function, passing `event.product` into it.

```
<v:AddProduct cats="{categories}"
   units="{units}"
   productAdded="addProduct(event.product)"
label="Add Product"/>
```

When a user tried to add a product to the application previously, you simply displayed a pop-up window. Now you actually call the addProduct() method which sends the data to the server and displays a pop-up if the product was added successfully.

27 Save DataEntry.mxml and run the application. Fill out the new product section and manually specify a name for a GIF product image. Notice the category you specified in the ComboBox and click Add Product. You will notice a pop-up window confirming that the new product was added. Go to the Update/Delete tab to see the new product in the Tree component.

When you run the DataEntry application and add a product to the Meat category, you should see the following after you expand the Tree component:

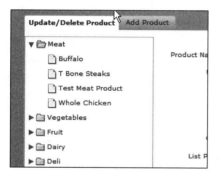

Using the Web Service Introspection Wizard

So far, you have called several methods of a web service, using both a web service defined in MXML and one defined in ActionScript. However, in all cases, the names of the method, the arguments provided to the method, and the type of result was explained in the text of this book. Determining this crucial information is the work of the Web Service Introspection Wizard.

In this section, you will examine the WSDL file you have used to date with the Introspection Wizard and identify the methods available. You will also use the wizard to generate code to access these web service methods. The generated code provides all the benefits of the MXML coded operations with the flexibility of the ActionScript created instance. Finally, you will replace the manual code created earlier in DataEntry.mxml with calls to the wizard-generated code.

1 If you have not done so already, start your local ColdFusion server.

2 Open DataEntry.mxml.

3 From the Data menu in Flex Builder, choose Import Web Service (WSDL).

4 Choose the FlexGrocer [main source folder] and click Next.

5 Choose "Directly from the client" as the method your application will use to access the web service.

To the right of "Directly from the client," the Flex Builder wizard notes that this requires a crossdomain file. A crossdomain file is a small XML file that exists on the server where the WSDL for this web services exists. Its job is to set the policy for clients using Flash player to access assets on the server. It allows the author and/or administrator of the web server to allow or prevent access based on the origin of the Flash movie.

6 Specify the URL of the WSDL, `http://localhost:8300/flexGrocer/cfcs/` `ProductManager.cfc?wsdl`, which is the same address you used in the previous sections. Click Next.

The wizard loads the WSDL file from the URL you specified and returns a list of the operations available, the arguments that each operation requires, and the expected return type.

7 Leave all the operations checked, and ensure the package name is `generated.webservices` and the main class is `ProductManagerService`.

These parameters tell the wizard to create a new class called ProductManagerService in the `generated.webservices` package that will have methods for updating, getting, deleting, and adding products via this web service.

8 Click Finish.

The wizard just generated a lot of code intended to facilitate communication with the web services on your behalf.

9 In the Flex Navigator window, browse to the generated/webservices directory.

You will see 16 files generated by the wizard to simplify both your access to the web service operations and to ensure that the correct arguments and return types are used for these operations.

10 From the Data menu, choose Manage Web Services.

Your project and the associated WSDL URL is listed.

11 Select the WSDL for your FlexGrocer project and choose update.

If the WSDL on the server changes, you can use this screen to update the generated code. The new code will overwrite the original files in the generated/webservices directory along with any changes you made manually.

12 Click finish and allow the wizard to regenerate the code. Then click OK on the Manage Web Services dialog box to exit.

You can regenerate this code whenever the WSDL changes. As you will see in the next sections, the calls to these web services are now encapsulated in other classes, further decoupling the use of these server-side resources.

Using the Generated Code in Your Application

The WSDL Introspection Wizard works best if used when you are starting a new project. It performs a lot of work on your behalf, generating the classes to access the web service and even the required value objects, such as a Product class.

Unfortunately, this is not the beginning of the Flex Grocer project. You have already performed some of the same work and have your own value object classes used by the remainder of the application. Therefore, this next section becomes a tutorial on two concepts; first, integrating the generated code into your application; and second, a process that often happens in projects developed from multiple distinct pieces over the course of time—the need to adapt or interface distinct elements together.

1 Open DataEntry.mxml.

2 Inside the script block, add an import for the `generated.webservices.ProductManagerService` class.

```
import generated.webservices.ProductManagerService;
```

This imports the main class created by the WSDL Introspection Wizard.

3 Create a new private variable in the script block called pm of type `ProductManagerService`.

```
private var pm:ProductManagerService;
```

4 Change the `creationComplete` handler in the Application tag to call `init()` instead of `unitRPC.send()`. The Application tag should appear as follows:

```
<mx:Application xmlns:mx="http://www.adobe.com/2006/mxml"
    layout="vertical"
    creationComplete="init()"
    xmlns:v="views.dataEntry.*"
    xmlns:m="managers.*">
```

5 At the bottom of the script block, create a new private function `init` with a return type of void. As the first line of this new method, invoke `unitRPC.send()`, which was previously called directly by the `creationComplete` handler.

6 Create a new instance of the ProductManagerService class in this method, and assign it to the pm variable. Your `init()` method should look as follows:

```
private function init():void{
    unitRPC.send();
    pm = new ProductManagerService();
}
```

7 Next, call the `addaddProductEventListener` method of the `ProductManagerService` and pass it a single argument of `addProductResult`, which is the result handler you created earlier to deal with results from the web service.

The WSDL Introspection wizard creates a new method for each operation in your WSDL to allow you to easily listen to the result event of just one operation. The method names created by the wizard always follow this format: 'add' + *operation name* + EventListener. In this case, the operation name was addProduct, so we receive a rather strange looking method name of *addaddProductEventListener()*. This line of code registers the *addProductResult()* method to be called when the result event for the addProduct operation occurs.

8 Add a listener to the `ProductManagerService` for the fault event, calling *addProductFault()* if this occurs. Your completed `init()` method should look like the following:

```
private function init():void {
    unitRPC.send();
    pm = new ProductManagerService();

    pm.addaddProductEventListener( addProductResult );
```

```
    pm.addEventListener("fault", addProductFault);
}
```

Unlike using the web service directly, the wizard-generated code only allows for a single fault event for all operations. This means that the same fault event will be broadcast regardless of the method of the `ProductManagerService` that you invoke.

9 Find the method named `addProductResult()` that handles the result of a successfully added product. Change the event type from `ResultEvent` to `AddProductResultEvent`.

The `AddProductResultEvent` was created by WSDL Introspection Wizard. It creates specific custom events for the result of each operation. Ensure the `import generated.webservices.AddProductResultEvent` was added automatically by Flex Builder when you changed the event type, or add it manually now.

10 Find the method named `addProduct()` where you created a WebService instance via ActionScript in the previous section and replace the contents of this method with a single call to `pm.addProduct`, passing the `product` as an argument.

```
private function addProduct(product:Product):void{
    pm.addProduct(product);
}
```

We are no longer invoking the web service code directly but are now asking the generated `ProductManagerService` instance to handle these details for us.

11 Attempt to run DataEntry.mxml. You will receive an error in the `addProduct()` method.

```
1067: Implicit coercion of a value type valueObjects:Products to an unrelated
type generated.webservices:Product.
```

As mentioned, the WSDL Introspection Wizard did a lot of repeat work on our behalf, including create its own version of the Product class. Right now the generated code expects a different Product class than the remainder of the application. The error specifically states that the `pm.addProduct` is expecting an instance of the Product class from the generated webservices directory, and we are attempting to give it one from the valueObjects directly.

Even though these two classes contain the same properties, they are different classes to the compiler and they are, as it states, unrelated.

You will resolve this using some new features of Flex Builder 3.

Refactoring with Flex Builder

Refactoring generally involves enhancing the readability and organization of code while keeping its original functionality unchanged. In Flex Builder 3, a very powerful new feature was added to facilitate that goal: renaming.

In most code editors, you can search and replace any string across many files. However, in our case, we actually have two Product classes that are both often referred to just as Product, albeit they are in different paths and are different classes. Searching and replacing for the word *Product* would create a mess of the code with unintentional changes to the wrong classes. However, using the renaming tool, we can choose to rename all references to one of these classes while leaving the other intact.

1 In DataEntry.mxml, comment out the `pm.addProduct(product)` line inside of the `addProduct()` method.

```
private function addProduct(product:Product):void{
   //pm.addProduct(product);
}
```

The code you intend to refactor must be able to successfully compile first. Right now this code fails because of the mismatched Product classes.

2 Open the Product.as file from the src/valueObjects directory.

3 Next, open the Product.as file from the src/generated/webservices directory.

4 Compare the two files visually.

The two files are similar. You created the version in the valueObjects directory and included an extra method for building a new product as well as a `toString()` method. The generated version was created by Flex based on the WSDL. Currently, these two versions are not related to each other in any way.

5 Switch to the generated/webservices/Product.as version and highlight the word Product in the line that says "public class Product."

6 Click the Source and choose Refactor > Rename from the submenu.

7 In the New name text box change the name *Product* to *WebServiceProduct*. Ensure that the UpdateReferences box is selected, and leave the Rename textual matches in strings box deselected. Click the Preview button.

You will see a list of all places where Flex Builder intends to change the term *Product* to *WebServiceProduct*.

8 Click OK. When Flex Builder completes the work, the Product class in the valueObjects directory will be exactly the same, but the Products class in the generated/webservices directory has been renamed and all references to it throughout the code have also been modified.

This provides a powerful new tool to help refactor your code as you write and develop.

Completing the Integration of the Generated Code

Before continuing, it should be noted that the previous section intentionally caused some issues. As mentioned in the these sections, if you were to rerun the WSDL Introspection Wizard, the code would be regenerated and you would overwrite the changes you just made using refactoring.

This wizard should only be used when starting a new project and not as an addition to an existing application where the value objects have already been defined. However, the purpose of this book is to expose you to the tool set and techniques behind Flex, not to build a well-architected FlexGrocer application that will be maintained for many years to come.

At this point, you have renamed one of the Product classes to WebServiceProduct. However, you have not solved the central issue: the two product classes are unrelated to each other. In this section, we are going to relate the two classes through inheritance, which will allow us to finish this portion of the application and complete the DataEntry add product feature.

1 Open the Product.as file from your src/valueObjects directory.

2 Remove all of the public variables listed in the beginning of the file, but leave the constructor and the instance methods.

3 Change the class definition of the Product class so that it extends from `WebServiceProduct`. Ensure that `generated.webservices.WebServiceProduct` is imported.

```
public class Product extends WebServiceProduct {
```

Now the valueObjects.Product class is a generated.webservices.WebServiceProduct. This change will allow us to pass an instance of our Product class to the generated web services successfully. The public properties you removed are now inherited from the generated class.

4 As the WebServiceProduct class now contains all of the properties for our product, it must be marked bindable. Add the `[Bindable]` metadata tag just above the class definition for the WebServiceProduct class.

```
[Bindable]
    public class WebServiceProduct {
```

5 Return to the DataEntry.mxml application and uncomment the call to `pm.addProduct(product);`.

6 Run the DataEntry application, and add a product from the Add Product tab to a specific category. Then return to the Update/Delete tab, and find your new product under the appropriate category.

With the Add Product feature working correctly, the update and delete capabilities now need to call the appropriate method on the web services; once that is accomplished the basic functions of the DataEntry screen will be complete.

Updating and Deleting Products

You have already completed the difficult work of setting up and integrating with the web service code. Now it is time to reap the rewards of the foundation by quickly adding update and delete capabilities to the DataEntry application.

1 Open the DataEntry.mxml.

2 Find the init() method where you created your `ProductManagerService` instance.

3 After the `pm.addaddProductEventListener` line, add the following code to listen for the result event of both the update and delete operations.

```
pm.addupdateProductEventListener(updateProductResult);
pm.adddeleteProductEventListener(deleteProductResult);
```

4 Your init() method should now look as follows:

```
private function init():void{
    unitRPC.send();
    pm = new ProductManagerService();

    pm.addaddProductEventListener(addProductResult);
    pm.addupdateProductEventListener(updateProductResult);
    pm.adddeleteProductEventListener(deleteProductResult);
    pm.addEventListener("fault", addProductFault);
}
```

5 Create a new private method named `updateProductResult()` that accepts a single event object of type `UpdateProductResultEvent`. Ensure that the generated.webservices.UpdateProductResultEvent class is imported successfully.

6 This method will closely mirror the `addProductResult()` method. However, the title of the pop-up will be *Product Updated*. Your method should look like as follows:

```
private function updateProductResult(event:UpdateProductResultEvent):void{
    showPopUp(Product.buildProduct(event.result);'Product Updated');
    prodMgr.refetchData();
}
```

7 Create a new method named deleteProductResult() that accepts a single event object of type DeleteProductResultEvent. Ensure that the generated.webservices.DeleteProductResultEvent class is imported successfully.

8 This method will closely mirror the addProductResult() method. However, the title of the pop-up will be *Product Deleted*. Your method should look like the following code:

```
private function deleteProductResult(event:DeleteProductResultEvent):void{
    showPopUp(Product.buildProduct(event.result),'Product Deleted');
    prodMgr.refetchData();
}
```

9 Find the UpdateDeleteProd MXML component in DataEntry.mxml. On the productUpdate event, call pm.updateProduct and pass event.product as the argument. On the productDelete event, call pm.deleteProduct, passing event.product as the argument. Your code should look like the following:

```
<v:UpdateDeleteProd label="Update/Delete Product"
    units="{units}"
    foodColl="{foodColl}"
    productUpdate="pm.updateProduct(event.product)"
    productDelete="pm.deleteProduct(event.product)"/>
```

10 Run DataEntry.mxml and test the add, update, and delete features, which now all work through the code generated for you by Flex Builder.

What You Have Learned

In this lesson, you have:

- Learned about server communication (pages 447–448)
- Configured an application to work locally (pages 448–450)
- Declared the specific operations on the <mx:WebService> tag (pages 450–452)
- Sorted the collection returned from the server as a result of the web service call (pages 453–456)
- Bound specific parameters to a web service operation (pages 456–457)
- Used a WebService ActionScript object to update data on the server (pages 458–463)
- Used the WSDL Introspection Wizard to examine a web service and generate code (pages 463–465)
- Used the Flex Builder refactoring tools to rename a class (pages 467–468)
- Integrated the existing DataEntry application with the generated code (pages 465–471)

What You Will Learn

In this lesson, you will:

- Upload a file to the server

- Use the `<mx:RemoteObject>` tag to place an order on the server

- Map a server object to an ActionScript class to transfer data between a client and server

- Learn about the Flex Data Wizards

Approximate Time

This lesson takes approximately 1 hour to complete.

Lesson Files

Media:

None

Starting Files:

Lesson18/start/Dashboard.mxml
Lesson18/start/DataEntry.mxml
Lesson18/start/valueObjects/OrderInfo.as
Lesson18/start/views/dataEntry/AddProduct.mxml
Lesson18/start/views/dataEntry/UpdateDeleteProd.mxml
Lesson18/start/EComm.mxml
Lesson18/start/views/ecomm/Checkout.mxml
Lesson18/start/views/ecomm/OrderConf.mxml

Completed Files:

Lesson18/complete/Dashboard.mxml
Lesson18/complete/DataEntry.mxml
Lesson18/complete/valueObjects/OrderInfo.as
Lesson18/complete/views/dataEntry/AddProduct.mxml
Lesson18/complete/views/dataEntry/FileUpload.mxml
Lesson18/complete/views/dataEntry/UpdateDeleteProd.mxml
Lesson18/complete/EComm.mxml
Lesson18/complete/views/ecomm/Checkout.mxml
Lesson18/complete/views/ecomm/OrderConf.mxml

Accessing Server-Side Objects

In the previous lesson, you learned to communicate with an application server using web services and Flex's `<mx:WebService>` tag. Web services use human-readable XML and are used extensively for communication between organizations around the world.

In this lesson you will learn to use Flex's `<mx:RemoteObject>` tag. Unlike the `<mx:WebService>` tag, the `<mx:RemoteObject>` uses a binary protocol called Action Message Format (AMF) to invoke methods of objects residing on the server. AMF can be used to communicate with an increasing number of server technologies, including Java, PHP, and ColdFusion.

The Ecomm application integrated with server-side order processing

In this lesson you will learn to access server-side objects to upload an image for each product, retrieve product data, and place an order. You will also learn to map value objects inside your Flex application to objects on the server, providing seamless integration of multiple tiers.

All external access from the application will be using the local web instance. Please refer to the appendix "Setup Instructions," to learn how to install, set up, and run the web server instance and application.

Uploading Files to the Server

An image for each product is displayed in the EComm application. Now that you can successfully add products to the application, you need a way to upload the associated images using Flex's file upload capabilities. In addition to adding new images, a user may want to change the image of a product during the update process. Rather than duplicating the same file upload code in two different places, you will create one reusable component to handle this task.

1 Right-click the src/views/dataEntry folder and select New > MXML Component. In the New MXML Component dialog box, set the filename to be **FileUpload.mxml**, set the base component to Canvas, clear the Height and Width fields, and then click Finish.

The component layout will be very basic; a button and the logic for uploading the file.

2 At the top of the file, place an `<mx:Script>` block to hold variables and functions.

```
<mx:Script>
  <![CDATA[
  ]]>
</mx:Script>
```

3 Inside the script block, add an `import` for `flash.net.FileReference`.

```
import flash.net.FileReference;
```

The FileReference class is used to both browse for a specific file as well as upload a file to a specified location.

4 Create a private variable called `fileRef`, of type FileReference.

```
private var fileRef:FileReference;
```

5 Create a private function called `fileBrowse()` and have it return `void`.

```
private function fileBrowse():void{
}
```

6 Inside the function, set the fileRef variable to a new FileReference instance.

```
private function fileBrowse():void{
   this.fileRef = new FileReference();
}
```

7 Add an event listener to the fileRef object that listens for the Event.SELECT event to occur and calls the selectHandler function.

```
private function fileBrowse():void{
   this.fileRef = new FileReference();
   fileRef.addEventListener(Event.SELECT, selectHandler);
}
```

The FileReference class contains many different events pertaining to choosing and uploading files. The Event.Select event fires after the user has selected the file in the dialog box and chooses OK. When working with built-in Flex components, it is a standard practice to use the event names stored as variables within the event class instead of the string value when assigning event listeners. In this case, instead of specifying the string value of 'select,' you used the variable Event.SELECT. Although both evaluate to the same thing, using the variable allows the Flex compiler to ensure you didn't type the string incorrectly. Further, if the underlying event changed in the future, your code would work correctly, or the compiler would aid you in tracking down the issue.

8 Add an event listener to the fileRef object that listens for the Event.COMPLETE event to occur and calls the completeHandler function.

```
fileRef.addEventListener(Event.COMPLETE, completeHandler);
```

9 Create a new variable called gifFilter of type FileFilter, and set it to a new instance of the FileFilter class, passing three arguments "Images", "*.gif" and "GIFF". Ensure that the flash.net.FileFilter class was imported by Flex Builder, or import it manually.

```
var gifFilter:FileFilter = new FileFilter("GIF Images", "*.gif", "GIFF");
```

The AddProduct component ensures that the filename of any image saved to the database ends in gif. By using a FileFilter here, you can guarantee that the user can only choose GIF files from their hard drive when browsing. Without this filter, the user could successfully choose and upload any file from their hard drive, only to be stopped later when they attempt to add a product with that image. Avoiding frustrating user experiences is a must.

The first argument of the FileFilter constructor is a description of the file to be uploaded. The second is the file extension of the file on a Windows machine. The third is a file type for Macintosh.

10 Call the browse() method on the fileRef object, passing the gifFilter variable surrounded by square brackets. This opens the dialog box to select a file.

```
private function fileBrowse():void{
   this.fileRef = new FileReference();
   fileRef.addEventListener(Event.SELECT, selectHandler);
         fileRef.addEventListener(Event.COMPLETE,completeHandler);

   var gifFilter:FileFilter = new FileFilter("GIF Images", "*.gif", "GIFF");
   fileRef.browse( [gifFilter] );
}
```

The gifFilter argument passed to the browse method was surrounded by square brackets. This is simply a shorthand way to create an array. Flex interprets that line of code as: Create a new array, add gifFilter to that array; and pass that array as an argument to the browse method of the FileReference instance called fileRef.

11 Create a private function called selectHandler() that accepts one argument called event of type Event. Have it return void.

```
private function selectHandler(event:Event):void {
}
```

You will use this function to initiate uploading the file to the server.

12 Inside the function, create a local variable called request of type URLRequest. URLRequest accepts a valid URL as its argument in its constructor. Set it to http://localhost:8300/flexGrocer/cfcs/fileUpload.cfm.

```
private function selectHandler(event:Event):void {
   var request:URLRequest = new URLRequest
   _("http://localhost:8300/flexGrocer/cfcs/fileUpload.cfm");
}
```

This URL points to a ColdFusion page in your local server that was written to accept file uploads.

❊ **NOTE:** When you upload a file via Flex, the file is uploaded as a form value with the name of Filedata.

13 Call the upload() method of the fileRef object, passing in the local request object as its only argument.

```
private function selectHandler(event:Event):void {
   var request:URLRequest = new URLRequest
   _("http://localhost:8300/flexGrocer/cfcs/fileUpload.cfm");
   fileRef.upload(request);
}
```

14 Create a private function called completeHandler() that accepts one argument called event of type Event. Have it return void.

```
private function completeHandler(event:Event):void {
}
```

15 Inside this method, broadcast an event of type Event named uploadComplete.

```
private function completeHandler(event:Event):void {
   dispatchEvent(new Event("uploadComplete"));
}
```

16 Directly under the Canvas tag that begins this component, but before the <mx:Script> block, insert an <mx:Metadata> tag that specifies you intend to broadcast an event named uploadComplete.

```
<mx:Metadata>
   [Event("uploadComplete")]
</mx:Metadata>
```

17 Inside the <mx:Script> tag, underneath the definition for the fileRef variable, create a new public get method (also called a getter) named fileName, which returns a string. Inside the method, return the fileRef object's name property. Your code should look like the following:

```
public function get fileName():String {
   return fileRef.name;
}
```

The FileReference class contains several read-only properties, including the name and extension of the file chosen when the user browsed their file system. Providing this public getter allows the code that uses this custom component to retrieve the filename that was selected by the user. Providing a getter but not a set method (a setter) creates a read-only property on a component.

18 Create a button to start the upload process. Set the label to Browse, and on the click event handler, have it call the fileBrowse() function.

```
<mx:Button click="fileBrowse()" label="Browse"/>
```

19 Save FileUpload.mxml.

Integrating the FileUpload Component with DataEntry

1 Open AddProduct.mxml from your src/views/dataEntry directory.

2 In the base VBox that wraps the file, create namespace v and point it to `views.dataEntry.*`.

```
<mx:VBox xmlns:mx=
    "http://www.adobe.com/2006/mxml" xmlns:v="views.dataEntry.*">
```

You now have a namespace to reference the FileUpload component.

3 Toward the bottom of the page, replace the button labeled Browse with your new FileUpload component. Prefix the component name with v.

```
<v:FileUpload/>
```

4 When the `uplodadComplete` event of the FileUpload component occurs, call a method name `handleUploadComplete` and pass it the event object.

```
<v:FileUpload uploadComplete="handleUploadComplete(event)"/>
```

5 Remove the `import` statement for `flash.net.FileReference` and the `fileBrowse()` function.

This code has been moved to the FileUpload component, so it is a good practice to remove it from this file, even though leaving it would not cause an issue.

6 Create a new method named `handleUploadComplete` that accepts an argument named event of type Event and returns void.

```
private function handleUploadComplete( event:Event ):void {
}
```

7 Inside the method, set the `text` property of the `imageName` field to the `fileName` property of the `event.currentTarget` cast as the FileUpload component.

```
private function handleUploadComplete( event:Event ):void {
    imageName.text = FileUpload( event.currentTarget ).fileName;
}
```

The FileUpload component broadcasts this event once the image has uploaded to the server. When that event occurs, you ask the component for the file name of the uploaded image to display in your form.

8 Save AddProduct.mxml.

9 Open UpdateDeleteProd.mxml from your src/views/dataEntry directory.

10 In the base HBox that wraps the file, create namespace v and point it to `views.dataEntry.*`.

```
<mx:HBox xmlns:mx=
    "http://www.adobe.com/2006/mxml" xmlns:v="views.dataEntry.*">
```

11 Toward the bottom of the page, replace the button labeled Browse with your new FileUpload component. Prefix the component name with v.

```
<v:FileUpload/>
```

12 When the `uplodadComplete` event of the FileUpload component occurs, call a method name `handleUploadComplete` and pass it the event object.

```
<v:FileUpload uploadComplete="handleUploadComplete(event)"/>
```

13 Remove the `import` statement for `flash.net.FileReference` and the `fileBrowse()` function.

This code has been moved to the FileUpload component, so it is a good practice to remove it from this file, even though leaving it would not cause an issue.

14 Create a new method named `handleUploadComplete` that accepts an argument named event of type Event and returns void.

```
private function handleUploadComplete( event:Event ):void {
}
```

15 Inside the method, set the `text` property of the `imageName` field to the `fileName` property of the `event.currentTarget` cast as the FileUpload component.

```
private function handleUploadComplete( event:Event ):void {
    imageName.text = FileUpload( event.currentTarget ).fileName;
}
```

The FileUpload component broadcasts this event once the image has uploaded to the server. When that event occurs, you ask the component for the file nameof the uploaded image to be displayed in your form.

16 Save UpdateDeleteProduct.mxml.

17 Open and run the DataEntry.mxml file. On either the Add or Update tab, click the Browse button. Select a file from your computer to upload.

When you click the Browse button, you should see a dialog box similar to the following pop-up window. The uploaded file should be in your flexGrocer/src/assets directory.

Using RemoteObject to Save an Order

In these next tasks, you will modify the EComm.mxml to place an order using the <mx:RemoteObject> tag after the user has finished going through the checkout process. RemoteObject is different from Web Services in several ways:

- RemoteObject uses the serialized binary protocol AMF instead of XML-based Simple Object Access Protocol (SOAP).

- RemoteObject requires a configuration file that is compiled with the application to determine the location of the remote service.

- RemoteObject enables you to map a defined ActionScript class, such as the Product value object, to a server class of the same definition.

Both the RemoteObject and WebServices classes enable you to talk to multiple server technologies. Over Web Services, the WSDL file defines what the SOAP message should look like, and the WSDL on the server is used by the server technology to translate the SOAP message into the specific technology. RemoteObject, or "remoting" (a slang term for the use of RemoteObjects) doesn't work that way. There is a configuration file, services-config.xml, that Remoting uses to determine how to make the calls to the server. This file acts much like the WSDL file does for WebService. To use remoting in your stand-alone version, you need to make sure it is in your compiler commands in Flex Builder.

It is necessary for you to specify the following via the configuration file:

- **Technology adapter:** This is the specific class that translates the generic AMF message into the specific technology. In the following snippet, you see an adapter, referenced by the id of cf-object, which points to an adapter that handles ColdFusion requests. It is also specified as default="true", which means that this adapter is to be used for each destination defined that has no specific adapter noted.

```
<adapters>
   <adapter-definition id="cf-object"
      class="coldfusion.flash.messaging.ColdFusionAdapter" default="true"/>
</adapters>
```

- **Channels:** This defines the location where the server with the remote services exists and what technology the server is using. You will use only AMF, but it is possible to use other types of channels in a Flex application as well. You should also note two things from the following snippet of code. First is that the gateway used by Flex 3 is /flex2gateway, which is using the AMF 3.0 specification, the same specification used by Flex 2. Second, note the <instantiate-types> tag, which must be set to false when connecting to ColdFusion.

```
<channel-definition id="my-cfamf" class="mx.messaging.channels.AMFChannel">
   <endpoint uri= "http://localhost:8300/flex2gateway/"
      class="flex.messaging.endpoints.AMFEndpoint"/>
   <properties>
      <polling-enabled>false</polling-enabled>
         <serialization>
            <instantiate-types>false</instantiate-types>
         </serialization>
   </properties>
</channel-definition>
```

- **Destination handles:** These are the grouping of adapters, channels, and custom properties that Flex will reference by the id, that are needed to make the connection and request to the remote service using Remoting. When dealing with Remoting, the most important tag to notice in the following code is the <source> tag. This can be used to specify the exact class that the destination is referencing, or it can be used to restrict which class directories Remoting can request. If you specify an exact class in the <source> tag, you will not need to pass in a source attribute in the <mx:RemoteObject> tag within your Flex code.

```
<destination id="ColdFusion">
   <channels>
      <channel ref="my-cfamf"/>
   </channels>
   <properties>
      <source>*</source>
   </properties>
</destination>
```

Update Flex Compiler Command

As noted, to have the stand-alone Flex Builder configuration work with RemoteObjects, you need to specify to the Flex Compiler which services-config.xml to use. The configuration file will store the location of your RemoteObjects.

> **TIP:** You will have to compile with different configuration files if the final server location is different than your development or staging environment, as each configuration file (when dealing with stand-alone deployments) will have a specific location in it. For ease of managing, it is best if you create a unique configuration file, as was done for this book, rather than modify the default one provided.

1 Go to Project > Properties > Flex Compiler screen. Enter **-services "*driveroot*/flex3tfs/ flexGrocer/src/assets/FlexGrocer_CF_Services.xml"** into the Additional Compiler Arguments box after any existing items in this field.

Assuming that you have installed the ColdFusion per the setup instructions (if not, then the directory structure will be different), you should see the following before you click OK:

2 Click OK to close the window.

Dispatch an Order Confirmed Event in the Checkout Process

Now you need to provide a way to confirm an order so the checkout process knows it can place the order.

1 Open OrderConf.mxml from the src/views/ecomm directory.

2 Define an event named `orderConfirmed`. This will be a generic event, so you don't need to specify a specific event type in the event definition. Place it between the `<mx:Metadata>` tags at the top of the page.

```
[Event(name="orderConfirmed")]
```

You will dispatch this event when the order is confirmed to let the checkout process know that it can now place the order.

3 Create a private function called `orderConfirm()` that returns void.

```
private function orderConfirm():void{
}
```

This function will be called when the order is confirmed, and then it will dispatch the `orderConfirmed` event.

4 Create a local variable, called o, of type Event. Set it equal to a new event with an event name of `orderConfirmed`.

```
private function orderConfirm():void{
   var o:Event = new Event("orderConfirmed");
}
```

The simplest way of dispatching an event on a component is to use the Event base class. This event only holds an event name and is used only to note that the event occurred. It does not pass additional data like some of the custom event classes you learned about previously.

5 Dispatch the locally created event, called o, via `this.dispatchEvent()` passing in o.

```
private function orderConfirm():void{
   var o:Event = new Event("orderConfirmed");
   this.dispatchEvent(o);
}
```

6 Call the `orderConfirm()` function from the Complete Order button's click handler.

```
<mx:Button label="Complete Order" click="orderConfirm()"/>
```

Create and Call Remote Object

In this exercise, you will configure the Checkout component to send order information directly to a ColdFusion component. You will also create and dispatch an event to notify other areas of the application that the user has completed his or her order successfully.

1 Open Checkout.mxml from the src/views/ecomm directory.

2 Inside the script block, add an `import` for the valueObjects.ShoppingCart class.

```
import valueObjects.ShoppingCart;
```

3 Below the imports, declare a public variable named `cart` that will hold the reference of the shopping cart of the application. Make it of type `ShoppingCart`.

```
public var cart:ShoppingCart = null;
```

The `cart` will be set by the component being included in the main application. This is a reference to the whole shopping cart.

4 Insert an `<mx:MetaData>` pair above the `<mx:Script>` block.

```
<mx:Metadata>
</mx:Metadata>
```

5 Define an event named `checkOutComplete`. This will be a generic event, so you don't need to specify an event type in the event definition.

```
<mx:Metadata>
   [Event(name="checkOutComplete")]
</mx:Metadata>
```

Upon the completion of the checkout, you will dispatch an event indicating that you successfully completed the checkout.

6 Below the `<mx:Script>` tags, insert an `<mx:RemoteObject>` tag. Set the `id` attribute to `srv`, set the `destination` attribute to ColdFusion, set `source` to FlexGrocer.cfcs.Order, and set `showBusyCursor` to `true`. Finally, set the default result handler `result` to `saveOrderResult`, passing along the event.

```
<mx:RemoteObject
   id="svc"
   destination="ColdFusion"
   source="FlexGrocer.cfcs.Order"
   result="saveOrderResult(event)"
   showBusyCursor="true"/>
```

This creates a RemoteObject component with the id of svc, which points to the Order ColdFusion component on the server. In this case the destination name is ColdFusion, providing a good indication of the server technology in use. However, the technology specified for the destination name in the services-config.xml file is a fool-proof way to find this information without relying upon a descriptive name. The showBusyCursor attribute equal to true is used to turn the cursor to a busy icon. It does not restrict the user from clicking buttons or using the application; it is just visual.

Because the RemoteObject requests are made external to the Flex application, you need to "listen" for the result back from the server. The RemoteObject class enables you to listen for the result at the RemoteObject itself via the result event. The event object that is returned to these methods is of type mx.rpc.events.ResultEvent.

> **TIP:** You can also define your operations on your RemoteObject just as you could with the <mx:WebService> tag. It follows the same rules.

7 Inside the script block, add an import for the mx.collections.ArrayCollection class.

```
import mx.collections.ArrayCollection;
```

You need this to reset the item's ShoppingCart value object.

8 Inside the script block, add an import for the mx.rpc.events.ResultEvent class.

```
import mx.rpc.events.ResultEvent;
```

9 Inside the script block, add an import for the mx.controls.Alert class.

```
import mx.controls.Alert;
```

You need this to be able to show an alert window to the user on order placement.

10 Create a private function called saveOrderResult(). Have it pass in one argument called event of type ResultEvent. Specify the functions return type as void.

```
private function saveOrderResult(event:ResultEvent):void{
}
```

11 Clear the items in the ShoppingCart, stored on cart.aItems, by setting the variable to a new ArrayCollection().

```
private function saveOrderResult(event:ResultEvent):void{
   this.cart.aItems = new ArrayCollection();
}
```

12 You want to show a message box, or an alert, with the order number generated for this new order. You will open the alert window with `Alert.show()` and pass it a single string argument. You will pass in a message using the `ORDERNUM` property of the event.result object.

```
private function saveOrderResult(event:ResultEvent):void{
   this.cart.aItems = new ArrayCollection();
   Alert.show("New Order Num: " + event.result.ORDERNUM );
}
```

If you need to create a simple alert window, you can call the static `show()` method of the Alert class. The `event.result` holds the result of the call to the server. In this case, the server returns a result that is an Object. It has all the same properties as an OrderInfo value object, plus the `ORDERNUM`, which holds the order number created.

13 Create a local variable, called o, of type Event. Set it equal to a new Event with an event name of checkOutComplete.

```
private function saveOrderResult(event:ResultEvent):void{
   this.cart.aItems = new ArrayCollection();
   Alert.show("New Order Num: " + event.result.ORDERNUM);
   var o:Event = new Event("checkOutComplete");
}
```

The simplest way of dispatching an event on a component is to use the Event base class. This event only holds an event name and is used only to indicate that the event occurred. It does not pass additional data like some of the custom event classes you learned about previously.

14 Dispatch the locally created event, called o, that was created via `this.dispatchEvent()` passing in o.

```
private function saveOrderResult(event:ResultEvent):void{
   this.cart.aItems = new ArrayCollection();
   Alert.show("New Order Num: " + event.result.ORDERNUM);
   var o:Event = new Event("checkOutComplete");
   this.dispatchEvent(o);
}
```

15 Set the ViewStack for the checkout process, checkoutNav, to display the billingInfo view.

```
private function saveOrderResult(event:ResultEvent):void{
   this.cart.aItems = new ArrayCollection();
   Alert.show("New Order Num: " + event.result.ORDERNUM);
   var o:Event = new Event("checkOutComplete");
   this.dispatchEvent(o);
   checkoutNav.selectedChild=billingInfo;
}
```

You need to set the process back to the beginning, so the next time you check out it will start from the beginning.

16 Create a private function called `completeCheckOut()` that will call the RemoteObject. Have it return void.

```
private function completeCheckOut():void{
}
```

This function will be called when the user confirms that the order is correct.

17 In the `completeCheckOut()` function, make a call to the `saveOrder()` method on the RemoteObject svc. Pass in `orderInfo` and `cart.aItems`.

```
private function completeCheckOut():void{
   svc.saveOrder(orderInfo, cart.aItems);
}
```

Calling a method on RemoteObject is accomplished the same way as you did with WebService. You call the actual method name on the RemoteObject you want to call using the remoteObject.methodName (arg1, arg2, and so on) format.

The Checkout component acts as a wizard, in that it collects the order information, address, and credit card data and puts it into an OrderInfo value object called `orderInfo`. You need to pass that information and the items in the shopping cart to the remote service.

18 Call the `completeCheckOut()` function from the OrderConf component's `orderConfirmed` event handler.

```
<v:OrderConf id="orderConf"
width="100%" height="100%"
   orderInfo="{orderInfo}"
   back="checkoutNav.selectedChild=billingInfo"
   orderConfirmed="completeCheckOut()"/>
```

19 Save the Checkout.mxml file.

Pass ShoppingCart into the Checkout Component

Your new Checkout component needs a reference to the user's shopping cart. You will now add that information to the component in EComm.

1 Open the EComm.mxml file.

The file is located in flexGrocer/src directory.

2 In the Checkout component, add an attribute of `cart` that is bound to the public variable of `cart`.

```
<v:Checkout id="checkout" cart="{cart}" width="100%" height="100%"/>
```

Change the Application State Back to Welcome

Once the user has completed the ordering process, you need to return them to the welcome screen. You will now use the event previously created to facilitate this change.

1 If you have not done so already, start your local ColdFusion server.

2 Capture the checkOutComplete event on the Checkout component and have it set the selectedChild on the ecommNave ViewStack equal to homePage.

```
<v:Checkout
    id="checkout"
    checkOutComplete="ecommNav.selectedChild=homePage"
    cart="{cart}" width="100%" height="100%"/>
```

This causes the EComm application to show the home page upon successful completion of the order.

3 Save EComm.mxml and run the application.

When you run the EComm application and check out, you should get an alert at the end noting that the order was placed. You should see the following:

Mapping ActionScript Objects to Server Objects

This exercise shows how you can map an ActionScript class to a Server object and pass an instance of that class between the client and server. The [RemoteObject()] metadata descriptor in a value object class makes this possible. However, this relies on two things: first, that both the server and client copies of the class that are to be transferred have the same number of properties; and, second, that like properties in each class have equivalent names.

There are several benefits of this approach. For starters, a method like buildProduct() of the Product class is no longer needed. When a Product object arrives from the server, it is automatically mapped to the ActionScript Product value object. This feature is only supported using remote objects.

Further, without the need to first build value objects from the results returned from the server, you can immediately use the result. For example, in your event handler, you can call event.result.someMethod(), assuming that someMethod() is a method on your value object. It is important to realize that this is not a requirement to pass data between Flex and the server via ActionScripts objects but instead a possibility for you to use when developing your applications.

> **TIP:** This is especially helpful to do when you have all the data in your application stored in ActionScript classes (value objects).

1 If you have not done so already, start your local ColdFusion server.

2 Open OrderInfo.as from the src/valueObjects directory.

3 Right above the class declaration, add a [RemoteClass] metadata attribute. Set the alias to FlexGrocer.cfcs.OrderInfo.

```
[RemoteClass(alias="FlexGrocer.cfcs.OrderInfo")]
public class OrderInfo {
```

The RemoteClass metadata attribute informs the server object that this ActionScript class maps to the class that can be found at FlexGrocer.cfcs.OrderInfo on the server. This alias is case sensitive. For the mapping to occur, Flex requires that there be an exact match in properties on the ActionScript class and the server object.

> **TIP:** Be aware that when you are mapping ActionScript classes to server objects, you must keep the definitions in sync. Any change on the server object that is not exactly matched on the client will cause Flex to simply translate the server object returned to a generic Object. That said, the best patterns to use this feature with are Proxy, Domain, or ValueObject.

4 After the last property declaration, declare a new public variable named `createDate`, which will hold the date that the order was created. Make it of type Date.

```
public var createDate:Date;
```

As previously emphasized, it is important to have an exact property match between the ActionScript class and the server object to which it is associated.

5 After this property, create another new variable named `orderNum` that will hold the order number, which will be created when the order is placed, to uniquely reference it. Make it of type String.

```
public var orderNum:String;
```

6 Below the property declarations, create a public function called `getOrderInfoHeader()`, which will return a message containing the order number and the date it was created. It will receive no arguments, using the value object properties instead, and will return a String.

```
public function getOrderInfoHeader():String{
    return "Order '" + orderNum + "' was created on " + createDate;
}
```

You will use this method to provide a message to users about the details of the order they just placed.

7 Save the OrderInfo.as file.

8 Open Checkout.mxml from the src/views/ecomm directory.

9 In the `completeCheckOut()` function, switch to call the `saveOrderWithVO()` function on the RemoteObject, svc, passing in the same arguments as before.

```
private function completeCheckOut(){
    svc.saveOrderWithVO(orderInfo, cart.aItems);
}
```

The method `saveOrderWithVO()` is another method that has already been written for you on the server. It is configured to accept a ValueObject rather than a generic Object, like `saveOrder()`;

10 In the `saveOrderResult()` function, change the text being passed into the `Alert.show()` function to be returned from the `getOrderInfoHeader()` method called directly on the event.result.

```
private function saveOrderResult(event:ResultEvent):void{
    this.cart.aItems = new ArrayCollection();
    Alert.show(event.result.getOrderInfoHeader());
    var o:Event = new Event("checkOutComplete");
    this.dispatchEvent(o);
    checkoutNav.selectedChild=billingInfo;
}
```

The remote service is returning an OrderInfo value object from the server. This means that event.result is of type OrderInfo rather than Object. As a result, you can call the getOrderInfoHeader() method you created to get a formatted description of the order.

11 Save the Checkout.mxml file.

12 Run EComm.mxml.

When you run the EComm application and check out, you should get an alert at the end noting that the order was placed using the new header message. You should see the following:

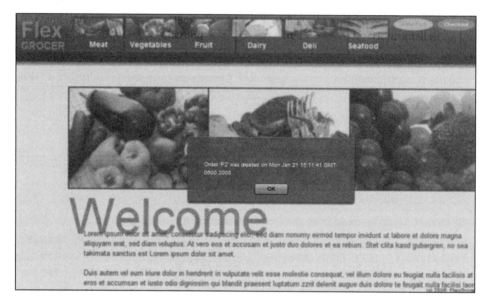

The Flex Builder Data Wizards

Flex Builder 3 ships with a series of data wizards that will create both the client and server side of a simple application. These applications serve as a useful learning tool when trying to understand the finer points of client communication.

The data wizards are accessed from the main application menu by choosing Data > Create Application from Database in Flex Builder 3. They demonstrate client and server communication for PHP, ASP.NET or J2EE (when used with LiveCycle Data Services or BlazeDS, an open-source Java remoting and messaging server released by Adobe). The wizards themselves only require a handful of steps to generate an application, assuming you already have one of the environments mentioned previously set up and running properly on your machine.

Although the process of configuring one of these servers simply to demonstrate the wizards is well outside the scope of this book, the following section is an overview of the steps and basic requirements to use these tools. If you do have access to a supported server environment, you are strongly encouraged to explore this option as it is a great learning device.

Creating a Server Project

The choice to use the data wizards starts when creating a new project. In earlier lessons, you created projects, but always left the combo box that specified the Application server type set to none. Valid options for this combo box that will allow you to work with the data wizards include ASP.NET, J2EE, or PHP.

You must be prepared to provide the project setup with crucial information such as the folder on your hard drive that acts as the web root and the URL that correspond to that web root. Flex Builder will suggest a directory under the web root to store your project output based upon the project name.

Clicking Finish will create the project and configure settings such as your output directory for use with the server. At this point, you have the necessary setup to run the data wizards.

Navigating to Data > Create Application from Database opens a dialog box asking which project you would like the data wizards to use. You may only choose a project that has been configured to use a server.

The dialog box needs to know the connection information for your database and which table and field inside of that table to use as a key or unique identifier. Flex Builder queries this information to help generate the code.

Flex Builder next requests information about the name and location of the server-side code it needs to generate. Throughout this book we have asked you to create the client-side portion of the code, as the server-side code had already been created on your behalf. This is a great opportunity to review and understand both sides of that equation.

The next screen asks which fields should be included in the client side DataGrid that Flex Builder intends to create, as well as the type of data contained in each field. Flex Builder also allows you to specify a filtering column. The data in this row will be added to a combo box. Only records that match the data in the combo box will be displayed in the DataGrid.

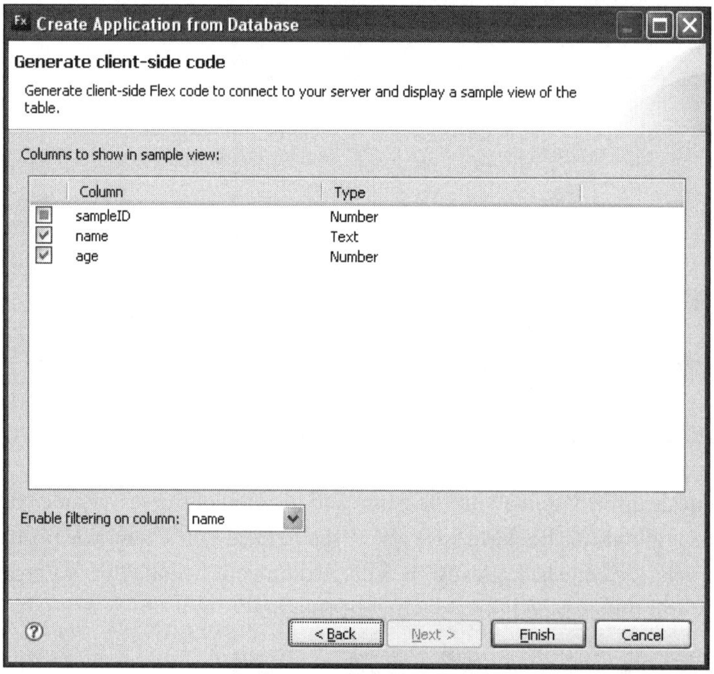

Clicking Finish causes Flex Builder to generate both the server-side and client-side code. The client-side code includes an MXML file with the controls and layout information, and an ActionScript file that contains the methods necessary to interact with the server. The server-side code contains methods that respond to requests from the client and interact with the database.

Assuming your environment is configured correctly and your web and database servers are running, you can run the created application.

Any data from the database and table you specified will be displayed in the grid, with the option to edit and filter it. The data wizards generate these small applications as learning tools for developers. We encourage you to review the generated code (and use the steps you will learn in Lesson 25, "Debugging Flex Applications,") to learn more about client-server communication in Flex.

What You Have Learned

In this lesson, you have:

- Uploaded a file to the server (pages 475–481)
- Used the <mx:RemoteObject> tag to place an order on the server (pages 481–489)
- Mapped a Server object to an ActionScript class to transfer data between a client and server (pages 490–492)
- Learned about the Flex Data Wizards (pages 492–497)

What You Will Learn

In this lesson, you will:

- Work with pie, column, and line charts
- Learn how to provide data to charts
- Specify chart axes
- Handle chart events
- Animate charts when data is set
- Apply styles to charts

Approximate Time

This lesson takes approximately 1 hour and 30 minutes to complete.

Lesson Files

Media Files:

Lesson19/assets/TypeChart.mxml
Lesson19/assets/ComparisonChart.mxml
Lesson19/assets/SalesChart.mxml

Starting Files:

Lesson19/start/Dashboard.mxml

Completed Files:

Lesson19/complete/Dashboard.mxml
Lesson19/complete/views/dashboard/ComparisonChart.mxml
Lesson19/complete/views/dashboard/SalesChart.mxml
Lesson19/complete/views/dashboard/TypeChart.mxml

LESSON 19

Visualizing Data

Visualizing data in a chart or graph can make interpretation of that data much easier for users. Instead of presenting a simple table of numeric data, you can display a bar, pie, line, or other type of chart using colors, captions, and a two-dimensional representation of your data.

Data visualization enables you to present information in a way that simplifies data interpretation and data relationships. Charting is one type of data visualization in which you create two-dimensional representations of your data. Flex supports some of the most common types of two-dimensional charts—such as bar, column, and pie charts—and provides you with a great deal of control over the appearance of charts.

A simple chart shows a single data series, in which a series is a group of related data points. For example, a data series might be monthly sales revenues or daily occupancy rates for a hotel. The following chart shows a single data series that corresponds to sales over several months:

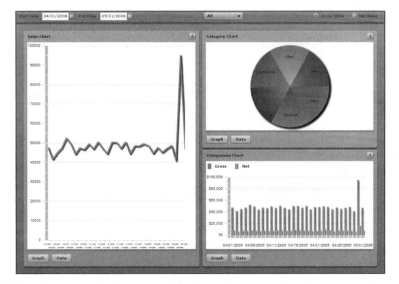

The Dashboard application shows rich interactive charts about the company's sales.

Exploring Flex Charting Components

Among the many powerful tools available with Flex is a robust set of Charting components. The Flex Charting components enable you to create some of the most common chart types and also give you a great deal of control over the appearance of your charts. After you understand the API for charts, it becomes easy to add rich interactive charts to any application. Throughout this lesson, you will add charts to the Dashboard application, enabling users to better visualize sales information for the FlexGrocer company. The new features introduced in charting for Flex 3 largely focus on richer user interactions. The latest features include:

- More options for selecting data from a chart. Users can now select multiple points, drag/select a box around points, and drag/drop data between charts and other components.

- More flexibility with fill colors. Developers can build conditional logic to programmatically change a charting element's colors based on data conditions.

- New enhancements with item labels and axis renderers, allowing for greater control over customizing charts.

Chart Types

Flex provides a number of different types of charts, including the following:

- Area
- Bar
- Bubble
- Candlestick
- Column
- HighLowOpenClose
- Line
- Plot

You can see the various types of charts being used in the Charting section of Adobe's Flex 3 Component Explorer: www.adobe.com/go/flex3_explorer_app

Chart Packaging

Although the Flex Charting components are available for all versions of Flex Builder, they are not included free of charge. Flex Builder 3 Standard includes a limited trial of the Charting components, and Flex Builder 3 Professional includes the full version and another package that makes these components available for developers using the Flex SDK.

Parts of a Chart

All Flex Charting components have a similar API, so after you learn to work with one type of chart, it should be pretty easy to pick up any of the others.

You use a number of different tags to define a particular chart, but in general, most charts follow this structure:

```
<ChartType>
    <!-- Define the axes. -->
    <mx:horizontalAxis>
        <mx:AxisType/>
    </mx:horizontalAxis>
    <mx:verticalAxis>
        <mx:AxisType/>
    </mx:verticalAxis>
    <mx:series>
        <mx:SeriesName/>
    </mx:series>

    <!-- Style the axes and ticks. -->
    <mx:horizontalAxisRenderer/>
    <mx:verticalAxisRenderer/>

    <!-- Add grid lines and other elements to the chart. -->
    <mx:annotationElements/>
    <mx:backgroundElements/>
</mx:ChartType>
<mx:Legend/>
```

In the pseudo code, you can see that a chart can contain a chart type, one or more series, one or more axes, renderers, and other elements.

The <ChartType> tag is the root tag for each chart. It is required and is used to determine what kind of chart will be used (such as LineChart, ColumnChart, PieChart, and so on). This tag can also be used to customize elements of the chart, such as the data to render, whether ToolTips should be shown as elements are moused over, and so on.

The series defines an array of Series classes, which are used to specify data to render in a chart. For each series of data, specific styles (such as fill, stroke, and so on) can be used to customize how that data is rendered. Because an array of Series is provided, a chart can contain multiple sets of data, such as you will implement in the comparison chart later in this lesson—graphing both Net and Gross sales. Every chart must have a series defined before any data will be rendered. Each chart type has its own Series class that can be used; for example, the series for an <mx:ColumnChart> is an <mx:ColumnSeries>, whereas the series for an <mx:PieChart> is an <mx:PieSeries>.

The Axis class is required for any of the rectangular two-dimensional charts (known as Cartesian charts), because it specifies what data should be rendered for the horizontal and vertical axes of the chart. Axis subclasses enable you to specify whether the Axis is numeric (`LinearAxis`) or string-based (`CategoryAxis`).

An AxisRenderer can optionally be used to describe how the horizontal and vertical axes of a chart should be shown. For example, an axis is responsible for rendering the labels, tick marks, and title along the axis. Among the items that can be specified with an AxisRenderer are Cascading Style Sheets (CSS), text properties, label rotation, and spacing (such as the capability to drop labels to make the axis fit better).

Other chart elements that can also be provided include annotationElements and backgroundElements, both of which are subclasses of the ChartElement class. The backgroundElements subclass enables you to add things such as background images, whereas the annotationElements subclass enables you to add items to further describe the chart, such as gridLines.

Laying Out Initial Charts

In this first exercise, you will use the Charting components to lay out the basics of three chart types: a type chart, sales chart, and comparison chart. The skeleton files for the three charts are provided for you in the Lesson19/assets directory.

Up to this point, each skeleton file contains only a DataGrid component with data relating to products sold. You will now start to add charts to visualize this data as well.

1 Open TypeChart.mxml from the Lesson19/assets directory and save it to your flexGrocer/src/views/dashboard directory.

2 Inside the first `<mx:VBox>` within the `<mx:ViewStack>`, add an `<mx:PieChart>`, with a `height` and `width` of 100% and a `dataProvider` bound to `dp`.

```
<mx:ViewStack id="chartStack"
   width="100%" height="100%">
   <mx:VBox width="100%" height="100%">
      <mx:PieChart id="chart"
         width="100%" height="100%"
         dataProvider="{dp}">
      </mx:PieChart>
   </mx:VBox>
   <mx:VBox width="100%" height="100%">
      <mx:DataGrid id="chartData" dataProvider="{dp}">
   ...
</mx:ViewStack>
```

This is the skeleton of a pie chart, which requires that you specify one or more series before it will be rendered. You will do this in a later exercise.

3 Save TypeChart.mxml.

As mentioned earlier, several elements are necessary before a chart will render. If you run the application now, no chart will appear. We need to provide more information, which you will do in the next exercise. The file at this point should resemble TypeChart_initial in the intermediate directory.

4 Open SalesChart.mxml from the Lesson19/assets directory and save it to your flexGrocer/src/views/dashboard directory.

5 Inside the first `<mx:VBox>` tag within the `<mx:ViewStack>` tag, add an `<mx:LineChart>` tag with a `dataProvider` bound to dp, and a `height` and `width` of 100%.

```
<mx:VBox width="100%" height="100%">
   <mx:LineChart id="chart"
      dataProvider="{dp}"
      height="100%" width="100%"/>
</mx:VBox>
```

This is the skeleton of a line chart. Before it works properly, a line chart requires one or more series as well as its axis. You will do this in a later exercise.

6 Save SalesChart.mxml.

The file at this point should resemble SalesChart_initial in the intermediate directory.

7 Open ComparisonChart.mxml from the Lesson19/assets directory and save it to your flexGrocer/src/views/dashboard directory.

8 Inside the first `<mx:VBox>` tag within the `<mx:ViewStack>` tag, add an `<mx:ColumnChart>` tag with a `height` and `width` of 100% and a `dataProvider` bound to dp.

```
<mx:VBox>
   <mx:ColumnChart id="chart"
      dataProvider="{dp}"
      width="100%" height="100%"/>
</mx:VBox>
```

This is the skeleton of the column chart, which requires you to specify one or more series, as well as a vertical axis, before it will work. You will do so in a later exercise.

9 Save ComparisonChart.mxml.

If you run the application now, no chart will appear because you need to provide more information, such as the series and axis data. The file at this point should resemble ComparisonChart_initial in the intermediate directory.

Populating Charts

Depending on the type of chart, one or more steps are necessary before a chart is drawn. All charts, regardless of type, require that you specify one or more series of data for the charts. The Cartesian charts also require that you specify the horizontal and/or vertical axes.

A series is a set of data provided to a chart. Depending on the type of chart you use, there are different Series classes to use.

Series Classes	
Series Class Name	**Description**
AreaSeries	The AreaSeries class defines a data series for an AreaChart control.
AreaSet	AreaSet is a grouping set that can be used to stack AreaSeries in any arbitrary chart.
BarSeries	The BarSeries class defines a data series for a BarChart control.
BarSet	BarSet is a grouping set that can be used to stack or cluster BarSeries in any arbitrary chart.
BubbleSeries	The BubbleSeries class defines a data series for a BubbleChart control.
CandleStickSeries	The CandleStickSeries class represents financial data as a series of candlesticks representing the high, low, opening, and closing values of a data series.
ColumnSeries	The ColumnSeries class defines a data series for a ColumnChart control.
ColumnSet	ColumnSet is a grouping set that can be used to stack or cluster ColumnSeries in any arbitrary chart.
HLOCSeries	The HLOCSeries class represents financial data as a series of elements representing the high, low, opening (optionally), and closing values of a data series.
LineSeries	The LineSeries class defines a data series for a LineChart control.
PieSeries	The PieSeries class defines the data series for a PieChart control.
PlotSeries	The PlotSeries class defines a data series for a PlotChart control.

Although it's not as common, many charts allow you to mix and match different series within the same chart, so it is possible to overlay a line chart above a column chart, for example.

Specifying the Charts' Series

In this section, you will make the charts functional by adding the required series elements.

1 Open Dashboard.mxml and change the `<v:ChartPod id="sales">` to use
   `<v:SalesChart id="sales">` instead. Change the `<v:ChartPod id="type">` tag
   to use `<v:TypeChart id="type">`, and change `<v:ChartPod id="comp">` to use
   `<v:ComparisonChart id="comp">`. Leave the rest of the attributes exactly as they were.

```
<v:SalesChart id="sales"
   width="100%" height="100%"
   title="Sales Chart"
   maximize="this.currentState='fullSales'"
   restore="this.currentState=''">
</v:SalesChart>
<mx:VBox id="rightCharts" width="100%" height="100%">
   <v:TypeChart id="type"
      width="100%" height="100%"
      title="Category Chart"
      maximize="this.currentState='fullType'"
      restore="this.currentState=''">
   </v:TypeChart>
   <v:ComparisonChart id="comp"
      width="100%" height="100%"
      title="Comparison Chart"
      maximize="this.currentState='fullComp'"
      restore="this.currentState=''">
   </v:ComparisonChart>
</mx:VBox>
```

You will start to make the charts functional, but you will need to call them from the
Dashboard application to see them function.

2 Add a new attribute to both the `<v:SalesChart>` and `<v:TypeChart>` tags, binding the
   selection.data of the grossOrNetGroup to the grossOrNet property.

```
<v:SalesChart id="sales"
   width="100%" height="100%"
   title="Sales Chart"
   grossOrNet="{grossOrNetGroup.selection.data}"
   maximize="this.currentState='fullSales'"
   restore="this.currentState=''">
</v:SalesChart>
<mx:VBox id="rightCharts" width="100%" height="100%">
   <v:TypeChart id="type"
      width="100%" height="100%"
      title="Category Chart"
      grossOrNet="{grossOrNetGroup.selection.data}"
      maximize="this.currentState='fullType'"
      restore="this.currentState=''">
   </v:TypeChart>
   ...
</mx:VBox>
```

This will pass the string GROSS or NET, whichever value the user selects from the radio buttons, into the SalesChart and TypeChart components. You don't need to pass this string to the ComparisonChart because it will ultimately show both net and gross sales at once.

3 Open TypeChart.mxml from the flexGrocer/src/views/dashboard directory.

Alternately, you can open TypeChart_initial from the intermediate directory and save it as **TypeChart.mxml** in your flexGrocer/src/views/dashboard directory.

4 Between the open and close <mx:PieChart> tags, add an <mx:series> tag pair. Within the <mx:series> tag, create an <mx:PieSeries> tag with the field attribute bound to grossOrNet.

```
<mx:PieChart id="chart"
    width="100%" height="100%"
    dataProvider="{dp}">
    <mx:series>
        <mx:PieSeries field="{grossOrNet}">
        </mx:PieSeries>
    </mx:series>
</mx:PieChart>
```

When using the <mx:PieSeries>, you need to specify which property to render in the chart. By binding that property to grossOrNet, the chart will show either the gross or net sales, based on which radio button the user selected in the main application.

Save and test the Dashboard application. At this point, the pie chart should be functional.

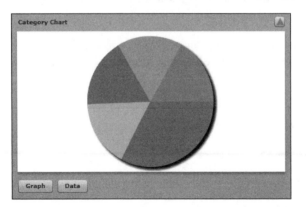

5 Add a labelPosition attribute to the <mx:PieSeries> tag, specifying insideWithCallout as the value.

```
<mx:PieSeries
    labelPosition="insideWithCallout"
    field="{grossOrNet}">
```

The label position specifies how to render labels. The valid values are as follows:

- **"none"**—Do not draw labels. This is the default.

- **"outside"**—Draw labels around the boundary of the pie.

- **"callout"**—Draw labels in two vertical stacks on either side of the pie. The pie shrinks if necessary to make room for the labels.

- **"inside"**—Draw labels inside the chart, centered approximately $\frac{7}{10}$ths of the way along each wedge. Shrink labels to ensure that they do not interfere with each other. If labels shrink below the calloutPointSize property, Flex removes them. When two labels overlap, Flex gives priority to labels for larger slices.

- **"insideWithCallout"**—Draw labels inside the pie, but if labels shrink below a legible size, Flex converts them to callouts.

Save and test the application again. Notice that the labels show the value, but not the category name, as might be expected.

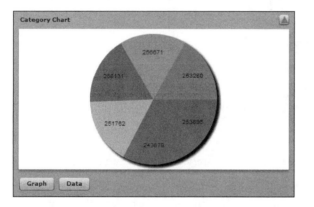

6 In the <mx:Script> block, create a new function called renderLabel(), which takes four arguments and returns a String. The function should return item.CATEGORY.

```
private function renderLabel(item:Object, field:String, index:int,
    ➥ pct:Number):String{
    return item.CATEGORY;
}
```

You will use this label function to tell the chart which field to render as its label. For a PieSeries, the label function is automatically passed four arguments:

- **item**—Contains the object being graphed. In your pie chart, to show the category name, you want to return the item.CATEGORY.

- **field**—A string that contains the field (NET or GROSS in your application) that is being graphed.

- **index**—The item number being graphed.

- **pct**—The percentage of the pie for this item.

7 Specify the labelFunction attribute of the <mx:PieSeries> to be renderLabel.

```
<mx:PieSeries labelPosition="insideWithCallout"
    field="{grossOrNet}"
    labelFunction="renderLabel">
```

Save and test the application. You should now see the labels rendering properly. This file should resemble TypeChart_labels.mxml in the intermediate directory.

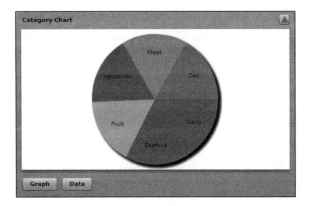

8 Open SalesChart.mxml from your flexGrocer/src/views/dashboard directory.

Alternately, you can open SalesChart_initial.mxml from the intermediate directory and save it as **SalesChart.mxml** in your flexGrocer/src/views/dashboard directory.

9 After the opening <mx:LineChart> tag, add an <mx:series> tag; within the <mx:series>, add an <mx:LineSeries> tag with the yField attribute bound to grossOrNet.

```
<mx:LineChart id="chart"
    dataProvider="{dp}"
    height="100%" width="100%">
    <mx:series>
        <mx:LineSeries yField="{grossOrNet}">
        </mx:LineSeries>
    </mx:series>
</mx:LineChart>
```

You are telling the LineChart that the selected property (either gross or net) will be the field that defines the value for the y-axis.

10 Save SalesChart.mxml and run the application.

The chart is now rendering. Notice, however, that the labels along the axis have no bearing on the data they represent. You will fix this in the next exercise when you specify the horizontal and vertical axes. This file should resemble SalesChart_labels.mxml in the intermediate directory.

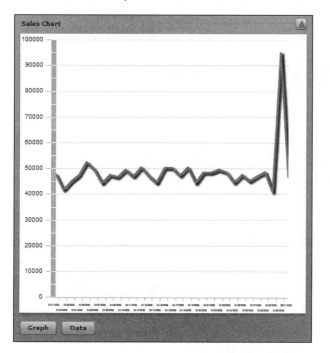

11 Open ComparisonChart.mxml from your flexGrocer/src/views/dashboard directory.

Alternately, you can open ComparisonChart_initial.mxml from the intermediate directory and save it as **ComparisonChart.mxml** in your flexGrocer/src/views/dashboard directory.

12 Specify two column series—one with a yField set to GROSS and one with a yField set to NET.

```
<mx:ColumnChart id="chart"
   dataProvider="{dp}"
   width="100%" height="100%">
   <mx:series>
      <mx:ColumnSeries yField="GROSS">
      </mx:ColumnSeries>
      <mx:ColumnSeries yField="NET">
      </mx:ColumnSeries>
   </mx:series>
</mx:ColumnChart>
```

This chart takes two different Series—one to plot a day's gross sales; the other to show the day's profit (net sales).

13 Save ComparisonChart.mxml and run the application.

The column chart is now rendering, showing columns for both gross and net sales. Notice, however, that the labels along the horizontal axis are index numbers, not the dates you would expect. You will fix this in the next exercise when you specify the horizontal axis. This file should resemble ComparisonChart_labels.mxml in the intermediate directory.

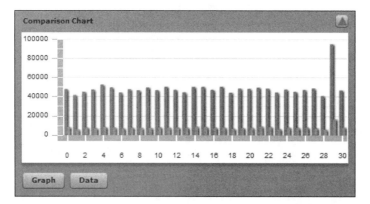

Adding Horizontal and Vertical Axes to Line and Column Charts

After data has been provided to the charts, you can refine how the axis labels are rendered by using the `<mx:horizontalAxis>` and `<mx:verticalAxis>` tags. These tags can be used to specify valid ranges for the chart and also to map the data on the chart.

Flex supports four Axis types:

- **CategoryAxis**—Maps a particular property of the objects in the chart to the axis. For example, a chart showing the total enrollment of a school based on the students' demographics could use a CategoryAxis to map the students' race property to the horizontal axis.

- **LinearAxis**—Maps numeric data to the points on an axis. This can allow for easily specifying valid numeric ranges, numbers to skip, and so on.

- **LogAxis**—Maps logarithmic data to an axis. To facilitate this, the Log axis has labels for each power of 10 (1, 10, 100, 1000, and so on).

- **DateTimeAxis**—Maps time-based values to an axis. This can also be used to set the format for the labels. This axis also allows you to disable particular dates from being shown, allowing for an easy creation of an axis that displays only work days or weekends, for instance.

 TIP: It is now possible to have multiple axes for a given chart, which allows multiple datasets to display alongside each other. To facilitate this, you create additional axes within a series, as shown here:

```
<mx:LineChart id="linechart" dataProvider="{myData}">
   <mx:horizontalAxis>
      <mx:CategoryAxis id="catAxis" categoryField="categoryFieldName"/>
   </mx:horizontalAxis>

   <mx:verticalAxis>
      <mx:LinearAxis id= "v1"/>
   </mx:verticalAxis>

   <mx:verticalAxisRenderers>
      <mx:AxisRenderer axis = "{v1}"/>
      <mx:AxisRenderer axis = "{v2}"/>
      <mx:AxisRenderer axis = "{v3}"/>
   </mx:verticalAxisRenderers>

   <mx:series>
      <mx:LineSeries yField="fieldName" form="curve" displayName="Display Name"
         ➥ itemRenderer="mx.charts.renderers.CircleItemRenderer">
      </mx:LineSeries>
      <mx:LineSeries yField="anotherFieldName" form="curve" displayName="Another
         ➥ Display Name" itemRenderer="mx.charts.renderers.CircleItemRenderer">
         <mx:verticalAxis>
            <mx:LinearAxis id = "v2" />
         </mx:verticalAxis>
      </mx:LineSeries>
      <mx:LineSeries yField="yetAnotherFieldName" form="curve"
         ➥ displayName="Yet Another Field Name" itemRenderer=
         ➥ "mx.charts.renderers.CircleItemRenderer">
         <mx:verticalAxis>
            <mx:LinearAxis id = "v3" />
         </mx:verticalAxis>
      </mx:LineSeries>
   </mx:series>
</mx:LineChart>
```

Flex assumes that any axis not specifically defined is mapping a numeric field to the axis. This is why, in the previous exercise, the horizontal axis showed the index number of the item instead of the date.

1 Open SalesChart.mxml from your flexGrocer/src/views/dashboard directory.

Alternately, you can open SalesChart_labels.mxml from the intermediate directory and save it as **SalesChart.mxml** in your flexGrocer/src/views/dashboard directory.

2 Add an `<mx:horizontalAxis>` tag pair inside the `<mx:LineChart>` tag. Within the `<mx:HorizontalAxis>` tags, add an `<mx:CategoryAxis>` with the `categoryField` attribute set to DTSALE.

```
<mx:LineChart id="chart"
   dataProvider="{dp}"
   height="100%" width="100%">
   <mx:horizontalAxis>
     <mx:CategoryAxis categoryField="DTSALE" id="catAxis"/>
   </mx:horizontalAxis>
   <mx:series>
     <mx:LineSeries yField="{grossOrNet}">
     </mx:LineSeries>
   </mx:series>
</mx:LineChart>
```

You are now telling the chart what data to plot along the horizontal axis. By specifying a CategoryAxis with a `categoryField` of DTSALE, you are mapping the DTSALE property across the x-axis. It would also be possible to use a DateTimeAxis instead of a CategoryAxis; if you had a situation in which you had more day data than you wanted to graph, you could use DateTimeAxis and specify a start and end date. In this case, you want to graph any data returned by the server, so a CategoryAxis is more appropriate.

3 Save SalesChart.mxml and run the application.

The dates now show across the bottom of the chart. Notice, however, that there are too many dates to effectively read the labels. If you change the dates in the ApplicationControlBar (at the top of the Dashboard application) to limit the search to only one week's worth of data, you can more clearly see that part of the problem is that the labels are too long and not particularly user-friendly.

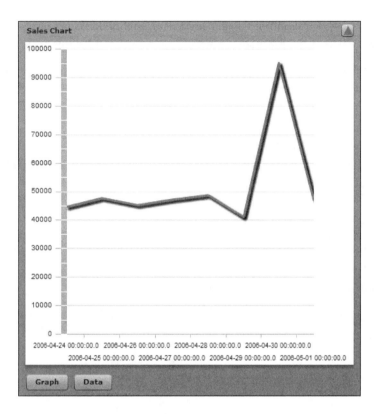

4 In the <mx:Script> block, add a function called renderDate(), which will format the labels on the horizontal axis as dates.

```
private function renderDate(value:Object, previousValue:Object,
    ➥ axis:CategoryAxis, item:Object):String{
    return mmddyyyy.format(value);
}
```

A label function for a CategoryAxis is automatically passed four arguments:

- **value**—The value of the property for the object being rendered. In this case, that value is the DTSALE property, which contains the date.

- **previousValue**—The value of the property for the previous column.

- **axis**—A reference to the axis.

- **item**—The whole data object.

In your case, all you need to do is return the formatted version of the date as a String. You can use the DateFormatter named mmddyyyy, which is already present in this file.

If you use the code completion feature, the import for CategoryAxis will be added automatically; otherwise, you will need to add it explicitly:

```
import mx.charts.CategoryAxis;
```

5 Specify renderDate as the labelFunction for the CategoryAxis.

```
<mx:CategoryAxis categoryField="DTSALE" id="catAxis" labelFunction="renderDate"/>
```

This tells the axis to use the renderDate() function when creating labels.

6 Save SalesChart.mxml and run the application.

You can now see the dates rendered properly. There are still too many dates shown at once, but you will fix that soon, when you learn about AxisRenderers. This file should resemble SalesChart_labelFunction.mxml in the intermediate directory.

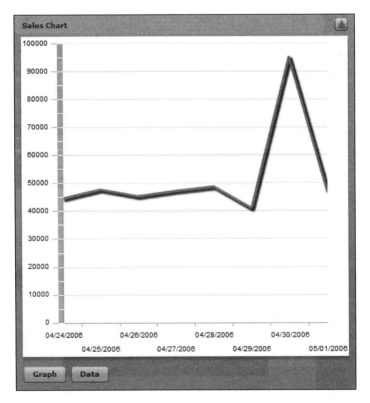

7 Open ComparisonChart.mxml from your flexGrocer/src/views/dashboard directory.

Alternately, you can open ComparisonChart_labels.mxml from the intermediate directory and save it as **ComparisonChart.mxml** in your flexGrocer/src/views/dashboard directory.

8 Add an `<mx:horizontalAxis>` tag pair inside the `<mx:ColumnChart>` tag. Within the `<mx:horizontalAxis>` tags, add an `<mx:CategoryAxis>` with the `categoryField` attribute set to DTSALE.

```
<mx:ColumnChart id="chart"
   dataProvider="{dp}"
   width="100%" height="100%">
   <mx:horizontalAxis>
      <mx:CategoryAxis id="hCatAxis" categoryField="DTSALE"/>
   </mx:horizontalAxis>
   ...
</mx:ColumnChart>
```

Just like the line chart, the column chart will use DTSALE as its field on the horizontal axis. You already discovered the need for a label function, so next you will add a label function for the horizontal axis.

9 In the `<mx:Script>` block, add a function called `renderDate()`, which will format the labels on the horizontal axis as dates.

```
private function renderDate(value:Object, previousValue:Object,
   ➥ axis:CategoryAxis, item:Object):String{
   return mmddyyyy.format(value);
}
```

Just as with the line chart, you use this function to format DTSALE as a date. If you use the code completion feature, the `import` for CategoryAxis will automatically be added; otherwise, you will need to add it explicitly.

10 Specify `renderDate` as the `labelFunction` for the CategoryAxis.

```
<mx:CategoryAxis id="hCatAxis"
categoryField="DTSALE"
   labelFunction="renderDate"/>
```

This tells the axis to use the `renderDate` function when creating labels.

11 Save ComparisonChart.mxml and run the application.

The comparison chart now shows the dates correctly. Next, you will add a labelFunction for the vertical axis as well.

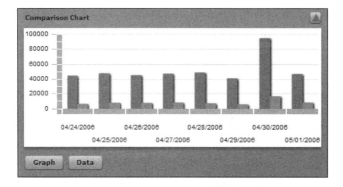

12 Just after the </mx:horizontalAxis> tag, add an <mx:verticalAxis> tag pair. Inside the vertical axis pair, add an <mx:LinearAxis> tag, to specify a labelFunction called renderDollars.

```
<mx:horizontalAxis>
    <mx:CategoryAxis id="hCatAxis" dataProvider="{dp}"
    categoryField="DTSALE" labelFunction="renderDate"/>
</mx:horizontalAxis>
<mx:verticalAxis>
    <mx:LinearAxis id="vLinAxis" labelFunction="renderDollars"/>
</mx:verticalAxis>
```

A LinearAxis will work fine for the vertical column because the values are all numeric. In the next step, you will create the renderDollars() function.

13 In the <mx:Script> block, create a function called renderDollars(), which accepts three arguments: value, previousValue and Axis.

```
private function renderDollars(value:Number, previousValue:Number,
    ➡ axis:LinearAxis):String{
    return dollars.format(value);
}
```

The labelFunction for a LinearAxis is automatically passed thee arguments: the value, the previous value, and a reference to the axis. If you use the code completion feature, the import for LinearAxis will be added automatically; otherwise, you will need to add it explicitly.

14 Save ComparisonChart.mxml and run the application.

The comparison chart now shows the dates and dollars correctly. The current file should resemble ComparisonChart_labelFunctions.mxml in the intermediate directory.

Adding Legends to Charts

Adding a legend to a Flex chart is incredibly easy. The <mx:Legend> tag requires only one argument, dataProvider, which is bound to the chart. You can use several other attributes to further customize the legend; a couple of the commonly used attributes are as follows:

- **labelPlacement**—Just like the labelPlacement of a check box or radio button, this indicates whether the label should be left, right, top, or bottom as compared with the colored square that identifies the data.

- **direction**—Indicates whether the items in the legend should be laid out vertically or horizontally.

1 Open ComparisonChart.mxml from your flexGrocer/src/views/dashboard directory.

Alternately, you can open ComparisonChart_labelFunctions.mxml from the intermediate directory and save it as **ComparisonChart.mxml** in your flexGrocer/src/views/dashboard directory.

2 Inside the <mx:VBox>, before the <mx:ColumnChart> tag, add an <mx:Legend> tag with the direction set to horizontal and the dataProvider bound to chart.

```
<mx:VBox>
    <mx:Legend direction="horizontal" dataProvider="{chart}"/>
    <mx:ColumnChart id="chart"
        dataProvider="{dp}"
        width="100%" height="100%">
    ...
</mx:VBox>
```

This should create a legend placed horizontally that appears before the chart inside the <mx:VBox>.

3 Find the <mx:ColumnSeries> tag for the GROSS column. Add a displayName attribute with the value Gross. Find the <mx:ColumnSeries> tag for the NET column. Add a displayName attribute with the value of Net.

```
<mx:series>
    <mx:ColumnSeries yField="GROSS" displayName="Gross">
    </mx:ColumnSeries>
    <mx:ColumnSeries yField="NET" displayName="Net">
    </mx:ColumnSeries>
</mx:series>
```

The displayName indicates what should be shown in the legend.

4 Save and run the application.

You should see a legend appear above the comparison chart. The current file should resemble ComparisonChart_legend.mxml in the intermediate directory.

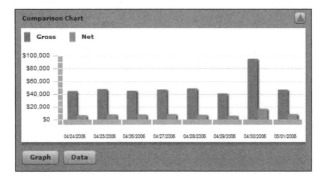

Limiting the Labels Shown on an Axis

When graphing large datasets, there is often too much data for every item to get its own label on the axis. To help you, there is an AxisRenderer you can use to customize the rendering of the axis.

The syntax for an AxisRenderer looks like this:

```
<mx:horizontalAxisRenderers>
    <mx:AxisRenderer id="{axisId}"
    canDropLabels="true|false"
    canStagger="true|false"
    showLabels="true|false"
    showLine="true|false"
    tickLength="Default depends on axis"
    tickPlacement="inside|outside|cross|none"
    title="No default"/>
</mx:horizontalAxisRenderers>
```

✱ **NOTE:** This is only a subset of the elements that can be set on an AxisRenderer.

1 Open ComparisonChart.mxml from your flexGrocer/src/views/dashboard directory.

Alternately, you can open ComparisonChart_legend from the intermediate directory and save it as **ComparisonChart.mxml** in your flexGrocer/src/views/dashboard directory.

2 Between the open <mx:ColumnChart> tag and the first <mx:horizontalAxis> tag, add an <mx:horizontalAxisRenderer> tag pair. Inside the pair, add an <mx:AxisRenderer> tag, setting the canDropLabels attribute to true.

```
<mx:ColumnChart id="chart"
  dataProvider="{dp}"
  width="100%" height="100%">
  <mx:horizontalAxisRenderers>
    <mx:AxisRenderer canDropLabels="true" axis="{hCatAxis}"/>
  </mx:horizontalAxisRenderers>
  <mx:horizontalAxis>
    <mx:CategoryAxis id="hCatAxis" dataProvider="{dp}" categoryField="DTSALE"
      ➥ labelFunction="renderDate"/>
  </mx:horizontalAxis>
  ...
</mx:ColumnChart>
```

This tells the horizontal axis that if there is not room for every label, it is okay to render the labels that fit. Labels will be rendered at regular intervals (such as every other item, every third item, and so on).

3 Save and test the application.

You should now see that regardless how many days, weeks, or months of data you view, the labels always render legibly.

Interacting with Charts

Like all elements in Flash Player, charts have a rich set of interactions that can be easily integrated into an application. Among the elements easily implemented are showing data tips as users mouse over elements of the charts, as well as enabling users to click elements in the chart to effect other changes throughout the application.

Mouse-Over Events

Mouse-over events are incredibly useful and simple to implement. All charts inherently support a property called showDataTips. By setting this to true for a chart, a tool tip-type element will appear, showing more data about the element the user is mousing over.

Click Events

Another easy-to-implement interaction is a click event. In this exercise, you will add data tips to the type and sales charts and enable users to filter the type and comparison charts by category when the user clicks a slice of the pie chart.

Selection Events

In addition to the ability to click on individual chart elements, Flex 3 includes the framework for selecting multiple elements, either by holding the Ctrl key (or Command key on a Mac) while selecting elements, or by dragging a box around a number of points within the chart.

Adding Chart Events

Using events, you will make your charts more interactive.

1 Open SalesChart.mxml from your flexGrocer/src/views/dashboard directory.

Alternately, you can open SalesChart_labelFunction.mxml from the intermediate directory and save it as **SalesChart.mxml** in your flexGrocer/src/views/dashboard directory.

2 Set the showDataTips attribute of the <mx:LineChart> tag to true and specify the dataTipFunction attribute equal to renderTips.

```
<mx:LineChart id="chart"
    dataProvider="{dp}"
    height="100%" width="100%"
    showDataTips="true"
    dataTipFunction="renderTips">
```

This tells the chart to show data tips when any element is moused over and to use the function renderTips() to determine what to show. You create renderTips() in the next step.

3   In the <mx:Script> block, create a function named renderTips(), which takes a single argument, called hd of type HitData, and returns a String.

```
private function renderTips(hd:HitData):String {
    var item:Object = hd.item;
    return "<b>"+mmddyyyy.format(item.DTSALE)+"</b><br>" +
    ➥ dollars.format(item[grossOrNet]);
}
```

If you use the code completion feature, the import for HitData will be added automatically; otherwise, you will need to add it explicitly.

4   Save and test the application.

Notice that as you mouse over elements in the line chart, nicely formatted data tips are now available. The completed file should look like SalesChart_dataTips.mxml in the intermediate directory.

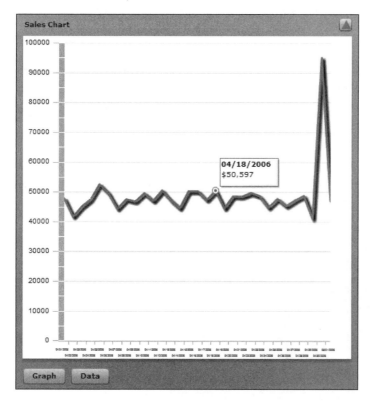

5 Open TypeChart.mxml from your flexGrocer/src/views/dashboard directory.

Alternately, you can open TypeChart_labels.mxml from the intermediate directory and save it as **TypeChart.mxml** in your flexGrocer/src/views/dashboard directory.

6 Set the showDataTips attribute of the <mx:PieChart> tag to true, and specify the dataTipFunction attribute equal to renderTips().

```
<mx:PieChart id="chart"
    dataProvider="{dp}"
    height="100%" width="100%"
    showDataTips="true"
    dataTipFunction="renderTips">
```

You create renderTips() in the next step.

7 In the <mx:Script> block, create a function named renderTips(), which takes a single argument, called data of type HitData, and returns a String.

```
private function renderTips(data:HitData):String{
    var gross:Number = data.item.GROSS;
    var net:Number = data.item.NET;
    return "Total Sales: " + dollars.format(gross)+ '\n' +
        ➥ "Total Profit: " + dollars.format(net);
}
```

Remember, you may need to explicitly import the mx.charts.HitData class, unless it was imported automatically for you.

Here, the renderTips() function takes a HitData object, finds the value for the gross and net properties, and builds a string, formatting them before returning it.

8 Save and test the application.

Notice that as you mouse over elements in the pie chart, nicely formatted data tips are now available. Next you will react to click events in the pie chart.

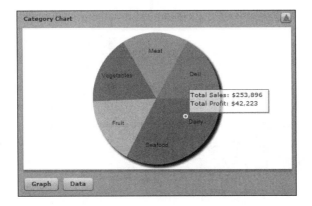

9 In the `<mx:PieChart>` tag, specify an `itemClick` attribute to call a function named
broadcastTypeChange() and pass it `event.hitData.item` as an argument.

```
<mx:PieChart id="chart"
    width="100%" height="100%"
    dataProvider="{dp}"
    showDataTips="true"
    dataTipFunction="renderTips"
    itemClick="broadcastTypeChange(event.hitData.item)">
```

itemClick is invoked when the user clicks an item in the chart. When this happens, a
ChartItemEvent object is created, which has a property called hitData. The hitData
property is an object describing the click. The item property of hitData contains a
reference to the item on which the user clicked. In the next step, you will write the
broadcastTypeChange() function, so an event is dispatched back to the main application
when the user clicks a category on this chart.

10 In the `<mx:Script>` block, create a function called broadcastTypeChange(), which takes
an argument called item of type Object, and returns void. This function will create an
instance of the ObjectDataEvent class and dispatch it.

```
private function broadcastTypeChange(item:Object):void{
    var o:ObjectDataEvent= new ObjectDataEvent("typeChange", item.CATEGORY);
    this.dispatchEvent(o);
}
```

ObjectDataEvent is an event written earlier that has a custom property called data that is
of type Object.

11 Declare an event named typeChange of type events.ObjectDataEvent in an `<mx:MetaData>`
tag at the top of the TypeChart.mxml component.

```
<v:MaxRestorePanel
    xmlns:mx="http://www.adobe.com/2006/mxml"
    xmlns:v="views.*">
    <mx:Metadata>
        [Event(name="typeChange", type="events.ObjectDataEvent")]
    </mx:Metadata>
    ...
</v:MaxRestorePanel>
```

12 Save TypeChart.mxml.

You need to make a change to Dashboard.mxml before you can test this latest change. TypeChart.mxml should now resemble TypeChart_events.mxml in the intermediate directory.

13 Open Dashboard.mxml from your flexGrocer/src directory.

This is the application that instantiates all three charts.

14 Find where TypeChart is instantiated. Add an attribute to handle the typeChange event and call a soon-to-be-written function called doTypeChange().

```
<v:TypeChart id="type"
    width="100%" height="100%"
    title="Sales By Type"
    grossOrNet="{grossOrNetGroup.selection.data}"
    typeChange="doTypeChange(event)"
    maximize="this.currentState='fullType'"
    restore="this.currentState=''"/>
```

When TypeChart dispatches a type change, you want the rest of the application to react and update itself accordingly.

15 In the <mx:Script> block, create a function called doTypeChange(), which takes an argument of type ObjectDataEvent. This function should use the Util class's static presetCombo() method to set the ComboBox control in the ApplicationControlBar container. Next, the selectedType property should be set to event.data.toString(). Finally, the function should send the dashboardWS.getSalesData web service.

```
private function doTypeChange(event:ObjectDataEvent):void{
    Util.presetCombo(catCombo,"name",event.data.toString());
    selectedType = event.data.toString();
    dashboardWS.getSalesData.send();
}
```

When an ObjectDataEvent is broadcast, you want the ApplicationControlBar to reflect the currently selected type, so you can use the presetCombo() function you saw earlier. If you recall from Lesson 18, "Accessing Server-side Objects," the getSalesData web service method takes three arguments: startDate, endDate, and selectedType. So, for the service to return the right data, you will first set selectedType and then send the service.

Don't forget, both the utils.Util and events.ObjectDataEvent classes need to be imported.

16 Save and run the application.

After the charts are drawn, if you click a slice of the pie in the type chart, the ComboBox updates, and new data loads from the server, showing only the sales for that type of product.

Adding Animations to Charts

Nearly limitless customizations can be applied to charts in Flex. The myriad customizations you can make include animating data into the chart or applying colors, gradients, and so on to the elements of a chart.

Three types of built-in animations can be easily applied to charts. They are all built as subclasses of the mx.charts.effects.SeriesEffect class. These classes can be used with a series showDataEffect or hideDataEffect attribute. The following are the classes:

- **SeriesInterpolate**—The SeriesInterpolate effect moves the graphics that represent the existing data in a series to the new points. Instead of clearing the chart and then repopulating it, it creates a nice smooth animation between the original data points and the new ones. You use the SeriesInterpolate effect only with a showDataEffect effect trigger. It has no effect if set with a hideDataEffect.

- **SeriesSlide**—The SeriesSlide effect slides a data series into and out of the chart's boundaries. The direction property specifies the location from which the series slides. If you use SeriesSlide with a hideDataEffect effect trigger, the series slides from the current position onscreen to a position off the screen in the indicated direction. If you use SeriesSlide as a showDataEffect, the series slides from offscreen to a position onto the screen, in the indicated direction.

- **SeriesZoom**—The SeriesZoom effect implodes and explodes chart data into and out of the focal point you specify. As with the SeriesSlide effect, whether the effect is zooming to or from this point depends on whether it is assigned to the showDataEffect or hideDataEffect effect triggers.

1 Open TypeChart.mxml from your flexGrocer/src/views/dashboard directory.

Alternately, you can open TypeChart_events.mxml from the intermediate directory and save it as **TypeChart.mxml** in your flexGrocer/src/views/dashboard directory.

2 Right before the `<mx:ViewStack>` tag, add an `<mx:SeriesInterpolate>` tag with an id attribute of interpolate and an elementOffset of 5.

```
<mx:SeriesInterpolate id="interpolate" elementOffset="5"/>
```

The elementOffset attribute specifies a number of milliseconds to delay before starting the effect.

3 Find the `<mx:PieSeries>` tag and add an attribute, showDataEffect="interpolate".

```
<mx:PieSeries field="{grossOrNet}"
   labelPosition="insideWithCallout"
   labelFunction="renderLabel"
   showDataEffect="interpolate" >
```

This attribute instructs the series to animate the data when it is added to the chart.

4 Save and run the application.

Notice the effects as data is rendered in the pie chart or any time the data changes. The completed file should closely resemble TypeChart_interpolate.mxml in the intermediate directory.

Customizing Chart Appearance with Styles

You can style a number of different elements in a chart, such as line colors, fill colors, fill gradients, alphas, and so on. One place they are often set is for each Series in a chart. As you have seen throughout this lesson, without setting any styles at all, Flex automatically assigns colors and renders the elements. However, if you want more control over the color choices, you can specify Series colors to whatever degree you need.

Specifying fill colors for a Series has this structure:

```
<mx:ColumnSeries displayName="net" yField="NET">
  <mx:fill>
    <mx:LinearGradient>
      <mx:entries>
        <mx:GradientEntry color="#0000FF"
          ratio="0" alpha="1"/>
        <mx:GradientEntry color="#0000DD"
          ratio=".1" alpha="1"/>
        <mx:GradientEntry color="#000022"
          ratio=".9" alpha="1"/>
        <mx:GradientEntry color="#000000"
          ratio="1" alpha="1"/>
      </mx:entries>
    </mx:LinearGradient>
  </mx:fill>
</mx:ColumnSeries>
```

Here, you see a four-color gradient fill being applied to a series of columns in a column chart. Notice that a gradient fill takes an array of GradientEntries, each with a color, ratio, and alpha, called entries. In this exercise, you will apply a gradient fill to the pie chart.

1 Open TypeChart.mxml from your flexGrocer/src/views/dashboard directory.

Alternately, you can open TypeChart_interpolate.mxml from the intermediate directory and save it as **TypeChart.mxml** in your flexGrocer/src/views/dashboard directory.

2 Between the open and close <mx:PieSeries> tags, add an <mx:fills> tag.

```
<mx:PieSeries field="{grossOrNet}"
  labelPosition="insideWithCallout"
  labelFunction="renderLabel"
  showDataEffect="interpolate" >
  <mx:fills>
  </mx:fills>

  ...
</mx:PieSeries>
```

In the next step, you will specify six different gradients to use for the data in the pie chart.

3 Inside the `<mx:fills>` tags you just created, specify six radial gradients, each with two colors. The first has a ratio of 0, and the second has a ratio of 1, as indicated in the following table.

First Color	First Color Ratio	Second Color	Second Color Ratio
#EF7651	0	#994C34	1
#E9C836	0	#AA9127	1
#6FB35F	0	#497B54	1
#A1AECF	0	#47447A	1
#996666	0	#999966	1
#339933	0	#339999	1

```
<mx:fills>
    <mx:RadialGradient>
        <mx:entries>
            <mx:GradientEntry color="#EF7651" ratio="0"/>
            <mx:GradientEntry color="#994C34" ratio="1"/>
        </mx:entries>
    </mx:RadialGradient>
    <mx:RadialGradient>
        <mx:entries>
            <mx:GradientEntry color="#E9C836" ratio="0"/>
            <mx:GradientEntry color="#AA9127" ratio="1"/>
        </mx:entries>
    </mx:RadialGradient>
    <mx:RadialGradient>
        <mx:entries>
            <mx:GradientEntry color="#6FB35F" ratio="0"/>
            <mx:GradientEntry color="#497B54" ratio="1"/>
        </mx:entries>
    </mx:RadialGradient>
    <mx:RadialGradient>
        <mx:entries>
            <mx:GradientEntry color="#A1AECF" ratio="0"/>
            <mx:GradientEntry color="#47447A" ratio="1"/>
        </mx:entries>
    </mx:RadialGradient>
    <mx:RadialGradient>
        <mx:entries>
            <mx:GradientEntry color="#996666" ratio="0"/>
            <mx:GradientEntry color="#999966" ratio="1"/>
        </mx:entries>
    </mx:RadialGradient>
```

```
<mx:RadialGradient>
    <mx:entries>
        <mx:GradientEntry color="#339933" ratio="0"/>
        <mx:GradientEntry color="#339999" ratio="1"/>
    </mx:entries>
</mx:RadialGradient>
</mx:fills>
```

Experiment and find colors that work best for you. You can add as many colors to the array as you want. Try switching between radial gradients and linear gradients to get a feel for how each works.

4 Save and run the application.

Notice the subtle gradient in each slice of the pie.

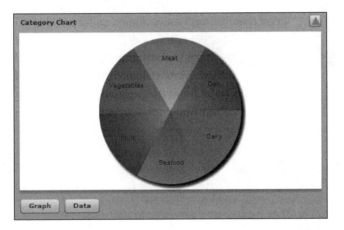

What You Have Learned

In this lesson, you have:

- Worked with the pie, column, and line charts (pages 500–503)
- Learned how to provide data to charts (pages 504–510)
- Specified chart axes (pages 510–517)
- Added chart legends and labels (pages 517–519)
- Handled chart events (pages 520–525)
- Animated charts when data is set (pages 525–526)
- Styled charts (pages 526–529)

What You Will Learn

In this lesson, you will:

- Understand the need for modularizing applications
- Understand the methods to modularize in Flex
- Create a Flex module and use it in your application
- Understand the pros and cons of RSLs
- Use the Flex framework RSL to reduce your application size
- Create a Flex Library project to facilitate the sharing of application code

Approximate Time

This lesson takes approximately 1 hour and 30 minutes to complete.

Lesson Files

Media Files:

None

Starting Files:

Lesson20/start/as/ecomm.as
Lesson20/start/EComm.mxml

Completed Files:

Lesson20/complete/as/ecomm.as
Lesson20/complete/Ecomm.mxml
Lesson20/complete/modules/CheckoutModule.mxml

LESSON 20

Creating Modular Applications

In previous lessons you added to the FlexGrocer application to create new functionality, add features, and work with data or application servers. The application has steadily grown in size from a single MXML file to over 30 files in multiple directories.

In this lesson, you will break the application down into smaller pieces to understand the methods available to a Flex developer to modularize and maintain an application as it grows in size.

EComm application with dynamically loaded checkout module

Introducing Modular Applications in Flex 3

In Lesson 4, "Using Simple Controls," you learned about the Embed directive and its ability to "bake" the required images directly into the SWF file at compile time. The process of baking these files into the final SWF provided several advantages. First, the files were preloaded at the start of the application. Second, when executed, the application didn't require Internet access to retrieve these files; this was useful for creating offline applications.

However, this strategy also has disadvantages. Baking images into your application increases the size of your SWF, causing it to download more slowly. Further, all users experience the download size penalty for these images regardless if they are used. For example, if we embedded all images for EComm directly into the application, even a user who never navigates to the Dairy category has still downloaded the Milk bottle image.

The source code for your Flex applications works in a very similar way. By default, all the class files, whether written in MXML or ActionScript, used by your application are baked into the SWF file. This has the same benefits as embedding an image: instant availability without the need to download. However, it is also subject to the same disadvantages.

As your application grows in complexity, its size and download time will continue to increase. Further, a user that never uses an area of the application must still download the classes that provide functionality to that area.

Fortunately, Flex provides a strategy to modularize, or break down, your larger application into smaller pieces. Using the Flex Module Loader, you can load and unload predefined pieces of the application at runtime, providing your users a smaller initial download size and allowing you to better encapsulate and separate logical portions of your application. In this lesson, you will use the Module Loader and the Flex Module Wizard to isolate the checkout portion of the EComm application into a module that will only be loaded if the user chooses to checkout.

Another different, but related, concern when developing Flex applications is duplication of code across multiple applications. In previous lessons, you developed three independent Flex applications: Dashboard, DataEntry, and EComm. Currently, these applications reside in the same directory and can easily share the same valueObject and views. However, as your application grows, you may need to have multiple projects sharing these classes. Although you could make a copy of the needed files, you would then need to maintain each copy separately. Flex offers a much better solution called a Library project. You will use this library both in your current applications and in the next lesson, when you will deploy a version of your application to the desktop.

Lastly, because your applications are independent, each currently bakes in its own copy of some overlapping classes such as HBox, VBox, LinkButton, and others. This unnecessarily punishes a user who uses both the EComm and Dashboard application by causing them to download the same code multiple times.

Flex also offers a solution for this problem, known as Runtime Shared Libraries (RSLs). They allow you to externalize shared assets that may be used across multiple applications and download them only once, reducing the cumulative download size of multiple applications. You will learn how RSLs can be used within your Flex applications and take advantage of the Flex framework RSL to significantly reduce the size of your applications.

Using Flex Modules

The checkout section of the EComm application is a great candidate to become its own Flex Module. While a necessary portion of the application for users that choose to buy products, users that are only browsing don't need this extra code on start-up. Further, once the section has become its own module, you will be able to make changes to this portion of the application separately from the rest of EComm.

1 In Flex Builder, create a new directory named modules in the src directory of your FlexGrocer application by choosing File > New > Folder and specifying **modules** as the Folder name. Click Finish to create the folder.

This folder will provide a convenient location to store any modules you create, separating them from the remainder of the application.

2 Open Checkout.mxml from your src/views/ecomm directory.

3 Note that the Checkout class currently extends VBox, indicating that the Checkout class uses a vertical layout.

This will be important when we create a new module in the following steps.

4 Choose File > New > MXML Module to launch the new module wizard within Flex Builder.

5 In the tree view area of the wizard, choose the newly created modules directory or type **FlexGrocer/src/modules** in the parent folder text input area.

6 Specify CheckoutModule as the filename for this new module and that the layout will be vertical to match the vertical layout of the current Checkout class.

7 Clear the width and height fields as, like our existing Checkout class, we will specify CheckoutModule width and height in EComm.mxml.

8 Ensure the Optimize size for the application radio button is selected and that EComm.mxml is selected in the ComboBox to the right.

Choosing EComm.mxml here tells the Flex compiler that we intend to use this module from within the EComm application. The compiler will attempt to ensure that classes used by both the main application and this module are not included more than once. This helps to reduce the download size of the module.

9 Click Finish. Flex Builder opens the new Module class in the editor.

Using the Module Class

The Module class, represented by the <mx:Module> tag in MXML, is the base class for any module that will interact with the Flex framework. Like the <mx:Application> tag, which serves as the root of your application, the <mx:Module> will serve as the root of any module that is loaded dynamically. Although there is only one <mx:Application> tag per application, you can have many different modules, each extending <mx:Module>.

The `<mx:Module>` tag also has a `layout` property that can be set to absolute, horizontal, or vertical to handle these various layout mechanisms. Right now, your `layout` property should be set to vertical as you indicated in the new module wizard.

As your next step, you will populate your new CheckoutModule with the code from the Checkout class.

1 Open Checkout.mxml from your src/views/ecomm. Copy all of the source code inside the main VBox tag. Do not include the VBox start and end tags.

This code will now make up our new module.

2 Switch to the CheckoutModule.mxml file and paste the copied code between the start and end of the `<mx:Module>` tag.

3 Add a namespace, using the letter v as a prefix, which will allow you to access the custom component in the src/views/ecomm folder used by the code you just copied.

The Module tag should appear as follows:

```
<mx:Module xmlns:mx=http://www.adobe.com/2006/mxml xmlns:v="views.ecomm.*"
➥ layout="vertical">
```

This completes the changes required to have a fully functional module. In the next exercise, you will add code to load this module into the EComm application.

Replacing the Checkout Code with a ModuleLoader Tag

Although the code for your module is complete, you still need to tell Flex when and where to load and display this module. You will need to remove the code that displays the old baked-in Checkout module, and then use a `<mx:ModuleLoader>` tag to dynamically load your new module.

1 Open EComm.mxml from the flexGrocer/src directory. Locate and remove the `<v:Checkout>` tag near line 78.

2 Add a `<mx:ModuleLoader>` tag where the `<v:Checkout>` tag was previously. Set the `id` property of the ModuleLoader to checkout, and set its width and height each to 100%.

```
    ...
            </mx:VBox>
        </mx:HBox>
        <mx:ModuleLoader id="checkout" width="100%" height="100%"/>
    </mx:ViewStack>
    ...
```

The ModuleLoader class is another type of container in Flex that specifically understands how to load and unload modules. As it is a descendant of the Container class, it can be placed directly into the ViewStack.

3 Set the url property of the ModuleLoader tag to modules/CheckoutModule.swf.

```
<mx:ModuleLoader id="checkout" url="modules/CheckoutModule.swf" width="100%"
➡ height="100%"/>
```

When Flex compiles the Checkout module you created in the previous exercise, it will become an independent SWF containing the code that you pasted into the module, as well as any other pieces included by your code (for example, the BillingInfo, CCInfo, and OrderConf views).

The name of the SWF is the same as the name of your module.

4 Select the FlexGrocer project in the Navigator pane and choose File > Properties.

5 From the options on the left side of the Properties panel, choose Flex Modules.

6 You will see your CheckoutModule listed. You can remove a module from your application or change which application the module is optimized to use from this screen. Click OK to exit.

7 Add a listener for the ready event to the ModuleLoader tag, calling handleModuleReady and passing it the event object.

The ready event is broadcast once the module has successfully loaded and is ready to use. Your CheckoutModule instance will be available as a special property of the ModuleLoader called child.

8 Open ecomm.as from the src/as/directory.

9 At the bottom of the file, add a new private method called handleModuleReady. It will take an event object of type ModuleEvent and return void. Inside the function, cast the child property of the checkout module loader to type CheckoutModule. Then set its cart property to the cart defined in this file as follow:

```
private function handleModuleReady( event:ModuleEvent ):void {
   CheckoutModule( checkout.child ).cart = cart;
}
```

Be sure that both mx.events.ModuleEvent and modules.CheckoutModule are imported. The child property of the checkout module loader contains your CheckoutModule instance. You need to ensure that this instance uses the same shopping cart as the rest of the application, so it is set once the module is ready to use.

10 Run the EComm.mxml file. The application should still work exactly as it did before.

If you add items to your cart and click Checkout, you may notice just a momentary pause before the Checkout screen is displayed. In this moment, Flex is loading the CheckoutModule for the first time and displaying it on the screen. The module is only loaded when it is needed, so users of this application will now only load the CheckoutModule and related code should they choose to enter the Checkout section of the application.

Understanding Runtime Shared Libraries (RSLs)

In the previous section, you used the ModuleLoader and Module class to separate a portion of the functionality of the EComm application into a separate SWF that was loaded only when needed. This section is also about separating applications into pieces, but this time it's for the purpose of sharing the code across *multiple* applications, instead of within a single application, to reduce the cumulative size of the application files.

Examining the three applications you built in previous lessons shows some commonality between them. All the applications use classes from the Flex framework, like VBox, HBox, and many others. DataEntry and EComm even share some code you wrote, such as custom events and valueObjects.

By default, every application you compile with Flex Builder is independent; it will contain a copy of each class it needs to function properly. However, as the following figure shows, this can lead to a lot of duplication across applications.

	DashBoard	DataEntry	EComm
Flex Framework Classes	VBox HBox Charting	VBox HBox Tree	VBox HBox HorizontalList
Common Application Code		ProductEvent Category Product	ProductEvent Category Product
	ChartPod	AddProduct	FoodList

As you can see, every application is really a combination of code from the Flex framework, code you write that may be common across the applications, and code that is unique to any given application.

Runtime Shared Libraries (RSLs) help this problem by allowing you to factor out common code, which can then be shared between your applications in the same domain. This common code is no longer baked into your application, but rather is kept in a separate library that is loaded at runtime. Further, the RSL can be cached on the client so it does not need to be downloaded every time your application is used.

Using RSLs, the previous figure could be rearranged to look like this:

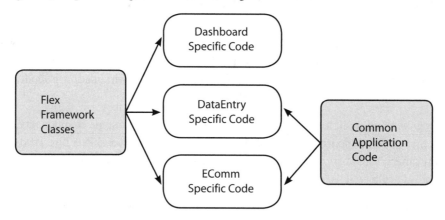

The code for the Flex framework, as well as any common application code, resides in separate files. This dramatically reduces the size of the Dashboard, DataEntry, and EComm applications as they no longer have major duplication.

To understand the dramatic effect of this change, here are the sizes in bytes of the Dashboard, DataEntry, and EComm application before and after the use of RSLs.

Application	As an independent application	When sharing code using RSLs	Amount reduced
Dashboard	417,792	163,840	253,952
DataEntry	430,080	167,936	262,144
EComm	434,176	135,168	299,008
Totals	1,282,048	466,944	815,104

We removed over 800 Kbytes of code between the three applications. This is very helpful, but there is a catch. The sizes in the table do not include the size of the shared code that we moved into a separate file. That file will have a size that needs to be considered when we are evaluating the benefit of using RSLs.

In this case, the RSL that contains the various framework items required is about 500 Kbytes. This RSL will need to be downloaded once and cached on the client. But this still means that the first time a user attempts to access your application, they will need to download the 500 Kbytes RSL and the application.

If a user works with all three of your application, RSLs are a huge advantage. Including the initial 500 Kbytes download, they will only have a cumulative download size of approximately 966 Kbytes, which is significantly less than the 1,282 Kbytes of the original applications. The subsequent downloading and switching between applications will be much faster.

Unfortunately, if you have users that only use a single application—EComm, for example— they will have a much worse initial download experience (500,000 + 135,168 bytes = 635,168 bytes as opposed to the original 434,176).

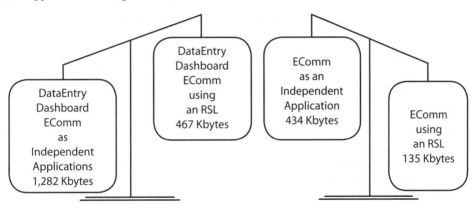

The reason for this increase is discussed in the next section, but it echoes the fact that RSLs are intended to reduce the cumulative size of several applications, not the size of a single application.

Understanding the Linker

Once the Flex compiler is done transforming your source code into a more base-level byte code, the linker takes over. The job of the linker is to assemble all the relevant pieces of byte code into a single SWF for execution.

It does this by resolving the required references for each class. In other words, if one of your class files uses a DataGrid, it is one of the linker's jobs to ensure the code for DataGrid, and all classes used by DataGrid, are available.

Conversely, if your code never uses a HortizontalList, the code for this component is not included. When you choose to have all of your classes merged (or baked) into your application, you only end up having the classes you truly need. This is extremely efficient.

However, when choosing to factor your code into a RSL, things become a little less efficient for a number of reasons. The primary issue we are concerned with here is that, to remove duplication in the applications, we add to the number of classes actually linked.

Earlier, we noted the following requirements from the Flex framework for each of our applications.

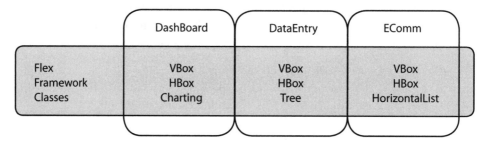

If we were to move all these classes into a single RSL, we would end up with an RSL that contained VBox, HBox, HorizontalList, Tree, and the Charting components. In other words, even though EComm doesn't use the Tree, the RSL would need to have that piece of code to make it viable for the other applications. This is one of the issues that causes an application linked with an external library to grow in size.

✱ **NOTE:** With some work, you can do a more specific job of determining whether individual files are merged into the project or reside in the RSL. In this example, you could specify that only the common files reside in the RSL, and that Charting, Tree, and HorizontalList reside in the specific application. For more information, read up on "About RSLs" and the load-externs compiler option in the Flex help files.

Using the Flex Framework RSL Caching

So far we have discussed a way to make your applications more modular and reduce their initial file size, as well as a technique for reducing the cumulative file size of many applications hosted within your domain.

With Flex 3, Adobe has taken that concept even further in an attempt to significantly reduce the cumulative file size of all Flex applications created by all developers using the RSL technique we discussed earlier in this lesson.

In this section, you will modify the existing FlexGrocer project to use a new feature of Flex 3 and Flash Player that allows the Flex framework to be cached and easily used across all of your applications.

Understanding the Purpose of the Framework Cache

In the last section, it was demonstrated that each of the applications within the FlexGrocer project contains its own copy of various framework classes, causing a user of these applications to download duplicate code, increasing the size of your application, and diminishing the user experience.

It was noted that a significant decrease in application size could be achieved by factoring out the common elements into a single Runtime Shared Library (RSL), which could be reused amongst the applications.

Now imagine the amount of duplicate code downloaded by all users of every Flex application on both the Internet and private networks throughout the world. When a user visits two separate websites that use Flex, the user is normally forced to redownload the applicable pieces of the framework.

To combat this problem and improve the user experience for everyone using a Flex application, Adobe has developed an RSL of the Flex framework that can be downloaded once by the user and then reused for any future Flex application.

When a user views a Flex application hosted at one website, Flash Player first checks for an appropriate version of the framework RSL in the player's cache. If the appropriate version is found, it is used; otherwise, it is downloaded and stored for future use. When the user later visits a Flex application at another website, Flash Player performs the same check, this time finding the framework in the cache.

Ultimately, the first time a user views a Flex application, they will have a longer initial download. However, each subsequent visit to any Flex application will be significantly faster.

Using Signed vs. Unsigned RSLs

You may have noticed that I said "player's cache" as opposed to "browser's cache" in the preceding paragraphs. Normal RSLs created by developers are referred to as unsigned RSLs and are stored in the Internet browser's cache, making them subject to deletion when the user chooses to clear that cache. Unsigned RSLs are also only applicable to the domain from which they are served. Two applications from one website can both use an RSL from that website, but an application from another website cannot.

The framework RSL provided by Adobe is digitally signed and referred to as a signed RSL. This provides two main benefits: the RSL is cached in Flash Player, not the browser; and the RSL can be used across domains without restriction.

When stored on a user's local hard drive, signed RSLs have a .swz extension. Unsigned RSLs have a .swf extension.

Examining the Current Size of the Applications

Before we begin to use the framework RSL, it is a useful exercise to note the current size of each application.

1 Expand the bin-debug folder in your project from the Navigator pane.

The bin-debug folder is where Flex Builder creates the output SWF files when you run or build the application.

2 Find and select the Dashboard.swf file.

3 Choose File > Properties.

The size of the Dashboard.swf file should be approximately 669 Kbytes, but can vary due to debugging options that you will learn about in later lessons.

4 Feel free to repeat this process for the other two application files.

Configuring Your Application to Use the Framework RSL

The following steps will allow you to use the signed framework RSL in the FlexGrocer application. The changes we make in this step apply to the entire project—EComm, DataEntry, and Dashboard will all be affected.

1 Select the FlexGrocer project in the Navigator pane and choose File > Properties.

2 From the options on the left side of the Properties panel, choose Flex Build Path.

This section contains information about additional source files and libraries that should be included in your Flex project.

3 Choose the Library Path tab at the top of the screen.

4 Change the combo box labeled "Default link type" from "Merged into code" to "Runtime shared library (RSL)."

5 Expand the item in the tree view called Flex 3.

The list will expand to show all the libraries currently available to Flex Builder to merge into your code.

6 Find and expand the framework.swc. Your screen should look like the following image.

7 Highlight the RSL URL node, and click the Edit button.

8 Ensure the "Use same linkage as framework" check box is selected.

This tells the Flex compiler to use the default link type you specified in step 4 for this item.

9 Ensure the Digests radio button is selected.

This tells Flash Player we want to use an SHA-256 hash to verify that we are loading the correct version of this library. In a trusted environment, we may choose to skip this step, but it would not be advisable to do so on the Internet at large.

Listed in the Deployment Paths grid, you will see two files. The first has a .swz extension; the second has a .swf extension. The .swz file is a special version of the digest mentioned earlier. It will be stored in the cache of Flash Player itself. If the user of your site is running an older version of Flash Player that cannot support this feature, they will use the second file. This second file is not verified by the digest and is not allowed into Flash Player cache, but it will still be cached by the web browser.

10 Click OK to return to the Library Path screen.

11 Click OK again to return to your project.

12 If you still have Build Automatically turned on, the project will begin rebuilding. If not, choose Clean from the Project menu in Flex Builder to initiate a rebuild of all your applications.

Examining the Difference Made by the Framework RSL

The framework RSL is now being used by your three applications, and their size will have reduced significantly as described previously. To examine this change, we need to look at the output of each file.

1 Expand the bin-debug folder in your project from the Navigator pane.

The bin-debug folder is where Flex Builder creates the output SWF files when you run or build the application.

2 Find and select the Dashboard.swf file.

3 Choose File > Properties.

The size of the Dashboard.swf file should be noticeably smaller than when performing this same exercise earlier in the lesson.

Feel free to repeat this process for the other two application files.

Creating a Library Project

In the introduction, we alluded to three aspects of modularization: creating runtime loadable modules that contain portions of the application that can be considered independent; using Runtime Shared Libraries, such as the framework cache, to ensure multiple applications do not needlessly redownload code; and creating libraries to share code between distinct Flex projects.

The last item, creating libraries, is arguably a subset of the Runtime Shared Library topic; however, it is being called out separately here to examine the process of creation in more detail.

In this exercise, you will create a new Flex Library project from a portion of the classes in the FlexGrocer project and reconfigure FlexGrocer to use this new library. This library will also be used in subsequent lessons when dealing with desktop deployment.

1 Create a new Flex Library project by choosing File > New > Flex Library Project.

2 In the Project name field, specify **FlexGrocerLibrary.**

3 Leave the other options at their defaults and choose Next.

4 In the Main source folder field enter **src**.

Flex Builder generally uses a src folder when creating Flex Projects but does not follow this convention when creating a library. To eliminate confusion and remain consistent, we will use a src folder in both cases.

5 Click Finish.

A new project will appear in your project list, representing this library. A library, unlike a standard project, is not run on its own. It is simply a collection of classes and assets used by other projects.

Adding Classes and Assets to the Library

You are going to begin moving files and folders to the library. Once you begin, your existing FlexGrocer project will no longer be able to compile until this process is complete. You may receive errors and warnings if Build Automatically is selected. This is a normal part of the process.

1 Inside the src folder of your new Library project, create five directories named:

assets
events
valueObjects
views
utils

These directories will contain classes that are moved from the FlexGrocer project.

2 Expand the src/assets directory of your FlexGrocer project and drag both the downArrow.gif and upArrow.gif to the new assets directory of the Library project.

You will be moving the classes that use these assets to the library shortly.

3 Drag the CategoryEvent.as and ObjectDataEvent.as files from the src/events folder of the FlexGrocer project to the src/event folder of the Library project.

4 Drag the Category.as file from the src/valueObjects folder of the FlexGrocer project to the src/valueObjects folder of the Library project.

5 Drag the Util.as file from the src/utils folder of the FlexGrocer project to the src/utils folder of the Library project.

6 Drag the MaxRestorePanel.as and the dashboard directory (including the ChartPod. mxml and the charts created in the last lesson residing within) from the src/views directory of the FlexGrocer project to the src/views folder of the Library project.

These files will now reside in the Library project and will be usable by multiple projects in the future.

7 Right-click the FlexGrocer Library project and choose Properties.

The Properties panel for a Library project is very different than a standard Flex project.

8 From the options on the left side of the Properties panel, choose Flex Library Build Path. On the classes tab, expand the src directory and select the check boxes next to events, utils, valueObject, and views.

This tab determines which of the classes in this project will be included in the final library. You just told the builder to include all classes under these directories.

9 Click the tab labeled Assets, and select the check box next to the Assets folder, then click OK.

Flex Builder will now ensure that the assets in this directory are baked into the library.

Using the FlexGrocerLibrary within the FlexGrocer Application

1 If you have not done so already, start your local ColdFusion server.

2 Right-click your FlexGrocer project and select Properties.

3 From the options on the left side of the Properties panel, choose Flex Build Path, and then choose the Library Path tab.

4 On the right side, click the Add Project button.

This button allows you to add Flex Library projects to your FlexGrocer project.

5 Choose the FlexGrocerLibrary from the dialog box and click OK.

Flex Builder will now use the contents of this library during the linking stage explained previously.

6 Click OK in the Properties dialog box.

7 If your builder is set to build automatically, it should begin rebuilding now. Otherwise, choose Project > Clean and rebuild both the FlexGrocerLibrary and FlexGrocer.

Once the build is complete, you should no longer receive any errors; however, you may receive a warning about a type selector. Flex is just letting you know that, despite listing a type selector for DateChooser in your CSS file, DateChooser is no longer being used in the FlexGrocer project. This is because you have moved the files using DateChooser to the library.

8 Run your Dashboard application. Everything should perform as it did previously; however, several of the key dashboard files are now in a separate library that will be usable by additional projects in the following lessons.

What You Have Learned

In this lesson, you have:

- Learned two methods to modularize Flex applications at runtime (pages 532–533)
- Created a Flex module and used it in the EComm application (pages 533–537)
- Learned about RSLs and cumulative size reduction (pages 537–540)
- Set up the Flex framework RSL and noted the reduced application size (pages 540–544)
- Created a Flex Library project for shared code (pages 544–547)

What You Will Learn

In this lesson, you will:

- Explore the deployment options for Flex applications
- Learn the liabilities of browser-based applications
- Learn how to use AIR to break out of the browser

Approximate Time

This lesson takes approximately 1 hour to complete.

Lesson Files

Media Files:

Lesson21/DashboardDesktop/start/src/assets/HelloWorld.air

Starting Files:

Lesson21/DashboardDesktop/start/src/Dashboard.mxml
Lesson21/DashboardDesktop/start/src/assets/FlexGrocerDesktop16.png
Lesson21/DashboardDesktop/start/src/assets/FlexGrocerDesktop32.png
Lesson21/DashboardDesktop/start/src/assets/FlexGrocerDesktop48.png
Lesson21/DashboardDesktop/start/src/assets/FlexGrocerDesktop128.png

Completed Files:

Lesson21/DashboardDesktop/complete/src/Dashboard.air
Lesson21/DashboardDesktop/complete/src/Dashboard.mxml
Lesson21/DashboardDesktop/complete/src/Dashboard-app.xml
Lesson21/DashboardDesktop/complete/src/assets/FlexGrocerDesktop16.png
Lesson21/DashboardDesktop/complete/src/assets/FlexGrocerDesktop32.png
Lesson21/DashboardDesktop/complete/src/assets/FlexGrocerDesktop48.png
Lesson21/DashboardDesktop/complete/src/assets/FlexGrocerDesktop128.png

LESSON 21

Deploying Flex Applications

Up to this point, you have been building and testing your application locally. When your application is complete and ready to be deployed, there are different options available to you. Your application can be deployed to a web server or to the desktop. One of the most interesting new features of Flex 3 is the ability to build applications for deployment to the desktop. With the Flex 3 release, Adobe has also released the Adobe Integrated Runtime (AIR), which is a platform for deploying cross-platform desktop applications. For years, web developers have been building applications to run in browsers, largely because they had no choice for deployment: web applications required a browser. Adobe introduced AIR to allow web developers to use technologies they know (HTML, JavaScript, Flash, and Flex) to build applications that can be deployed directly to the desktop. In this lesson, you will create a desktop version of the Dashboard application that can be installed directly on a Windows or Macintosh operating system and run without a browser.

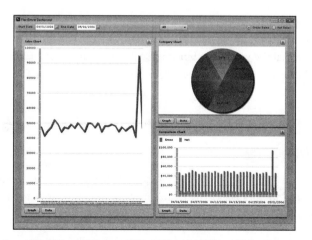

The FlexGrocer Dashboard that you have been building all along has now been deployed as a desktop application.

Compiling a Deployment Version of Your Application

Throughout this book, each time your application was recompiled, it was stored in the bin-debug directory. The reality is this published version contains the application, as well as the added information to allow it to work with the debugger (which you will explore in Lesson 25, "Debugging Flex Applications"). The reality is the debugging framework can add an extra 40 to 70 percent to the file size of the application, and this extra size provides no additional functionality to the end users.

Fortunately, it is extremely easy to create the "release" version of the application using Flex Builder. By simply clicking the Export Release Build button,

or choosing Project > Export Release Build,

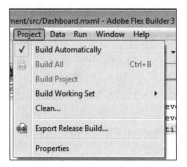

the export dialog box opens, allowing you to specify the project and application to export and the directory to which it will be exported (this defaults to bin-release). If you were to try this now, you would see that the version in bin-release is approximately 528,371 bytes, while the version in bin-debug is approximately 858,976 bytes (63 percent larger!).

Breaking Out of the Browser with the Adobe Integrated Runtime (AIR)

Another option now available to Flex Developers is deployment for the desktop. Although many web developers do not necessarily realize it, there are limitations to browser-based applications that other desktop applications do not have. For instance:

- Browsers do not allow applications to interact with the file system.

- Browser-based applications have very limited choices for storing client-side data: cookies in HTML applications, and Shared Objects in Flash Player applications.

- Browser-based applications cannot run as background services; if running, they are always running in an open browser.

- Browser-based applications offer only a very limited offline application; they rely heavily on being connected to the Internet.

- Many keyboard shortcuts are intercepted by the browser. Browser-based applications cannot map these shortcuts to other meanings within the application.

AIR offers an alternative for web developers. They can use the technologies they know and build an application outside of the web browser. AIR applications can escape all of the browser's limitations:

- AIR applications have direct access to the file system.

- AIR applications can support dragging and dropping of items from the operating system directly into the application.

- In AIR applications, with the windowing API, the look and feel of the application can be completely customized or even hidden away, allowing for "background" applications.

- AIR offers a robust API to allow for easy development of partially connected applications.

- AIR applications exist outside the browser, so there are no "off-limits" keyboard shortcuts.

- AIR offers an embedded database, allowing for even greater client-side storage possibilities.

Getting Started with AIR

The first step in using or building an AIR application is to have its runtime available. The runtime acts like a virtual machine for AIR applications, providing a base layer between the application and the user's operating system. It is this runtime that allows an AIR application to be written once and to run identically across operating systems.

Installing the AIR Runtime

Most end users will have the runtime installed automatically when they install their first AIR application. However, developers may often find themselves needing to install the runtime independently.

Installing on Windows

1. Download the AIR runtime installer for Windows from the Adobe site (www.adobe.com/go/getair).

2. Double-click the AIR.msi file. An installation window opens.

3. When the installation is complete, click OK.

Installing on Mac OS

1. Download the AIR runtime installer for Macintosh from the Adobe site (www.adobe.com/go/getair).

2. Double-click the AIR.pkg file. The Install Adobe Integrated Runtime 1.0 window opens.

3. Click the Continue button, in the lower-left corner of the window. The Select a Destination page of the installer opens.

4. Select the destination volume, and click the Continue button. The Easy Install button opens.

5. Click the Install button in the lower-left corner of the window. If the installer displays an Authenticate window, enter your Mac OS username and password.

6. After the installation is completed, click the Close button in the lower-right corner of the installation window.

Installing a First Application

Once you have the AIR runtime installed, it is simple to run a new AIR application on your system. Each AIR application is represented by the .air file extension. To install one of these applications, simply double-click the AIR file. To see how this works, follow these steps:

1. Find the HelloWorld.air file in the Lesson21/DashboardDesktop/start/src/assets directory. Double-click the file.

2. In the dialog box that appears, choose a directory to which the application will be installed.

3. After the installation is complete, the application is launched automatically. It can also be accessed through the OS's normal means: On Windows, select Start > Flex 3 TFS> Hello World Application. On a Mac OS, double-click the application's icon, which is installed in the subdirectory you specified during installation.

As you can clearly see, installing and running an AIR application is no different than installing and running any other desktop application on your computer.

Creating an AIR Application

Two main files are needed to create an AIR application: one is the MXML application, and the other is an application.xml file that defines the deployment options for an application. Listing 1 shows a simple HelloWorld application defined in MXML. Listing 2 shows the corresponding application.xml file, which can be used to package and deploy the HelloWorld application.

Listing 1 – HelloWorld.mxml

```
<?xml version="1.0" encoding="utf-8"?>
<mx:WindowedApplication xmlns:mx="http://www.adobe.com/2006/mxml">
   <mx:Label text="Hello World" fontSize="40"/>
</mx: WindowedApplication >
```

Listing 2 - HelloWorld-app.xml

```
<?xml version="1.0" encoding="UTF-8"?>
<application xmlns="http://ns.adobe.com/air/application/1.0">
   <id>HelloWorld</id>
   <filename>HelloWorld</filename>
   <name>HelloWorld</name>
   <version>v1</version>
   <description></description>
   <initialWindow>
      <content>HelloWorld.swf</content>
      <title>Hello World</title>
   </initialWindow>
</application>
```

Creating a New AIR Project

You will create a new Flex Builder project to house the desktop version of the Dashboard. Although it is possible for Flex and AIR applications to coexist in the same project, it requires advanced manipulation of the Flex Builder project files. Rather than go through these steps and run the risk of corrupting your other Flex Builder project, it is easier to create a new project and leverage the SWC you created in Chapter 20, "Creating Modular Applications." To get started, you need to create a new project.

1 Create a new subdirectory in your flex3tfs directory, called DashboardDesktop.

2 Create a subdirectory of DashboardDesktop named src.

3 Copy Dashboard.mxml from your Lesson21/DashboardDesktop/start/src/ directory into your src subdirectory of DashboardDesktop directory.

4 Open Flex Builder.

5 From the top menu, choose File > New > Flex Project.

6 Name the project Dashboard.

7 Deselect the Use Default Location option, and instead specify the DashboardDesktop directory you created in step 1 as the project directory.

8 For the application type, specify Desktop application (runs in Adobe AIR).

9 Choose the None option from the Application server type combo box, and click Next.

10 Leave the default choice, which specifies bin-debug as the output folder, and click Next.

11 Leave src specified as the Main source folder, leave Dashboard.mxml specified as the Main application file, and create a new unique ID for the application, something like com.flexgrocer.dashboard.desktop for example.

▼ CAUTION! In real-world AIR applications, it is crucial that each application has its own unique ID. Internally, this ID is used to register the application with the operating system, so if a user tries to install an AIR application that has already been installed, it knows to ask whether the user wants to uninstall, reinstall, or run the application.

12 Click Finish.

By completing this wizard, you have created your application.xml file (named Dashboard-app.xml). Don't be alarmed by the errors you may see in the Problems panel; in the next steps, you will fix those by importing a library.

Making the Dashboard Application into an AIR Application

In Lesson 20, "Creating Modular Applications," you created a library project with all the files necessary to run the Dashboard application. (This can also be found in the Lesson20/ FlexGrocerLibrary directory). By making this project available to the Dashboard application, you should have all the functionality you need for your Dashboard Desktop.

To use the library project you created in Lesson 20, you need to add it to the build path for your new project.

1 Reference the FlexGrocerLibrary library project from your application. To do this, you need to have the FlexGrocerLibrary project that was created in Lesson 20 open. If you still have it as part of your workspace, make sure it is open; otherwise, right-click it and choose Open project. If you don't still have it in your workspace, create a new Flex Library project (as discussed in Lesson 20) that points to the FlexGrocerLibrary subdirectory for the FlexGrocerLibrary folder of Lesson 20.

2 From the menu, choose Project > Properties. Click the Flex Build Path selection on the left side, then choose the Library Path tab on the top right.

3 Click the Add Project button, and choose the FlexGrocerLibrary project from the list.

If that project doesn't appear in the list, close the dialog box and make sure the library project is open in your workspace.

Flex Builder is now treating all the classes in the library as if they were local to your project. By simply adding the library project to the path for your project, its classes, such as MaxRestorePanel, ComparisonChart, and so on, become available to you.

4 Open Dashboard.mxml from your DashboardDeskop/src directory.

5 Change the root node (and the corresponding closing tag) of this file from `<mx:Application>` to `<mx:WindowedApplication>`.

6 Find the TypeChart tag, and change its `id` from `type` to `typeChart`. You also need to update the references to this instance inside the `typeRPCResult` function (around line 38), as well as two places in the states (around lines 156 and 159).

While `type` is not a reserved word in Flex, it is in AIR, so to avoid a name collision, you need to rename this pod `typeChart`.

7 Test your application directly from Flex Builder by clicking the Run button located in the top tool bar. This will launch your application.

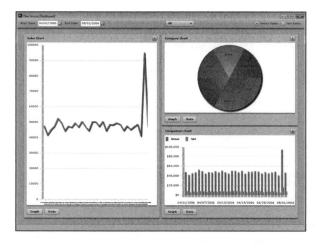

Customizing the Application with the Application.xml file

When you first created the application, an additional XML file was created in the same directory. This XML file, known to AIR developers as their Application.xml file, has a number of application specific properties set in it. Here, you can see the basic structure of the file:

```
<?xml version="1.0" encoding="UTF-8"?>
<application xmlns="http://ns.adobe.com/air/application/1.0
   <id>your-custom-id</id>
   <filename>name-of-packaged-file</filename>
   <name>name-displayed-by-operating-system</name>
   <version>v1</version>
   <description>displayed-in-installer</description>
   <copyright>Copyright-info</copyright>
   <initialWindow>
      <content>Copyright</content>
      <title>title-displayed-in-standard-chrome-header</title>
      <systemChrome>standard</systemChrome>
      <transparent>false</transparent>
      <visible>true</visible>
      <minimizable>true</minimizable>
      <maximizable>true</maximizable>
      <resizable>true</resizable>
      <width>500</width>
      <height>500</height>
      <x>150</x>
      <y>150</y>
      <minSize>300 300</minSize>
      <maxSize>800 800</maxSize>
```

```
    </initialWindow>
    <installFolder>path-in-which-to-install</installFolder>
    <programMenuFolder>path-in-program-menus</programMenuFolder>
    <icon>
        <image16x16>16x16-icon.png</image16x16>
        <image32x32>32x32-icon.png</image32x32>
        <image48x48>48x48-icon.png</image48x48>
        <image128x128>128x128-icon.png</image128x128>
    </icon>
    <customUpdateUI/>
    <allowBrowserInvocation/>
    <fileTypes>
        <fileType>
            <name>com.example</name>
            <extension>xmpl</extension>
            <description>Example File</description>
            <contentType>example/x-data-type</contentType>
            <icon>
                <image16x16>16x16-icon.png</image16x16>
                <image32x32>32x32-icon.png</image32x32>
                <image48x48>48x48-icon.png</image48x48>
                <image128x128>128-icon.png</image128x128>
            </icon>
        </fileType>
    </fileTypes>
    <name>name-displayed-by-operating-system</name>
</application>
```

In the next few steps, you will customize the application.xml file for your FlexGrocer Desktop Dashboard.

1 Copy FlexGrocerDesktop16.png, FlexGrocerDesktop32.png, FlexGrocerDesktop48.png, and FlexGrocerDesktop128.png from the Lesson21/DashboardDesktop/start/src/assets directory to your DesktopDashboard/src directory.

2 Open src/Dashboard-app.xml.

3 The application name node is specified on line 24 of the file, and is used to specify the name that the operating system will display to the user. By default, Flex Builder will use the id you specified for the name, but a more descriptive name would be better. So, add the text FlexGrocer.com Desktop Dashboard to the node.

```
<name>FlexGrocer.com Desktop Dashboard</name>
```

Specify the same name for the title node, which will be seen in the installer.

```
<title>FlexGrocer.com Desktop Dashboard</title>
```

> ✱ Note: By default, there was no title, as the title tag was commented out. To add the title, you need to uncomment the title tag.

4 Add a meaningful description, which will be seen by end users while they are installing the application.

```
<description>A desktop version of the FlexGrocer.com reporting dashboard
</description>
```

5 (Optional) Add any copyright information.

```
<copyright>© 2006 All rights reserved</copyright>
```

6 Find the `title` node that is located within the initialWindow node. Uncomment it, and add the title **FlexGrocer.com Dashboard**.

```
<title>FlexGrocer.com Dashboard</title>
```

7 The content node will automatically be populated with the name of the SWF generated by your application. As this is automated, you will see a string which is replaced by the compiler, such as [This value will be overwritten by Flex Builder in the output app.xml].

8 The string that is specified is exactly what the compiler is looking to replace, so do not change this line in any way.

9 Scroll past the `systemChrome`, `transparent`, and `visible` nodes. These can all be used to customize the look and feel of your application, but are not covered in this book. A bit lower, uncomment the `icon` node, you will specify a series of icons to be used by the application. The files you copied in step 1 provide 16x16, 32x32, 48x48, and 128x128 icons as PNGs.

```
<icon>
    <image16x16>FlexGrocerDesktop16.png</image16x16>
    <image32x32>FlexGrocerDesktop32.png</image32x32>
    <image48x48>FlexGrocerDesktop48.png</image48x48>
    <image128x128>FlexGrocerDesktop128.png</image128x128>
</icon>
```

10 Save the Dashboard-app.xml file, and test the application.

11 As the application runs, you should see the title you specified in the title bar of the application.

Exporting the AIR File

Now that you have built an application that runs on the desktop, you can have Flex Builder package it into an installer, so it can be easily distributed.

1 Select the Dashboard project, and choose Project > Export Release Version.

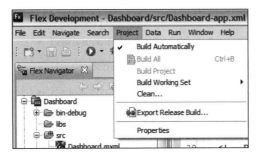

2 Leave all the default choices, and click Next.

3 If you have an existing certificate, you can browse to it; assuming you don't have one, click the Create button.

When you export your application, you need to decide how you will digitally sign it. There are several options:

- You can sign the application using a Verisign or Thawte digital certificate.

- You can create and use a self-signed digital certificate.

- You can package an intermediate application without a signature.

✳ **NOTE:** An Intermediate AIR file (.airi), cannot be installed by end users, and exists only for debugging for a developer. These files can only be run using the ADT command-line tool.

For this application, you will be creating a self-signed certificate.

4 Complete the entries for Publisher name, Organizational unit, Organizational name, Email, Country, Password, and Confirm Password. Then choose your country—US is selected by default; to change it, click the Choose button, and select the country name from the list. Next, enter a password in the Password and Confirm password fields. Then, select the encryption type for the certificate (1024 or 2048 bit keys). Lastly, specify a file name for your certificate, and click OK.

5 The Create Self-Signed Digital Certificate window will close, and leave you with the Digital Signature screen filled out. Click Next to continue.

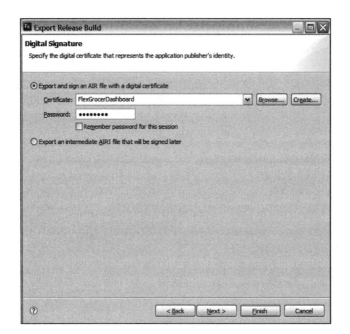

6 The final screen of the process allows you to specify which files will be included in the exported file. At a minimum, you need the SWF and app.xml file specified, but you can optionally include any other files from your project. For this project, you will also want to include the files for the icons. Confirm the icon files you want to include are selected, and click Finish.

7 When the export process completes, a file named Dashboard.air is created in your project root.

8 Find the new AIR file (it should be in the root of your new project directory) and double-click it. The Dashboard application installer launches, allowing you to install the application.

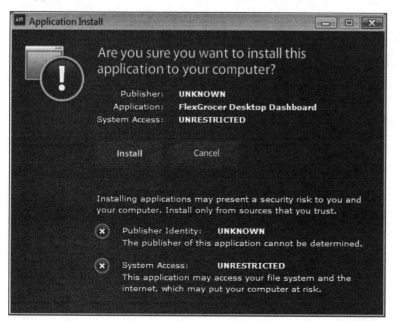

9 Click the Install button, leave the default choices on the next screen, and click Continue.

10 When the installer finishes, you should see an icon for the Dashboard on your desktop and in your operating system's Programs menu.

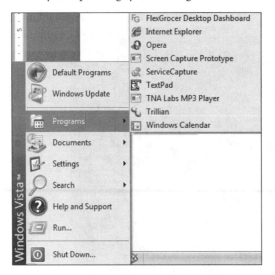

As you can see, it is quite easy to take an existing Flex application and convert it to an AIR application.

What You Have Learned

In this lesson, you have:

- Learned the limitations of browser-based applications (pages 550–551)
- Installed the Adobe Integrated Runtime (pages 551–552)
- Installed an AIR application (page 552)
- Created an AIR application (pages 553–559)
- Built an AIR installer (pages 559–564)

What You Will Learn

In this lesson, you will:

- Use prebuilt behaviors in Flex to fade in the display of a component
- Use prebuilt transitions in Flex to smooth out changes from one state to another

Approximate Time

This lesson takes approximately 45 minutes to complete.

Lesson Files

Media Files:

None

Starting Files:

Lesson22/start/EComm.mxml
Lesson22/start/as/ecomm.as
Lesson22/start/views/ecomm/GroceryDetail.mxml

Completed Files:

Lesson22/complete/EComm.mxml
Lesson22/complete/as/ecomm.as
Lesson22/complete/views/ecomm/GroceryDetail.mxml

Creating Transitions and Behaviors

You can apply dynamic effects to your application using behaviors and transitions that can include animation and/or sounds. These effects can be based on application or user triggers, which cause behaviors or transitions to occur. Content is the most important consideration, but animations and sound can also greatly enhance the user experience—especially in dynamic presentation interfaces.

Behaviors are dynamic effects that can be applied directly to Flex components, whereas transitions are dynamic effects applied to view states. Animations can often enhance the user's experience when navigating throughout an application. In this lesson, you will modify the FlexGrocer application so that the transitions between states are smoother and components display using a fade-in effect.

Grocery item details will display using a WipeRight transition.

Introducing Behaviors and Transitions

Behaviors and transitions enable you to add animation and sound to objects in your Flex application.

Using Behaviors on Components

Behaviors are prebuilt animations and sounds that can be applied directly to components, including user-defined components. Transitions are simply effects applied to application states used within an application. Some examples of effects that can be applied to components or application states include the following:

- Fading in/fading out
- Dissolving in/dissolving out
- Moving or resizing a component
- Rotating a component
- Zooming
- Wiping left/right/up/down
- Using other visual effects such as glow and iris
- Using sound effects

Content is, of course, the most important part of the FlexGrocer application, and at first glance it may seem that adding animation is not necessary. However, animation can greatly enhance the user experience. In the FlexGrocer application you have built to this point, many transitions between components and application states are not optimal and appear jerky and sudden. Animation in the FlexGrocer application will serve many useful purposes, including these:

- Drawing the users' attention to items changing on the screen and giving visual cues about where their attention should be focused
- Enhancing the users' experience with movement and animation
- Using effects to suggest to users which elements of an application are interactive

When you click a grocery category in the FlexGrocer application, the appropriate component just appears. In this lesson, you will use a prebuilt fade-in effect to smooth out the display of the custom component and to draw the end users' attention to the right place.

When applied to components, behaviors have two parts:

- **Trigger**: An action such as a user clicking a button, a component coming into focus, or a component becoming visible

- **Effect**: A visible or audible change to the component that occurs over a period of time

Components have triggers, but they do not do anything until you associate them with an action. The trigger is *not* an event. A button has both a mouseDownEffect trigger and a regular mouseDown event. The trigger itself is what causes the event to fire, whereas events specify a specific custom event handler that fires when the event occurs. When you use a mouseDownEffect trigger, you do not specify an event handler; you specify the behavior that you want to occur. It is possible to specify multiple effects when a trigger is fired. For example, when a user presses the mouse button, you could have a window resize and fade out. The triggers you can use with behaviors include the following:

- focusInEffect

- focusOutEffect

- hideEffect

- mouseDownEffect

- mouseUpEffect

- rolloutEffect

- rolloverEffect

- showEffect

To apply an effect to a component, you set the trigger name property equal to the name of the Effect class. You can declare only one effect when you define the trigger inline in the component, and you cannot customize the effect in any way. Here is an example of applying an effect to a List control when it is first displayed:

```
<mx:List id="myList" showEffect="Fade"/>
```

If you want to customize the event, you can define a reusable tag and specify the available property, in this case `duration`, which instructs Flex to perform the effect over a duration of milliseconds, as follows:

```
<mx:Dissolve id="myDissolve" duration="2000"/>
```

You can then apply the customized effect to the targets by using data binding, as follows:

```
<mx:Button id="sendButton" mouseDownEffect="{myDissolve}"/>
```

You can apply multiple effects (with the same trigger) to a component by using the `<mx:Parallel>` and `<mx:Sequence>` tags. The `<mx:Parallel>` tag specifies that the effects will occur all at the same time, whereas the `<mx:Sequence>` tag specifies that the events will occur in order. It is possible to nest `<mx:Parallel>` and `<mx:Sequence>` tags within one another to generate more complex animations. You will use these tags to build complex effects later in this lesson.

Using Transitions on View States

Transitions enable you to apply effects to view states, which then enable you to vary the content and appearance of a component in response to a user interaction. Transitions are great for creating much smoother changes between states. Transitions are different from behaviors; they apply to application states, whereas behaviors apply to components. You can apply one or more effects to one or more components in a view state, and you are not limited to the same effects when expanding or collapsing a state. The following properties are available in the Transition class:

- `fromState`: A string that specifies the view state you are changing from when you apply the transition.

- `toState`: A string that specifies the view state you are in when you apply the transition.

- `Effect`: The Effect object you want to play when you apply the transition. You can use an `<mx:Parallel>` tag or an `<mx:Sequence>` tag to define multiple effects.

To use transitions, you must surround one or more `<mx:Transition>` tags with an `<mx:transitions>` tag block, in lowercase. The reason for the case difference is that the `<mx:transitions>` tag represents a property of the Application, which can then contain one or more Transition objects.

```
<mx:transitions>
   <mx:Transition id="myTransition1"
      fromState="state2" toState="state3">
         <mx:Dissolve duration="800"/>
   </mx:Transition>
```

```
    <mx:Transition id="myTransition2"
       fromState="*" toState="*">
    [..]
    </mx:Transition>
    <mx:Transition id="myTransition3"
       fromState="state1"
       toState="state2">
    [..]
    </mx:Transition>
  </mx:transitions>
```

By using the <mx:transitions> tag, you can have multiple <mx:Transition> tags applied.

If you define multiple effects within a specific Transition object, you must use the <mx:Parallel> or <mx:Sequence> tags. You can use the targets property of the <mx:Parallel> or <mx:Sequence> tags to apply these effects to multiple components within a state. Parallel effects trigger at the same time, whereas sequence effects trigger in order. You can be more specific about which components you want the effect to apply to by using the targets property, as shown here:

```
    <mx:transitions>
      <mx:Transition id="myTransition1"
         fromState="state1
         toState="state2">
         <mx:Sequence targets="{[VBox1, VBox2, VBox3]}">
            <mx:Move targets="{[VBox1, VBOX2]}"
               duration="400" />
            <mx:Dissolve duration="800"/>
         </mx:Sequence>
      </mx:Transition>
      <mx:Transition id="myTransition2"
         fromState="state2"
         toState="state3">
         [..]
      </mx:Transition>
      <mx:Transition id="myTransition3"
         fromState="*"
         toState="*">
         <mx:Parallel targets="{[VBox1, VBox2, VBox3]}">
            <mx:Iris duration="400" />
            <mx:Move duration="400" />
         </mx:Parallel>
      </mx:Transition>
    </mx:transitions>
```

After you have set up the transition, you can trigger it by setting the `currentState` property in a `click` event. When a view state is triggered, Flex searches for and runs the Transition object that matches the current and destination view state. If more than one transition matches, Flex will use the first transition defined in the `<mx:Transitions>` tag.

Implementing Effects on a Component

In this exercise, you will add a dissolve behavior that smoothes the transition when the user clicks a grocery category to display the list of items in that category.

1 Be sure to go back to work with your regular FlexGrocer project, not the DashboardDesktop project. Also, be sure that ColdFusion is running in a console window as application data is now dynamically retrieved. As a reminder, go to the cfusionFlexTFS/bin folder in a console window and enter **jrun –start cfusion**.

You will work with the code you finished in Lesson 20, "Creating Modular Applications," which is in your FlexGrocer project.

2 Open EComm.mxml and run the application. Click a grocery category.

The file is located in your flexGrocer/src directory. If you skipped Lesson 19, when this version was created, you can open this file from Lesson22/start and save it in your flexGrocer/src directory.

Notice that the transition from the home page to the list of grocery products is immediate and appears rather jerky. You will add a dissolve behavior that will greatly improve the user experience.

3 In EComm.mxml, directly below the `<mx:CurrencyFormatter>` tag, add an `<mx:Dissolve>` tag, assign it an `id` of `bodyDissolve`, and set the `duration` attribute to 2000, as follows:

```
<mx:Dissolve id="bodyDissolve" duration="2000"/>
```

This creates an effect that you can later reference from a trigger on a component. As you learned earlier, the triggers that you can use are `focusInEffect`, `focusOutEffect`, `hideEffect`, `mouseDownEffect`, `mouseUpEffect`, `rolloutEffect`, `rolloverEffect`, and `showEffect`.

4 Locate the invocation of the custom FoodList component that you built earlier. Add a `showEffect` trigger and set up a binding to the `bodyDissolve` behavior you created in the previous step. Your final invocation of the `<mx:FoodList>` component should look as follows:

```
<v:FoodList id="prodTile"
    width="100%" height="100%"
```

```
prodByCategory="{prodByCategory}"
itemAdded="addToCart(event.product)"
showEffect="{bodyDissolve}"/>
```

FoodList is where the list of grocery items are displayed based on the category the user clicks. You want to apply a dissolve behavior here that will create a better transition for the user. The FoodList component changes when the user clicks an item in the category. You want the dissolve effect to display when the FoodList component changes. The showEffect trigger is fired only when the visible property of a component is changed. In this case, you need to manually set the visible property.

5 Open the ecomm.as file in the src/as folder and locate the displayProdByCategory() method. Modify the method so that it checks if the prodTile has been created and if it has sets the visible property of the prodTile container to false. Then set the visible property of the prodTile container to true as the last line of the method. Your final displayProdByCategory() function should look as follows:

```
private function displayProdByCategory(event:CategoryEvent):void{
   if (prodTile) {
      prodTile.visible=false;
   }
   if (event.cat != null){
      var prodArray:Array=catProds.getProdsForCat(event.cat.catID);
      prodByCategory=new ArrayCollection(prodArray);
   }else{
      prodByCategory=new ArrayCollection();
   }
   if (prodTile) {
      prodTile.visible=true;
   }
}
```

Checking if a variable exists is a common practice in Flex. You may remember that Flex defers instantiation of any Components until they are needed. This line could be executed before the prodTile list was created and would then cause a runtime error.

By manually setting the visible property of the FoodList component—which has an id of prodTile—from false to true, you will fire the showEffect trigger you added in the previous step. This will cause the dissolve effect to be used each time a new category is selected, which is exactly the behavior you want!

6 Run the EComm application.

You should see the dissolve effect display when you click a category.

Adding Effects to View States

In this exercise, you will add a transition that will be applied when a view state within a component is displayed. In this case, you will add the transition when the user rolls over the food item to display the details.

1 Open GroceryDetail.mxml in src/views/ecomm.

The file is located in your flexGrocer/src/views/ecomm directory. If you skipped Lesson 16, "Customizing the Look and Feel of a Flex Application," when this version was created, you can open this file from Lesson22/start/views/ecomm and save it in your flexGrocer/src/views/ecomm directory.

This is the component that contains all the view states displayed when the user rolls over a food item.

2 Below the `<mx:Script>` tag, add an `<mx:transitions>` tag block. Inside that tag block, nest an `<mx:Transition>` tag block. Assign the `<mx:Transition>` tag an id of foodTransition. Specify the fromState attribute as an asterisk (*) and the toState attribute as an asterisk (*). Your code should appear as follows:

```
<mx:transitions>
    <mx:Transition id="foodTransition"
        fromState="*"
        toState="*">
    </mx:Transition>
</mx:transitions>
```

The fromState is simply a string that specifies the view state that you are changing from when the transition is applied. In this case, you specify an asterisk (*), which means any view state. The toState is a string that specifies the view state that you are changing to when the transition is applied. In this case, you specify an asterisk (*), which means any view state.

3 Within the `<mx:Transition>` tag block, nest an `<mx:WipeRight>` effect and specify the duration property as 500. Also, add the target to be bound to foodBox.

```
<mx:transitions>
    <mx:Transition id="foodTransition"
        fromState="*"
        toState="*">
            <mx:WipeRight duration="500" target="{foodBox}"/>
    </mx:Transition>
</mx:transitions>
```

Remember that the <mx:Transition> tag defines the effects that make up a transition. You can specify the duration of the WipeRight effect so the text will gradually "roll in" when the end user rolls over the appropriate grocery item.

4 Locate the <mx:VBox> tag in the <mx:AddChild> tag in the expanded view state. Give this VBox an id equal to foodBox.

```
<mx:VBox id="foodBox"
    width="100%"
    x="200"
    styleName="standardBlack">
    ...
</mx:VBox>
```

This is the target you bound to in the WipeRight effect.

5 Run the EComm application. Select a category from the horizontal list and roll over a grocery item.

When you roll over each item, you should see the item description and other item information displayed from left to right.

What You Have Learned

In this lesson, you have:

- Learned what different effects are available (pages 568–570)
- Learned how to use transitions on view states (pages 570-572)
- Learned how to apply effects to components (pages 572–573)
- Learned how to add effects to view states (pages 574–575)

What You Will Learn

In this lesson, you will:

- Instantiate a FlexPrintJob object and then use the start(), addObject(), and send() methods to produce printed output

- Implement code to gracefully exit the printing process if the user cancels the print job at the operating-system level

- Use the PrintDataGrid control for printing data from a DataGrid

- Create a container that is not visible on the screen and is used for formatting printed output

- Create a custom component that is not visible on the screen and is used for formatting printed output

- Scale printed output on a page using static constants of the FlexPrintJobScaleType class

Approximate Time

This lesson takes approximately 2 hours to complete.

Lesson Files

Media Files:

None

Starting Files:

Lesson23/printing/start/src/PrintingTask1.mxml
Lesson23/printing/start/src/PrintingTask2.mxml
Lesson23/printing/start/src/PrintingTask3.mxml
Lesson23/printing/start/src/PrintingTask4.mxml
Lesson23/start/views/ecomm/OrderConf.mxml

Completed Files:

Lesson23/printing/complete/src/PrintingTask1.mxml
Lesson23/printing/complete/src/PrintingTask2.mxml
Lesson23/printing/complete/src/PrintingTask3.mxml
Lesson23/printing/complete/src/PrintingTask4.mxml
Lesson23/printing/complete/src/views/PrintView.mxml
Lesson23/complete/views/ecomm/OrderConf.mxml
Lesson23/complete/views/ecomm/PrintReceipt.mxml

Printing from Flex

In many (if not most) cases, you will not want your printed output to look exactly like the screen display. Adobe Flex gives you functionality to build containers and components to format printed output that does not have to resemble the screen display at all. Two classes, FlexPrintJob and PrintDataGrid, are key to implementing printing.

No longer do web applications have to print receipts and itineraries that are poor resemblances of the real things.

Flex Grocer Thanks You!

Billing Information

Arthur Customer   Delivery Date 08/22/2006

 600 Townsend St.

San Francisco

CA

94103

A printed receipt from the checkout process

Introducing Flex Printing

Printing from web applications has often been problematic. A user would have to print from the browser and see a replica of the screen with odd page breaks and formatting. Now with Flex, you have the power to build containers and components that will print exactly as you would like and that do not have to be visible on the screen display at any time. The printed output does not have to be related to the screen display in any way.

Two classes are key to implementing this functionality:

- **FlexPrintJob:** A class that you instantiate to print one or more objects. The objects can be containers or custom components that you build specifically for displaying printed material. The class will also automatically split large objects over multiple pages and scale output to fit on a particular page size.

- **PrintDataGrid:** A subclass of the DataGrid control with appearance and functionality better suited for printing. The PrintDataGrid class has properties and methods that support printing grids that contain multiple pages of data.

The basic process for printing in Flex is as follows:

1. Instantiate an object from the FlexPrintJob class.

2. Start the print job using the FlexPrintJob's `start()` method.

3. Add an object or objects to be printed using the FlexPrintJob's `addObject()` method.

4. Send the job to the printer using the FlexPrintJob's `send()` method.

5. Clean up objects no longer needed after printing.

Printing for the First Time from Flex

In this exercise you will print for the first time from Flex. In this case you will focus on the steps needed to enable printing; what you print will be of lesser importance. You will print a VBox container that contains a Label and a Button control.

1 Choose File > New > Flex Project. Set the Project name to be **flex3tfs_Printing**.

2 Set the Project location to be flex3tfs/Lesson23/printing/start.

3 For the Application type select Web application.

4 Set the Server technology to None, and then click Next.

5 Leave the Output folder as bin-debug, and then click Next.

6 Leave the Main source folder as src.

7 Click the Browse button for the Main application file, select SortingADG.mxml, and then click OK.

You are creating a new project because some of the work in this lesson will not be directly involved with any of the three applications you are working on from the FlexGrocer site.

Notice that this file has a VBox that contains a Label and a Button control. The Button has a click event that calls a function named doPrint(). The skeleton of the doPrint() function is supplied in a script block.

8 At the top of the script block, import the mx.printing.FlexPrintJob class.

Remember that you could have skipped this step; when you used the class for data typing a variable, it would have been automatically imported for you.

9 As the first line of code in the function, create a variable local to the function named pj, data typed as FlexPrintJob, and set it equal to a new FlexPrintJob.

```
var pj:FlexPrintJob=new FlexPrintJob();
```

This instance of the FlexPrintJob class is where all the printing will center around.

10 On the pj FlexPrintJob object instance, invoke the start() method.

```
pj.start();
```

This initializes the FlexPrintJob object and causes the underlying operating system to display a print dialog box.

11 On the pj object, invoke the addObject() method passing the id of the VBox, printContainer, as a parameter.

```
pj.addObject(printContainer);
```

This adds the VBox to the list of objects to be printed.

12 On the pj object, invoke the send() method.

```
pj.send();
```

This sends the added objects to the printer to start printing.

▶ **TIP:** The send() method is synchronous, so the code that follows it can assume that the call completed successfully.

13 Ensure that your function appears as follows:

```
private function doPrint():void{
    var pj:FlexPrintJob=new FlexPrintJob();
    pj.start();
    pj.addObject(printContainer);
    pj.send();
}
```

Between the calls to the start() and send() methods, a print job is spooled to the under-lying operating system. You should limit the code between these calls to only print-specific methods. For instance, there should not be user interaction between those two methods.

14 Run the application. Click the button labeled Print Page in the Flex application to print the contents of the VBox.

You have now implemented a simple print job in Flex.

15 Run the application again. Click the Print button and this time cancel the print job. (Depending on your environment, you might have to be very quick to cancel the print job.)

Notice that the screen clears when you do this. You need to have Flex gracefully handle when the user cancels the print job.

16 In the function, wrap the invocation of the start() method in an if statement. Check to see whether the print job has started by checking if the value returned from the invocation is not equal to true. If the print job has not started, simply return from the function. Your code should appear as follows:

```
private function doPrint():void{
    var pj:FlexPrintJob=new FlexPrintJob();
    if(pj.start() != true){
        return;
    }
    pj.addObject(printContainer);
    pj.send();
}
```

This causes Flex to gracefully exit back to the application page if the user cancels the print job.

17 Run the application again, and cancel the print job after clicking the Print button.

You should see that the application remains visible this time.

Using the PrintDataGrid in a Nonvisible Container

As mentioned in the lesson introduction, sometimes what the screen displays is not what you want printed. The layout you see is designed for the computer monitor and is wider than it is long, while a printed page is usually longer than it is wide. You can build a container that is not visible to the user on the monitor but that is printed when the user asks for a hard copy. The PrintDataGrid class is often used in this case because it is tailored to have a better printed appearance than the normal DataGrid, as well as being able to print across multiple pages instead of displaying scroll bars like the normal DataGrid.

The normal DataGrid appears on the left of the following figure, and the PrintDataGrid appears on the right.

Price	Product	Price	Product
1.98	Bananas	1.98	Bananas
3.95	Stawberries	3.95	Stawberries
4.95	Swiss Cheese	4.95	Swiss Cheese
1.19	Yogurt	1.19	Yogurt

1 Open the file PrintingTask2.mxml from the flex3tfs_Printing project. Run the application.

Notice that this file contains a Form container with some default information in the TextInput controls, followed by a DataGrid. Your goal in this task is to display the name and e-mail address above the DataGrid when printed. Of course, you will not display the exact Form, but you will place the user information in a Label control and display it above the PrintDataGrid container with the same data as the normal DataGrid.

2 Below the Form, insert a VBox that will be used as the print container. It should have the following properties and associated values:

```
id:                printVBox
backgroundColor:   #FFFFFF
width:             450
height:            250
paddingTop:        50
paddingLeft:       50
paddingRight:      50
visible:           false
```

The VBox property values are special in two ways. First, the backgroundColor and padding have the values they do for better appearance when printing. The white background is best for printing, and the large amount of padding will keep the output from getting too close to the edges of the paper.

Second, at application startup this VBox will not be visible. Although setting the VBox visible property to false makes the VBox disappear, the VBox will still occupy space on the screen, which will just look like blank space at the end of the page.

3 In the VBox, insert an <mx:Label> with an id of contact.

This is where you will bind the user name and e-mail address gathered in the form.

4 Following the Label control, insert a <mx:PrintDataGrid> tag with an id of myPrintDG and a width and height of 100%.

You will tie the dataProvider of the normal DataGrid to myPrintDG.

5 Check to be sure that your VBox appears as follows:

```
<mx:VBox id="printVBox"
    backgroundColor="#FFFFFF"
    height="250" width="450"
    paddingTop="50" paddingLeft="50" paddingRight="50"
    visible="false">

    <mx:Label id="contact"/>
    <mx:PrintDataGrid id="myPrintDG"
        width="100%"
        height="100%"/>
</mx:VBox>
```

In a function that is called on the Button click, you will dynamically modify this VBox and content with values you want displayed when printing.

6 In the script block, import the mx.printing.FlexPrintJob class.

Remember that you could have skipped this step; when you used the class for data typing a variable, it would have been automatically imported for you.

7 At the bottom of the script block, create a private function named doPrint() data typed as void. In the function, create a new FlexPrintJob object local to the function named pj. Also insert an if statement that gracefully handles the situation if the user cancels the print job, which you learned in the last exercise. At this point, your function should appear as follows:

```
private function doPrint():void{
    var pj:FlexPrintJob = new FlexPrintJob();
    if(pj.start() != true)
    {
        return;
    }
}
```

In most circumstances you can assume that the beginning of functions you build to handle printing will start in this way.

8 Fill the `contact` Label from the VBox with the customer name and customer e-mail con-catenated together with the literal text Contact: preceding them.

```
contact.text="Contact: " + custName.text + " " + custEmail.text;
```

Here you are taking information gathered from the form and reformatting it for the printed output.

9 Set the `dataProvider` of the PrintDataGrid equal to the `dataProvider` of the normal DataGrid.

```
myPrintDG.dataProvider=prodInfo.dataProvider;
```

You want to display the same data in the PrintDataGrid as the data in the normal DataGrid, and making them use the same `dataProvider` is a sure way to make that happen.

10 Add the VBox to the print job using the `addObject()` method, and then send the print job to the printer using the `send()` method.

```
pj.addObject(printVBox);
pj.send();
```

11 Check to be sure that your function appears as follows:

```
private function doPrint():void{
    var pj:FlexPrintJob = new FlexPrintJob();
    if(pj.start() != true)
    {
        return;
    }
    contact.text = "Contact: " + custName.text + " " + custEmail.text;
    myPrintDG.dataProvider = prodInfo.dataProvider;
    pj.addObject(printVBox);
    pj.send();
}
```

You now have a function that can print your VBox.

12 Add a `click` event that calls the `doPrint()` function to the button in the Form with the label Print.

```
<mx:Button id="myButton"
    label="Print"
    click="doPrint()"/>
```

This allows the user to print when wanted.

13 Run the application. Click the Print button in the Flex application.

You should be able to both print and cancel the print job. When you print, you will see the VBox printed with the appropriate properties' values and content.

cost	listPrice	name	unitName
6	9.98	T Bone Steak	pound
0.99	1.59	Milk	each
0.99	1.19	Yogurt	each
2.5	3.95	Grapes	pound
1.25	1.99	Bell Peppers	each
1.09	1.95	Bananas	bunch

Contact: Sally Shopper sally@shopper.com

Building the Printable View in a Separate Component

In the last exercise, a separate container (a VBox) was used on the main application page and was configured especially for printing. If the printing configuration was very long and complex, it would probably not be a workable solution; a separate custom component would be better. In this task, you will do just that: build a custom component whose job is to hold the printable version of whatever data you want the user to print. Just like the previous task, the component will not be visible on the screen. However, this component will not create extra blank space on the screen; it will be built just for printing.

1 Right-click the views folder in the flex3tfs_Printing project and choose New > MXML Component. Set the Filename to be **PrintView.mxml**, and the Based On component should be a VBox. Set the width to 450 and the height to 250. Click Finish.

This is the skeleton of the custom component that will be used just for printing.

2 Set the following properties for the VBox:

```
backgroundColor:    #FFFFFF
paddingTop:       50
paddingLeft:        50
paddingRight:       50
```

3 In the VBox, insert an <mx:Label> with an id of contact.

This is where you will bind the user name and e-mail address gathered in the form.

4 Following the Label control, insert an <mx:PrintDataGrid> tag with an id of myPrintDG and a width and height of 100%.

You will tie the dataProvider of the normal DataGrid to this PrintDataGrid.

5 Check to be sure that your custom component appears as follows:

```
<?xml version="1.0" encoding="utf-8"?>
<mx:VBox xmlns:mx="http://www.adobe.com/2006/mxml"
    height="250" width="450"
    backgroundColor="#FFFFFF"
    paddingTop="50" paddingLeft="50" paddingRight="50">

    <mx:Label id="contact"/>
    <mx:PrintDataGrid id="myPrintDG"
        width="100%" height="100%"/>
</mx:VBox>
```

Of course, the custom component could be as complex as needed to meet your printing needs.

6 Open the file PrintingTask3.mxml from the flex3tfs_Printing project.

Note that this application file has the Form used in PrintingTask2, as well as the skeleton of the doPrint() function created.

7 In the doPrint() function, create a new FlexPrintJob object local to the function named pj. Insert an if statement that gracefully handles the situation if the user cancels the print job. At this point, your function should appear as follows:

```
private function doPrint():void{
    var pj:FlexPrintJob = new FlexPrintJob();
    if(pj.start() != true)
    {
        return;
    }
}
```

Flex Builder will automatically add the import for mx.printing.FlexPrintJob to the file when you specify the type of the variable pj. You can also import it manually by adding it to the top of the script block.

8 At the top of the script block, import the custom component you built earlier in this task.

```
import views.PrintView;
```

You will instantiate an instance of this class shortly, so you must import it.

9 In the function just below the if block, create an instance local to the function of the PrintView custom component class named myPrintView.

```
var myPrintView:PrintView=new PrintView();
```

This is the instance of the custom component you will use for printing.

10 Use the addChild() method to add the newly created myPrintView object as a DisplayObject of the application.

```
this.addChild(myPrintView);
```

The addChild() method is a method of the mx.core.Container class, which is the parent of the Application class. The method adds a child DisplayObject object to the specified container.

▶ **TIP:** Remember that you cannot give an instance name to the application (or any tag used as a base tag of a component), so you refer to the application by using the keyword this.

11 Fill the contact Label from the PrintView component with the customer name and customer e-mail concatenated together with the literal text Contact: preceding them. Remember that you must reference the Label through the myPrintView object.

```
myPrintView.contact.text = "Contact: " + custName.text + " " + custEmail.text;
```

12 Set the dataProvider of the PrintDataGrid equal to the dataProvider of the normal DataGrid. Remember that you must reference the PrintDataGrid through the myPrintView object.

```
myPrintView.myPrintDG.dataProvider = prodInfo.dataProvider;
```

13 Add the myPrintView object to the print job using the addObject() method, and then send the print job to the printer using the send() method.

```
pj.addObject(myPrintView);
pj.send();
```

14 To "clean up" after printing, remove the myPrintView object.

```
removeChild(myPrintView);
```

15 Check to be sure that your function appears as follows:

```
private function doPrint():void{
   var pj:FlexPrintJob = new FlexPrintJob();
   if(pj.start() != true)
   {
      return;
   }
   var myPrintView:PrintView=new PrintView();
   this.addChild(myPrintView);
   myPrintView.contact.text = "Contact: " + custName.text + " " + custEmail.text;
   myPrintView.myPrintDG.dataProvider = prodInfo.dataProvider;
   pj.addObject(myPrintView);
   pj.send();
   removeChild(myPrintView);
}
```

Just to reiterate, this function instantiates the custom component, adds it as a display object to the application (even though it is not actually displayed to the screen), sets the data values, prints, and finally cleans up after itself.

16 Run the application. Click the Print button in the Flex application.

You should be able to both print and cancel the print job. When you print, you will see the custom component with the appropriate properties' values and content.

Contact: Sally Shopper sally@shopper.com

cost	listPrice	name	unitName
6	9.98	T Bone Steak	pound
0.99	1.59	Milk	each
0.99	1.19	Yogurt	each
2.5	3.95	Grapes	pound
1.25	1.99	Bell Peppers	each
1.09	1.95	Bananas	bunch

Scaling the Printed Output

You might want to scale the output to fill a certain dimension of the printed page or pages. You have five dimension-formatting choices when adding an object to the print job with the addObject() method. All your options are static constants from the FlexPrintJobScaleType class. This means that to use them, you import the class and then use the constant in the form FlexPrintJobScaleType.CONSTANT. The options are as follows:

- **MATCH_WIDTH**: Scales the printed object to fill the page width. If the height exceeds the width, the output will span multiple pages. This is the default setting.

- **MATCH_HEIGHT**: Scales the printed object to fill the page height. If the width exceeds the height, the output will span multiple pages.

- **SHOW_ALL**: Scales the printed object to fit on a single page, filling one dimension. It selects the smaller of the MATCH_WIDTH or MATCH_HEIGHT and then fills that dimension.

- **FILL_PAGE**: Scales the printed object to fill at least one page. It selects the larger of the MATCH_WIDTH or MATCH_HEIGHT scale types.

- **NONE**: Does not scale the printed object. The printed page has the same dimensions as the object on the screen.

1 Open PrintView2.mxml from the flex3tfs_Printing/project/views folder. Notice that only two columns of the PrintDataGrid are displayed, and the width and height of 100% is removed from the previous PrintView custom component.

These changes are made so they don't interfere with the scaling.

2 Open the file PrintingTask4.mxml from the flex3tfs_Printing project.

This file should be identical to the one you left off with in the last task.

3 Run the application. Click the Print button from the Flex application to print the page.

This will give you a baseline to compare other printouts to.

4 In the script block, import the class mx.printing.FlexPrintJobScaleType.

You must import this class to use its static constants.

5 In the addObject() method, pass a second parameter of FlexPrintJobScaleType.MATCH_WIDTH. Run the application, and click the Print button in the Flex application to print the page.

```
pj.addObject(myPrintView, FlexPrintJobScaleType.MATCH_WIDTH);
```

You see there is no difference between the first and second printouts, confirming that MATCH_WIDTH is the default setting.

Contact: Sally Shopper sally@shopper.com

Name	Cost
T Bone Steak	6
Milk	0.99
Yogurt	0.99
Grapes	2.5
Bell Peppers	1.25
Bananas	1.09

6 Change the scale to FlexPrintJobScaleType.MATCH_HEIGHT in the addObject() method. Run the application, and click the Print button in the Flex application to print the page.

Because the MATCH_HEIGHT was specified as the scale, and the width of the object was greater than the height, the output was spread over multiple pages.

Contact: Sally Shopper sal ly@shopper.com

Name	Cost
T Bone Steak	6
Milk	0.99
Yogurt	0.99
Grapes	2.5
Bell Peppers	1.25
Bananas	1.09

7 Change the scale to `FlexPrintJobScaleType.NONE` in the `addObject()` method. Run the application, and click the Print button in the Flex application to print the page.

Because `NONE` was specified, the printed output matches the screen, and the output is smaller than your baseline printing from step 3.

The `NONE` value produced the smaller printed output on the right in the following figure.

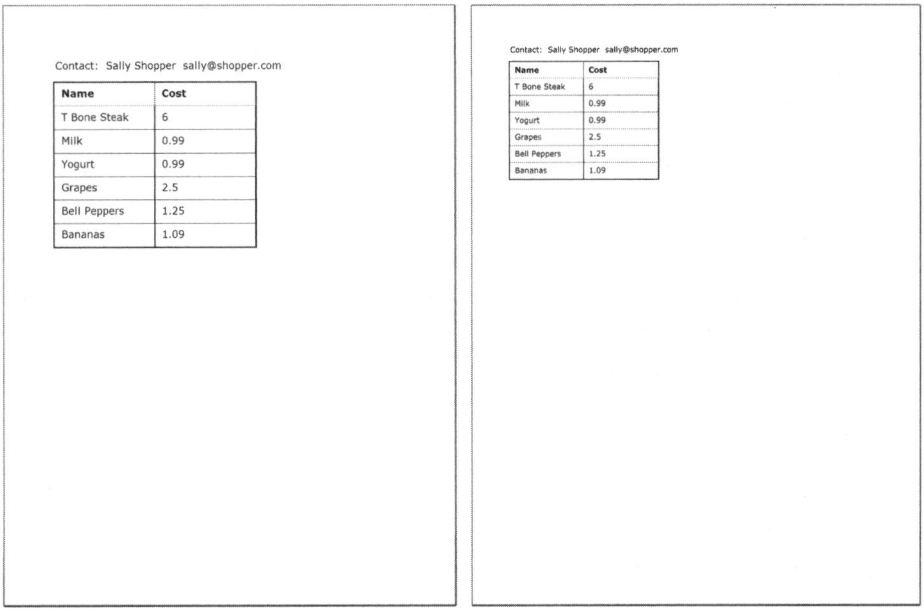

Printing a Receipt from the Checkout Process

In this task, you will put your new knowledge about printing to work in the EComm application. You will add a button to the order confirmation page to give the customer an option to print a receipt. In this case, you will create a custom component to print the receipt.

1 Back in the normal FlexGrocer project, open src/views/ecomm/OrderConf.mxml.

This is the page in which you will add the Print Receipt button.

2 Add a Button control beneath the last button on the page with a `label` of Print Receipt and add a `click` event that calls a method named `doPrint()`.

```
<mx:Button label="Print Receipt" click="doPrint()"/>
```

This printing process will be similar to what you did in the previous exercise in this lesson.

3 At the bottom of the script block, create a private function named doPrint() data typed as void. In the function, create a new FlexPrintJob object local to the function named pj. Also insert an if statement that gracefully handles the situation if the user cancels the print job. Your function should appear as follows:

```
private function doPrint():void{
    var pj:FlexPrintJob = new FlexPrintJob();
    if(pj.start() != true)
    {
        return;
    }
}
```

This is the standard way to start printing functions. The FlexPrintJob class was automatically imported when you created the pj instance; otherwise, add an import for mx.printing.FlexPrintJob to your script block.

4 At the top of the script block, import a custom component you will build later in this exercise named PrintReceipt, which will be created in the views/ecomm folder.

```
import views.ecomm.PrintReceipt;
```

You will instantiate an instance of this class, so you must import it.

5 In the doPrint() function just below the if block, create an instance local to the function of the PrintReceipt custom component class named theReceipt.

```
var theReceipt:PrintReceipt=new PrintReceipt();
```

This is the instance of the custom component you will use for printing.

6 Use the addChild() method to add the newly created theReceipt object as a DisplayObject of the current file.

```
this.addChild(theReceipt);
```

This adds an instance of the PrintReceipt class, which you will develop shortly, to the current container.

7 Assign the orderInfo variable to a similarly named property you will create in the theReceipt object.

```
theReceipt.orderInfo=orderInfo;
```

Here you are taking information gathered from the billing information form and assigning it to a property of the custom component. You will display some of this information on the receipt.

8 Add the theReceipt object to the print job using the addObject() method, and then send the print job to the printer using the send() method.

```
pj.addObject(theReceipt);
pj.send();
```

9 To "clean up" after printing, remove the myPrintView object.

```
this.removeChild(theReceipt);
```

10 Check to ensure your function appears as follows:

```
private function doPrint():void{
   var pj:FlexPrintJob = new FlexPrintJob();
   if(pj.start() != true){
      return;
   }
   var theReceipt:PrintReceipt=new PrintReceipt();
   this.addChild(theReceipt);
   theReceipt.orderInfo=orderInfo;
   pj.addObject(theReceipt);
   pj.send();
   this.removeChild(theReceipt);
}
```

This completes the code needed on the OrderConf.mxml page. Now, you need to build the custom component used. From the code you have written, you know that the custom component must be called PrintReceipt.mxml, and it must have a property named orderInfo. You also will display whatever you want the printed receipt to contain.

11 Right-click the views.ecomm folder in the FlexGrocer project, and choose New > MXML Component. Set the Filename to be **PrintReceipt.mxml**. and the Based On component should be a VBox. Set the width and height to be 450. Click Finish.

This is the skeleton of the custom component that will be used just for printing.

12 Set the following properties for the VBox:

```
backgroundColor: #FFFFFF
paddingTop:      50
paddingLeft:     50
paddingRight:    50
```

13 Insert a script block and import the valueObjects.OrderInfo class.

This is the datatype that will be used for the property you are about to create.

14 In the script block, create a bindable, public variable name `orderInfo`, data typed as OrderInfo.

This is the property that was assigned a value in the printing function.

15 Following the script block, insert a Label with the `text` set equal to the literal text Flex Grocer Thanks You!, a `fontSize` of 20 and a `width` of 100%.

This will be printed at the top of the receipt.

16 Next, copy the complete Form block from the OrderConf.mxml page and paste it below the Label. Remove the Label from this new copy of the Form that reads Checkout Page 3 of 3.

Remember that what you print does not have to match what the screen looks like. In this case, the Label that indicates where you are in the checkout process makes no sense to be printed, while the rest of the information from the Form should be part of the printed receipt.

17 Also copy the `<mx:DateFormatter>` tag from OrderConf.mxml and paste it just below the script block.

This is used to format the date in the form.

18 Run the EComm.mxml application. Go through the ordering process. On the last page, click the Print Receipt button.

▶ **TIP:** Remember that you must have the ColdFusion instance started for EComm to function correctly.

You will see that the receipt prints.

Flex Grocer Thanks You!

Billing Information

Arthur Customer   Delivery Date   08/22/2006

600 Townsend St.

San Francisco

CA

94103

What You Have Learned

In this lesson, you have:

- Printed a container that is contained on the main application page that is specifically formatted for printed output (pages 579–581)

- Printed data from the PrintDataGrid control for better appearance (pages 582–585)

- Printed data from a custom component that is specifically formatted for printed output (pages 585–588)

- Scaled printed output in multiple ways to fit on a page (pages 589–591)

- Printed a receipt at the end of the checkout process (pages 591–595)

What You Will Learn

In this lesson, you will:

- Create a new shared object on the client machine
- Write a complex data structure to the shared object
- Read data from an existing shared object
- Use data from an existing shared object to populate form controls

Approximate Time

This lesson takes approximately 45 minutes to complete.

Lesson Files

Media Files:

   None

Starting Files:

   Lesson24/start/views/ecomm/Cart.mxml
   Lesson24/start/views/ecomm/Checkout.mxml
   Lesson24/start/valueObjects/ShoppingCart.as

Completed Files:

   Lesson24/complete/views/ecomm/Cart.mxml
   Lesson24/complete/views/ecomm/Checkout.mxml
   Lesson24/complete/valueObjects/ShoppingCart.as

Using Shared Objects

An important part of most applications is the capability to persist data, such as remembering information about a specific user. Persisting user data can be done at the server by associating a user with a login ID and then passing specific information back to a server. The information is then written to a database and can be loaded back into the application when needed.

Using Adobe Flex, it is also possible to persist data on the client side, actually within Flash Player using the SharedObject class. Shared objects are similar to HTTP cookies, but are much more powerful because you can store complex data structures in them. In this lesson, you will use the SharedObject class to store information about which grocery items a user is interested in purchasing.

The Save For Later button writes items in the shopping cart into a shared object on the local machine for later retrieval.

Introducing Shared Objects

Whether you decide to persist data on the client or on the server depends largely on the type of data you have and its purpose. Data that needs to be stored permanently for business reasons, such as contact information for a customer, should be stored on the server. Information that persists primarily as a convenience for users, such as application preferences or a shopping cart the user wants to save for later, should be stored on the client to save the overhead of transmitting the data back to the server and putting it in a database.

Shared objects are the Flex equivalent of web cookies, but are much more powerful. Using ActionScript, you can write code to store data as a shared object on a user's machine. Properties assigned to a shared object are stored in the file as soon as the SWF file is removed from Flash Player by exiting the browser or moving onto a different web page or application. It is also possible to manually store the information at runtime, such as when an event occurs.

Data in a local shared object can be referenced from within the Flex application just like any other object.

Shared objects have the following characteristics:

- They are stored on the end user's machine in a location that varies depending on the platform.

- They have the extension .sol.

- By default, they can be up to 100 KB in size. The user can adjust the size limit and can deny or approve storage of larger objects.

- They can contain complex data structures.

- They cannot contain methods or functions.

- The end user must manually delete them or write code to delete them programmatically. Clearing cookies from the browser does not delete Flex shared objects.

- Like cookies, shared objects cannot be read from different domains. Flash Player has the capability of reading shared objects only if the shared object was created from the same domain as the SWF file.

✱ **NOTE:** When you test applications in the Flex Builder authoring environment, you can access only shared objects created by the same application because testing an application opens it as a local file and does not establish a domain.

Creating Shared Objects

The static `getLocal()` method of the SharedObject class retrieves an existing shared object; if a shared object does not exist, it creates a new one. All shared objects are written as soon as the SWF file is removed from Flash Player. If you need to write a shared object sooner, you can use the static `flush()` method.

The following ActionScript code creates a shared object:

```
var soMy:SharedObject = SharedObject.getLocal("myCookie");
```

A file called myCookie.sol is created on the user's machine. The shared object is manipulated in ActionScript as soMy.

To populate the shared object with data, you assign your variables as properties of the `data` property of the shared object. This is the shared object's only built-in property. The following ActionScript code stores the user Jeff in a shared object:

```
soMy.data.user = "Jeff";
```

To store complex data structures in a shared object, that object must be instantiated within the shared object. The following code creates an array inside a shared object and places an existing, populated array, `employees`, into that object:

```
soMy.data.aUsers = new Array();
soMy.data.aUsers = employees;
```

Although shared objects are automatically written as soon as the SWF file is removed from Flash Player, you can write shared objects to disk at other times; for example, using the `flush()` method in response to an event such as a user clicking a button. The syntax is as follows:

```
mySharedObject.flush(minimumDiskSpace);
```

The `minimumDiskSpace` parameter specifies the size of the .sol file to be created, instead of simply letting the file size be set by the actual size of the data being written. Using this technique to create an .sol file larger than the current data being written builds in the flexibility for the data size of the shared object to fluctuate without the user being prompted for approval at every slight change.

For example, if a shared object is currently 100 bytes but you expect it to grow to a maximum size of 500 bytes, create it with a value of 500 for the `minimumDiskSpace` parameter:

```
soMy.flush(500);
```

After the user responds to the dialog box, this method is called again and returns either `true` or `false`.

Because local objects are persisted on the client, you need to consider disk space constraints. By default, Flex can save shared objects up to 100 KB in size. Each application can have an unlimited number of shared objects, and the 100 KB limit is per shared object. When you try to save a larger object, Flash Player displays the Local Storage dialog box, which enables the user to allow or deny storage for the domain that is requesting access.

The user can also specify permanent local storage settings for a particular domain. Although the Flash Player application is playing, right-click, choose Settings, and then open the Local Storage panel. The panel that opens is shown here.

Additionally, if the user selects a value that is less than the amount of disk space currently being used for locally persistent data, Flash Player warns the user that any locally saved shared objects will be deleted.

Reading Shared Objects

When Flash Player tries to read the shared object, one of two possible outcomes occurs:

- A new shared object is created if one with the same name does not already exist (from the same domain).

- If the shared object does exist, the contents are read into the data property of the shared object.

Just as with cookies, it is a best practice to test for the existence of a shared object before referencing it. The following code snippet shows how to test for the existence of a user property:

```
if (soMy.data.user != undefined){
    //statements
}
```

After you know that the object exists, you can reference its properties as you can those of any other object in ActionScript. For example, to populate a Text control with the ID of txtUserName from a shared object, you can use the following code:

```
var soMy = sharedObject.getLocal("myCookie");
if (soMy.data.user != undefined){
   txtUserName.text = soMy.data.user;
}
```

All object properties can be referenced from a shared object just as you can do with any other object. However, you cannot store methods in a shared object. For example, to reference the length property of the Array object contained in the shared object, you can use the following code:

```
for (var i:int = 0; i < soCart.data.aCart.length; i++){
   //statements
}
```

Building a SharedObject to Store Shopping Cart Data

In this exercise, you will add a new button that, when clicked, will read the data from the end user's shopping cart and write that information to a shared object on his or her client machine. This will enable users to access their shopping cart data any time before they have actually gone through the purchasing process. You will also examine the resulting .sol file on the client machine.

1 From the FlexGrocer project, open the file src/views/ecomm/Cart.mxml.

In this file, you will add a Save For Later button. When clicked, this button will read the shopping cart data and write this data to a shared object on the client machine.

2 Immediately after the <mx:Script> block, add a <mx:Button> tag with the label of Save for Later.

```
<mx:Button label="Save for Later"/>
```

This code displays a button control with the label of Save for Later immediately above the current DataGrid.

3 Add a click event to the <mx:Button> tag that will call the saveCart() method of the cart object.

```
<mx:Button label="Save for Later" click="cart.saveCart()"/>
```

The cart object, an instance of the ShoppingCart class, has already been created in the script block. You will add a saveCart() method to this class, which will read the data from the user's shopping cart and write this data to a shared object.

4 Save the changes to Cart.mxml, and open up the src/valueObjects/ShoppingCart.as file.

It makes sense to place the saveCart() method in the ShoppingCart class because this is where the shopping cart data, aItems, that will be written to the shared object is stored.

5 At the top of the class, add an import statement that will import the flash.net.SharedObject class. Within the class, declare a new, public, bindable shared object with the name of soCart. At the end of the ShoppingCart class, add the skeleton of a new public() method with the name of saveCart() data typed as void.

```
import flash.net.SharedObject;
public class ShoppingCart {
   [Bindable]
   public var soCart:SharedObject;
   public function saveCart():void{
   }
   …
}
```

You will be using the data structure written to the client machine, the shared object, to populate the DataGrid when the application first starts. Therefore, it is important to declare the shared object itself as Bindable.

6 In the saveCart() method, using the static getLocal() method of the SharedObject class, declare a new shared object with the name of soCart. Pass the parameter of cartInfo to the getLocal() method.

```
public function saveCart():void{
   this.soCart = SharedObject.getLocal("cartInfo");
}
```

This will create a new shared object and write a file to the end user's machine with the name of cartInfo. The extension of the file created will be .sol.

7 In the saveCart() method, declare a new Array with the name of aCart in the data property of the SharedObject.

```
public function saveCart():void{
   this.soCart = SharedObject.getLocal("cartInfo");
   this.soCart.data.aCart = new Array();
}
```

To assign data to a shared object, you must use the data property. This is the only property of the shared object class and is how all data can be set and retrieved. If you are storing complex data structures in the shared object, the object itself must be instantiated within the object.

8 Immediately after declaring the Array, create a new variable with the name of len that will obtain the length of the aItems ArrayCollection and build the skeleton of a for loop that will loop through the aItems ArrayCollection:

```
var len:int = aItems.length;
for (var i:int = 0;i < len;i++){
}
```

Remember that the current contents of the shopping cart are stored in the aItems ArrayCollection. You are building a for loop to loop through the aItems array and populate the client-side shared object with that information.

9 Inside the for loop, populate the soCart.data.aCart array inside the SharedObject with the aItems ArrayCollection. Use the getItemAt() method to access the data in the Array-Collection. The final saveCart() method should look as follows:

```
public function saveCart():void{
    this.soCart = SharedObject.getLocal("cartInfo");
    this.soCart.data.aCart = new Array();
    var len:int = aItems.length;
    for (var i:int = 0;i < len;i++){
        this.soCart.data.aCart[i] = this.aItems.getItemAt(i);
    }
}
```

This will place the values from the ArrayCollection into the shared object. The SharedObject class can store only native ActionScript data structures such as an array of objects. An ArrayCollection cannot be stored in a shared object, nor can objects created using the value object pattern. These data structures will be converted to arrays of objects.

10 Save ShoppingCart.as.

11 Make sure your ColdFusion server is running, and then run the EComm application. Add some items to the shopping cart and view the cart. Click the Save for Later button.

When you click the Save For Later button, you will write a .sol file to the client machine. When you call the SharedObject.flush() method or simply close your browser, all the information in the shopping cart will be written to this file.

12 The storage location of local shared objects depends on the operating system. If you are using Windows, browse to *driveroot:*/Documents and Settings/{*username*}/ApplicationData/Macromedia/Flash Player/#Shared Objects. From this point, search for cartInfo.sol.

▶ **TIP:** The path might include some odd directory names because you are not browsing the MXML file, but running it from Flex Builder.

▶ **TIP:** On Macintosh OSX, shared objects are stored in /Users/{*username*}/Library/Preferences/Macromedia/Flash Player.

Inside the .sol file you will see the data structure of the shopping cart. This is the file that Flash Player can read and use to populate controls.

Reading Data from an Existing Shared Object

In this exercise, you will read the information from the existing shared object and use this information to populate the DataGrid control that is displaying the information.

1 Open src/views/ecomm/Cart.mxml.

You will populate the DataGrid, located in Cart.mxml, from the shared object that has already been written to the client machine.

2 At the top of Cart.mxml, locate the `<VBox>` root tag and add a `creationComplete` event that will call the `loadCart()` method from the cart object.

```
<mx:VBox xmlns:mx="http://www.adobe.com/2006/mxml"
    creationComplete="cart.loadCart()">
```

It makes sense to call the method that will populate the DataGrid on the `creationComplete` event to be sure that the DataGrid is available for use.

3 Save Cart.mxml and open src/valueObjects/ShoppingCart.as.

You will write the `loadCart()` method in the ShoppingCart class because the `aItems` ArrayCollection that populates all the controls is built in this class. You will build the ArrayCollection from the data structure stored in the shared object.

4 At the end of the class, add a skeleton of the `loadCart()` method, data typed as `void`, and use the `getLocal()` static method of the SharedObject class to read the existing cartInfo SharedObject. Store the shared object in a variable with the name of `soCart`.

```
public function loadCart():void{
    this.soCart = SharedObject.getLocal("cartInfo");
}
```

5 Add conditional logic that ensures that the `aCart` variable is not undefined.

```
if ( this.soCart.data.aCart != undefined ){
}
```

The `data` property of a new shared object does not contain any properties until you add them. Before you attempt to use the `aCart` data that might be stored in the shared object, you need to ensure that it exists.

6 Within the conditional logic, create a new local variable with the name of `len` and obtain the length of the `aCart` array stored in the `data` property of the `soCart` SharedObject, as follows:

```
var len:int = this.soCart.data.aCart.length;
```

`data` is the only property of the SharedObject class and is where all the data stored in the shared object is accessed. You are accessing the array in this case and can use all Array properties and methods.

7 Next, set up a looping structure that will loop through the `aCart` array stored in the `soCart` shared object.

```
for (var i:int=0;i<len;i++){
}
```

This will loop through the `aCart` array stored in the shared object. You will loop through this data structure and place the resulting data structure in the `aItems` ArrayCollection, which has already been bound to all the controls. Data stored in shared objects can be only native ActionScript data structures, so you will need to convert these objects into the value objects that `aItems` is expecting.

8 Create a new instance of the Product class using the static `buildProduct()` method. Pass the method the Product object stored inside the `aCart` array.

```
var myProduct:Product = Product.buildProduct (this.soCart.data.aCart[i].product);
```

The `buildProduct()` method will build a new Product value object based on the Product class you wrote earlier. You must do this because all value objects stored in a shared object are automatically converted into native data structures. Unless you convert these objects back into the appropriate value objects, you will receive a type coercion error when you try to place the objects into the `aItems` array, which is linked to the visual controls.

9 After building the Product object, define a new quantity of type `int` from the `quantity` property stored in the shared object.

```
var myQuantity:int = this.soCart.data.aCart[i].quantity;
```

To define a new ShoppingCartItem, you must define a Product object, which you did in the previous step. You also must define a quantity, which is stored in the shared object. The `quantity` property in the shared object is untyped, and the ShoppingCartItem requires a variable that has the type of `int`, so you must define it again here.

10 Define a new ShoppingCartItem, and pass to the constructor the `myProduct` Product object you created in the previous two steps.

```
var myItem:ShoppingCartItem = new ShoppingCartItem(myProduct, myQuantity);
```

The `aItems` array is an ArrayCollection of ShoppingCartItem value objects, and you must re-create these value objects to avoid type coercion errors because these value objects are not stored as value objects in the shared object. They are stored as a native ActionScript array of objects.

11 Still within the `for` loop, call the `addItem()` method on the class you are currently working on and pass it the `myItem` ShoppingCartItem. The final `loadCart()` method should
look as follows:

```
public function loadCart():void{
   this.soCart = SharedObject.getLocal("cartInfo");
   if ( this.soCart.data.aCart != undefined ){
      var len:int = this.soCart.data.aCart.length;
      for (var i:int=0;i<len;i++){
         var myProduct:Product =
            ➥ Product.buildProduct(this.soCart.data.aCart[i].product);
         var myQuantity:int = this.soCart.data.aCart[i].quantity;
         var myItem:ShoppingCartItem =
            ➥ new ShoppingCartItem(myProduct, myQuantity);
         this.addItem(myItem);
      }
   }
}
```

To build the *aItems* ArrayCollection, you will use the `addItem()` method of the
ShoppingCart. This method checks to see whether the item is already in the cart,
manages the quantity of each item, and updates the subtotals of each item.

12 At the end of the class, add a skeleton of the `clearCart()` method data typed as void. Within
the method, call the *aItems*.`removeAll()` method. Check if the *soCart* exists, and if it does,
call the `clear()` method on *soCart*, and then call the `calcTotal()` method of this class.

```
aItems.removeAll()
   if (soCart) {
      soCart.clear();
   }
calcTotal();
```

This method empties all the items from the *aItems* ArrayCollection, clears the contents
of the *soCart* shared object, and forces the shopping cart to recalculate the total. You will
call this method when the user finishes the ordering process.

13 Open src/modules/CheckoutModule.mxml.

You will change the `saveOrderResult()` method to use your new `clearCart()` method.

14 Find the `saveOrderResult()` method. Change the first line, which currently sets the
cart.aItems to a new ArrayCollection, to call your `clearCart()` method on the cart
object instead. The final `saveOrderResult()` method should look as follows:

```
private function saveOrderResult(event:ResultEvent):void{
   this.cart.clearCart();
   Alert.show(event.result.getOrderInfoHeader());
```

```
    var o:Event = new Event("checkOutComplete");
    this.dispatchEvent(o);
    checkoutNav.selectedChild=billingInfo;
}
```

15 Save all open files. Run the EComm application. Add some items to the shopping cart and view the cart. Click the Save For Later button. Close the browser, restart the application, and view the cart again. Click on a product category, add another item to your cart, and view the cart again.

When you restart the application and view the shopping cart, you should see that the shared object has been read and has populated the DataGrid with the items previously in the shopping cart. This information was written to the client machine in the shared object.

What You Have Learned

In this lesson, you have:

- Learned how to create and read shared objects using the SharedObject class (pages 598–601)
- Saved shopping cart data into a shared object (pages 601–604)
- Read shopping cart data from a shared object (pages 604–607)

What You Will Learn

In this lesson, you will:

- Learn how to use the `<mx:TraceTarget>` tag to view client/server communication

- Use the debugger in Flex Builder in new ways

- Handle errors using the `try-catch-finally` statements

Approximate Time

This lesson takes approximately 1 hour and 30 minutes to complete.

Lesson Files

Media Files:

None

Starting Files:

Lesson25/start/DataEntry.mxml
Lesson25/start/EComm.mxml
Lesson25/start/as/ecomm.as

Completed Files:

Lesson25/complete/DataEntry.mxml
Lesson25/complete/EComm.mxml
Lesson25/complete/as/ecomm.as

LESSON 25

Debugging Flex Applications

Bugs occur when developing applications. In this lesson, you will take two approaches to these bugs. The first part of the lesson gives you insight into how to find bugs and apply what you have learned in the rest of the book to correct them. In the rest of the lesson, you learn how to handle bugs that slip by and programmatically catch them at runtime using error handling with the **try-catch-finally** statements.

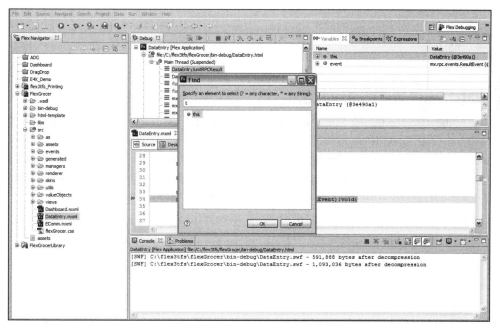

Using the debugger to search for properties beginning with the letter t.

Introducing Debugging Techniques

Finding and correcting bugs is part of application development. This lesson will give you additional tools to eliminate bugs from your applications. This lesson is different from other lessons in that you will not write code, but instead use debugging tools with existing code to learn about ways to help debug your applications.

In the first section of the lesson, you will use the `<mx:TraceTarget>` tag to give you insight into what communication is happening between the client and server when using functionality that accesses server-side data, such as RemoteObject and HTTPService.

Next, you will see some new ways to use the debugger that you have not yet explored in this book. You will also get some more explanation and vocabulary about Flex Builder's built-in debugger.

Finally, you will learn how to handle errors that occur during runtime. Most likely, you will not be able to correct every bug and anticipate every way a user will interact with your application. So, it is possible that runtime errors could occur. To handle these errors, you will learn how to use `try-catch-finally` statements to gracefully catch, and recover from, run-time errors.

> ✳ **NOTE:** You need to have ColdFusion running in the console window for the following exercise.

Watching Client/Server Data Exchange

One of the most frustrating debugging tasks can occur when dealing with data exchange on the server side. In some cases, you will not be able to tell if the problem exists in how you are handling the data once it has been received at the client, or if you simply are not getting back the expected data. The `<mx:TraceTarget>` tag, along with debugging your application, will give you a wealth of information about the traffic passing between client and server.

1 From the FlexGrocer project, open EComm.mxml. Just after the opening `<mx:Application>` tag, insert an `<mx:TraceTarget/>` tag. Debug the EComm application by selecting it from the Debug menu.

> **TIP:** You might want to insert the <mx:TraceTarget> tags on the far-left margin, ignoring best practice indentation. Because you do not want this debugging tag in your production code, it is easy to locate and remove when it is sitting on the left margin.

2 Return to Flex Builder and double-click the Console view. Notice the HTTPService information in the Console view.

```
[SWF] C:\flex3tfs\flexGrocer\bin-debug\EComm-debug.swf - 1,231,127 bytes after
➥ decompression
'0C43236E-46E3-E632-438D-3573BDC724AF' producer set destination to 'ColdFusion'.
'63C5E353-518F-1463-C894-3573BE15DD03' producer set destination to 'DefaultHTTP'.
'direct_http_channel' channel endpoint set to http:
'63C5E353-518F-1463-C894-3573BE15DD03' producer sending message
➥ 'A5E7E4ED-6D21-40C1-C45F-3573BF5D1C27'
'direct_http_channel' channel sending message:
(mx.messaging.messages::HTTPRequestMessage)#0
    body = (Object)#1
    clientId = (null)
    contentType = "application/x-www-form-urlencoded"
    destination = "DefaultHTTP"
    headers = (Object)#2
    httpHeaders = (Object)#3
    messageId = "A5E7E4ED-6D21-40C1-C45F-3573BF5D1C27"
    method = "GET"
    recordHeaders = false
    timestamp = 0
    timeToLive = 0
    url = "http://localhost:8300/flexGrocer/xml/categorizedProducts.cfm"
'63C5E353-518F-1463-C894-3573BE15DD03' producer connected.
'63C5E353-518F-1463-C894-3573BE15DD03' producer acknowledge of
➥ 'A5E7E4ED-6D21-40C1-C45F-3573BF5D1C27'.
```

This information can give you a confirmation of the HTTPService request information.

3 Terminate the current debugging session by clicking the red square in the Console view. Double-click the Console view to restore the normal debugging perspective. Remove the <mx:TraceTarget> tag and save the EComm.mxml application.

TraceTarget is for debugging and should not be left in your production code.

Learning More About the Debugger

So far in this book, you've used the debugger built into Flex Builder in a limited way on a number of occasions. In this exercise, you will learn more about the debugger and how it can help you find errors in your application and more fully understand your application.

Learning More Details About Setting Breakpoints

In earlier lessons, you created breakpoints by double-clicking in the marker bar (next to the line numbers in an editor) to toggle breakpoints on and off. Here are more details about creating breakpoints:

- You can add breakpoints only on executable lines of ActionScript code. This means you can set breakpoints on lines that contain the following:

  - MXML tags that contain an event handler. For example,
    `<mx:Button click="clickHandler()"/>`

  - ActionScript code enclosed in an `<mx:Script>` block

  - Executable ActionScript in an ActionScript file

- If you set a breakpoint on a line that does not meet one of the listed criteria, Flex Builder will automatically scan down 10 lines to try and find a valid line to place a breakpoint. If it does, the breakpoint will be moved. If it cannot find a valid line for a breakpoint within 10 lines, the breakpoint will be ignored when debugging.

- The moving of the breakpoints will happen when you start your debugging session; if you set another breakpoint during a debugging session, it will be moved immediately.

After you hit a breakpoint and are in Flex Builder in the Flex Debugging perspective, you have a number of options for controlling application flow and breakpoint manipulation. On top of the Debug view, you see options for controlling your debugging session.

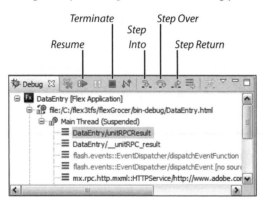

Here are the most common commands:

- **Resume**: Resumes execution of an application that has been interrupted by a debugging session. You can either run the application to completion or to another breakpoint set in the editor.

- **Terminate**: Stops the debugging session.

- **Step Into**: Steps into the called function and stops at the first line of the function.

- **Step Over**: Executes the current line of the function and then stops at the next line of the function.

- **Step Return**: Continues execution until the current function has returned to its caller or until another breakpoint is reached.

Inspecting Variables and Their Associated Values in the Debugger

After you have hit a breakpoint, you have a number of ways to inspect values of variables at the current state of the application. In a previous lesson, you used the Variables view to check the value of a variable. In the Variables view, you can check the values of the current object context, located in the this variable. If you happen to be in a function, you can also check the variables defined in that function by inspecting the variables labeled with an *L* in the circle in front of the variable. The following figure shows a debugging session stopped in an event handler where the event is passed to the function as a parameter, and hence scoped local to the function.

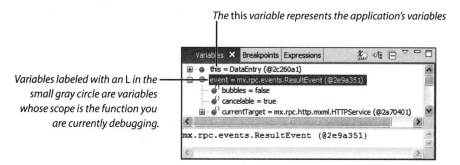

The this *variable represents the application's variables*

Variables labeled with an L *in the small gray circle are variables whose scope is the function you are currently debugging.*

In Variables view, there can be hundreds of variables to inspect. There is a feature in Flex Builder to help you find a variable from that long list: the Find Variable option. You can use either Ctrl+F or right-click in the Variables view and select Find Variable to bring up the interface. As you type in the data-entry section, the variables matching your entry will be listed. You can then click the variable you want to be highlighted in the Variables view.

If you are watching one variable or a small set of variables, a better option is to use the Expressions view. In the Expressions view, you can enter variables (or expressions) to watch; when debugging, the values of the variables appear in the Expressions view. You don't have to search for them in a long list of values in the Variables view.

1 From the FlexGrocer project, open DataEntry.mxml. Locate the unitRPCResult() event handler, which is called when the HTTPService successfully returns unit information. Place a breakpoint on the line of code that assigns the unit variable a value from the event object by double-clicking in the gray column to the left of the line numbers.

```
30          private function unitRPCResult(event:ResultEvent):void{
31              units=event.result.allUnits.unit;
32          }
```

2 Debug the DataEntry.mxml application. Be sure that you are viewing the Flex Debugging perspective in Flex Builder.

You will either be automatically taken back to Flex Builder after you debug the application, or else you might have to click the blinking Flex Builder button in the Task Manager to get back to Flex Builder. If you are prompted to go into the Flex Debugging perspective, click OK.

3 Assume that you want to check the value of the units variable to be sure that the values are properly assigned. The first thing to do is to be sure that the event object contains the correct data. Use the Variables view, and drill into the event object to see that the data is returned correctly.

In this case, the path to the XML data returned by the HTTPService is event→result→allUnits→unit. There you see the ArrayCollection returned.

4 Now you know that the data is being retrieved correctly. Next, you want to be sure it is assigned to the units variable. Click the Expressions view tab, right-click in the Expressions view, and select Add Watch Expression. Enter **units** and then click OK. Notice that the variable is defined because it is declared as an ArrayCollection in the application. Drill down into the variable; you will see it does not have any values.

The reason why the units variable has no values yet is because the breakpoint stops execution before the line is executed. You must run the line of code before the assignment is made.

5 In the Debug view, click the Step Over button; you will see that the debugging session is now sitting on the closing brace of the function and that units now has the correct values.

✸ **NOTE:** Do not terminate the debugging session because you will shortly see that you can add breakpoints during an active debugging session.

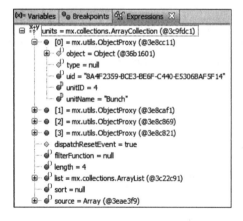

6 Now assume that you want to be sure the data returned from the Data Manager, which retrieves data for the variables categories and foodColl, is also correct. Place a breakpoint on the closing brace of the categorizedProductDataLoaded() method.

```
34          private function categorizedProductDataLoaded():void{
35              categories = new ArrayCollection(prodMgr.getCats());
36              foodColl= prodMgr.getCategorizedProducts();
37          }
```

7 Be sure that you have not terminated the debugging session and then click the Resume command. You will see that the debugging session has now highlighted where you set the second breakpoint. Double-click the Variables view tab to make it full screen.

Because there are so many properties in the Variables view, it is often helpful to make it full screen when looking for variables and their associated values.

8 In the Variables view, be sure to expand the variable to see all the variables within the scope. Right-click in the Variables view and select Find Variable. Start typing **categories** until you can see that variable highlighted in the Variables view in the pop-up window. Select categories, and click OK to close the Find Variable window. Then check to be sure the correct data stored in an ArrayCollection is in categories. Right-click in the Variables view again, and select Find Variable. Start typing **foodColl** until you can see that variable in the pop-up window. Select foodColl, click OK to close the Find Variable window, and then ensure that the correct XML data is in foodColl.

Notice that you can see the values of the variable selected in the Variables view in the Detail pane. When you select foodColl, you can see the actual XML in the Detail pane— either to the right of or below the variable display.

Name	Value
⊞ ● _DataEntry_UpdateDeleteProd1	views.dataEntry.UpdateDeleteProd (@3b51851)
⊞ ■ _documentDescriptor_	mx.core.UIComponentDescriptor (@3c03fb9)
⊟ ■' foodColl	XML
⊟ ■' <catalog>	
⊞ ● <category catID="1" catName="Meat" name="Meat">	
⊞ ● <category catID="2" catName="Vegetables" name="Veç	
⊞ ● <category catID="3" catName="Fruit" name="Fruit">	
⊞ ● <category catID="4" catName="Dairy" name="Dairy">	
⊞ ● <category catID="5" catName="Deli" name="Deli">	
⊞ ● <category catID="6" catName="Seafood" name="Seafo	

```
<catalog>
  <category catID="1" catName="Meat" name="Meat">
    <product catID="1" catName="Meat" cost="4" description="Delicious, low fat Buff
    <product catID="1" catName="Meat" cost="2.25" description="Cat meat" imageName=
    <product catID="1" catName="Meat" cost="3.55" description="Croc meat" imageName
    <product catID="1" catName="Meat" cost="2.25" description="It's dog meat" image
    <product catID="1" catName="Meat" cost="6" description="Thick and delicious, th
    <product catID="1" catName="Meat" cost="1.5" description="This free range chick
  </category>
  <category catID="2" catName="Vegetables" name="Vegetables">
    <product catID="2" catName="Vegetables" cost="2.16" description="Firm and no bi
    <product catID="2" catName="Vegetables" cost="1.69" description="Juicy and tend
    <product catID="2" catName="Vegetables" cost="1.25" description="Yellow Peppers
  </category>
  <category catID="3" catName="Fruit" name="Fruit">
    <product catID="3" catName="Fruit" cost="0.95" description="Bunches of Banans,
    <product catID="3" catName="Fruit" cost="1.34" description="Sweet, juicy grapes
    <product catID="3" catName="Fruit" cost="2.5" description="Crisp, sweet, great
  </category>
  <category catID="4" catName="Dairy" name="Dairy">
```

You can change the location of the Detail pane by choosing the option from the Variables View menu (a downward-facing triangle) and selecting the Orientation option of your choice from the Layout menu.

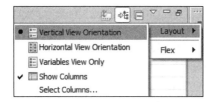

9 Be sure you are still in a debugging session, and assume that you want to verify the data being returned from a component that updates a product. Set a third breakpoint on the productUpdate event handler in the MXML that creates the UpdateDeleteProd component.

```
<v:UpdateDeleteProd label="Update/Delete Product"
   units="{units}"
   foodColl="{foodColl}"
   productUpdate="pm.updateProduct(event.product)"
   productDelete="pm.deleteProduct(event.product)"/>
```

Remember MXML becomes ActionScript when you compile your application. This means you can set a breakpoints in MXML as well.

This breakpoint will behave a bit differently from the second one you set. When you resumed the application to continue to the second breakpoint, you did not have to interact with the application; loading data happened on start-up. When you resume, you will have to interact with the application for the third breakpoint to be hit.

10 Select the Resume command from the Debug view. Return to the browser where the application is running and select a product from the Tree on the Update/Delete Product tab. Make a change to the product information and then click Update. Be sure that you are viewing the Flex Debugging perspective in Flex Builder. In the Variables view, check to be sure that event.product has your new value.

> **TIP:** Of course you could have terminated the debugging session, cleared the first two break-points, and then set a single breakpoint on the productUpdate() function. But by following that procedure, you would not have seen that you can select Resume, return to the application, and get to the next breakpoint in a single debugging session.

11 Terminate the debugging session, and close any open files.

You will be working with a different main application in the next exercise.

Handling Errors with try-catch

No matter how careful you are when developing your applications, there will be times when runtime errors occur. You might make a mistake in development, or perhaps users will use your application in a way that you never anticipated. It is considered a poor practice to allow any errors that would be generated to be seen by users. Instead, you should anticipate where a runtime error could occur, and then handle those situations using try-catch statements. Runtime errors, also called exceptions, can be caught, and you can choose what should hap-pen when they occur, depending on the type of exception caught and the situation. Exception handling gives your applications the chance to recover gracefully from runtime errors, instead of the user encountering an error while using the application.

The new ActionScript 3.0 compiler reports syntactical errors to you in Flex Builder and pre-vents your application from being built. These types of errors are not the type to be dealt with using try-catch. Runtime errors occur when a user is running your application; these are errors caused during playback of the SWF file.

In earlier versions of Flash Player, more often than not, Flash Player failed silently. This was not a good situation for you as the developer because you were not given a clue about why the application did not work—you just knew it had failed. So, runtime errors are a good thing for you as a developer but not for interacting with the application.

Using the try-catch Syntax

The general syntax for using try-catch is the following:

```
try{
    //possible error producing code;
}
catch (e:ErrorType){
    //code to execute when error is caught;
}
```

A simple example designed to guarantee an error is as follows:

```
<mx:Script>
    <![CDATA[
        import mx.collections.ArrayCollection;
        private var newAC:ArrayCollection=new ArrayCollection();
        private function test():void{
            try{
                var myVar:Object=newAC.getItemAt(10);
            }
            catch (e:Error){
                errorLabel.text="error caught";
            }
        }
    ]]>
</mx:Script>
<mx:Label id="errorLabel" text="error Label"/>
<mx:Button label="Cause a Problem" click="test()"/>
```

In this case, when the button is clicked, the label would display "error caught", and no exception error would be displayed in the browser running the application.

You can also access properties and methods of the error object (the e variable in the previous code example) in the catch statement. Those available properties and methods are as follows:

- message (property): Contains the message associated with the Error object.

- name (property): Contains the name of the Error object.

- getStackTrace() (method): For debugger versions of Flash Player, only; this method returns the call stack for an error as a string at the time of the error's construction.

- toString() (method): Returns the string "Error" by default or the value contained in Error.message, if defined.

By using the trace() statement in the catch block, you can see what appears in the Console view for each property and method:

```
catch (e:Error){
    trace(e.message);
    trace(e.name);
    trace(e.getStackTrace());
    trace(e.toString());
}
```

name

messge   *getStackTrace()*

Console ⊠

EComm [Flex Application] file:/C:/flex3tfs/flexGrocer/bin-debug/EComm.html

```
Error #1009: Cannot access a property or method of a null object reference.
TypeError
TypeError: Error #1009: Cannot access a property or method of a null object reference.
        at EComm/displayProdByCategory()[C:\flex3tfs\flexGrocer\src\as\ecomm.as:47]
        at EComm/__catView_categorySelect()[C:\flex3tfs\flexGrocer\src\EComm.mxml:49]
        at flash.events::EventDispatcher/dispatchEventFunction()
        at flash.events::EventDispatcher/dispatchEvent()
        at mx.core::UIComponent/dispatchEvent()
        at views.ecomm::CategoryView/broadcastCategoryEvent()[C:\flex3tfs\flexGrocer\src\vi
        at views.ecomm::CategoryView/loadState()[C:\flex3tfs\flexGrocer\src\views\ecomm\Cat
        at mx.managers::HistoryManagerImpl/browserURLChangeHandler()
        at flash.events::EventDispatcher/dispatchEventFunction()
        at flash.events::EventDispatcher/dispatchEvent()
        at mx.managers::BrowserManagerImpl/browserURLChange()
        at mx.managers::BrowserManagerImpl/browserURLChangeBrowser()
        at Function/http://adobe.com/AS3/2006/builtin::apply()
        at <anonymous>()
        at flash.external::ExternalInterface$/_callIn()
        at <anonymous>()
TypeError: Error #1009: Cannot access a property or method of a null object reference.
```

toString()

> ✱ **NOTE:** Remember that when using the trace() statement, you must Debug, not Run, your application to see the results in the Console view.

Understanding the Error Types

So far, both code examples use the Error class, which is the base class for all error classes in ActionScript. There are number of error classes. One set is defined by ECMAScript, and the others are ActionScript specific:

Error Classes	
ECMAScript Errors	**ActionScript Specific Errors**
Error	ArgumentError
EvalError	SecurityError
RangeError	VerifyError
ReferenceError	EOFError
SyntaxError	IllegalOperationError
TypeError	IOError
URIError	MemoryError
	ScriptTimeOutError
	StackOverFlowError

Using Multiple catch Blocks

You can use these error types with a single catch block, or you can have multiple catch blocks associated with a single try statement. So, if you have a piece of code that might throw different kinds of errors, and you want to handle the different errors with different code, you can use multiple catch blocks. Here are some rules to remember if you are doing this:

- The first catch block with a matching error type will be executed.
- Only one catch block will be executed.
- Never place a catch block with the type Error before other catch blocks. Because Error will match all errors, you guarantee that the other catch blocks will never be used.

Here are a few examples to further clarify the rules to remember:

Example Using Only One catch Block

```
<mx:Script>
  <![CDATA[
      import mx.collections.ArrayCollection;
      private var newAC:ArrayCollection=new ArrayCollection();
      private function test():void{
        try{
          var myVar:Object=newAC.getItemAt(10);
        }
        catch (e:EvalError){
          errorLabel.text="EvalError class";
        }
        catch (e:RangeError){
          errorLabel.text="RangeError class";
        }
        catch (e:Error){
          errorLabel.text="Error base class";
        }
      }
  ]]>
</mx:Script>
<mx:Label id="errorLabel" text="error Label"/>
<mx:Button label="Cause a Problem" click="test()"/>
```

When the button is clicked, the label would display the RangeError class. The code in the try block would cause the error. The first catch block is looking for an EvalError, which would not be a match, so processing would continue. The second catch block is a RangeError, which is a match, so the corresponding string would be displayed. The third catch block with the base Error class is also a match, but because a previous catch block was used, the Error catch block is skipped.

Example Showing Bad Practice of Using the Error Base Class in the First catch Block

```
<mx:Script>
  <![CDATA[
      import mx.collections.ArrayCollection;
      private var newAC:ArrayCollection=new ArrayCollection();
      private function test():void{
        try{
          var myVar:Object=newAC.getItemAt(10);
        }
        catch (e:Error){
          errorLabel.text="Error base class";
        }
```

code continues on next page

```
               catch (e:EvalError){
                  errorLabel.text="EvalError class";
               }
               catch (e:RangeError){
                  errorLabel.text="RangeError class";
               }
            }
         }
   ]]>
</mx:Script>
<mx:Label id="errorLabel" text="error Label"/>
<mx:Button label="Cause a Problem" click="test()"/>
```

When testing this code, the label would display the Error base class. The code in the try block
would cause the error. The first catch block is looking for the Error base class, which would
match any kind of error, so the corresponding string would be displayed. Because the first
catch block is executed, the second and third catch blocks are ignored. This demonstrates the
rule that you should never place a catch block with the type Error before other catch blocks.
In this example, the specific error type, RangeError, was used to show that it was never evalu-
ated because of order of the catch blocks.

Using the finally Statement

ActionScript, like many languages that implement some kind of try-catch syntax, offers
a finally statement. The finally statement should be placed after all of your catch blocks,
and the code it contains will be executed whether an error occurs in the try statement or
not. In the example code shown, the errorLabel would display the RangeError class, and the
finallyLabel would display "finally executed".

```
<mx:Script>
   <![CDATA[
        import mx.collections.ArrayCollection;
        private var newAC:ArrayCollection=new ArrayCollection();
        private function test():void{
           try{
              var myVar:Object=newAC.getItemAt(10);
           }
           catch (e:RangeError){
              errorLabel.text="RangeError class";
           }
           finally{
              finallyLabel.text="finally executed";
           }
        }
   ]]>
</mx:Script>
```

```
<mx:Label id="errorLabel" text="error Label"/>
<mx:Label id="finallyLabel" text="finally Label"/>
<mx:Button label="Cause a Problem" click="test()"/>
```

In this example, even if you commented the assignment statement in the try statement, and no error occurred, the finally statement would still be executed, and the finallyLabel would display the corresponding text.

Using the throw Statement

There might be times when you want to manually generate an error. This means that something has occurred in your application that, although it is not a runtime error, you want to raise an exception so it can be handled in your normal exception-handling scheme. For instance, you might have a situation in which the number of products ordered is more than those in stock. You could programmatically take care of the situation, but you might also want to handle the problem by raising (also referred to as throwing) an exception.

One approach would be to use an existing error class and put in a message you could later examine to check the error. In the following code example, in the try statement, the throw statement is used to raise an exception of type Error, and the error is then caught and the custom message is displayed.

```
<mx:Script>
  <![CDATA[
      import mx.collections.ArrayCollection;
      private var newAC:ArrayCollection=new ArrayCollection();
      private function test():void{
        try{
          throw new Error("This is a custom message on a throw statement");
        }
        catch (e:Error){
          errorLabel.text=e.message;
        }
      }
  ]]>
</mx:Script>
<mx:Label id="errorLabel" text="error Label"/>
<mx:Button label="Cause a Problem" click="test()"/>
```

In this code example, the errorLabel would display "This is a custom message on a throw statement".

Creating Your Own Error Classes

When wanting to throw an error, the next step would be to throw an error of a class you have created. Perhaps you will look for that specific class in your catch, and/or it will contain a special code to alert you of a particular exception. The following ActionScript class defines a custom error class that extends the base Error class. You add an instance variable named customCode that will hold the error code that will be generated in a specific situation you have defined. By the package name, errorClasses, you see that this class was saved in a directory named errorClasses.

```
package errorClasses {
    public class CustomError extends Error {
        public var customCode:int;
        public function CustomError(message:String,customCode:int){
            super(message);
            this.customCode=customCode;
        }//end constructor
    }//end class
}//end package
```

To use this custom class, you'll need to import the class and then throw it when a certain condition occurs. When you instantiate it, you'll need to pass both a custom message as the first parameter and a custom integer code as a second parameter. The following code example shows just that:

```
<mx:Script>
    <![CDATA[
        import errorClasses.CustomError;
        private function test():void{
          try{
             throw new CustomError("Custom message",123);
          }
          catch (e:CustomError){
             errorLabel.text=e.message;
             codeLabel.text=String(e.customCode);
          }
        }
    ]]>
</mx:Script>
<mx:Label id="errorLabel" text="error Label"/>
<mx:Label id="codeLabel" text="code Label"/>
<mx:Button label="Cause a Problem" click="test()"/>
```

When the button is clicked, the errorLabel displays "Custom message", and the codeLabel displays 123, both of which are arbitrary example values.

✱ **NOTE:** Because of security constraints, users of Microsoft Internet Explorer cannot build and preview this next exercise. History Management is used, and it does not work in Internet Explorer when previewing a local file, meaning that it does not work when previewing local files on your hard drive. However, it will work if the file is on a web server or accessed through an HTTP URL as opposed to the file:// URL that is used during normal development. If you are using Internet Explorer, you need to preview these files from a web server. History Management does work in Firefox and Netscape browsers when previewing a local file.

1 From the FlexGrocer project, open the file src/as/ecomm.as. Locate the displayProdByCategory() method, and remove all if statement logic so it appears as follows:

```
private function displayProdByCategory(event:CategoryEvent):void{
   prodTile.visible=false;
   var prodArray:Array=catProds.getProdsForCat(event.cat.catID);
   prodByCategory=new ArrayCollection(prodArray);
   prodTile.visible=true;
}
```

You are removing the logic that prevents a runtime error from occurring. You will replace the if logic with try-catch-finally.

2 Run the EComm.mxml application. Click one of the categories, and notice that a runtime error appears.

```
■ Adobe Flash Player 9                                                    ⊠

An ActionScript error has occurred:

TypeError: Error #1009: Cannot access a property or method of a null object reference.
        at EComm/::displayProdByCategory()
        at EComm/__catView_categorySelect()
        at flash.events::EventDispatcher/flash.events:EventDispatcher::dispatchEventFunction()
        at flash.events::EventDispatcher/dispatchEvent()
        at views.ecomm::CategoryView/::broadcastCategoryEvent()
        at views.ecomm::CategoryView/loadState()
        at mx.managers::HistoryManager$/http://www.adobe.com/2006/flex/mx/internal::load()
        at mx.managers::HistoryManager$/http://www.adobe.com/2006/flex/mx/internal::loadInitialState()
        at mx.managers::InitLocalConnection/loadInitialState()

                                                       Dismiss All    Continue
```

3 In the function, surround the contents of the function with a `try` block; then trace the `message` property of the error in a `catch` block. Debug the application. Click one of the categories.

```
private function displayProdByCategory(event:CategoryEvent):void{
   try{
      prodTile.visible=false;
      var prodArray:Array=catProds.getProdsForCat(event.cat.catID);
      prodByCategory=new ArrayCollection(prodArray);
      prodTile.visible=true;
   }catch(e:Error){
      trace(e.message);
   }
}
```

You should see in the Console view that the `trace` statement displays the same message as in the first line of the runtime error.

4 Remove the `trace` statement.

Even though the `trace` statement will display only information when debugging an application, there is no need to leave the code in the function.

5 Move the code which sets the prodTile's visible property to try to be immediately after the line which sets it to false. Next move the remaining contents from the try block to the finally block, so your code appears as it does here:

```
private function displayProdByCategory(event:CategoryEvent):void{
   try{
      prodTile.visible=false;
      prodTile.visible=true;
   } catch(e:Error) { }
   finally{
      var prodArray:Array = catProds.getProdsForCat(event.cat.catID);
      prodByCategory=new ArrayCollection(prodArray);
   }
}
```

This will catch the error and populate the ArrayCollection. So, instead of an error being thrown and the application crashing, the application is ready to use.

6 Save ecomm.as and run the Ecomm.mxml application. Click one of the categories.

Rather than an error being displayed, the area below the toolbar is blank.

What You Have Learned

In this lesson, you have:

- Used the <mx:TraceTarget> tag to watch data passed between client and server (pages 610–611)

- Learned new details about Flex Builder's built-in debugger (pages 611–619)

- Handled runtime exceptions using the `try-catch-finally` statements (pages 619–629)

What You Will Learn

In this lesson, you will:

- Learn about garbage collection
- Profile a Flex application
- Understand the different views of the Flex Profiler
- Learn to identify memory leaks within an application
- Learn to identify performance problems

Approximate Time

This lesson takes approximately 1 hour and 30 minutes to complete.

Lesson Files

Media Files:

None

Starting Files:

Lesson26/profiler/start/src/ProfilerTest.mxml
Lesson26/profiler/start/src/components/ImageDisplay.mxml
Lesson26/profiler/start/src/managers/UpdateManager.as

Completed Files:

Lesson26/profiler/complete/src/ProfilerTest.mxml
Lesson26/profiler/complete/src/components/ImageDisplay.mxml
Lesson26/profiler/complete/src/managers/UpdateManager.as

LESSON 26

Profiling Flex Applications

Lesson 25, "Debugging Flex Applications," taught you about tools and techniques used to find errors within an application. This lesson teaches you about the tools and techniques used to identify another set of problems that don't prevent an application from functioning immediately, but cause an application to run more slowly or use more memory than it should.

In this lesson, you will learn about both memory and performance profiling, two techniques facilitated by the new Profiler feature in Flex Builder 3 Pro. (**Note:** The new profiling feature is only available to users of Flex Builder 3 Pro. An evaluation version of Flex Builder 3 Pro is available from www.adobe.com/go/flex/. Flex Builder Standard users will not be able to access the profiler screens.) To understand the need for this tool, you need to learn some details about how Flash Player executes code in Flex and how it allocates (gives) and frees (takes back) memory.

Using Live Objects view in an executing application

Flash Player Memory Use

This lessons deals with a lot of memory-related issues. So far in this book, we have largely ignored the details behind the process of memory and garbage collection because it can be immensely complicated to understand completely. However, it is necessary to have at least a high-level understanding to use the Flex Profiler as an effective tool, so we'll discuss these issues in a simplified way that is intended to provide some understanding rather than convey complete technical correctness.

Flash Player Memory Allocation

Flash Player is responsible for providing memory for your Flex application at runtime. When you execute a line of code that creates a new instance of the DataGrid class, Flash Player provides a piece of memory for that instance to occupy. Flash Player in turn needs to ask your computer's operating system for memory to use for this purpose.

The process of asking the operating system for memory is slow, so Flash Player asks for much larger blocks than it needs and keeps the extra available for the next time the developer requests more space. Additionally, Flash Player watches for memory that is no longer in use, so that it can be reused before asking the operating system for more.

Passing by Reference or Value

There are two broad groups of data types that you need to understand when dealing with Flash Player memory. The first group is referred to as primitives, which include Boolean, int, Number, String, uint. These types are passed by value during assignment or function calls.

So, if you were to run the following example:

```
var a:Number;
var b:Number;
a = 5;
b = myAge;
a = 7;
```

It would create two numbers, and assign their values separately. From a very high level, Flash Player memory would look like this:

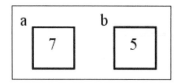

The second group is objects, which pass by reference.

Running the following example:

```
var a:Object;
var b:Object;
a = new Object();
a.someVar = 5;
b = a;
b.someVar = 7;
```

It would create a single Object instance with two references, or ways to find the object. From a very high level, Flash Player memory would look like this:

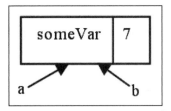

This point is so important that it is worth a walkthrough of the code. First, we create two variables named a and b. Both variables are of type Object. Next, we create a new Object instance and assign it to the variable a. It can now be said that a refers to the new object. When we set a.someVar to the value 5, we are setting that property inside the object that a refers to. Next, we assign a to b. This does not make a copy of the object, but rather simply ensures that a and b both now refer to the same object. Finally, when we set b.someVar to the value 7, we are setting that property inside the object that both a and b refer to. Since a and b both refer to the same object, a.someVar is exactly the same as b.someVar.

Flash Player Garbage Collection

Garbage collection is a process that reclaims memory no longer in use so that it can either be reused by the application or, in some cases, given back to the operating system. Garbage collection happens automatically at allocation, which is often confusing to new developers. This means that garbage collection does not occur when memory is no longer in use, but rather occurs when your application asks for more memory. At that point, the process responsible for garbage collection, called the Garbage Collector, attempts to reclaim available memory for reallocation.

The Garbage Collector follows a two-part procedure to determine which portions of memory are no longer in use. Understanding this procedure will give you the insight necessary to develop applications that use memory appropriately and to understand the information presented by the Flex profiler.

The first part of the garbage collection procedure is referred to as *reference counting*, and the second is referred to as *mark and sweep*. Both rely upon different methods of ensuring that the memory in question is no longer referenced by other objects in use.

As was demonstrated earlier, when you create a new object, you usually also create a reference, or a way of referring to, that object. Looking at this code snippet, you can see we create a reference named canvas to our new Canvas instance and one named lbl to our newly created Label. We also add the Label as a child of the Canvas.

```
var canvas:Canvas = new Canvas();
var lbl:Label = new Label();
canvas.addChild(lbl);
```

All components also maintain a reference to their children, and all component children maintain a reference to their parent. This means the references from the previous code snippet look like the following image:

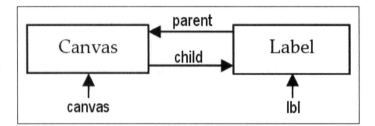

The previous small snippet demonstrates at least four references that we need to keep in mind.

- canvas is a reference to an instance of Canvas

- lbl is a reference to an instance of Label.

- lbl.parent is a reference to the Canvas instance.

- canvas.getChildAt(0) returns a reference to the Label instance.

The following application is used to illustrate how both parts of the garbage collection procedure determine what is free for collection.

```
<?xml version="1.0" encoding="utf-8"?>
<mx:Application xmlns:mx="http://www.adobe.com/2006/mxml"
    creationComplete="onCreation(event)">
  <mx:Script>
    <![CDATA[
      import mx.controls.TextInput;
      import mx.controls.Label;
      import mx.controls.ComboBox;
```

```
import mx.containers.Canvas;
import mx.controls.DataGrid;
import mx.containers.VBox;
import mx.containers.HBox;

private function onCreation( event:Event ):void {
    var hBox:HBox = new HBox();

    var vBox:VBox = new VBox();
    vBox.addChild( new DataGrid() );
    vBox.addChild( new ComboBox() );

    hBox.addChild( vBox );
    this.addChild( hBox );

    var canvas:Canvas = new Canvas();
    canvas.addChild( new Label() );

    var textInput:TextInput = new TextInput();
}
            ]]>
        </mx:Script>
    </mx:Application>
```

The application calls the onCreation() method when the creationComplete event occurs. This method creates a new HBox, with a VBox inside of it. The VBox contains a DataGrid and a ComboBox instance. The HBox is later added as a child of the application. A Canvas instance is then created with a Label instance as a child and finally a TextInput is instantiated. However, it is important to note that neither the Canvas instance nor the TextInput is ever added to the application via the addChild() method. The following figure shows the important references just before exiting the onCreation() method.

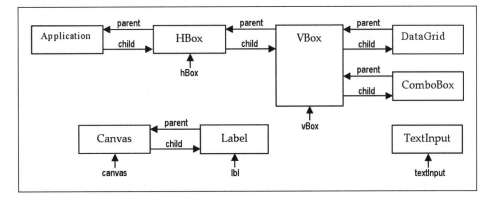

The diagram shows the references created in the onCreation() method, including the variables canvas, lbl, hBox, vBox, and textInput. However, these variables are defined within the onCreation() method. This means the variables are local to the method; once the method finishes execution, those references will disappear, but the objects created within this method will continue to exist.

As we mentioned previously, references are the metric that the Garbage Collector uses to determine the portions of memory that can be reclaimed. If the developer does not have a reference to an object, he or she has no way to access it or its properties. If there is no way to access the object, then the Garbage Collector reclaims the memory it used to occupy.

The first method that the Garbage Collector uses to determine if references to an object exist is called *reference counting*. Reference counting is the simplest and fastest method to determine if an object can be collected. Each time you create a reference to an object, Flash Player increments a counter associated with the object. When you remove a reference, the counter is decremented. If the counter is zero, the object is a candidate for garbage collection.

Looking at the example code, the only object with a zero reference count is the TextInput. After the onCreation() method is completed, the TextInput is left without any references. Once again, if there is no way to reference an object, then the object may be collected. This example also reveals a problem with reference counting: the circular reference.

If you examine the Canvas and Label, each has a reference to the other, meaning that each has a reference count greater than zero. However, there are no other references to either of these components in the application. If Flash Player could identify this fact, the memory for both of these components could be reclaimed. This is the reason for the second method used within the garbage collection procedure, called *mark and sweep*.

Using this method, Flash Player starts at the top level of your application and marks each object to which it finds a reference. It then recurses down into each object and repeats the process, continuing to dive further until it runs out of objects to mark. At the end of this process, neither the Canvas nor Label would be marked, and would become candidates for garbage collection. Although this method produces definitive results, it is very slow compared to reference counting, so it is not run continually. Working together, these two methods can be used to achieve higher levels of performance and garbage collection accuracy.

Garbage Collection

Now that you understand how garbage collection decides to reclaim memory, you can begin to establish practices to let the Garbage Collector do its job. Simply stated, you need to ensure you remove all references to an object when you no longer need it. Leaving an accidental reference to an object prevents that memory from ever being reclaimed; the inability to reclaim this memory can cause your memory to continue to grow as the application continues to execute. This is commonly referred to as a memory leak.

As you first learned in Lesson 10, "Creating Custom Components with ActionScript 3.0," visual children are added to components using the addChild() method. Children can also be removed using the removeChild() or remoteChildAt() method. The first method requires you to provide your own reference to the child needing removal, such as removeChild(hBox), whereas the second method allows you to specify the index of the child within its parent, removeChildAt(0). The second simply uses the reference maintained by the parent to identify the child. These methods ensure that both the parent and child references are cleared from within the components.

In our previous example, if you removed the HBox from the application with the removeChild() method, the HBox and every other object contained within it would become available for collection, as there are no other references to the child. This is fairly simple to explain; however, there is a caveat. There are other ways that references are created and maintained besides the variables and properties we have discussed so far.

In fact, the most common cause of memory leaks when programming in Flex is the use of event listeners without proper care.

Understanding leaks caused by event listeners

In Lesson 9, "Using Custom Events," you learned about the addEventListener() method, which allows you to programmatically listen to an event being broadcast. We need to dive a little deeper into this concept and develop a high-level model of this functionality to understand its implications to garbage collection.

Objects that wish to be notified when an event occurs register themselves as listeners. They do this by calling the addEventListener() method on the object that broadcasts the event (called the broadcaster or dispatcher). The following example shows a simple case:

```
var textInput:TextInput = new TextInput();
textInput.addEventListener('change', handleTextChanged);
```

In this case, the TextInput is expected to broadcast an event named change at some point in the future, and you want the handleTextChanged method to be called when this occurs. When you call addEventListener() on the TextInput instance, it responds by adding a reference to the object (the one that contains the handleTextChanged method) to a list of objects that need to be notified when this event occurs. When it is time to broadcast the change event, the TextInput instance loops through this list and notifies each object that registered as a listener.

In memory this looks something like this:

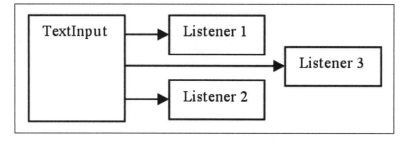

The important thing to take away from this discussion is that each object that broadcasts an event maintains a reference to every object listening for the event to be broadcast. In terms of garbage collection this means that, in certain circumstances, if an object is listening for events, it may never be available for garbage collection.

> ✴ **NOTE:** For more information on event dispatching, please refer to the IEventDispatcher inter-
> face in the Flex 3 livedocs.

Your main weapon to combat this problem is diligence. Much like any child that is added with addChild() can be removed with removeChild(), addEventListener() has a parallel function named removeEventListener() that stops listening for an event. When removeEventListener() is called, it also removes the reference to the listener kept by the broadcaster, potentially free-ing up the listener for garbage collection.

In an ideal world, the number of addEventListener() and removeEventListener() calls in your application should be equal. However, there are times when you have less control over when objects are no longer needed and using removeEventListener() is simply not feasible. Shortly, you will see an example of a situation similar to this in the test application for this lesson. In these situations, we can use a concept called *weak references*.

Using weak references with listeners

Weak references, like most of the items in this lesson, are an advanced topic that requires quite a bit of understanding to use correctly. Instead of covering this topic completely, we will explain the high-level portions that are important in this context.

When adding an event listener to a broadcaster, the developer can specify that the event lis-tener should use weak references. This is accomplished by specifying extra parameters to the addEventListener() method.

```
var textInput:TextInput = new TextInput();
textInput.addEventListener('change', handleTextChanged, false, 0, true);
```

Previously, you were taught to use the first two parameters of the addEventListener() method: the name of the event and the method to call when the event occurs. However, there are three other parameters that can be specified. In order, these parameters specify whether the event listener should use capture, its priority relative to other listeners for this event, and finally whether weak references should be used. The first two are beyond the scope of this lesson, but the last one is critical to garbage collection.

 NOTE: For more information on the other addEventListener arguments, please refer to "Registering event handlers" in Flex 3 programming elements.

Specifying a value of true (the default is false) for the fifth parameter of the addEventListener() method specifies that the reference established by this listener is to be considered weak. All the references that we have discussed so far in this lesson are considered strong references, which we will simply say are references considered by the Garbage Collector when deciding if an object is available for collection. Conversely, weak references are ignored by the Garbage Collector, meaning that an object with only weak references will be collected.

As a more concrete example, if an object had a strong reference and three weak references to it, it could not be collected as garbage. However, if the strong reference was removed, the weak references would be ignored and the object could be collected.

In practice, this means that specifying the weak reference flag on addEventListener() calls is almost always a good practice. It prevents the case where listening to an event is the only reason that an object is not collected.

Memory Profiling a Flex Application

Memory profiling involves examining the memory used, as well as the memory currently in use, by objects in your application. Those objects could be simple classes, like Strings, or complex visual objects, like DataGrids. Using memory profiling, you can determine if an appropriate number of your objects exist and if those objects are using an appropriate amount of memory.

Reviewing the ProfilerTest Application

In this exercise you will use a new sample project that has been poorly designed with memory leaks and performance issues. Using the Flex Builder Profiler, you will learn the basic interface and identify a memory leak caused by an event listener issue. You will then fix the issue and verify the results with the Profiler.

1 Choose File > New > Flex Project. Set the Project name to be **ProfilerTest**.

2 Set the Project location to be flex3tfs/Lesson26/profiler/start.

3 For the Application type select Web application.

4 Set the Server technology to None, and then click Next.

5 Leave the Output folder as bin-debug, and then click Next.

6 Leave the Main source folder as src.

7 Click the Browse button for the Main application file, select ProfilerTest.mxml, and then click OK.

8 Click Finish.

You have now created a project to run the application for profiling practice.

9 Run the ProfilerTest.mxml application.

10 Click one of the categories on the left and the products should appear on the right.

11 Now click the Toggle View Only button below the categories.

The Add to Cart button in each of the products should toggle between visible and hidden as you click this button.

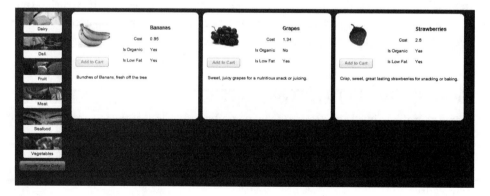

12 Click several more categories.

Note the momentary pause that occurs each time you click a category before the new products display on screen.

13 Close the browser, and return to Flex Builder.

14 Open the src/managers/UpdateManager.as file, src/component/ImageDisplay.mxml file, and src/ProfilerTest.mxml file inside of Flex Builder.

At this point, you know enough Flex and ActionScript to look through this code on your own. Here is a brief high-level description of the code and the interaction of the objects. Using this description, review the code and ensure you can identify all of the major points.

UpdateManager.as

Sometimes you want to ensure that only one instance of a specific object exists in an application. For example, there can only be one `<mx:Application>` tag in any Flex application. The UpdateManager is one of these objects. We want to ensure that we create just one UpdateManager and that every other object in the system uses this single instance, so it follows a specific design pattern called the singleton pattern. The details of this pattern and how it works are inconsequential to this lesson. It is just important to understand that there will only be one UpdateManager in the entire application at any time.

The UpdateManager's job is to broadcast an event called `toggleViewOnly` to its listeners whenever the UpdateManager's `toggleViewOnly()` method is called.

ImageDisplay.mxml

This class defines each of the boxes that display product information on the right side of the screen. It displays critical information, such as the product name and price, and defines the Add to Cart button, which is initially hidden.

Each ImageDisplay has a bindable public property called `product`, which contains information about the product being displayed. It also listens to the UpdateManager's `toggleViewOnly` event and responds by changing the visible state of the Add to Cart button.

ProfilerTest.mxml

This is the main application for your profiling tasks. It has a VBox with images for each category of food product on the left side and a repeater tag that displays several ImageDisplay instances dependent upon the selected category.

When a category image is clicked, the `handleNavClick()` method is called and passed the name of the category. The `handleNavClick()` method constructs a filename based upon the category and calls `loadNewXMLData` to load that XML file using an HTTPService. If the data loads successfully, the result is passed to the `dataProvider` of the repeater, which creates the appropriate number of ImageDisplay instances and passes each instance their data via the public product `property`.

When the Toggle View Only button is clicked, the `toggleViewOnly()` method of the updateManager is called to notify its listeners.

Profiling the ProfilerTest Application

In this exercise, you will use the memory profiling capabilities of the Flex Profiler to identify a memory leak in the ProfilerTest application. You will capture and review memory snapshots, identify reference relationships between objects, and determine the object responsible for the memory leak.

1 Click the Profile Application button (immediately to the right of the debug button).

The application begins launching, but focus will then be given back to the Flex Builder window and a Configure Profiler window will appear.

2 Ensure that "Enable memory profiling" and both "Watch live memory data" and "Generate object allocation stack traces" are selected.

Memory profiling will drastically slow down your application as it collects a significant amount of data about when, where, and how often objects are created. These options should only be selected when attempting to diagnose a memory leak or verify that a leak does not exist.

Fx Connection Established ✕

Configure Profiler

The profiling session is suspended. Configure the profiler settings before continuing.

Connected from:
    localhost

Application:
    file://C:\flex3tfs\Lesson26\profiler\start\bin-debug\ProfilerTest.swf

☑ Enable memory profiling
    ☑ Watch live memory data
    ☑ Generate object allocation stack traces
☑ Enable performance profiling

⑦   Resume | Suspend

3 Click Resume. The Eclipse perspective changes to Flex Profiling.

4 The Profiling perspective begins displaying information regarding memory usage, cumulative and current object instances, as well as cumulative and current memory use for each object type.

The upper-left corner of the screen shows the application currently being profiled. This area also shows memory snapshots, a concept you will explore shortly, and several icons on the upper right that you will learn to use.

The upper-right corner shows a graph of current memory usage along with peak memory usage. One clear indicator of a memory leak in an application is that the memory never truly peaks. If your application continues to grow with continued use over time, you likely have a memory leak.

The bottom of the screen currently contains a view called Live Objects. This view shows the class, package, and cumulative and current instances of each object type, as well as the cumulative and current memory used by those objects.

On the right side of the screen at the same level as the Live Objects tab, you will see a series of icons that you will explore shortly.

5 Switch to your web browser running the ProfilerTest application, and click the Dairy category.

With the memory profiling enabled, the entire application moves much more slowly than before.

6 Once the products from the dairy category appear on the right, switch back to Flex Builder and look at Live Objects view. You should now see the ImageDisplay class listed in the left-most column. The cumulative instances and the instances should both say 3.

When you clicked on the Dairy category, the application created a new HTTPService and loaded XML data for this category. The data was then passed to the repeater's `dataProvider` property, which created an instance of the ImageDisplay for each product in the category.

The Cumulative Instances column shows the total number of times this class has been instantiated since the application started. The Instances column shows the number of instances that are still in memory at this time. The difference between the Cumulative and Instances column is the number of instances that have been garbage collected at some point.

7 Click through each of the other categories in the application to display the products contained within them. Switch back to the Flex Profiler and view the instance information for the ImageDisplay class.

The ImageDisplay class will now show 18 cumulative and current instances. This indicates that none of these instances have been garbage collected yet. This could indicate a memory leak.

8 Directly above the column named Memory in the Live Objects grid, there are a series of icons arranged horizontally. The first of these icons causes the Garbage Collector to execute immediately. Click this icon now.

As mentioned in the earlier section, garbage collection runs automatically during allocation; however, it is difficult for the developer to understand precisely when garbage collection last ran. The Flex Profiler gives you the ability to run garbage collection as needed.

9 Review the cumulative and current instances for the ImageDisplay class again.

The number of instances is now 18. As you just forcibly ran garbage collection, and there are only three ImageDisplay instances displayed on the screen currently, it now seems certain that there is a problem. ImageDisplay instances that are no longer used are not being garbage collected. As you know from the earlier sections of this lesson, the only thing that would prevent garbage collection is a remaining reference to these ImageDisplay instances.

10 Click the icon immediately to the right of the garbage collection icon to take a memory snapshot.

A memory snapshot saves the current state of the memory at the moment you click the snapshot button. The snapshot does not update the Live Object view, but allows you to analyze the memory in a much deeper way.

11 Double-click the words Memory Snapshot underneath your running application in the upper-left corner of the window.

After analyzing the data, a new tab opens next to the Live Object tab with the snapshot information. It is possible to take multiple snapshots and even save this data for review as you attempt to resolve problems within your application. The following figure shows the results of a new memory snapshot.

NOTE: When you a take a memory snapshot, the Flex Profiler implicitly runs garbage collection first. Clicking the memory snapshot icon is the same as clicking Run garbage collection and then Memory Snapshot.

12 Inside the Memory Snapshot tab, double-click the ImageDisplay class.

You see 18 separate listings for each of the ImageDisplay objects in memory when this snapshot was taken, each with a number in parentheses. The number in parentheses is the total number of references to the current object.

13 Click the first component:ImageDisplay label.

The right side of the screen shows the Allocation trace. This information shows where in the program flow this object was first created. In this case, you see that this particular object was created in a method in Container.as, which was called from Repeater.as, which was called from ProfilerTest.mxml. The line number of each of these calls is also recorded.

At this point, you know that the object was created because of the Repeater call, which is correct, but you do not know which other object has a reference that is preventing this object from being garbage collected.

14 Click the tree open indicator next to the component:ImageDisplay label.

This causes the tree to expand and show all objects in the system that contain references to the current object and the property name within that object that holds the reference. This list can be extensive. As we discussed, there are many circular references between parent and child that are not factors during the mark and sweep phase of garbage collection; so, we are looking for items here that could still be a factor.

At this point, we will make an assumption. Although there may be memory leaks in the code written and provided by Adobe, it is unlikely that you will be able to do much about those. The memory leak you are seeing involves objects written in your code. Therefore, to limit the scope of information we need to search, we are going to focus on things outside of the Adobe-provided Flex framework. In other words, you will ignore any objects that exist in the mx.* path.

15 You will be focusing your search for references on the remaining items. Open each of the subitems labeled Function, and examine the children of these references.

Most of the children will say components:ImageDisplay. These references exist mainly as a result of data binding; however, these are not of particular interest as we know the Garbage Collector can handle circular references. You should also quickly find a listing for managers:UpdateManager and a property of [listener0]. This one is important.

Instance	Property	ID
▷ mx.core:UITextField (4)	mx.core:UITextField:_doc...	73826
▷ mx.controls:HScrollBar (17)	http://www.adobe.com/...	73604
▷ mx.core:UITextField (4)	mx.core:UITextField:_doc...	75511
◢ Function (2)	[savedThis]	61451
▷ managers:UpdateManager (20)	[listener0]	41027
component:ImageDisplay	component:ImageDispla...	48922
▷ mx.controls:FormItemLabel (8)	http://www.adobe.com/...	50221
▷ mx.core:UITextField (5)	mx.core:UITextField:_doc...	50699
▷ mx.core:UITextField (4)	mx.core:UITextField:_doc...	75117
▷ mx.binding:Binding (5)	http://www.adobe.com/...	49115
▷ mx.core:UITextField (4)	mx.core:UITextField:_doc...	50550
◢ Function (2)	[savedThis]	48950
component:ImageDisplay	mx.core:UIComponent:a...	48922
component:ImageDisplay	[listener0]	48922
▷ mx.core:UITextField (4)	mx.core:UITextField:_doc...	58066
▷ mx.controls:Label (9)	http://www.adobe.com/...	50856
▷ mx.containers:Form (10)	http://www.adobe.com/...	49751
▷ mx.core:UIComponentDescriptor (2)	document	49387
▷ mx.controls:VScrollBar (17)	http://www.adobe.com/...	74921

16 Examine several of the other ImageDisplay class instances.

Each will show a similar result with a reference from UpdateManager.

17 Terminate this profiling session by either choosing it in the upper-left corner of the screen and clicking the Stop button or simply closing your web browser.

18 We do not intend to save the results; so once this session is terminated, click the red X to remove the session information.

At this point you know that the UpdateManager has a reference to each of the ImageDisplay classes. The profiler also gave you the clue that this reference was due to an event listener. Using this information, you should be able to quickly find the issue.

Fixing the ImageDisplay Class

In this exercise, you will fix the memory leak identified in the previous exercise by modifying the event listener to use weak references.

Switch back to the Flex Development perspective in Flex Builder.

1 Open the ImageDisplay.mxml class.

2 Find the code that adds an event listener to the UpdateManager instance. It is on line 17.

If you review the remainder of the code in this class, you will note that there is no removeEventListener() call. As was noted earlier, ideally the number of addEventListener() calls should match the number of removeEventListener() calls. In this case, we have limited control and understanding of when our class is no longer needed, so we are going to opt for making the addEventListener() call use weak references.

3 Change the code that adds the event listener to use weak references. The new line of code should read as follows:

```
updateManager.addEventListener('toggleViewOnly',
handleViewOnlyChanged, false, 0, true);
```

The reference in the UpdateManager instance created for each ImageDisplay will no longer count during garbage collection.

4 Save ImageDisplay.as.

5 Profile your application again using the same setting as before.

6 Once the application has launched, click each of the product categories to see all of the products.

7 Return to Flex Builder and click the Run Garbage Collector icon.

The Live Objects view should now show 18 cumulative instances but only three current instances, meaning the other 15 have been garbage collected and this memory leak has been fixed.

This section merely touched upon the power of the memory Profiler. For more information, read "Using the Profiler" in the Flex Builder 3 documentation provided by Adobe.

Performance Profiling a Flex Application

Performance profiling is used to find aspects of your application that are not responsive or where performance can be improved. When profiling for performance, you are generally looking for methods that are executed very frequently or methods that take a long period of time each time they are executed. The combination of those two factors usually provides a good indication of where your time should be spent optimizing or potentially refactoring.

In this exercise, you will use the same poorly designed sample project. Although you have already fixed the major memory issue, the performance issues remain. Using the Flex Builder Profiler, you will identify one of the slowest portions of the application and optimize it. You will then verify the results with the Profiler.

Profiling the ProfilerTest Application

In this exercise, you will use the performance profiling capabilities of the Flex Profiler to identify the methods and objects responsible for the slow response of the ProfilerTest application. You will capture a performance profile and review it to identify methods taking a disproportionate amount of time to execute.

1 Click the Profile Application button (immediately to the right of the Debug button).

The application begins launching, but focus will then be given back to the Flex Builder window and a Configure Profiler window will appear.

2 Ensure that only "Enable performance profiling" is selected.

3 Click Resume and the Eclipse perspective changes to Flex Profiling.

The Profiling perspective when only capturing performance metrics is rather boring. Nothing will actually happen here until we are ready to dive into performance profiles.

4 Select the running application, and click the icon that looks like an eraser. This resets the performance statistics.

In this case, we are not trying to gauge start-up time, so we are resetting our performance statistics after the application has started but before we interact with it.

5 Switch to your web browser and navigate through each of the six product categories.

Be sure to wait for the previous category to load before clicking on the next.

6 Switch back to the Flex Profiler and select the running application.

7 Click the icon with a clock and a pair of glasses to capture a performance profile.

A performance profile will appear under the running application, much as the memory profile did in the previous section.

8 Click the red stop icon to stop profiling the running application, then close your web browser.

9 Double-click the performance profile to open the Performance Profile view.

The Performance Profile view shows the method and package along with other crucial information.

- **Calls**: The number of calls to this method during the capture

- **Cumulative time**: The cumulative time spent in the calls to this method and any subsequent methods called within this method

- **Self Time**: The cumulative time spent in this method, but not subsequent method calls within this method

- **Avg. Cumulative and Avg. Self**: The averages of each of the previous time types

✳ **NOTE:** Within the Methods column, there is a lot of additional information, including many items in square brackets. We can't dive into the level of detail here to address each of these, so for additional information read the section entitled "About Profiling" in the Adobe help documentation.

10 Click the Cumulative Time column to sort from longest to shortest.

Method	Package (Filtered)	Calls	Cumulative Time...	Self Time (ms)
[io]		0 (0.0%)	629 (29.49%)	9 (0.42%)
DirectHTTPMessageResponder.completeHandler		6 (0.0%)	608 (28.5%)	0 (0.0%)
ProfilerTest.handleDataResult		6 (0.0%)	598 (28.04%)	0 (0.0%)
ImageDisplay.initialize	component	18 (0.0%)	502 (23.53%)	0 (0.0%)
[mouseEvent]		0 (0.0%)	322 (15.1%)	285 (13.36%)
[enterFrameEvent]		0 (0.0%)	160 (7.5%)	10 (0.47%)
[mark]		0 (0.0%)	101 (4.74%)	96 (4.5%)
<anonymous>		0 (0.0%)	95 (4.45%)	20 (0.94%)

file:///C:/flex3tfs/Lesson26/profiler/start/bin-debug/ProfilerTest.swf (Sun Feb 10 19:11:31 CST 2008 - Sun Feb 10 19:11:52 CST 2008)

The top three items are the completeHandler for the HTTP Response, the handleDataResult method of ProfilerTest and the ImageDisplay's initialize method. However, the Self Time for each of these methods is almost nonexistent. The returned data from the server causes the application to create a new instance of the ImageDisplay class, which is far from optimized. So, it would seem that creating those ImageDisplay classes is where all of your performance loss occurs.

Fixing the ProfilerTest Class

In this exercise, you will address the source of the largest performance issue identified in the last exercise, creation of ImageDisplay instances. You will use a property of the Repeater class to limit object recreation and significantly increase the responsiveness of the application.

1 Switch back to the Flex Development perspective in Flex Builder.

2 Open the ProfilerTest.mxml class.

3 Find the repeater in the application on line 65.

4 Repeaters have a property called `recycleChildren`. Set it to `true`.

When set to `true`, the repeater reuses the children it already created instead of creating new ones. As you saw in the previous example, right now you create three new children every time you click a category. Reusing those children will save a significant amount of time.

5 Save the ProfilerTest.mxml file, and reprofile your application, using the steps in the previous exercise.

You will see a significant reduction in time for these methods and an increase in performance.

Ultimately, performance profiling is about optimizing the items that cost the most amount of time. It is an iterative process that continues until the application performs as required.

The ProfilerTest application can be optimized significantly further. Right now, it is extremely slow laying out and organizing its children, and lacks any intelligence when reloading data that has already been loaded once. Continuing to optimize an application like this is a great exercise to learn these tools.

What You Have Learned

In this lesson, you have:

- Learned about memory allocation and garbage collection (pages 632–639)
- Profiled a Flex application for memory and performance (pages 639–641)
- Identified a memory leaks within the application (pages 642–648)
- Identified a performance problem (pages 648–651)

This appendix contains the requirements and instructions for you to complete the exercises in this book. It covers the following:

- Hardware requirements
- Software requirements
- Software installation

Hardware Requirements

Windows

- Intel Pentium 4 processor or equivalent
- 1 GB of RAM recommended
- 750 MB of available hard disk space to install

Macintosh

- G4 1.25 GHz PowerPC or Intel-based Mac
- 1 GB of RAM recommended
- 750 MB of available hard-disk space to install

Software Requirements

- Microsoft Windows XP (with Service Pack 2) or Microsoft Vista Home Premium or higher or OS X 10.4.7 through 10.4.10, OS X 10.5.x
- Java Virtual Machine:
  - Windows: Sun JRE 1.4.2, 1.5, or 1.6, IBM JRE 1.5
  - Macintosh: JRE 1.5 or JRE 1.6 from Apple
- For the Flex Builder plug-in, Eclipse 3.2.2 or higher is required
- A recent version of one of the following browsers:
  - Internet Explorer
  - Mozilla Firefox
  - Safari
  - Netscape Navigator
  - Opera

✸ NOTE: Due to security constraints, History Management does not work in Internet Explorer when previewing a local file, meaning that it does not work when previewing local files on your hard drive. However, it will work if the file is on a web server or accessed through an HTTP URL as opposed to the file:// URL that is used during normal development. If you are using Internet Explorer you will need to preview these files from a web server. History Management does work in Firefox and Netscape browsers when previewing a local file.

- The latest version of Adobe Flash Player, or at least version 9.0.30 (During the installation of Flex Builder 3 your Flash Player will be upgraded to an appropriate version of 9.)

➤ TIP: To check your Flash Player version, go to www.adobe.com, right-click the main ad banner, and select About Macromedia Flash Player; or go to www.adobe.com/software/flash/about.

Software Installation

There are two phases of the installation:

- Installing Flex Builder
- Installing lesson files

APPENDIX A

Setup Instructions

Be sure to complete the installation of all required files before working through the lessons within the book.

Installing Flex Builder

If you do not yet have Flex Builder 3 installed, step through the following directions for installation.

1 Browse to the URL www.adobe.com/products/flex, and click the Download Free Trial link.

2 Download Flex Builder 3 for your operating system.

3 Install Flex Builder 3, accepting all the default options. The trial period on Flex Builder 3 is 60 days.

Installing Lesson Files

Once again, it is important that all the required files are in place before working though the lessons within the book.

1 From the CD included with your book, copy the flex3tfs directory to the root of your drive.

In this directory, there is a subdirectory named flexGrocer, in which you will be doing most of your work. Also included are directories for each lesson in the book with starting code and completed code for the work you do in the lesson.

Installing the ColdFusion Server

Windows

1 Navigate to the Windows directory on the CD provided with the book.

2 Uncompress the cfusionFlexTFS.zip directly to the root of your drive.

Macintosh

1 Navigate to the Mac directory on the CD provided with the book.

2 Uncompress the cfusionFlexTFS.zip directly to the root of your drive.

All files are uncompressed to a directory named cfusionFlexTFS. This is a fully configured version of ColdFusion Developer Edition along with necessary server files for Lessons 17 and above. The files directly related to this book are located in *driveroot:*/cfusionFlexTFS/servers/cfusion/cfusion-ear/cfusion-war/flexGrocer.

✱ NOTE: The server code for this book relies upon the files and directory structure created during the installation process described. If you install the files in a location other than the default, you must update the path information of two files within the ColdFusion server: fileUpload.cfm on line 2 and ProductManager.cfc on line 125, both originally located at /cfusionFlexTFS/servers/ cfusion/cfusion-ear/cfusion-war/flexGrocer/cfcs, with your modified installation directories. You will also need to use your new installation path in the section "Update Flex Compiler Command" of Lesson 18, "Accessing Server-Side Objects."

Starting the ColdFusion Server

1 To ensure that the installation worked correctly, start the configured ColdFusion server by opening another console window (DOS Command prompt), moving to the *driveroot:*/ cfusionFlexTFS/bin directory, entering **jrun –start cfusion** (**./jrun –start cfusion** on the Mac) and pressing enter. Be sure that ColdFusion starts and that no errors are shown.

2 To stop the service, press Ctrl+C or close the console window. To restart the service, if you are still in the console, just press the up arrow and it will bring back to the prompt the previously typed entries.

Starting in Lesson 17, ColdFusion needs to be running to complete the exercises in the lessons.

Installing Flash Debug Player

At various times in the book, you will be using features of Flash Debug Player. If you happen to receive a notice saying you do not have Flash Debug Player installed, follow these steps to install it:

Windows

1 Locate the player install directory:
applicationInstallDirectory/Adobe/Flex Builder 3/Player/win.

✱ NOTE: In a default installation this directory is:
Windows: C:\Program Files\Adobe\Flex Builder 3\Player\win.

2 To install Flash Debug Player for Internet Explorer, run the program Install Flash Player 9 ActiveX.exe. For other versions of web browsers, run the program Install Flash Player 9 Plugin.exe.

Macintosh

1 Locate the player install directory:
applicationInstallDirectory/Adobe Flex Builder 3/Player/mac.

✱ NOTE: In a default installation this directory would be:
/Applications/Adobe Flex Builder 3/Player/mac.

2 To install Flash Debug Player, run the program Flash Player 9 Silent Installer.

▶ TIP: In rare instances, you might run the appropriate installer and still get the message that you don't have the debug version of the player. In this case, uninstall the version you currently have by using the information located at the following URL: http://kb.adobe.com/selfservice/viewContent.do?externalId=tn_14157.

Index

A

absolute layout, 20, 33
absolute positioning, 53
acceptDragDrop() method, 337, 341
Accordion container, 394, 397
Action Message Format (AMF), 448, 474, 481–482
ActionScript, 11
  building user forms, 84
  components, 256–277, 258, 258–261, 261–267, 268–269, 269–270, 270–276
  custom classes, 101–106, 106–109, 108, 109–113
  displaying summary data, 312–316, 318–320
  event handling, 91–93, 96
  grouping data, 309–312
  mapping objects to server objects, 490–492
  running application, 24
  styles, 416
  web services access, 458–463
  XML class in, 129
ActionScript Virtual Machine (AVM2), 11
actualSize() method, 271
adapters, FMS, 482
Add Project button, 546, 555
Add to Cart button, 148, 224–225, 641
addaddProductEventListener() method, 466–467, 470
addChild() method, 262–267, 587, 592, 637
addChildAt() method, 263
addData() method, 335, 342
addEventListener() method, 250, 637–639, 647–648
addItem() method
  DragSource class, 338, 343
  ProductEvent class, 249
  ShoppingCart class, 111–113, 147–148, 150
  ShoppingCartItem class, 153, 159, 606

addItem(object) method, ArrayCollection, 127–128
addItemAt() method, 125, 127
addObject() method, 580–581, 584, 587, 589–591, 593
AddProduct component, 196, 243–244, 352–353, 382–386, 476
addProduct() function, 462–463, 467
addProductFault() method, 461–462, 466
addProductResult() method, 461, 467
AddressValidator class, 387–391
addToCart() method
  ArrayCollection class, 146
  passing product to, 226–228
  ProductEvent class, 247–249
  ShoppingCart class, 112–113
  ViewStack class, 357
addtoTextArea event handler, 92–93
Adobe
  Authorized Training Partner program, xxiii
  Flash Debug Player, 656
  Flash Platform. see Flash Platform
  Flash Player. see Flash Player
  Flash Remoting, 448
  importing skins created in CS3, 434–437
Adobe Flex 3 Language Reference (ASDocs), 180, 413
Adobe Integrated Runtime (AIR), 550–552
ADT command-line tool, 561
AdvancedDataGrid control
  custom styles, 302–306
  grouping data, 306–312
  sorting, 299–302
  summary information, 312–320
AdvancedDataGridColumn
  inline editing control, 289–290
  inline MXML item renderer, 290–297
  overview of, 287–289
  set and get functions, 298–299

AIR (Adobe Integrated Runtime), 550–552
.air file extension, 552
.airi (Intermediate AIR file), 561
AJAX (Asynchronous JavaScript and XML), 9
alerts, 487, 492
alpha channels, 71
AMF (Action Message Format), 448, 474, 481–482
anchors, in deep linking, 403
animations, 525–526, 568–570
annotationElements, charts, 502
Application containers, 40, 268–269
Application object, creationComplete, 94
application property, 227
ApplicationControlBar container, 40–42, 210, 268–269, 422
applications
  appearance. see layouts; skins; styles
  loosely coupled, 70, 169, 233
  running, 23–29
  tightly coupled, 233
AreaChart control, 504
AreaSeries class, 504
AreaSet class, 504
ArrayCollection class
  addItem(), 127–128
  addItemAt(), 125, 127
  createCursor() method, 152, 155–157
  data binding, 135, 145–146, 152
  getItemAt(), 603
  sorting items in, 148–150
  using arrays vs., 122
  using cursors, 152–160
  web service results, 453
  XML data, 122–125, 141–145
arrays, in CSS, 428
ASDOC (Adobe Flex 3 Language Reference), 180, 413
assets, adding, 545–546
Asynchronous JavaScript and XML (AJAX), 9
attribute operator (@), 133
attributes, 130

AVM2 (ActionScript Virtual
    Machine), 11
axes, limiting labels shown on,
    518–519
Axis class, 502, 510–511
AxisRenderer class, 502, 518–519

B
back() function, 369
backgroundColor style, 27, 417
background-color style, CSS,
    417, 421–422
backgroundElements, charts, 502
backgroundImage style, 27, 438
backgroundSize style, 27
BarChart control, 504
BarSeries class, 504
BarSet class, 504
<Base state>, 55, 57, 75
base view state, 55, 57, 64
beginFill() method, Graphics
    class, 440
behaviors, 567–570
billingAddress property, 359,
    361, 364, 368
billingCity property, 359, 361,
    364, 368
BillingInfo component, 378–379,
    384–386, 389, 428–429
billingInfoReturn event,
    385–386, 389
billingName property, 359, 361,
    364, 368
billingState property, 359, 361,
    364, 368
billingZip property, 359, 361,
    364, 368
[Bindable] metadata tag, 103,
    105–106, 112, 282
[Bindable] property, 147
bindings. see data binding
BlazeDS, xvii
bodyDissolve behavior, 572–573
Border class, 438
borderBox style, 426
borderMetrics property, 438
bottom constraints, 47
bottomBranding property, 423
breakpoints, 120, 331, 367
    setting, 612–613, 616–619

broadcastCategoryChange()
    method, 407
broadcastCategoryEvent()
    method, 399–401, 404, 406
broadcastEvent() method,
    ProductEvent class, 243
broadcastTypeChange()
    function, 523
Browse button, 84
browse() function, 83–84, 477
BrowserManager class, 403–408
browsers
    AJAX limitations, 9
    deep linking, 403–408
    History Management. see
        History Management
    requirements for this book, 652
btStateDown property, 259,
    264–265
btStateUp property, 259, 264–265
BubbleChart control, 504
bubbles property, Event class,
    252–255
BubbleSeries class, 504
bubbling phase, event flow,
    250–255
Build Automatically option, 23–24
buildObject() method, 107
buildProduct() function,
    459–461
buildProduct() method,
    Product class, 181, 342
    building method to create
        object, 107–108
    shared objects, 605
    using web service, 461
business managers, RIA
    advantages, 7
Button class, 259
Button controls/component
    creating, 262–263
    layout, 43–44, 46
    printing receipt, 591

C
calcTotal() method, 159, 161,
    606
callLater() method, 407
CandleStickSeries class, 504
canLoadWSDL() function, 461
Canvas container
    constraints, 47–52
    dragging item from, 339–344

layout rules, 40, 42
sizing and positioning, 268–269
capture phase, event flow, 250
cardExpirationMonth property,
    359, 366
cardExpirationYear property,
    359, 366
cardNumber property, 359, 366
CardNumberSource property, 380
cardType property, 359, 366
CardTypeSource property, 380
Cart component
    adding inline editing, 289
    adding products, 225–227
    building SharedObjects, 601
    creating MXML item renderer,
        291, 293–297
    display, 287–289
    reading data from
        SharedObjects, 604–607
    styles, 427–428
Cartesian charts, 502, 504
cartFormat format, 339–342
cartGrid style class, 427
cartView state, 357
Cascading Style Sheets. see CSS
    (Cascading Style Sheets)
case-sensitivity
    CSS property syntax, 417
    MXML, 18
    state names, 57
casting objects, 180
catch blocks
    bad practice, 623–624
    creating own error classes, 628
    finally statement, 624–625,
        627–628
    multiple, 622
    single, 623
    trace statement, 621–622
catDataLoaded event, 235
categories, displaying, 207–210
categorizedProductData
    Loaded() function, 193,
    209–210, 233–234, 236, 616
CategorizedProductManager
    component
    configuring to work locally, 449
    creating, 184–191
    declaring events, 235–236
    dispatching events, 233–235
    displaying categories, 210
    overview of, 192–195
    web services, 459–460

category nodes, XML, 130
Category value object class, 182–183
CategoryAxis, 510, 512–515
CategoryEvent class, 237–241
categoryID property, 127
categorySelect() function, 216
categorySelect() method, 240, 399–400
categoryText style class, 425
CategoryView component
    adding deep linking, 403–408
    building and using CategoryEvent, 237–240
    custom History Manager, 398–402
    displaying categories, 207–210, 215–222
catHandler() method, 126–127
catID property, Category class, 182–183
catName property, Category class, 182–183
catRPC HTTP Service, 126
catSelected property, CategoryView, 215–216, 221–222
CCInfo component
    completing checkout process, 365–370
    setting styles, 414–419, 421, 429–430
    using Validator classes, 379–381
ccInfoReturn event, 366
CDATA tags, 83
<![CDATA[ ]]> block, 92
CD-ROM, accompanying book, xxi–xxii
cells, styling, 305–306
certificates, 561
channels, RemoteObject, 482
character data, displaying, 92
ChartPod component, 197–198, 266–267, 276, 281–282
charts
    animations, 525–526
    components, 500–502
    events, 520–525
    initial layout, 502–503
    interacting with, 520
    labels on axes, 518–519
    legends, 517–518
    overview of, 499

populating, 504, 504–510, 510–517
styles, 527–529
<chartType> tag, 501
CheckBox control, 83, 136–138, 289
Checkout button, 48–49, 356, 367, 369, 379, 381
Checkout component
    adding to application, 354–358
    completing checkout, 366–370
    implementing checkout process, 358–365
    mapping ActionScript to server objects, 491–492
    with RemoteObject, 485–488
    returning to welcome screen, 489
    using CheckoutModule, 533–537
    using ViewStack, 365
checkout process
    orderConfirmed event in, 484
    printing receipt, 591–595
checkOutComplete event, 485, 489
CheckoutModule, 533–537
child nodes, 130, 131
chrome, containers, 263–267
class keyword, 103
class library, 70
class selectors, CSS, 417–419, 422–423, 441–442
classes
    adding to Library Project, 545–546
    creating ActionScript components, 258–261
    naming, 108
ClassReference directive, 441
clear() method, 606
clearCart() method, 606
click events
    ActionScript functions handling, 91–92
    charts, 520
    doPrint() function, 584
    event handling and, 90–91
    Update button, 179
client/server systems, 4
clone() method, Event class, 237, 239, 242
close event, 176

code hinting, 25–26, 91, 108
coercing objects, 180
ColdFusion server
    configuring to work locally, 448–450
    installing, 655
    setup instructions, 448
    starting, 655
    using web services, 450–463
    WSDL Introspection wizard and, 463–465
collections, 123–125. see also ArrayCollection class
Color style property, 413
color, chart, 527–529
ColumnChart control, 503–505, 509–510, 515–516
columns
    AdvancedDataGrid, 299–303
    ColumnChart control. see ColumnChart control
    DataGrid. see DataGridColumn
ColumnSeries class, 504, 509–510
ColumnSet class, 504
columnSpan property, 317
ComboBox control
    calling web service methods, 456–457
    dataProvider property, 123, 380
    layout, 82
    populating, 125–128
    setting in ApplicationControlBar, 275, 524
    setting styles, 414–419, 422
commitProperties() method, 262
Common Object Request Broker Architecture (CORBA), 447
ComparisonChart component, 503, 509–510, 515–519
Compile to SWF option, 432
compiler arguments, 101
compilers, choosing, 17–18
COMPLETE event, 476–477
Complete Order button, 370
completeCheckOut() function, 488, 491
completeHandler() function, 478
complex controls, 70

components. *see also* MXML custom components; skins
ActionScript 3.0, 256–277, 258, 258–261, 261–267, 268–269, 269–270, 270–276
behaviors, 568–570
effects, 574–575
History Management for, 395
printable view in separate, 585–588
Components view, 31, 41–42, 71–72
compRPCResult() method, 284, 455
computer applications, evolution of, 4–6
ConfirmScreen object, 180–181, 244
constants, FlexPrintJobScaleType class, 589
constraint-based layouts, 47–54
ConstraintColumn class, 52–54
ConstraintRow class, 52–54
constructors, 102, 104, 110, 242
Container class, 262, 264, 535, 587
containers
  assigning width, 61–62
  chrome, 263–264
  layout area, 263–264
  layout rules for children, 40
  sizing and positioning, 268–269
  using constraints, 47–54
Continue button, 369, 381
ControlBar container, 40, 60–62, 266–267, 282. *see also* ApplicationControlBar container
controller, MVC architecture, 170
controls
  complex, 70
  simple, 69–87, 70–71, 71–74, 75–78, 78–80, 80–85, 85–87
Controls folder, 30
cookies, 7
copyright constraints, 49
CORBA (Common Object Request Broker Architecture), 447
cost property, 104–105
Create Self-Signed Digital Certificate window, 561
createChildren() method, overriding, 262–267

createCursor() method, ArrayCollection class, 152, 155–157
createPopUp() method, 176, 180
creationComplete event
  building data structure, 93–96
  creating data manager, 185
  deep linking, 405
  grouping data, 311
  HTTPService calls, 285–286
  populating controls, 126, 136
  retrieving XML data, 120
Creative Suite (Adobe CS3), 434–437
credit card information form, 365–370
CreditCardValidator class, 374, 380–381
cross-domain policy files, 119, 464
CS3 (Adobe Creative Suite), 434–437
CSS (Cascading Style Sheets)
  with AxisRenderer, 502
  changing at runtime, 431–433
  Flex Builder 3 tools for, 419–421
  inheritance, 416
  setting styles, 417–419, 421–431
  specifying arrays, 428
  using standards, 413
Cumulative Instances column, 644
Cumulative Time column, 650
curly brackets ({ }), 79–80, 91
CurrencyFormatter class, 374, 375–378
current property, cursor, 157
currentIndex property, Repeater component, 211–212
currentItem property, Repeater component, 211–212
currentState property, 57, 66, 75
cursor property, ArrayCollection class, 152–160
cursors, working with, 152–160

D

Dashboard application
  adding HTTPService calls, 283–286
  adding radio buttons and date fields, 85–87
  configuring to work locally, 449
  creating/using components, 184–191, 195–196

customizing with application. xml file, 557–559
in Design mode, 30–35
populating ComboBox control, 125–128
in Source mode, 59–62
turning into AIR application, 556–557
using view states, 64–66
web services in, 450–458
DashboardDesktop directory, 553–554
data binding
  assigning values to properties, 91
  curly brackets, 79–80
  data structures, 78–80, 145–146
  Text controls, 71
data manager, 184–195
data property, 362, 599, 602
data transfer objects (DTOs), 101–106
data visualization. *see* charts
data wizards, 492–497
DataEntry application, 18, 24–35
  configuring locally, 449
  data manager, 191–195
  FileUpload component, 480–481
  Form layout container, 81–85
  History Management, 397
  web services, 458–463
dataField attribute, DataGrid, 287–289
dataForFormat() method, 330–331, 336, 338, 342
DataGrid control
  AdvancedDataGrid. *see* AdvancedDataGrid control
  columns in, 282
  dataProvider property, 123
  displaying dataset via, 281–282
  displaying shopping cart, 287–299
  drag and drop support, 325–332
  with item renderer, 290–297
  PrintDataGrid subclass, 582–585
  reading data from SharedObjects, 604
  retrieving data from HTTPService, 283–286
DataGridColumn, 287–299
dataProvider property, 128, 202, 207–208, 217

datasets, 201–228
　displaying categories, 207–210
　displaying product details using
　　state, 223–225
　HorizontalList component,
　　203–204
　itemRenderer, 205–206
　labelFunction, 204–205
　overview of, 202–203
　Repeater component, 211–215,
　　215–222
　shopping cart functionality,
　　225–228
　TileList component, 203–204
DataSource object, 330
dataTipFunction attribute,
　charts, 520, 522–523
Date class, 359
date fields, 86
Date object, 285
DateChooser control, 361, 547
DateField control, 361
DateFormatter class, 374, 377–378
dates, charts, 511–516
DateTimeAxis, 511, 512
DateValidator class, 374
debugging, 608–629
　inspecting values of variables,
　　613–619
　overview of, 610
　setting breakpoints, 612–613
　terminating session after, 100
　using try-catch. see try-
　　catch statements
　watching client/server data
　　exchange, 610–611
Debugging perspective
　defined, 22
　setting breakpoints, 612–613
　switching between
　　perspectives, 22, 100
　viewing, 99–100, 121, 331, 615,
　　618
declarations, event, 235–236
Declared Method, WebService
　tag, 451
deep linking, 393–394, 403–408
defaultLeafIcon, 318
deferred instantiation, ViewStack,
　357
Delete/Update buttons, 175–181
deleteProd() method, 160, 247
deleteProductResult()
　method, 471

deleting products, web services,
　468–469
deliveryDate property, 359, 378
Deployment Paths grid, 543
deployment, Flex applications,
　549–564
　AIR application, 550–551,
　　551–552, 553–564
　compiling deployment version,
　　550
　getting started, 551
descendant accessor operator (..),
　134
Design mode
　in CSS, 420
　Detail view in, 75–76
　displaying images, 71–74
　layout in, 41–46
　linking to simple controls, 79
　toggling with Source mode,
　　41, 59
　using constraints in, 50–54
　viewing application in, 21
　working in, 30–35
destination handles, 482
Detail view, 75–78
Development perspective, 22, 100
DHTML (Dynamic HTML), 6–7, 9
Digests radio button, 543
digital signatures, 560–561
direction attribute, 82
direction property, 136
directory structure, 102, 167
disabledColor style property,
　413
disabledSkin attribute, 433, 439,
　441
disk space constraints, 600
dispatchEvent() method,
　233–235, 249
DisplayObject class, 272
DisplayObjectContainer class, 264
displayProdByCategory()
　function, 221–222, 573
displayProdByCategory()
　method, 240–241, 402, 627
dissolve effect, 572–573
doBillingInfoReturn()
　function, 364, 366
doCCInfoReturn() function,
　366–367, 369
doClick() function, 97
doDrag() method, 334, 336, 343
doDragDrop() function, 330–331,
　337–338, 342

doDragEnter() function, 336,
　341
doMaximize() method, 265–266
doPrint() function, 580–581,
　583, 586–588, 591–592
doProdAdd() method, 244,
　382–383
doProdDelete() method, 179,
　181
doProdUpdate() method, 179,
　180–181, 243
doRestore() method, 265–266
dot (.) operator, 131–132
doTypeChange() function, 524
doValidation() method,
　388–390
downSkin attribute, 433, 439, 441
Drag and Drop Manager, 324–325
drag and drop operations
　between DataGrid and List,
　　328–332
　to shopping cart, 339–344
　between two DataGrids,
　　325–328
　using, 323
　using Drag and Drop Manager,
　　324–325
　using nondrag-enabled
　　component, 333–339
drag initiator, 324, 329
drag proxy, Drag and Drop
　Manager, 324–325, 331
drag source, Drag and Drop
　Manager, 324
dragComplete events, 329
dragDrop events, 329, 330, 337
dragEnabled property, 325–327
dragEnter events, 329, 334,
　336–337
dragExit events, 329
draggableColumns property,
　DataGrid, 287–288
dragImage, 343–344
dragIt() function, 335, 339–340,
　342–344
DragManager class, 334, 340–344
dragOver events, 329
DragSource class
　creating object to hold data, 325
　dataForFormat(), 330–331
　dragging item, 339–344
　format property, 324
　methods, 334

using nondrag-enabled component, 333–339
viewing row data, 328
drawEllipse() method, 440
driveroot, 17
drop targets, 324–325, 328
dropEnabled property, 326–328
DTOs (data transfer objects), 101–106
dumb terminals, 4
Dynamic HTML (DHTML), 6–7, 9

E
E4X (ECMAScript for XML) operators, 129–134, 135, 141–145
Eclipse platform, 11, 652
ECMAScript for XML (E4X) operators, 129–134, 135, 141–145
EComm application, 35, 41–48, 55–59, 79–80, 169–170
editable attribute, 288–290
editorDataField attribute, 289
Effect property, Transition class, 570
effects, 569–570, 572–575
Element selectors, CSS, 417–418
EmailValidator class, 374
@Embed directive, 71, 74, 259
[Embed] metadata tag, 259–260
endFill() method, 440
enhanced constraints, 52–54
error classes, 622–624, 626–628
error handling. see try-catch statements
escape character (//), 383
EvalError class, 623
event bubbling, 250–255
Event class, 236–237, 252
Event data type, 138
event flow, 250–255
event handlers, naming, 98
event handling, 232–255
  with ActionScript functions, 91–92
  CategoryEvent class and, 237–238
  charts, 520–525
  creationComplete event, 93–96
  custom event classes, 236–237
  declaring for components, 235–236

dispatching events, 233–235
event flow and bubbling, 250–255
example of, 90–91
FileReference class, 476
overview of, 90
passing data when calling functions, 92
ProductEvent class, 241–245, 245–247, 247–249
remote server calls, 448
setting breakpoints, 612
for simple controls, 70
using data from Event object, 96–100
Event object, 96–100
[Event] metadata tag, 235–236
EventDispatcher class, 233–235
EventListeners, 637–639
expanded state, 75, 426
Export Release Build button, 550
exporting, AIR file, 559–564
Expression, Microsoft, 12
Expressions view, 614, 616
Extensible Application Markup Language (XAML), 12

F
FaultEvent, 462
fields property, Sort class, 310, 319
fileBrowse() function
  building user forms, 83–84
  creating component, 172–173
  integrating FileUpload, 480
  uploading files to server, 475, 478
FileFilter class, 476–477
FileReference class, 83–84, 475–478
FileUpload component, 475–481
fillAlphas style value, 27
fillColors style value, 27, 527–529
finally statement, 624–625, 627–628
Find Variable window, 617
findAny() method, 156
findFirst() method, 156–157
findLast() method, 156
Flash Debug Player, installing, 656
Flash Platform, 10

Flash Player
  event flow and bubbling, 250–255
  History Management, 394
  memory use, 632–639
  programmatically drawing skins, 437–443
  reading SharedObjects, 600–601
  as RIA technology, 10
  security sandbox restrictions of, 119
  software requirements for, 652
Flash Player 9 (FP9), 11
Flash Remoting, 448
Flex
  defined, 22
  early versions of, xvi
  as RIA technology, 10–11
  sizing and positioning in, 268–269
  version 2, xiv
Flex Builder 3
  creating projects, 16–20
  CSS tools for, 419–421
  data wizards, 492–497
  importing skins created in CS3, 434–437
  installing, 654
  overview of, 11
  Pro vs. Standard, xxiv, 631
  refactoring with, 468–469
  requirements, 652
  workbench, 21–23
  working with DataGridColumn, 295
Flex Compiler command, 483
Flex Debugging perspective. see Debugging perspective
Flex Development perspective, 22, 100
Flex framework, 11–12, 69, 71, 105
Flex Layout Manager, 61
Flex Module Loader, 532
Flex Modules, 533–537
Flex Properties view, 32–34, 72–73, 79–80
Flex SDK, 11, 432
/flex2gateway, 482
FlexGrocerLibrary
  creating Library Project, 544–545
  customizing application, 557–559
  turning Dashboard into AIR application, 555–557

FlexPrintJob class, 579, 580–581
FlexPrintJobScaleType class,
     589–591
flow-driven programming model,
     90
flush() method, 599, 603
Focus Manager class, 85
focusInEffect trigger, 569, 572
focusOutEffect trigger, 569, 572
fontFamily style property, 413
fontSize style property, 414
fontStyle style property, 414
fontWeight style property, 414
foodColl variable,
     UpdateDeleteProd, 172,
     174–175, 192–195
FoodList component, 216–222,
     248–249, 254–255
for each...in loop, 143–144, 186
Form containers, 80–85, 582–585
format() method, 376–378
format, Drag and Drop Manager,
     324, 330–331
formatString property,
     Formatter class, 377
Formatter classes, 374–378
FP9 (Flash Player 9). see Flash
     Player
framework RSL, 541–544
fromState property, 570, 574
fullComp state, 65
fullType state, 65
Fully Declared Method, WebService
     tag, 450

G
garbage collection, 633–639
gateway, Flex, 482
get method, 478
get quantity () function, 296
getCategorizedProducts()
     function, 190
getCategorizedProducts()
     method, 193
getCats() function, 189
getChildAt() method, 264
getChildByName() method, 272
getData() method, 284–286, 456
getExplicitOrMeasuredHeight
     () method, 271
getExplicitOrMeasuredWidth()
     method, 271

getFocus() method, Focus
     Manager, 85
getItemAt() method, 146, 159,
     603
getItemInCart() method, 150,
     154–155, 161
getLocal() method, 599, 602,
     604
getOrderInfoHeader() method,
     491–492
getProdsForCat() function, 189
getRepeaterItem() method,
     212–213
getSalesData() method, 452
getStackTrace() method, 621
getTypeSalesData() method,
     451
GIF files, 476–477
graphical skins, 434, 437
Graphics class, 437, 440
graphics property,
     ProgrammaticSkin class, 440
GroceryDetail component
     adding effects to view states,
          574–575
     adding products, 247–249
     display based on categories, 217
     dragging items, 339–344
     event bubbling, 254
     styles, 425–426
     using CurrencyFormatter,
          375–378
groceryInventory property, 220
grouping data, AdvancedDataGrid,
     306–312
Grouping object, 310
grouping property, 310
GroupingCollection class, 308,
     309–312
groupName property, 86–87
GroupWithActionScriptADG.mxml,
     309–312
GroupWithTagsADG.mxml,
     307–309

H
handleDataResult() method,
     650
handleNavClick() method, 641
handleUploadComplete()
     method, 479–480
hardware requirements, for this
     book, 651

hasFormat() function, 336–337
HBox containers, 40, 44, 50
HelloWorld application, 552–553
hideEffect trigger, 569, 572
History Management
     custom History Manager,
          398–402
     historyManagementEnabled
          property, 397
     within Navigator container,
          396–397
     overview of, 393–396
     security restraints, 627, 652
history.swf file, 394
HistoryManager class, 395,
     398–402
HLOCSeries class, 504
Homepage component, 354–358,
     424–425
homePageButton class selector,
     441–442
homePageText style class, 424
homePageTitle style class, 424
horizontal center constraints, 47
horizontal layouts, 20
horizontalAlign style values, 27
HorizontalList component
     displaying categories, 207–210
     implementing itemRenderer,
          205–206
     implementing labelFunction,
          204–205
     overview of, 203–204
horizontalScrollPolicy
     property, 208
HTML (Hypertext Markup
     Language), 6–7, 9
HTTPService class
     adding calls to Dashboard,
          283–286
     XML data retrieval, 116–122,
          122–125, 135–136
Hypertext Markup Language
     (HTML), 6–7, 9
hyphen (-), 417

I
IBrowserManager interface, 405
ICollectionView interface, 282
ICursorView interface, 152

IDs
    assigning to text controls, 70
    unique for AIR applications, 554–555
if statements, 336
if-else statements, 304–305
IFlexDisplayObject interface, 180
IFrames, 9
IHistoryManagerClient interface, 395, 398
Image class, 73, 343
Image control, 71–74
ImageDisplay class, 644–645, 647–648
ImageDisplay.mxml, 641
ImageName property, 104
import statements
    ArrayCollection, 124
    building SharedObject, 602
    creating components with, 171, 173, 184
    populating ComboBox control, 126
    transforming XML data into ArrayCollection of custom, 142
    using classes with, 105–106, 111–112
indicatorGap style, 429
inheritance, 233, 416, 422
init() method, 285, 466, 470–471
initApp() function, 405
initDG() function, 309–311, 319–320
Intermediate AIR file (.airi), 561
Internet Explorer, security constraints, 396, 627, 652
IsError property, ValidationResult, 389
isItemInCart() method, 150, 154–155
IsLowFat property, 107, 144, 224
IsOrganic property, 107, 144, 224
IT organizations, benefits of RIAs to, 8
italicized text, in this book, xxi
item renderer, MXML, 290–297
itemAdded() function, 219, 226
itemAdded() method, 248
itemEditor attribute, DataGridColumn, 289
itemRenderer property, 205–210
IViewCursor interface, 152–153

J
Java Virtual Machine, 652
Java, Remote Method Invocation, 447
JavaScript, and AJAX, 9
JPEG files, 208–209

K
keyboard shortcuts, xxi
keywords, xxi

L
Label button, 368
Label controls
    building printable view, 586
    CurrencyFormatter, 376–377
    in Design mode, 42–45
    in Detail view, 77–78
    display in categories, 217–218
    PrintDataGrid, 582–583
    Text control vs., 34
    using cursor, 159–160
label property, 81, 98, 128, 136, 148
labelField property, 123–125, 128, 137, 204
labelFunction property, 204–205, 295
labelFunctionName method, DataGrid, 295
lastResult variable, 117–118
Layout Manager, 268–269
layouts, 39–67. see also UIs (user interfaces)
    of application pages, 20
    Charting components, 502–503
    constraint-based, 47–54
    in Design mode, 41–46
    in Source mode, 59–62
    using containers, 40
    working with view states, 55–59, 63–66
left constraints, 47
legends, chart, 517–518
lesson files in this book, installing, 654
Library Project, 532, 544–547
line numbers, 23
LinearAxis, 510, 516
LineChart controls, 508–517, 520–521
LineSeries class, 504, 508, 511–512

LinkBar controls, 349–351
LinkButton controls, 51, 57–59
linkers, RSL, 539–540
List controls
    adding items as, 148
    drag and drop operations, 325, 328–332, 339–344
    populating with HTTPService data, 123–125
ListBase class, 202
Live Objects view, 643–645
LiveCycle Data Services, xiv
load event, WebService tag, 450
load() method, 343
loadCart() method, 604, 606
loadstate() method, 395–396, 400–401
loadWSDL() function, 461
Local History, 28
Local Storage dialog box, 600
LogAxis, 510
logoBottom class selector, 422
logoTop class selector, 422
loosely coupled applications, 70, 169, 233

M
Macintosh
    installing AIR, 552
    installing ColdFusion server, 655
    installing FlashDebug player, 656
    location of local shared objects, 603
    location of manifest file, 20
    system requirements, 651, 652
mainframes, 4
manageAddItem() method, 150, 153–154
manifest file, 20
mapping, 490–492
marginLeft style property, 414
marginRight style property, 414
mark and sweep, 634, 636
Maximize event, 260, 276
MaxRestorePanel class, 258–261, 264–267, 270–276
measure() method, 262, 269–270
memory
    Flash Player, 632–639
    profiling Flex application, 639–641, 642–647, 647–648

Memory Snapshot, 644–645
message boxes, Checkout component, 487
message property, 621
methods, private vs. public, 388
microcomputers, evolution of, 4
Microsoft
  Expression, 12
  Internet Explorer security constraints, 396, 627, 652
  Windows. *see* Windows
  Windows Presentation Foundation, 12
modal pop-up windows, 175–181
model-view-controller (MVC) architecture, 170, 202–203
modular applications
  Flex framework RSL caching, 540–544
  Flex Modules, 533–537
  library project, 544–547
  overview of, 532–533
  runtime shared libraries, 537–540
Module class, 534–535
ModuleLoader class, 535–537
modules directory, 533
mouseDown event, 335
mouseDownEffect trigger, 569, 572
mouseMove event, 339
mouseOver events, 75, 223, 520
mouseUpEffect trigger, 569, 572
move() method, 274
multipleSelection property, DataGrid, 331
MVC (model-view-controller) architecture, 170, 202–203
mx.collections.ICollectionView class, 282
mx.core.Application class, 227
<mx:AddChild> tag, 63–64, 76, 224–225, 426
<mx:AdvancedDataGrid> tag, 303–305, 307–309, 311
<mx:AdvancedDataGridColumn> tag, 303
<mx:AdvancedDataGridRenderer Provider> tag, 317
<mx:Application> tag, 19, 27, 35, 79–80
<mx:ApplicationControlBar> tag, 60, 66, 85
<mx:AxisRenderer> tag, 519

<mx:Button> tag, 294, 296, 601
<mx:Canvas> tag, 223, 339–344
<mx:cellRenderer> tag, 292
<mx:ChartPod> tag, 276
<mx:CheckBox> tag, 136
<mx:ColumnChart> tag, 503, 515–518
<mx:ColumnSeries> tag, 518
<mx:ComboBox> tag, 128
<mx:Component> tag, 292
<mx:ControlBar> tag, 197, 266
<mx:CreditCardValidator> tag, 380–381
<mx:CurrencyFormatter> tag, 375–378
<mx:DataGrid> tag, 282, 287–288, 292, 427
<mx:DataGridColumn> tag, 288, 289, 291, 293, 296
<mx:dataProvider> tag, 168, 307–309
<mx:DateField> tag, 86
<mx:DateFormatter> tag, 377–378, 594
<mx:Dissolve> tag, 572
<mx:fields> tag, 314
<mx:fills> tag, 527–529
<mx:FoodList> component, 573
<mx:Form> tag, 80–81, 177–178, 430
<mx:FormHeading> tag, 80–81, 429, 431
<mx:FormItem> tag, 80, 82–84, 136–137
<mx:Grouping> tag, 308
<mx:GroupingCollection> tag, 308
<mx:GroupingField> tag, 308, 313
<mx:HBox> tag, 171–173, 291, 361, 428–431, 480
<mx:horizontalAxis> tag, 510–517
<mx:horizontalAxisRenderer> tag, 518–519
<mx:HorizontalList> tag, 207–210, 215–222, 398
<mx:HTTPService> tag, 283
  data manager component, 185–188, 191
  populating controls, 126, 135–136

retrieving XML data, 120, 141–143
using web service, 450–452, 460
<mx:Image> tag, 73–74, 75–78, 217, 291, 343
<mx:itemRenderer> tag, 292–297
<mx:Label> tag, 25, 86, 224, 355, 423–426, 429–431, 583, 586
<mx:Legend> tag, xxiv
<mx:LineChart> tag, 503, 512–514, 520–521
<mx:LineSeries> tag, 508
<mx:LinkButton> tag, 60, 85
<mx:List> tag, 168, 226
<mx:Metadata> tag, 235–236, 362, 368, 478, 485
<mx:Model> tag, 79–81, 83, 94–96, 106, 178–179
<mx:Module> tag, 534–535
<mx:ModuleLoader> tag, 535–537
<mx:operation> tag, 450–452
<mx:Panel> tag, 60, 197–198
<mx:Parallel> tag, 570
<mx:PieChart> tag, 502–503, 505, 522–529
<mx:PieSeries> tag, 505–508, 527–529
<mx:PrintDataGrid> tag, 583
<mx:RadioButton> tag, 86–87
<mx:RadioButtonGroup> tag, 86–87
<mx:RemoteObject> tag, 474, 481–482, 485–488
<mx:RemoveChild> tag, 63, 227
<mx:rendererProviders> tag, 317
<mx:Repeater> tag, 217
<mx:request> tag, 450–452
<mx:RestorePanel> tag, 281–282
<mx:RichTextEditor> tag, 136
<mx:Script> block, 83, 91–92, 95, 612
<mx:Sequence> tag, 570
<mx:series> tag, 508
<mx:SetProperty> tag, 63–64, 220–221
<mx:SetStyle> tag, 426
<mx:Spacer> tag, 85–86, 275
<mx:State name-"expanded"/> tag, 76
<mx:State> tag, 63–64, 221
<mx:States> tag, 63–66

<mx:Style> tag, 417–419, 421–431, 434
<mx:summaries> tag, 313
<mx:SummaryField> tag, 314
<mx:SummaryRow> tag, 313
<mx:TabNavigator> tag, 351–353
<mx:Text> tag, 78, 108, 224, 291, 424
<mx:TextInput> tag, 82, 136
<mx:TitleWindow> tag, 176–177
<mx:TraceTarget> tag, 610–611
<mx:Transition> tag, 570–571, 574–575
<mx:transitions> tag block, 570–572, 574
<mx:Tree> tag, 172–173
<mx:UIComponent> tag, 185
<mx:VBox> tag, 293–294, 363, 426, 479, 575
<mx:verticalAxis> tag, 510–517
<mx:ViewStack> tag, 349–351, 355, 360, 423, 502
<mx:WebService> tag, 450–452
<mx:WipeRight> effect, 574
<mx:XMLListCollection> tag, 135
<mx:ZipCodeValidator> tag, 379
MXML. *see also* XML
    adding and controlling view states, 63–66
    compiling to ActionScript class, 106
    creating projects, 18–20
MXML custom components, 165–198
    building, 167–170, 258
    creating Category value object, 182–183
    creating UpdateDeleteProd, 171–175
    creating/using data manager, 184–195
    creating/using for Dashboard application, 196–198
    implementing AddProd, 195–196
    retrieving product information, 175–181
    UIComponent, 166
myCookie.sol file, 599
myLabel control, 71, 335
myPrintView object, 587
myStyleFunc() function, 303–305

N

name collision, 104–105
name property, 440, 621
naming conventions
    ActionScript classes, 102
    code hinting for class names, 108
    components, 167
    event handlers, 98
    projects, 17–18
    states, 57
    value objects, 104
navigateToURL() function, 394
navigation, 347–371
    adding Home page and Checkout page, 354–358
    checkout process, 358–370
    deep linking, 403–408
    History Management, 394–396, 396–397, 398–402
    overview of, 348–351
    TabNavigator, 351–353
navigator containers, 348
Navigator view, 21–22, 432
new keyword, 107
nodes, XML, 130
nondrag-enabled components, 333–344
NumberFormatter class, 374
NumberValidator class, 374
numChildren() method, 264
NumericStepper controls, 290

O

ObjectDataEvent class, 362–363, 524
object-oriented programming (OOP), 101
onCreation() method, 635–636
OOP (object-oriented programming), 101
Open Perspective button, 22
OrderConf component, 367–369, 377–378, 430–431, 484, 591–595
orderConfirm() function, 484
orderConfirmed event, 484
OrderInfo class, 359–360, 364–369
OrderInfo.as file, 490–491
Outline view, 45, 419
overSkin attribute, 433, 439, 441
setStyle() method, 416

P

package keyword, 103
paddingTop, Left, Bottom and Right style values, 27
page-based architecture, 4–7
Panel containers, 40, 60–61
parentheses [()] operator, 132–133
parseURL() method, 405–408
pattern regular expression, 384–386
performance
    DataGrid costs, 281
    Performance Profile view, 650
    TileList vs. Repeater, 215
period (.), 382
perspectives
    Debugging. *see* Debugging perspective
    defined, 22
    Development, 22, 100
    increasing space allotted to, 100
    Profiling, 643, 649
PhoneFormatter class, 374
PhoneNumberValidator class, 374
PieChart control
    adding chart events, 522–525
    defined, 504
    initial layout, 502–503
    specifying series classes for, 505–508
PieSeries class, 504, 506–507
PlotChart control, 504
PlotSeries class, 504
plus sign (+), 209
populateForm() function, 138–139, 172–173
populateForm() method, 138–139
pop-up window, 175–181, 461
PopUpManager class, 175–181, 245
position attribute, 64
pound sign (#), 416
predicate filtering, 132–133
presetCombo() method, 524
presetList() method, Util class, 139
preventDefault() method, 332
primitive data types, 632
Print button, 581
Print Page button, 581
PrintDataGrid class, 579, 582–587

printing in Flex, 578–595
  building printable view,
    586–588
  checkout process receipt,
    591–595
  for first time, 579–581
  overview of, 579
  scaling printed output, 589–591
  using PrintDataGrid, 582–585
PrintReceipt class, 592–595
PrintView.mxml, 585–588
private methods and properties,
  public vs., 388
Pro, Flex Builder 3, vs. Standard,
  xxiv, 631
Problems panel, 235
Problems view, 29
process() method, 362–363, 381,
  384, 386, 389
prod property, 180
prodArray, 145
prodbyCategory property,
  217–222
prodByCategoryHandler()
  function, 185, 189–190,
  459–460
prodbyCatRPC HTTPService, 136
prodHandler() method, 95–96,
  106, 108–109, 112, 142–145,
  145–146
prodName attribute, 138–139
Product class, 103–106, 109–113,
  225–228
product data type, 110
product property, ProductEvent
  class, 241–242
Product() method call, 459
Product.as file, 458–459
ProductEvent class
  adding product to cart, 247–249
  creating events, 241–245
  event bubbling, 253–254
  removing product from cart,
    245–247
ProductManagerService class,
  464–467
ProductName component,
  290–292
productRemoved event, 247
productUpdate() function, 619
Profile Application button, 642,
  648
ProfilerTest component
  defined, 641

memory profiling, 642–647
  performance issues, 651
  performance profiling, 648–650
  reviewing, 639–641
profiling, 630–651
  Flex Builder 3 Pro vs. Builder
    Standard, xxiv, 631
  memory, 632–639, 639–641,
    642–647, 647–648
  overview of, 631
  performance, 648–651
Profiling perspective, 643, 649
programmatic skins, 437–443
ProgrammaticSkin class, 438–443
projects
  creating, 16–20
  naming, 17–18
  running application, 23–29
properties
  accessing in top-level
    application, 227
  assigning values to, 91
  code hinting for class, 108
  component, 172, 174
  creating ActionScript class,
    102–105, 107–111
  name collision, 104–105
  private vs. public, 388
  style, 413–414, 417–419
pseudocode, 150, 157–159
public methods and properties,
  private vs., 388
public() method, 602
push() method, 144

Q

quantity property, 109–111

R

radio buttons, 85–87
RadioButtonGroup, 85–87
RangeError class, 623–624
rawChildren property, 264–267
reading, data from SharedObjects,
  600–601, 604–607
reCalc() method, 110–111, 158,
  298
RectBorder class, 438
refactoring, 468–469
reference counting, 634–636
reference, passing by, 633
refetchData() function, 460,
  462

refresh() method, 149–150,
  308, 310
RegExp class, 382
register() method, 395
registerWithHistoryManager()
  method, 399
regular expressions
  using new custom Validator
    class, 387–391
  validating data with, 382–386
relativeTo attribute, 64
Remote Method Invocation (RMI),
  447
Remote Procedure Calls (RPCs), 447
remote XML data, 115–162
  overview of, 115–116
  populating ArrayCollection,
    122–125
  populating ComboBox control,
    125–128
  populating Tree control, 129,
    129–134, 129–140,
    134–140
  retrieving with HTTPService,
    117, 117–118, 119,
    119–122
  shopping cart manipulation,
    147–148, 148–150, 150–
    151, 152–160, 160–162
  transforming into
    ArrayCollection, 141–145
  using data binding, 145–146
  using source attribute, 95
remoteChildAt() method, 637
[RemoteClass] metadata tag,
  490
RemoteObject components. see
  also <mx:RemoteObject>
  tag
  creating and calling, 485–488
  defined, 474
  dispatching orderConfirmed
    event, 484
  passing cart into Checkout
    component, 488
  returning to welcome screen,
    489
  saving order, 481–482
  Update Flex Compiler
    command, 483
Remove button, 160–162,
  245–246, 292–297
remove() method, 161
removeAll() method, 606

removeChild() method, 637
removeEventListener()
    method, 638, 647
removeItem() method, 161, 246,
    294
removePopUp() method, 176–177
renaming tool, 468–469
renderDate() function, 513–514,
    515
renderDollars() function, 516
rendererProviders, 316–318
renderLabel() function, 225,
    295, 507
renderPriceLabel() function,
    295–296
renderTips() function, 521–522
Repeater class, 651
Repeater component
    addressing components built
        by, 214–215
    displaying items in categories,
        215–222
    general syntax for, 211
    looping over dataset, 211–212
    retrieving data from, 212–213
    TileList performance vs., 215
resetForm() method, 138, 140,
    172–173
restore event, 260, 276
result event handler, 117–118,
    120, 453–455
ResultEvent class, 119–122, 126
Resume command, 613, 618
RIAs (Rich Internet Applications)
    benefits of, 7–8
    evolution of, 4–6
    page-based architecture vs., 6–7
    technologies, 9–12
RMI (Remote Method Invocation),
    447
rolloutEffect trigger, 569, 572
rollOverColor property, 414–416
rolloverEffect trigger, 569, 572
root node, XML, 130, 131
rowCount variable, 124
rows, AdvancedDataGrid styles,
    303–305
RPCs (Remote Procedure Calls), 447
RSLs (Runtime Shared Libraries)
    defined, 533
    linker, 539–540
    overview of, 537–539
    using Flex framework caching,
        540–544

Run button, 24
runtime
    application at, 23–29
    changing CSS at, 431–433
    installing AIR at, 551–552
    populating text fields at, 70–71
Runtime Shared Libraries. see RSLs
    (Runtime Shared Libraries)

S

SalesChart component
    adding chart events, 520–521
    adding horizontal axis, 512–514
    initial layout, 503
    series classes for, 505–506,
        508–509
salesRPCResult() function, 283,
    452, 455
sandbox restrictions, Flash Player,
    119
save() method, 399–400
saveCart() method, 601–603
saveOrder() method, 488
saveOrderResult() method,
    486, 491, 606–607
saveOrderWithVO() function,
    491
saveState() method, 395–396,
    400–401
scalar values, 91
scaling printed output, 589–591
search() method, String class,
    383, 385
security restrictions
    Flash Player, 119
    Microsoft Internet Explorer,
        627, 652
Select event, 476
selected attribute, CheckBox
    control, 83
selectedChild property, 350,
    356–357
selectedDate property,
    DateChooser, 361
selectedIndex property,
    ViewStack, 127–128, 350,
    356–357, 400–401, 406
selectedItem property, 246, 400
selectedNode variable, 138
selectHandler() function,
    476–477
selection events, charts, 520

selectionColor property,
    414–416
selectors, CSS styles, 417–419
send() method
    HTTPService calls, 116–117, 120,
        126–127, 136, 142, 285
    print jobs, 580–581, 593
    web service calls, 456–458
Series classes, 501, 504–510
SeriesInterpolate effect, 525
SeriesSlide effect, 526
SeriesZoom effect, 526
server-side objects, 474–497
    Flex Builder data wizards and,
        492–497
    mapping ActionScript objects
        to, 490–492
    uploading files to server,
        475–481
    using RemoteObject, 481–482,
        483, 484, 485–488, 488,
        489
services-config.xml file, 481–482,
    483
set quantity () function, 298
setActualSize() method,
    272–274
setCat() function, 456–457
setChildByName() method, 272
setFocus() method, 85
setFragment() function, 406
setState() method, 260–261,
    266
setStyle() method, 265, 416,
    434
setTitle() method, 407–408
SHA-256 hash, 543
shared objects, 597–607
    building SharedObject, 601–603
    characteristics of, 598
    creating, 599–600
    reading, 600–601, 604–607
Shift+Tab keys, 227
ShoppingCart class
    building SharedObject to store
        data, 601–603
    configuring Checkout
        component, 485–488
    loadCart() method, 604
    removeItem() method,
        160–161
    shared objects, 601–604

ShoppingCartItem class
  adding items, 147–148, 150–
    151, 225–228, 247–249
  building, 109–113
  dragging items, 339–344
  placing products, 225–228
  removing items, 245–247
  shared objects, 605–606
  sorting items in ArrayCollection,
    148–150
  updating with set and get
    functions, 298–299
  using cursor to locate item,
    152–160
Show Line Numbers, 23
show() method, 487
showCart() function, 356–357
showCloseButton property, 176
showEffect trigger, 569, 572–573
showFault() method, 284
showPopUp() method, 179–181,
    244–245, 461
showProducts() function, 358
signed RSL, 541
Silverlight, 12
simple controls. *see* controls,
    simple
sizing
  enhanced constraints, 54
  Flex mechanisms for, 268–269
  Image control, 73
  measure() method, 269–270
SkinArtwork, importing, 434–437
skins
  defined, 413
  graphical, 434
  importing from CS3, 434–437
  programmatic, 437–443
  skinning components, 433–443
slash (/), 26
slashes and period (//.), 382–383,
    385
SOAP messages, 481
SocialSecurityValidator class, 374
software
  installation, 654–656
  requirements for this book, 652
.sol file, 603
Sort class, 148–150
SortByDateField() method,
    453–454
sortExpertMode property,
    AdvancedDataGrid, 299–302
SortField class, 148–150

SortingADG.mxml application,
    299–301
SortingExpertADG.mxml, 301–302
sortItems() method, 150, 156
sounds, applying behaviors as, 568
source attribute, <mx:Model>
    tag, 95, 116
Source mode
  building Detail view, 75–78
  displaying images, 73
  layout in, 59–62
  toggling Design mode and,
    41, 59
  using constraints, 50–51
  viewing application in, 21
source property, 73, 379
<source> tag, Remoting, 482
Spacer button, 368
Standard, Flex Builder 3, vs. Pro,
    xxiv, 631
standardBlack style class, 426
standardBlackBold style class,
    426, 429, 431
standardOrange style class, 425
standardOrangeBold style class,
    429–431
start() method, 580–581
States view, 32, 55–57, 75
states, coding, 223–225
static methods, 107–109
Step Into command, 613
Step Over command, 613
Step Return command, 613
string concatenations, 209
StringValidator class, 374
StyleCellADG.mxml, 305–306
StyleColumnADG.mxml, 302–303
styleFunction property,
    AdvancedDataGrid, 303–305,
    306
StyleManager, 433
styleName property, 423–425,
    428–429
StyleRowADG.mxml, 303–305
styles, 412–433
  AdvancedDataGrid, 302–306
  applying, 413–414
  changing CSS at runtime,
    431–433
  chart, 527–529
  defined, 413
  Flex Builder tools for CSS,
    419–421
  inheritance, 416

programmatic skins vs., 437
  setting via CSS files, 421–431
  setting via tag attributes,
    414–416
  setting with <mx:Style> tag,
    417–419
  skins applied as, 434
subclassing, 374
subdirectories, 167
subtotal property, 110
summaries property, 320
summary data, AdvancedDataGrid
  with ActionScript, 318–320
  overview of, 312–316
  with rendererProviders, 316–318
  with tags, 312–316
SummaryField objects, 315
summaryFunction property, 315
summaryPlacement property,
    313–314, 319
SummaryRow class, 318–320
SummaryWithActionScriptADG.
    mxml, 318–320
SummaryWithTagsADG.mxml,
    312–318
super() function, 388
.swf extension, 540–544
SWF files
  baking images/source code into
    application, 532–533
  creating from CSS files, 432–433
  displaying images, 71–74
  generating when running
    application, 24
  importing skins created in CS3,
    434–437
switch statement, 439–440
.swz extension, 540–544
system events, 90

T
TabNavigator component,
    351–353, 394, 397
tabs, removing excess, 227
tags
  displaying summary data,
    312–316
  grouping data, 307–309
  setting styles inline, 414–416
  terminating, 26
  variable or function help, 95

target phase, of events, 250
target property, Event object, 97, 100
Terminate command, 613
Text controls
  defined, 70
  in Design mode, 30–35
  in Detail view, 76–78
  Label control vs., 34
  linking to simple controls, 79–80
  overview of, 70–71
text property
  Detail view, 77
  displaying summary data, 316
  event handling, 90–91
  methods, 108
  radio buttons, 86
  Text controls, 70
  Tree control, 138–139
textAlign style property, 414
TextandPic component, 425
TextArea controls/components, 53–54, 70
textDecoration style property, 414
textIndent style property, 414
TextInput controls, 70, 83, 582–585
theReceipt class, 592
this keyword, 399
throw statement, 625
tightly coupled applications, 233
Tile containers, 40
TileList components, 123, 203–206, 215
Title Window class, 175–181
toggleState() function, 223
toggleViewOnly() method, 641
top constraints, 47
toState property, 570, 574
toString() function, 105–106, 183, 298
toString() method, 107–109, 395–396, 621
trace statements
  building value object, 106
  creationComplete event, 96
  debugging, 621–622, 627–628
  transforming data into ArrayCollection, 144
  web services, 462
trace() function, 111
transitions
  behaviors vs., 568
  on components, 572–574

defined, 567
view states, 570–572, 574–575
Tree control/component
  creating, 172–173
  dataProvider property, 123
  E4X operators, 129–134
  populating with XML data, 134–140
  testing data manager, 195
  using XML data, 129
tree open indicator, 646
triggers, 569
try-catch statements, 619–628
  creating own error classes, 626–628
  error types, 622
  finally statement, 624–625
  multiple catch blocks, 622
  overview of, 619–620
  single catch block, 623
  syntax, 620–622
  throw statement, 625
  using Error base class, 623–624
type property, 97, 100
type selectors, CSS, 417–418
TypeChart component
  animations, 526
  events, 522–525
  initial layout, 502–503
  specifying series classes, 505–508
  styles, 527–529
typeRPCResult() method, 284, 451

U
<u:AddressValidator> tag, 390
UIComponent class, 166, 184, 233
uint data type, 109–110
UIs (user interfaces)
  dynamic updates, 10
  layout, 39–67, 40, 41–46, 47–54, 55–59, 59–62, 63–66
  page-based architecture limitations, 4
  RIAs, advantages of, 6
  WPF, 12
Undeclared Method, WebService tag, 451
unit nodes, 130, 132
unitID property, 124, 139–140
unitRPC.send() method, 466

unitRPCResult() function, 120, 124, 615
units property, UpdateDeleteProd component, 172, 174
Universal Resource Identifier (URI), 20
unloadStyleDeclaration() method, 433
unsigned RSL, 541
Update/Delete buttons, 175–181
UpdateDeleteProd component
  creating, 171–175
  integrating FileUpload, 479–480
  popping up information, 175–181
  ProductEvent class, 243–244
  with TabNavigator control, 352–353
  testing data manager, 194–195
  updating and deleting products, 471
  using web services, 460
updateDisplayList() method, 270–276, 438–440
updateItem() method, 154, 157–158
UpdateManager, 641, 646–648
updateProductResult() method, 470–471
updateURL() method, 406–408
updating products, Web services, 470–471
upload() method, fileRef, 477
uploadComplete event, 478, 479–480
uploading file, to server, 475–481
upSkin attribute, 433, 439, 441
URI (Universal Resource Identifier), 20
URL-based navigation. see deep linking
URLRequest type, 477
user events, 90
user interfaces. see UIs (user interfaces)
Util class, 119, 138, 139

V
<v:ChartPod> tags, 198
<v:FileUpload/> tag, 479–480
<v:MaxRestorePanel> tag, 267
<v:SalesChart> tag, 505
<v:TypeChart> tag, 505

validate() method, 381
ValidationResult class, 387
ValidationResultEvent, 381
Validator class, 374, 378–391
value objects, building, 101–106
var statement, 172
Variables view, 613, 615, 617–618
VBox containers
    building Detail view, 76–77
    Design mode layout, 44–45
    rules for children, 40
    sizing and positioning, 268–269
    Source mode layout, 61–62
    using constraints with Parent
        container, 50
vertical center constraints, 47
vertical layouts, 20
View Cart button, 48–49, 227,
    356–357
view states
    adding and controlling with
        MXML, 63–66
    adding effects, 574–575
    controlling, 57–59
    defined, 55
    using transitions, 570–572
    working with, 55–56
views
    Design mode, 32–34
    Flex Builder 3, 21
    MVC architecture, 170
ViewStack class
    adding home and checkout
        page, 354–358
    built-in tools, 349–353
    checkout process, 358–365,
        365–370
    checkout process setup, 487
    overview of, 348
    runtime errors, 348–349
visible property, 108, 224–225
visualizing data. see charts
void data type, 111–112, 127, 138
void keyword, 84

W
weak references, 638–639,
    647–648
Web Service Description Language
    (WSDL), 450, 461
Web Service Introspection wizard,
    463–467
Web services
    calling methods, 456–458
    in DataEntry application,
        458–463
    event model remote server calls,
        448
    handling results, 452–455
    local configuration, 448–450
    overview of, 446–447
    refactoring with Flex Builder,
        468–469
    server communication, 447–448
    setup instructions, 447
    updating and deleting products,
        470–471
    using generated code, 465–467,
        469–470
WebService() method, 452
welcome screen, 489
win variable, UpdateDeleteProd,
    178–180
Windows
    AIR installation, 552
    ColdFusion server installation,
        655
    FlashDebug Player installation,
        656
    hardware requirements for this
        book, 651
    location of local shared objects,
        603
    manifest file location, 20
    software requirements for this
        book, 652

Windows Presentation Foundation
    (WPF), 12
WipeRight effect, 574–575
workbench, Flex Builder 3, 21–23
WPF (Windows Presentation
    Foundation), 12
WSDL (Web Service Description
    Language), 450, 461
WSDL (Web Service Description
    Language) Introspection
    wizard, 463–467
wsdl parameter, WebService tag,
    450, 461

X
XAML (Extensible Application
    Markup Language), 12
XML. see also MXML; remote XML
    data
    and AJAX, 9
    E4X operators, 130–134
    terminology, 129–130
    transforming into
        ArrayCollection, 141–145
XML class, ActionScript, 129
XMLDocument class, 129
XMLHttpRequest, 9
XMLListCollection, 134–140, 194

Y
yesNoToBoolean() method, Util,
    138–139, 144

Z
ZipCodeFormatter class, 374
ZipCodeValidator class, 374,
    378–379, 390